DRAWING PORTRAITS

A COMPLETE GUIDE

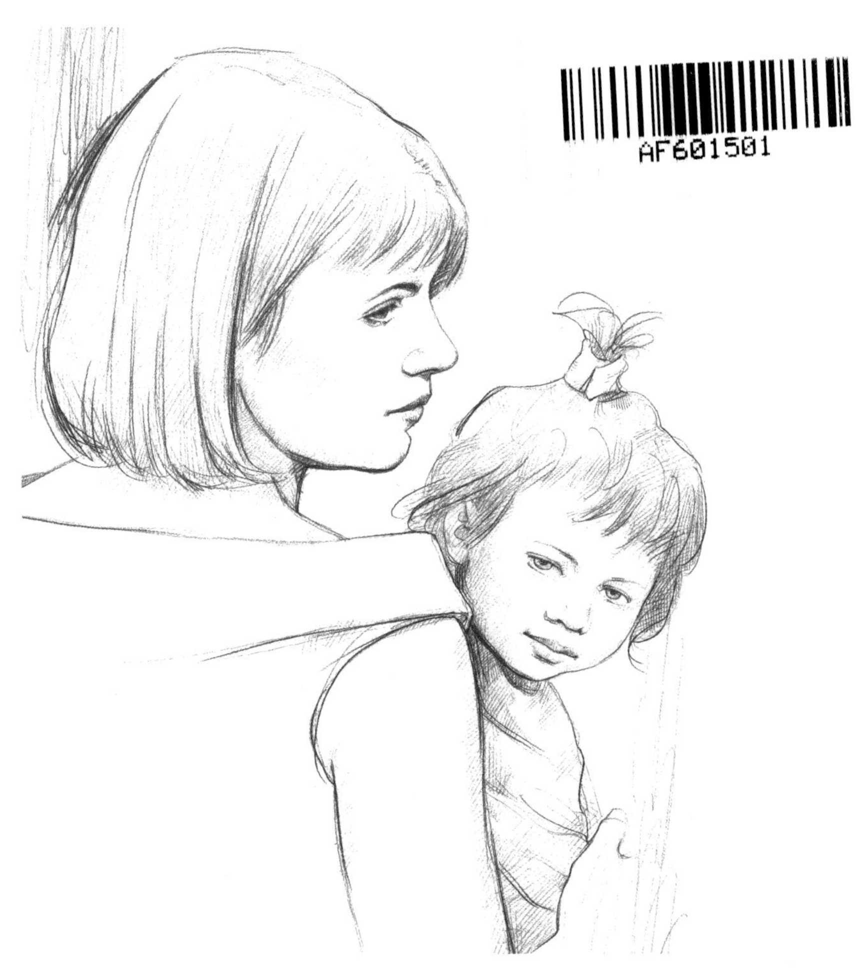

First published in 2026
Search Press Limited
Wellwood, North Farm Road,
Tunbridge Wells, Kent TN2 3DR

1 2 3 4 5 6 7 8 9 10

This book features content from the following books by Giovanni Civardi, published by Search Press:
1. *The Art of Drawing: Drawing Portraits* (2002)
2. *The Art of Drawing: Heads and Faces* (2012)
3. *Drawing Using Grids: Portraits with Character* (2018)
4. *The Art of Drawing: Portraits of Babies and Children* (2017)
5. *Drawing Using Grids: Portraits of Babies and Children* (2018)
6. *The Art of Drawing: Sketching People* (2011)

All titles originally published in Italy by Il Castello Collane Techniche, Milano

English translations from Italian of the above, by Julie Carbonara (1), Paul Enock at Cicero Translations (2), Burravoe Translation Services (3, 4 and 5), and Cicero Translations (6).

ISBN: 978-1-80092-419-2
ebook ISBN: 978-1-80093-377-4

Bookmarked Hub
For further ideas and inspiration, and to join our free online community, visit www.bookmarkedhub.com

Publishers' notes
The Publishers and author can accept no responsibility for any consequences arising from the information, advice or instructions given in this publication.

For errata, please visit our website (www.searchpress.com) or the Bookmarked Hub (www.bookmarkedhub.com).

GPSR information can be found at www.searchpress.com
Printed in China, AP052026.

GIOVANNI CIVARDI

DRAWING PORTRAITS

A COMPLETE GUIDE

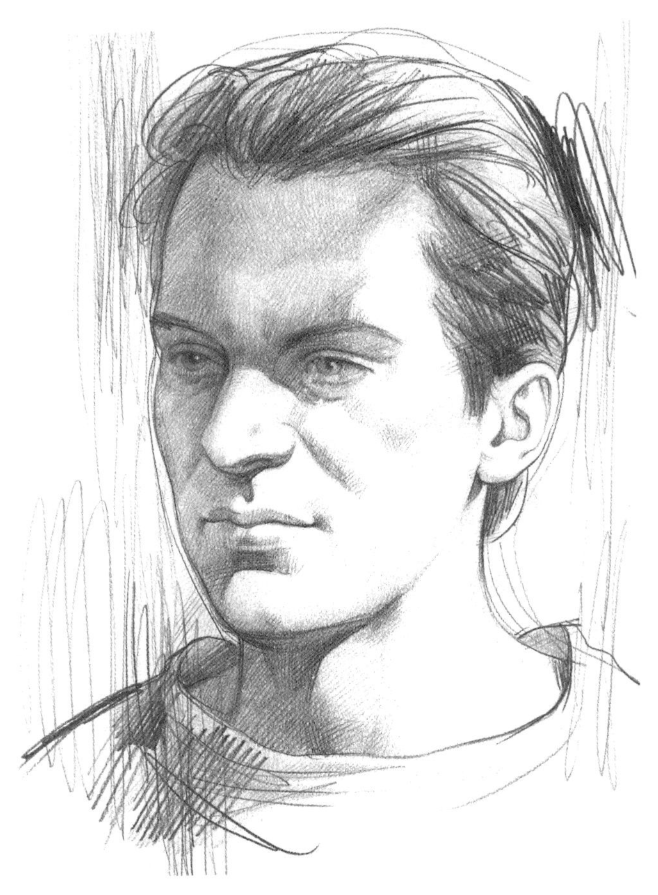

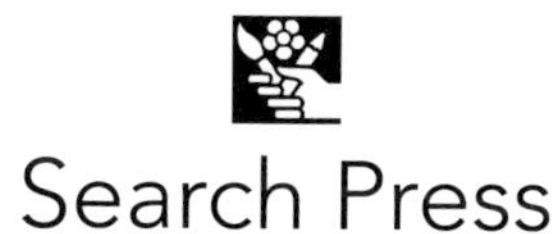

Search Press

CONTENTS

III: DRAWING PORTRAITS OF BABIES AND CHILDREN 204

IV: SKETCHING FACES AND FIGURES 342

CHAPTER 1: DRAWING PORTRAITS

INTRODUCTION

Drawing is a tool for learning to see – both literally, in the case of what is around us, and metaphorically, in what arises from our projects and our emotions. Through drawing we can decide to gather information about a visual situation or extract the most important, expressive elements from the situation.

At root, the character and qualities of a form are more important than the simple superficial method by which it is expressed. The various drawing techniques are chosen and used to translate these aspects in the most interesting, effective graphic manner.

As a subject, the human face is extremely well-suited to experimenting along these paths of drawing and expression, as the artist searches for what he or she finds most stimulating or most suited to their aesthetic style and the formal characteristics of the model.

A portrait is commonly perceived as the representation of a human being's features, whether the face, head and shoulders or the whole body. It has always been an important theme in figurative arts and a favourite with artists, who have found in it not just a professional genre well rewarded and socially appreciated for its symbolic or celebratory value, but also an interesting opportunity to investigate the human condition in its physical and, most of all, psychological aspects. It is this latter aspect which tends to predominate nowadays, as photography has greatly undermined the function of the drawn and painted portrait as the only way to reproduce and hand down for posterity an individual's physiognomic features. But this 'documentary' aspect was, of course, only part of the artistic portrait.

Using my experience as a portrait painter, illustrator and teacher, I have tried to simplify and sum up the main problems one usually comes across when first tackling a 'generic' head drawing and, subsequently, an actual portrait or likeness. Some subjects of particular importance, e.g. drawing hands, portraits of children and elderly people, the full figure portrait, and heads with unusual features have to be dealt with specifically and are covered in more detail later in the book.

This first chapter covers tools, techniques, practical considerations, anatomy, details of the face, composition, lighting and actual method, stressing the 'overall' view of the head. These basic technical principles can only direct you in your first experiences and should be seen as suggestions on which to build your own study. Your subsequent artistic development will depend on how committed you are to observation and how regularly you practise drawing. Before approaching your first drawings, you can of course resort to studying the drawings of other artists and taking photographs of your subject. However, as soon as you feel confident in sketching the basic outlines of the head, I advise you to try and draw from life, getting a patient friend to sit for you. In the last section of this book I have put together some portrait studies which I have drawn at different times and which give an indication of how to go about tackling different subjects.

MATERIALS AND TOOLS

Many artists have made sketches on paper napkins, till receipts, on the pages of newspapers and books or scraps of packing paper – even on the walls of their studios or on the backs of painted canvasses. However, it is clear that, except in emergencies, a slightly more suitable material is preferable. This may be a bound notebook with blank pages, perhaps small in size (9 × 14cm / 3½ × 5½in) or medium-sized (13 × 21cm / 5 × 8¼in), or a typical album-sized artist's drawing pad. Sketchbooks and sketchpads may be made up and bound by the artists themselves, using the size and quality of paper that best suits their purpose. You can do this by simply folding and joining sheets of paper together and enclosing them in a hard cover (an indispensible support, given that we draw holding the sketchbook in one hand).

Commercially available **sketchbooks** have the advantage of being pocket size, making it easy to have them ready to hand at all times. The papers also come in various weights, colours and qualities: light-grade paper is suitable for pencil sketches, a slightly heavier paper will take pen strokes and coloured crayons, while wet techniques (watercolour, wash, etc.) require paper that is heavier still, although excessive applications of water will cause even these surfaces to pucker.

It is a good idea to insert a sheet of thin paper between facing pages that have been drawn on in order to avoid smudging or staining, especially if drawn using soft graphite. The same care should also be taken while sketching in order to prevent the hand that is resting on the paper from moving material around.

What is a sketch? There are various interpretations as well as different purposes or ends, but the term is commonly used to refer to a fairly quick, spontaneous drawing of something from life that is represented swiftly and with a few essential strokes. In addition, a sketch can be a note, made in graphic form, of a sensory experience; it can constitute the starting point of a project; it can be a means of gathering visual information ahead of a large-scale work; it can be a preliminary study for a complex, composite work or, lastly, it can be made in order to study the form of a subject either viewed as a whole or focusing in on particular details. For all these purposes, the sketchbook becomes a precious tool for artists as well as their richest source of information and recollection.

A sketch is made quickly and should always be fluent, free and concise – characteristics that clearly differ from those of a more elaborate or fully finished drawing. Suitable tools, therefore, are the simplest ones that can be picked up and used immediately, as long as they suit the artist's style and technical preferences.

The pencil Ordinary pencils may be used: those with the lead enclosed in a wooden sheath, or mechanical pencils with graphite leads that are inserted into a button-operated sleeve. These have very fine leads with diameters between 0.5mm and 0.7mm. These are rather fragile but have the advantage of not needing to be sharpened. Different shades of graphite are represented on a conventional scale ranging from the hardest (9H) to the softest (9B) with the middle of the range being represented by HB or B. Soft graphite leads deliver a full, pliable mark on the paper which is ideal for spontaneous drawings 'in one go', but which can also be applied to a sheet of paper upwards of 20 × 30cm (8 × 12in). Medium and hard leads are suited to making sharper and more detailed sketches (which are nonetheless fast and concise), even working on a very small scale.

Woodless graphite sticks and crayons These are small sticks made entirely of graphite with a diameter roughly between 5 and 15mm (¼ and ⅝in), which can be held directly or using a purpose-made metal handle. They are usually manufactured out of graphite paste ranging from soft to very soft (from B to 9B), which is why they really only come into their own when used on rather large surfaces. They also allow you to indicate large areas of shade with a few forceful and concise strokes.

Charcoal This is a very delicate and soft tool, especially when made out of carbonized twigs. It can produce drawings with strong, clear-cut lines, or drawings that are extremely vague in their rendering of shade. However, due partly to the fact that charcoal is a very brittle material, it is poorly suited to drawing small-scale sketches in a sketchpad or sketchbook. More suitable for this purpose, though, is the kind of charcoal made of compressed lamp black, as this leaves a very dense mark on the paper and its properties of line drawing are similar to those of soft graphite sticks.

Coloured pencils These have characteristics similar to those of lead pencils, being easy to handle and leaving clear, soft lines. As they come in a wide range of shades for each colour, they offer a quick and easy means of noting details of colour in complex subjects, for example in a portrait or when depicting figures dressed in garments with striking colours.

Pen and ink These tools are also widely used and are very suitable for making quick and concise sketches. However, they are more demanding than a pencil because they leave an indelible mark on the paper. This is why they require the artist to be daring, as well as to possess a great deal of sureness of hand so that the end product is not muddled, blotchy or overly tentative. The opportunity for tracing faint guidelines in pencil, which can then be erased later on, is not really feasible for sketches of the human figure, which by definition have to be (and so appear) spontaneous and fluent, as well as being free of jarring 'second thoughts'. The classic tool set for drawing in pen and ink comprises a penholder, nib and bottle of coloured or black India ink. While unrivalled in its versatility, this does not adapt very well to impromptu sketches, especially of figures and faces spotted in outdoor situations. There are at least two reasons for this: first, the charge of ink in the nib is used up in a few strokes and this slows down the speed of the sketch, and secondly, the metallic nib can get caught in the fibres of sketchpad paper (which is often fairly light and low grade in quality) producing unwelcome spots or tearing. The bamboo pen presents similar problems, although it is a little more amenable to this kind of work. Pens, on the other hand, such as ballpoints, fountain pens, felt-tipped and technical drawing pens, are much more suitable in this case.

Continued overleaf ›

Drybrush technique A good alternative to a pen is a small paintbrush with natural hair or synthetic bristles. Once the brush has been dipped in the ink and suitably dried on a rag or piece of tissue, it is possible to draw on the paper with a very soft and flowing stroke, the width of which can be greatly varied, and also to fill in areas with blocks of shade that can be either opaque and solid or light and grainy. In order to exploit drybrush technique to its full potential, the paper of the sketchpad should be of sufficient weight and slightly textured, and the size of the brush used suitable for the sketch you intend to execute. As soon as work is completed, the brush should be washed thoroughly in water.

Watercolours and lavis (ink wash) These media are seldom used for impromptu sketching of the human figure because they do not lend themselves very well to this kind of spontaneous, unpredictable 'note taking'. Indeed, even the minimum amount of equipment required becomes cumbersome with both the artist and subject assuming fleeting poses in a public place. At most, large areas can be blocked in, either in colour, using watercolours, or by the monochrome lavis technique of diluting black ink (or any other colour) with water. Touches of colour and shade can also be added and worked on afterwards, with the pencil sketch already finished and both the time and the means available for supplementing and enriching it. It is, however, advisable to be aware that such a procedure can easily 'weigh down' the sketch and remove its freshness.

Other tools In order to gain experience in using them and to experiment with new or unconventional effects, you might like to try out other media – although they might not be among the most convenient for executing the kind of sketches we have in mind here. Examples include oil or acrylic paint; on either coloured paper or canvas panel or perhaps on a surface coated with china clay; or using metal tools to produce a drawing in ink. It has now also become possible to sketch using an electronic pen on a portable laptop.

Accessories This is, of course, a basic overview. Pencil and paper are all you really need to make an impromptu sketch of human figures in an outdoor scene. Nonetheless, it could be useful to have at least a plastic eraser to hand – not so much for erasing mistakes as for removing excess marks or spots of graphite from the paper – and a bulldog clip to hold the pages of the sketchbook while you are working.

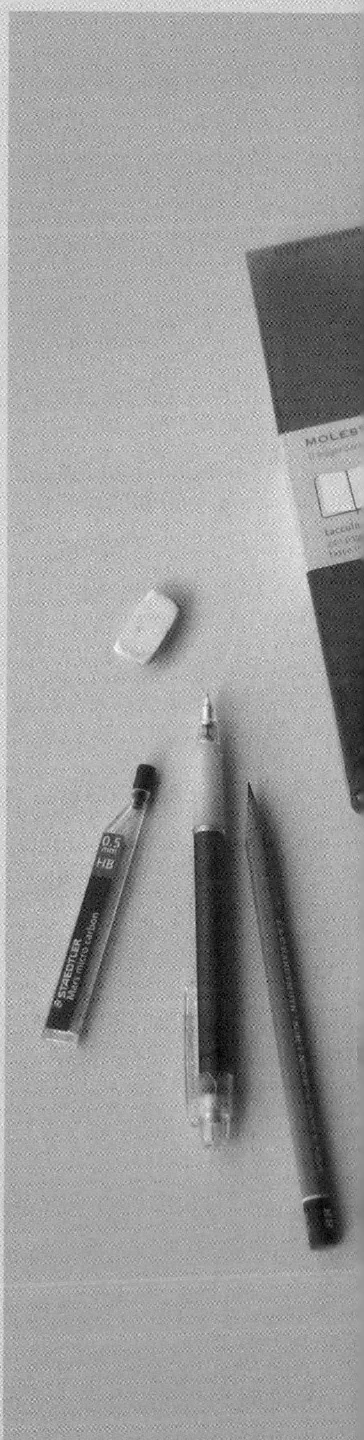

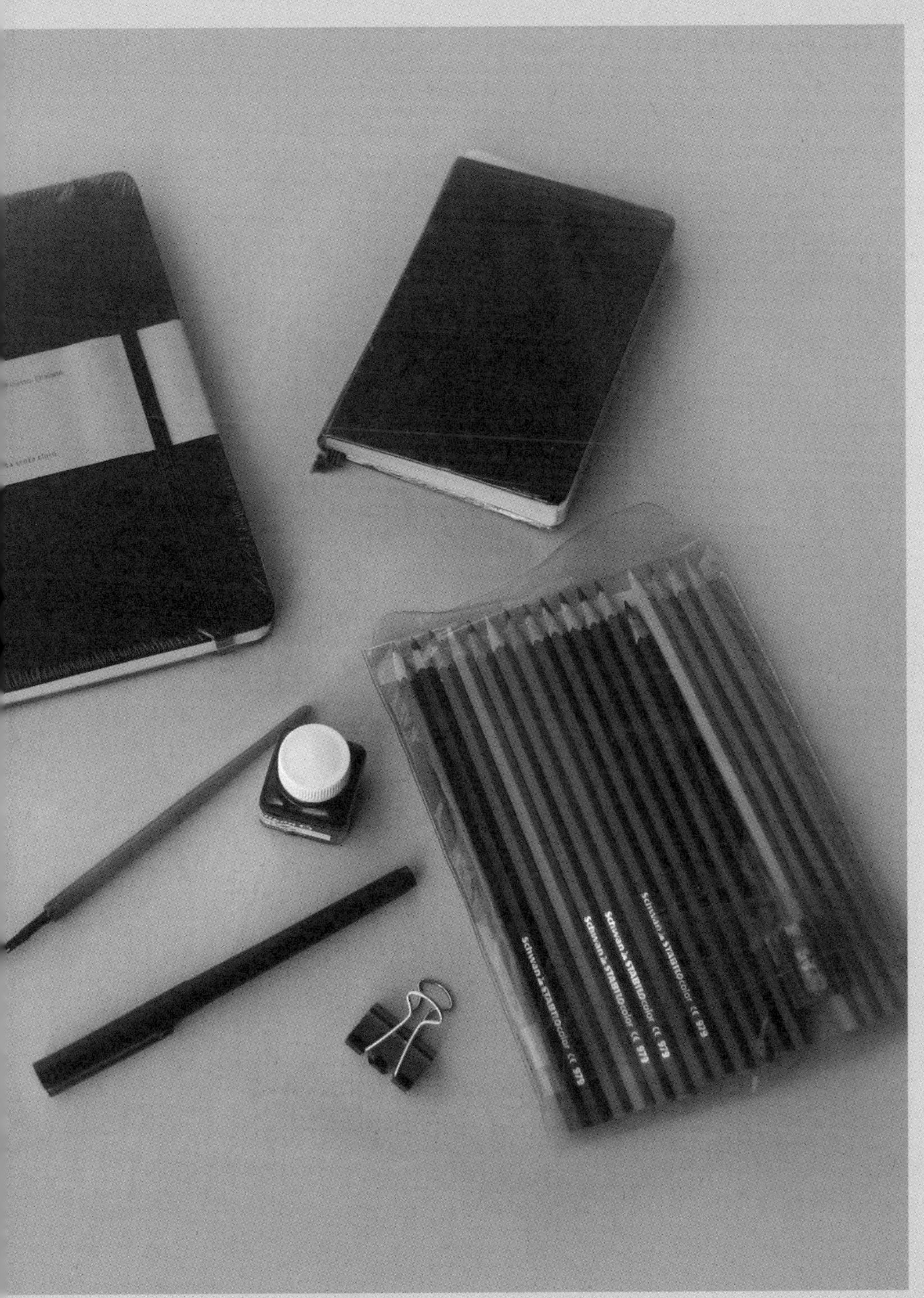
Schwan STABILOcolor CE 973
Schwan STABILOcolor CE 973
Schwan STABILOcolor CE 973

TOOLS AND TECHNIQUES

You can draw a portrait using any of the popular media mentioned on the previous spread. Each one of them, however, will produce different effects, not only due to the specific characteristics of the medium and the technique used, but also in relation to the characteristics of the surface on which it is drawn: smooth or rough-textured paper, card, white or coloured paper, etc. The drawings shown on these two pages demonstrate how different media effectively render the complex tonal values of the human face and body. Each of the techniques offers its own characteristic properties that enable artists to give free rein to their creative impulses.

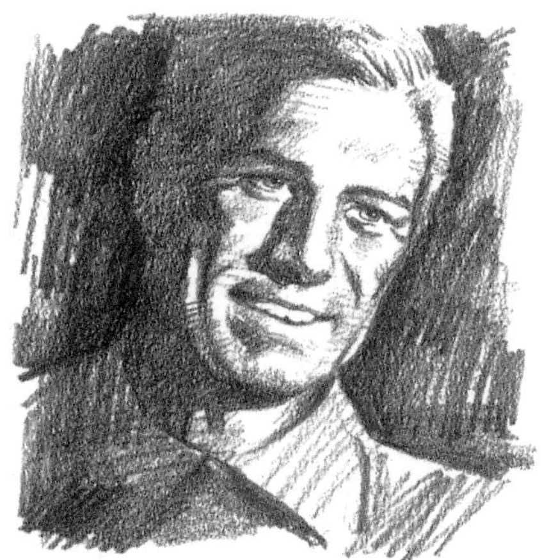

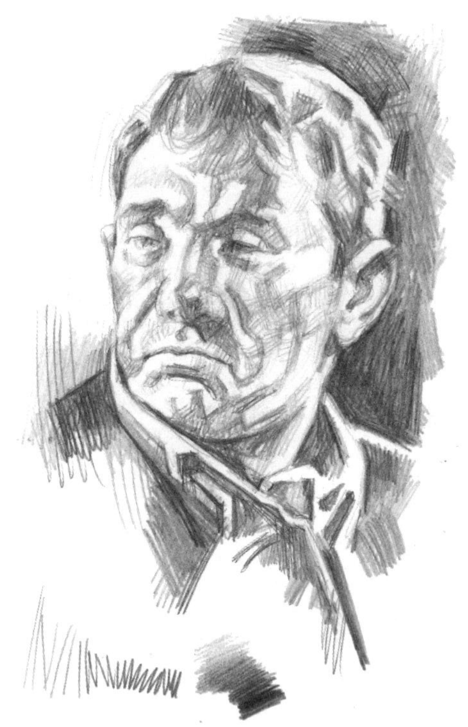

Pencil (B and 2B) on rough-textured paper

Pencil is the most widely used medium for any type of drawing and, with figures and portraits, it allows you to be spontaneous and is very convenient to use. It can be used for complex drawings or for small studies and quick reference sketches: for the latter very fine leads are suitable, while for the former you can use thicker and softer-grade graphites. Graphites (leads that are held in mechanical, clutch pencils) as well as pencils (wood-encased graphites) are graded according to their consistency: from 9H, the hardest, which gives thin and faint lines, to 6B, very soft, which gives thick and dark lines with ease.

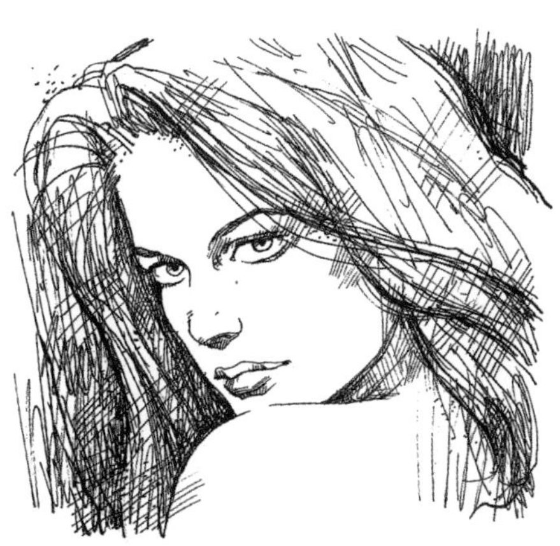

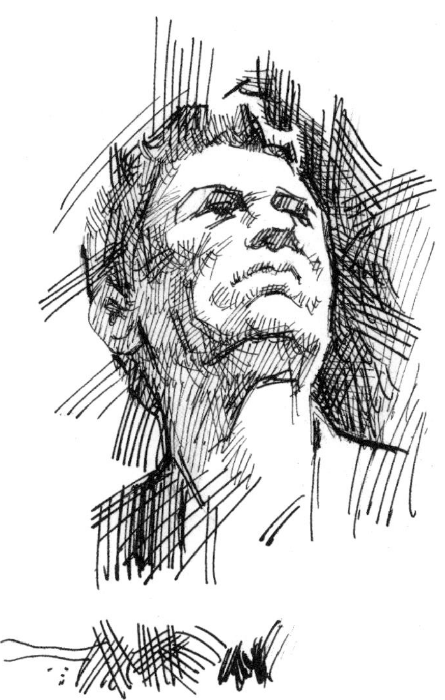

Pen and black Indian ink on smooth paper

Ink is widely used by artists. It can be applied either with a brush or with a pen, but special effects can be achieved using bamboo reeds, large nibs, fountain pens, technical pens, felt-tip pens or ball-point pens. Tones can usually be graded by drawing fairly dense lines over one another at right angles (cross-hatching). It is advisable to use smooth, good quality paper or card, so that the surface won't fray or absorb ink in an irregular way.

Pen and ink can be used to create very small drawings, also relative to the thickness of the nib or type of tool (such as felt-tip pen, ball-point pen and bamboo). Sometimes very fine lines can be achieved by placing the back of the pen nib on the paper.

Dry brush

This technique involves the application of ink using a semi-dry brush: when placed on absorbent paper, the bristles spread out and then trace thin parallel lines of a light intensity. The effects differ depending on whether smooth or rough paper is used. The mid and dark tones are obtained by overlapping strokes, similar to drawing with a pen or pencil. In place of India ink, any other diluted pigment can be used (watercolour, gouache and oil) and then spread using a fairly dry brush.

Monochromatic watercolour on medium-textured paper

Watercolours, water-soluble inks and water-diluted Indian ink are ideal for portrait study, although they are closer to painting than to drawing, as they are applied with a brush and require a tonal vision which is both concise and expressive. For quick studies you can use water-soluble graphites or colour pencils (to blend strokes easily, wipe them with a water-soaked brush) and it is advisable to use heavy card so that the moisture will not cause the surface to cockle and become irregular.

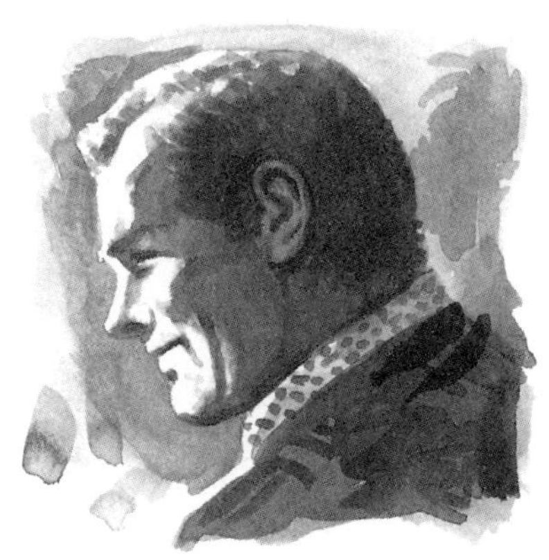

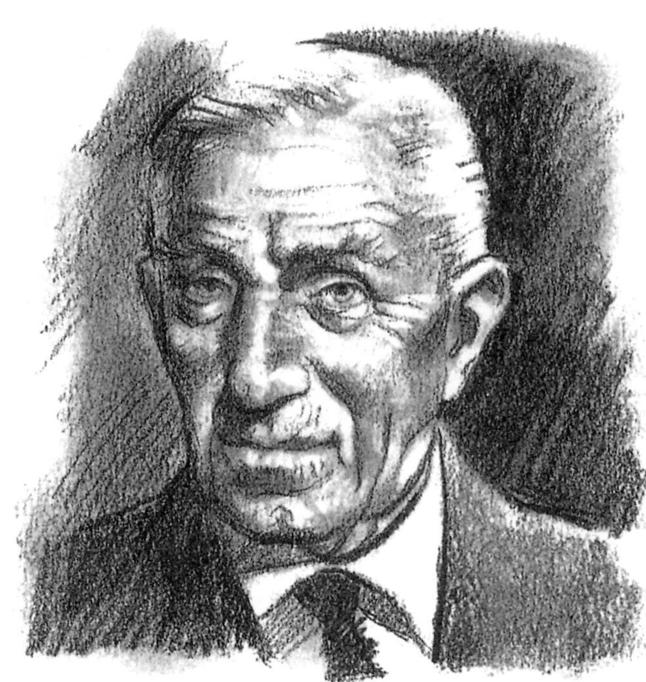

Compressed charcoal on paper

Charcoal is perhaps the ideal medium for portrait study as it is very easy to control when applying tones but also allows you to achieve fairly sharp detail. It should, however, be used 'broadly', concentrating on the overall rendering of the 'shapes': this exploits its greatest assets, as it is both versatile and evocative. You can use either compressed charcoal or willow charcoal but be careful, in either case, not to smudge the sheet. Charcoal strokes can be blended and smudged by gently rubbing with a finger, and tones can be softened by blotting with a soft eraser (kneadable putty eraser). The finished drawing should be protected by spraying with fixative.

When diluted with the appropriate proportions of water, ***watercolour paint, water-soluble inks, aquarelle pencils and Indian ink*** *will all produce a rich range of subtle tones, which are well-suited to executing studies of the human face and head. The method could follow the classic techniques of watercolour painting, or these media can be used as tonal supplements for drawings made in pencil or ink. A single watered-down colour can also achieve nuances of tonal gradation, (as with the lavis technique). The same effects can be obtained by using Indian ink (half-tone) – with the objective of concentrating attention on the play of light and shade on the structural form, rather than on obtaining chromatic effects. Watercolour technique requires a progression from lighter to increasingly darker tones to retain the transparency of the colours; the gradual building up of layers of paint still allows the luminous whiteness of the paper to shine through.*

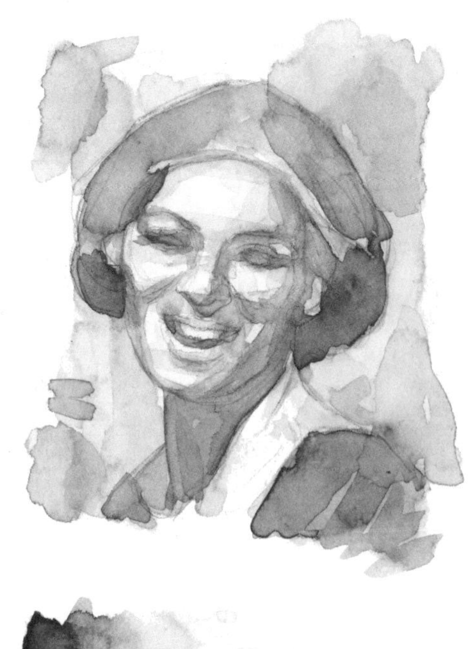

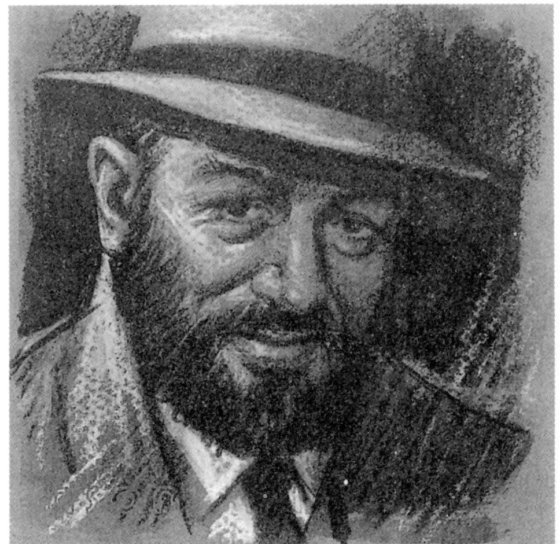

Pen and ink, watercolour, white pastel on coloured paper

'Mixed' media involves using different materials to achieve a drawing with unusual effects. Although still 'graphic' materials, their more complex application requires good control and a good knowledge of the media themselves if we are to avoid muddled results of little aesthetic meaning. Mixed media are very effective on textured and coloured, or dark, supports.

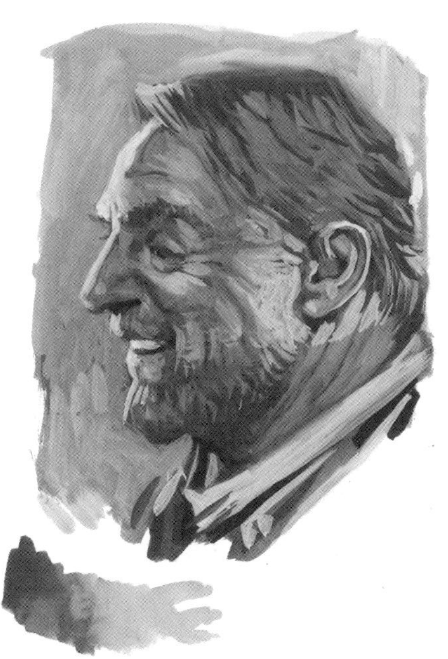

Gouache (or tempera) *is a very attractive medium that can take on graphic qualities, offering properties midway between those of watercolours and those of oils or acrylics. As with watercolour, the paint is diluted to the required density using water (although if white is added this will also lighten the shade of a colour) before being applied using a brush made from hair. As with oil paint, a thinned wash will permit the application of a quick-drying glaze, while paint laid down in a thicker consistency – which will also dry relatively quickly – will cover and hide underlying layers in one go. This allows you to work both spontaneously with free-flowing brushstrokes and also to execute high-resolution, clear and detailed work. Gouache paint can be applied to just about any surface that has some key and is not water-repellent. This includes paper, card, canvas, canvas-board and many others. The surface of the finished work has a pleasing matt look. Gouache lends itself to mixed-media work with pen and ink, graphite, charcoal and coloured pencil.*

I have divided the process of creating a portrait into five (hopefully self-explanatory) consecutive steps for depicting the shape of the head. This is one of the many intuitive and structured approaches to executing a work; approaches which have nonetheless proven themselves to be very useful in helping artists to start portraying any type of subject successfully.

The procedure consists of the following stages:

Step 1 Set down a concise but accurate indication of the overall dimensions and the main proportional relationships.
Step 2 Indicate the structural volumes.
Step 3 Fill in the areas of shadow in a simplified way.
Step 4 Modulate the light and dark tones more fully.
Step 5 Continue to work on tone and detail until the desired effect has been achieved. Once the use of the medium, the method and the way of 'seeing' has been mastered, each artist will then find his or her own personal style of expression and way of working.

PRACTICAL ADVICE

It is useful to outline very briefly some advice on portrait 'practice'. In the subsequent chapters some of these subjects will be developed with the help of diagrams and examples.

TYPES OF PORTRAIT

Given the great variety of poses a human being can take on and the psychological wealth which characterizes every personality, the artist has to assess what 'pose' to suggest to the model so that these elements are displayed in the most suitable way to achieve a likeness.

In addition, all individuals have their own characteristic posture and typical movements which are part of their 'being'. On the other hand, there are elements of physical behaviour and social convention which allow us to place the subject in the profession and 'status' they belong to or aim for. One can therefore differentiate between two types of portrait: 'formal', where the subject's pose follows traditional configurations, and where a lot of attention is paid to **composition** (see pages 58–63), the environment and the, at times symbolic, décor; and 'informal', where the model's pose is spontaneous as he or she is captured in a casual pose or while carrying out some regular activity in a normal environment. It is an effective and modern way of portraying people which is a legacy of 'instant' photography and requires a lot of skill and good taste from the artist. Expressive portraits also belong to this category; that is those where the subject is, for instance, caught smiling or in motion.

FRAMING

Whatever the type of portrait, you need to choose how to represent the subject. Do you wish to draw just the head (or part of the face), or the whole figure. To make the portrait more expressive it can be useful to draw just part of the body including, for instance, not just the head but also the shoulders, the torso and the hands. Draw a lot of sketches to find the best pose and a composition which is effective, well balanced, and not monotonous. Avoid dispersing the visual interest of the viewer and bear in mind that the focal point must be the face and, above all, the eyes. Note that the hands can be as expressive as the face, because of their 'movement', as well as their shape and their role in the composition. Therefore, if you think your model's hands have character, do not hesitate to include them in the drawing.

SUBJECTS

To portray a human being you need not just to be able to capture and draw their features, but also to hint at the character and the mood of the model: this encapsulates the artistic quality of a portrait. I have found it useful to include some advice specific to the different types of subjects you are likely to draw. Always obtain from your subject permission to portray them and, if need be, to exhibit the drawings you have done.

Children (See pages 40–47 and 204–341)
A child's head is proportionally bigger than that of an adult, especially in the skull, which is far bulkier than the face. Eyes and ears look big but the nose is small and upturned; the bone structure is minute and the jaw rounded. Drawing children is difficult because they are restless and don't like being looked at. In many instances you will find useful a photograph taken by surprise to avoid 'grimaces'. Children's delicate features need weak and diffused lighting: strong artificial light or direct sunlight create strong shadows which may alter the physiognomy and cause them to half-close their eyes.

Women In portraits of women, as well as searching for the subject's personality, there is also a tendency to enhance the aesthetic aspect. Choose informal poses, spontaneous if the subject is young, or more austere and serene if she is more mature. Avoid, however, affected or excessively 'theatrical' poses. In many cases you will find it useful to draw the whole figure so that clothes and background can help to convey the subject's personality.

Men The male portrait was traditionally more formal, representing an 'official' image linked not just to the subject's physical features, but also to their social standing. Sometimes side lighting, with its interesting contrasts, helps characterize the features and shapes of the male face. Young subjects often turn out better if drawn in spontaneous poses and expressions, while mature men are better suited to more composed and 'dignified' poses. Make sure that the model does not cross his arms in front of him or appear authoritarian and off-putting.

Self-portrait (See page 82) Almost all artists have drawn, painted or sculpted their own portrait. If you do the same, you will find that it will help to considerably improve your portraiture skills. Position yourself in front of a mirror and study your reflected face experimenting with different types of lighting and poses and then choose the pose you find most comfortable and which shows the 'real you'.

The elderly (See pages 32–39) Elderly people, both men and women, are very interesting to draw because their faces, marked by the passage of time and characterized by their everyday expressions, tell a 'story' of life and experiences. For this reason it is easier to capture their physiognomic traits, than it is with young people, and achieve a true likeness. Choose poses suited to the wisdom and tolerance which should come with old age.

Avoid strong and direct light on the model. Even if effective, it can easily lead you to draw an unflattering portrait and can unpleasantly emphasize any irregularities of the skin. Note the 'anatomic' changes in elderly people's heads: wrinkles on the forehead, near the eyes and the mouth, and on the neck; whitening and thinning of the hair; hollowing of the eyeballs; lengthening of the ears, and so on.

THE SIZE OF THE DRAWING

In a portrait drawing the dimensions of the face should not be more than two-thirds of the real face to avoid altering the proportions. Make sure the face is not at the very centre of the drawing surface, but slightly higher and to one side (see page 58).

CHOOSING THE POSE

(See pages 59–63 and 65) Usually, a portrait reproduces the head and shoulders, i.e. the torso, but it could also include the arms, the hands or the whole body.

If you draw from life, make sure the model sits in a natural and comfortable position, and that their face is more or less level with yours. The pose should be relaxed, but clearly convey the subject's character to enable you to capture the psychological, as well as the physical likeness. It's better to choose a pose which highlights the physical features of the subject, so place yourself at a distance of about 2m (6½ft) to offset any foreshortening effects.

As a rule, the three-quarter view is considered the most effective, but profile or full face can also be interesting.

LIGHTING

(See pages 66–68) Lighting should be gently diffused, and from just one source (window or lamp) positioned slightly higher than the subject and from the side. This will highlight facial features, but will do so gently, preventing the formation of ugly shadows under the nose, the lips and around the eyes. Avoid intense artificial light (for instance, from a spotlight) as well as direct sunlight, both of which create such effects; they emphasize the tiniest creases in the skin and affect the subtlety of the modelling. In addition, they force the model to contract their facial muscles giving a frozen, unnatural expression.

CLOTHING

Clothes have considerable importance, particularly in a full-figure portrait, both for their compositional and aesthetic function, and because they not only supply information about the personality, social status, and emotional state of the subject, but also about the era and background. Therefore, leave your model free to choose what to wear and limit yourself to suggesting some items of clothing which, because of their shape and arrangement, can make the composition of the drawing more effective. Arrange the folds and notice how different they look depending on whether the fabric is light and soft (lots of little folds) or heavy and stiff (a few thick folds), although in both cases they radiate from the top of the 'centres of tension': shoulders, elbows, knees, etc. Draw the folds which, due to their direction and size, are the most significant and ignore the minor ones which could create confusion. In some circumstances, partial nudity (shoulders, breast or back, for instance) can enhance the portrait of female subjects with a particularly vivid and strong personality.

Continued overleaf ›

HAIR

(See pages 56 and 212–213) Hair (as a whole and in relation to colour, quantity and style is essential to characterize a face. The artist can use its look to improve the composition of a portrait, by weakening or enhancing, by contrast, the model's physiognomic traits.

If you draw female subjects (whose hair is usually thick), go for simple, tidy, well-cut hair. Hair should be treated as a whole. Capture its colour and overall form and try to pick out the most significant locks. Of these, assess areas of shadow and light, and lines of separation and disregard small, insignificant highlights and single hairs – you will need just a few fine, sharp strokes to suggest them. Use a fairly soft pencil to draw thick confident lines, in various directions, to achieve unusual 'weave-like' effects. Draw the hairline very carefully, making it irregular and soft and pay particular attention to the forehead and the temples.

THE BACKGROUND

A portrait requires a background which is plain and unobtrusive, in shades which don't clash with one another or weaken the subject's appearance. Before you start, decide whether a light background (the white of the paper, for instance) or a dark one is suitable. In some cases the subject's surroundings (workplace, house, garden, etc.) can act as background – treat it as if it were a landscape or an interior – making sure, however, that it doesn't overshadow the face or the figure.

TECHNICAL AIDS

Photography is useful to record spontaneous and fleeting images of the subject, to have a point of reference when it isn't possible to organize sittings, and to portray children. Take photographs yourself (modern cameras make this easy even if you are not an expert) as they should be a source of reference rather than images to copy passively. Allow for perspective distortion and, to avoid or reduce it, do not get too close to the subject. If possible, use natural lighting and avoid the flash, which is unsuitable for portraiture.

Sketches Get used to doing plenty of little sketches to study the main lines of the face and figure of the subject you are drawing (especially if you are working from life). Gauge the best composition, the most suitable lighting, the most convenient dimensions, etc. by walking around your subject. These sketches, even if done quickly, require careful observation, almost a commitment to 'explore' the aesthetic possibilities offered by the model. It may be from them that a successful portrait depends. After you have become more experienced at drawing the face, you may want to start painting it; then you will find it useful to do a preliminary study, more complex than the sketches, to help you sort out any aesthetic problems and to note down all the information which you will need for the definitive work.

HOW TO ACHIEVE A LIKENESS

As we know, portraying a human subject means perceiving and representing both the physical and the psychological aspect of the model. To achieve a physical likeness (see page 70), pay particular attention to the overall shape of the head (drawing 'from the general to the particular') and exactly evaluate your subject's proportions, both in the face as a whole and between its elements (eyes, nose, mouth, etc.). To achieve a psychological likeness, converse with your model, try to understand their character, preferences, habits, and observe the environment where they live and work. Of course this is not always possible, but it can be very useful to give you an idea of the most suitable pose and which aspects of their character are worth highlighting or bringing to the fore.

Enlarging Whether you are planning an accurate drawing, or you are attempting to paint a colour portrait, you will need to trace on the final support (paper, canvas, card, etc.) the outline which will serve as a base for the work. To this effect, you can, at least to start with, take advantage of a number of methods to effortlessly enlarge a sketch or even a photograph to the desired dimensions. You can use an ordinary slide projector to magnify the image on to the support and trace the face or figure's main contours.

Alternatively, you can use an episcope: an optical tool which allows you to enlarge and project images from opaque supports (photographic prints, sketches or reduced photocopies of drawings and paintings, etc.). These are practical devices, almost 'tricks' which may even harm one's artistic growth if one becomes too dependent on them. More appropriate, therefore, is the 'grid of squares' method, which is well known even at school level. Draw a grid of squares on the image to be enlarged (whether a drawing or photograph) and then transfer that same grid, with the same number of squares, enlarged, onto the larger surface.You can then easily transfer strokes within individual squares, keeping them in proportion.

The working environment If you have your own studio, or at least a room in the place where you live, and you are determined to devote yourself body and soul to portraiture, you will find some furnishing accessories to be useful. For example: a chair, an armchair or a small couch for the subject to be comfortable and relaxed upon while posing; a lamp which will allow you to adjust the intensity of the lighting so that the model is properly lit; a radio or a small TV to make posing less of a burden for your sitter (and for you). Remember to allow for frequent breaks and to take advantage of these intervals to study your subject with different expressions and in different poses.

You can place your support on an easel or the tilting surface of a special table, but often it will be sufficient to place it on a stiff board (made of wood, cardboard or MDF), 50 × 60cm (19¾ × 23½in), and which you can rest on your knees. This simple equipment, together with your favourite drawing media, will come in useful when working outdoors, in public places or (and I hope this will happen soon) when going to the house of someone who has commissioned you to do a portrait.

Portrait study, oil on canvas, 30 × 40cm (12 × 15¾in)

This portrait was not drawn from life but from the photograph on the left. Look carefully at the two images to find out to what extent the photographic information has been adhered to, highlighted or disregarded in the drawing.

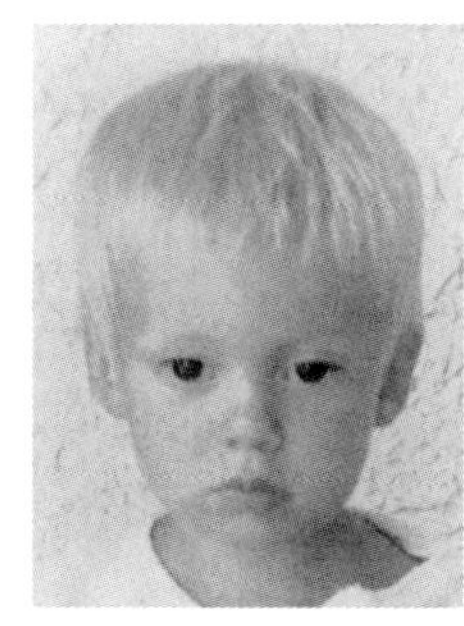

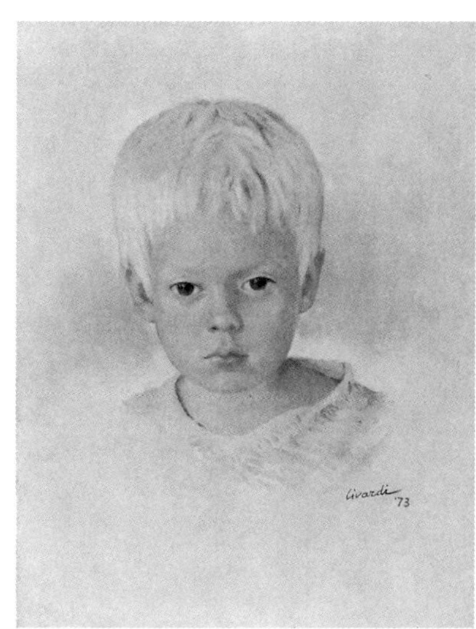

ANATOMY AND EXTERNAL MORPHOLOGY

If the artist knows at least the basics of anatomical structure, portrayals of the human head will be much easier and more precise. Indeed, the shape of the cranium – which differs slightly between the sexes – determines the overall shape of the head and influences individual facial characteristics.

BONE AND ARTICULAR STRUCTURE

The skull, in a broad sense, has two parts: the cranium (braincase), which is ovoid in shape; and the facial block, which houses some of the sensory organs (eyes, nose) along with the start of the digestive and respiratory routes, and is a pyramid shape. The bones are almost all joined to each other with fixed joints that do not allow movement. The only mobile bone is the mandible, which moves within the limits permitted by the temporomandibular joint.

The human cranium is made up of numerous bones that are fused together to form its two component parts: the cranial vault and the facial block. The only moveable bone is the jawbone, which, hinged on its two condyles, is articulated in relation to the cranial vault. The muscles of the facial system are also numerous. Acting on the jawbone are the masticator muscles, including the masseter and temporal muscles, while the much finer cutaneous muscles act on the skin alone, performing such physiological functions as moving the lips or the eyelids. These latter muscles are responsible for the gestural movements of our faces, creating all the nuances of expression by which our physiognomy communicates our psychological states. Both the shape and the size of the cranium are subject to change during our stages of maturation and ageing and this has far-reaching effects on the head's proportions and on individual characteristics (see the diagrams on pages 208–211). Added to this, different evolutionary and environmental influences have led to differences in the cranial shapes depending on ethnicity, as shown below.

The neck should not be overlooked when drawing, painting or modelling the human head, and its muscular structure and dimensions require careful consideration. An accurate copy of the neck conveys the dynamics of the subject's pose and lends vitality and expressiveness to the face. While the head as a whole could be geometrically likened to an ovoid in shape, the neck is comparable to a cylinder with two prominent muscle bundles running down its sides: the sternocleidomastoid muscles with the trapezius muscle at the back of the neck.

The external anatomical forms are arranged in layers over the bony structure and are influenced by it to a great extent.

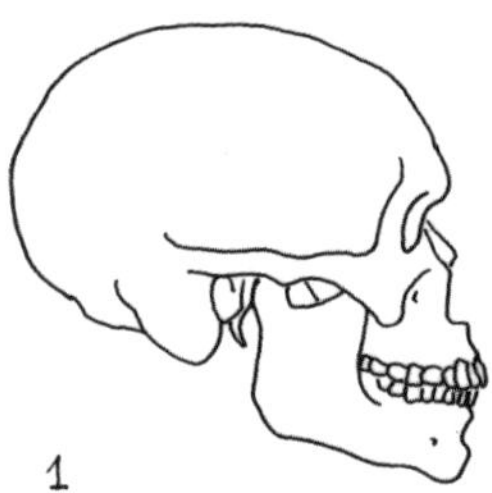

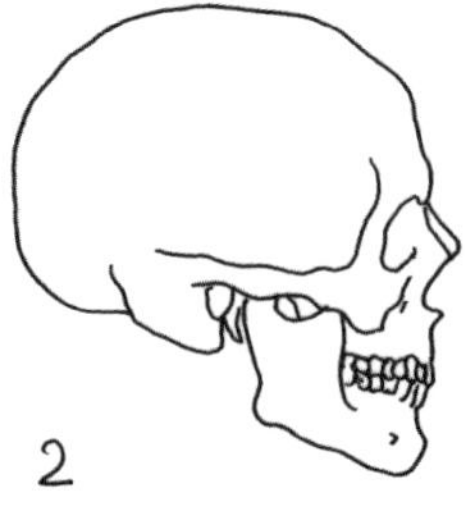

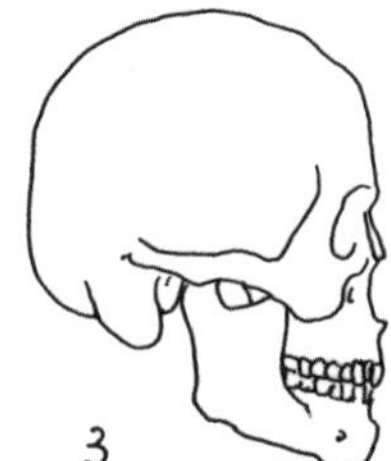

Outlines of crania belonging to the three major human groups (male, lateral view):

1 *Negroid*
2 *Caucasoid*
3 *Mongoloid.*

THE BONES

The shape of the skull determines by and large the external morphology of the head and can be divided into two parts: the brain case and the facial block, which comprises several bones tightly joined together to achieve a solid structure.

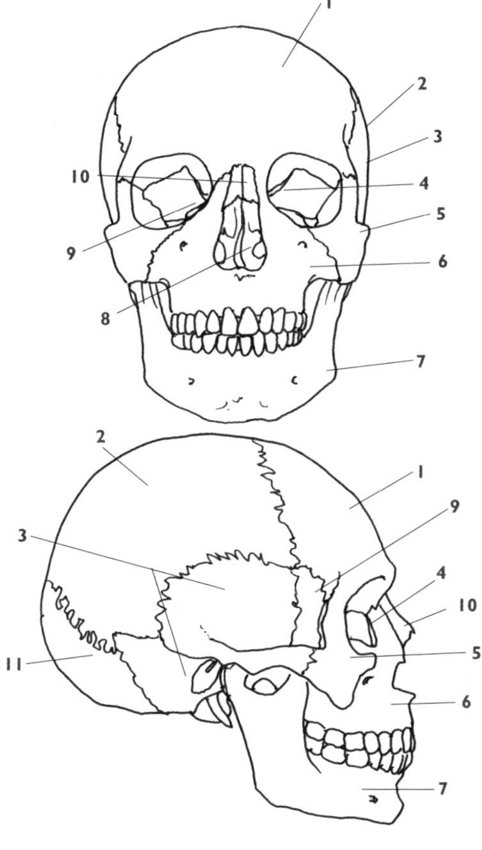

BONES

1 *frontal bone*
2 *parietal bone*
3 *temporal bone*
4 *lacrimal bone*
5 *zygomatic bone*
6 *maxilla*
7 *mandible (jawbone)*
8 *vomer*
9 *sphenoid*
10 *nasal bone*
11 *occipital bone*

Left, views of the cranium

If you get the opportunity to observe a real skull or to buy a plastic one, practise drawing its main outline. Render it from different angles, as I have shown in these quick sketches below, and apply the principles of perspective and structural simplification.

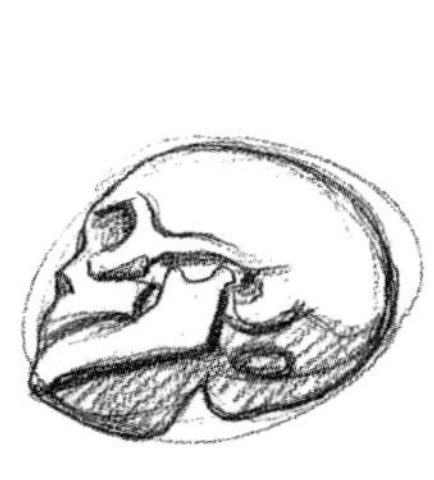

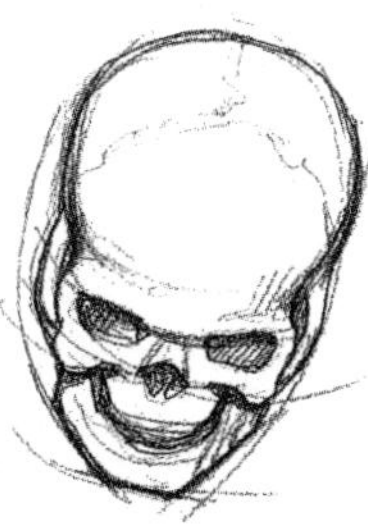

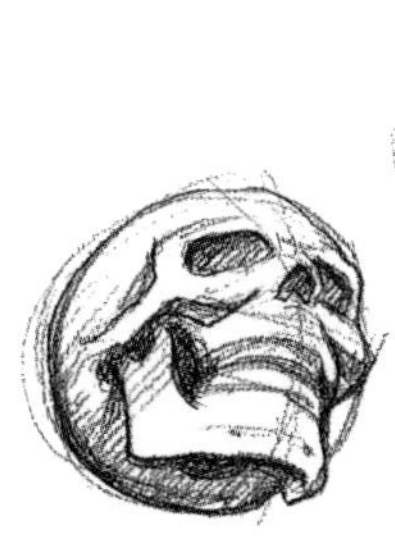

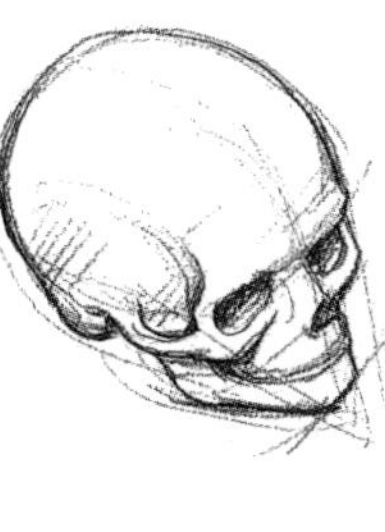

When we look at a living person, the bone structure of the head appears in direct, immediate proportion to the external forms, as the soft tissues – the muscles, skin and subcutaneous tissues and so forth – faithfully cover the surface, increasing and adding to it to various degrees.

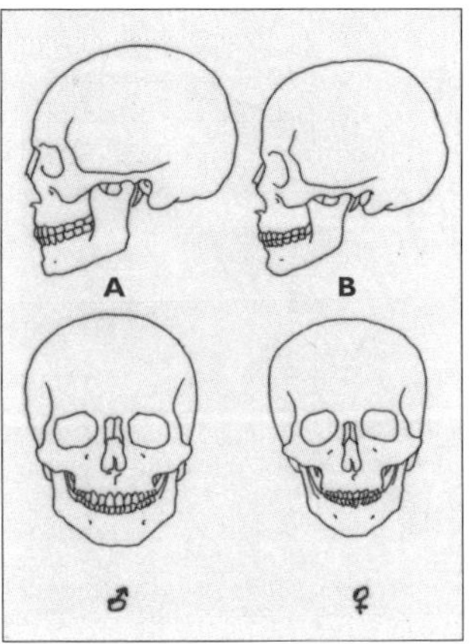

Side view and front view of a typical male adult skull (A) and a typical fvemale skull (B).

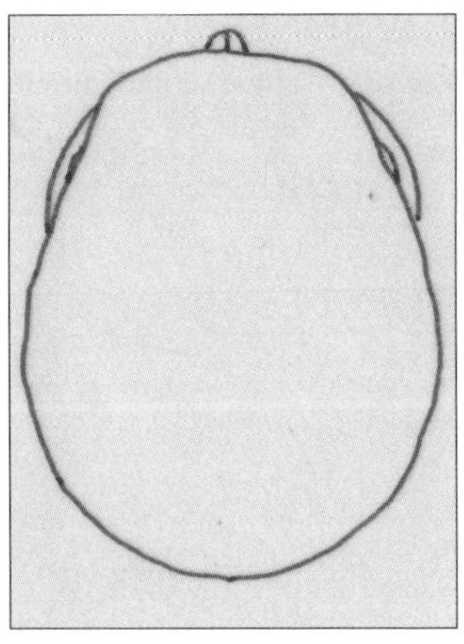

View of the skullcap in a zenithal projection: note that the width of the frontal lobe is smaller than the occipital lobe.

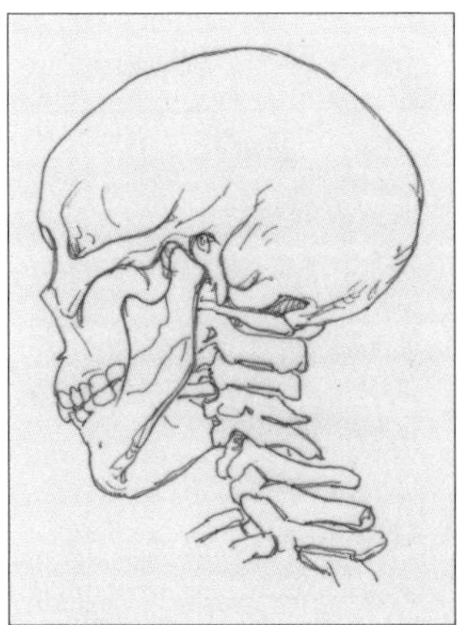

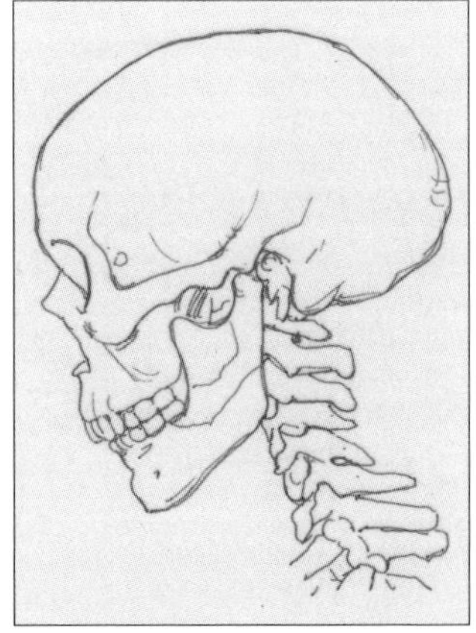

The skull in an oblique-posterior (above left) and lateral (above right) projection. It is joined to the cervical part of the spine, which is the support axis for the muscles running along the neck. The sum of the movements allowed by each vertebral joint contributes to the extension, flexion, and lateral extension and flexion of the head.

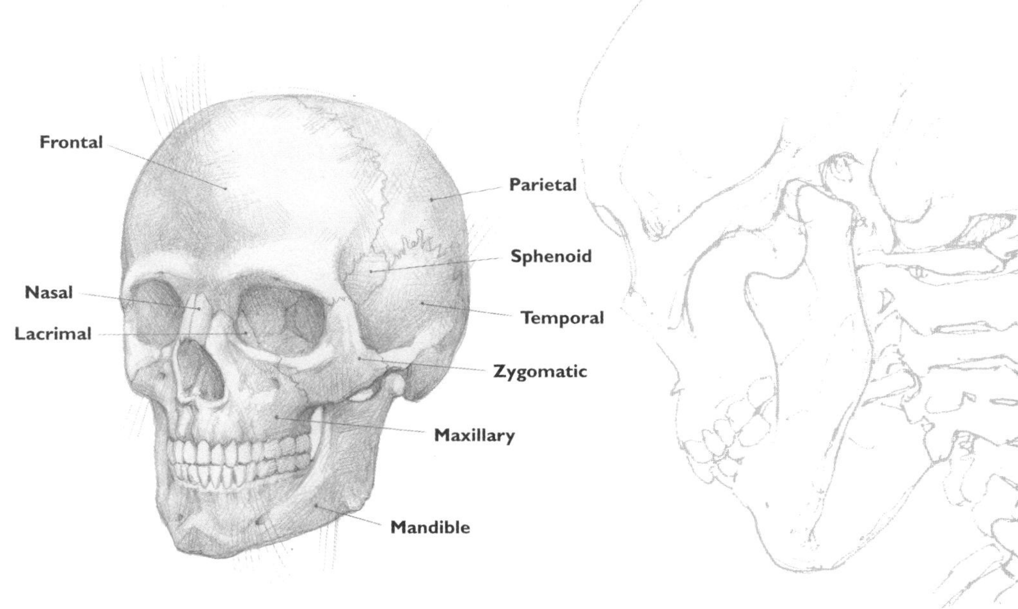

Oblique-frontal projection of the skull in toto*, with an indication of the bones that determine the outer appearance.*

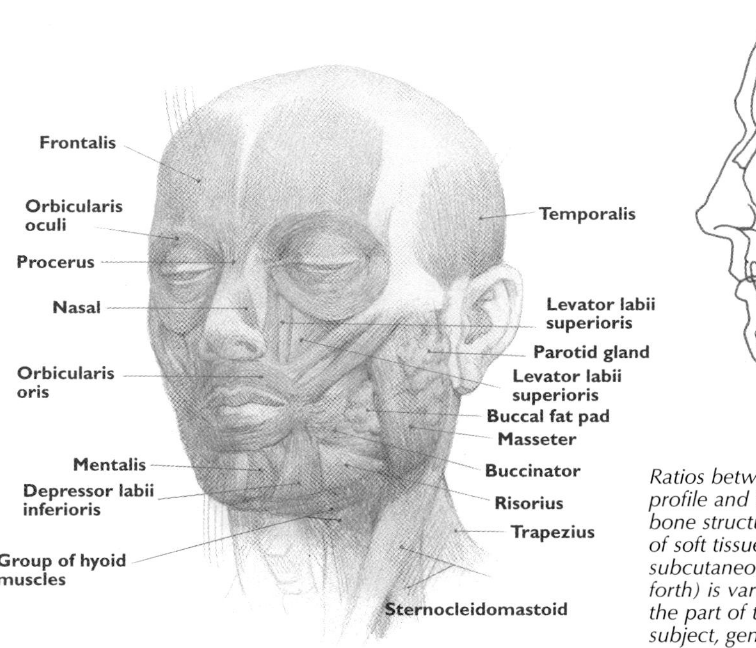

Oblique-frontal projection of the outermost muscles of the head and neck.

Ratios between the in vivo *face profile and the corresponding bone structure: the thickness of soft tissues (muscles, skin, subcutaneous layers and so forth) is variable in relation to the part of the face, age of the subject, gender, state of health and nutrition, etc. The eyeball has a precise ratio to the orbital cavity that houses it.*

Muscles are discussed in more detail overleaf.

THE MUSCLES

There are two types of muscles that cover the skull: the mimetic muscles, which allow facial expressions and are connected with the skin, mainly spread over the facial block; and the masticatory muscles, which dictate the mobility of the jaw (temporal muscle, masseter muscle, pterygoid muscles and so forth). They become stratified on the cranial bones whose external shape they follow pretty closely, as they are very thin.

Also study the main neck muscles – inevitably, they appear in nearly every portrait. Many neck muscles are connected to the base of the skull and are used to rotate, flex or extend the head. A thin, long muscle (the platysma) runs under the skin of the neck and works on the jaw, lowering it.

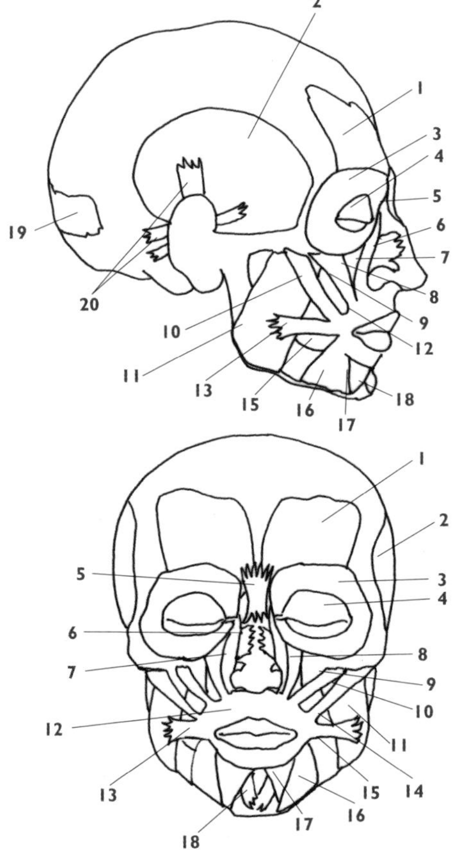

MUSCLES

1 *Occipitofrontalis*
2 *Temporal fascia*
3 and 4 *Orbicularis oculi*
5 *Procerus*
6 *Nasalis*
7 *Levator labii superioris*
8 *Levator labii superioris (infraorbital)*
9 *Zygomaticus minor*
10 *Zygomaticus major*
11 *Masseter*
12 *Orbicularis oris*
13 *Risorius muscle*
14 *Levator anguli oris*
15 *Buccinator*
16 *Triangularis*
17 *Quadratus labii inferioris*
18 *Mentalis*
19 *Occipitalis*
20 *Auricular muscles*

Left, views of the main superficial muscles.

Here I show the connection between the bone structure and the external morphology of the male head. Carefully examine the position of the ear, the eye and the lips. The thickness of the section between the bone surface and the external surface of the head is determined by the layer of muscle, the adipose tissue and the skin.

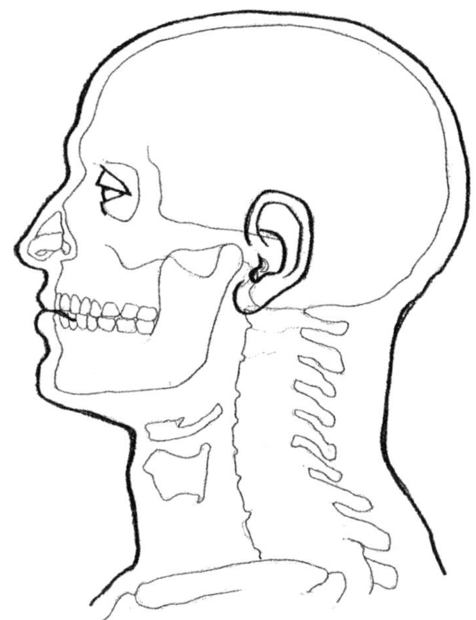

THE FEATURES OF THE FACE

The **eyes** are the most immediately significant part of the face: the eyelids cover the eyeballs following their spherical form and, when opened, reveal the iris, the pupil and those parts of the whites of the eyes which indicate direction of gaze.

Lips are extremely mobile and expressive, manifesting a large range of our emotions and revealing some aspects of individual character. The lips rest on the half-rounded protuberances of our jawbones and the parting between upper and lower lip runs along a line at approximately mid-height of the upper incisor teeth.

Ears are complex objects but can be simplified with a few lines describing the basic concentric shapes of the exterior auditory cone. Our ears have very precise individual characteristics that become more and more marked with advancing age.

The **nose** is a prominent feature and should be rendered with solidity but also with fine judgement when evaluating its size and projected shadows.

Hair on the masculine face requires careful treatment – as does the hair of the head, which should be depicted in terms of its larger areas of mass and gloss with only a few sparing fine precise lines suggesting the hair's softness, its colour and styling.

These features are explored in more detail on pages 48–56 and 214–217.

HEADS AND FACES OF ADULTS

The faces of adults in their prime (20–50 years of age) are a rich source of study material for the artist, especially for artists who are setting out to tackle the great themes of the portrait and the human figure. The reasons for this are many: the facial features have by this age become definite and well delineated; the anatomical structure and proportions of the face fully conform to standard types; the expressive characteristics of the face now appear with their full range of meaning.

People's heads vary enormously in size, in their characteristics and in their shapes, but they can all be brought within a useful proportional framework, which is helpful for simplifying the face's forms and coordinating its structures. If we draw two horizontal lines – one passing along the line of the eyebrows and the other touching the base of the nose on a 'generalized' person's head, whether male or female, we will find that the face, from the hairline on the forehead down to the base of the chin, can be divided into three sections. In the frontal view, two vertical lines passing through the centres of the pupils will enclose the narrower forms of the nose and lips.

Body build varies from person to person but, in general, there are three main types: 'short-limbed', for a short and compact stature, 'long-limbed', for tall and thin and 'average build' for builds somewhere between these two. The head, too, will follow the characteristics of body type, with many nuanced variations in between: as we all know from experience, people's heads and faces may vary between the above categories to take on the shapes generally described as round, square, wide and low-cast or long and narrow.

Even though the framework below applies to the faces of adult males and females alike, it is worthwhile noting some typical differences between the two sexes in the overall shaping of the head. A woman's head tends to be more rounded in form, with a lower and less expansive distribution of facial features and the female forehead tends more to the vertical, while the angle of the jawbone is more rounded than that of the male. Women tend to have more abundant heads of hair and their necks tend to be more slender than those of men.

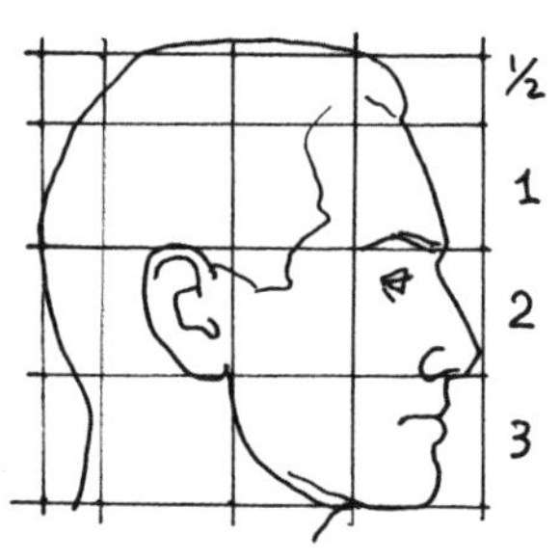

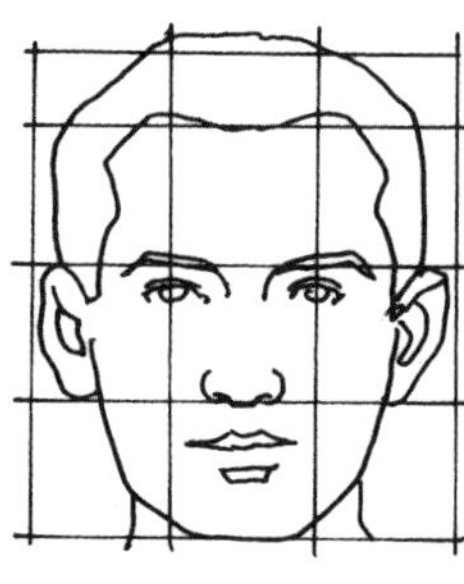

A

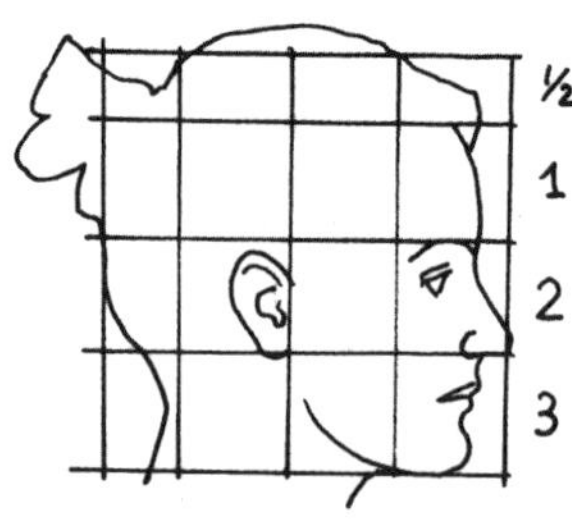

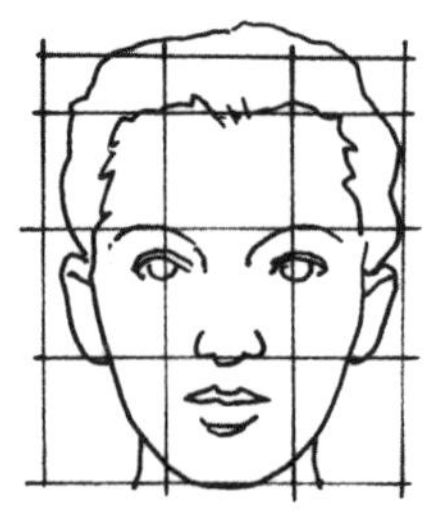

B

'Standard' proportions of the adult head and face:

A *male*

B *female*

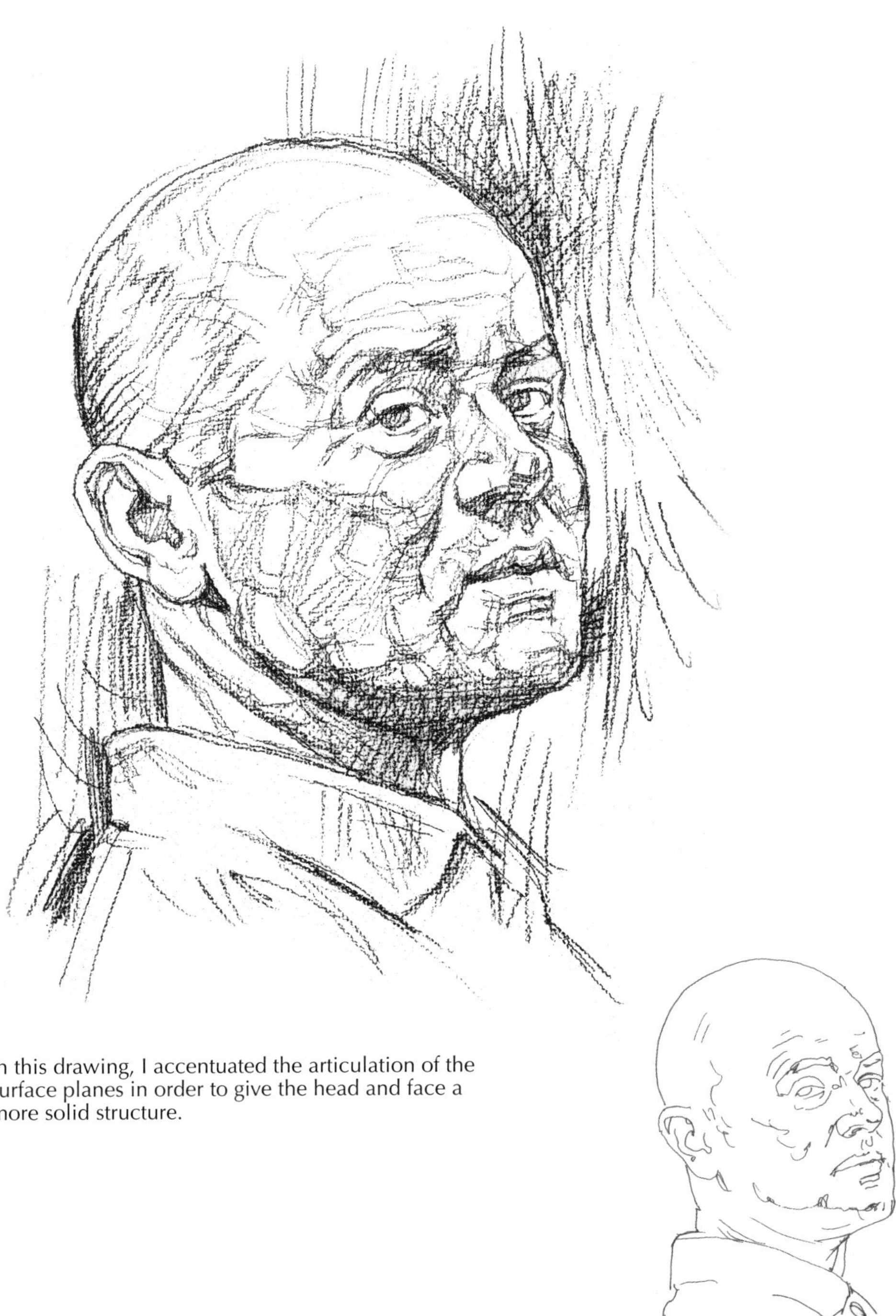

In this drawing, I accentuated the articulation of the surface planes in order to give the head and face a more solid structure.

DRAWING THE ADULT HEAD

PROPORTIONS

When drawing the head it is necessary to make sure that the proportions, i.e. the relative dimensions between its various constituent elements (eyes, ears, nose, mouth) are indicated correctly and precisely. Pay close attention to the overall structure of the head and evaluate its main characteristics as it is mainly from these that a good likeness depends. Details alone, even if minutely reproduced, almost invariably result in a vague and unsatisfactory portrait, when placed in a general context which lacks accuracy.

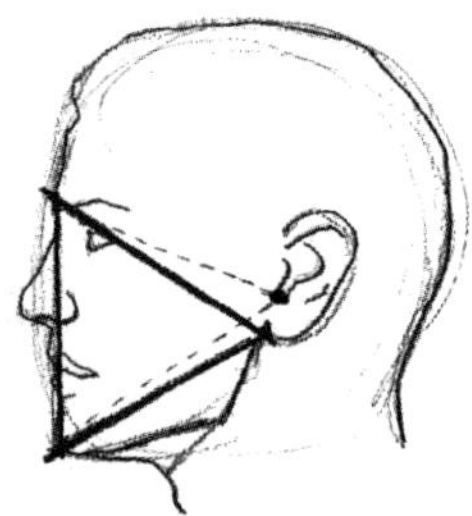

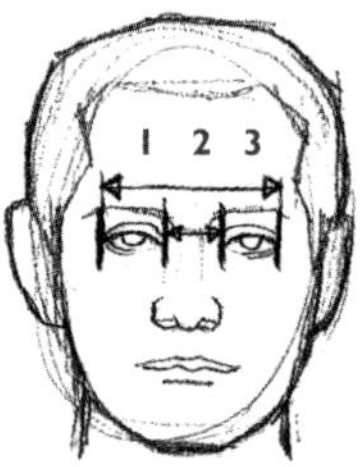

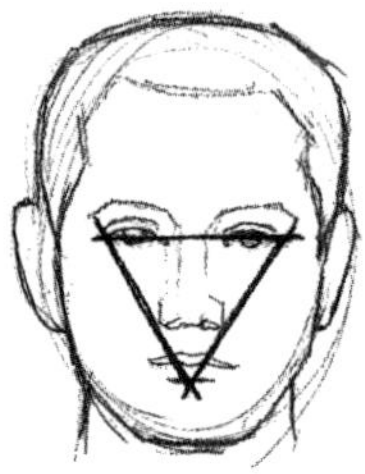

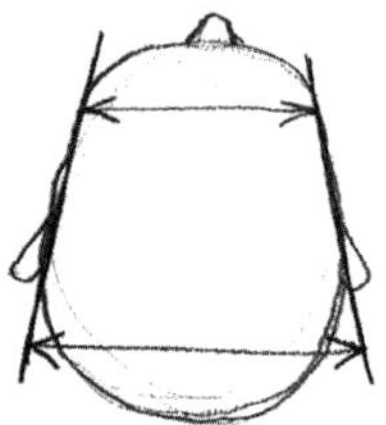

If studied carefully the diagrams above will provide you with the simple and essential points of reference and proportions of a 'typical' head seen in frontal and lateral projections. Compare them with those of your model and assess whether they correspond or differ. The height of the face can be divided into three portions of equal size, which correspond to the height of the forehead (up to the hairline), that of the nose, and that of the lower part of the face.

In addition, note that if you join the three points located above the bridge of the nose, on the chin and at the corner of the jaw (near the earlobe), you have an equilateral triangle. The same figure is obtained if you join together the outer corners of the eyes and the base of the lower lip. The width of the eye viewed from the front is a useful reference for measuring the distance between the eyes (according to an old academic maxim 'between eye and eye there is an eye') and the width of the base of the nose level with the nostrils. Notice how, viewed from the top, the head's shape is an oval, broader at the back.

Each head follows a structural plan and spatial ratio between the individual elements that comprise it. When we draw a head (whether generic or individual) therefore, we must take the following into consideration:

- *A head has an overall ovoid shape and therefore constitutes a volume.*
- *The head's components are arranged symmetrically along the median axis.*
- *In oblique views, or from top or bottom, the linear perspective helps in the three-dimensional representation of the head* in toto.
- *Facial elements are arranged according to constant proportional ratios that are applicable roughly to all adults.*

PERSPECTIVE

Perspective is a graphic method which helps to represent spatial depth on a flat surface. Therefore, to be represented correctly, the head too needs to be drawn (like any other object) bearing in mind the rules of perspective.

The diagrams shown below will be enough, I think, to remind you of some of the basic principles, such as the horizon line, the viewpoint and the vanishing points. If you imagine the head within a cube whose edges touch its most protruding points, you will find it easy to 'put in perspective', fairly correctly the details of the face. You can then conduct a more accurate study considering the 'geometrized' head represented by two ovoids and a cylinder (see diagrams on page 30).

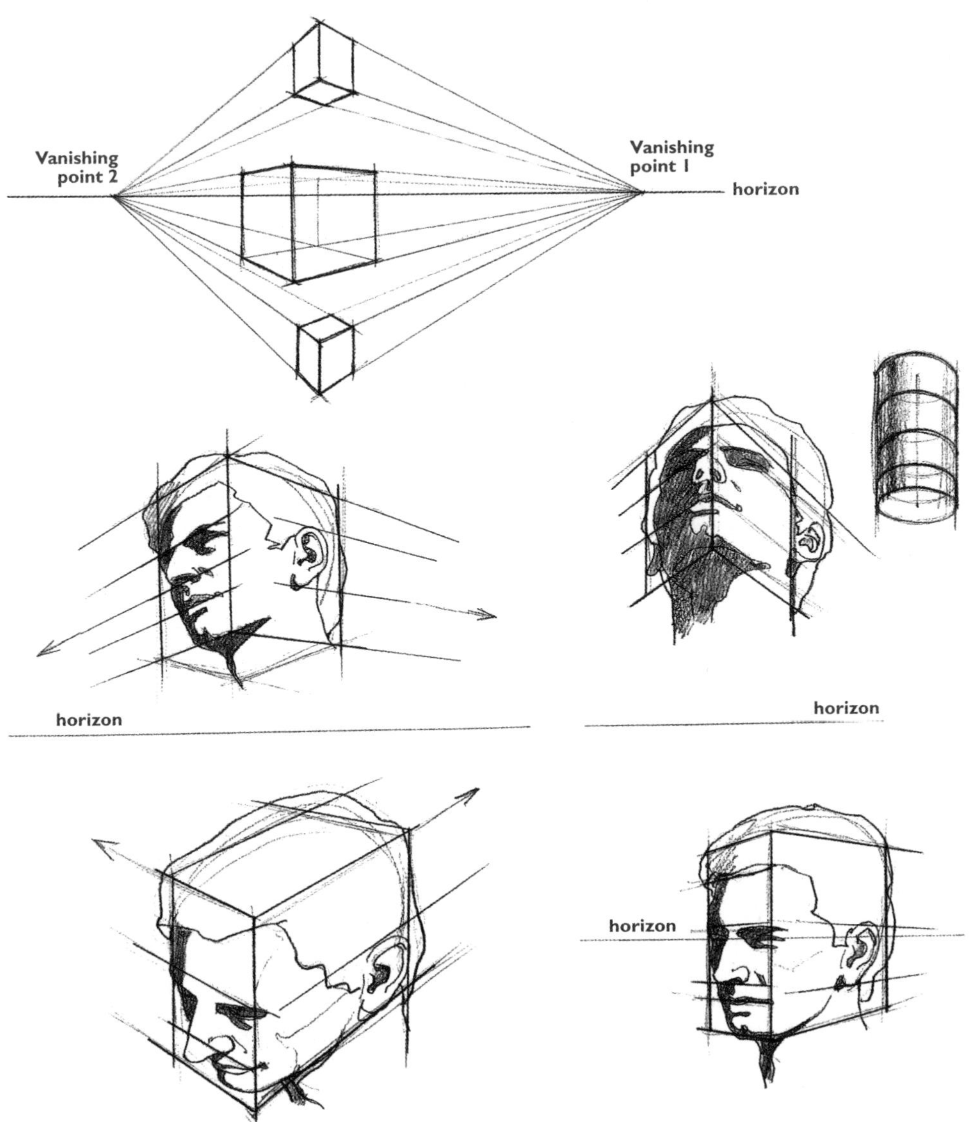

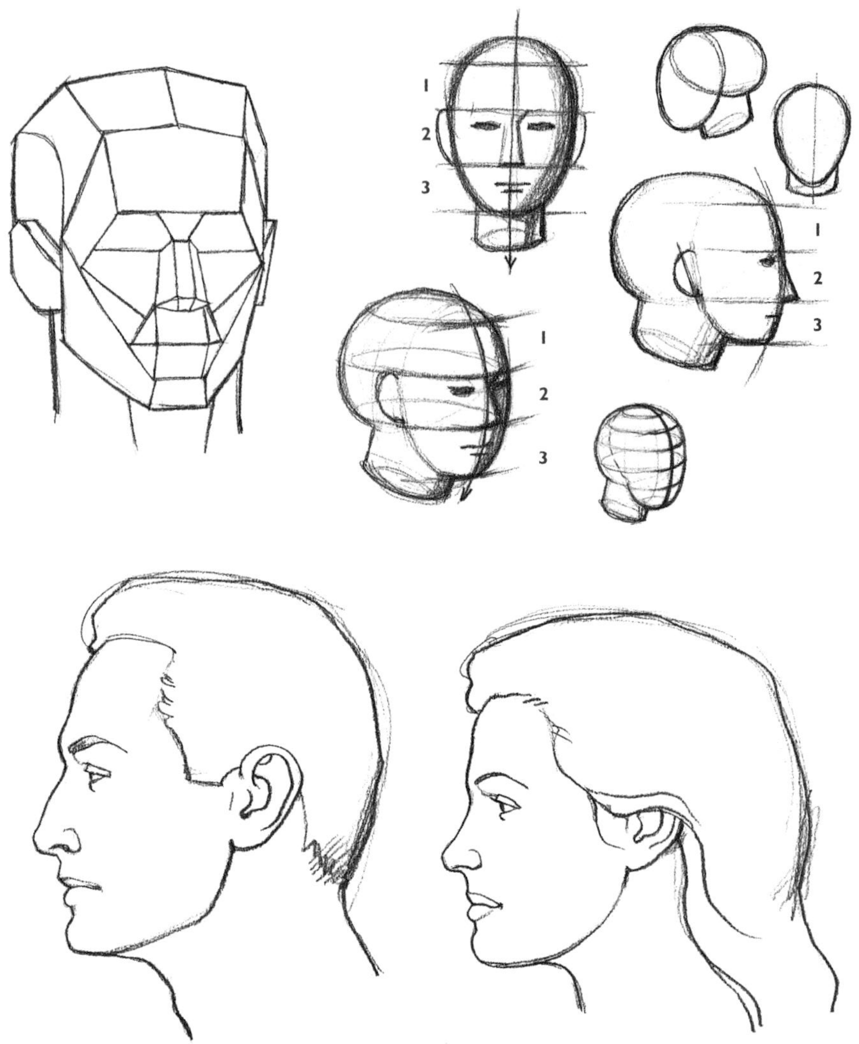

STRUCTURAL SKETCHES

As mentioned on the previous page, the head can be compared to the geometric shape of an ovoid and this, at the beginning at least, makes drawing it simpler, as far as proportions, as well as light and shadows are concerned. Notice how the two ovoids which represent the face and the skull can be superimposed. However, the roughly round shape of the head can also be divided into flat areas. As a whole, these 'surface planes', are useful for concisely shaping areas of light and shadow. Try drawing surface planes on to photographs which show heads in a variety of positions, and learn to recognize diagrams similar to the ones above.

When you first start drawing the head, which is a very complex shape, you are likely to encounter great difficulties and won't know where to start from. A traditional and scholastic, but very useful, approach is the one mentioned on these pages and which is developed further on pages 70–75. Bear in mind that in portraiture it is essential, first of all, to capture the overall individual characteristics of the model's head and then study the characteristics of the details and how they relate to one another.

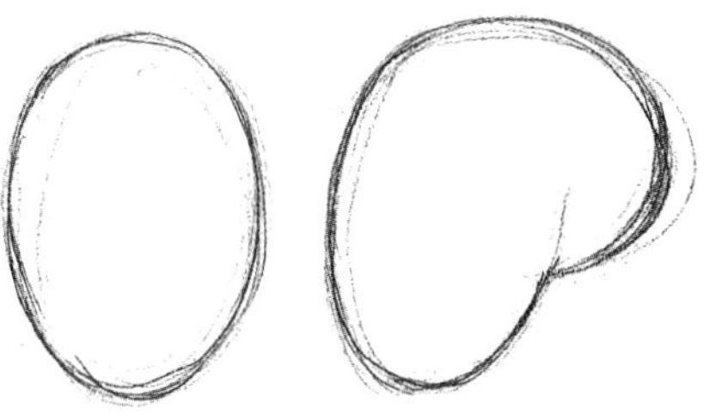

Stage 1

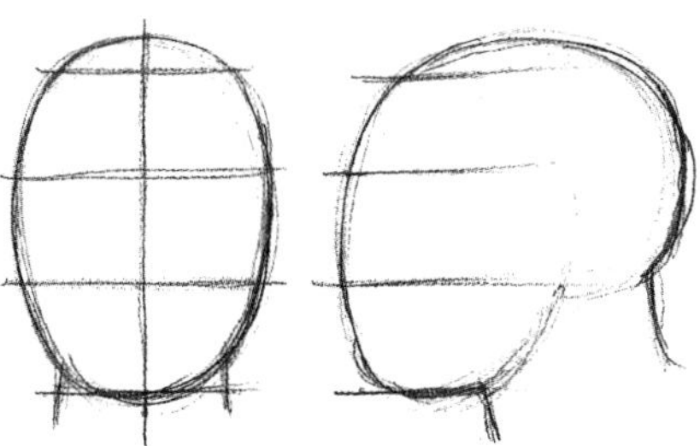

Stage 2

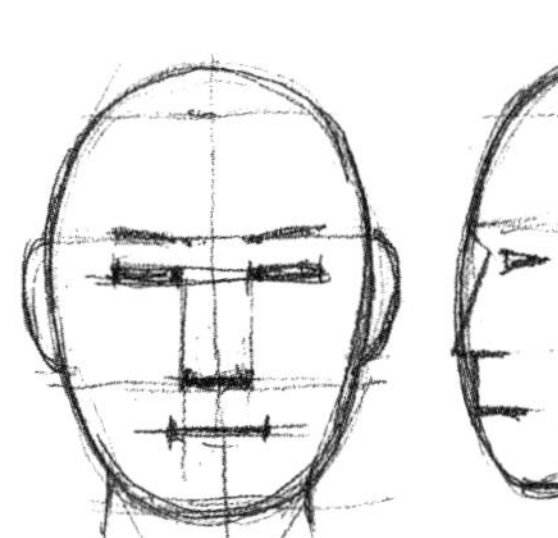

Stage 3

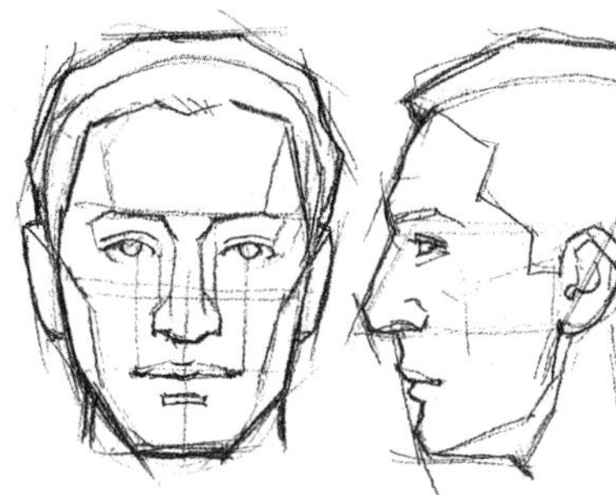

Stage 4

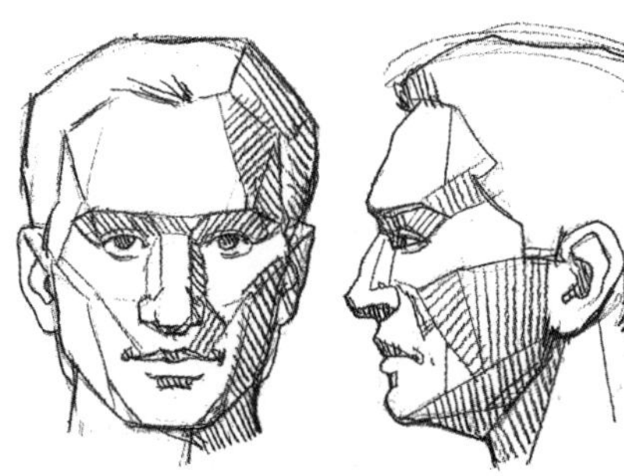

Stage 5

In these diagrams, limited to the front and side projections of a man's head, I have illustrated the various stages of structure.

Stage 1
Outline on the page the area you expect the head to occupy: draw a simple oval shape.

Stage 2
Indicate the proportions by way of four horizontal parallel lines more or less equidistant to suggest the three parts in which the face can be divided.

Stage 3
Carefully work out the position of the eyes, nose, mouth and ears by measuring their relative distances.

Stage 4
Thoroughly study how the elements of the head relate to one another, hinting at the 'planes', the hair, etc., coming close, little by little, to the natural shapes.

Stage 5
Continue to elaborate assessing also the light effects, that is, applying the 'chiaroscuro' – the contrast of light and shade in a drawing.

HEADS AND FACES OF OLDER PEOPLE

The time-worn faces of older people, marked by the ups and downs of life, make a welcome and much appreciated subject for the artist, offering many aspects for study through a variety of lines, mass, light, shade and form. As the face ages, it changes. This is only partly due to the presence of wrinkles, which become progressively more numerous and obvious. There is no need to reproduce every line on the face, or even to highlight any, which can all too easily lead to an involuntary caricature. It will suffice to make a good analysis of the directions taken by the main lines on the skin and the play of light and shade that they produce. Wrinkles may result from pockets of fat forming beneath the skin, as well as from the skin losing its elasticity, but they are also signs of oft-repeated facial gestures – some of them bearing witness to expressions that have characterized the face throughout its lifetime.

Knowledge of anatomy pays its greatest dividends when drawing the face of an older person. One of the signs of age is how the cranial and facial bones tend to rise to the surface (especially around the cheekbones and the orbits of the eyes), while the facial muscles begin to waste and deposits of fat form pockets around the eyelids and under the chin. Hair turns white and thins; the nose and ears have continued to lengthen gradually over a lifetime and lose their thickness; the folds of the neck become more pronounced; dark patches of various hues appear on the skin, and so forth. Even the face's proportions undergo a degree of change as loss of teeth and the thinning of the jawbone reduce the dimensions of the lower part of the face.

Older people make perfect models. They can be drawn unawares (while fully maintaining their spontaneity of expression and attitude), or asked to sit for a portrait; they will often be less impatient than younger models and be able to hold a calm, relaxed pose for an extended period of time.

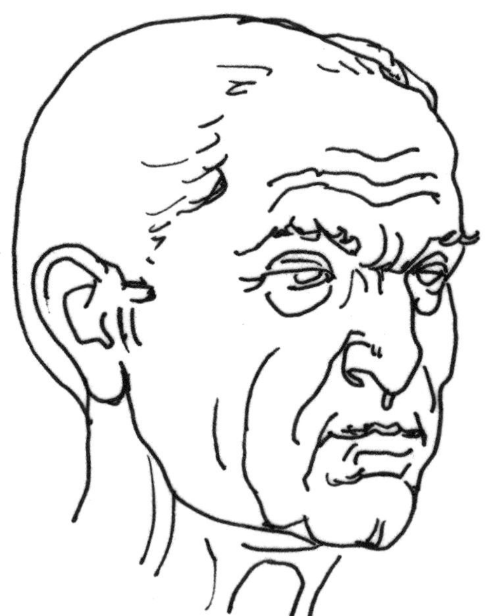

Drawing of the directions of the principal and most common folds and lines of the face: wrinkles are fairly superficial furrows, while folds are more substantial and pronounced. These are formed, in particular, on the forehead, around the eyes, at the sides of the nose and of the mouth, under the chin and in front of the ears.

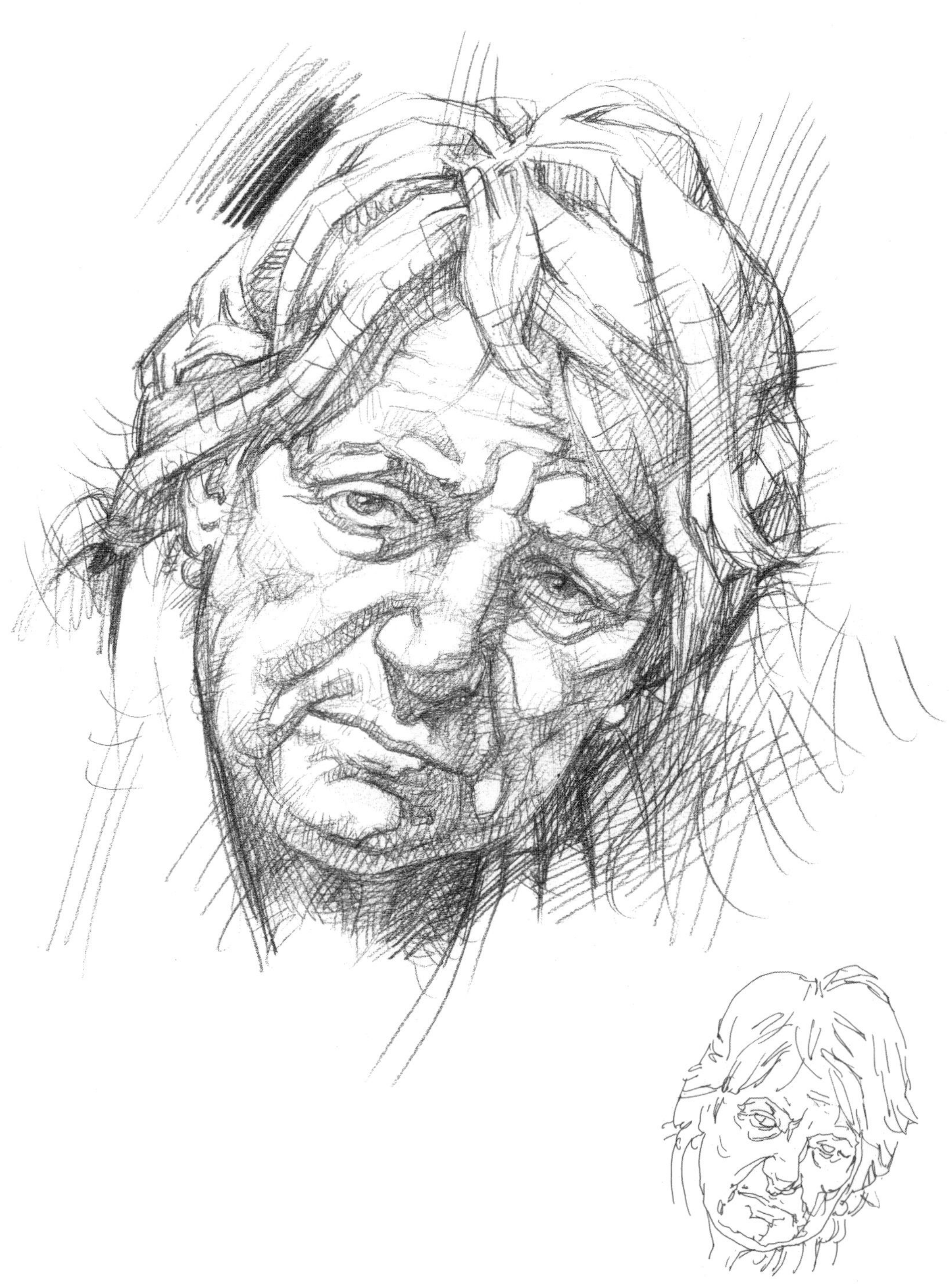

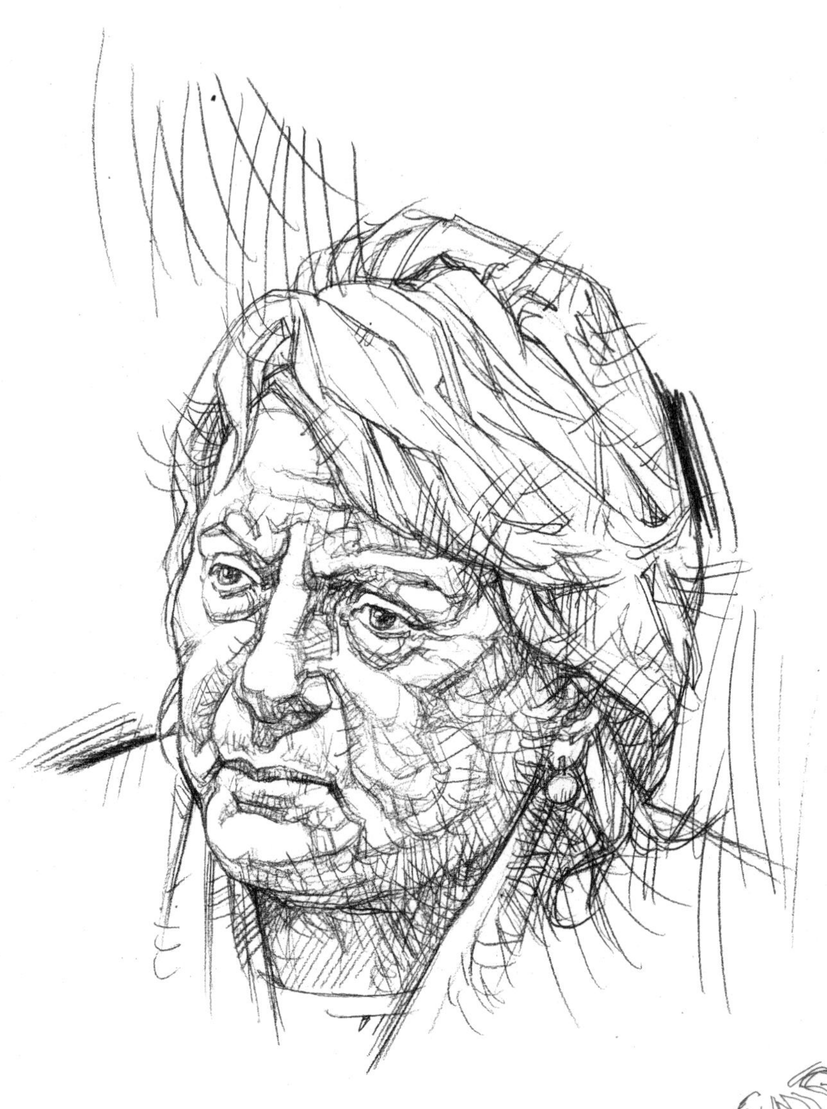

A face that has lived a long life tells us much about its owner, about character and the kind of life that has been lived. Wrinkles, creases and subcutaneous veins are in evidence and their arrangement is an important factor in portraying the model's physiognomy and in suggesting personality.

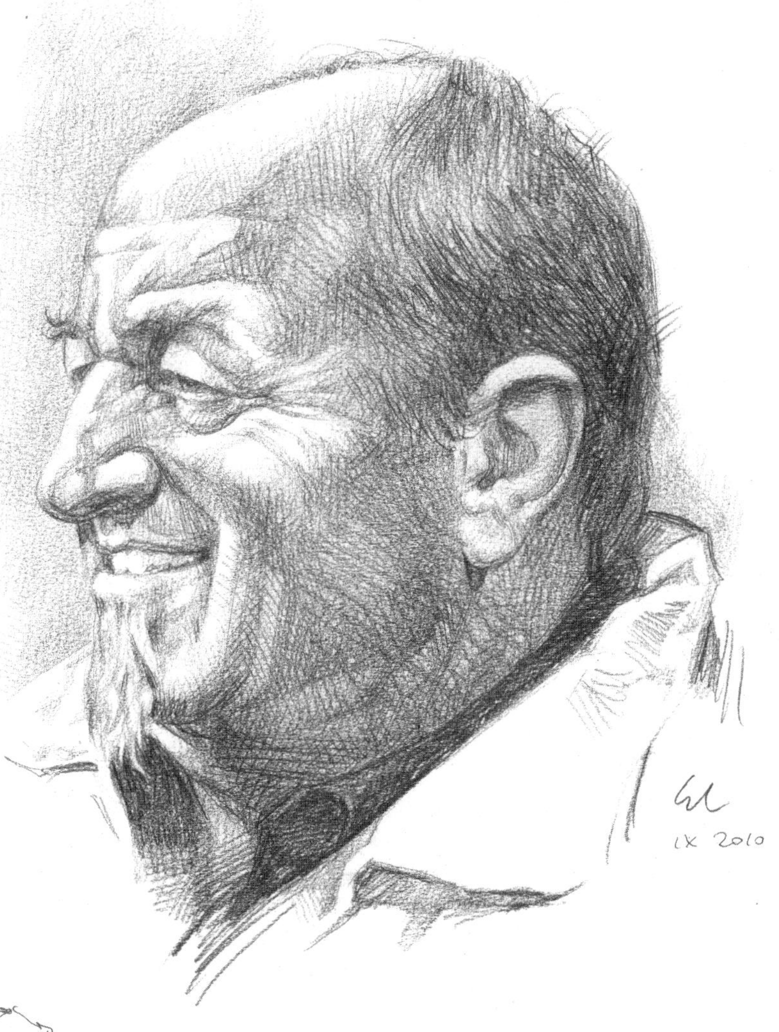

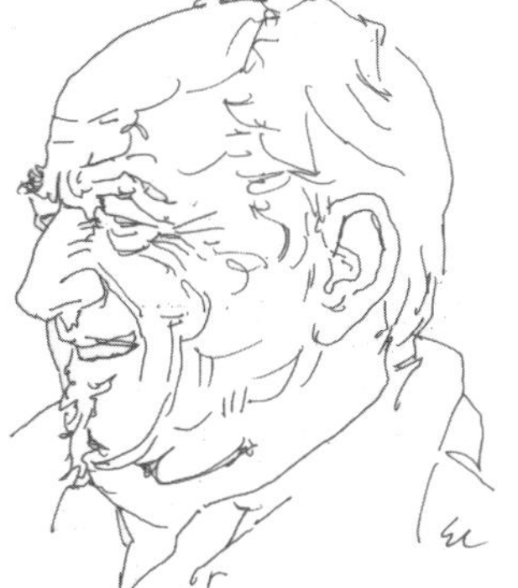

Particularly in the case of male subjects, the hair becomes sparser and recedes from the forehead and temples towards the apex of the head. Against this, the eyebrows thicken and characteristically long and vigorous hairs may appear in the nostrils and ears – at the entrance to the auditory canal. A three-quarters view of the head is an effective one, whether for a portrait or for an expressive sketch, as it sets off the rich modulations of shade and volume to good effect.

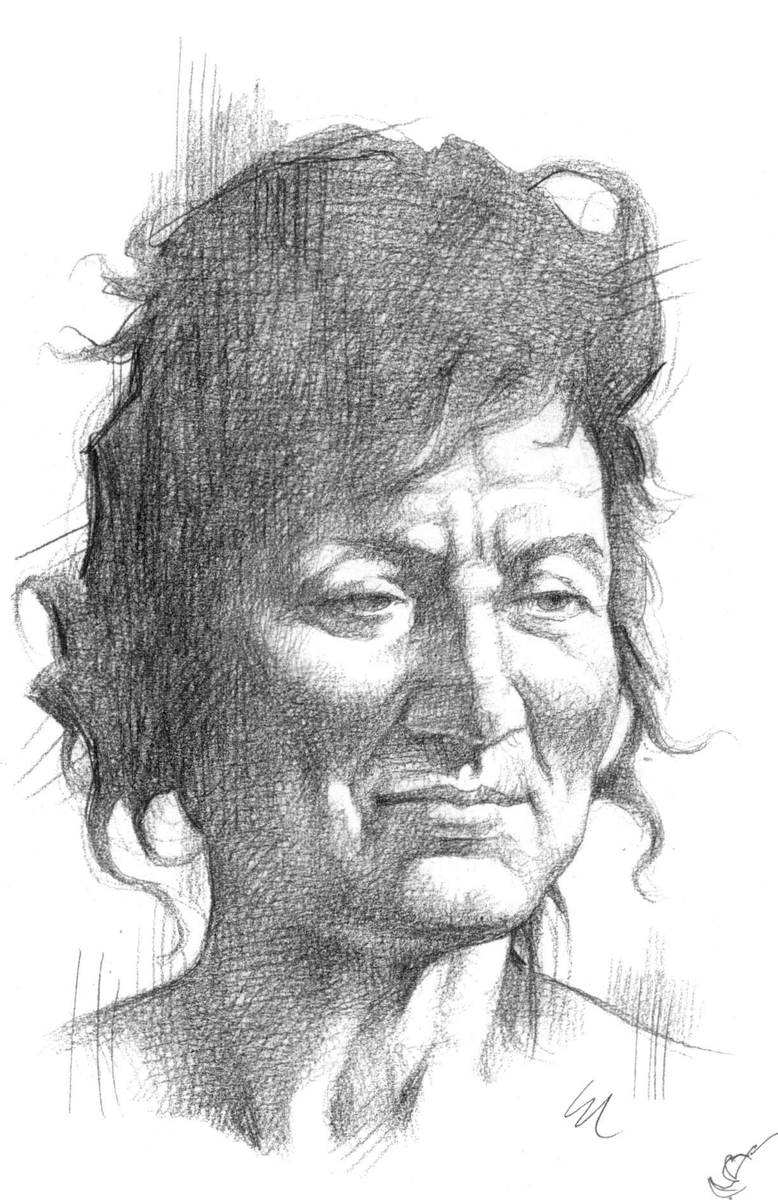

When drawing an older female face, it is a good idea to tone down the signs of old age. This is not for the sake of pleasing the model (if they are sitting for a portrait), but rather to attain more delicate and gradual effects of shading, uninterrupted by excessively deep marks.

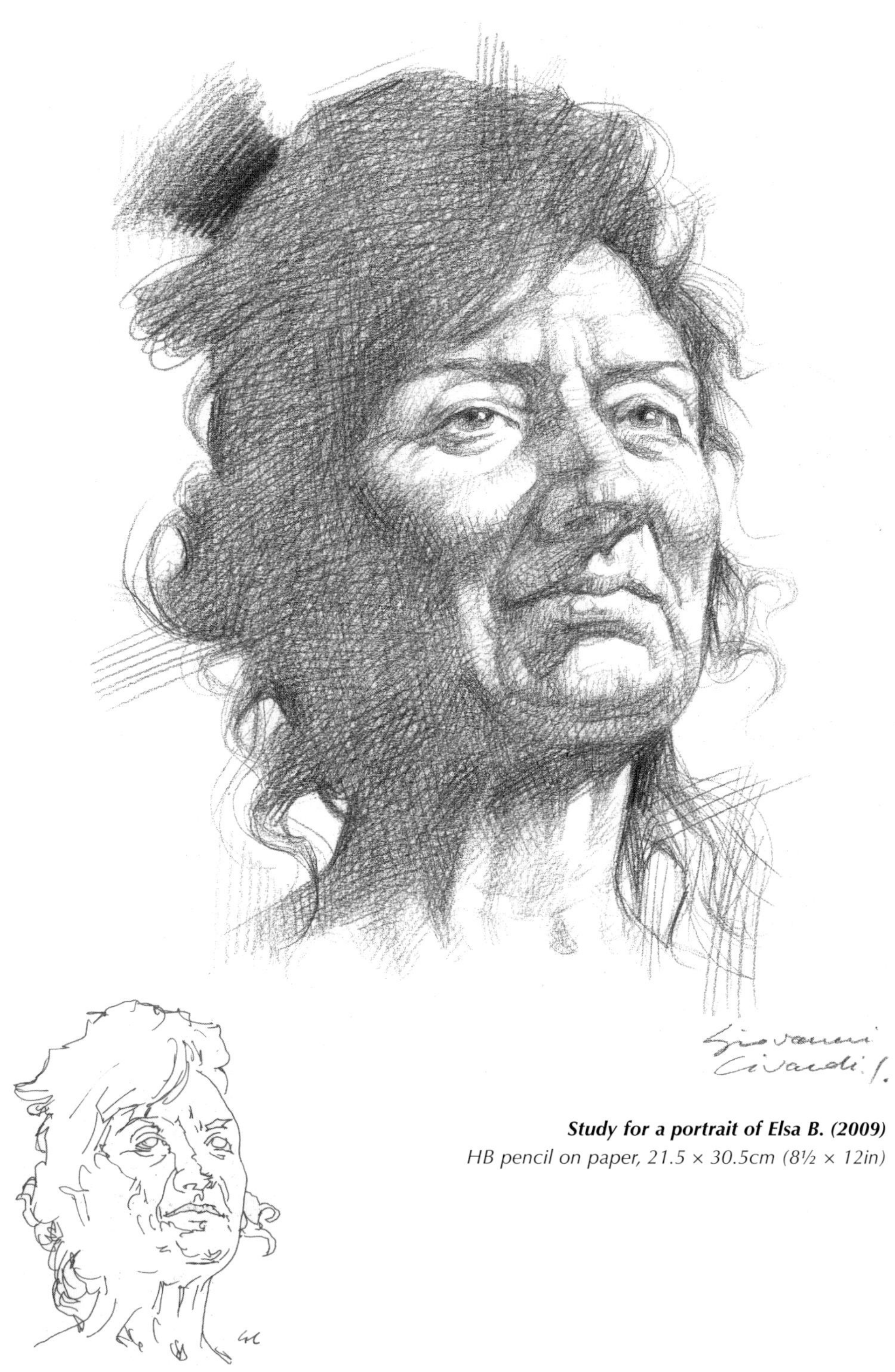

Study for a portrait of Elsa B. (2009)
HB pencil on paper, 21.5 × 30.5cm (8½ × 12in)

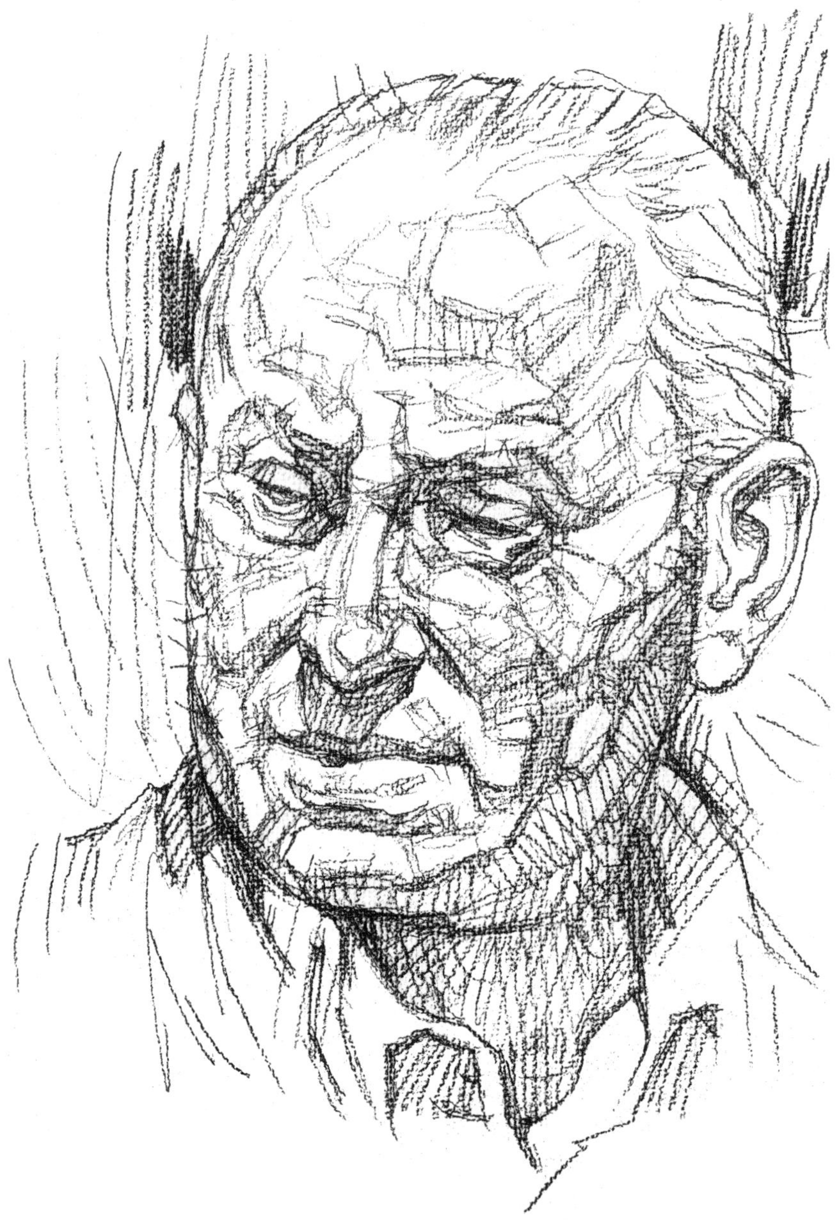

With an older man, the modulation of facial features is much more rich and complex than on a younger individual. This means that the planes into which the surface of the face may be broken down are much more numerous, and this will affect the way light and shade falls on the face.

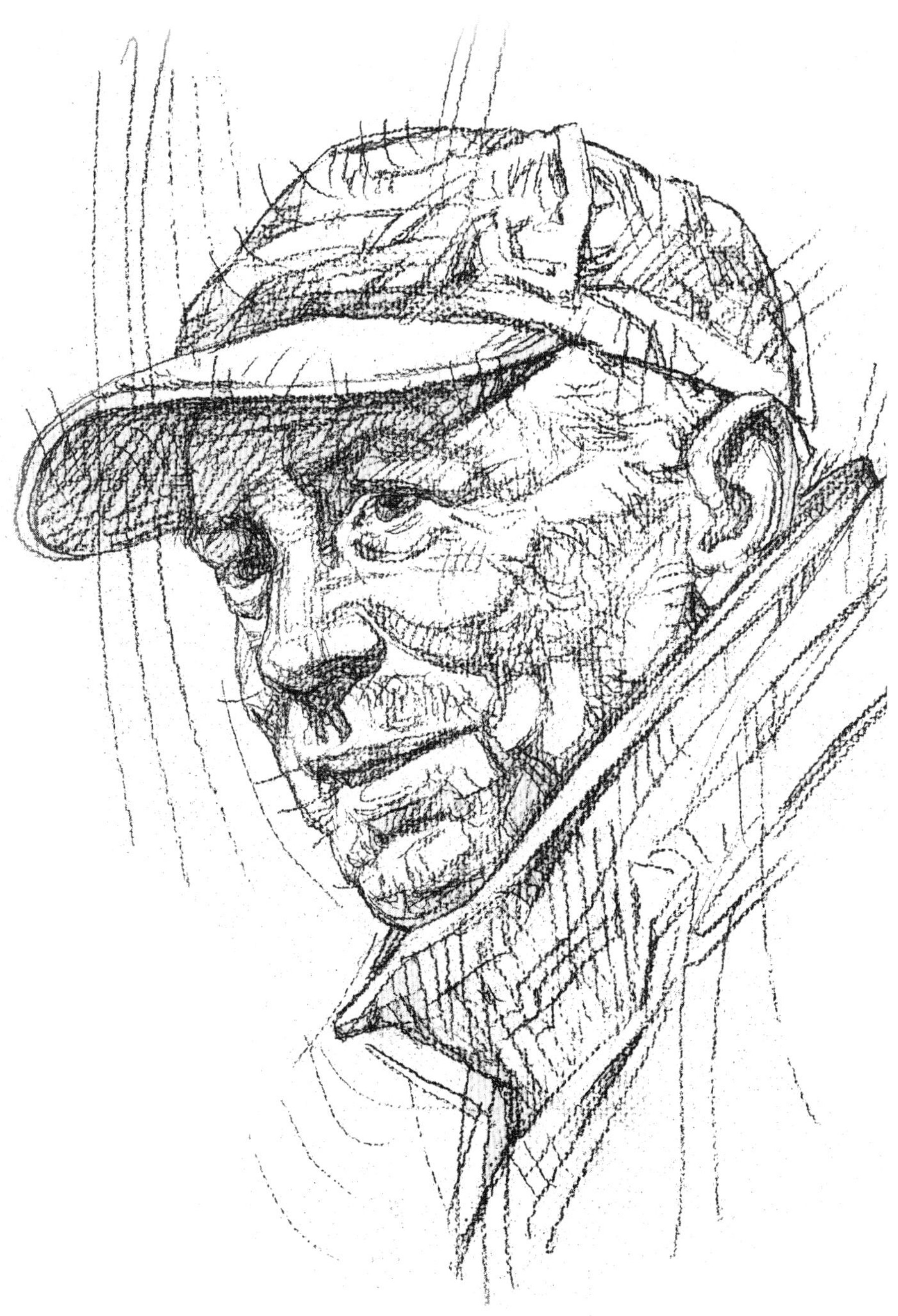

HEADS AND FACES OF INFANTS AND YOUNGSTERS

Always pursue your dreams – but stop before you reach them…

A drawing of the head and face of a child or an adolescent is based more on an analysis of proportions than on muscle anatomy. The proportions of an infant's head are indeed very different from those of an adult and they vary visibly as the child grows. The cranial vault is very rounded at birth, its size dwarfing that of the face, and this has the effect of making the eyes appear much larger.

The gradually changing proportions of head and face provide a visual indicator of the child's age. Particular attention should be paid, for example, to the length and shape of the nose, the position of the line formed by the eyebrows, the proportions of the ears (which may seem oversized) and the neck (which is slender and tubular in appearance), as well as the small, rounded chin. Make a mistake in your observation of the proportions and you run the risk of creating a drawing of an adult in miniature.

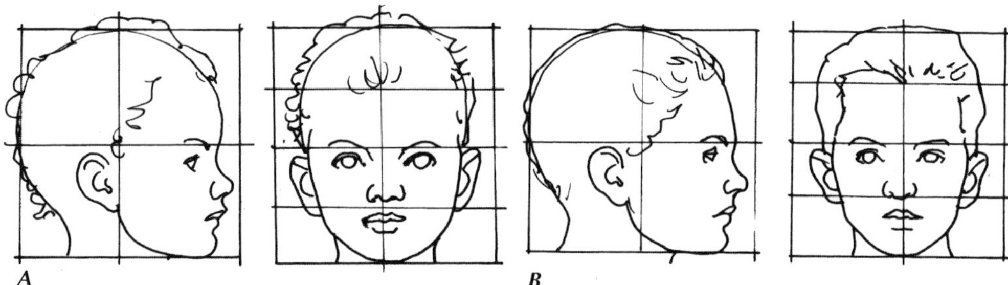

Grid for the proportions of the head and face of a child: at around two years old (A) and around seven to eight years old (B). The proportional relations remain similar for the sexes until at least adolescence.

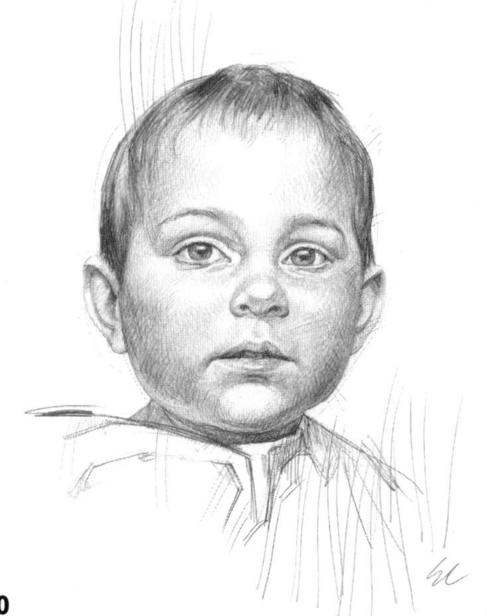

Portrait of N. (2010)

HB pencil on paper, 22 × 31cm (8¾ × 12¼in), with a structural guide in pen and ink

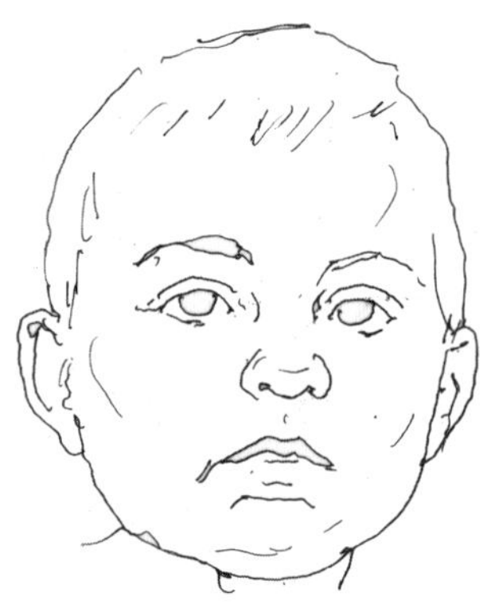

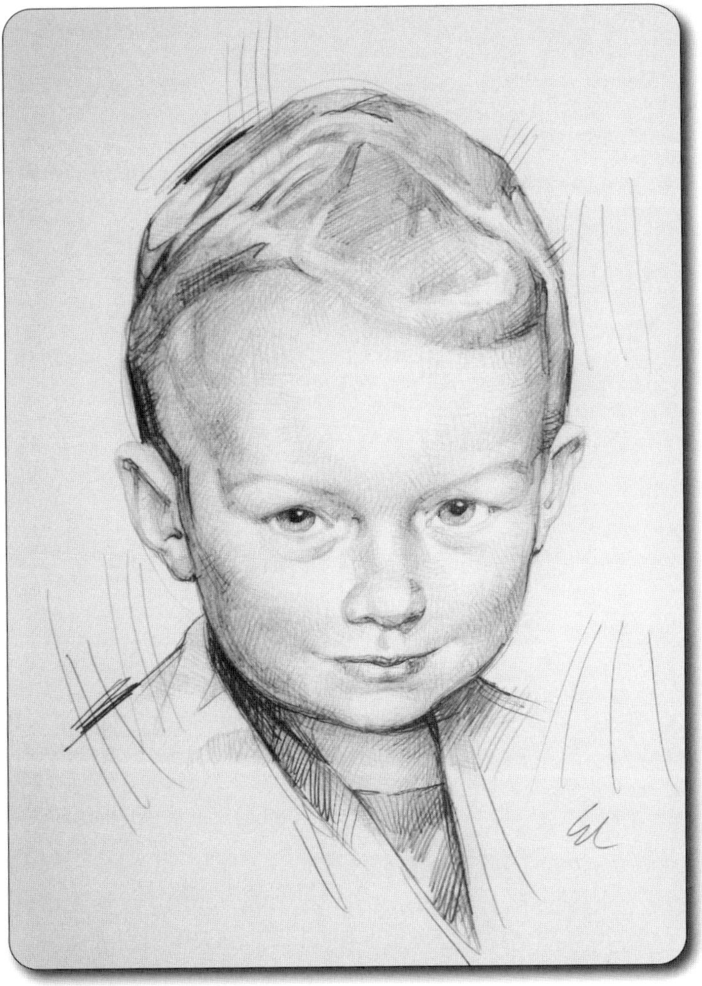

Portrait of W. (2010)
HB pencil on paper, 22 × 31cm (8¾ × 12¼in), with a structural guide in pen and ink

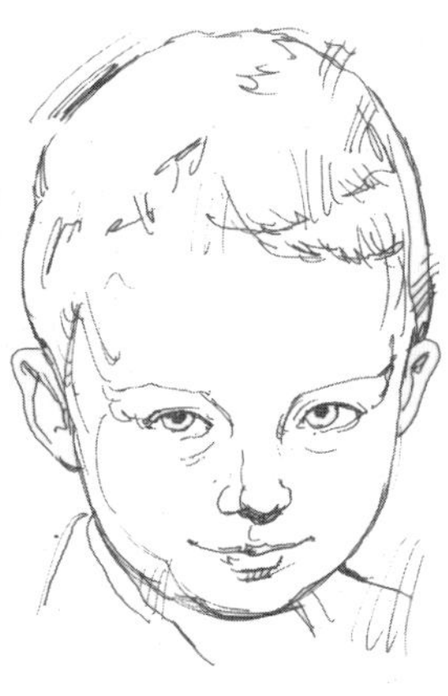

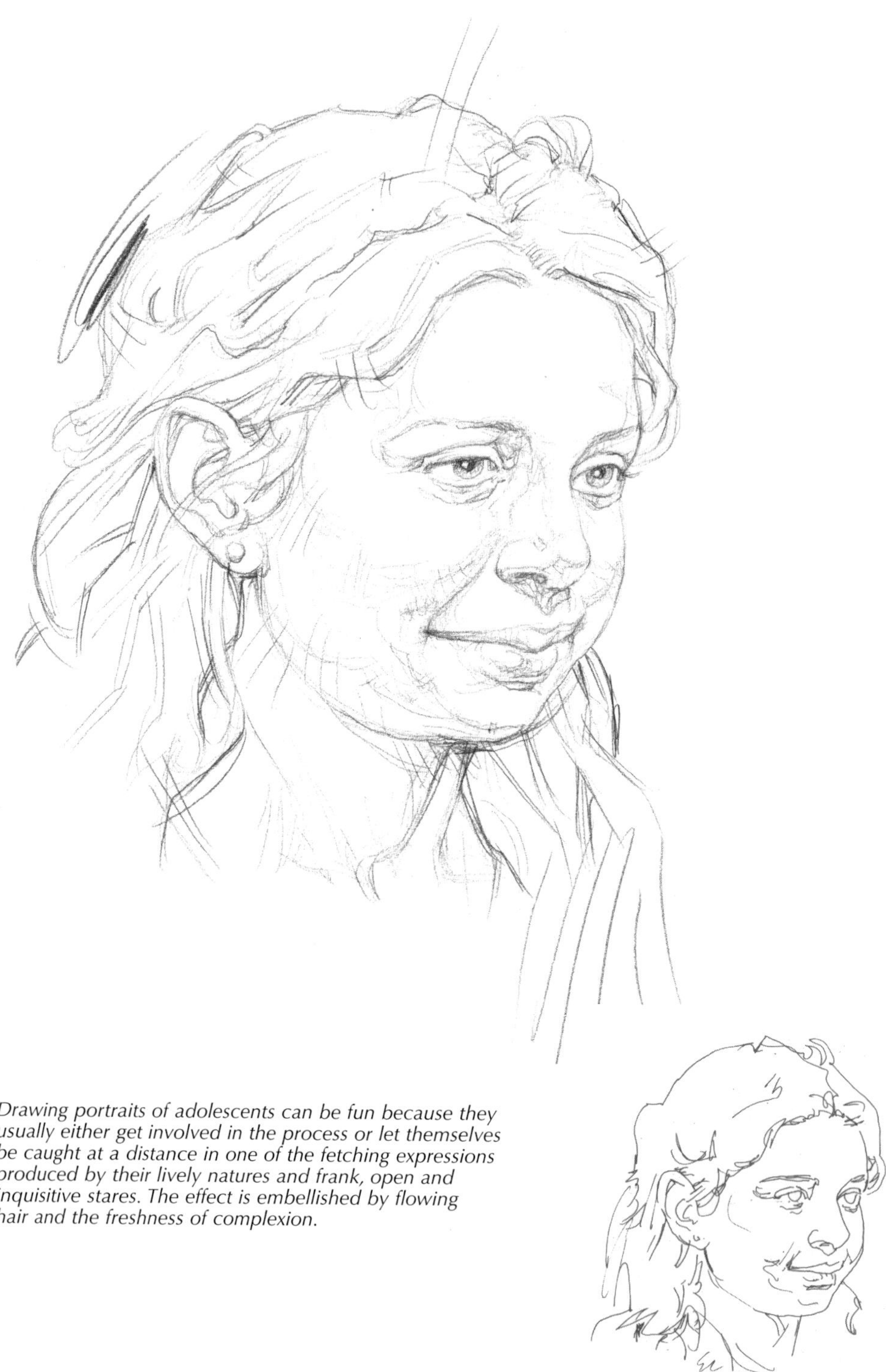

Drawing portraits of adolescents can be fun because they usually either get involved in the process or let themselves be caught at a distance in one of the fetching expressions produced by their lively natures and frank, open and inquisitive stares. The effect is embellished by flowing hair and the freshness of complexion.

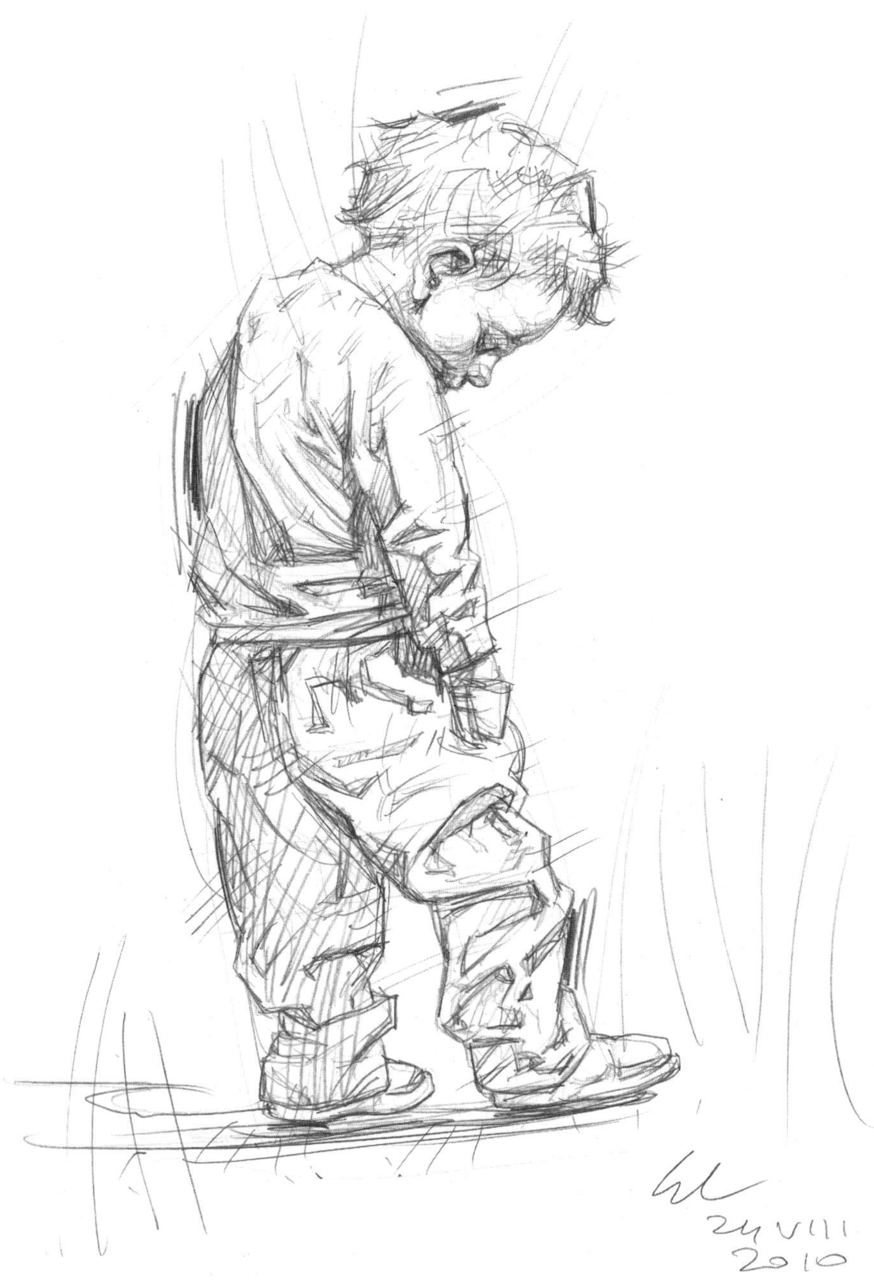

Little Pilgrim to Lourdes (2010)

HB pencil on paper, 22.5 × 31.5cm (9 × 12½in)

The face forms only a part (albeit the most significant part) of our bodily expression; sometimes it is nice to include the entire pose, suggesting it in a few summary lines.

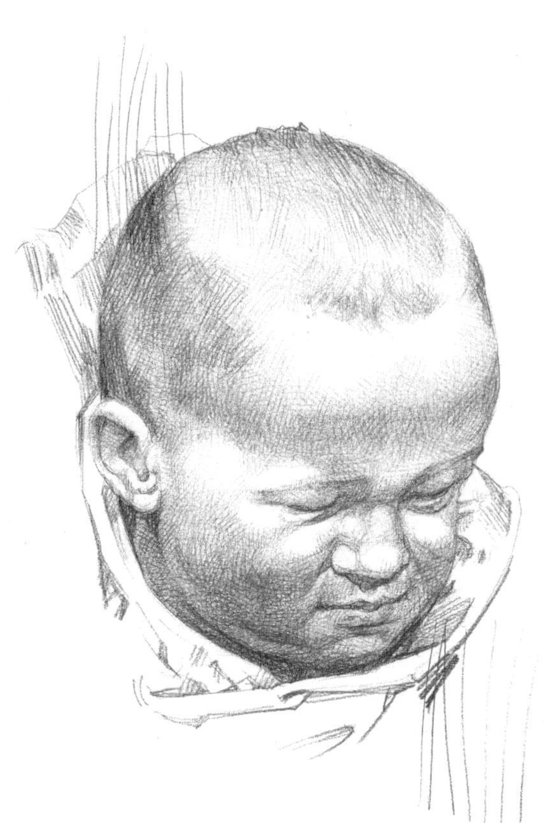

Some features of a child's face reveal characteristic traits for their age: a compact mouth and small teeth; the jutting upper lip; the small, rounded chin and substantial, protruding, smooth-surfaced cheeks. But while the face as a whole might seem to have a smooth, curvaceous look, avoid over-emphasizing this aspect – it is better to apportion each structure its due dimensions.

A preliminary structural sketch is useful for working out the 'structural gist' of the facial features in a simplified and concise way. I have included examples of such thumbnails, which are always executed before the main drawing.

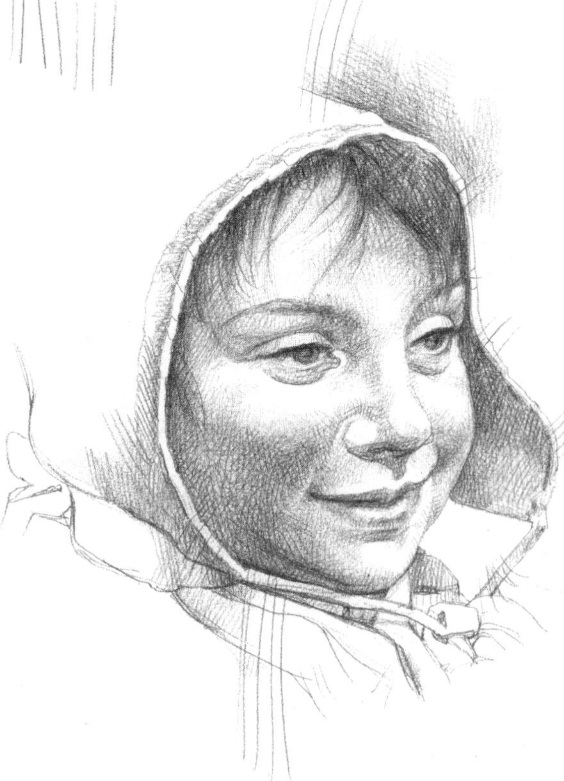

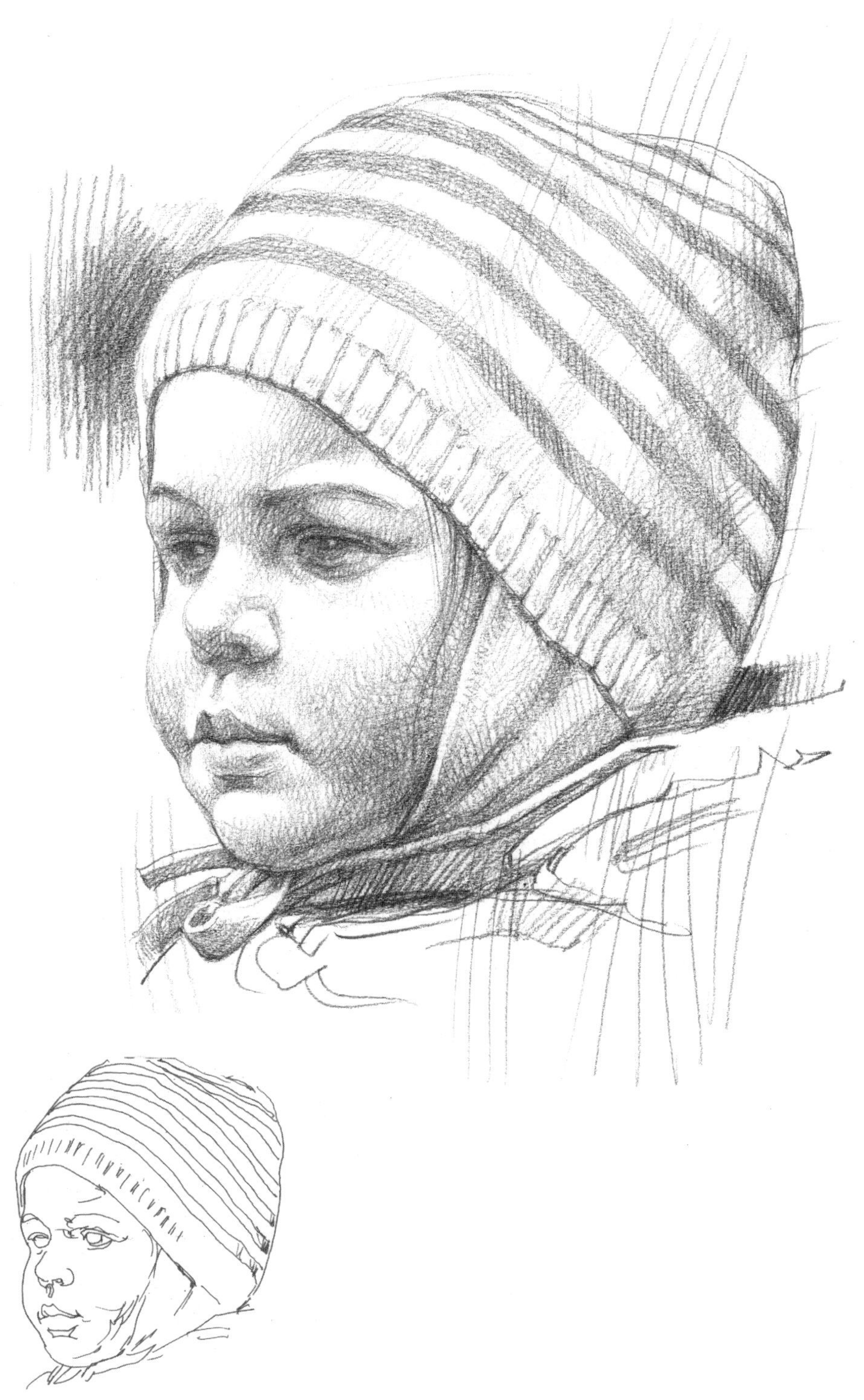

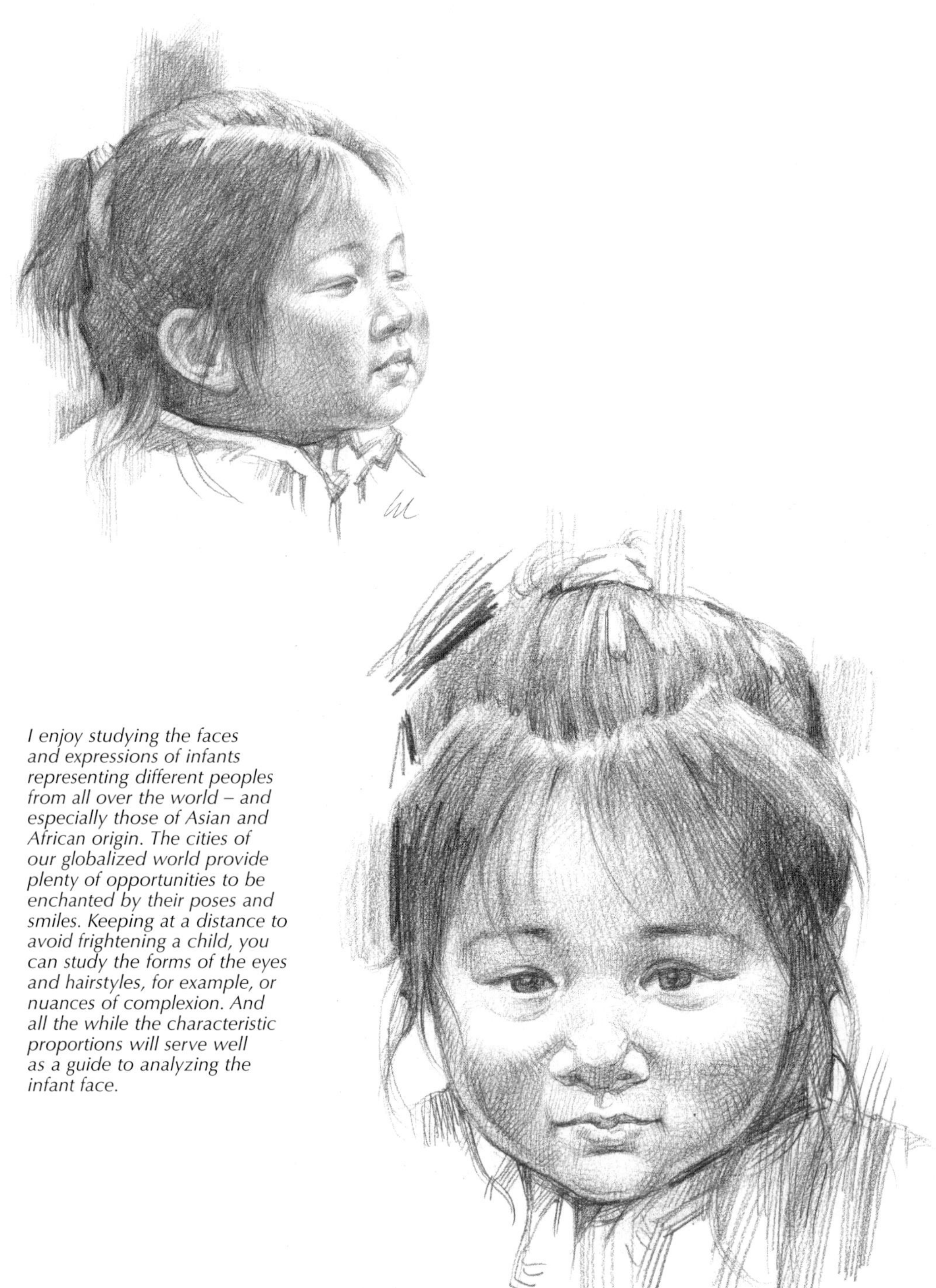

I enjoy studying the faces and expressions of infants representing different peoples from all over the world – and especially those of Asian and African origin. The cities of our globalized world provide plenty of opportunities to be enchanted by their poses and smiles. Keeping at a distance to avoid frightening a child, you can study the forms of the eyes and hairstyles, for example, or nuances of complexion. And all the while the characteristic proportions will serve well as a guide to analyzing the infant face.

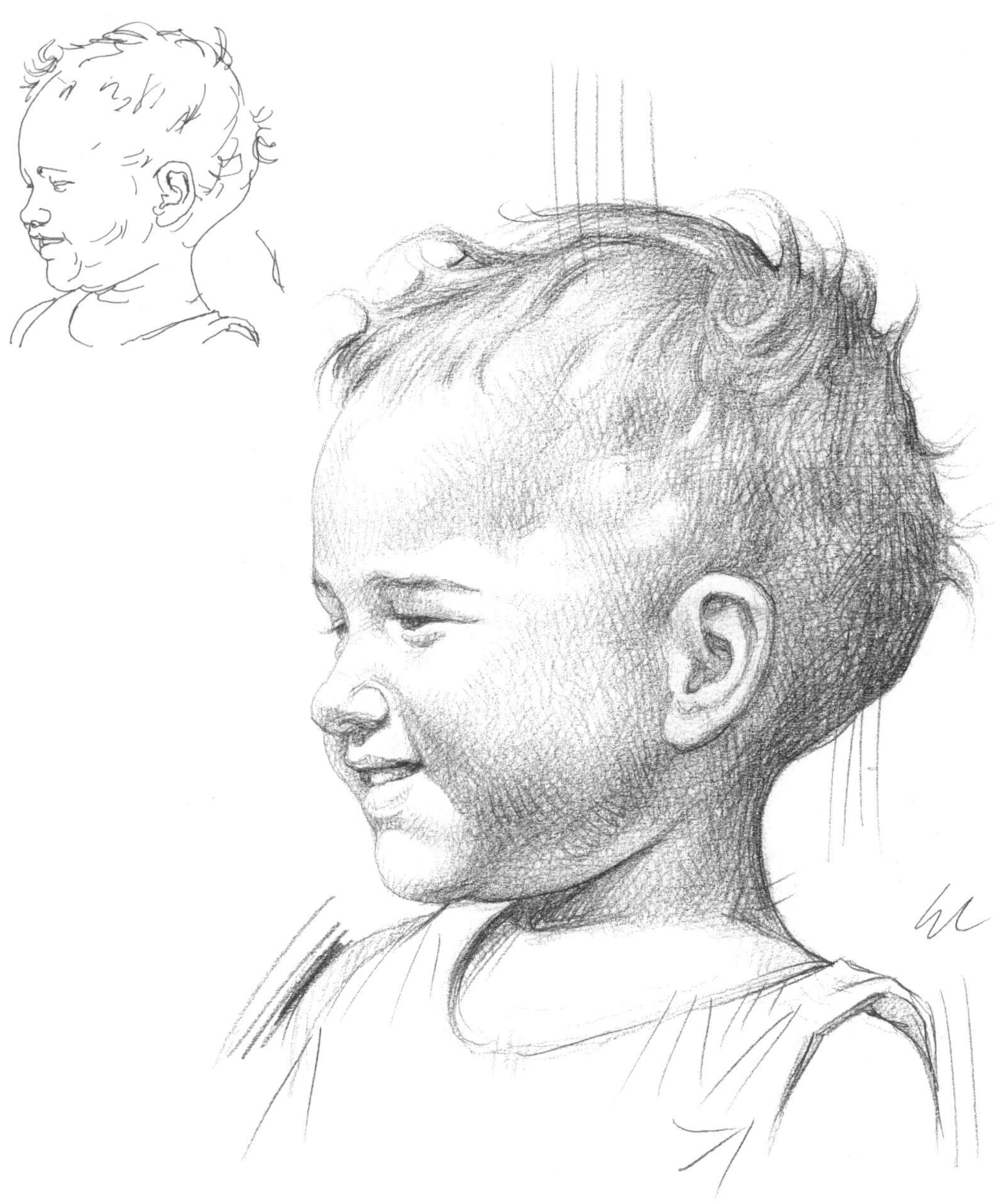

When portraying very young children (for instance, up to the age of six or seven) photographs will be an essential aid because children are always in movement and both their expressions and their moods change with lightning speed. This means that, at best, you can execute only quick sketches. However, photographs should only serve as an instrument for recording visual impressions and capturing fleeting poses.

The art of drawing babies and children is explored in more depth later in this book, from pages 204–341.

FEATURES OF THE FACE

THE EYE

Once you have examined the overall structure of the head, you need to analyze carefully the individual details of the face, i.e. the nose, mouth, eyes and ears. It makes sense to be able to recognize the basic morphological, i.e. 'structural' characteristics of each one, as by following them and precisely reproducing individual variations you will obtain a very good likeness.

The eye is, perhaps, the most expressive element and it is therefore essential to draw it in the correct position and to the exact shape. Notice that the white section of the eyeball (the sclera) is not pure white but actually changes colour due to the effect of its own shadow and the one cast by the eyelid. Be careful to draw both eyeballs (and therefore both pupils) looking in the same direction as the expressiveness of the eyes depends on this.

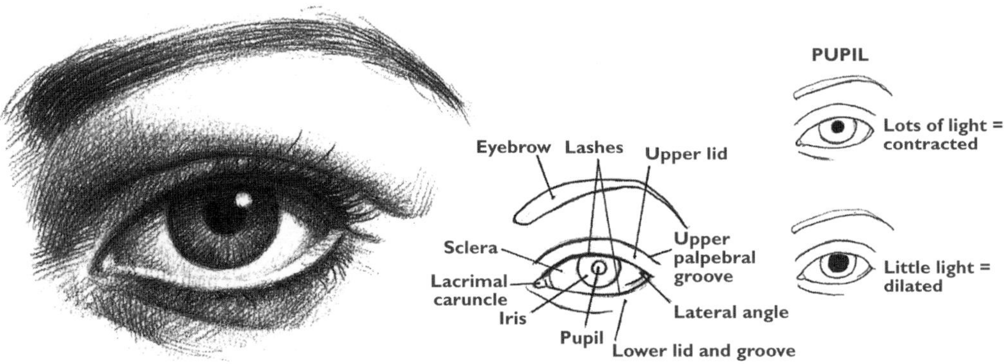

The diagrams below should be sufficient to show the spherical structure of the eye, how the eyelids rest on it and, finally, the stages to go through to draw it correctly.

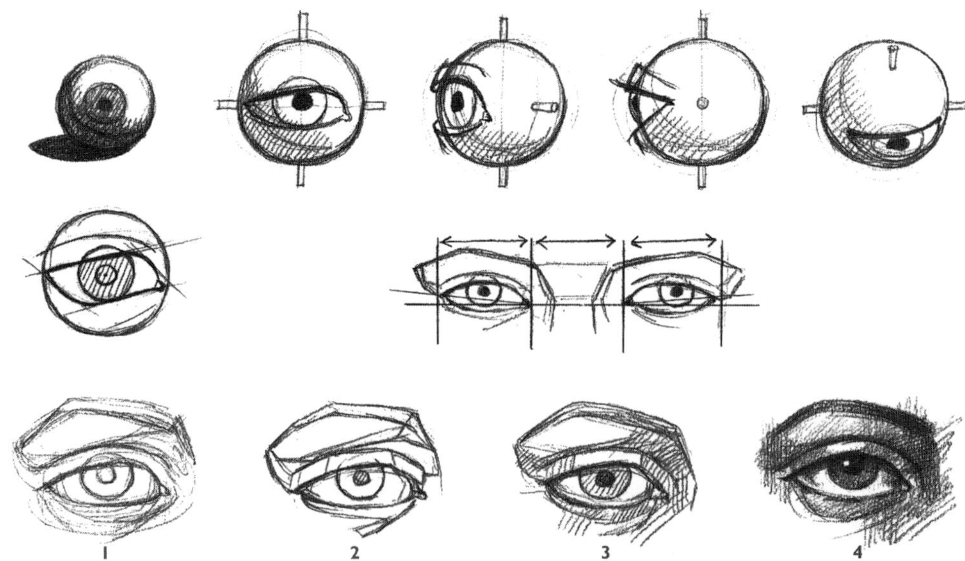

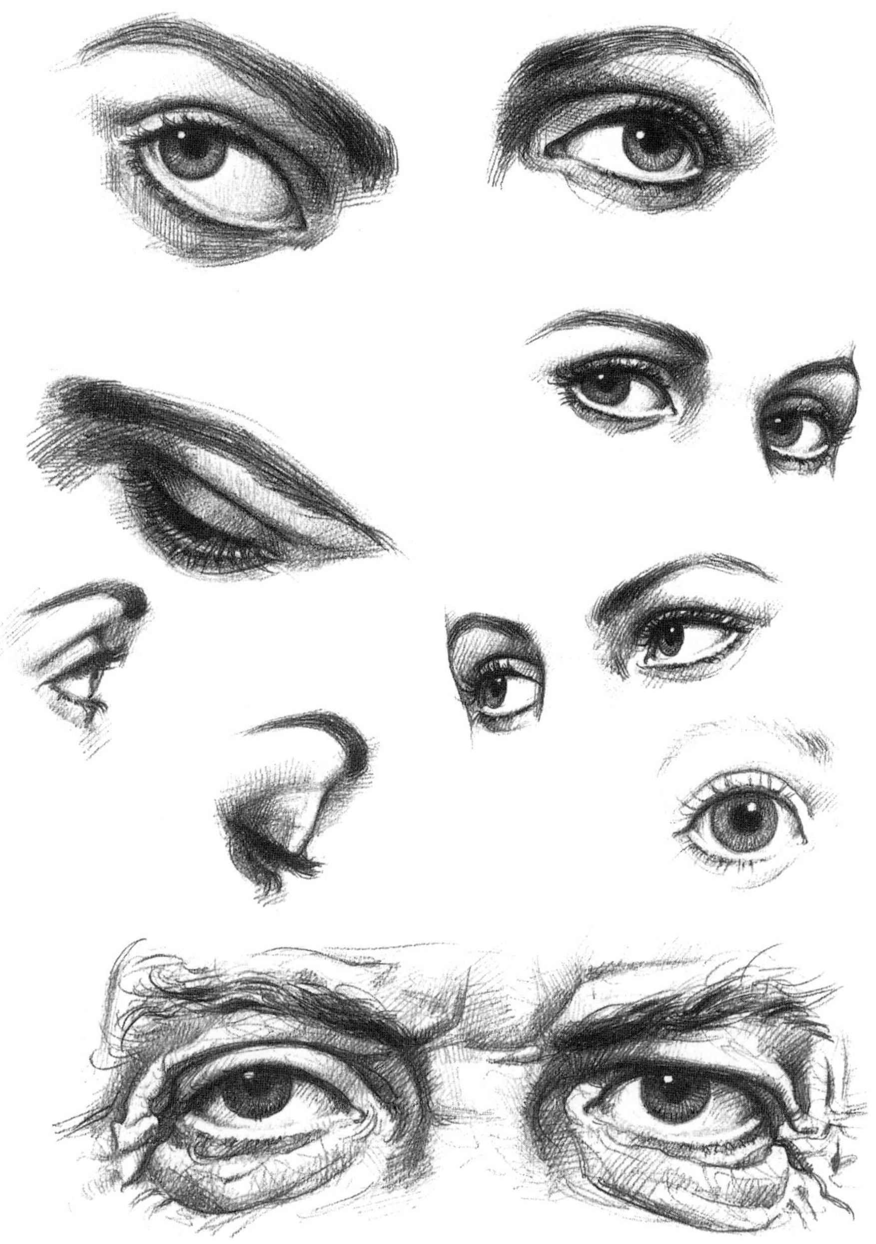

Practise drawing eyes in various positions and from different viewpoints, as shown by the examples on this page. The female eye usually has long and thick eyelashes, while the eyebrows are well outlined and thin. The iris of a child looks very big compared with the eyelids.

Elderly people show several deep wrinkles radiating from the corners of the eyes, the lower eyelids become 'baggy', and eyebrows become irregularly thick and bushy.

THE EAR

The ear is supported mainly by thin cartilage arranged in circumvolutions. Although its morphological characteristics vary greatly, its overall shape recalls a seashell and is fairly similar in both sexes. Ears are often partly hidden by one's hair and their expressive character depends on their precise position on the sides of the head, as I have shown in the sketches below.

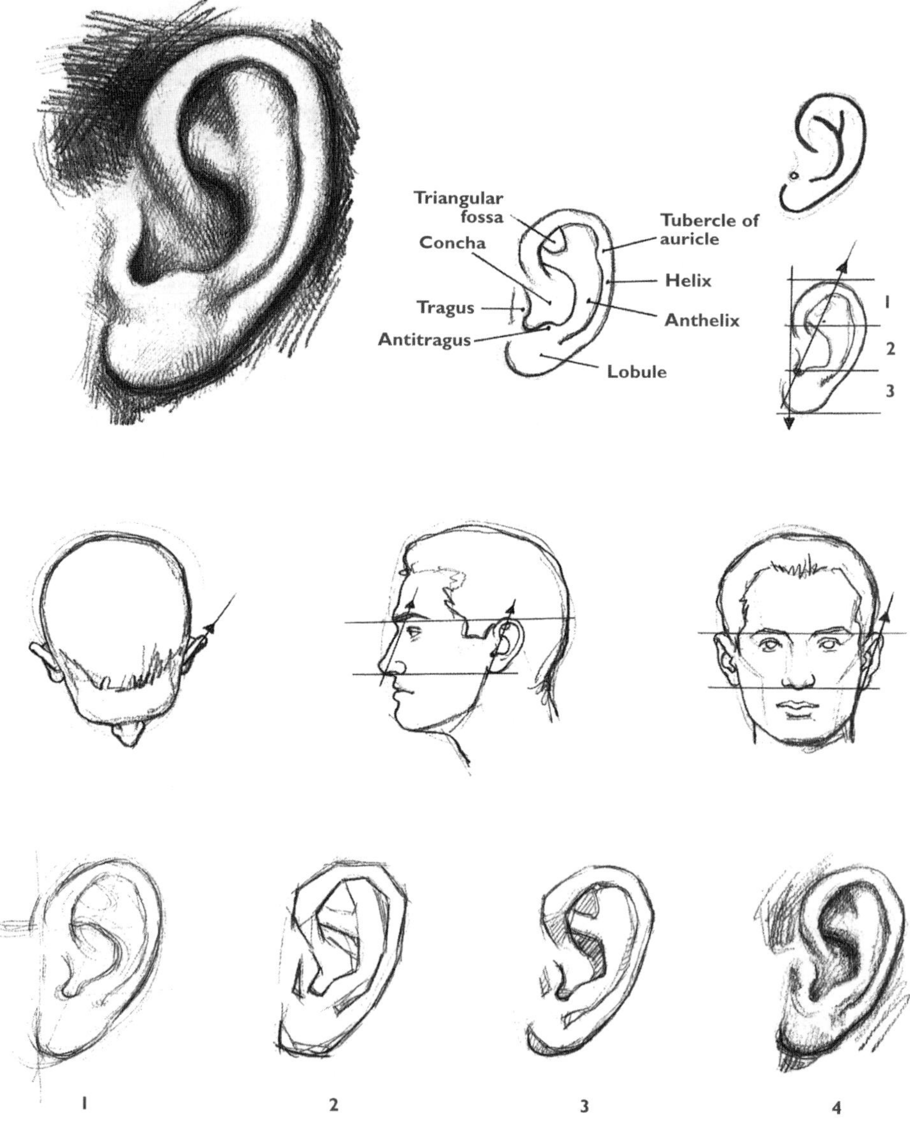

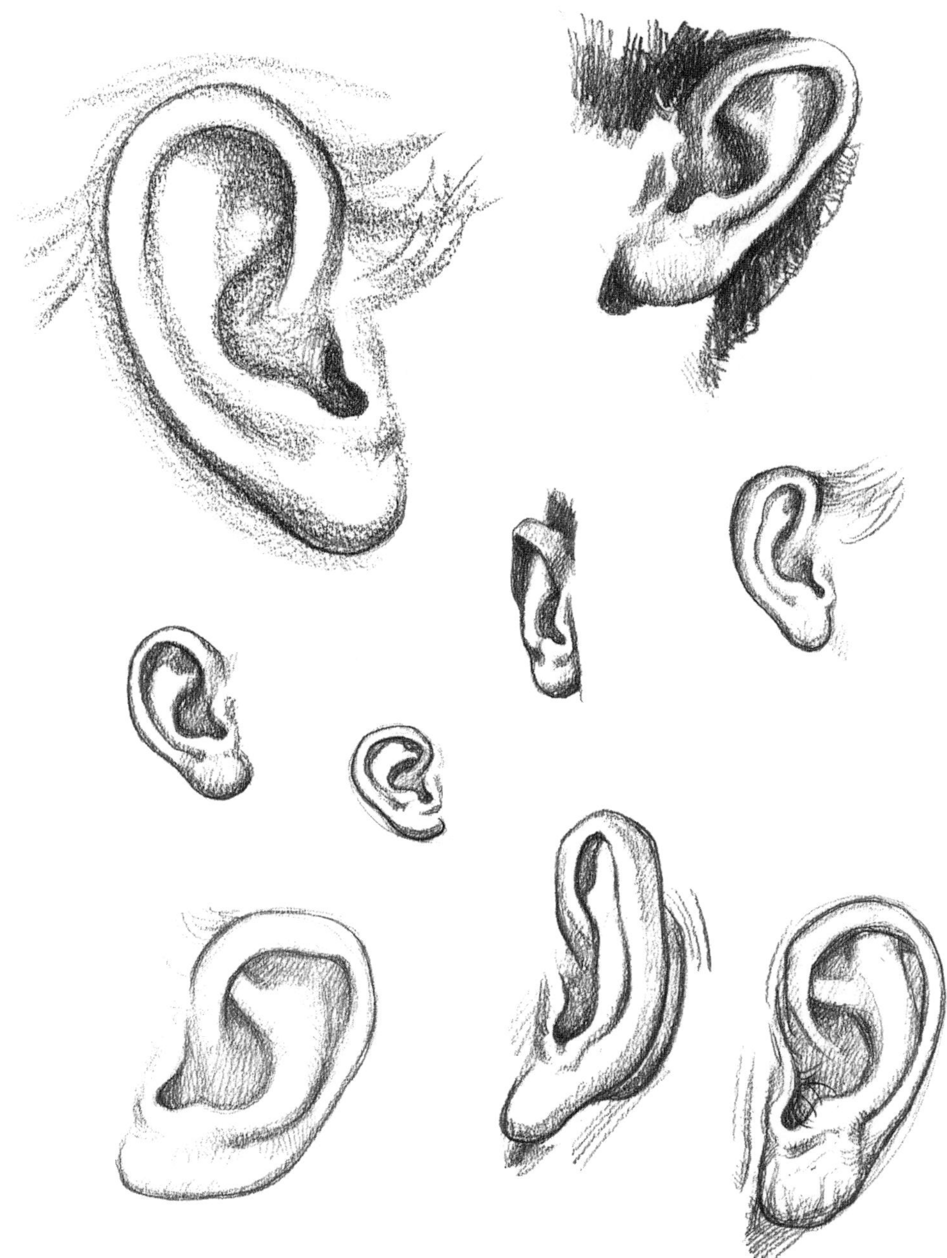

In an adult, the height of the ear corresponds, on average, to that of the nose; in a child it looks rather big in relation to the head; and in an elderly person it tends to lengthen because of the thinning and weakening of the cartilage tissue.

THE NOSE

The nose is rather difficult to represent as it sticks out of the face and its appearance therefore varies depending on the viewpoint. Its pyramid-like shape is partly due to two small bones in close proximity, and partly to cartilage, and this can be seen clearly on its dorsum. Observe the sketches shown on these two pages and practise drawing the nose in various positions, referring to photographs if it makes it easier to understand its structure. Notice that the dorsum moves away from the bridge to reach maximum projection at the tip and its sides slope towards the cheeks.

The triangular base hosts the nostrils, oval-shaped and slightly converging towards the tip, and delimited by the alae of the nose. Try to work out the most important areas of light and shadow (the maximum amount of light is usually on the dorsum and the tip, while the most intense shadow is at the base, near the nostrils) and indicate just those, to avoid making the drawing too 'heavy'.

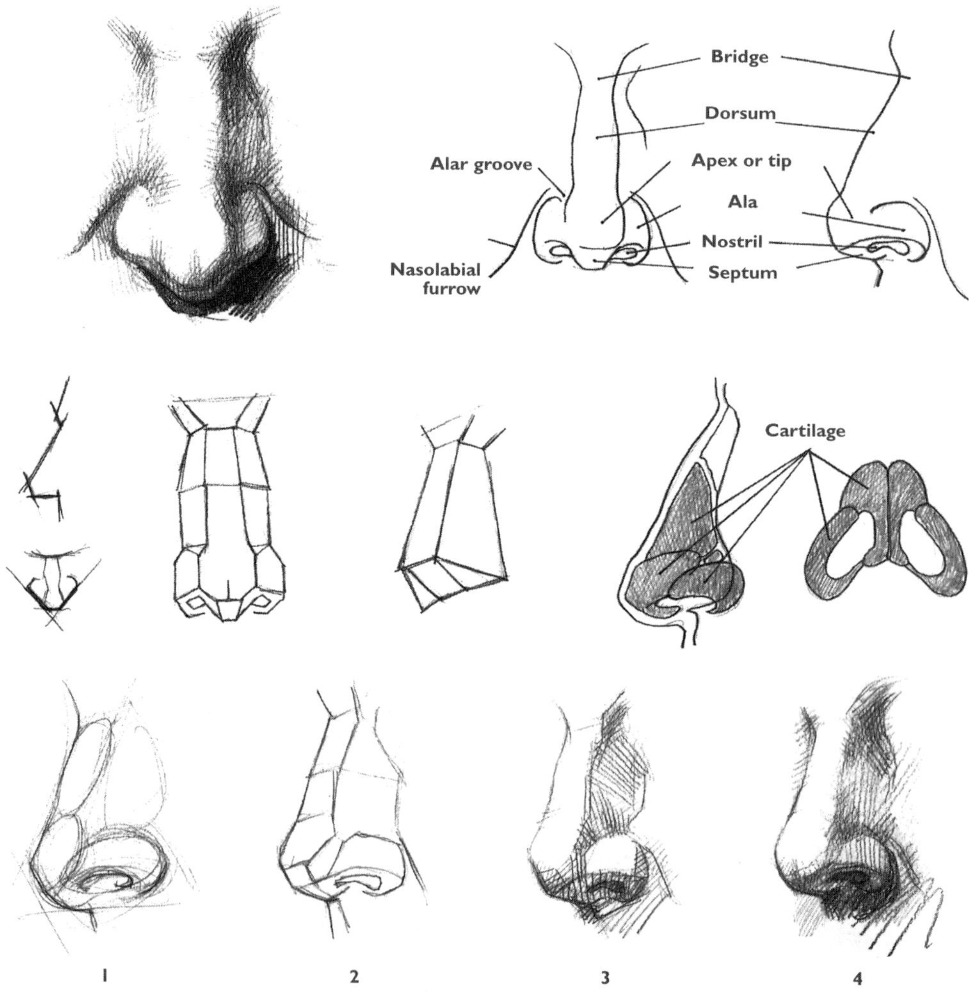

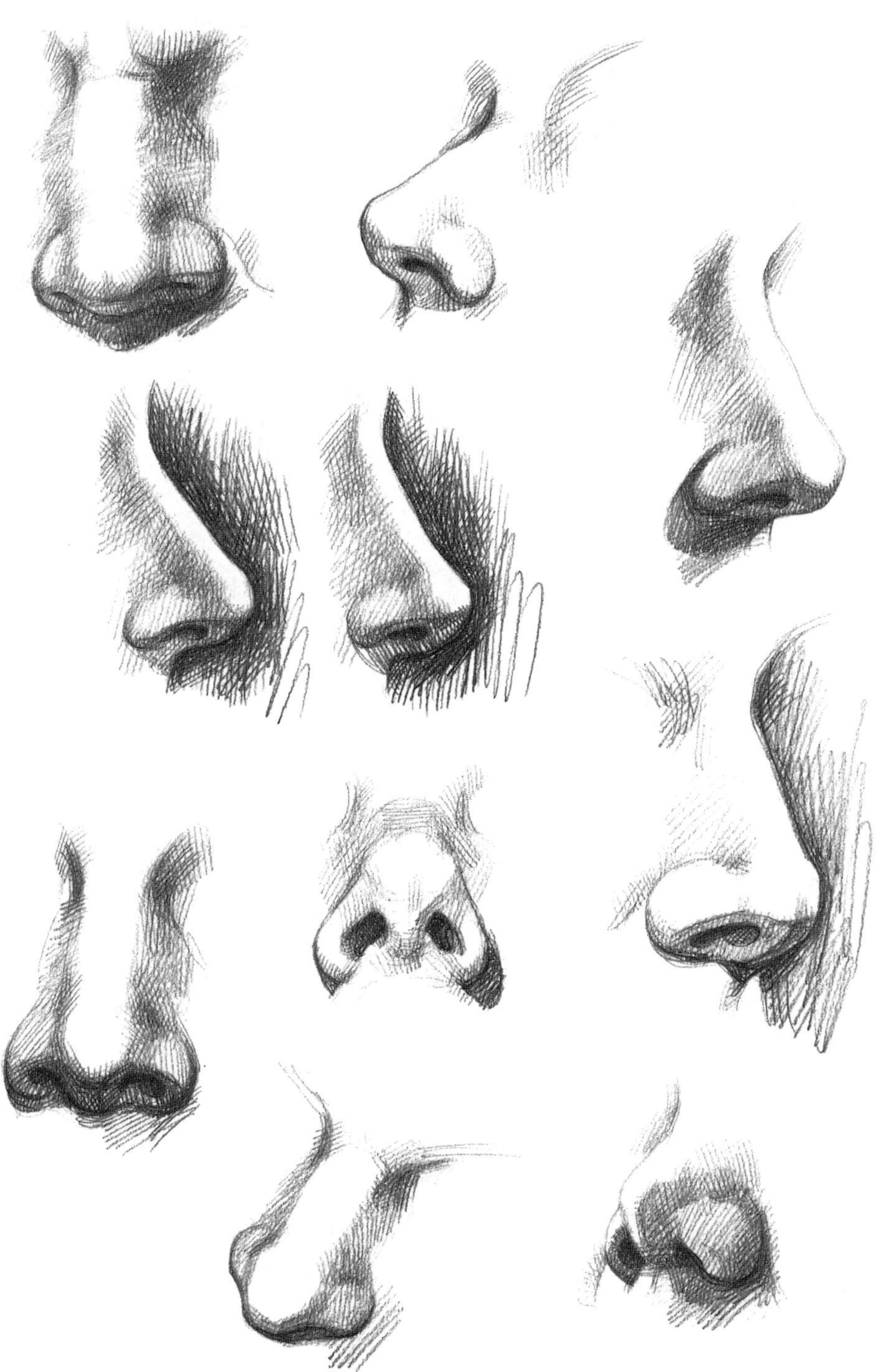

THE MOUTH

After the eyes the mouth is the second most expressive element of the face. The pinkish colour of the lips is due to the tissue they are made of, transitional between the mucous membrane (found inside the mouth) and the skin. When drawing the lips make sure that, above all, you carefully draw the line which separates them – ensure that it lies on the semi-cylindrical surface of the jaw bones and follows the rules of perspective I have already mentioned on page 29. The simple sketches shown below indicate some of the basic characteristics of labial morphology. Notice, for instance, that the upper lip is usually thinner and more protruding than the lower.

Lips are extremely mobile and can be stretched, puckered and projected depending on the expression and action being taken.

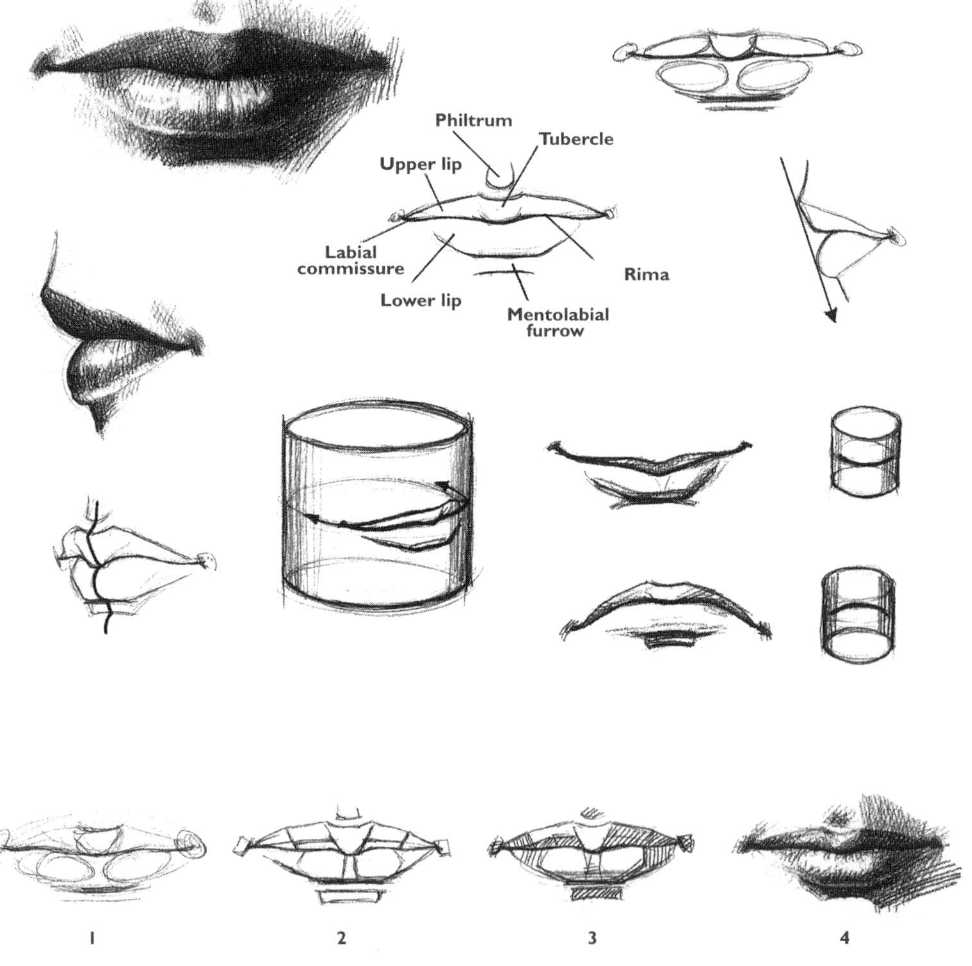

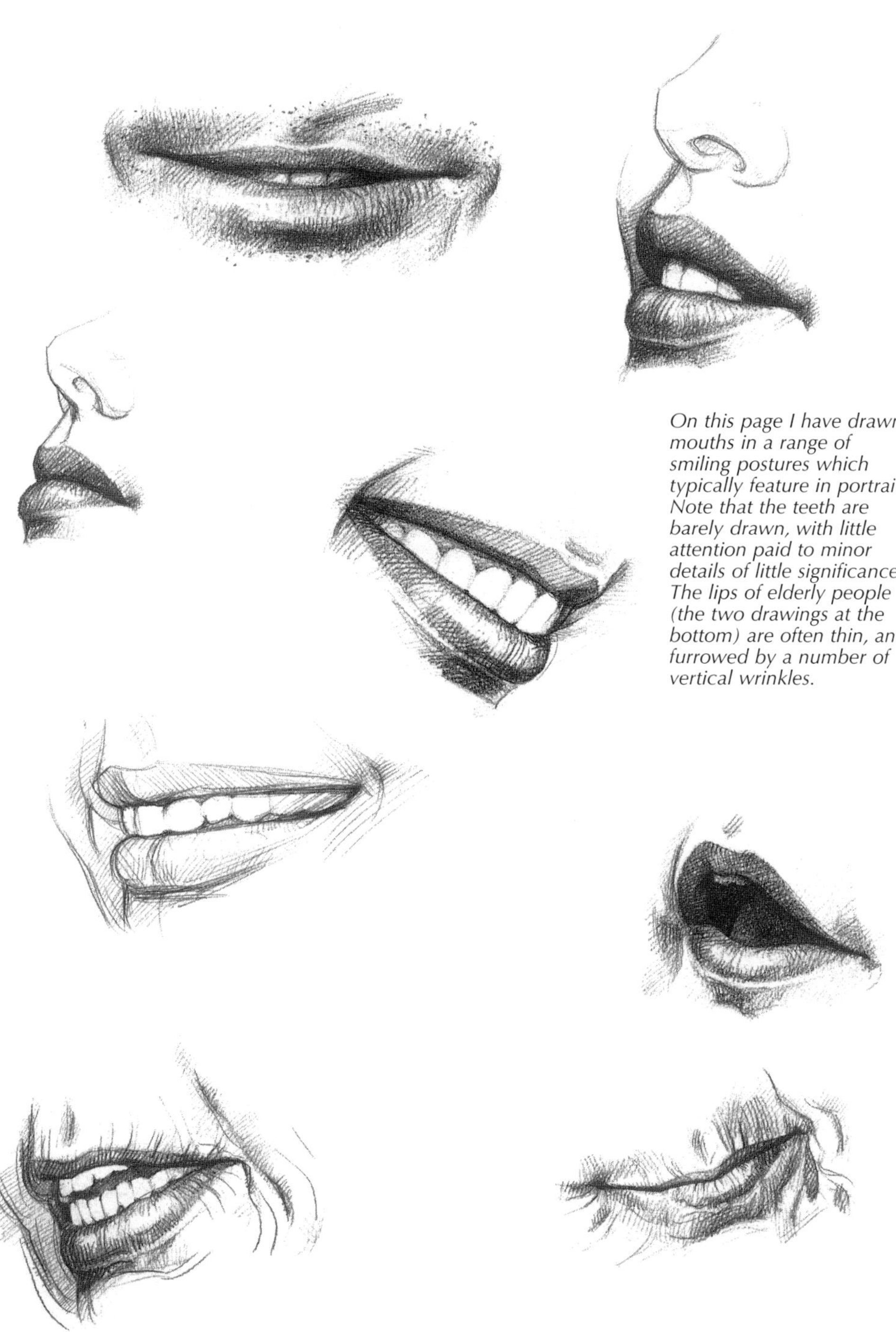

On this page I have drawn mouths in a range of smiling postures which typically feature in portraits. Note that the teeth are barely drawn, with little attention paid to minor details of little significance. The lips of elderly people (the two drawings at the bottom) are often thin, and furrowed by a number of vertical wrinkles.

HAIR AND BEARD

From an anatomical point of view, hair on the head and face can be considered secondary facial elements, but from an aesthetic point of view they are extremely relevant. Hair type and style contribute to characterizing the individual and showing the ethnic, biological, social and cultural group to which he or she belongs.

When drawing this part of the head, it is advisable to consider the line, colour, volume and direction of the main locks. In fact, it is useful to consider these shapes as sets of small masses rather than individual hairs. Hint at, rather than describe, the effects of depth, *chiaroscuro* and volume on these masses.

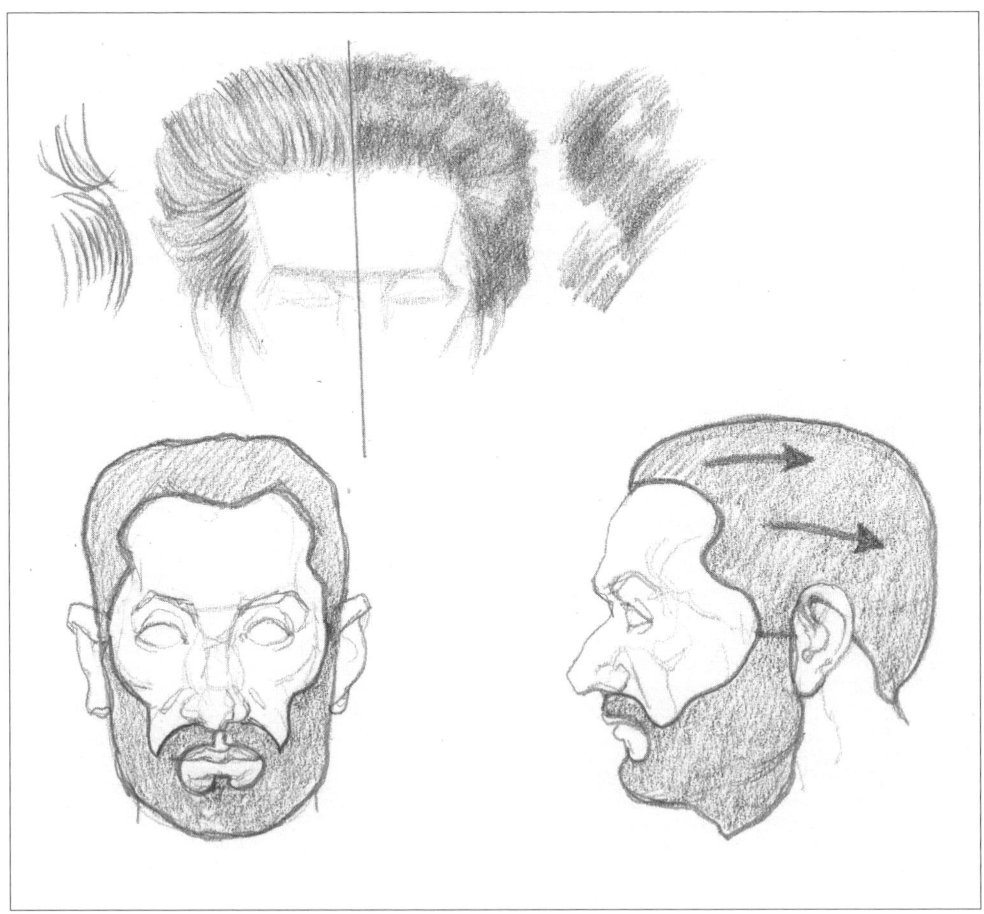

SOME EFFECTS OF AGE

The face almost always develops character and interest for the artist as the subject ages, in relation to his or her lifestyle or profession. These changes and adaptations mainly affect the skin, creating contrasts of volume, shadows, lines and intersections of grooves on the face, which are extremely attractive and effective for suggesting character in a drawing.

There are many well-known examples. Wrinkles – the folds and channels in skin caused by loss of elasticity and habitual expressions – produce alternating *chiaroscuro* tones and direction of lines, that are graphically rather effective. They usually appear on the forehead, around the eyelids, on the side of the nose, around lips and on the neck.

Nose cartilage alters in volume and consistency over time, causing the lobe to lengthen and droop. Earlobes also become longer and one or two vertical lines appear near the tragus. Other, less immediately noticeable changes occur, of which we are all aware. These include the consistency and colour of hair; the appearance of small, dark age spots on the face; the adaptation of lips to dentures and many more.

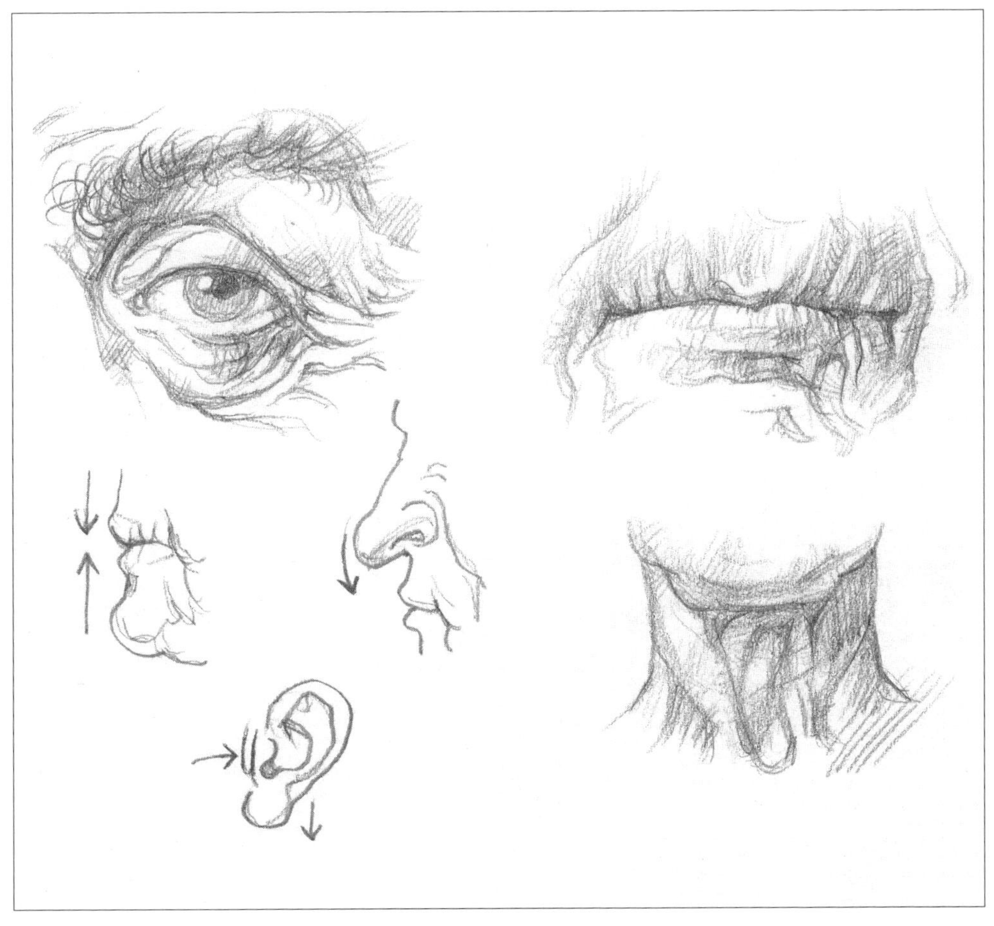

PORTRAIT COMPOSITION

Composition involves arranging on the drawing surface the elements which make up the image we are set to represent. There are no firm rules (except, perhaps, the one concerning the 'golden section') but rather principles relating to our visual perception, i.e. unity, contrast and balance. Portrait composition dictates that we make some choices straight away: deciding whether to draw the full figure or just the head, and in this case, whether full-face, profile, three-quarter; deciding whether to place the model in some sort of setting or isolate them against a neutral 'background'; deciding the size of the drawing and whether it should be portrait- or landscape-style; and so on. You need to get used to doing lots of little sketches to evaluate these problems, as I suggest in the following pages. In the meantime look carefully at the sketches below, which use 'tricks of the trade' to direct you when you start, but don't allow yourself to be tied down by traditional and stereotyped formulas – do experiment with original and unusual compositions.

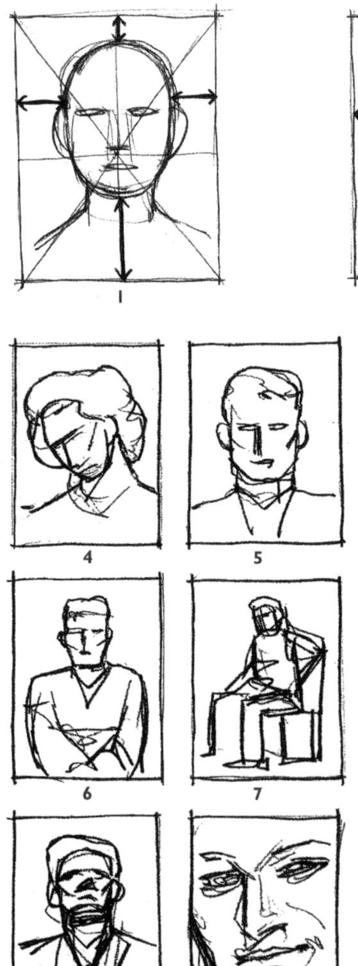

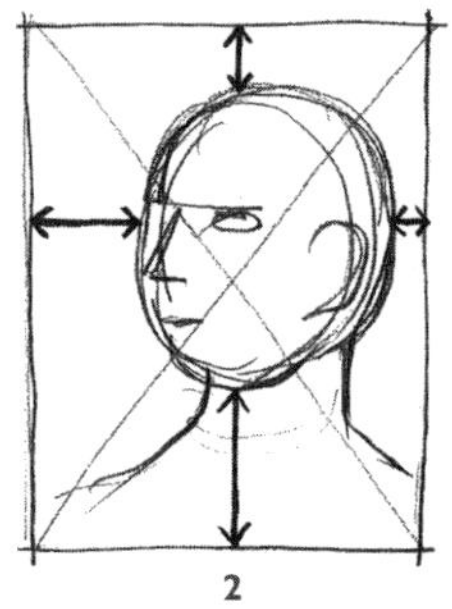

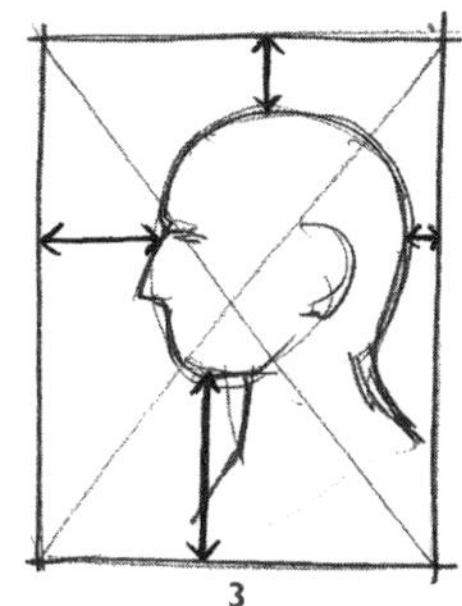

1 *In a full-face portrait you should not place the head right at the geometric centre of the page, but slightly higher, leaving more or less the same amount of space at the sides. Make sure, however, that the top of the head does not get too close to the edge of the page.*

2 *In a three-quarter portrait it's better to leave more room between the front of the face and the edge of the page, rather than at the back.*

3 *A profile portrait looks better if you leave lots of space in front of the face. Avoid, if possible, 'cutting' the head's back profile or making it fit with the edge of the page.*

4 *A bowed head can express a depressed mood.*

5, 6 and 7 *A full-face portrait showing the subject in the foreground can radiate strength and self-confidence.*

8 *An image viewed from below can make the face look fierce and the attitude authoritarian. It is therefore not recommended for a portrait.*

9 *An unusual and evocative effect can be achieved by having the face take up the whole page.*

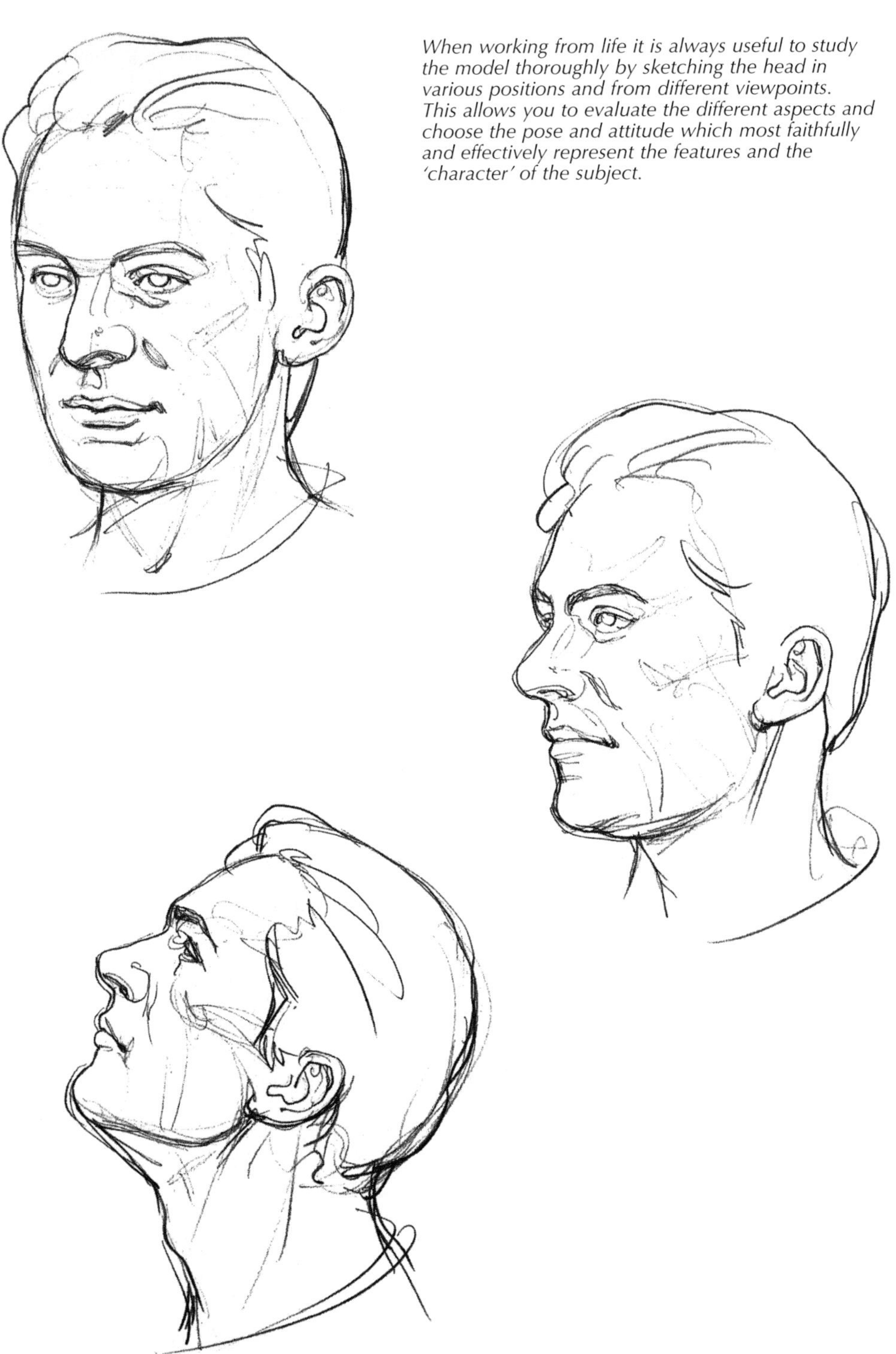

When working from life it is always useful to study the model thoroughly by sketching the head in various positions and from different viewpoints. This allows you to evaluate the different aspects and choose the pose and attitude which most faithfully and effectively represent the features and the 'character' of the subject.

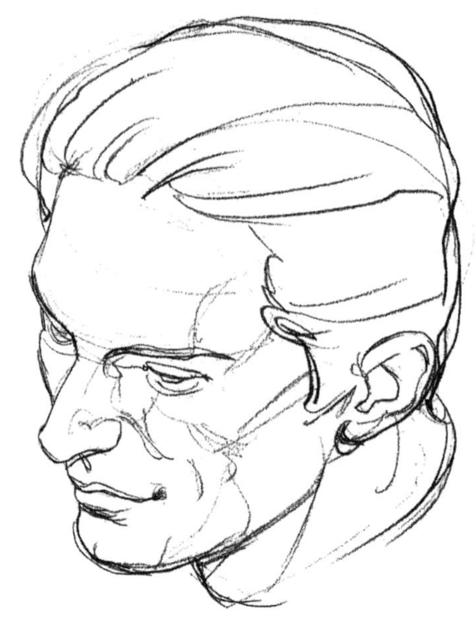

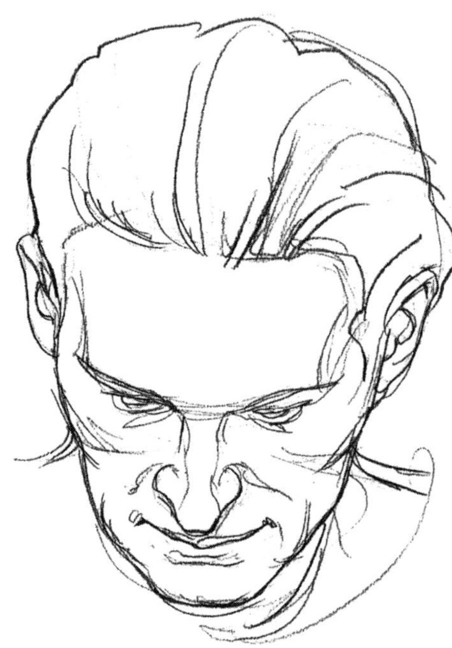

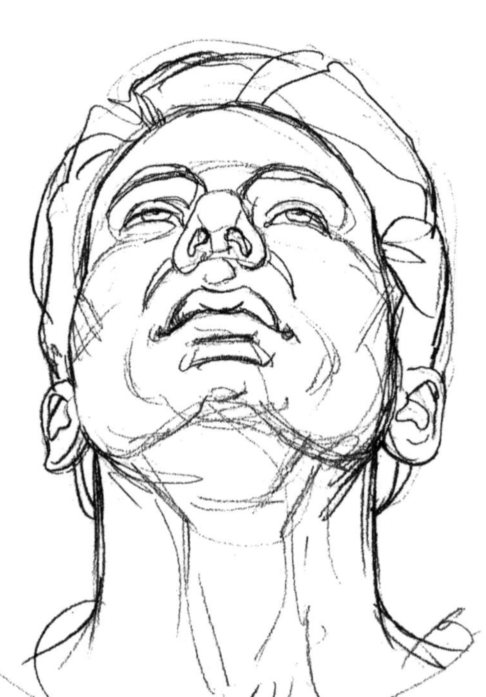

To work in a more relaxed way you canuse photographs to start with, but drawing from life is definitely more effective. In addition, it enables you to explore new compositional routes, 'going around' the model to catch every little expressive nuance and to master the overall shape, which is so important to achieving a likeness. Render these studies by way of simple, 'clean' strokes, aiming for the overall structure of the head rather than chiaroscuro *effects.*

The same advice outlined in the previous pages also applies to the full-figure portrait. On this page you can see two of the studies I did (in pen and ink) for an oil portrait. The model's pose and the final composition are summed up in the drawing on page 63.

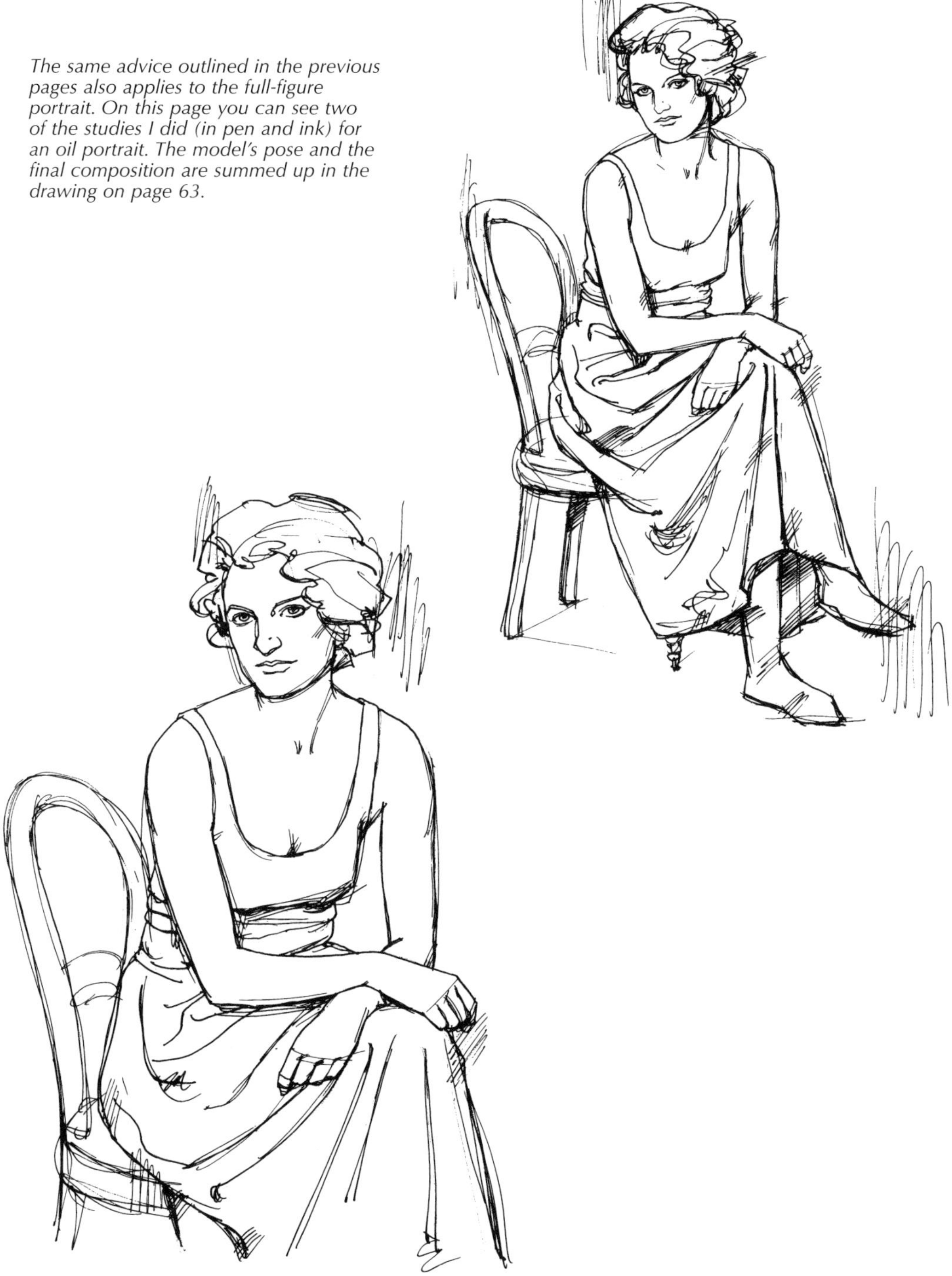

In full-figure portraiture the hands, as well as the face, have great importance and you need to find a pose which is expressive, yet conveys the whole. It is this latter aspect that I have tried to explore with the drawings shown on these pages.

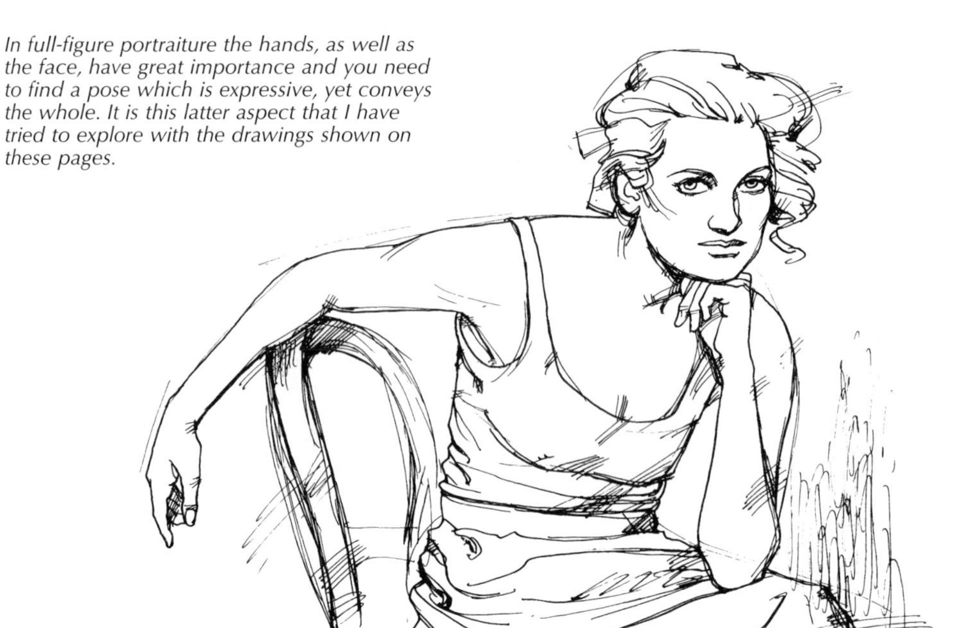

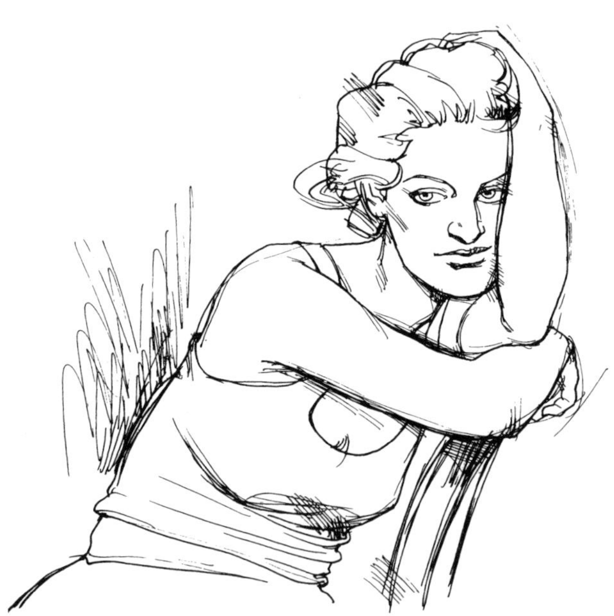

You will find more instruction on drawing full-figure portraits in the last chapter of this book, pages 342–400.

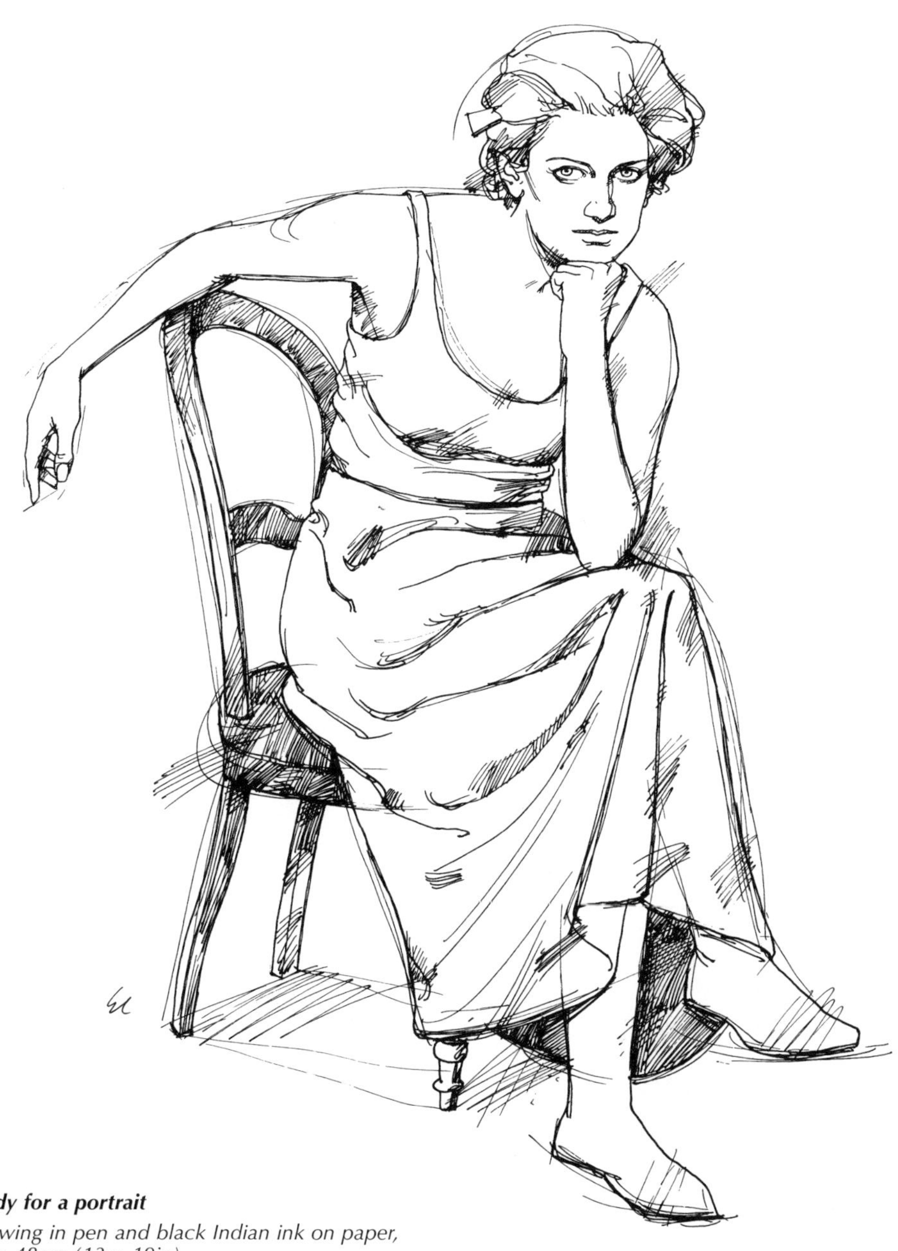

Study for a portrait

Drawing in pen and black Indian ink on paper, 33 × 48cm (13 × 19in)

The right arm resting on the chair contrasts with the vertical direction of all the other parts of the figure and makes the composition more 'dynamic'.

DRAWING PORTRAITS: GETTING STARTED

Depth of thought is redeemed by lightness of touch.

USING PLASTER CASTS

When setting out to study the human head, it can be very helpful to use a plaster cast that faithfully reproduces a high-quality, realistic piece of sculpture. This may seem to be an outmoded and rather boring way of practising, but if it is done with thought and artistic freedom, the technique can still prove very useful, even today. This is because drawing from plaster casts allows the student to work slowly, without the urgency imposed by using a live model. In this way students can develop a keen ability in observing forms by exploring proportional relationships and volumes and acquire the technical mastery to express these observations effectively through variation of tone.

USING PHOTOGRAPHS

Photography is a very useful and sometimes indispensible resource in situations in which drawing is not possible or when the model is surprised in a crowded place or caught performing a rapid, unrehearsed and unrepeatable movement. In such circumstances, photography (an art form in itself) makes an instant record of fleeting expressions and minute facial details, its form and the play of light, which would be impossible to jot down in a rapid sketch.

Photographs allow the portraitist to carry on with his work in the studio, at leisure, when the model is not there. It is by no means a matter of simply copying the photographic image, but to put the objectively recorded information to good use in attaining an authentic and living likeness, combining data gathered from direct observation of the model (as and when possible) and from photographs depicting the model. The artist's task is to create an atmosphere within an image that, in summarizing observed reality, goes beyond it. In short, photography is not a substitute for direct observation or for making sketches from life: it should be seen as a tool in the hands of the graphic artist and utilized as such.

When you use a camera to take photographs for reference or for documentation, it is advisable to make allowances for the optical limitations of this mechanical instrument. Human vision is binocular, but cameras 'see' the world through a single lens and so variations in focal length can lead to distortions in a face's proportions and the perspective in which it is seen. Such distortions may be minimal, but they are there nonetheless and can be compensated for either by retaking the photograph from the correct distance or by using appropriate telephoto lenses. Photographic film and digital images are less sensitive than the human eye, especially in the case of colour pictures, and they nearly always produce images in which either the shadows are too dark or the light areas too bright. For this reason, when taking photographs for a portrait, direct sunlight and poorly lit interiors are both best avoided; it is better to opt for diffuse daylight conditions.

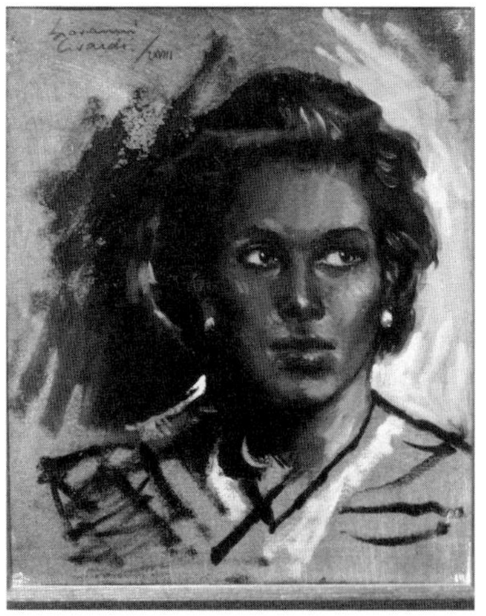

Portrait study (1968)
Oil on canvas, 21 × 26cm (8¼ × 10¼in)

POSING THE MODEL

In order to create a portrait or a detailed study of a person's head, the subject in question has to adopt and maintain a pose suited to bringing out the characteristics of his or her face and which at the same time creates an interesting composition.

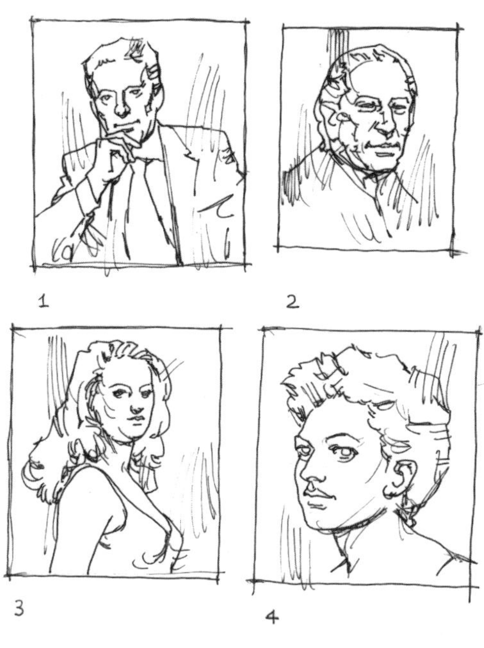

CLASSIC OR FORMAL PORTRAIT

In this case, the subject assumes a static, calm or reflective pose – i.e. one inspired by the mainstream tradition of representative portraiture. A three-quarter view of the face is usually chosen under somewhat diffused lighting with a part of the torso included in the composition with the aim of attaining a balanced arrangement in terms of structure and/or tone.

Consider how the subject is placed on the support. A central position is the obvious choice for formal paintings.

INFORMAL PORTRAIT

The artist may decide to break away from the normal traditions and seek out new and unusual ways of organizing the picture space. The subject may, then, appear 'surprised' in a chance position with a spontaneous, one-off expression, suggesting to the viewer that they are witnessing the person in a passing, unstable position. This kind of composition is usually the result of an impromptu sketch made of somebody seen incidentally.

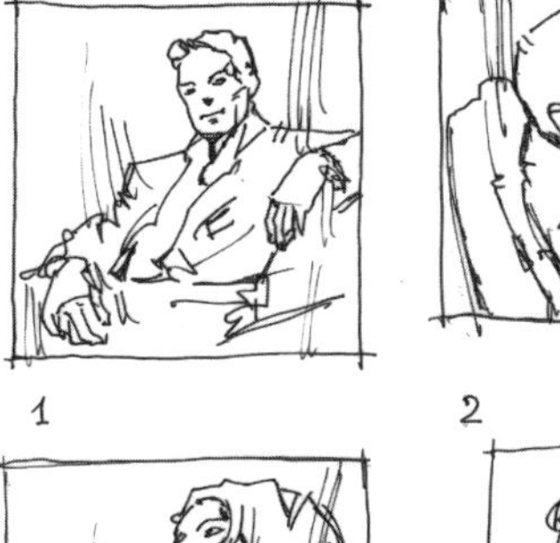

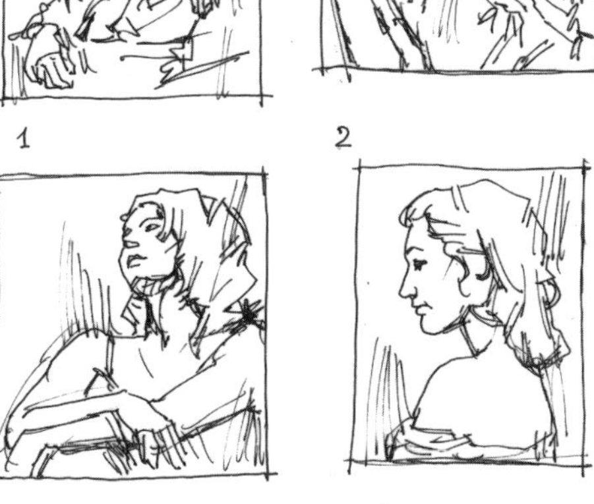

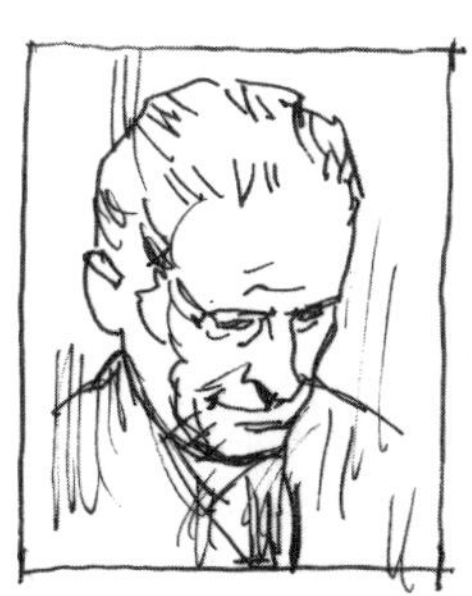

LIGHTING

When drawing a portrait it is very important to consider the direction, quality and intensity of the light falling on the model, as it is thanks to light and shadows that we get a sense of the shape and the plastic form of the face. Usually when drawing a portrait artificial light, which is easy to adjust and constant, is preferable to sunlight, which varies greatly in intensity and direction. Good lighting must highlight as best as possible the physiognomic characteristics of the subject. Therefore avoid using a light source which is too intense and close. It is better to use slightly diffused lighting, which doesn't create dark shadows, especially under the nose, the lips and the eyes.

The photographic examples on these pages are of a sculpture I moulded and show situations which are slightly unusual or extreme, but are useful to highlight the effects, both positive and negative, of different lighting on the face. The most suitable lighting for a portrait has the source slightly higher than the subject and midway between the front and the side. To make the light more diffused you can place a finely frosted glass in front of the source or use one of the well known photographic devices.

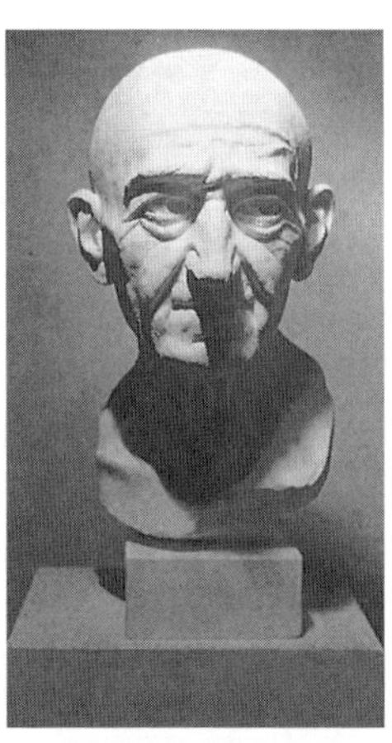

Top lighting *is very effective but you have to be careful not to create excessively dark shadows under the eyebrows, the nose, and the chin. The surface-grazing light can exaggerate the reliefs and depressions of the skin.*

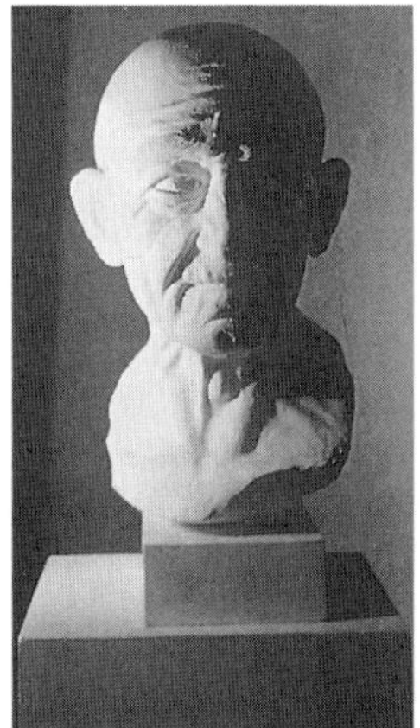

Side lighting *is not suitable for portraiture as it divides the face into two contrasting halves: one lit, one in shadow. Sometimes it can be useful to convey strong relief.*

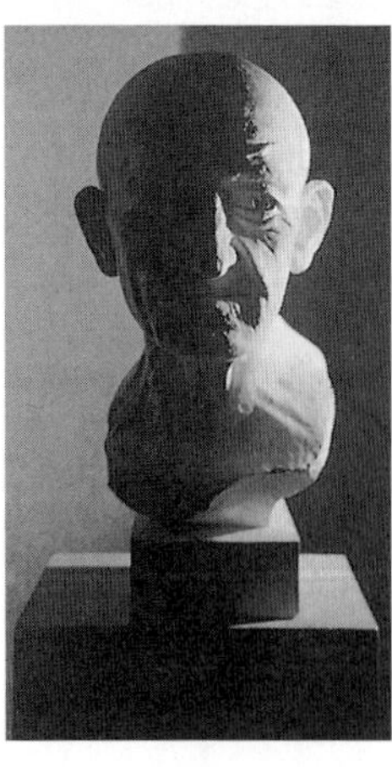

Side/back lighting *should not be used for a portrait as it cancels most of the shape of the face. It can be used, however, when the head is in profile. Note, in this example, a device adopted in drawing – the dark part of the head is silhouetted against the light background and the light part against the dark background.*

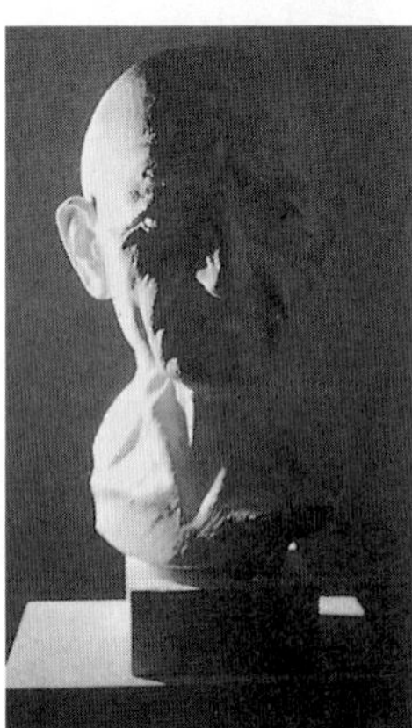

Almost back lighting *also called 'effect lighting', is not used in portraiture as it makes the model's features hardly recognizable. The backlit image, however, can work for a portrait where the face is in profile.*

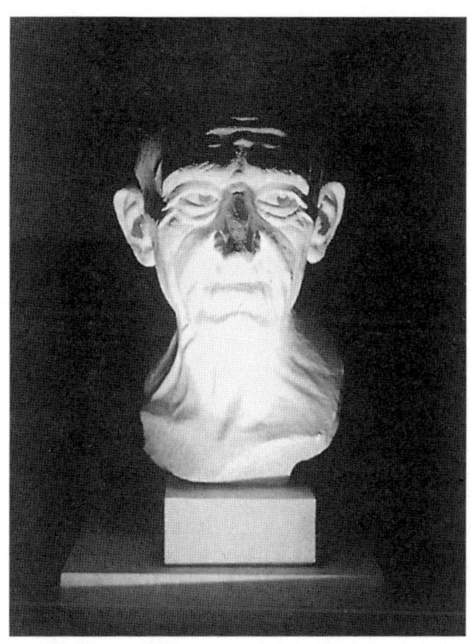

Lighting from below *is very 'dramatic' and is hardly ever used in portraiture as it alters the likeness and distorts the characteristics of the face.*

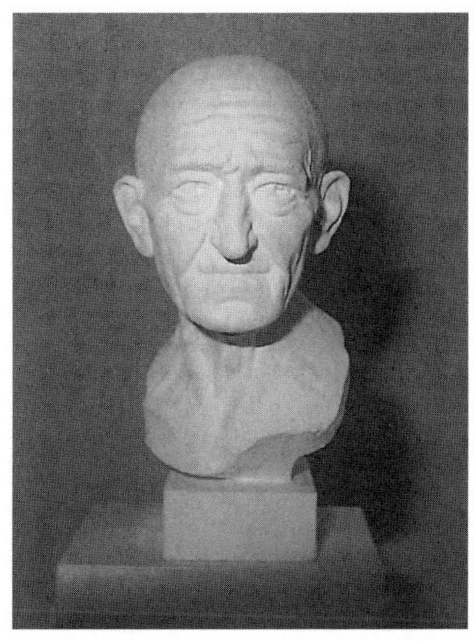

Front lighting *is simple, but flattens the details of the face; it is very suitable, however, for 'linear' and decorative portraits.*

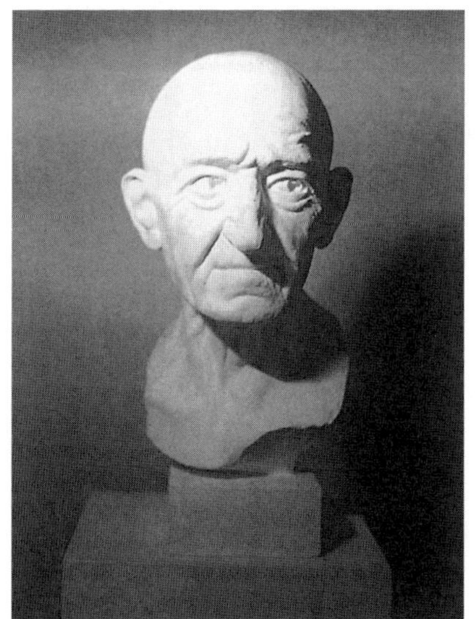

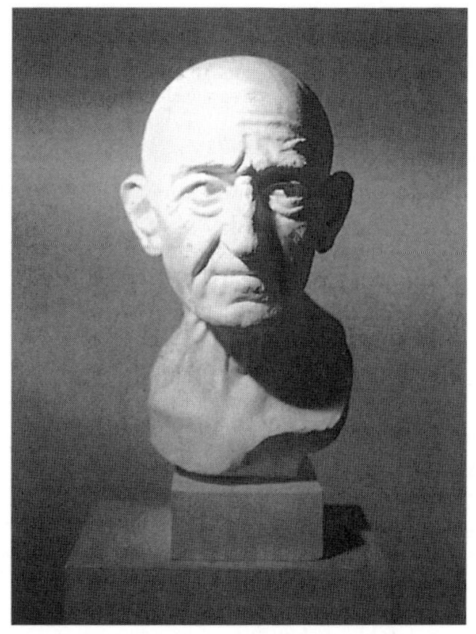

Angled lighting *from above, midway between front and side is the type of lighting most widely used in portraiture as it properly highlights the physiognomic characteristics and effectively conveys the plasticity of the face. These two photographs vary slightly in the inclination and distance of the light source from the subject.*

Lighting on the face can be natural or artificial. When sketching people in the street or other public places, you have to adapt to the lighting found in situ and try to turn it to your best advantage, or at least use it as a spur for better ideas. But when you are painting from a model in the studio, the intensity of the illumination and the most suitable kind of lighting to use are of central importance. For example, when creating a 'resemblance portrait', lighting schemes 1, 2, 3 and 5, below, would be the most advisable, while the other schemes would be suitable when seeking a dramatic effect, more probably in 'generic' face studies.

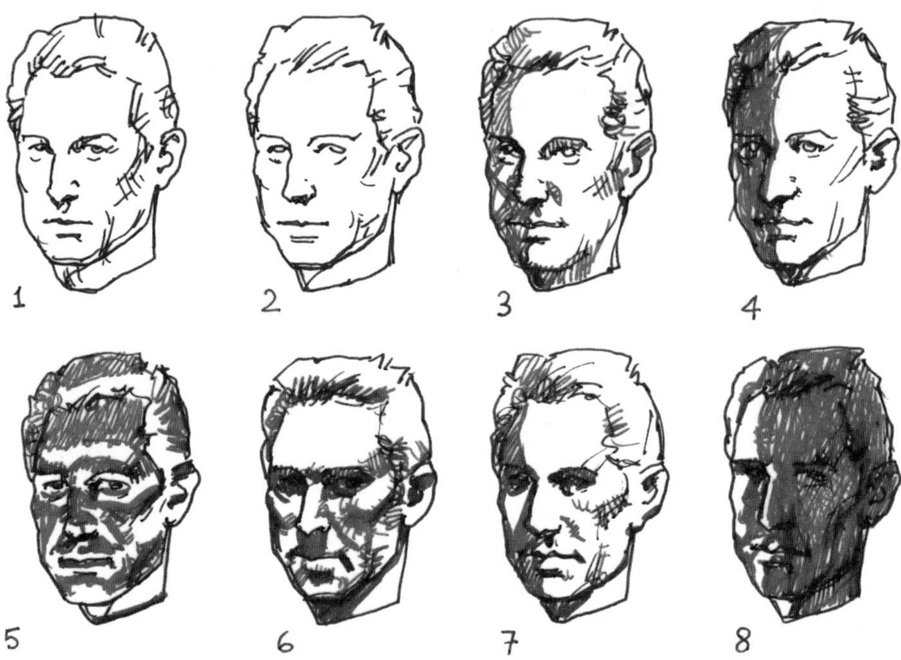

Some illustrated options for lighting the face:

1 *Diffuse lighting*

2 *Frontal illumination*

3 *Three-quarter lighting (with the light slightly to one side)*

4 *Lateral lighting (lighting from one side)*

5 *Illumination from below*

6 *Illumination from above*

7 *Three-quarter/lateral lighting from above*

8 *Three-quarter lighting from behind*

PAGES FROM A SKETCHBOOK: SKETCHES AND STUDIES FROM LIFE

Public places offer many favourable opportunities for observing the faces of strangers in their many forms, with various expressions and in different positions. An artist should get into the habit of making quick sketches of such subjects from life and keep a sketchbook and pencil to hand for recording faces and their details. These sketches can be just small 'annotations' jotted down as if for an anonymous portrait. This type of sketching trains the hand and strengthens essential skills of observation. The finished works can be used as suggestive material for more careful compositions. Here are some pages from the sketchbooks I took with me on a trip to Paris. The drawings were made in various situations and you may notice how I used these rapid sketches of strangers' faces as the basis for the portraits you will encounter later on in this book. See also pages 350–351.

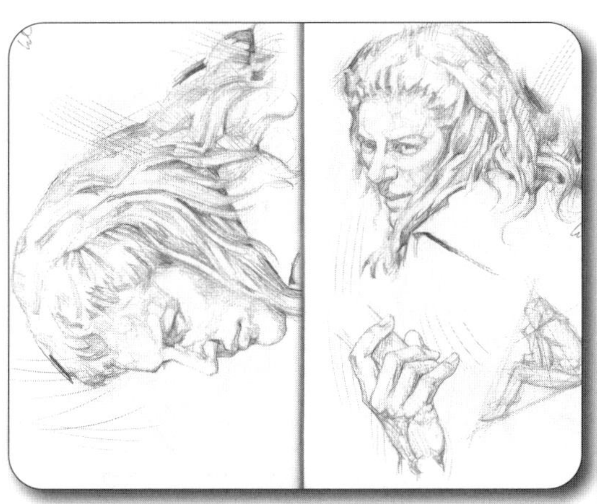

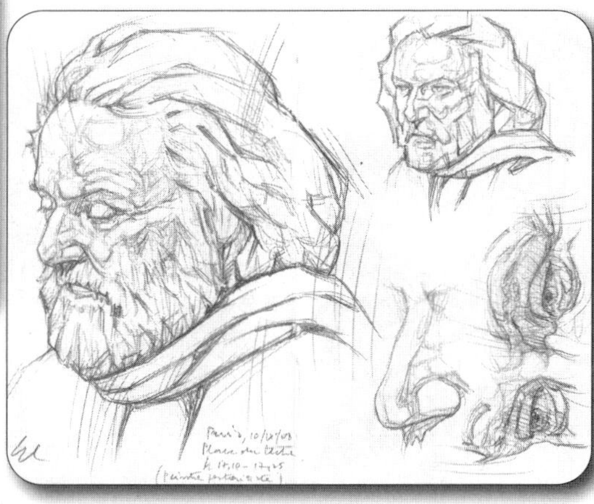

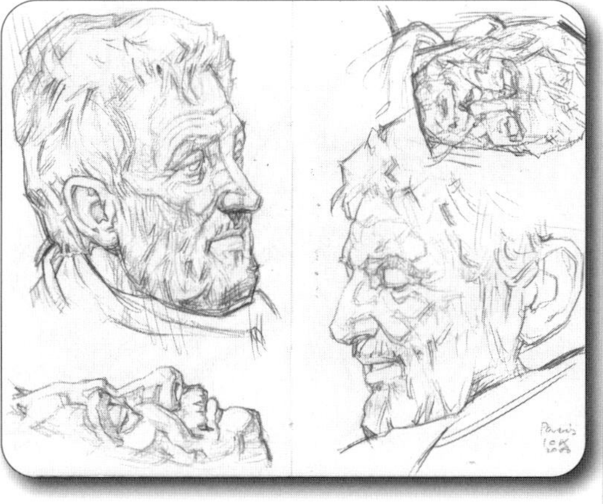

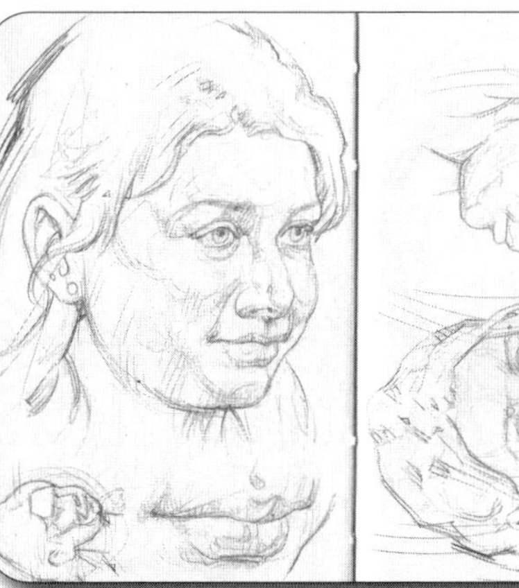

THE DRAWING METHOD

In this chapter, up to page 75, I illustrate the stages one has to go through to draw a portrait. The method indicated is rather formal, but useful to those new to portrait drawing. Once familiar with the elements which are essential to characterize a face, it will be easier and more spontaneous to move gradually from the first sketch to a more complex drawing and find your own, more immediate and personal, way forward. My advice is to do some of these exercises using live models and photographs, and to try to understand how each stage helps you tackle and solve a specific problem and how you get to draw a head correctly, at least from a formal point of view. Use sheets of white paper at least 30 × 40cm (12 × 15¾in) in size and pencils of various grades, as I have indicated.

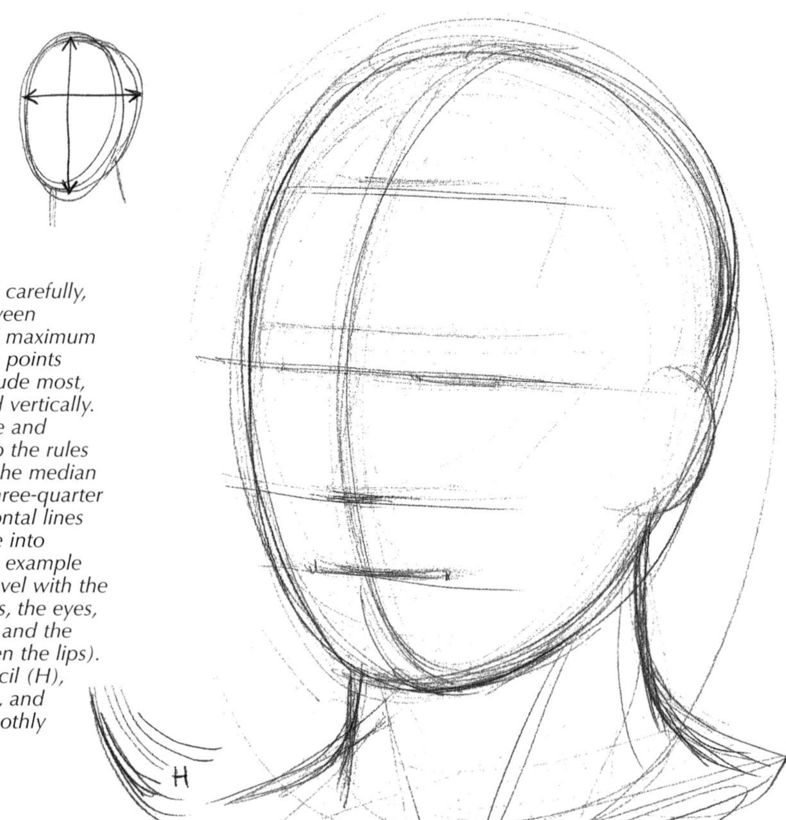

Stage 1

Observing the model carefully, find the relation between maximum height and maximum width by locating the points of the face that protrude most, both horizontally and vertically. Sketch the oval shape and indicate, according to the rules of perspective, both the median line (curved in this three-quarter view), and the horizontal lines which divide the face into different parts. In this example I have drawn them level with the hairline, the eyebrows, the eyes, the base of the nose, and the rima (the line between the lips). Use a fairly hard pencil (H), which won't smudge, and draw the strokes smoothly and lightly.

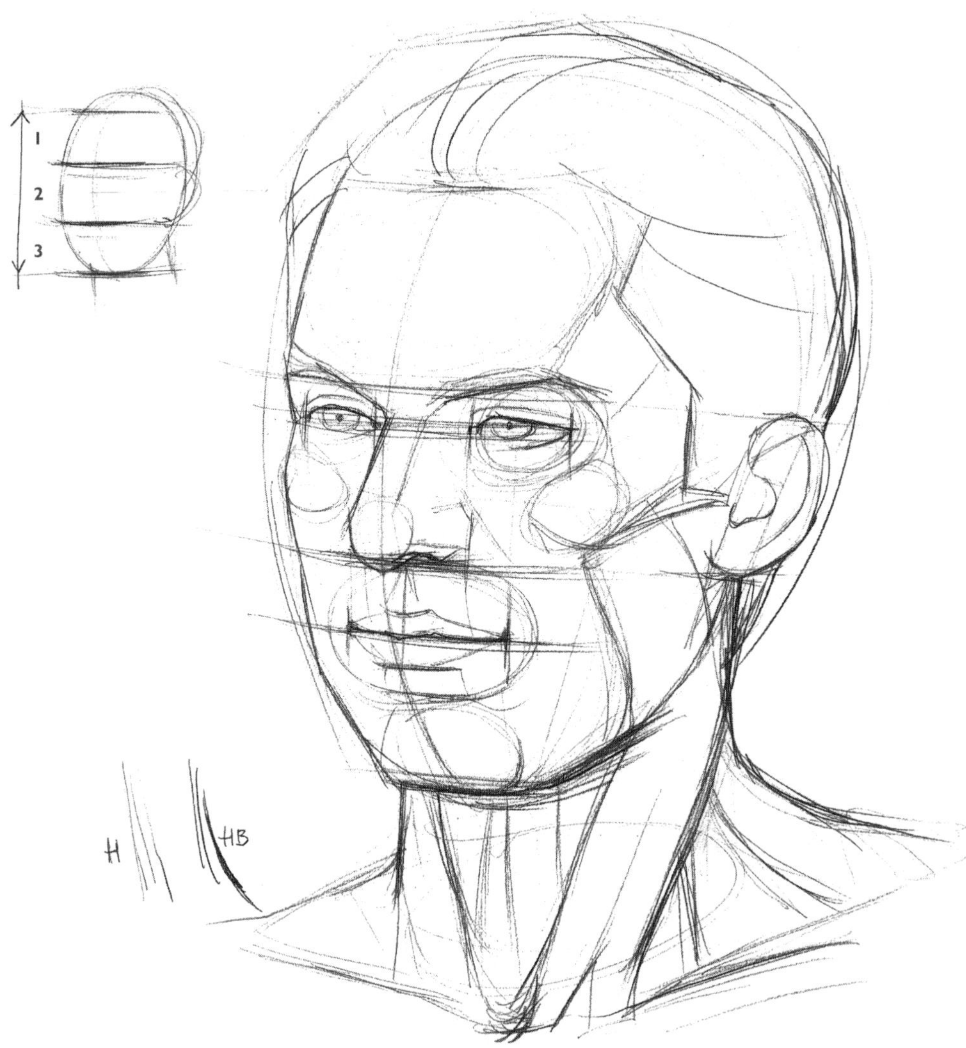

Stage 2

Continue to refine your sketch and carefully position the details of the face, i.e. the eyes, the nose, the mouth and the ears. Note that the subdivision of the face into three sections is approximate. Try to find in each individual the specific relative proportions and stick to them to achieve a likeness. This stage is very important as it lays the ground for the subsequent development of the drawing. Also try to recognize and lightly sketch the main anatomic structures (the subcutaneous bones, the surface muscles, etc). Here, for example, I have indicated the protruding cheekbones and frontalis bone, the position of the orbicularis oris, masseter and sternocleidomastoid muscles. Again, draw light strokes with an H pencil or, if you prefer, an HB.

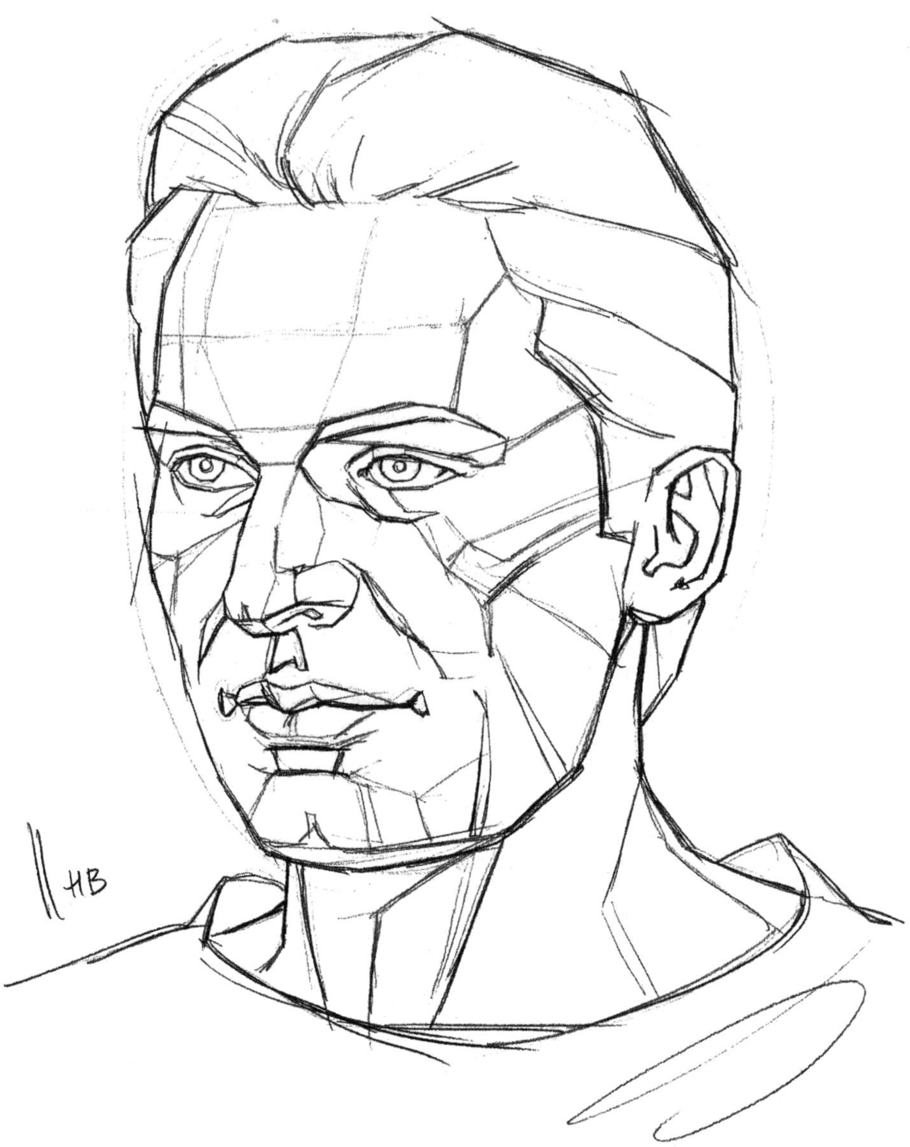

Stage 3

At this stage it's better to concentrate on recognizing the 'surface planes', i.e. those areas which are subtly distinguished by the different effect of the light. Concisely outline the areas (both lit and in shadow), as this can help you give an overall feeling of a solid, three-dimensional structure to the drawing. Be careful not to overdo the straight strokes to avoid a 'hard', angular shape. However, a certain 'dryness' can help to simplify the tonal planes in view of the subsequent stages. Use a medium-grade pencil, such as HB.

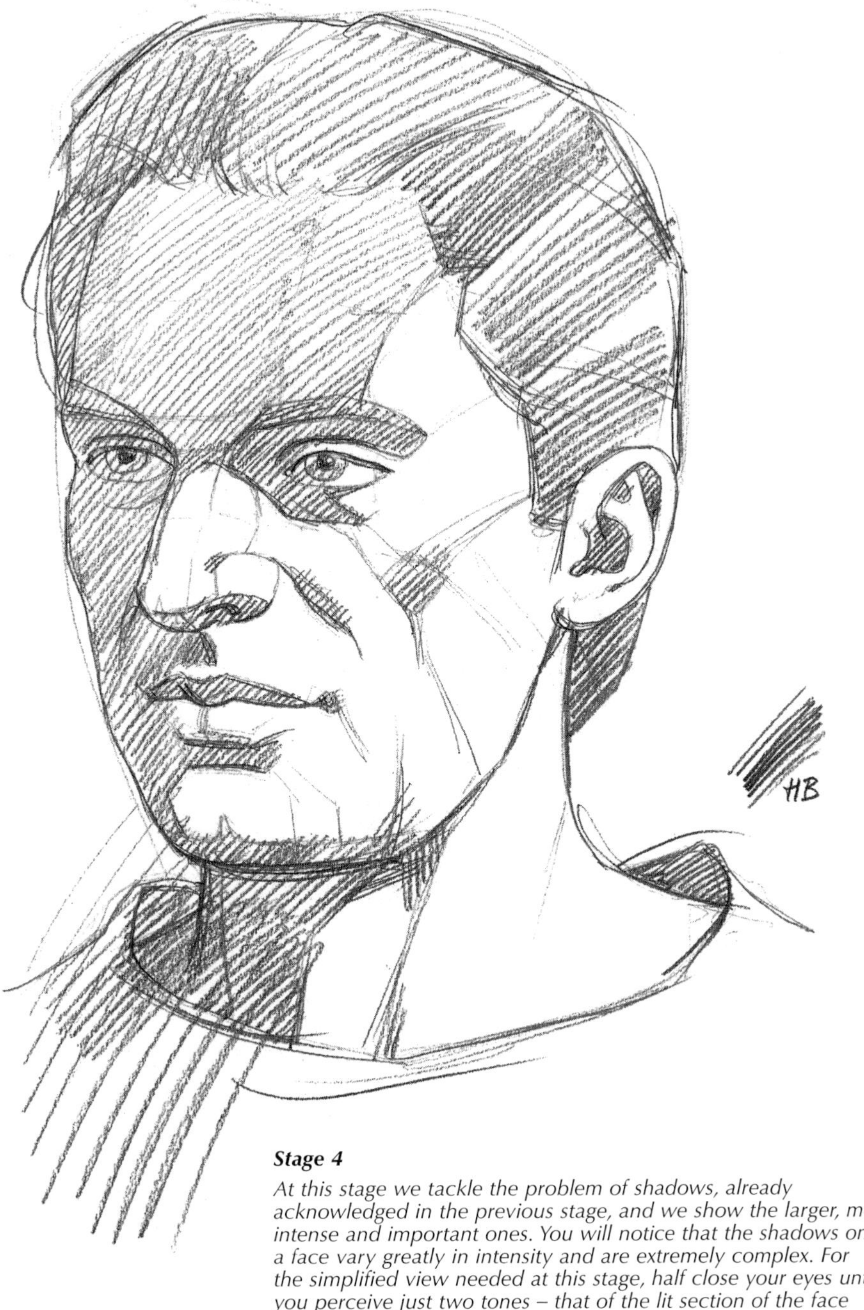

Stage 4

At this stage we tackle the problem of shadows, already acknowledged in the previous stage, and we show the larger, more intense and important ones. You will notice that the shadows on a face vary greatly in intensity and are extremely complex. For the simplified view needed at this stage, half close your eyes until you perceive just two tones – that of the lit section of the face and that of the areas in shadow. Again use a HB pencil lightly and rather evenly.

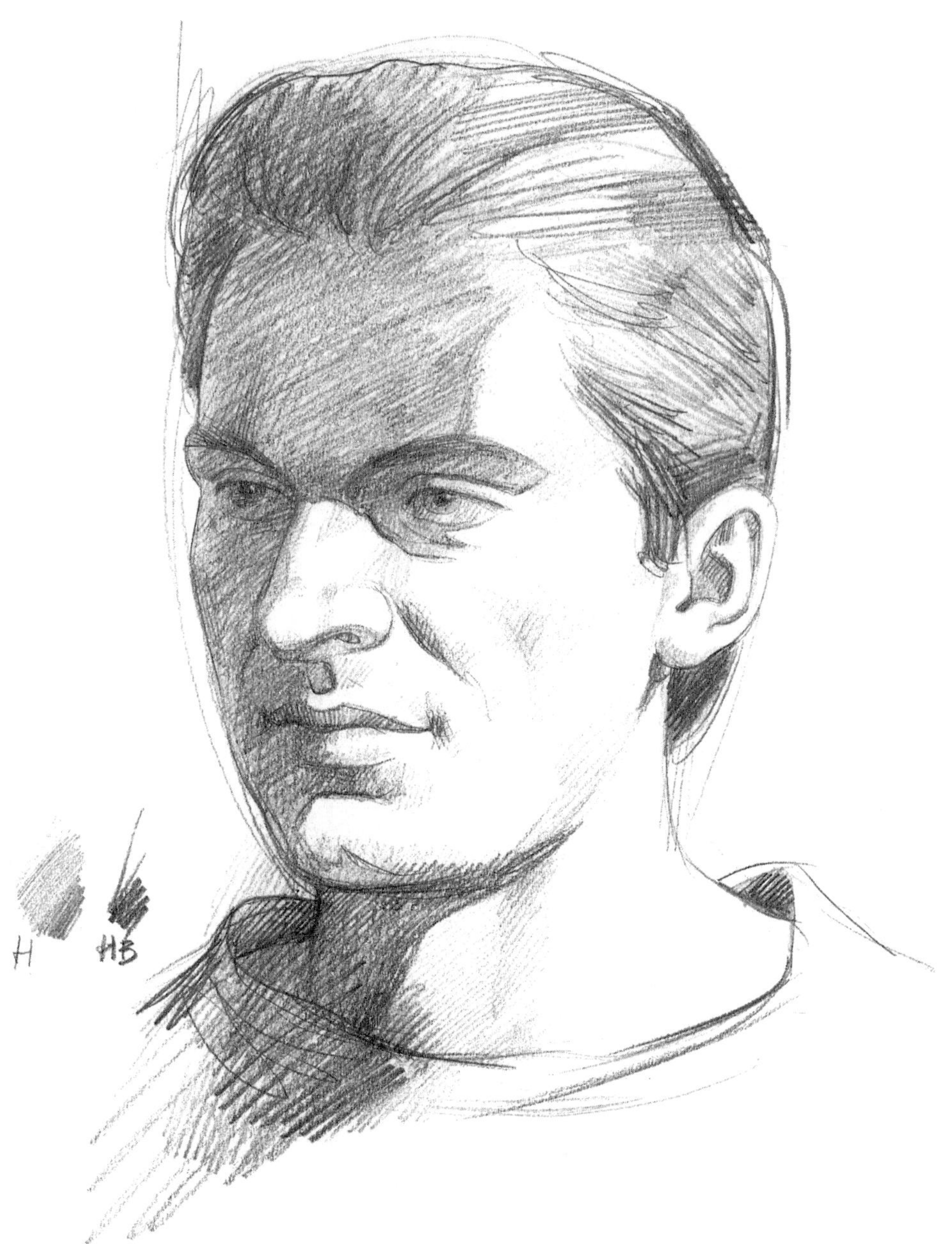

Stage 5

At this stage and, if necessary, in the next ones, proceed to fashion the surface shapes of the face, looking for the intermediate tones (which in the previous stage were left out and incorporated in the overall area of shadow). In addition, define the most significant details, for instance the eyes and the lips, enhancing or lightening the tonal values which define them. Again, use an HB pencil, varying the intensity of the stroke by increasing or decreasing the pressure on the paper. H pencil can be used to indicate areas of very weak tone.

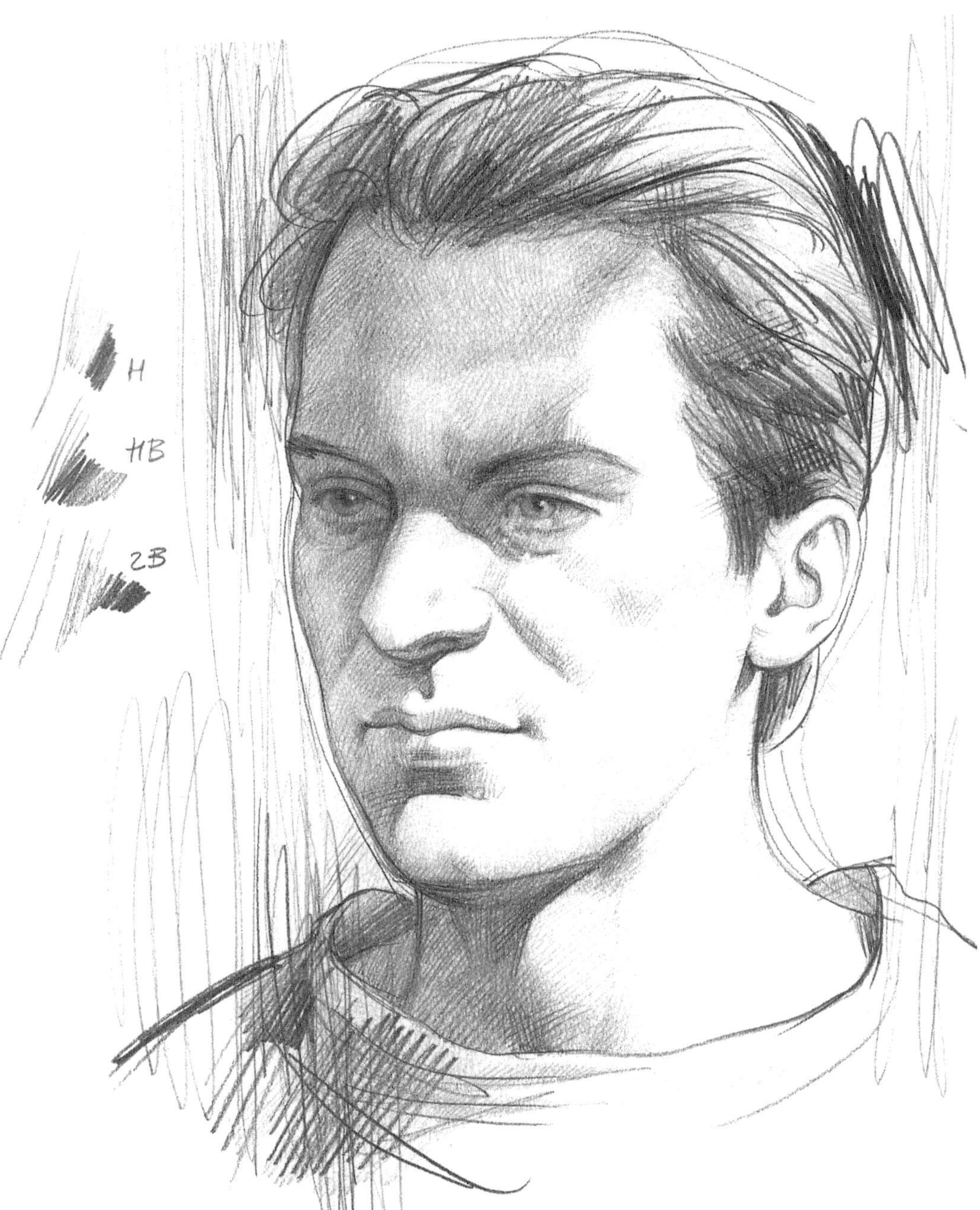

The drawing, now at an advanced stage, preserves traces of the previous stages. Do not erase them; rather 'soften them up', further perfecting the tones and blending them. It is impossible (and useless) to try to reproduce in a drawing all the tonal shades one finds in life. Therefore don't overdo the 'finishing touches' and the insignificant detail because a good drawing is always the result of careful selection and intelligent, sensitive simplification. Shadows can be intensified in places with a 2B pencil, which is rather soft.

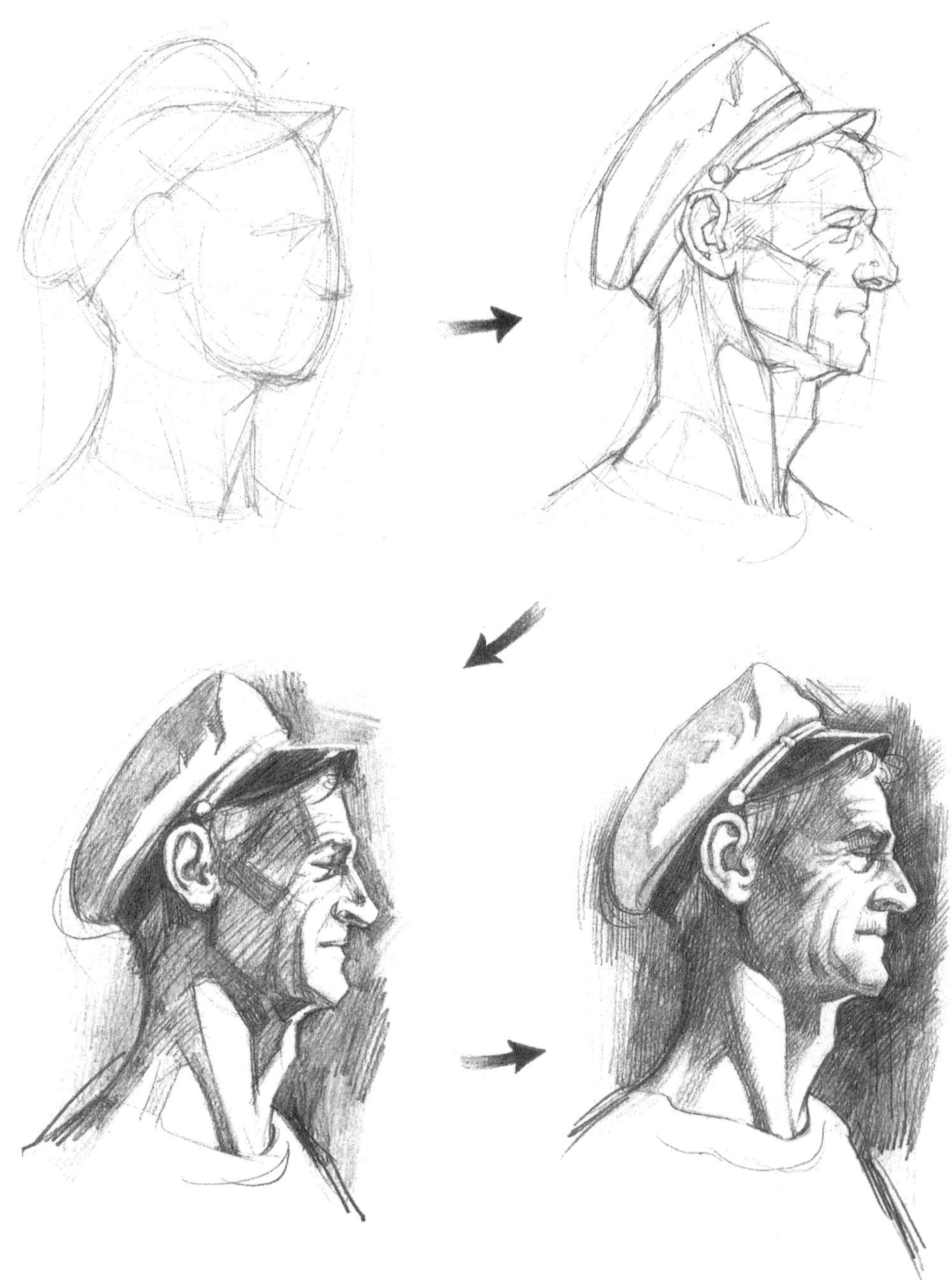

The sketches above are restructures (done 'afterwards' for the purpose of demonstration) of some of the stages which I follow as a rule, by now almost instinctively, when I draw a portrait.

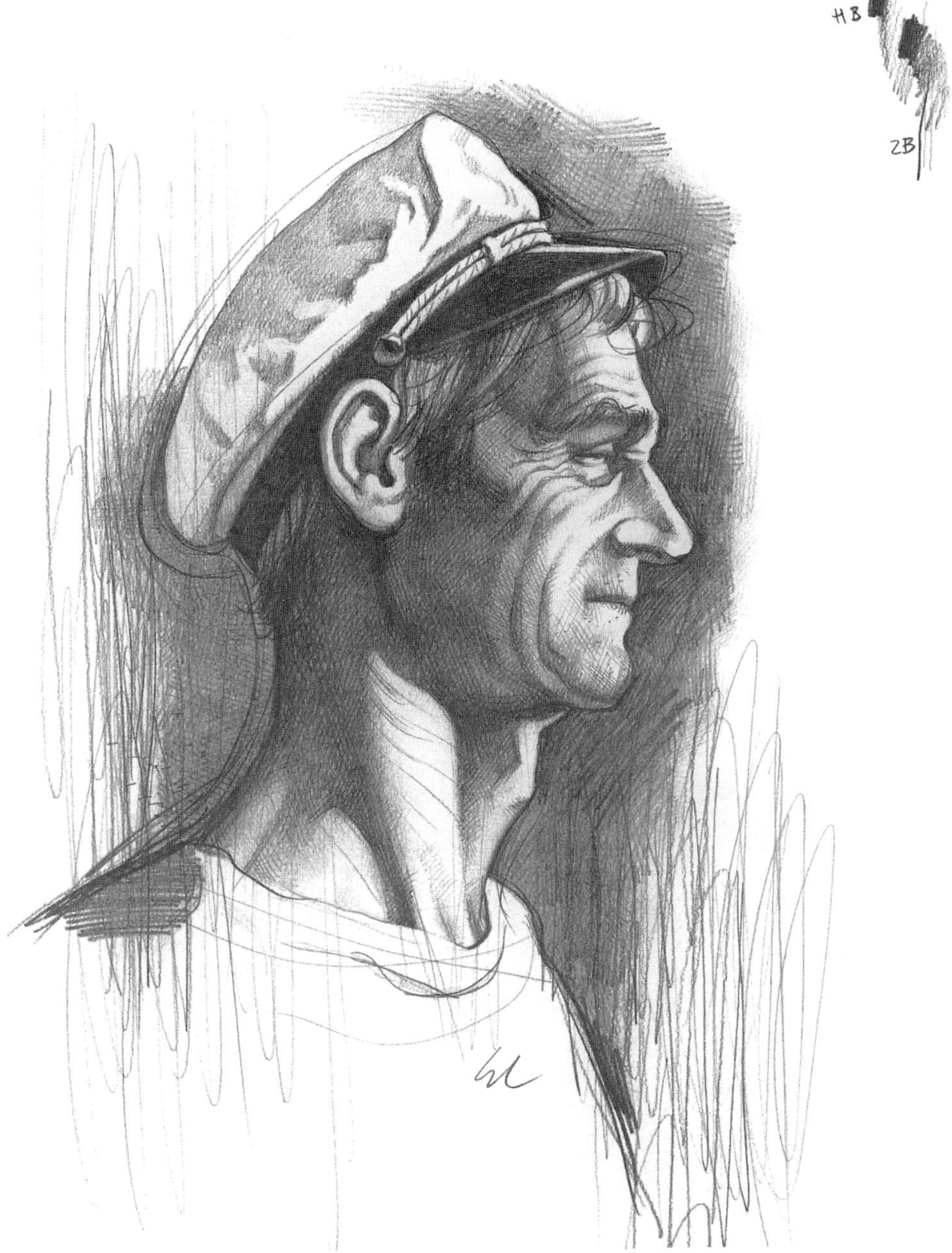

Portrait study

HB pencil (with some 2B added on) on medium-textured paper, 33 × 48cm (13 × 19in)

Charcoal is suitable for portraiture because it allows you to draw the tones of the face quickly and effectively. The method is slightly different from that followed with a pencil: with a few light strokes outline the head, then fill and blend with your fingers or a wad of cotton wool (stage 1); exercising more pressure on the charcoal, darken the areas of the face which appear in shadow and blend again (stage 2); then gradually try to find the different tones of chiaroscuro, *darkening some areas, lightening others more exposed to the light (stages 3 and 4). To erase or lighten tones use a kneadable putty eraser, gently pressing it and rubbing lightly. Do not grade the shading excessively or you will 'weaken' the drawing and give it a photographic, affected look. Rather, pay attention to the large masses and the main features of the face.*

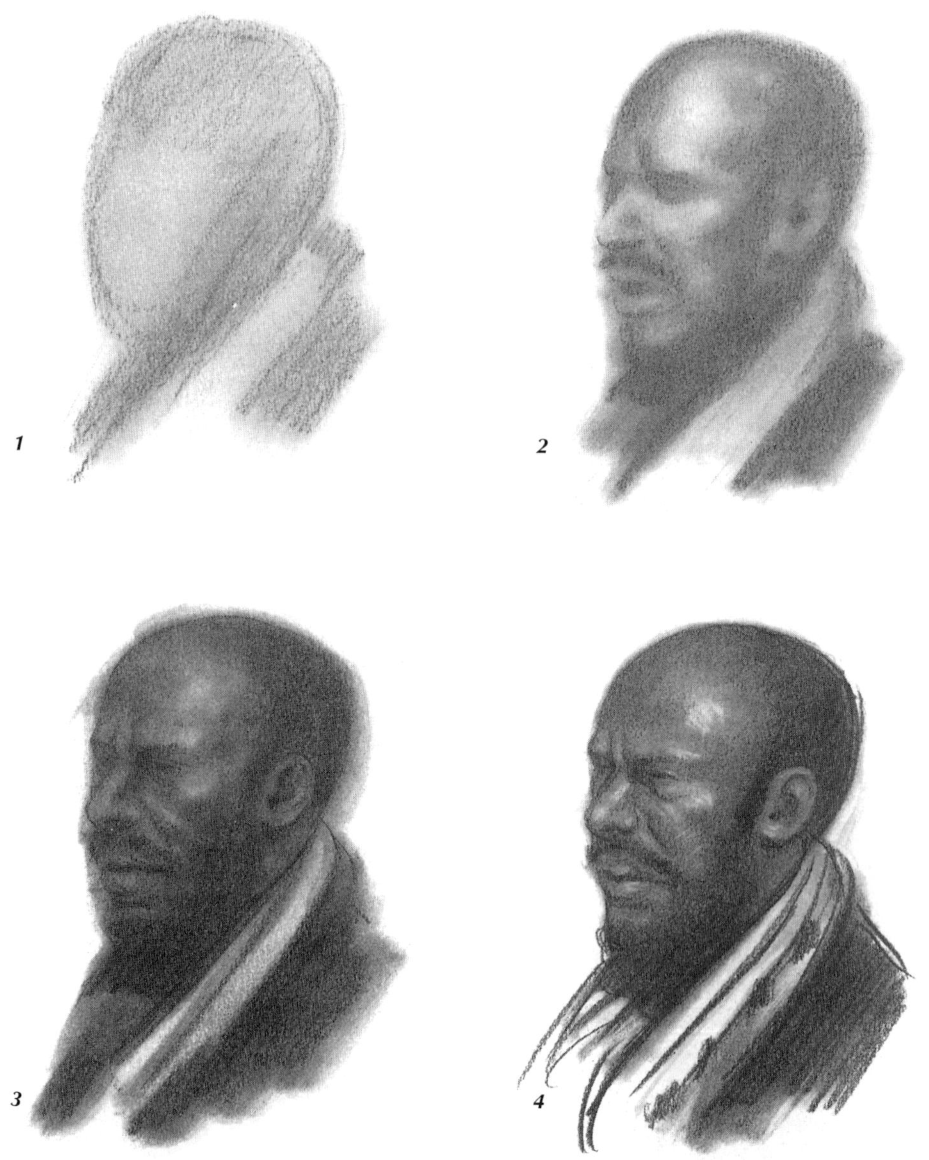

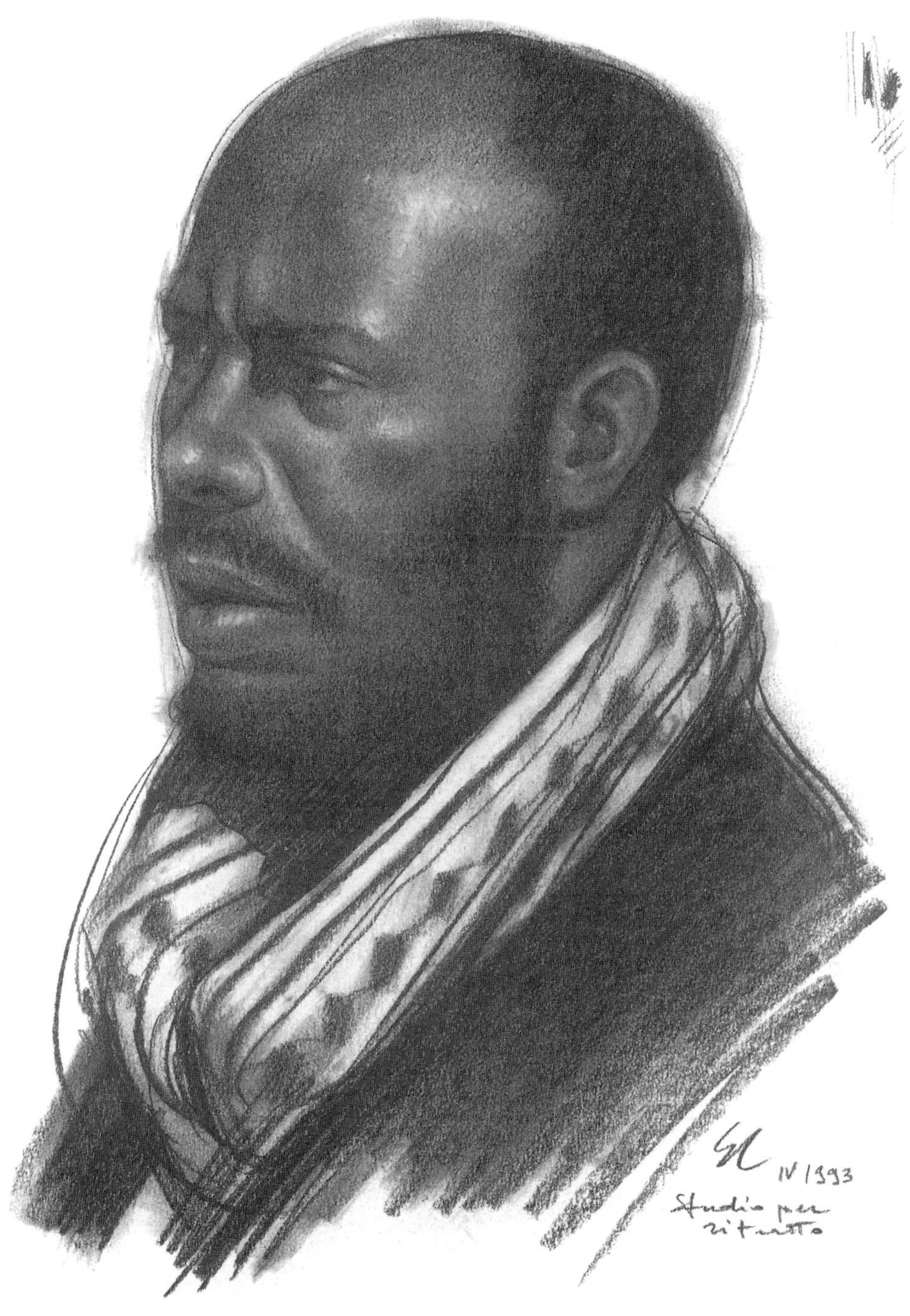

Portrait study

Compressed sepia charcoal on medium-textured paper, 33 × 48cm (13 × 19in)

PORTRAIT STUDIES

In this section I have put together a series of portraits. Almost all of them are studies for oil paintings or for more elaborate drawings and I chose them because the intermediate stages of implementation, more than the 'finished' works, are the ones which show how to recognize and tackle the problems of composition, pose, anatomy and working technique.

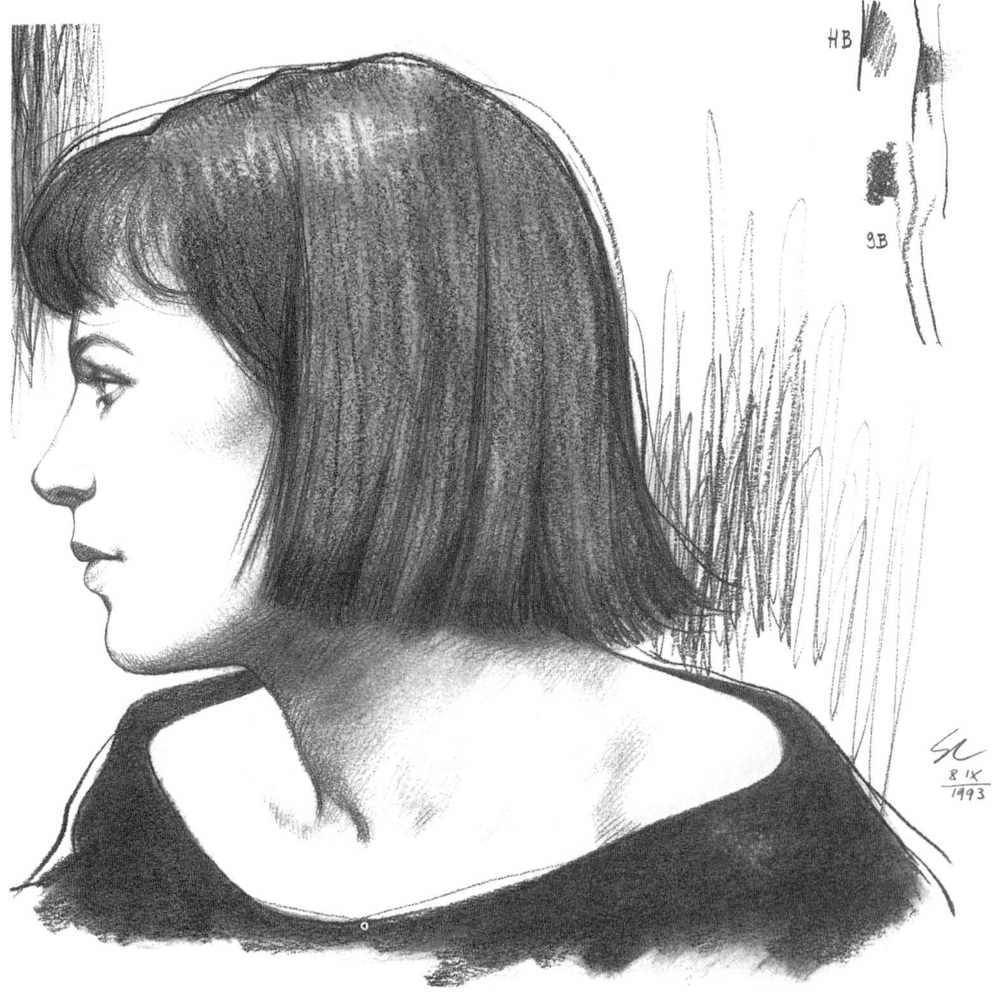

H, HB and 9B pencil on 30 × 40cm (12 × 15¾in) paper

The portrait in profile works well with young subjects: the hair contrasts with the features and creates interesting effects of composition. For the hair I used HB pencil, lightly blended with a finger, and added darker accents with a 9B, drawing some 'flat' strokes using the side of the point.

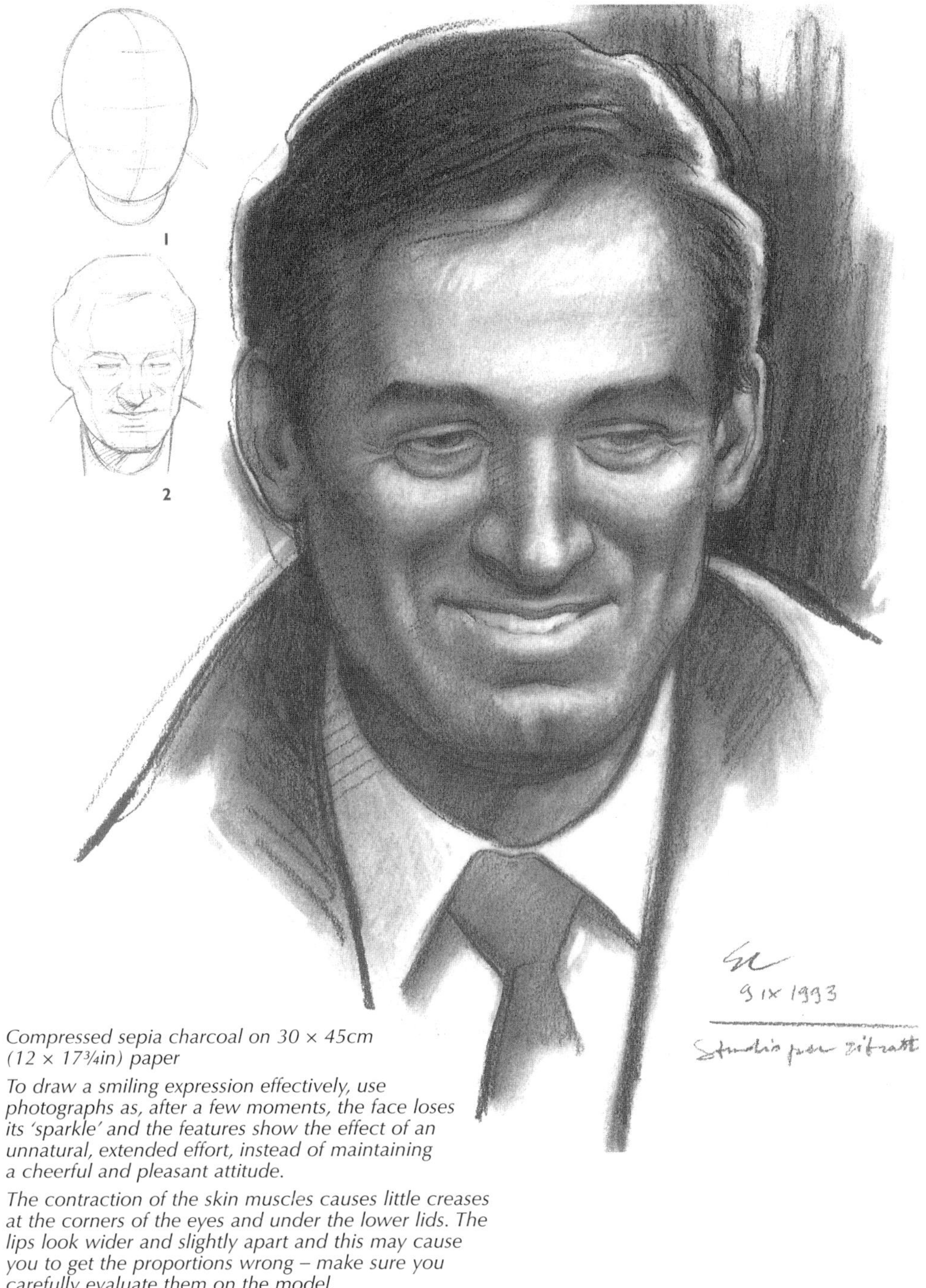

Compressed sepia charcoal on 30 × 45cm (12 × 17¾in) paper

To draw a smiling expression effectively, use photographs as, after a few moments, the face loses its 'sparkle' and the features show the effect of an unnatural, extended effort, instead of maintaining a cheerful and pleasant attitude.

The contraction of the skin muscles causes little creases at the corners of the eyes and under the lower lids. The lips look wider and slightly apart and this may cause you to get the proportions wrong – make sure you carefully evaluate them on the model.

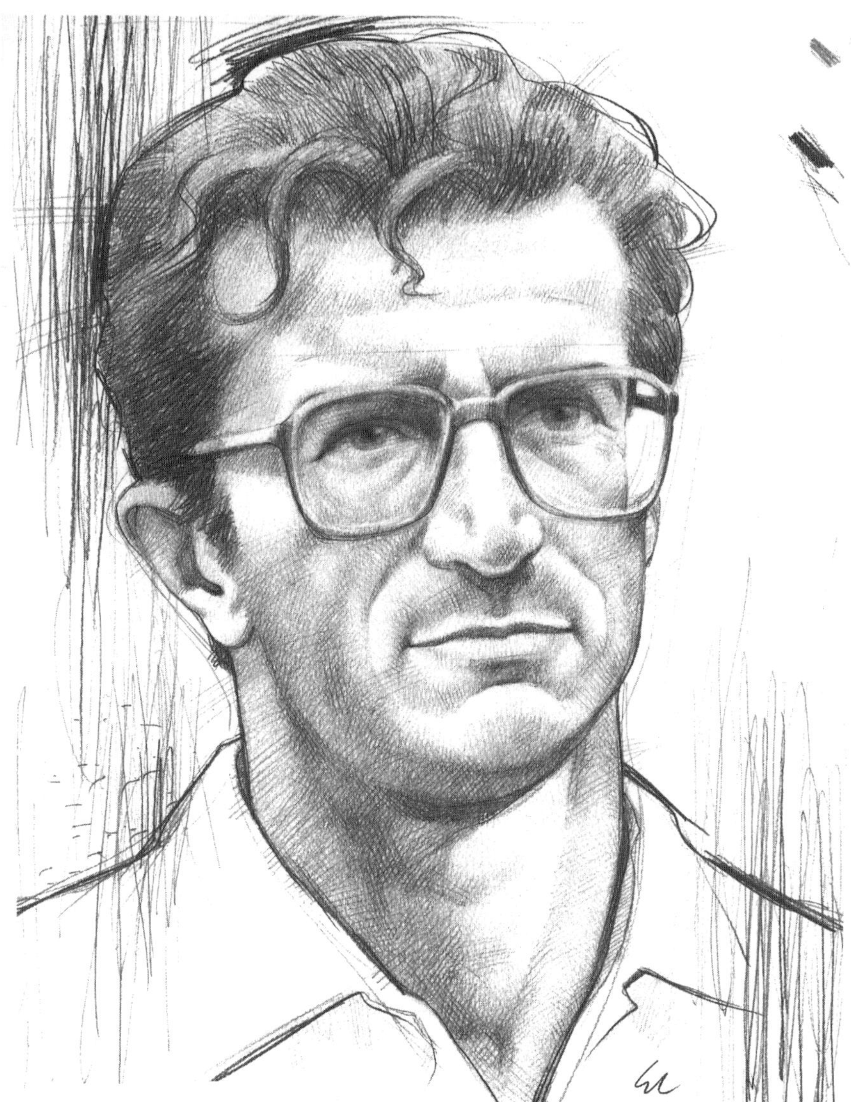

Self-portrait

HB and 2B pencil on paper, 33 × 48cm (13 × 19in)

The one model you can study whenever you like and in any condition is the one you see in the mirror. Practise drawing your mirror image and don't worry too much if, in the end, you don't recognize yourself fully in that self-portrait. Posing is tiring and, after a short while, your usual expression will look 'drawn' and hard. You could, of course, use photographs, but if you draw from life, the result is more gratifying. Above all try to get the relative proportions of the whole head and then insert the details. Glasses, if worn, become part of the physiognomy of the face and a defining characteristic. Lenses can distort the size and shape of the eyes, enlarging them or making them smaller. Also bear in mind the shadows cast by the frame.

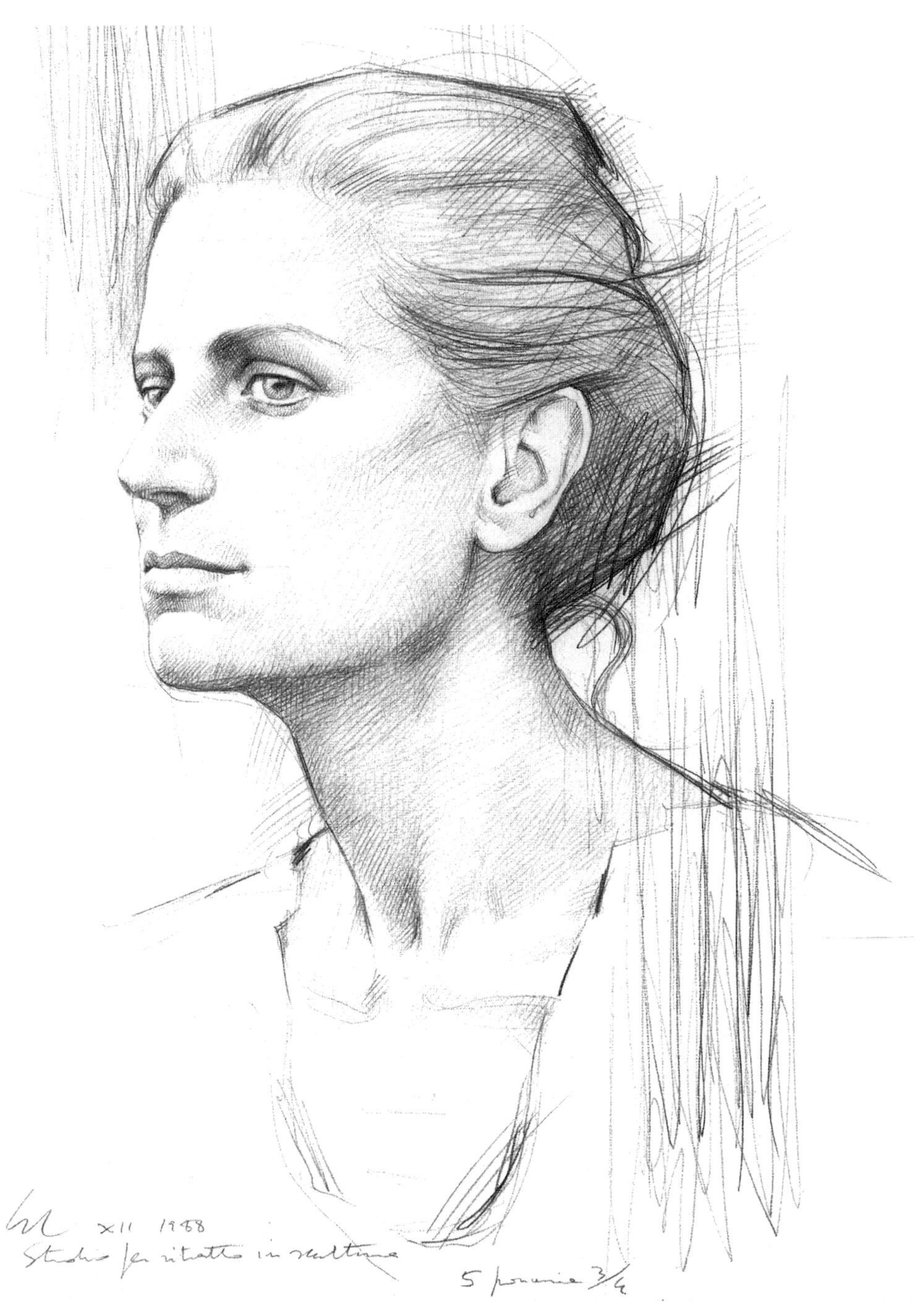

HB pencil on paper, 30 × 40cm (12 × 15¾in)

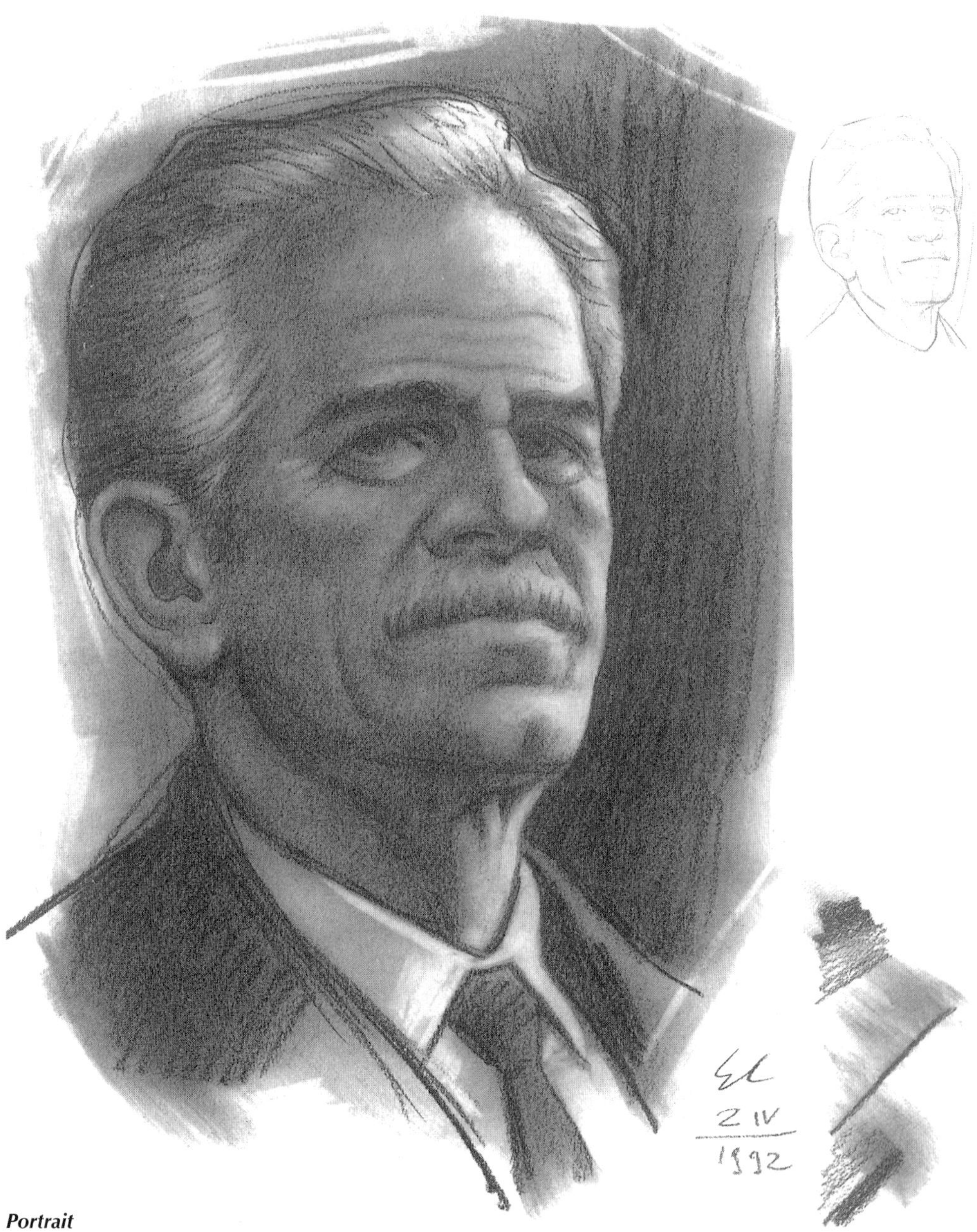

Portrait

Charcoal on paper, 33 × 48cm (13 × 19in)

To draw this study I used weak side lighting as it seemed particularly suited to highlighting the 'severe' character of the subject. The sketch shown on top indicates the basic lines drawn to find the proportions.

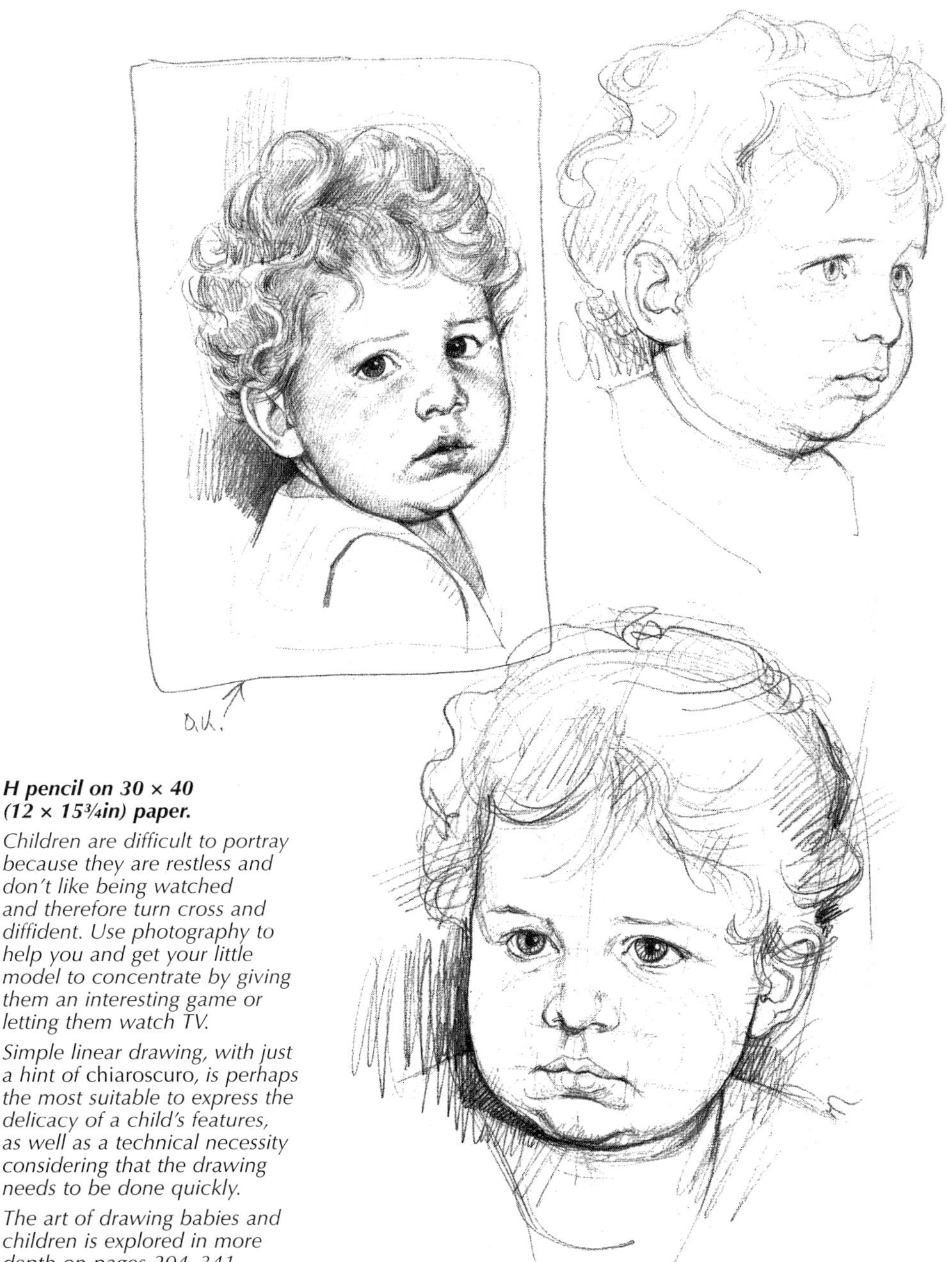

H pencil on 30 × 40 (12 × 15¾in) paper.

Children are difficult to portray because they are restless and don't like being watched and therefore turn cross and diffident. Use photography to help you and get your little model to concentrate by giving them an interesting game or letting them watch TV.

Simple linear drawing, with just a hint of chiaroscuro, is perhaps the most suitable to express the delicacy of a child's features, as well as a technical necessity considering that the drawing needs to be done quickly.

The art of drawing babies and children is explored in more depth on pages 204–341.

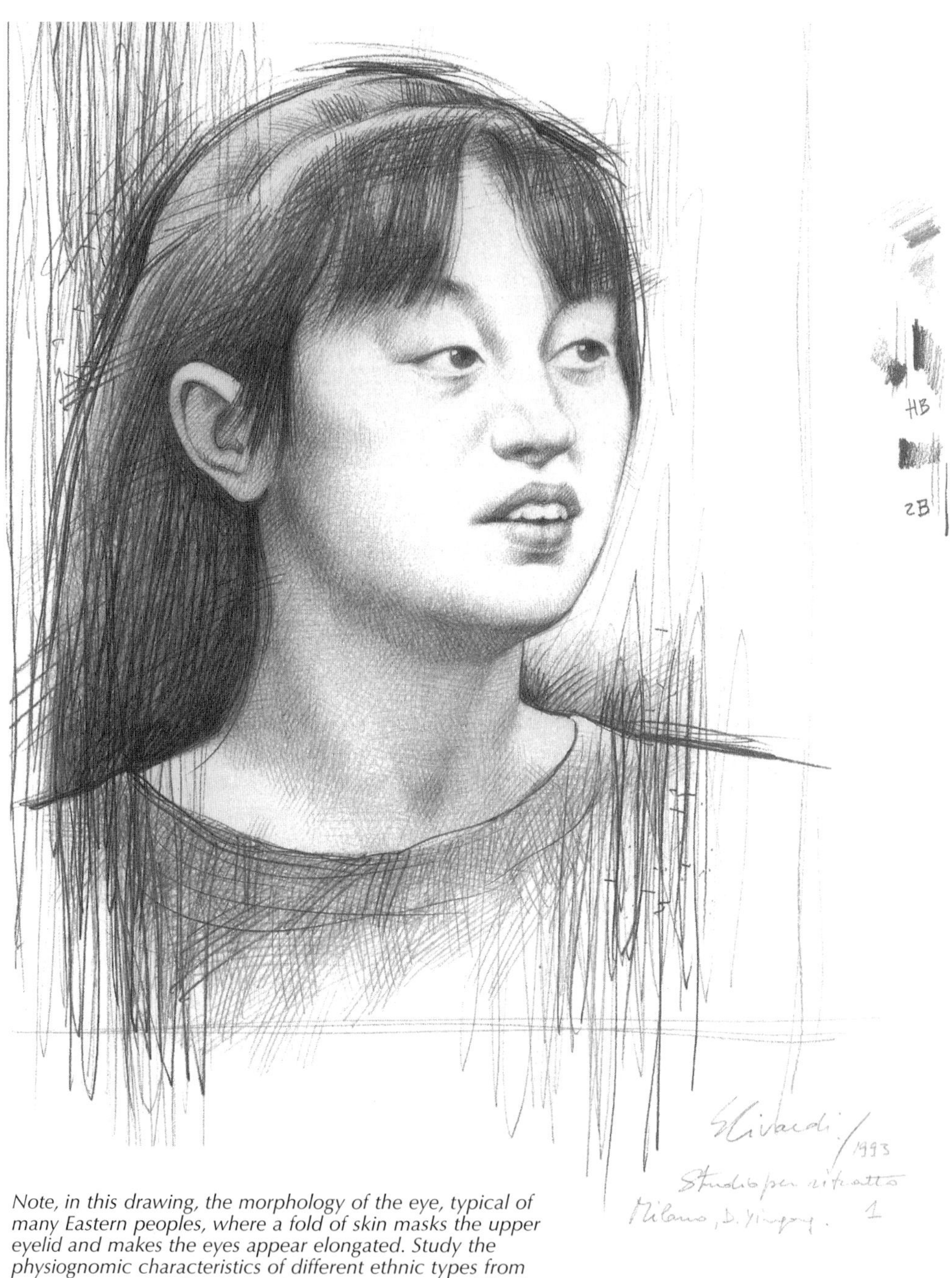

Note, in this drawing, the morphology of the eye, typical of many Eastern peoples, where a fold of skin masks the upper eyelid and makes the eyes appear elongated. Study the physiognomic characteristics of different ethnic types from your own practise drawing, as it can sometimes be difficult, at least to begin with, to get a good likeness.

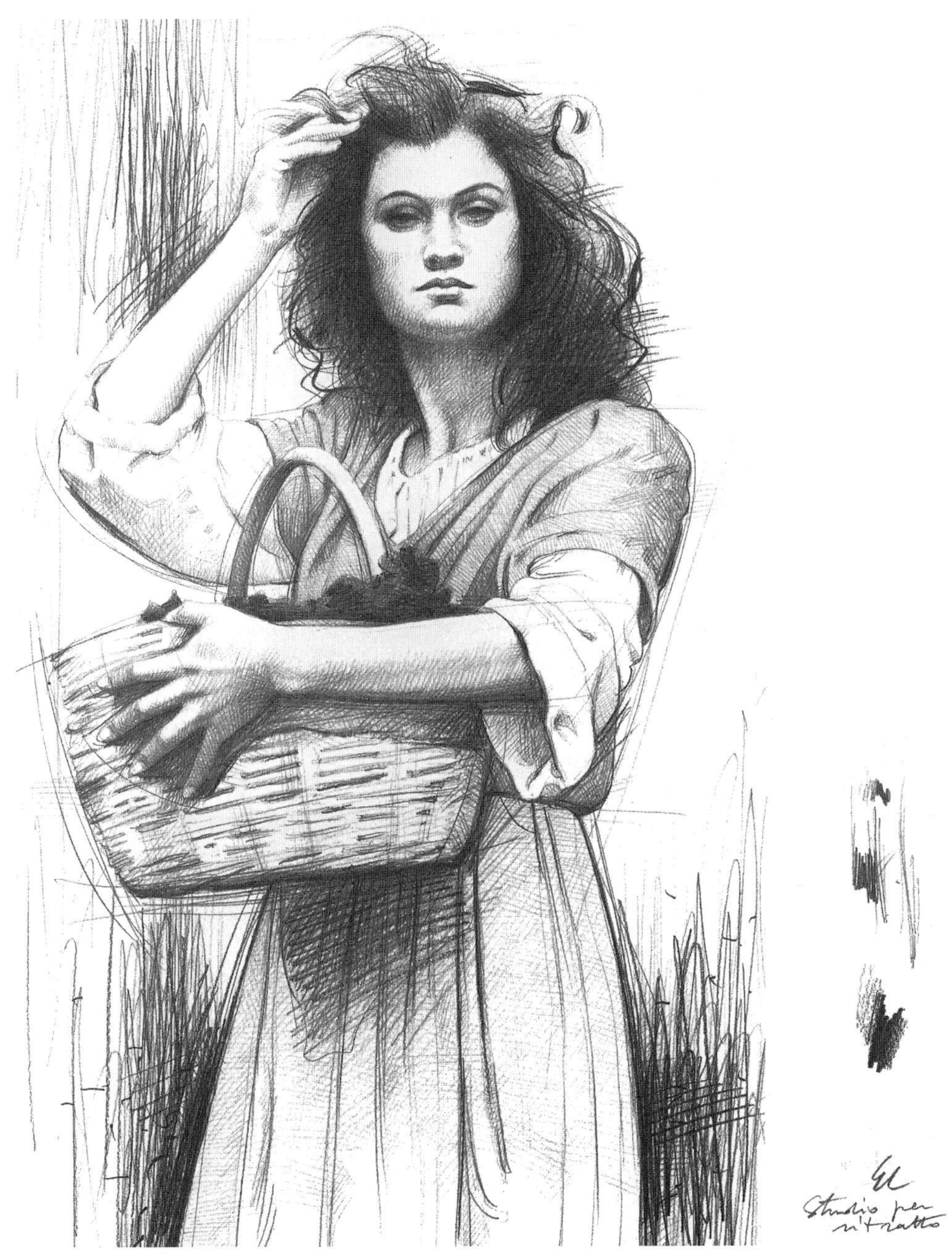

Pencil on paper, 35 × 45cm (14 × 17¾in).

It is sometimes worthwhile introducing elements which can make a portrait less 'formal', as for example the basket in this study. This has enabled me to catch the subject in a pose both informal and spontaneous, almost 'immediate'.

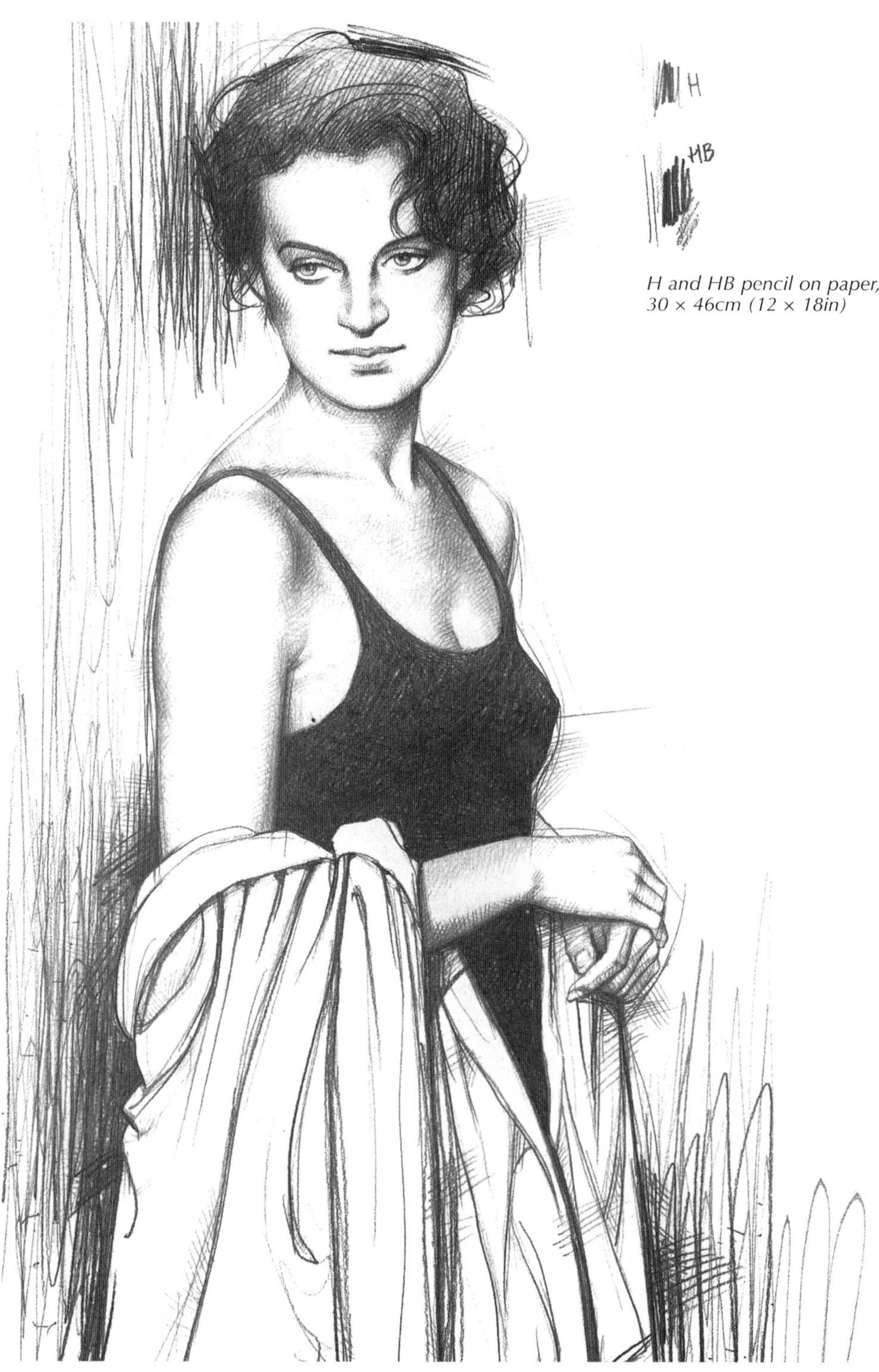

H and HB pencil on paper, 30 × 46cm (12 × 18in)

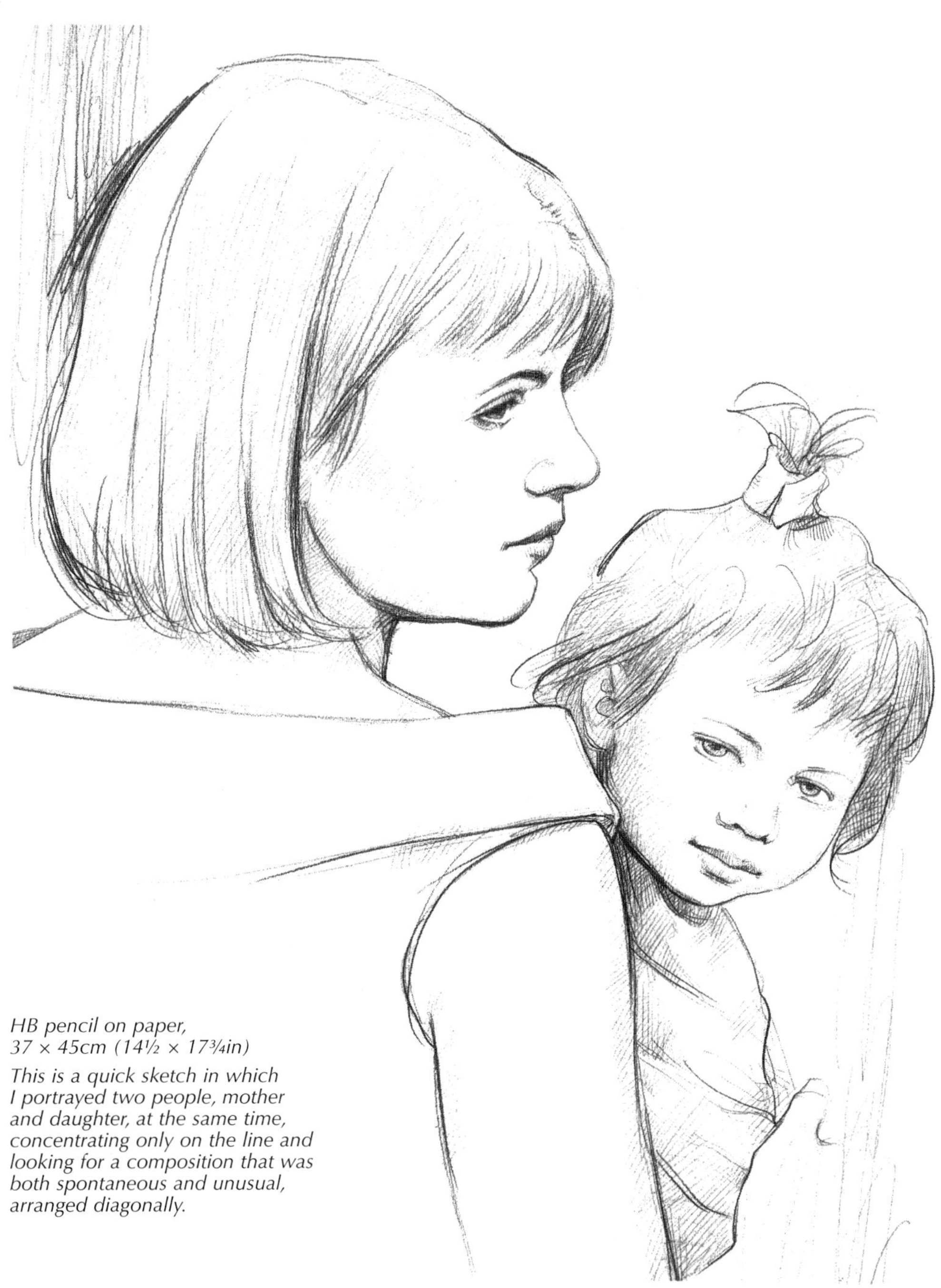

HB pencil on paper, 37 × 45cm (14½ × 17¾in)

This is a quick sketch in which I portrayed two people, mother and daughter, at the same time, concentrating only on the line and looking for a composition that was both spontaneous and unusual, arranged diagonally.

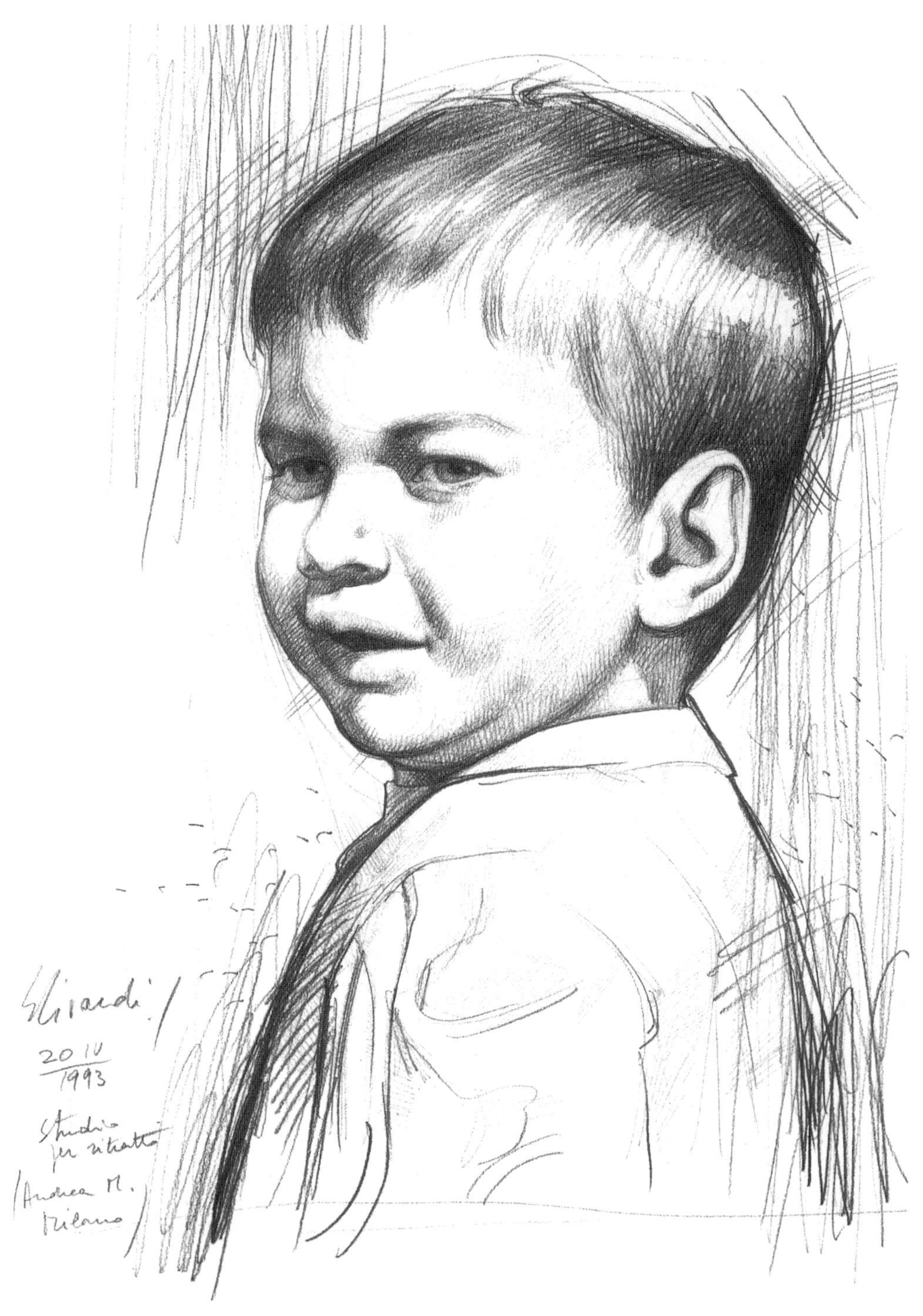

B pencil on paper, 34 × 48cm (13¼ × 19in)

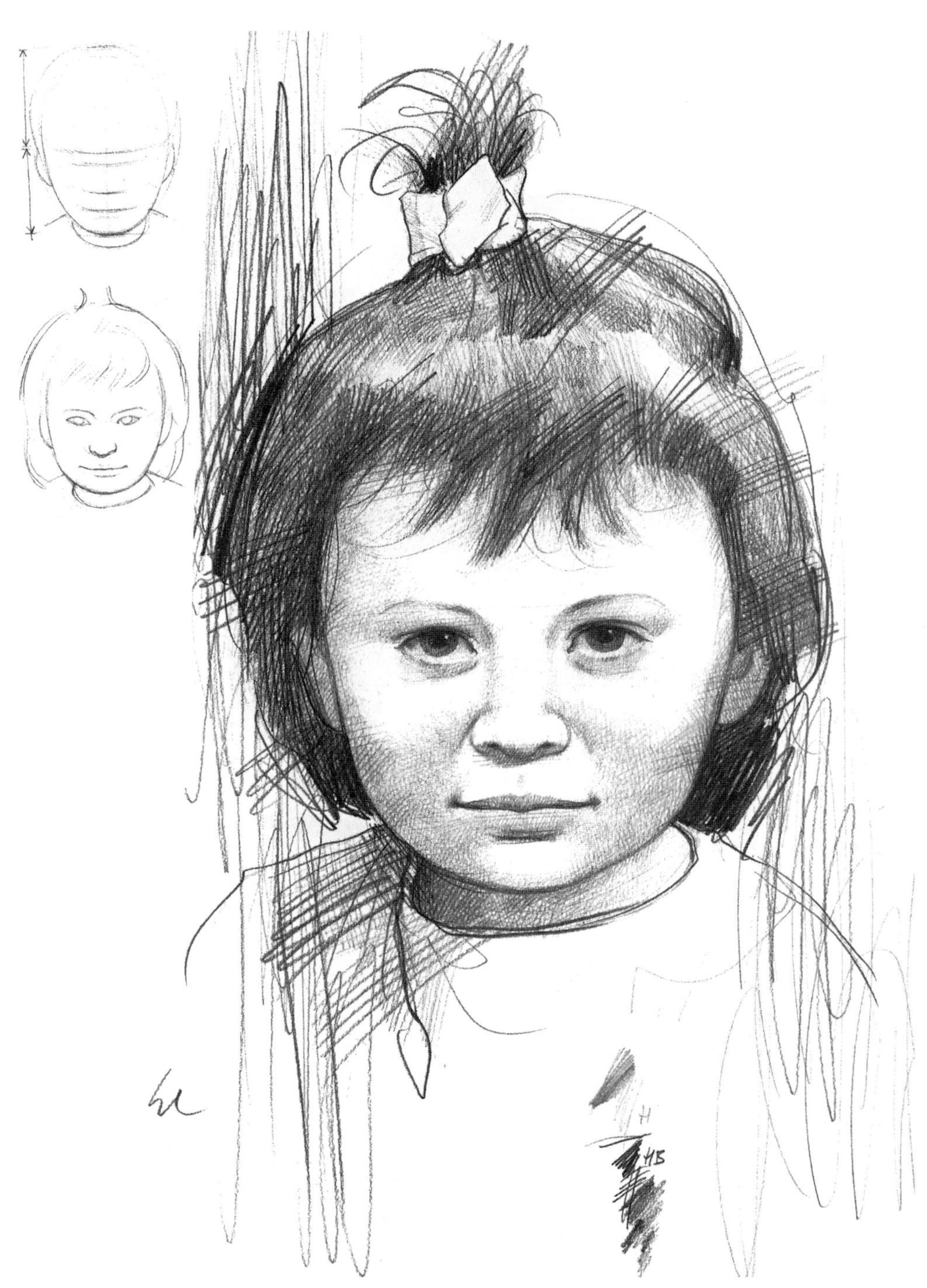

H and HB pencil on paper

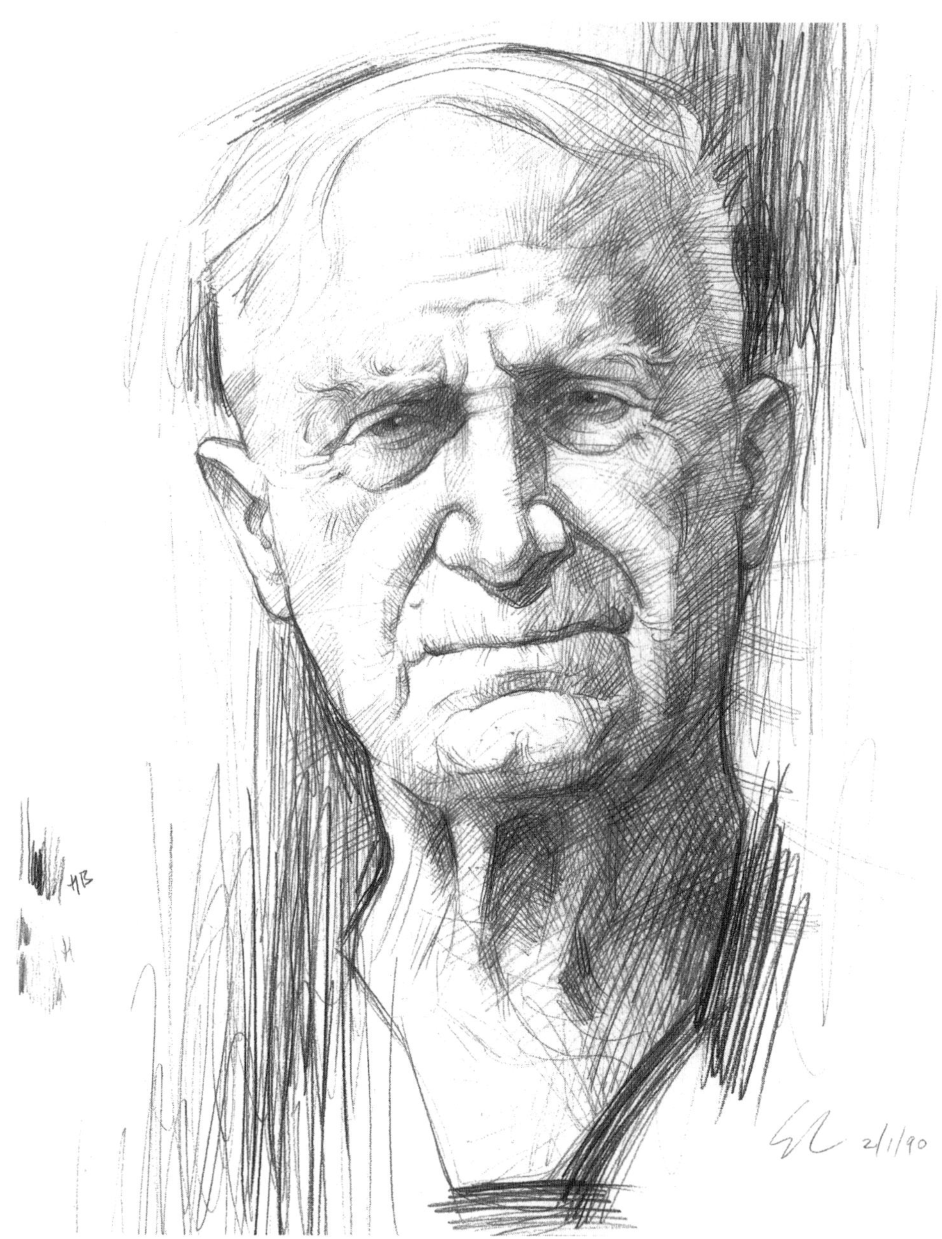

The drawings on these two pages are studies that I drew from life for a carved portrait. I walked around the model observing his features from different viewpoints (you can see the profile on page 94), and I partly neglected the chiaroscuro effects as I was interested, most of all, in understanding the volumetric structure of the head.

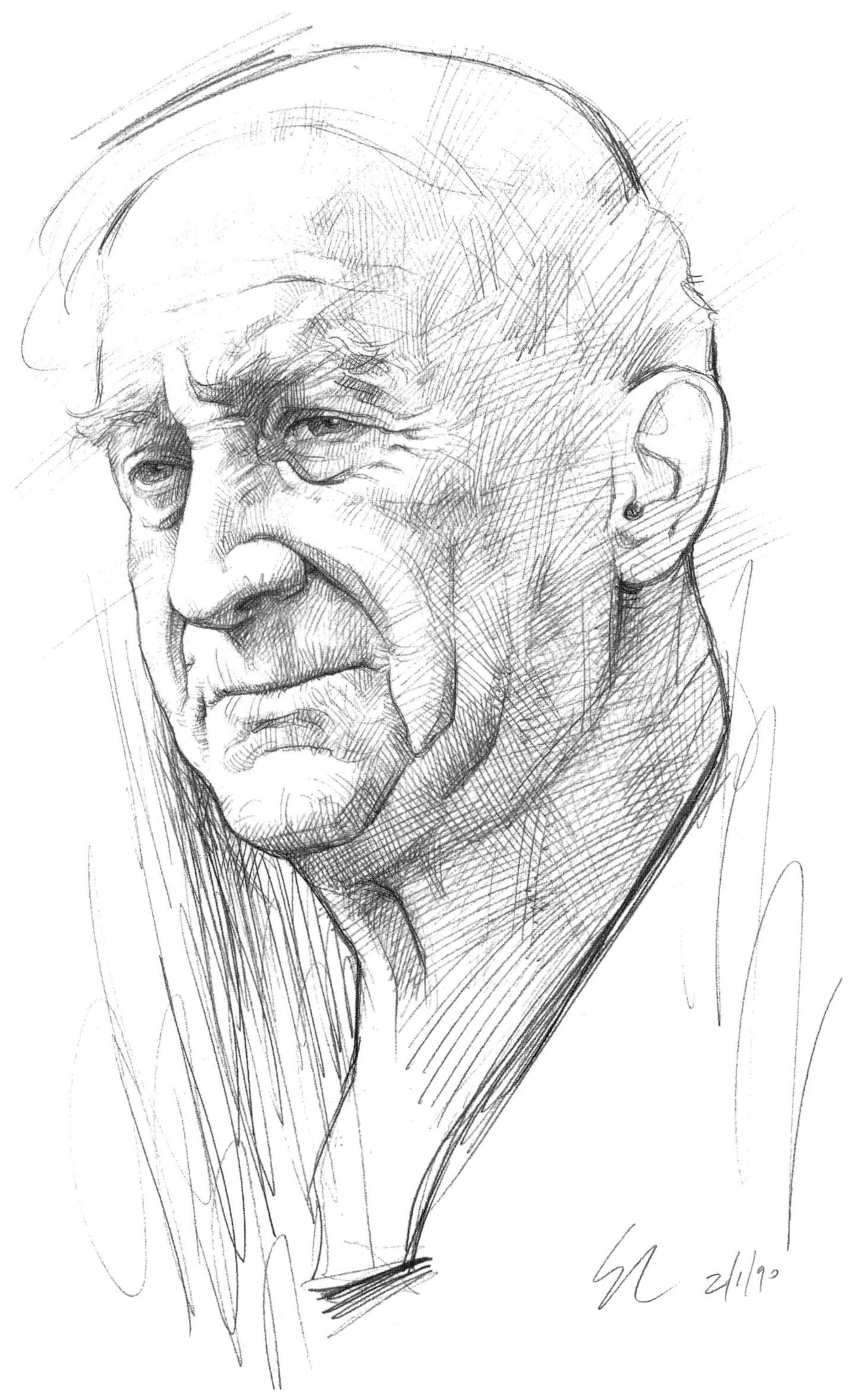

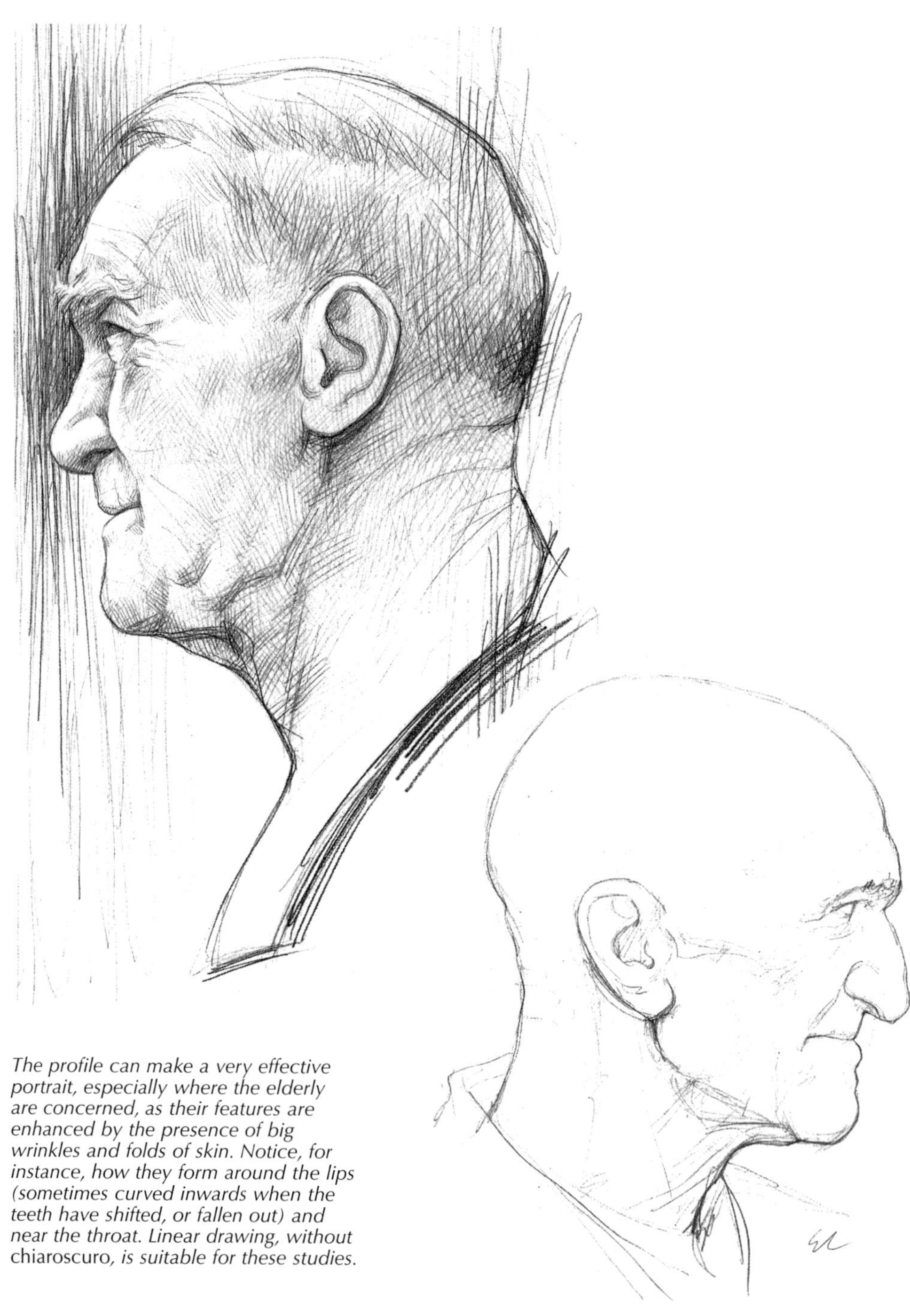

The profile can make a very effective portrait, especially where the elderly are concerned, as their features are enhanced by the presence of big wrinkles and folds of skin. Notice, for instance, how they form around the lips (sometimes curved inwards when the teeth have shifted, or fallen out) and near the throat. Linear drawing, without chiaroscuro*, is suitable for these studies.*

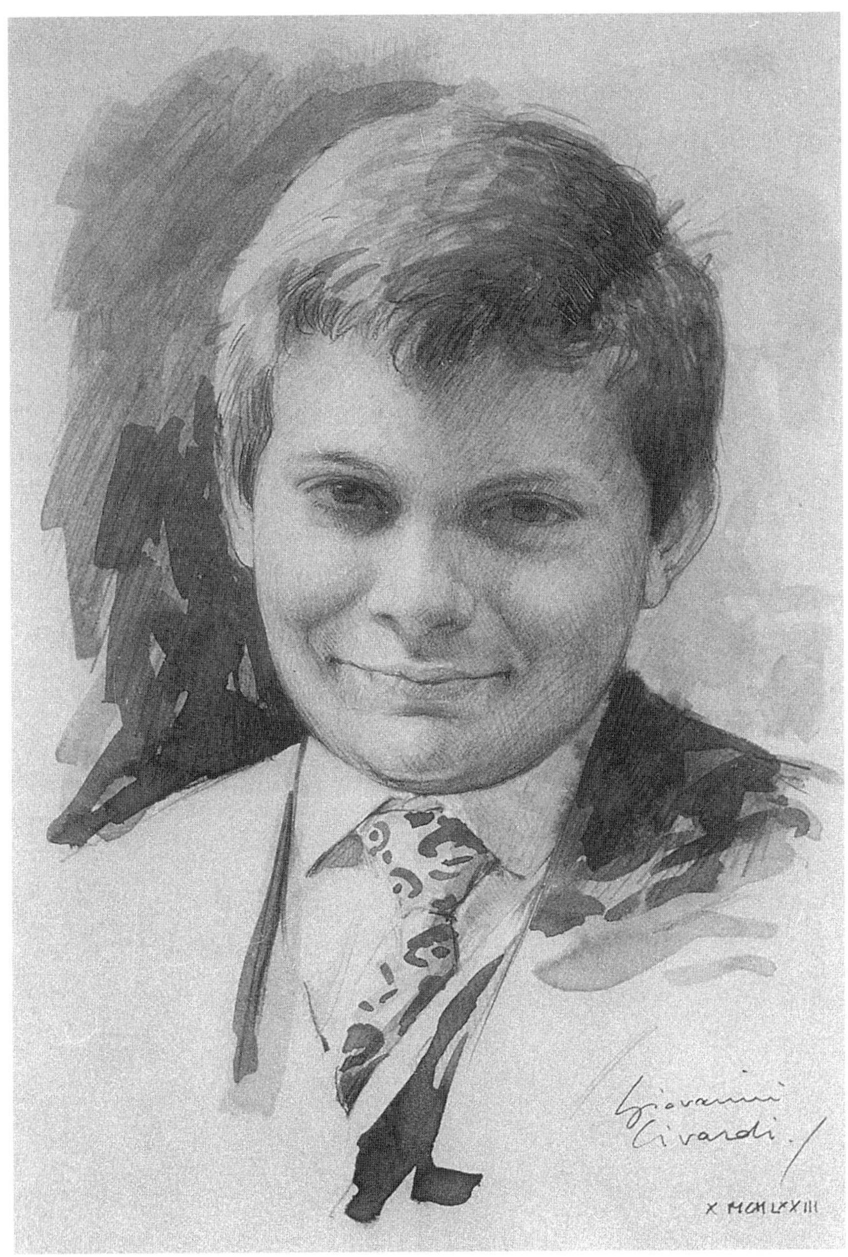

This portrait study was drawn with HB graphite on card, 15 × 20cm (6 × 8in). I enhanced some shadow areas with water-diluted Indian ink applied with a round brush. Finally, I 'glazed' the whole surface in order to soften and even the tones.

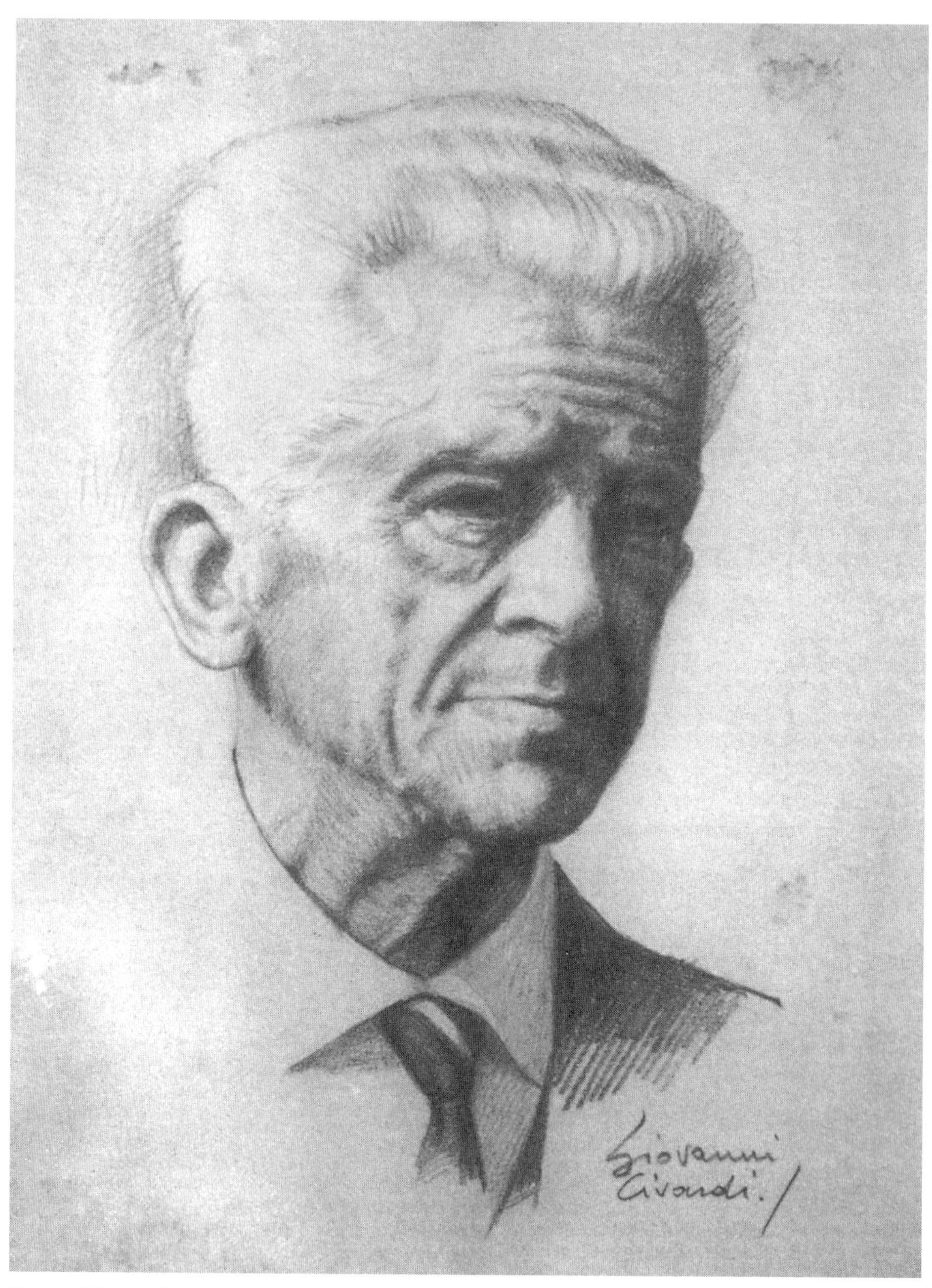

Portrait, HB pencil on grey card, 14 × 18cm (5½ × 7in)

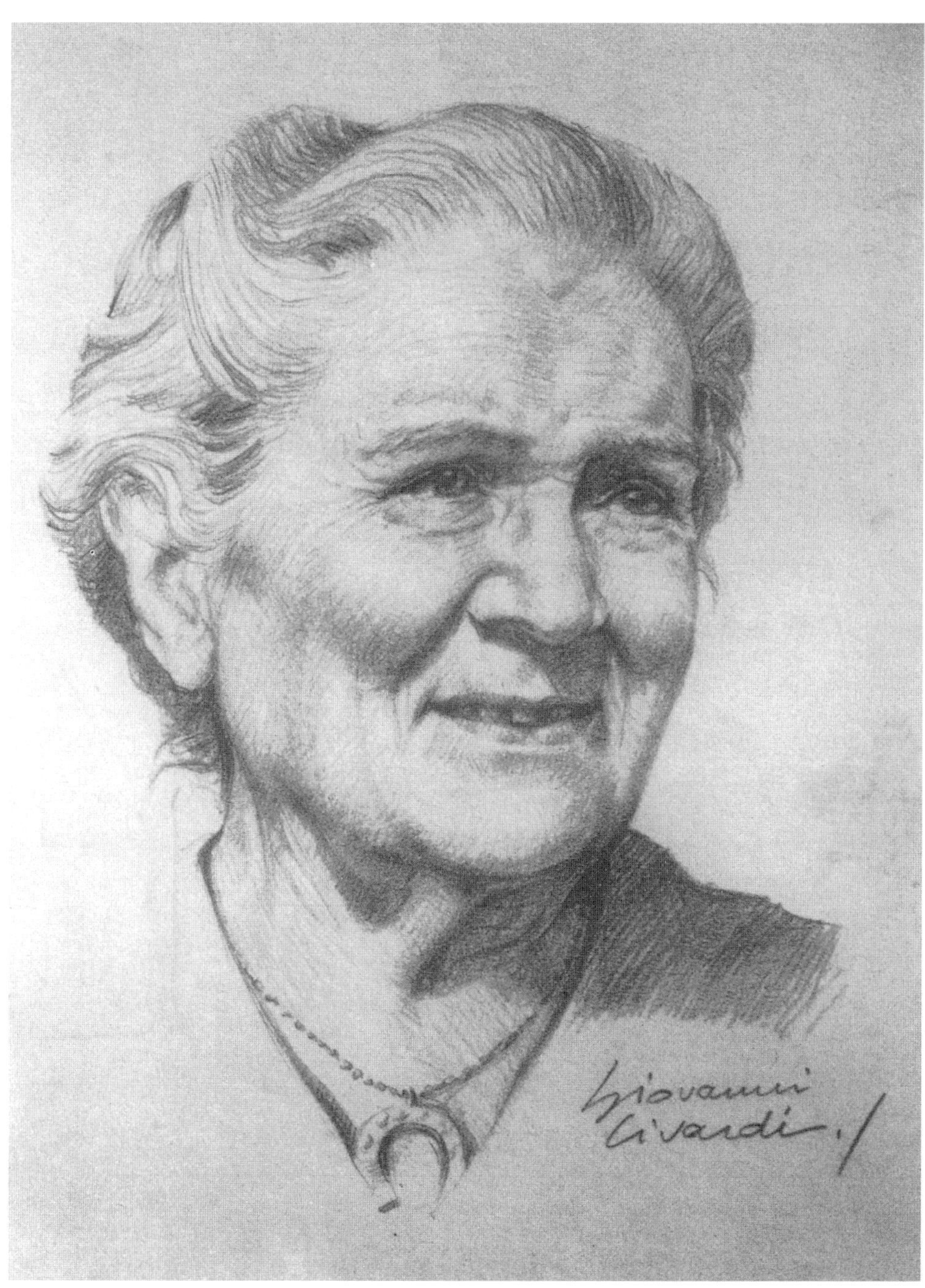

Portrait, HB pencil on grey card, 13.5 × 18cm (5¼ × 7in)

CHAPTER 2: CAPTURING CHARACTER AND EXPRESSION

INTRODUCTION

The human face and figure have always been central to artistic practice. A portrait should not only identify specific individuals by their physical features but also express their personalities, thoughts and emotions via their expressions. When we think of somebody, the first thing we call to mind will nearly always be the features of that person's face in one of its characteristic expressions. The impulse to draw this face may come from a desire we have to capture the traits that render the face unique and allow the person's character to show through. A person's physical appearance and their personality are intimately linked and what distinguishes a portrait, in the most widely used sense of the word, from a figure study or generalized depiction of a face is this descriptive treatment given to a person's idiosyncratic characteristics.

An extremely useful way to train and improve your observational abilities in this respect is to make drawings and sketches. The best method for carrying out a portrait or study of somebody's head (and such studies will frequently turn out as 'accidental portraits') is to examine the anatomical form and structure of the head, analyzing its overall proportions as well as those of each facial feature and relating these to each other. The drawing precision and exact positioning of the facial features are two essential elements for guaranteeing what many consider the fundamental attribute of any portrait – its resemblance to the subject. Additionally, the artist's empathetic perception of the mood and character of the model will help with the overall portrait.

In this book, I have attempted to direct the attention of fellow artists to the graphical and aesthetic opportunities that are present in every face. The faces of complete strangers, of people you know nothing about and who you encounter by chance, can attract interest through their characteristic features alone. What is usually meant by the term 'a face with character' is one that has distinctive features, proportions or expressions that make it instantly recognizable: all of these are elements which will spur the artist's investigative curiosity and aesthetic sense.

In brief, for artists who develop the habit of using their pencil to fill their sketchbooks with studies such as these, simply noticing passers-by in any public place will guarantee a plentiful supply of attractive and interesting faces.

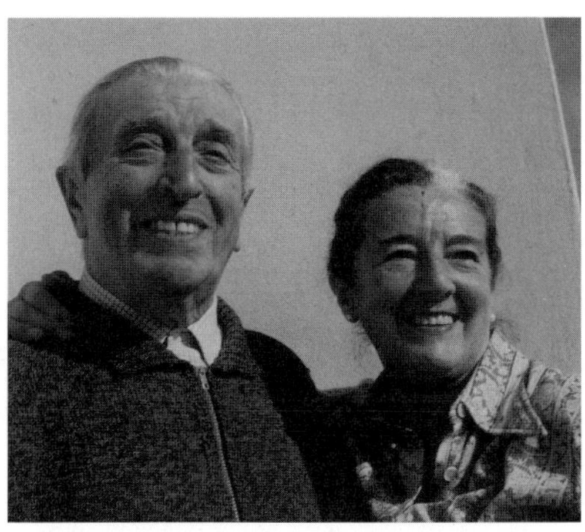

To my father, to my mother

METHODS OF CAPTURING CHARACTER

Everything appears to be ready – but something is still missing…

There are various possible approaches to the task of drawing a face; each one is the fruit of tradition and experience as well as of individual artistic attitudes and personal preference. These many approaches can be broadly summarized under the banners of two opposing routes that are centred around two distinct ways of seeing, two diverging accounts of how we perceive what is before us.

The first of these routes could be dsescribed as 'inductive', so-called because the artist begins by choosing one facial feature to develop – typically one or both of the eyes – and then proceeds to add the other features, while making the necessary measurements for correlating the proportions of one aspect with another.

The second route, which could be called the 'deductive' approach, begins with an overall assessment of the shapes of the head or face seen as a whole, and moves in from the general to the specific, locating the individual details, each in turn, in their correct position within the overall scheme.

Each of these approaches has its advantages, and in practice they alternate and combine with each other. If one approach or another should prevail, this will be in response to the subject's particular features, the pose or the psychological exploratory 'pathway' followed by the artist. The 'inductive' approach, for example, calls for patience and discipline in comparing the relative dimensions of the facial features and assessing the distances between them: the whole is reached via an accumulation of the scattered parts and this means that even the slightest error in judging a distance will be enough to throw the entire outcome into disarray. The deductive approach is perhaps to be preferred because it is more in keeping with the artistic vision, which sees forms first as wholes and then proceeds to investigate the way in which they are put together.

A face is considered 'characterful' when it immediately and markedly shows the physiognomic traits that describe the personality, peculiarities of behaviour and expression in a person. The features become interesting for the artist ('plastically interesting', we might say), both individually and as parts of a whole, as they lead to a marked individual expressiveness. This is founded upon the shape and anatomical characteristics of the main areas of the face – eyes, nose, and so forth – influenced by the subject's gender, age or ethnicity.

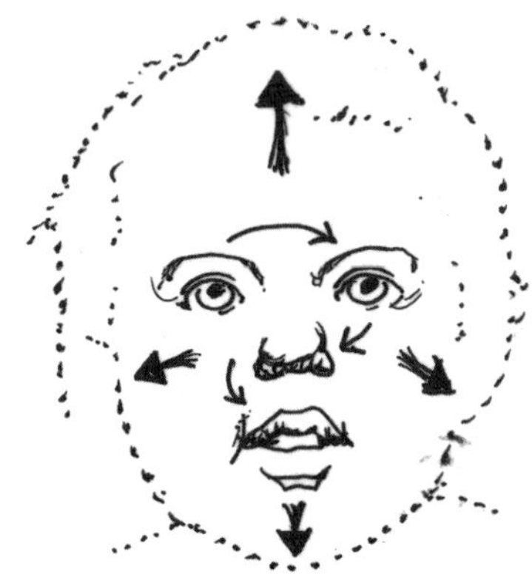

From the specific to the general: (the inductive approach) – working from the centre outwards to the overall outline.

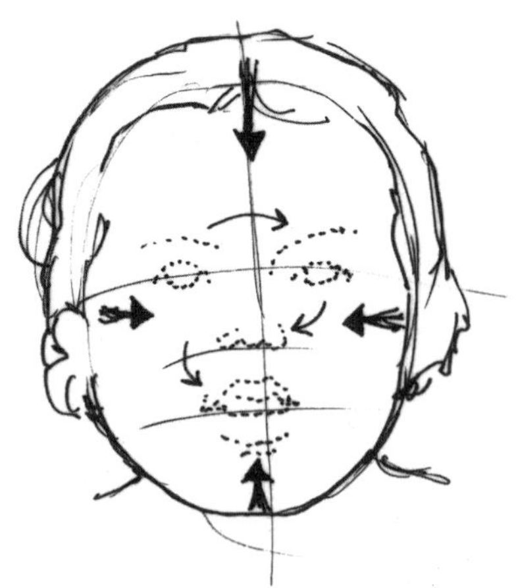

From the general to the specific: (the deductive approach) – working from overall outline inwards to the central details.

Other matters affecting the choice of approach include the way the face is perceived, the aesthetic effect the artist is trying to achieve and which drawing medium is the most suitable for obtaining this effect. The face may be perceived synthetically, i.e. concentrating on its larger principal structures at the expense of internal details, or it may be perceived analytically, i.e. giving a full rendering of every tiny detail making up its overall form, leading to a definitive representation of individual particulars in an almost scientific way. Either of these tendencies can be given a more or less linear treatment. At one extreme, depiction is realized by means of line alone: almost scalpel-like, the line investigates the face's forms and structures without any help from tonal nuance. At the other extreme, using *chiaroscuro*, it is only the modulation between areas of light and dark that render the form without using any directly drawn outline. When combined, these two approaches will complement each other.

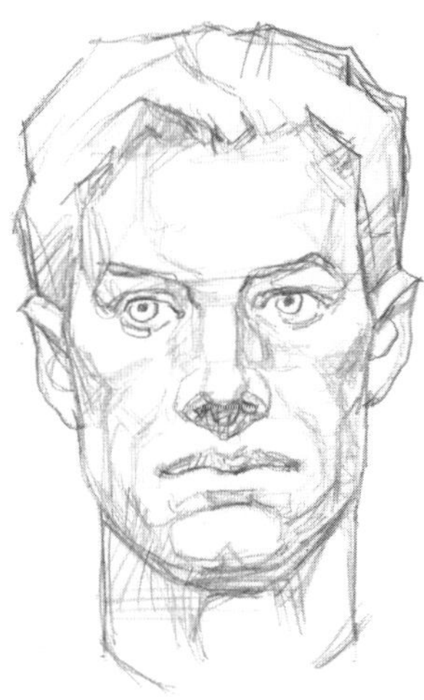

Synthetic (using large masses)

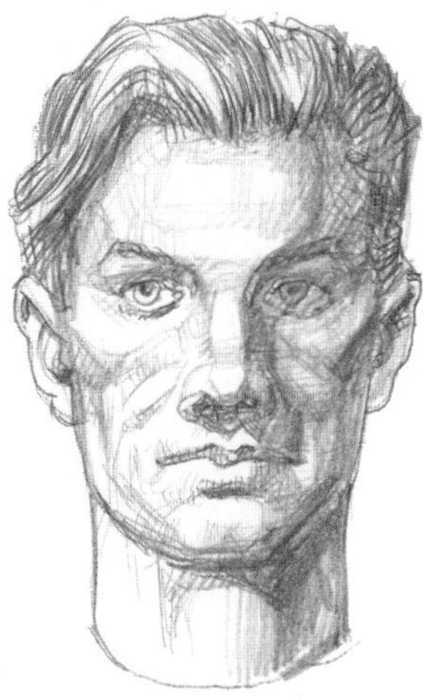

Analytic (using details)

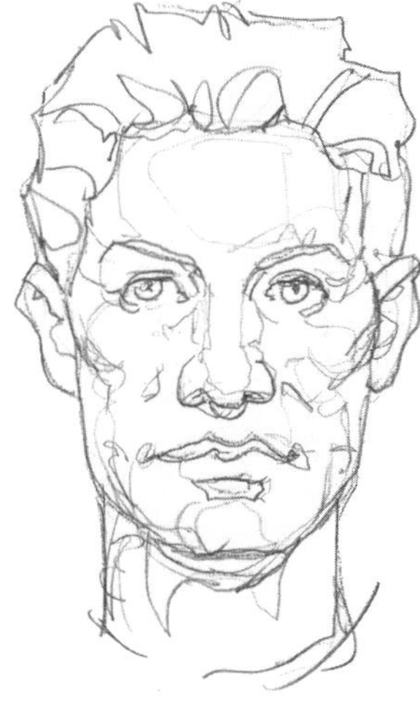

Linear (using lines only)

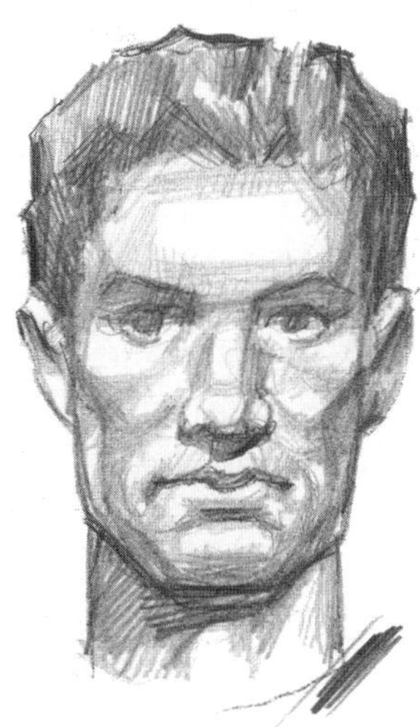

Tonal (using modulations of light and dark only)

APPROACHES TO DRAWING

There are different ways to draw a portrait – different 'paths of creation'. The artist's psychological and stylistic approach, might, for example, lead them through searching for a 'rational' structure of the shapes. Alternatively, the artist might prefer an emotional, suggestive path.

When drawing 'characterful' faces, it is advisable to reflect a while on the modes and results of visual perception. For example, from the first weeks of its life, a new-born baby is attracted to and learns to recognize the typical shape of a human face: simplified to an oval with a regular, constant relation, and marks that suggest two eyes, a nose, and a mouth. Similarly, many right-handed people, regardless of cultural background, tend to 'read' an image from left to right, while others have the opposite preferential perception of our visual centre of interest.

Two of the most simple, traditional approaches are referred to below: linear and tonal. Either can be applied in a pure form or they can be combined and integrated with each other and conveyed into a third, mixed approach.

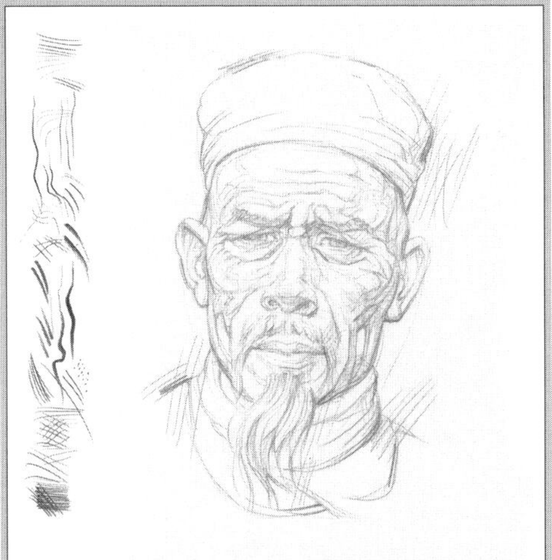

LINEAR

With this approach, tone becomes subordinate to line, or is missing entirely: line defines the shape.

Line does not exist in nature, but it is the oldest, most intuitive drawing convention to define the shape of an object through its overall outline and the outline of each element that is a part of it.

The line can be thin and even or modulated, thick, angled, interrupted, crossed or thickened, and used as part of a tonal weave that the artist wishes to suggest.

The linear procedure refers to the way of using drawing tools and is independent from them, although some are more suitable than others: hard graphite, nib and ink, and felt-tip pens are particularly well-suited.

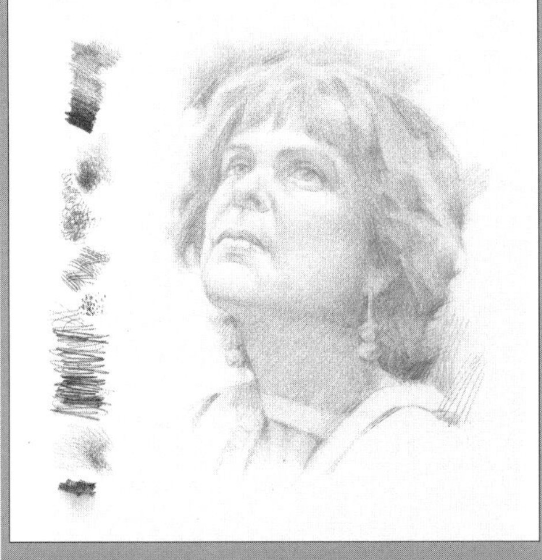

TONAL

Here, the line is subordinate to tone or is missing: tone describes the shape.

Tone is the degree of shade that distinguishes the light, illuminated areas of an object from the dark ones, in shadow. The range of monochrome shade is achieved in chiaroscuro. *The most suitable tools are the ones that lend themselves to a 'expressive' portrayal of the portrait, such as soft graphite, charcoal, and watercolour.*

See page 150 for a comparison of linear and tonal procedures applied to the same subject.

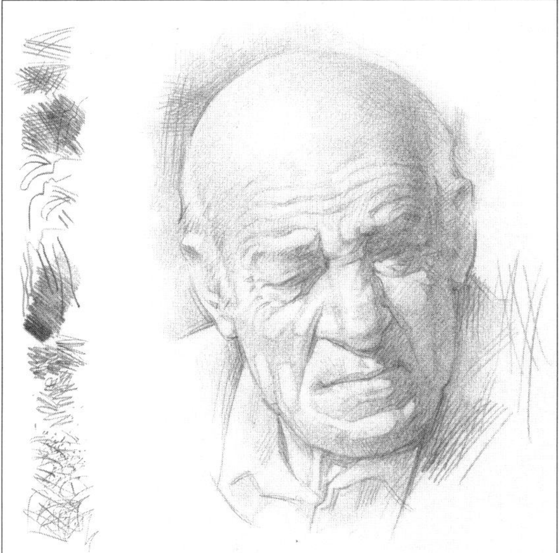

MIXED

Integration between line and tone. This is the most intuitive and traditional procedure, often used in realistic portraits. Both line and tone are brought together to define the shapes and volumes of the face and to express the chiaroscuro effects.

With this approach, each artist can find full freedom of style and choice, through the use of varied tools and marks.

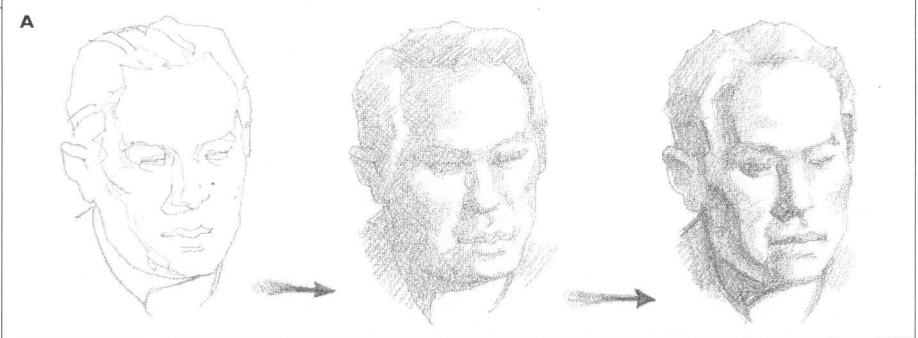

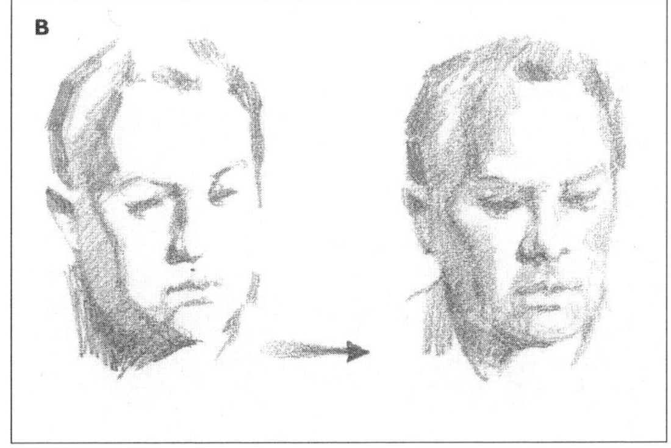

Figure A, above, shows the steps of an analytical way of working (during which the form and shape is gradually developed – see page 105): linear structure on the left, followed by the addition of the main tones of shade in the centre, followed in turn by modulation of the chiaroscuro for the finished image on the right. In combination with a grid, this is the procedure I followed for almost all the portraits shown in this chapter.

Figure B shows an alternative way of working: the development stages of a portrait based solely on the play of tones (see pages 104–105 and 148). Indications of only the main shade area are on the left of the image, while the right-hand side shows elaboration of the intermediate tones and 'accents' to complete the drawing.

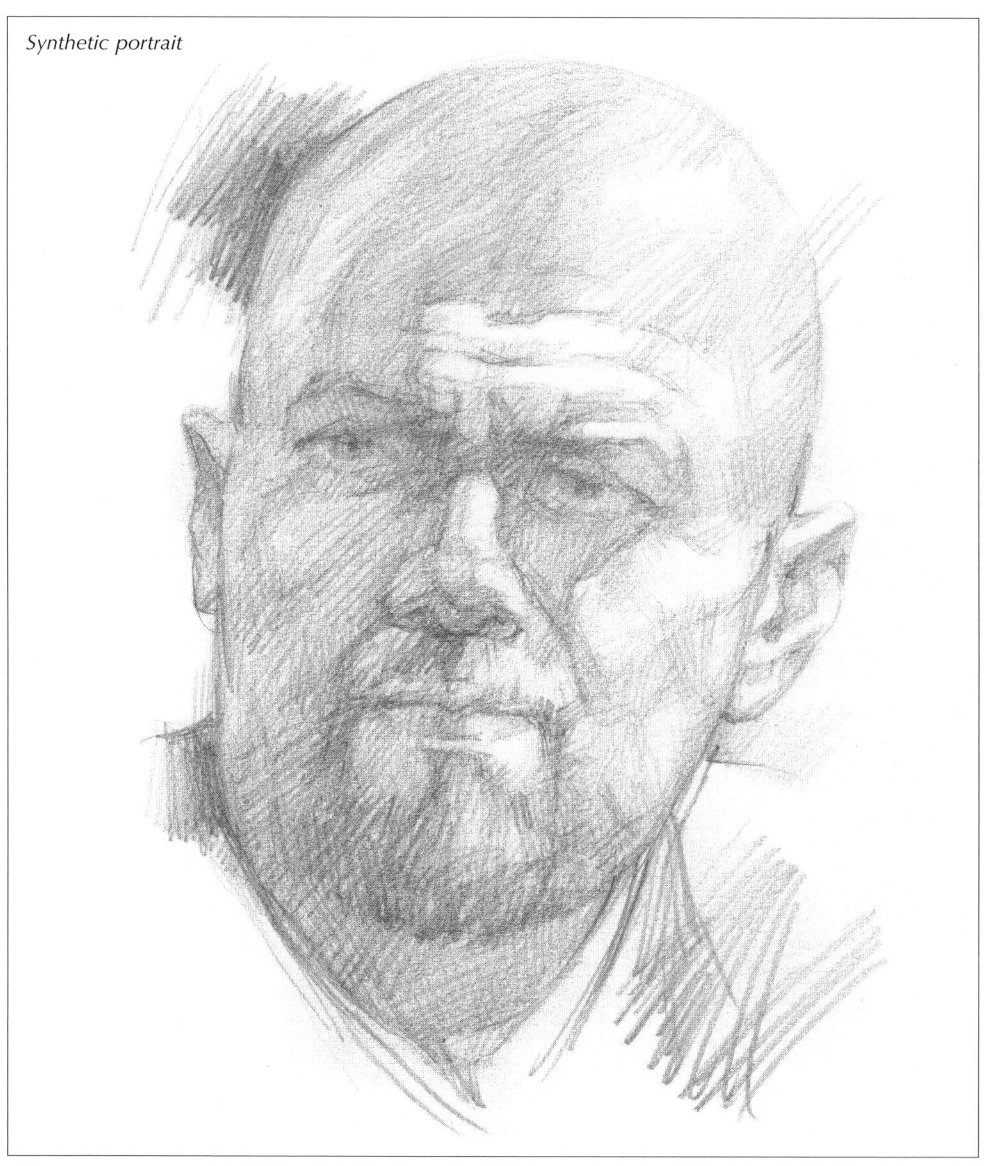

Synthetic portrait

The approaches referred to on the two previous pages can lead to very different graphic results. These are not a direct result of the use of a particular technique, but will vary according to the artist's aims and aesthetic choices, and the visual perception of shapes by the artist. These choices lead the artist to portray what they are seeing in different ways.

A **synthetic portrait**, as in the example above, leads to an 'abbreviated' drawing, we might say – although not an approximate one. Such a portrait concentrates on elements of tone and shape chosen as being essential and sufficient for an effective, suggestive, and evocative portrayal of a head.

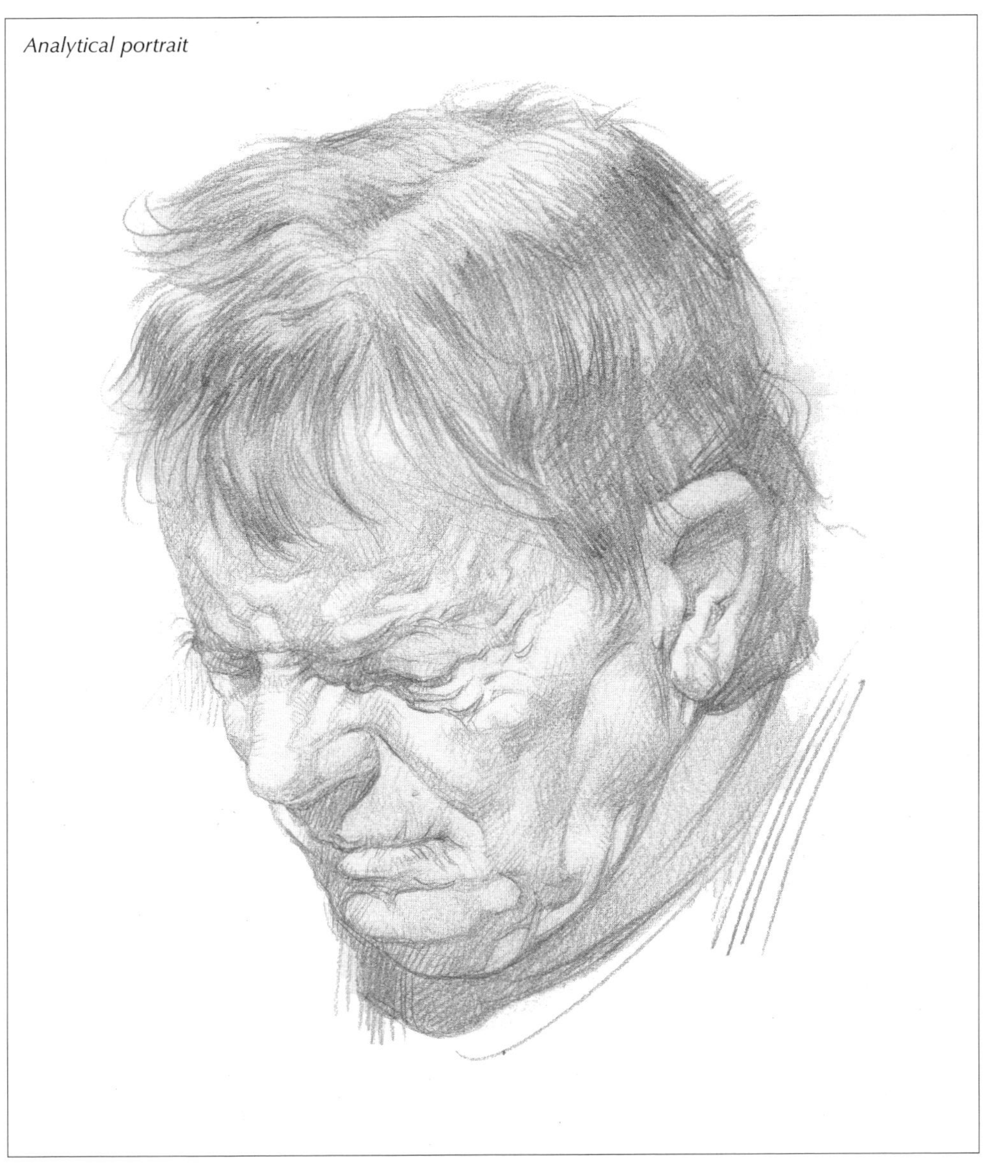
Analytical portrait

It is therefore an approach that requires a capacity to make a summary observation of the main parts, and an ability to clean the drawing of secondary detail in favour of a strong, expressive character.

An **analytical portrait**, in contrast, produces a clear, detailed, and faithfully described drawing that incorporates all the details of structure, shape and *chiaroscuro* of the head. The final shape is obtained by layering increasingly precise details that are connected to each other. It is therefore a gradual, structured drawing that requires good analysis and attention to detail and a lot of patience in execution.

DEDUCTIVE AND INDUCTIVE PATHS

Earlier I mentioned some traditional approaches to drawing. For the most part, the portraits in this section of the book have been produced using a deliberate combination of the linear and tonal techniques and according to the 'analytical' procedure of the gradual structure of shapes (see page 103).

This combination can be broken down into two different parts: observing and reproducing the shapes. There are then two paths to take: deductive – that is, working from the general to the particular; and inductive, where your starting point is the particular, which is then developed into the general. (See page 100.)

The deductive sequence proceeds from the 'general' to the 'particular' and the subject of the drawing is evaluated as a whole – that is, the overall outlines are drawn first of all, larger than the shape to be portrayed (**Step 1:** overall shape and dimensions); then inside these lines, the details in their correct ratios are added (**Step 2:** proportions); volume elements and tonal areas are then identified (**Step 3:** planes and structure); and finally the shading of tones, the details, volumetric sizes are inserted (**Step 4:** volume and tonal modulation).

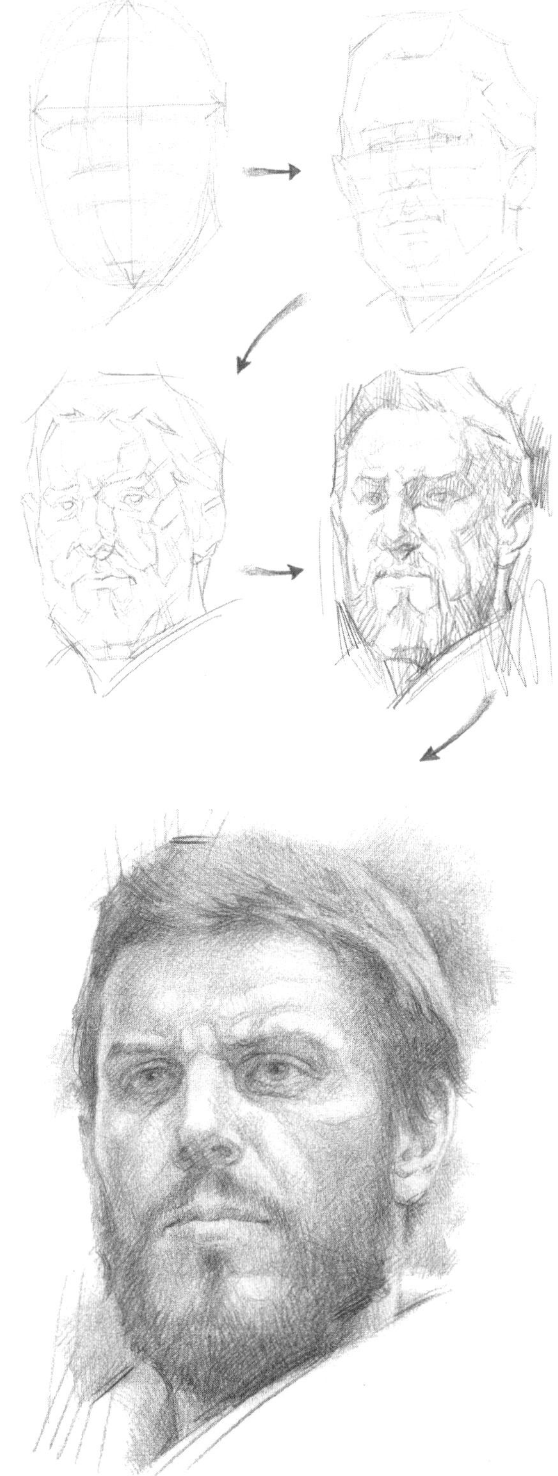

Deductive sequence

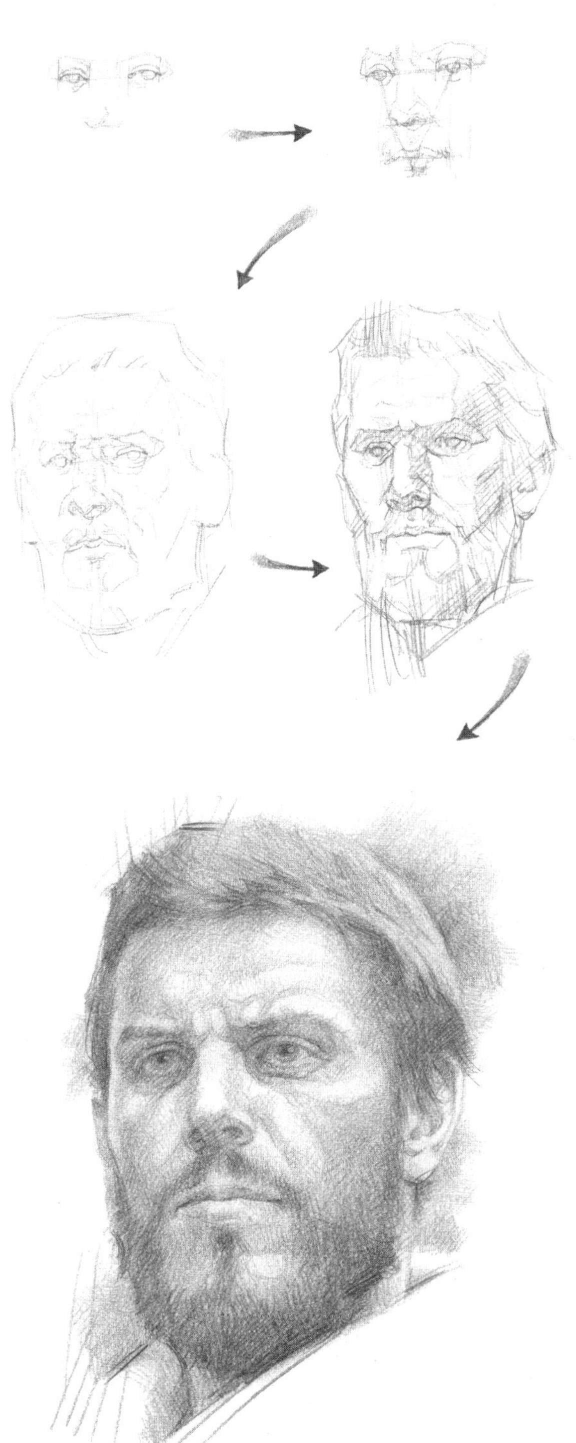

The inductive sequence (from the particular to the general) is more innovative and less restrictive, but also more demanding for the artist as it requires a good level of awareness of proportions and ratios.

After an initial evaluation of the area that the subject will occupy on the sheet, a significant detail (usually an eye, when portraying a human face) is chosen as a reference element of measurement and position to which all the other elements will then correlate, in a kind of expansion of shapes up to the outline that surrounds them.

The drawings on this page and the next should be clear enough to describe the main steps to follow in each case. The final result is the same for both paths.

Inductive sequence

STEP-BY-STEP EXAMPLES: PENCIL

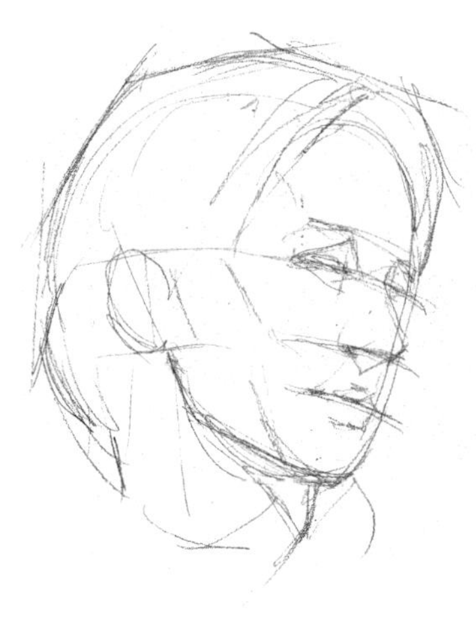

Step 1

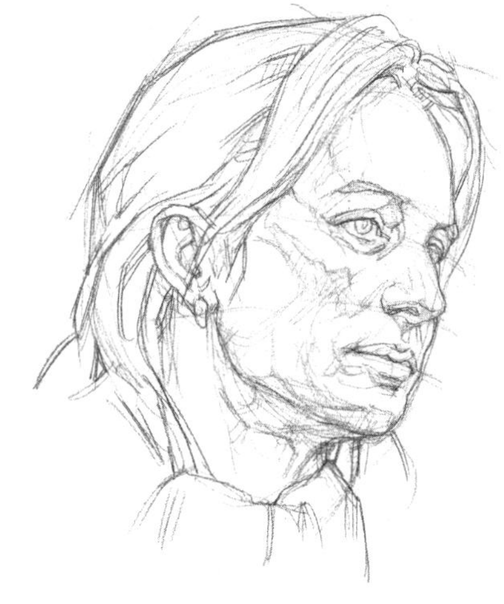

Step 2

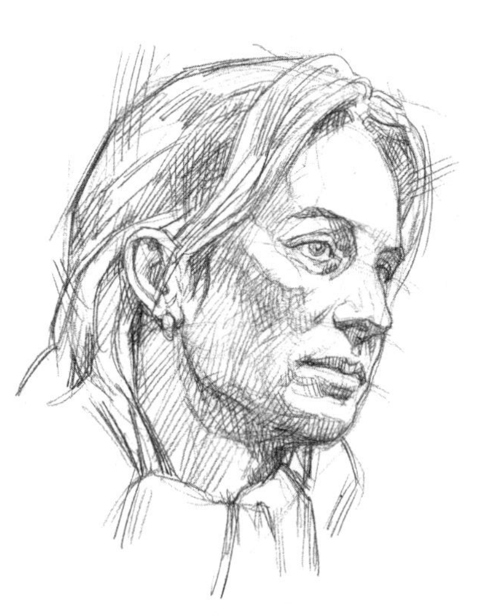

Step 3

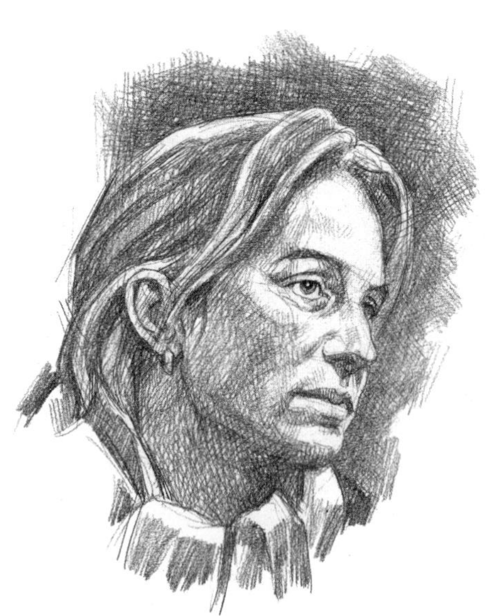

Step 4

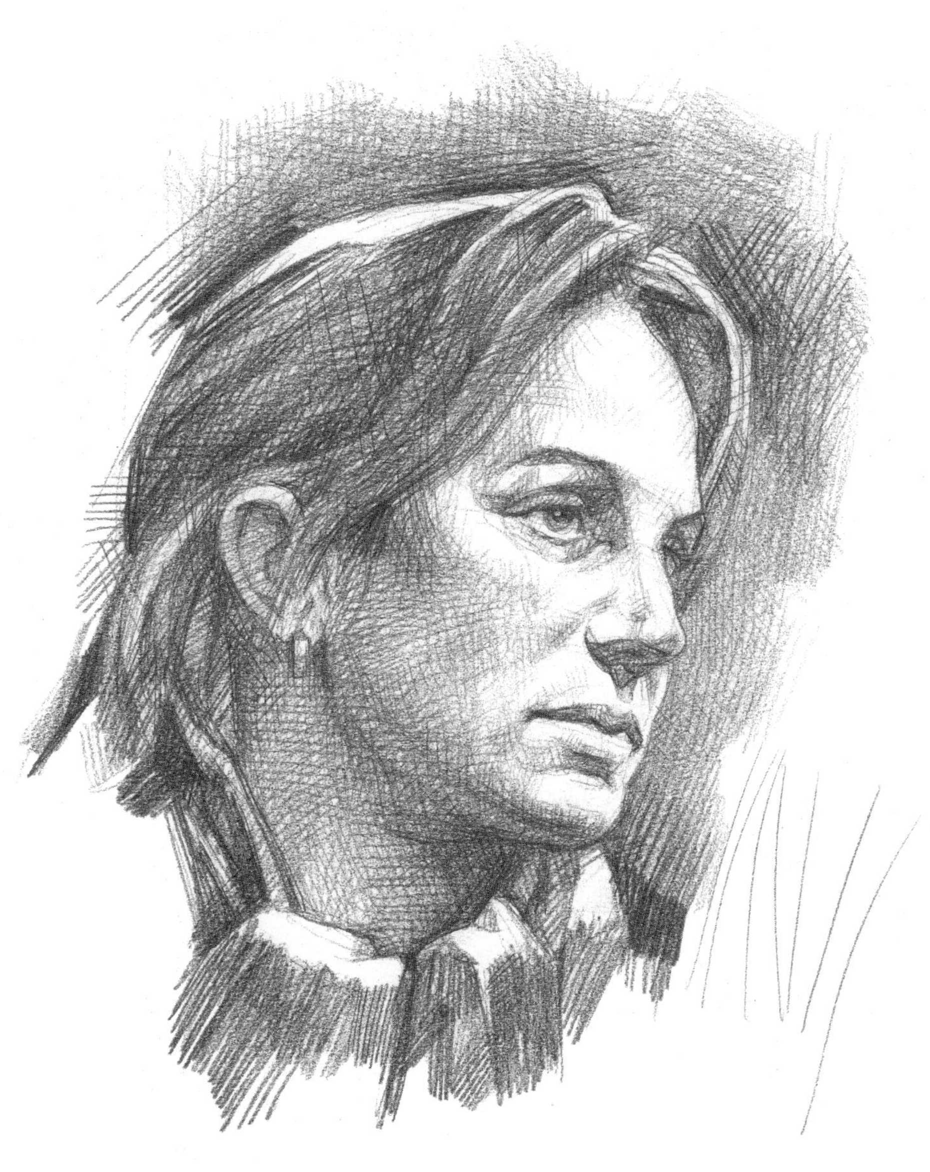

Step 5
HB and B pencils on paper, 21.5 × 30.5cm (8½ × 12in)

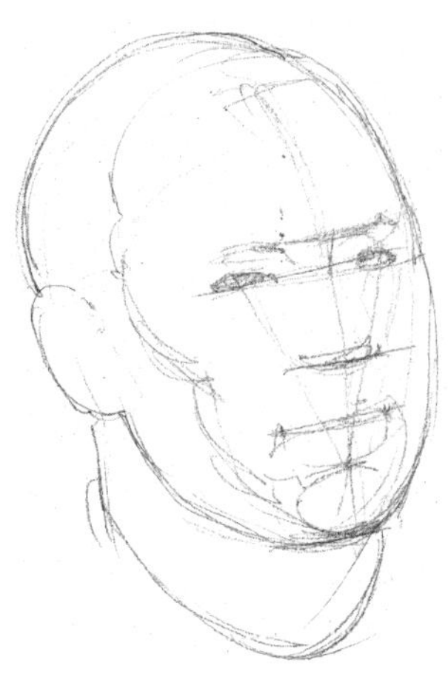

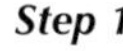

Step 1

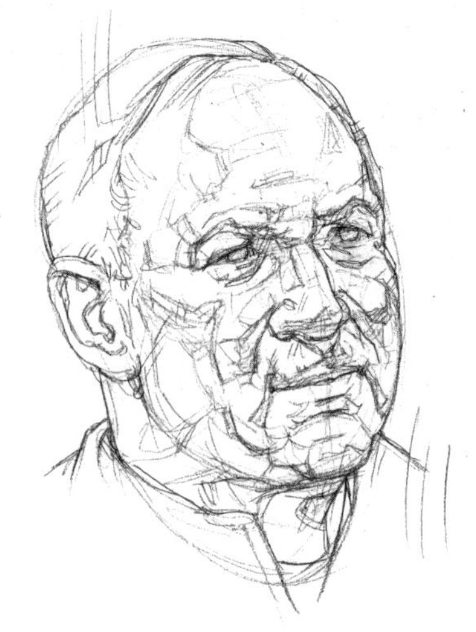

Step 2

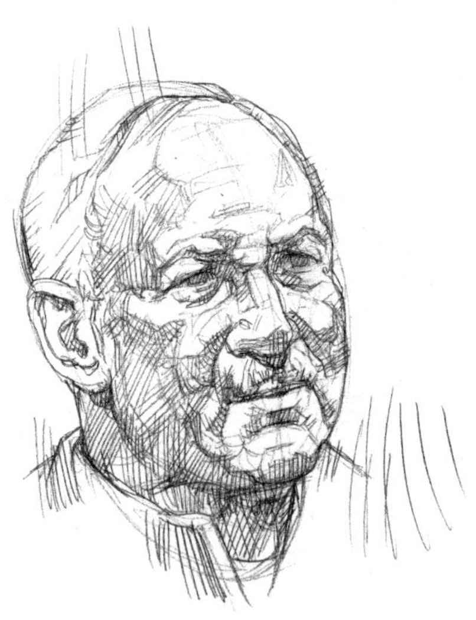

Step 3

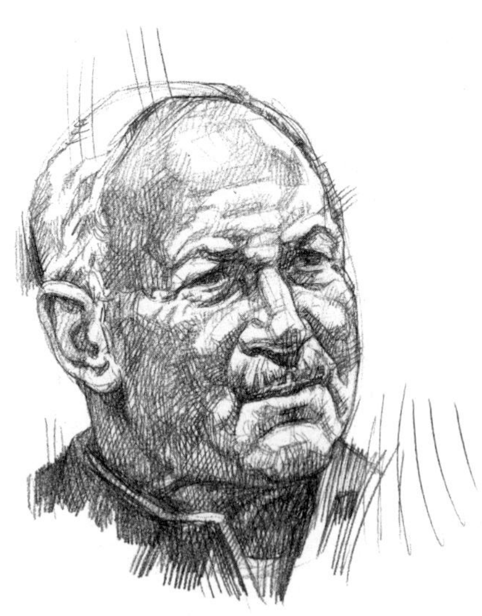

Step 4

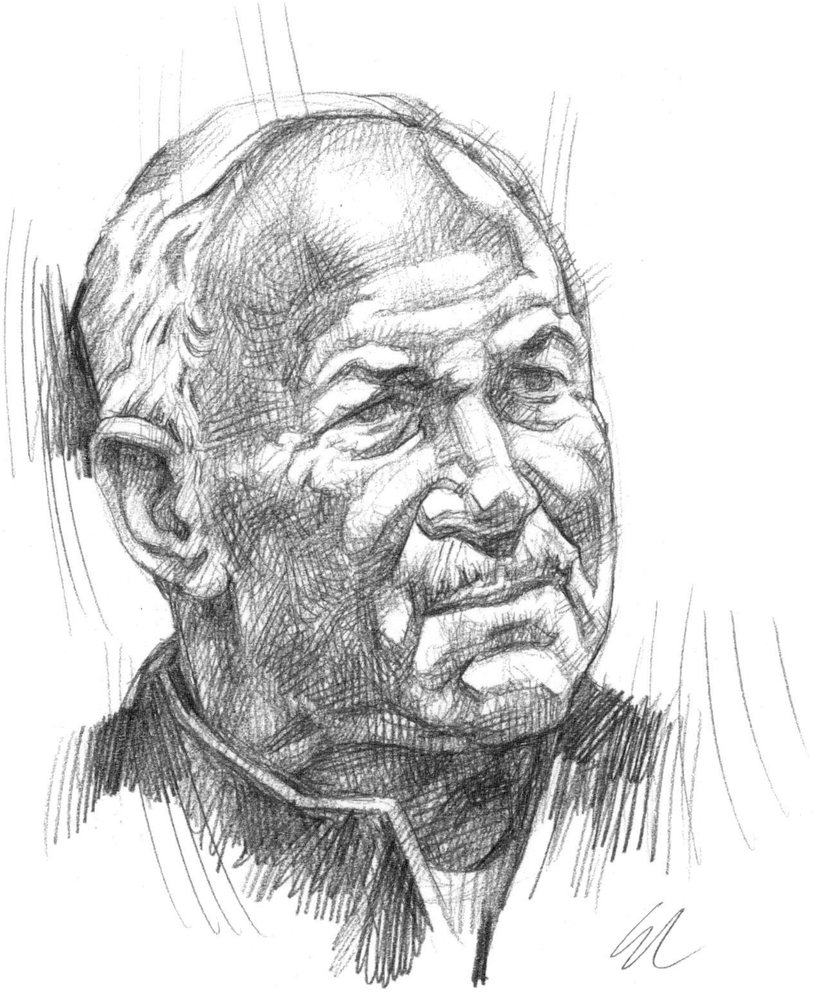

Step 5

HB and B pencils on paper, 21 × 30cm (8¼ × 12in)

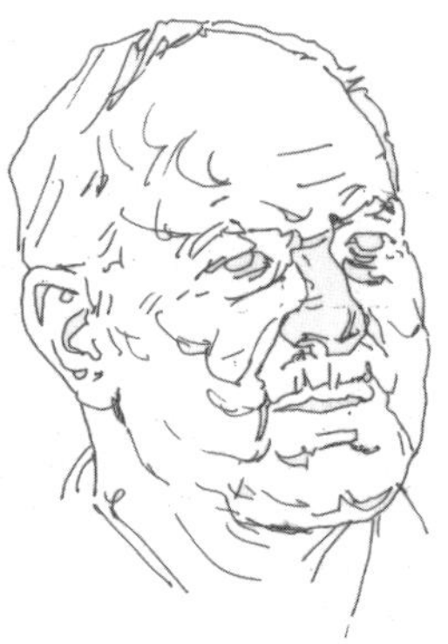

Preliminary outline in pen and ink on paper

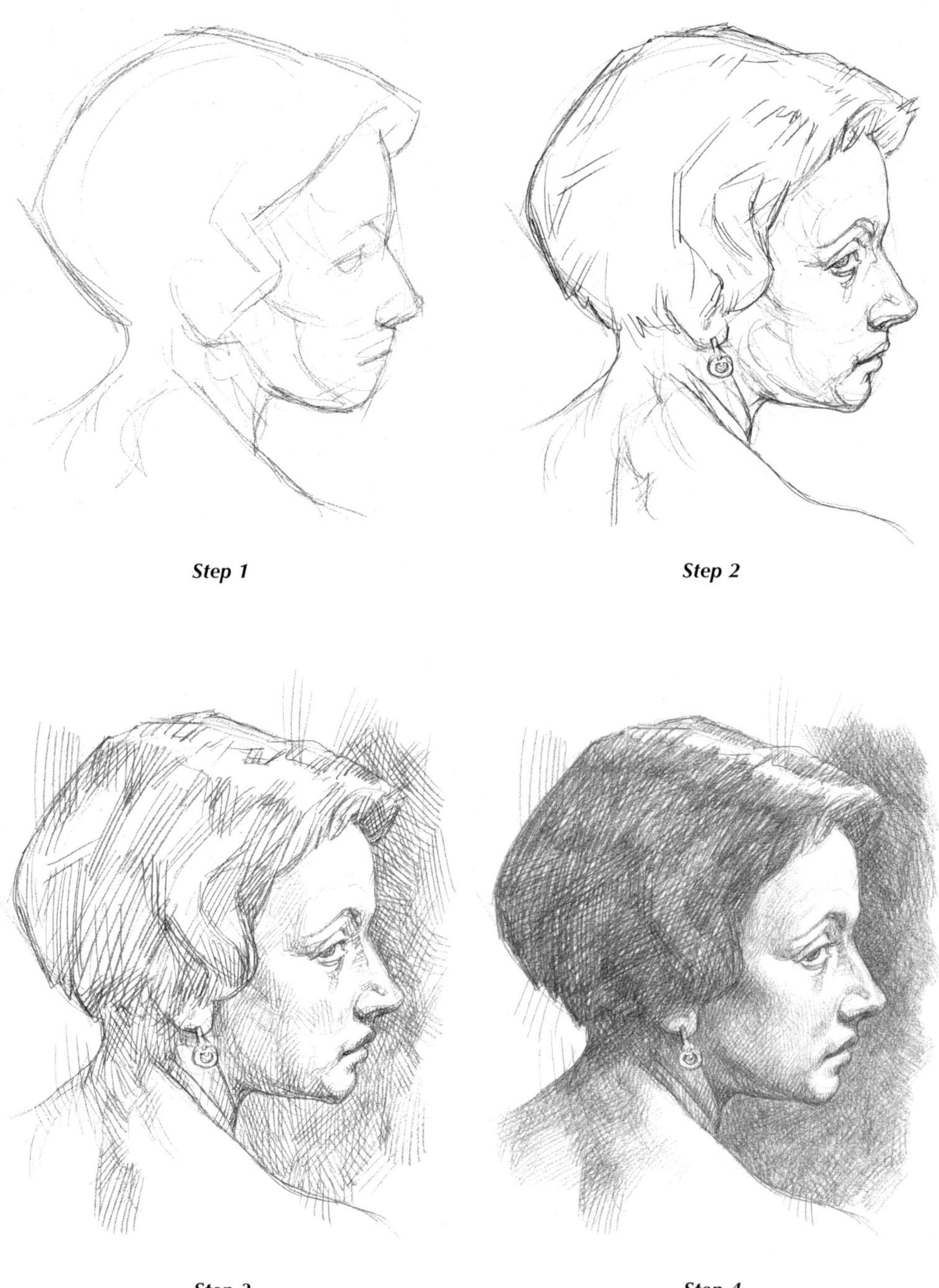

Step 1

Step 2

Step 3

Step 4

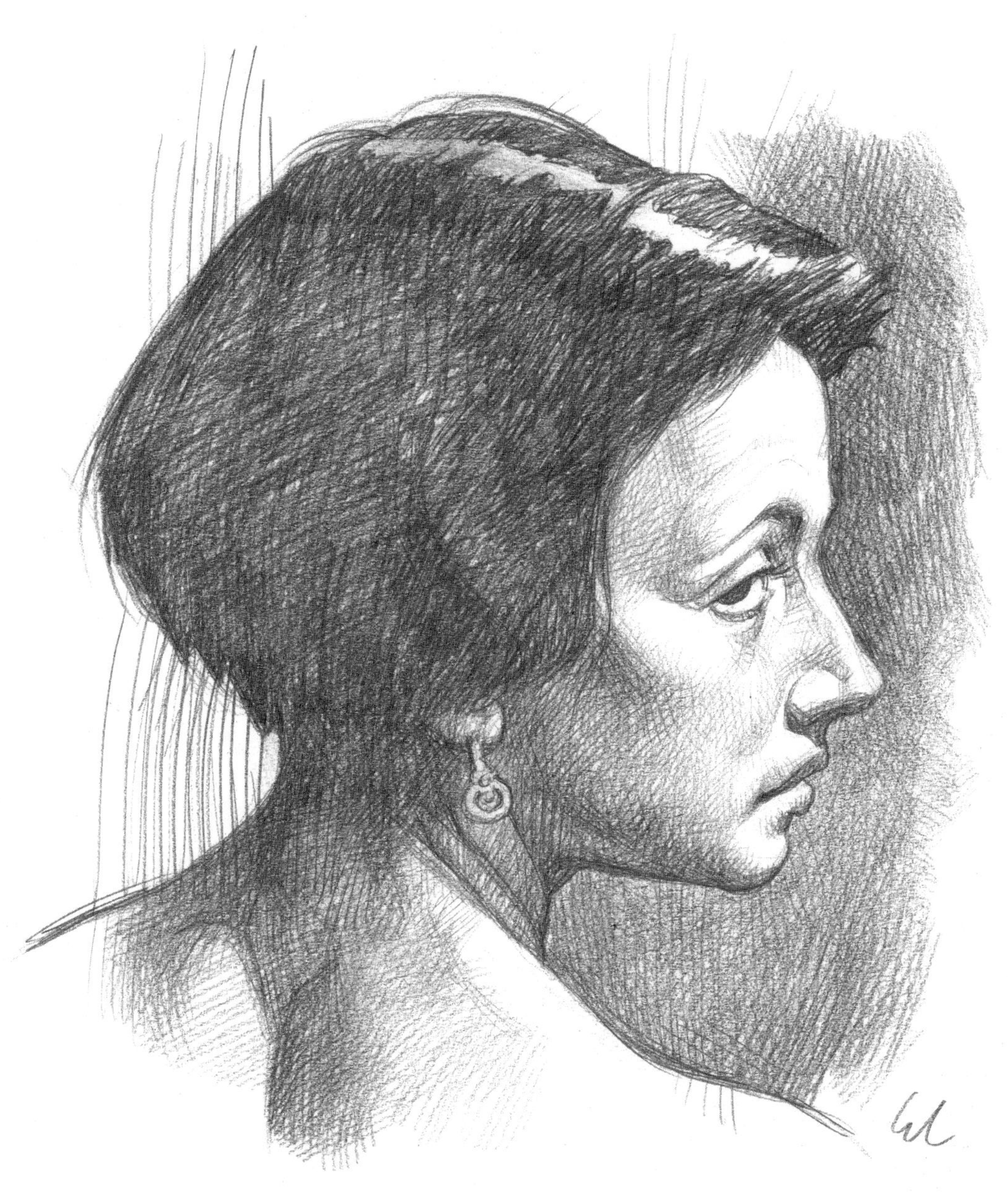

Step 5
HB pencil on paper, 30 × 21cm (12 × 8¼in)

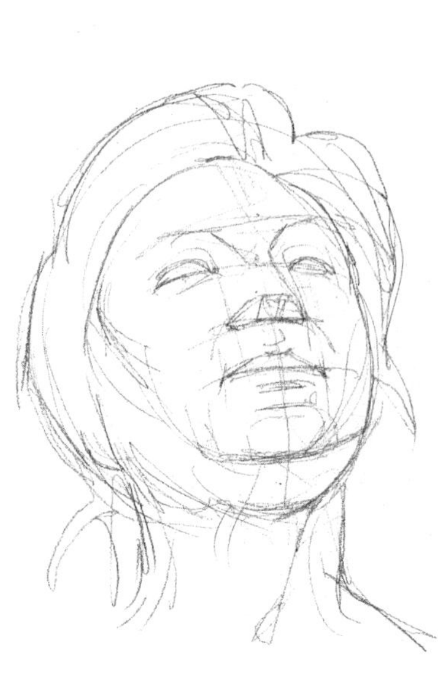

Step 1

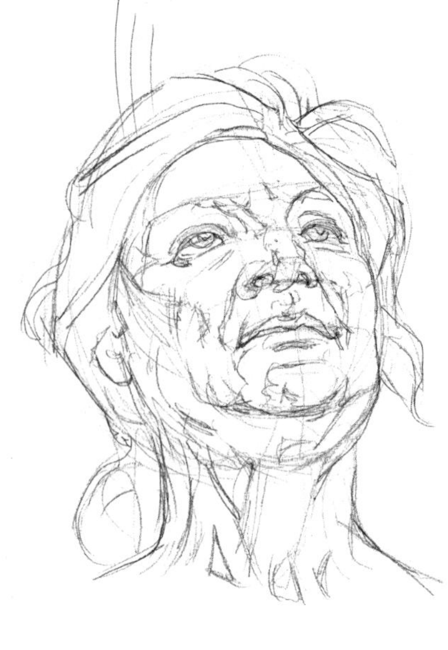

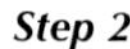

Step 2

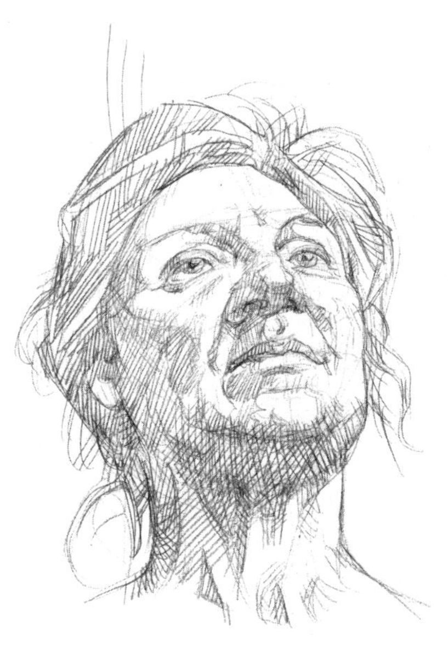

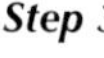

Step 3

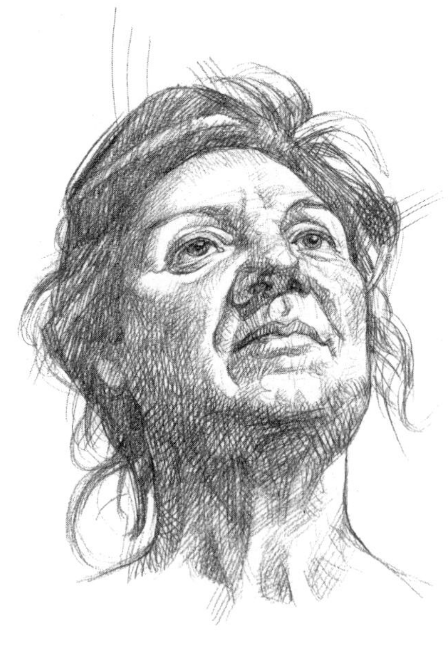

Step 4

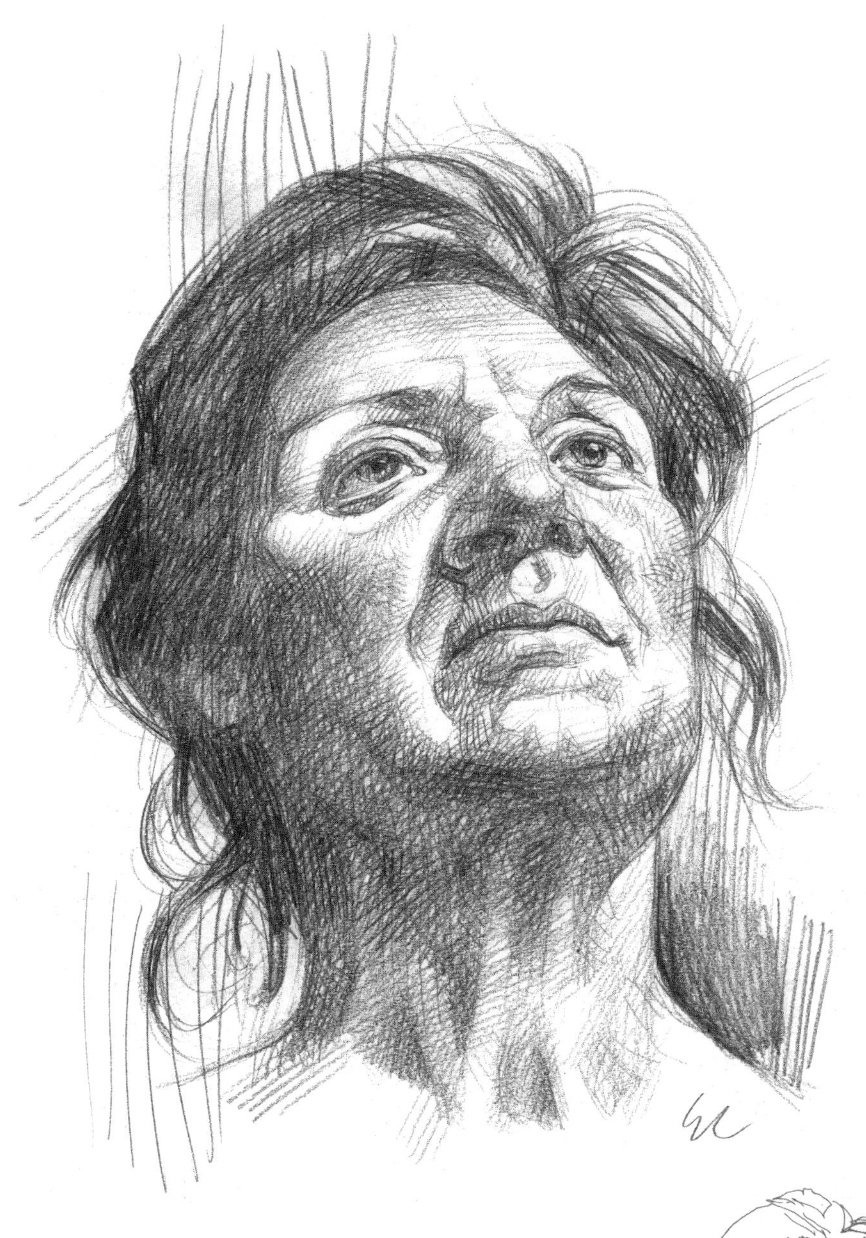

Step 5
HB and B pencils on paper, 21 × 30cm (8¼ × 12in)

Preliminary outline in pen and ink on paper

STEP-BY-STEP EXAMPLES: WATERCOLOUR

When using watercolours, the colours should be added to the picture in successive layers, using the same method as when achieving transparency effects, and moving from pale tones to darker ones. The initial drawing (***Step 1***) should be very brief and the outline drawn very lightly so that it will not show through the colour.

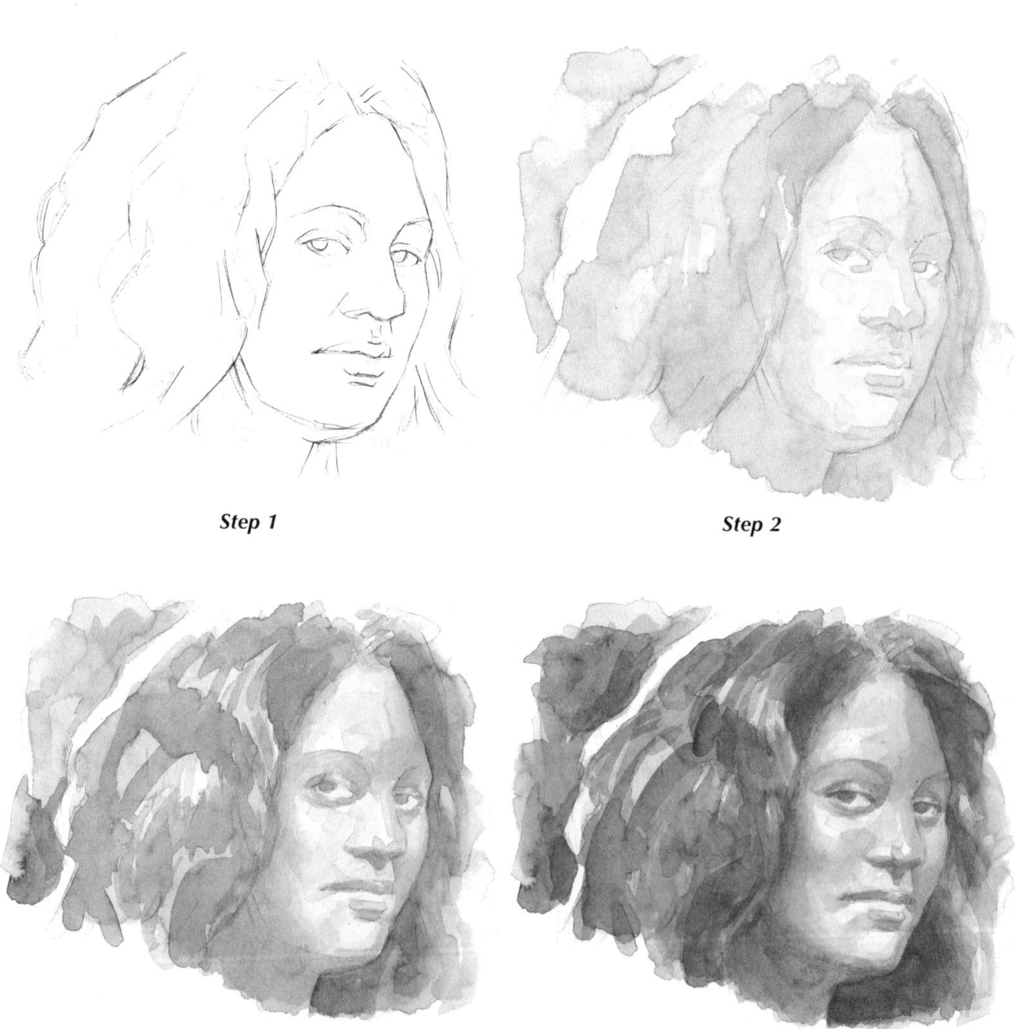

Step 1

Step 2

Step 3

Step 4

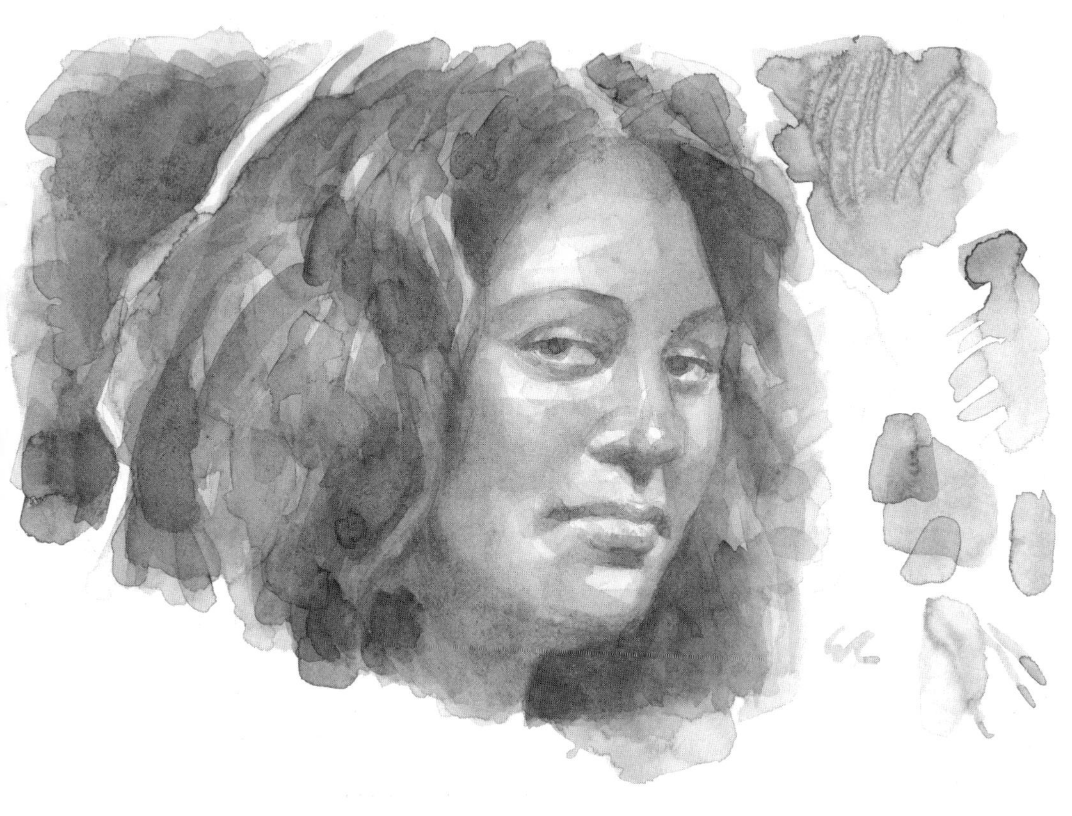

Step 5
Monochrome watercolour (sepia) on paper,
30.5 × 21.5cm (12 × 8½in)

In the initial drawing, it is best to avoid any rubbing out or drawing over existing lines because this could damage the paper's surface and lead to an uneven spread of paint. An alternative is to prepare the initial sketch on tracing paper and then trace just the essential outlines onto the surface of the finished work.

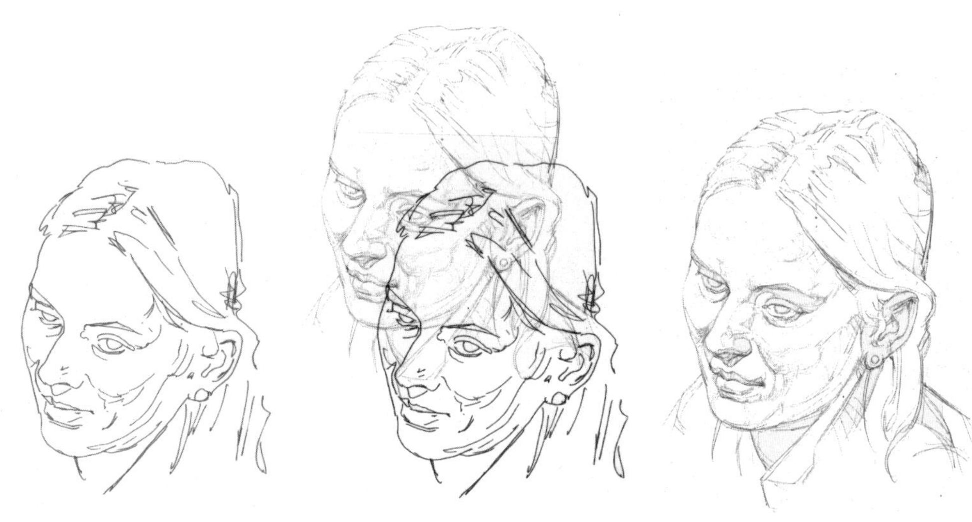

Traceable drawing and its application for ***Step 1***

Step 1

Step 2

Step 3

Step 4

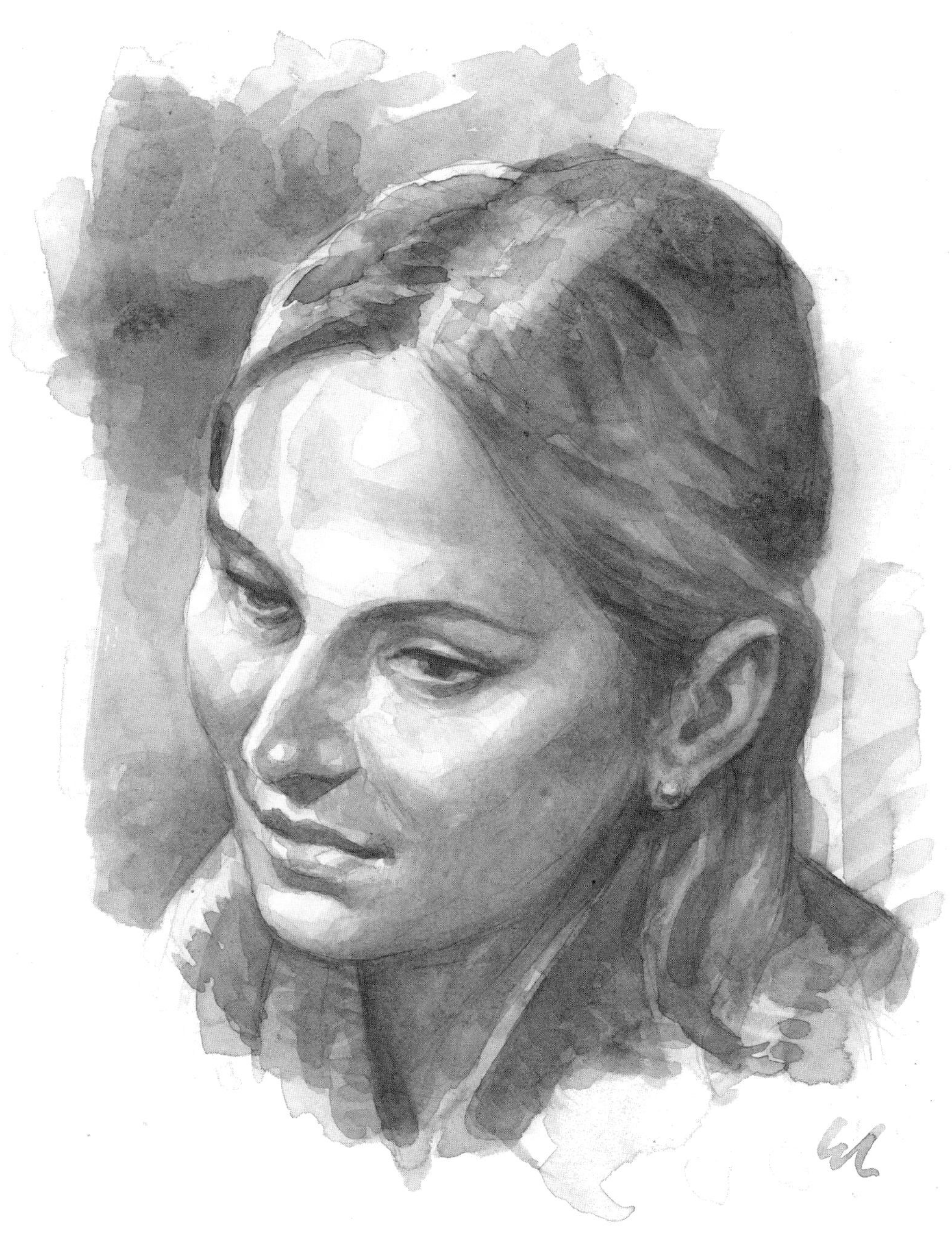

Step 5
Monochrome watercolour (raw sienna) on paper,
21 × 30cm (8¼ × 12in)

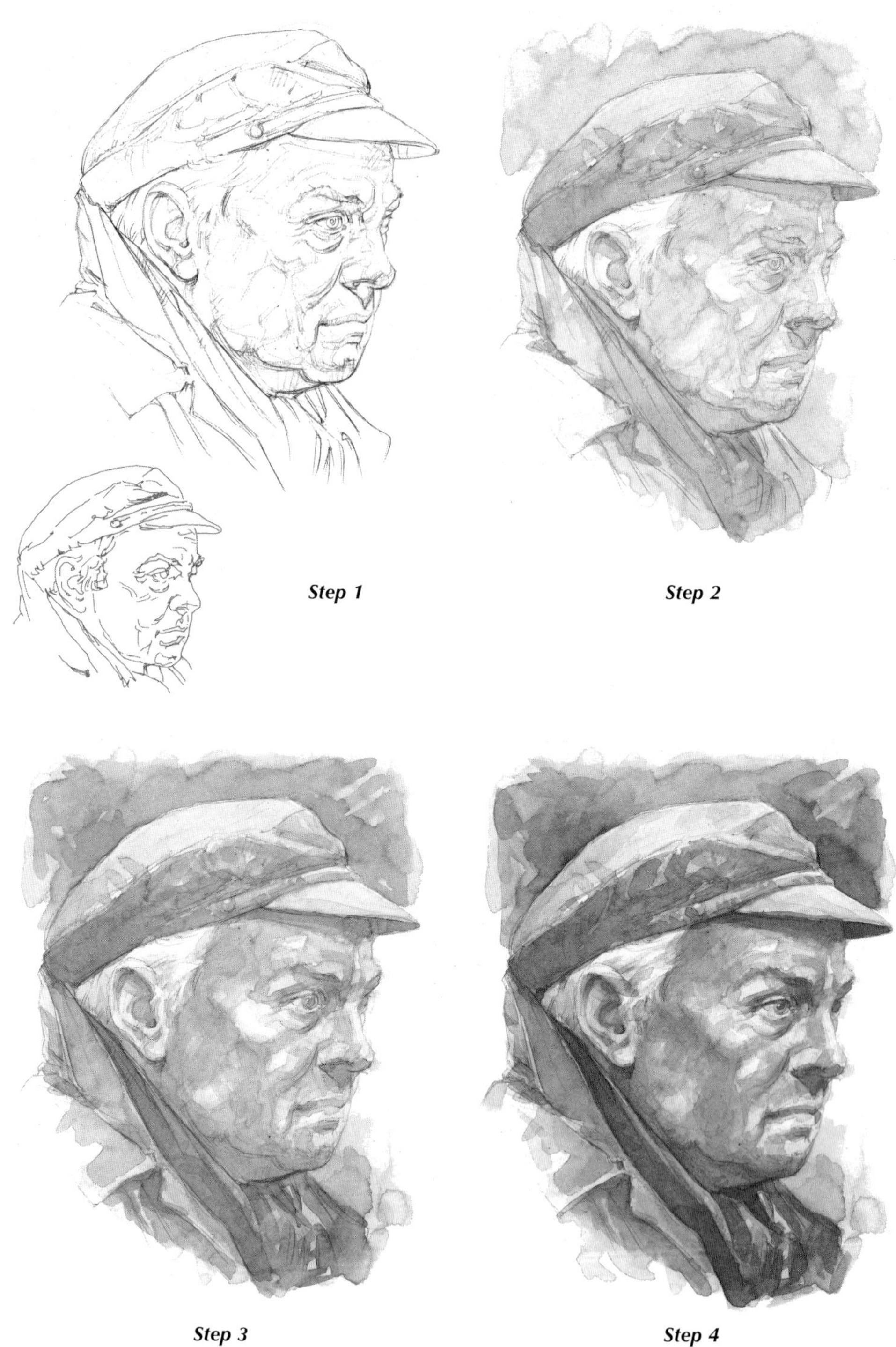

Step 1

Step 2

Step 3

Step 4

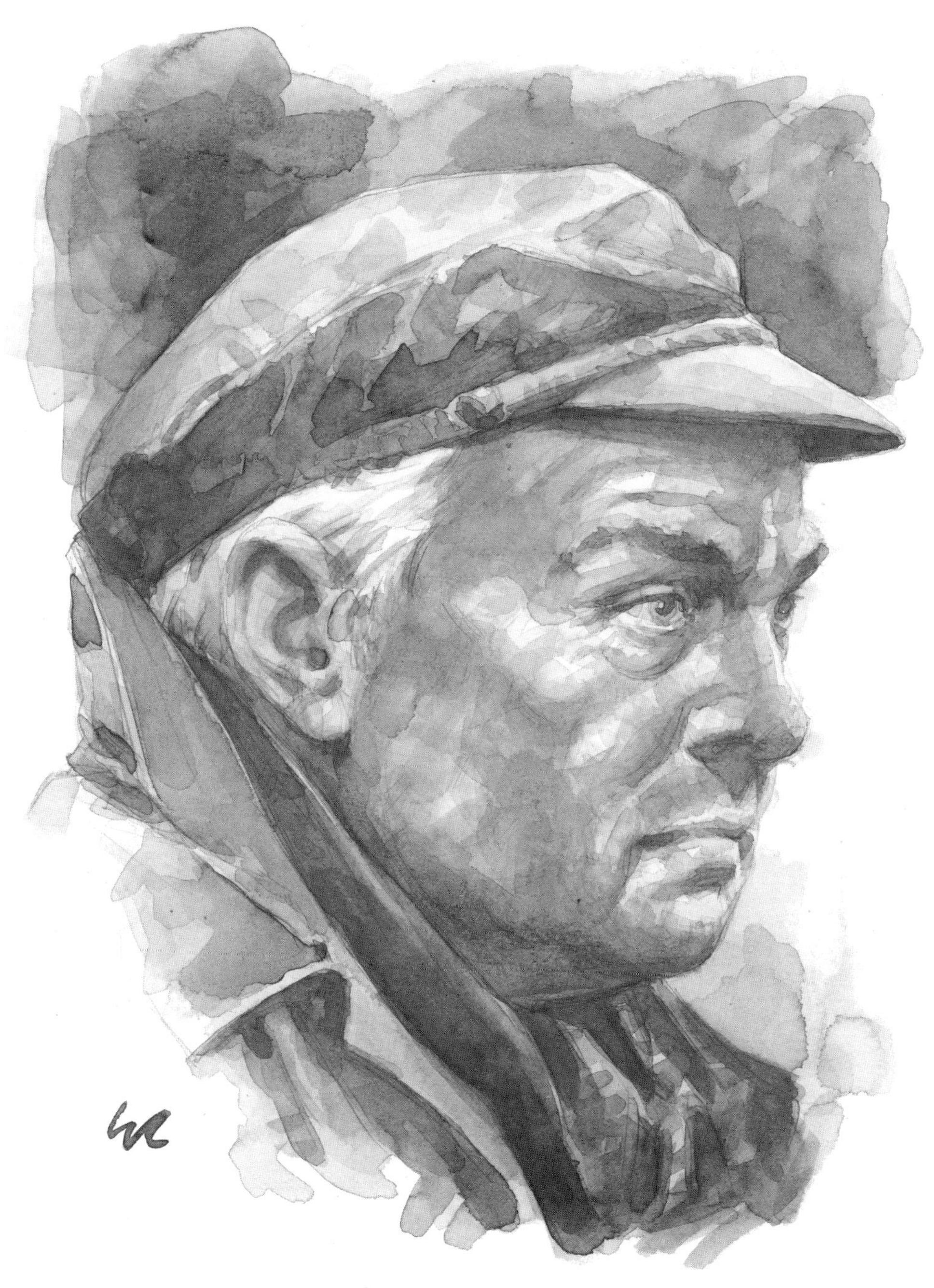

Step 5

Monochrome watercolour (raw umber) on paper,
21 × 30cm (8¼ × 12in)

STEP-BY-STEP EXAMPLES: GOUACHE

Gouache paint covers well (see page 15), especially if applied quite thickly. For this reason you can allow yourself to use bold strokes in the initial stages even when working directly on the final surface, and it is possible to work both from dark to light and from light to dark tones.

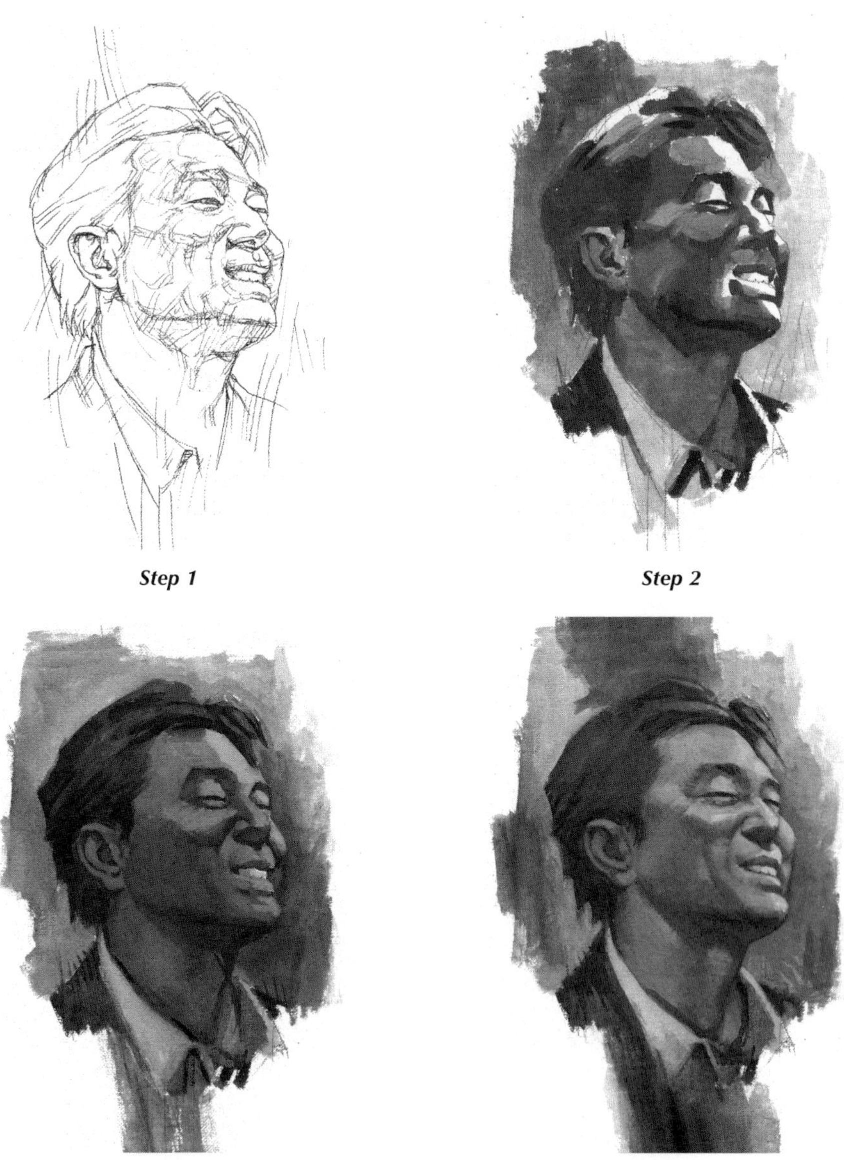

Step 1

Step 2

Step 3

Step 4

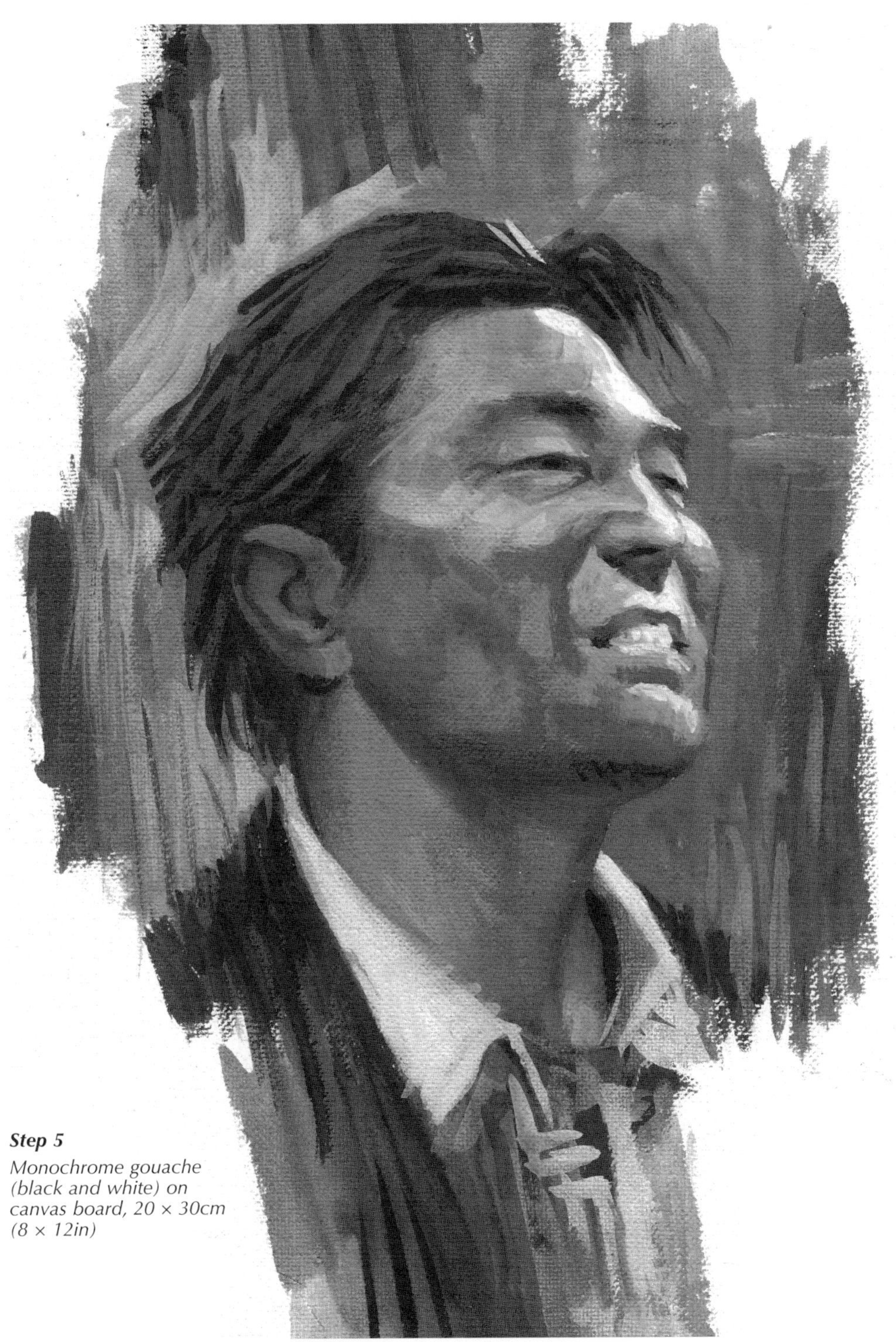

Step 5

Monochrome gouache (black and white) on canvas board, 20 × 30cm (8 × 12in)

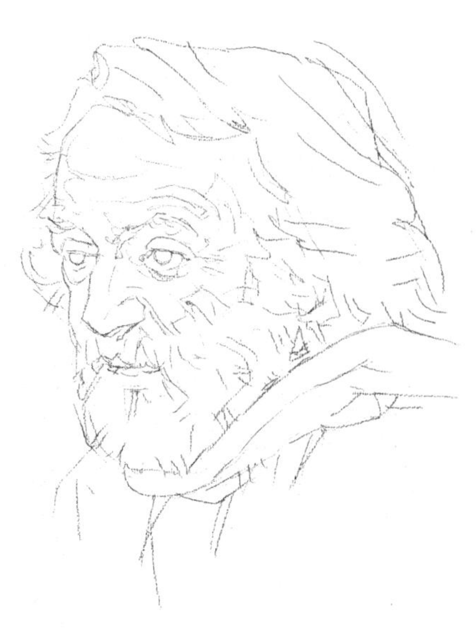

Step 1

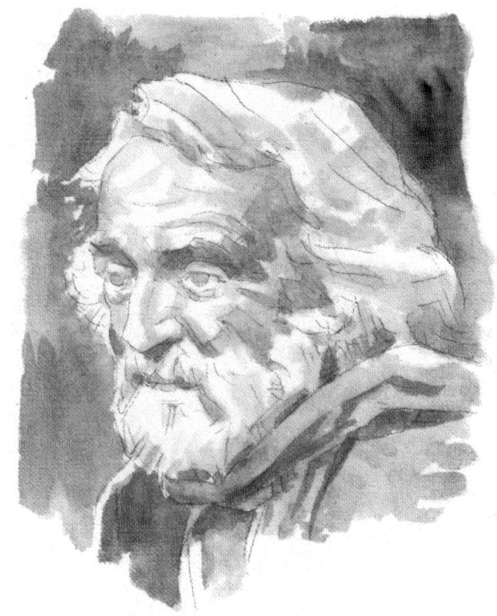

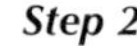

Step 2

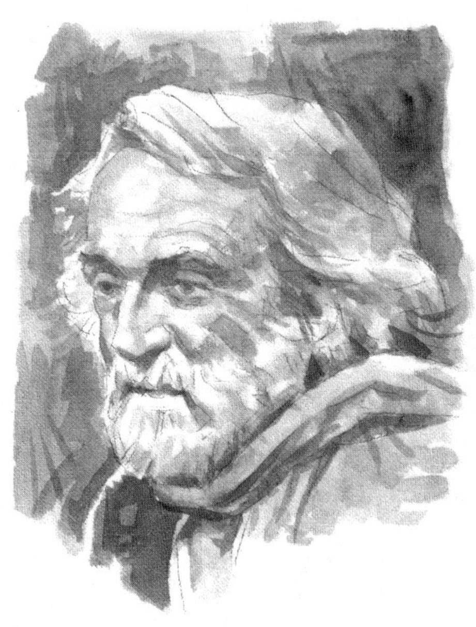

Step 3

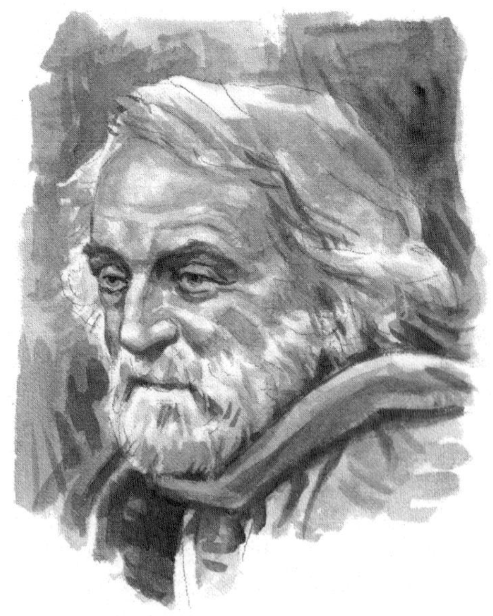

Step 4

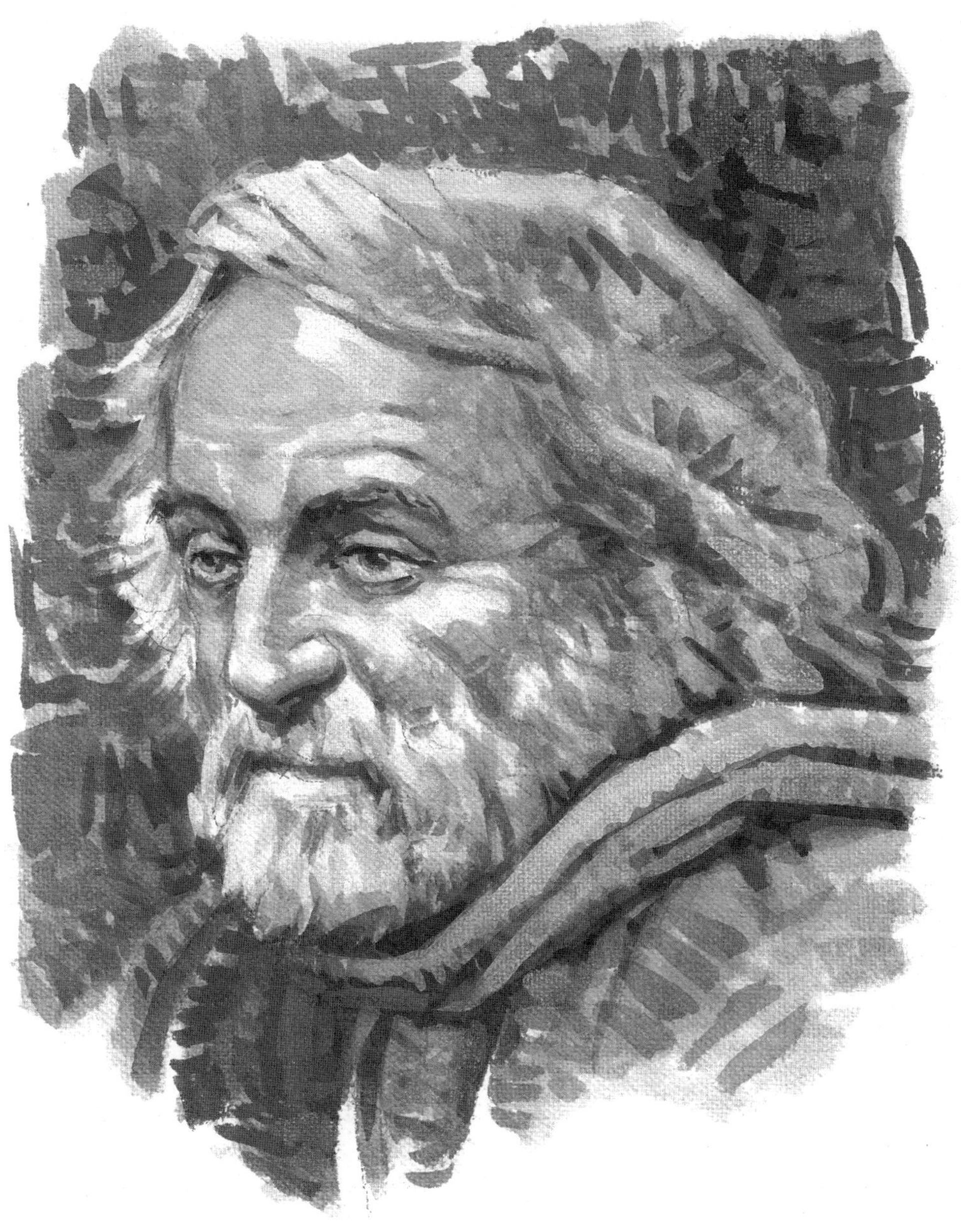

Step 5

Monochrome gouache (black and white) on canvas board, 20 × 30cm (8 × 12in)

For this painting, I used a highly diluted, watery paint to attain effects similar to those of watercolour. In a few places (on the scarf, in the hair and on the eyes, for example) I used slightly thicker paint.

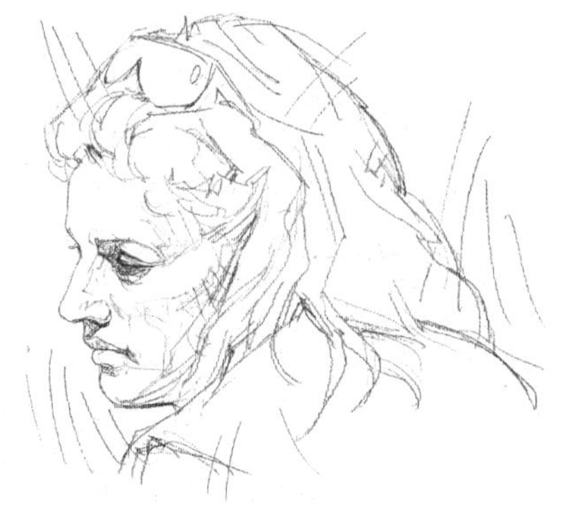

Step 1

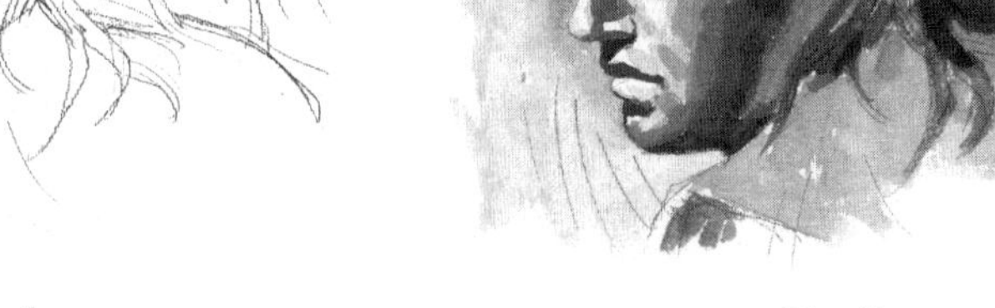

Step 2

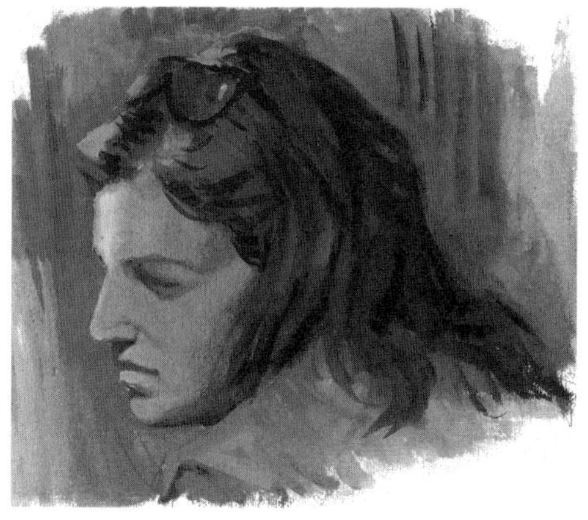

Step 3

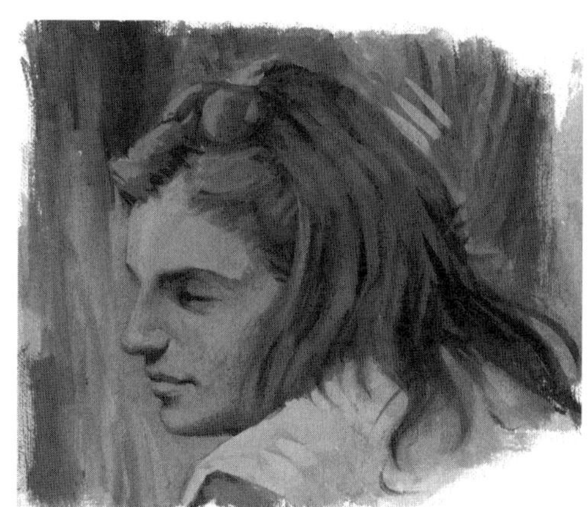

Step 4

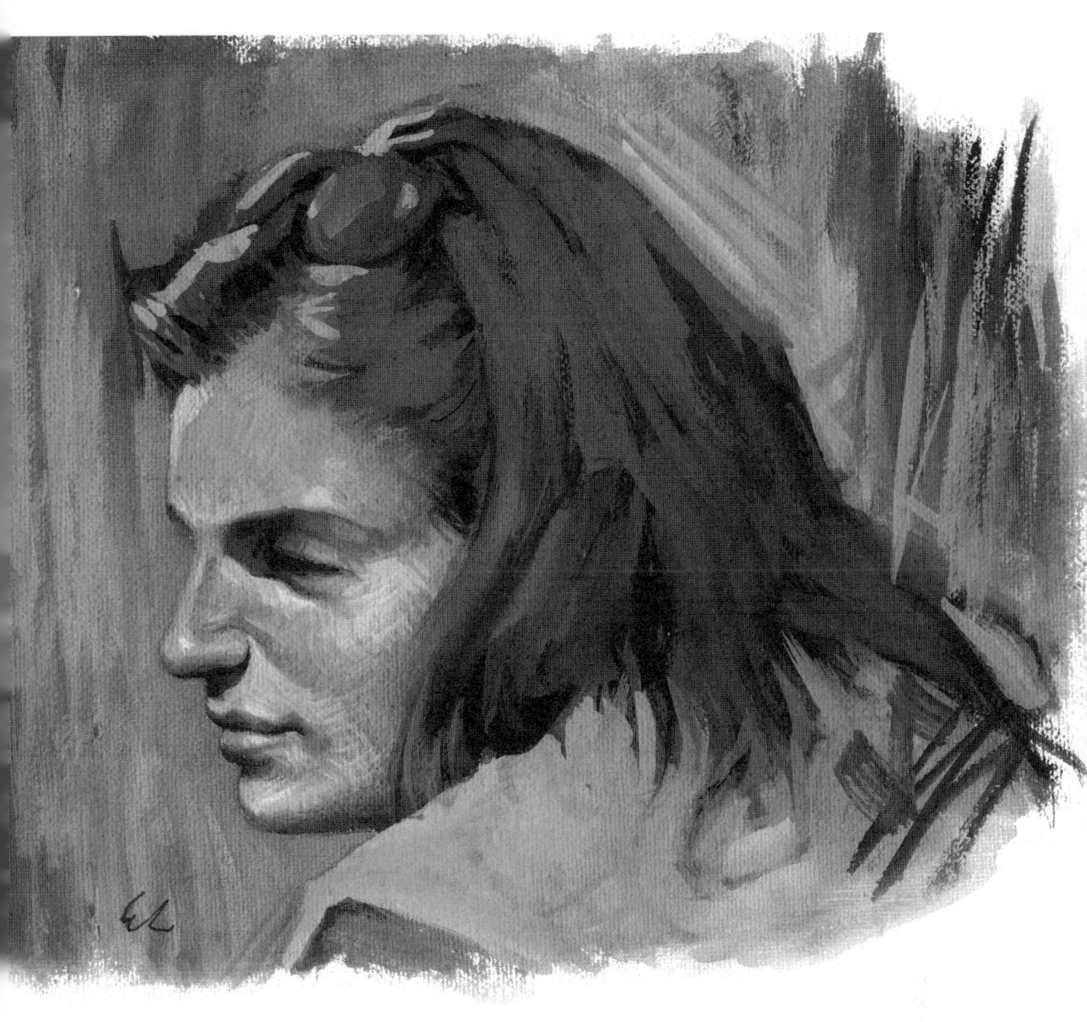

Step 5
Monochrome gouache (black and white) on canvas board, 30 × 20cm (12 × 8in)

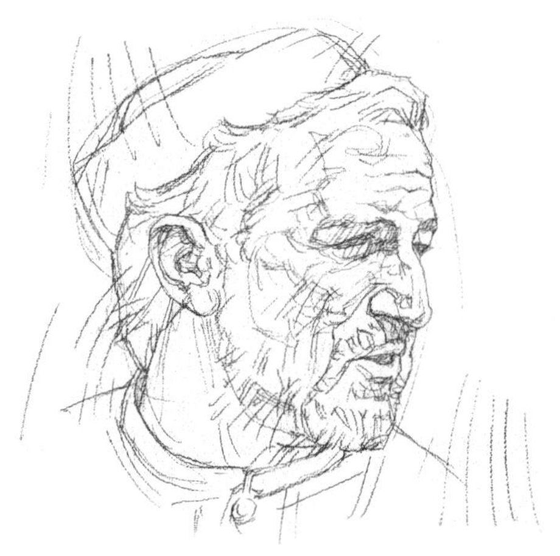

Step 1

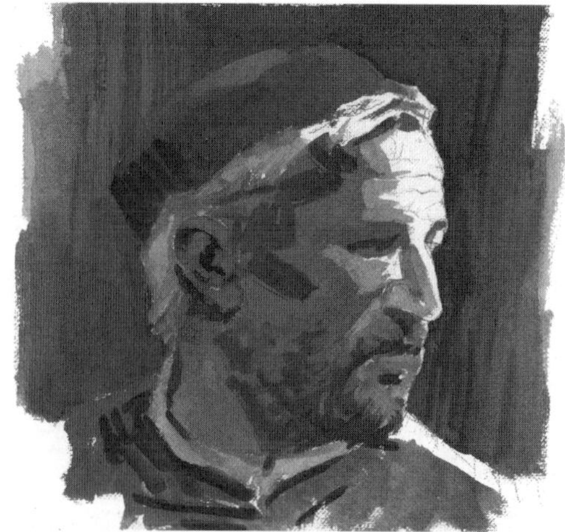

Step 2

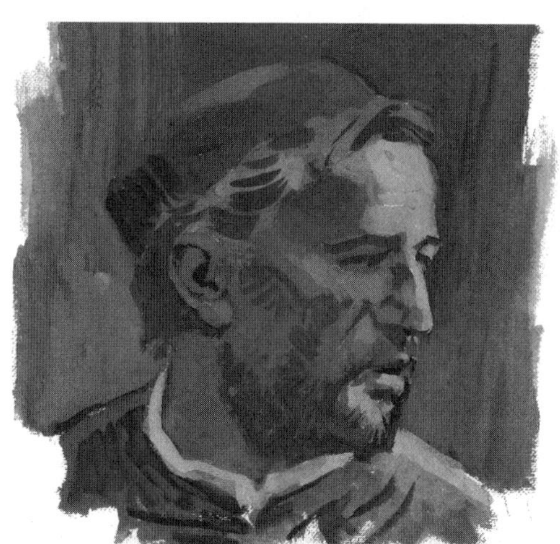

Step 3

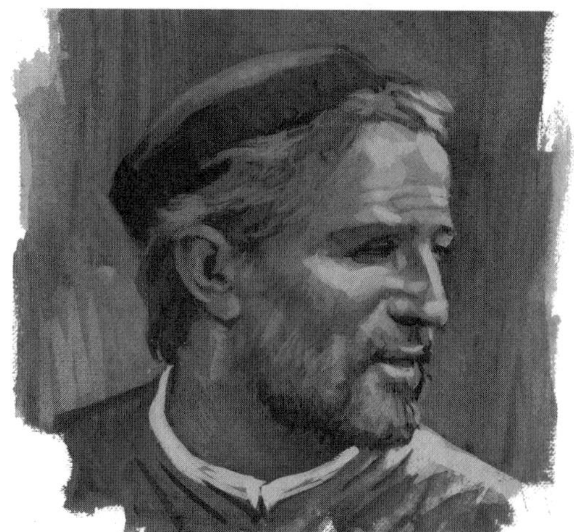

Step 4

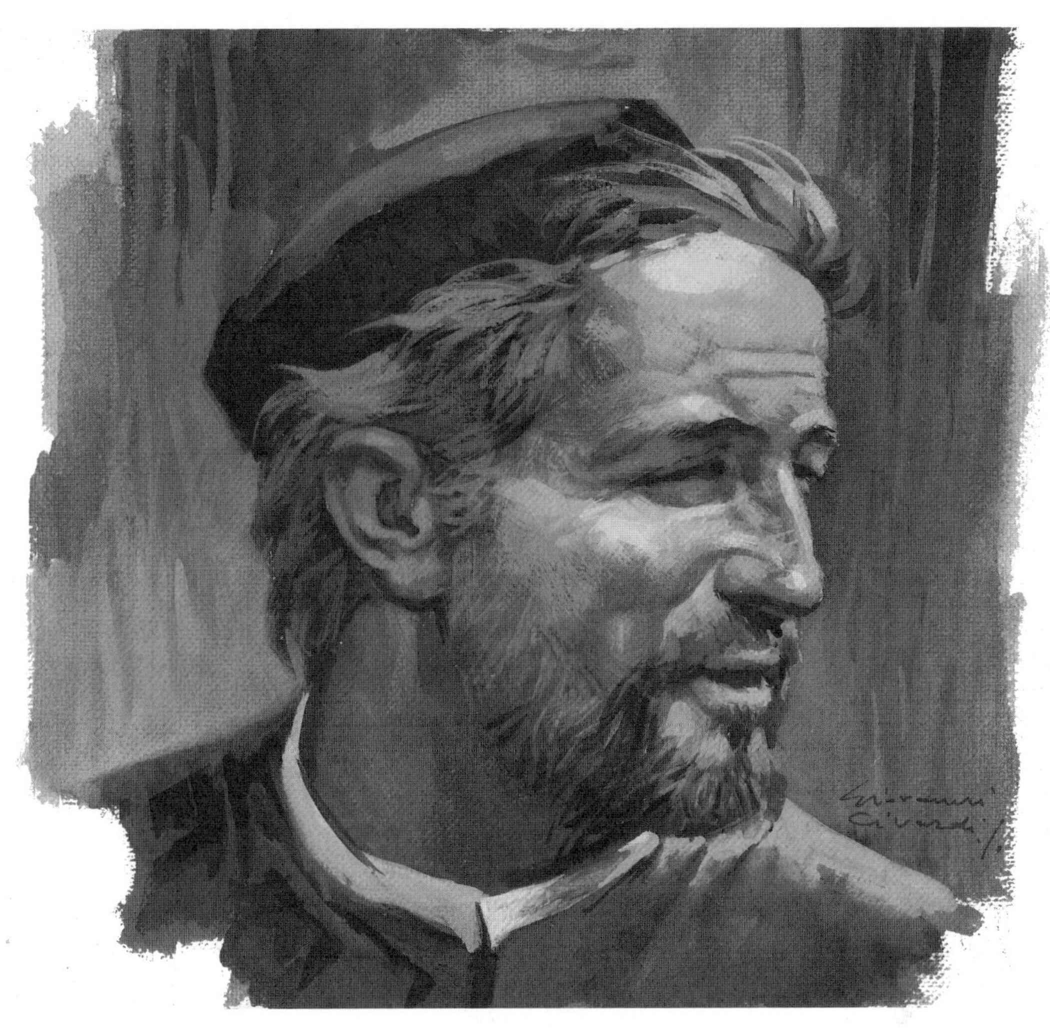

Step 5
Monochrome gouache (black and white) on canvas board,
30 × 20cm (12 × 8in)

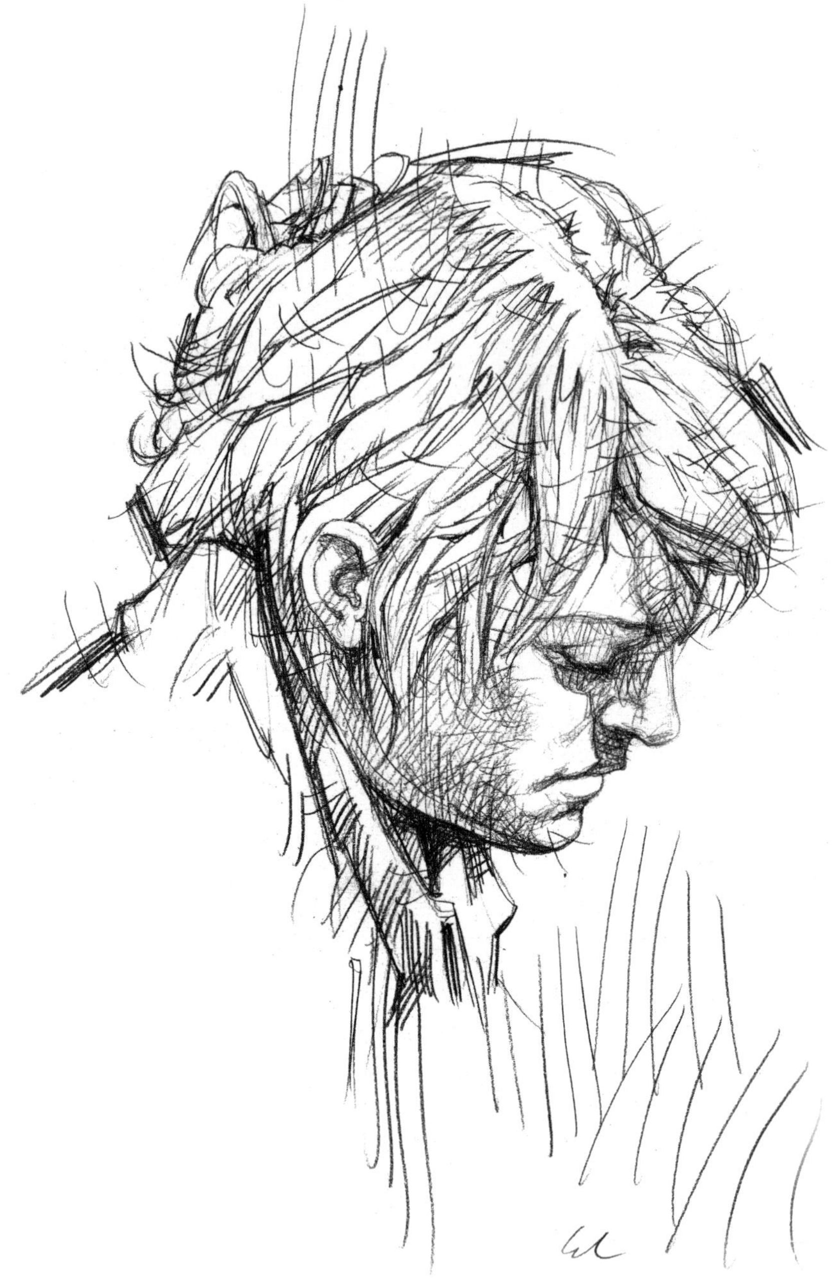

HB mechanical pencil on canvas board, 20.5 × 30.5cm (8 × 12in)

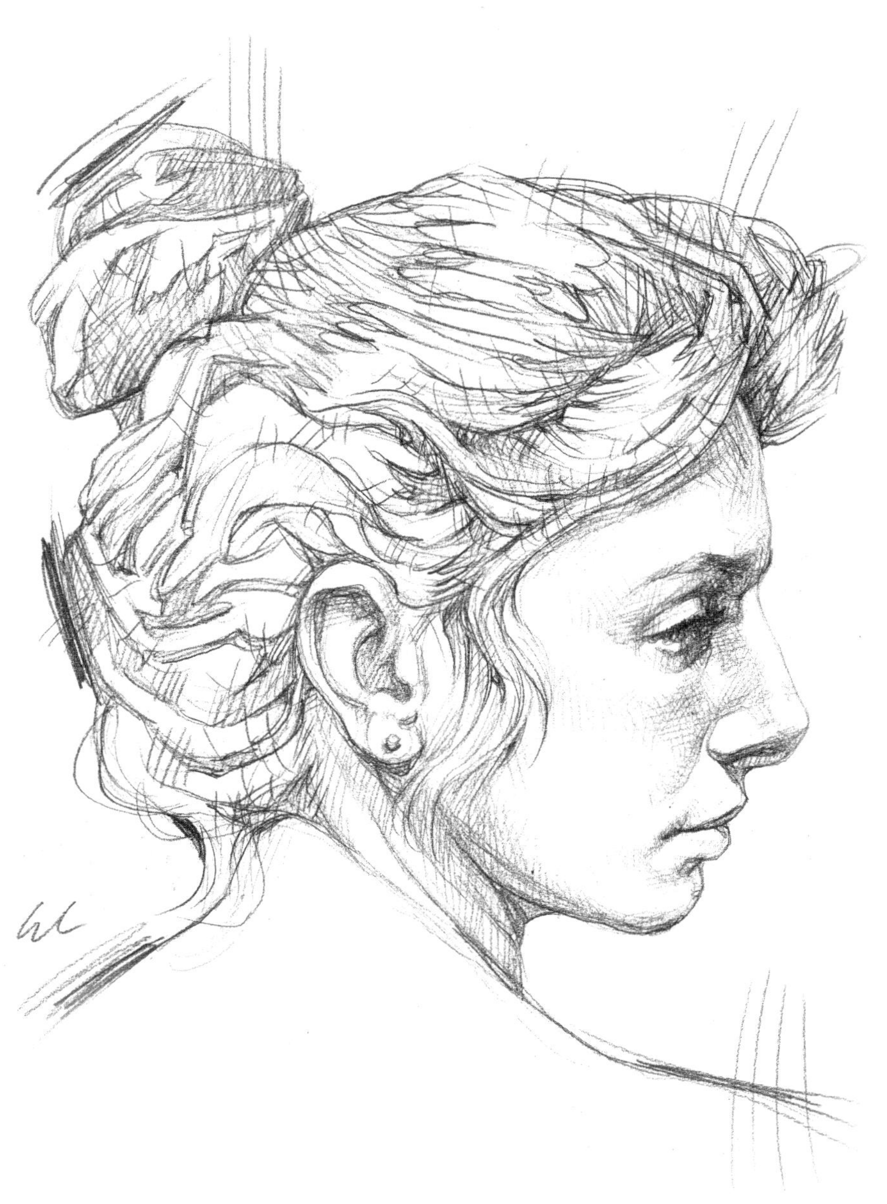

Portrait of Rosanna F. (2010, second version)
HB pencil on paper, 31 × 21cm (12¼ × 8¼in)

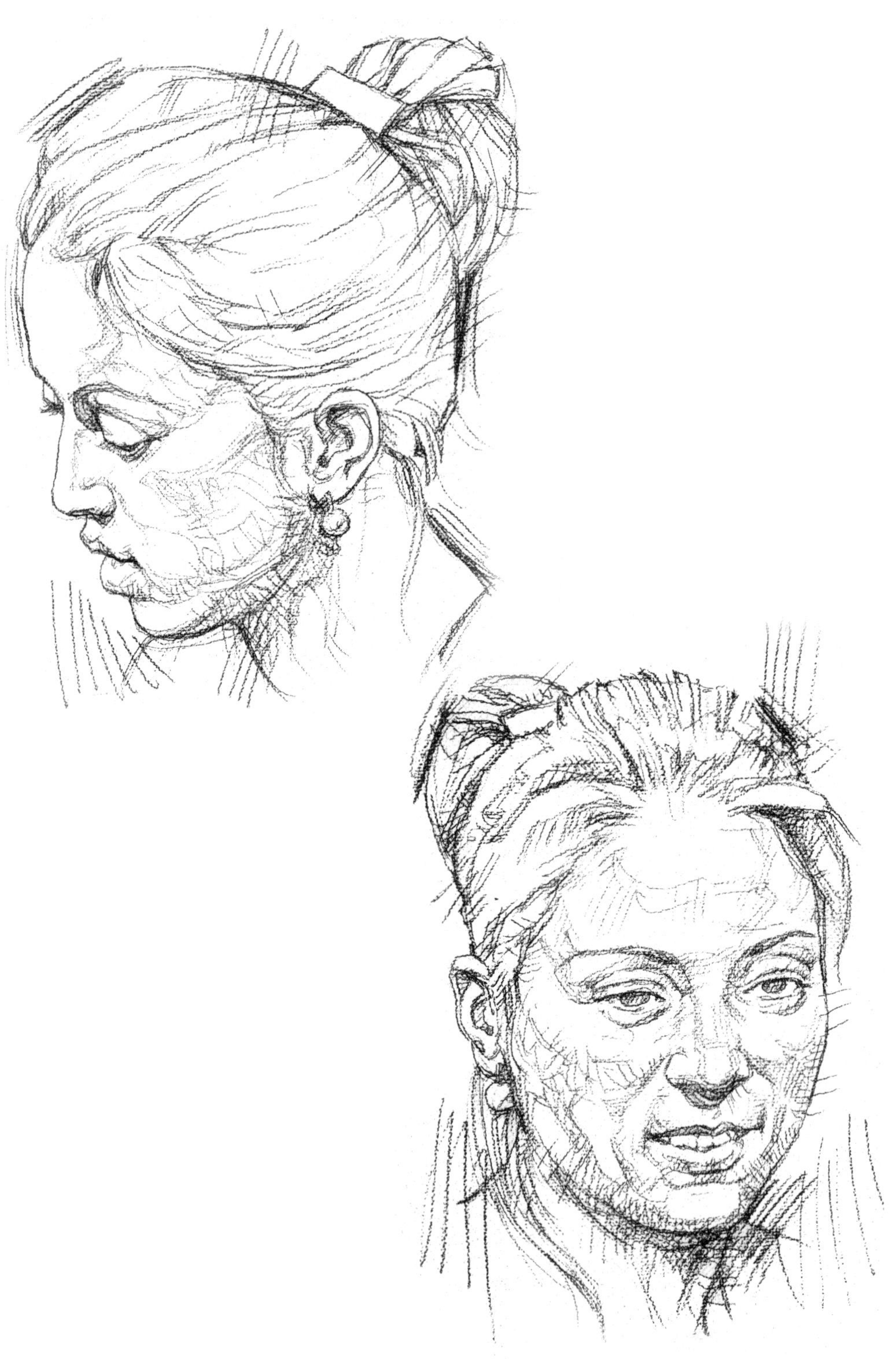

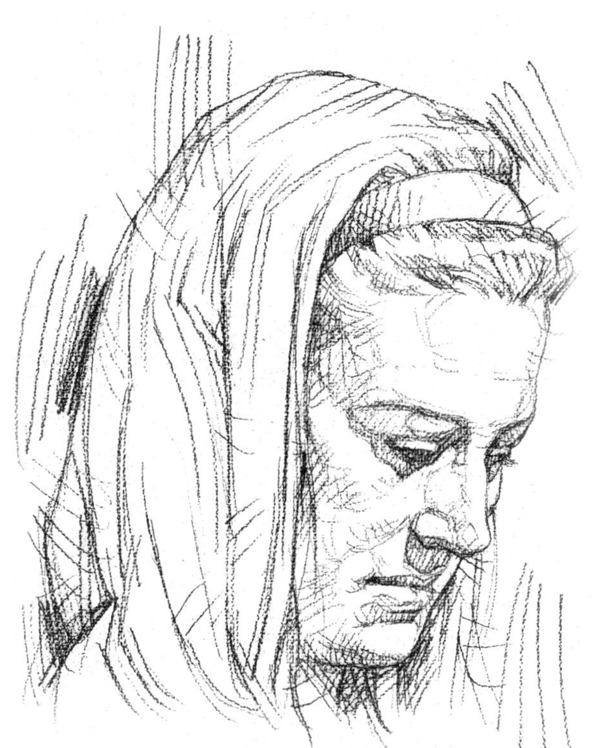

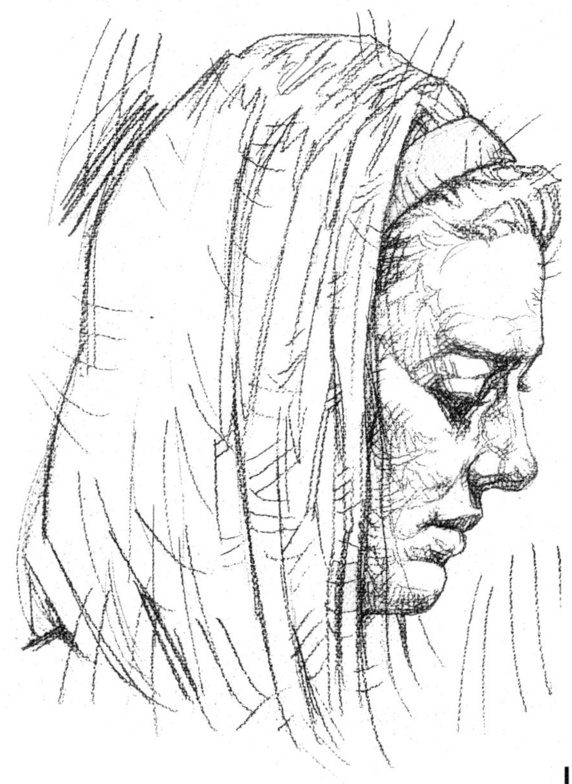

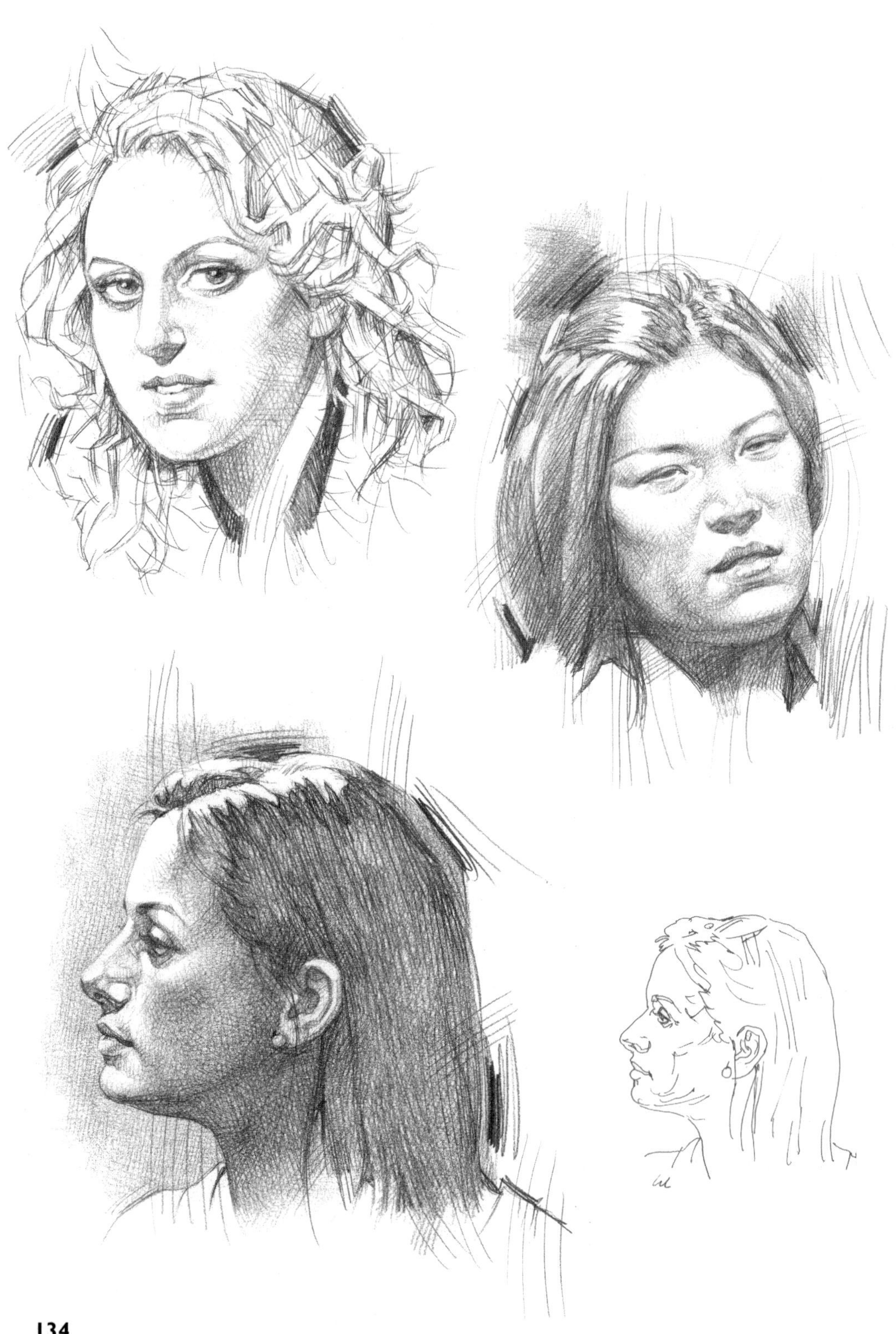

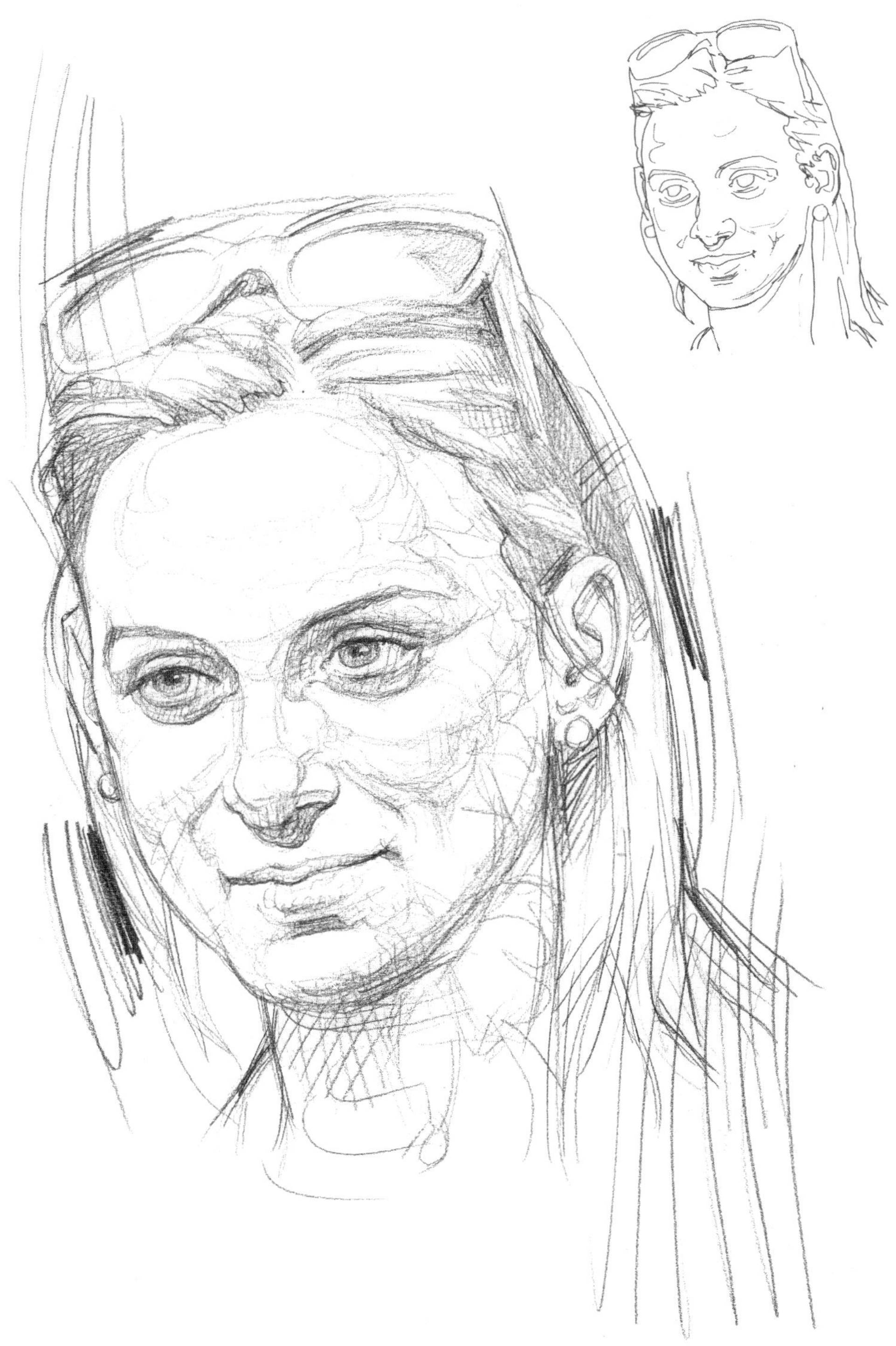

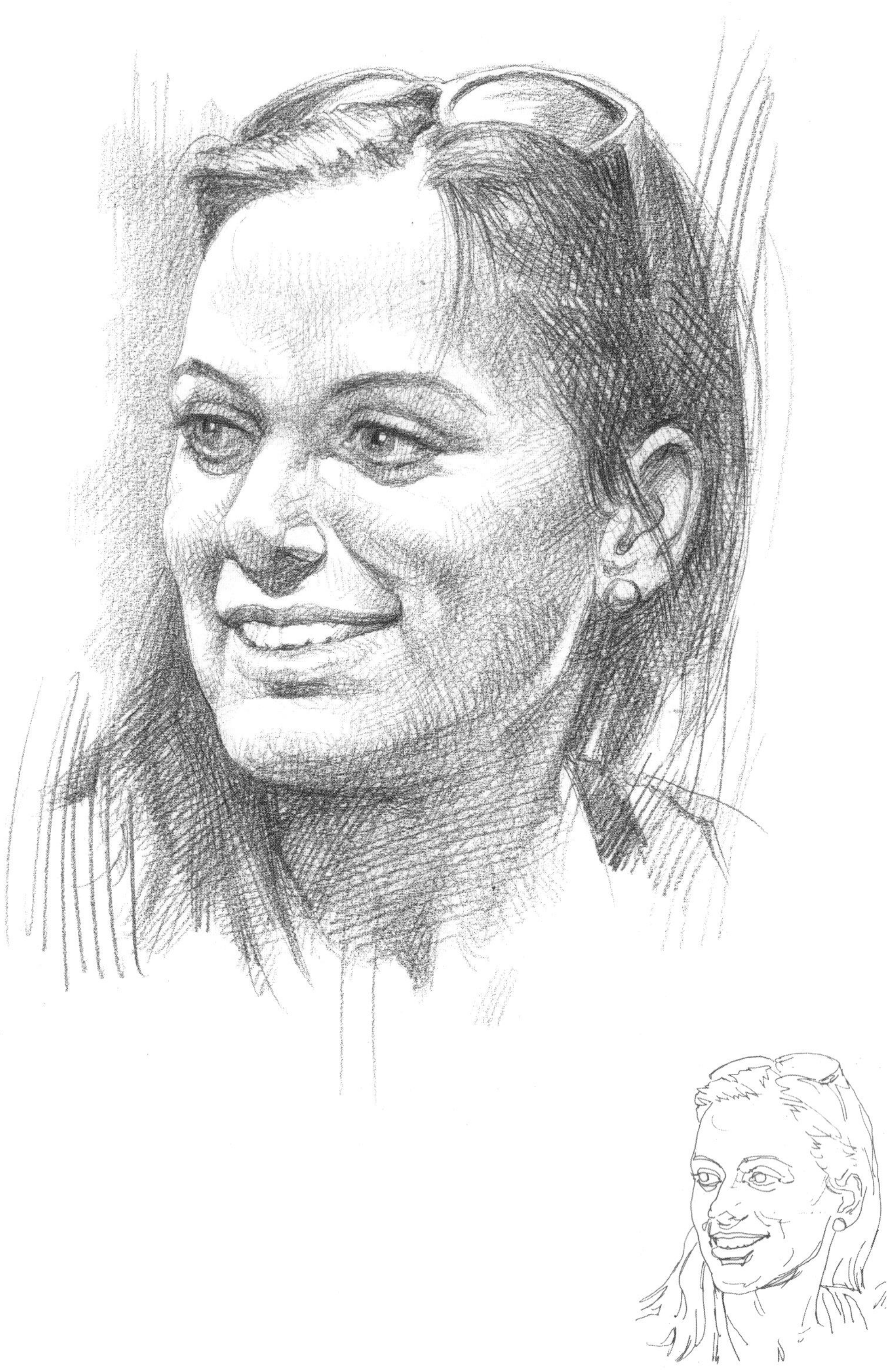

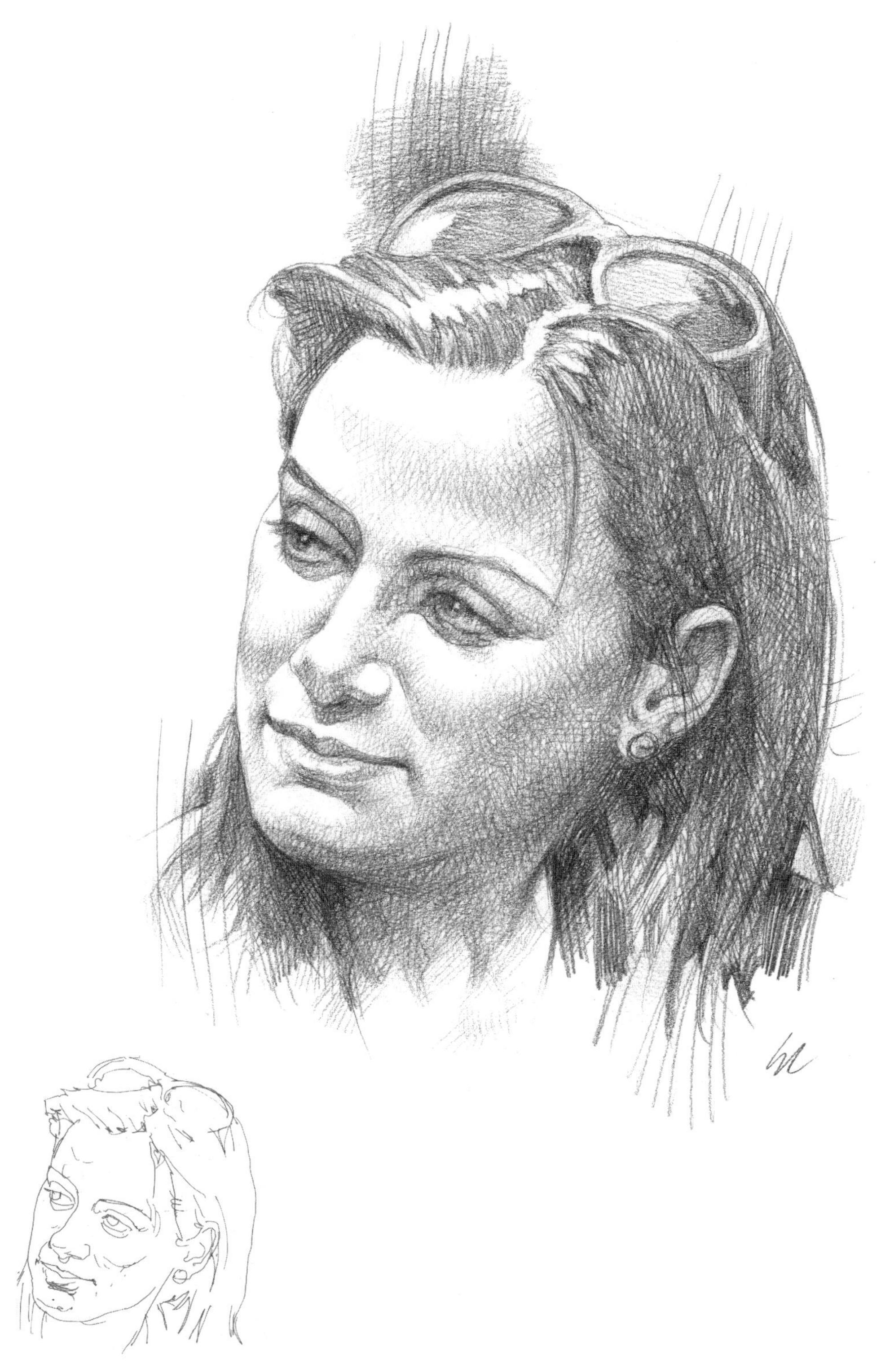

DRAWING PORTRAITS WITH CHARACTER USING GRIDS

Many artists have used models whose faces could symbolically represent the physical and psychological characteristics that were closest to those of the protagonists of their historical, mythological or religious paintings. This was common in the seventeenth and eighteenth centuries, but is fundamentally no different from what happens today when theatre or cinema actors are chosen for their matching physical appearance to the characters they play.

In this section of the book, I have collected a series of heads – drawings that could be used as preparatory studies or else be purely aesthetic, autonomous in meaning – that I have drawn live or from photographs after being attracted by some characterful features in the faces.

There are many paths of artistic experience: in drawing these faces, I chose to stay within the boundaries of figurative tradition: searching solely for a frank, descriptive translation of the forms instead of offering more personal, 'artistic' interpretive styles. This leaves those who wish to practise drawing full liberty in elaborating on the basic physiognomy. In short, these pictures are intended to be used to stimulate the artist's interest, and encourage you to search for other subjects in the environment you live in or visit.

Although photography is invaluable for capturing fleeting expressions, unusual or random gestures, and unrepeatable situations, it is best to proceed with the portrait from life where time and practicality make it possible: there is a substantial difference between reality as seen and its photographic reproduction, if for nothing else than the lack of spatial depth.

Of the many 'mechanical' approaches – which includes photocopying, projection, photographic and digital zooming – that can be used to reproduce a flat reference picture (whether drawing or photograph), that of using the grid is the simplest and oldest method and the one that most respects the honest practices of the manual skill of painting. It is also the one that provides both great precision and full freedom of execution and development when completing the requisite steps.

Reality gives us the model in its three spatial dimensions, while photographic reproduction mechanically transforms space into a two-dimensional surface, similar to the one on which an illustrator or painter works upon. When starting to draw, using a grid can aid the conceptual changeover between reality and the simplification suggested by the flat image, helping the artist to express volume.

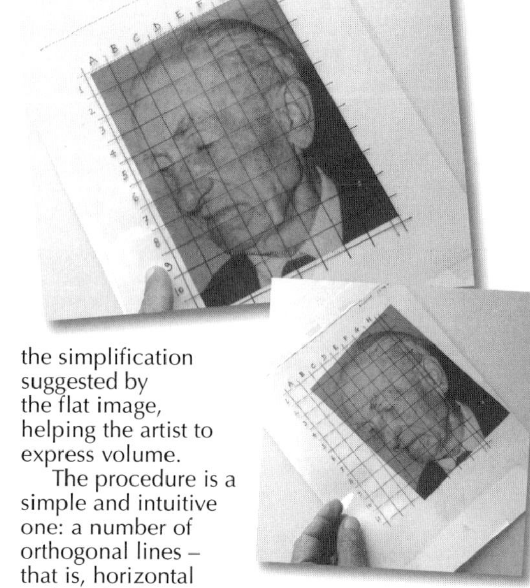

The procedure is a simple and intuitive one: a number of orthogonal lines – that is, horizontal and vertical – are drawn directly (or on tracing paper) onto the reference picture to form a grid of evenly-sized squares. A similar grid is then traced onto a drawing support (e.g. a sheet of paper, board, or canvas) using light pencil lines. The outline segments of the subject can then be copied from each square on the reference picture to the corresponding square on the grid on the drawing support, until all the outlines have been completed. Before completing the new picture with freer procedures, I recommend you erase the grid lines.

Depending on the desired result, you can vary this technique. Using more squares on the reference grid will give you less to copy from each square, making things more precise – though at the cost of having more individual squares to copy. The size of the squares on the support can vary from those on the reference picture in order to obtain a larger (or smaller) grid.

I hope that the ancient procedure of drawing a grid, or mesh, is used as an initial gateway or temporary support to help lay the technical bases – observation, proportion, shading and so forth – from which to proceed with the portrait and elaborate the most significant expressive style (as, in the end, all faces are 'characterful').

Grids drawn directly onto a photograph or drawing (left) and on tracing paper (right) over a photocopy.

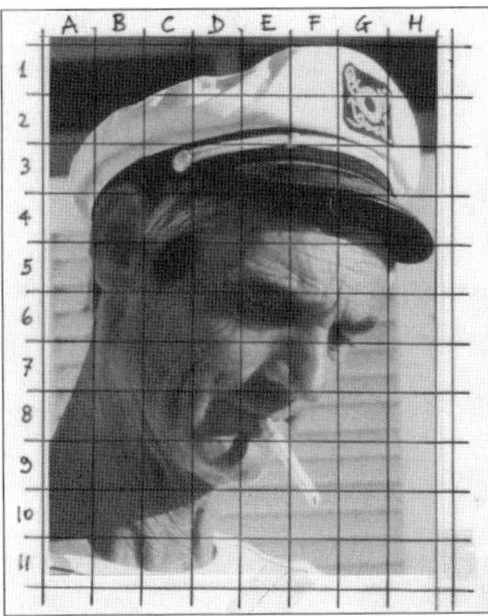

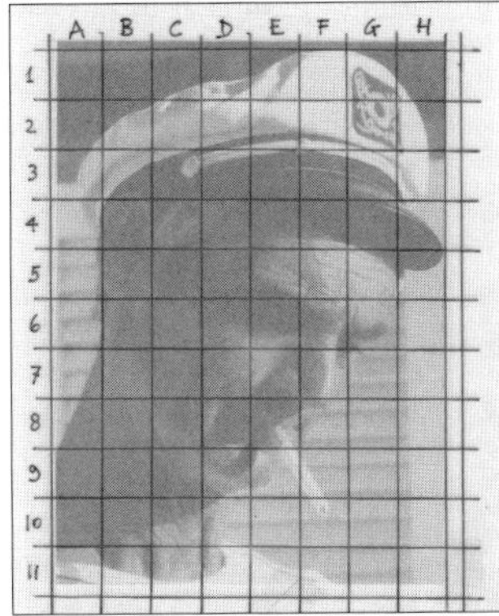

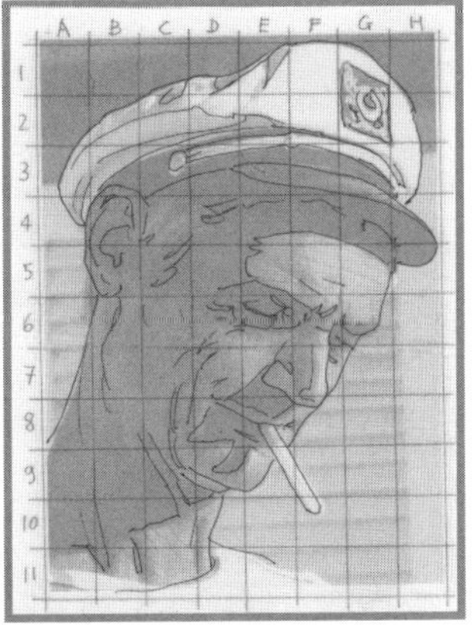

A

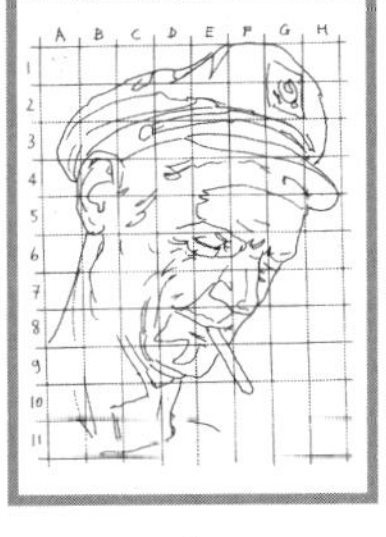

B

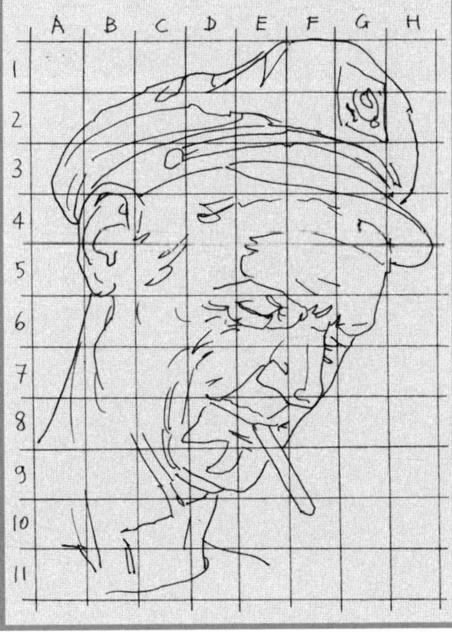

C

Above

Here, figure A shows the synthetic outline of the main shapes and outlines. Figure B shows these reproduced on a smaller grid, for a reduction in size; while Figure C shows them reproduced on a larger grid. The numerical and alphabetical sequences placed at the sides of the grid are useful for helping to find the right squares.

PORTRAIT GALLERY

The drawings printed in this section (from pages 142–201) have been chosen to provide ideas and elements to practise, in order to be able to observe and study the proportions and shapes of a 'characterful' human face.

The style that I used in drawing them is somewhat 'neutral', which reflects the intention to provide the objective elements of each face, so that the artist wishing to draw it can start from these elements and elaborate his own interpretation, according to the styles and techniques that he believes most suitable and fitting for his own aesthetic sensibilities.

Each portrait is accompanied by a rapid preliminary study of the main tones and their connections: they are all drawings created quickly, using very soft lead pencils and a much freer style (almost a sketch or visual note rather than the one I then applied to the portrait itself).

The 'grid' is usually drawn on the reference picture that is to be reproduced, but I preferred to use transparent paper and trace only the key facial features onto it – just enough to begin the process of developing the character of the face.

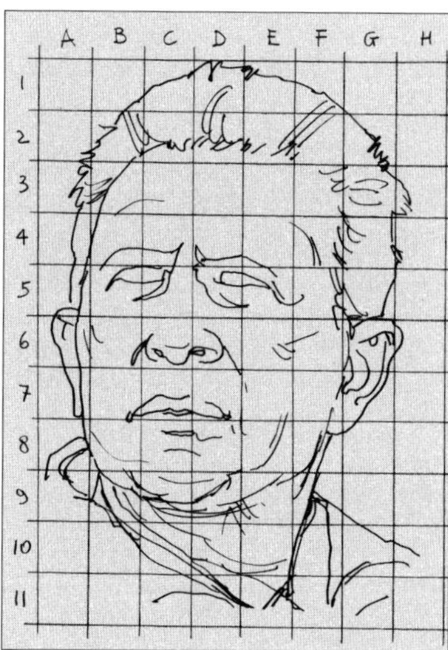

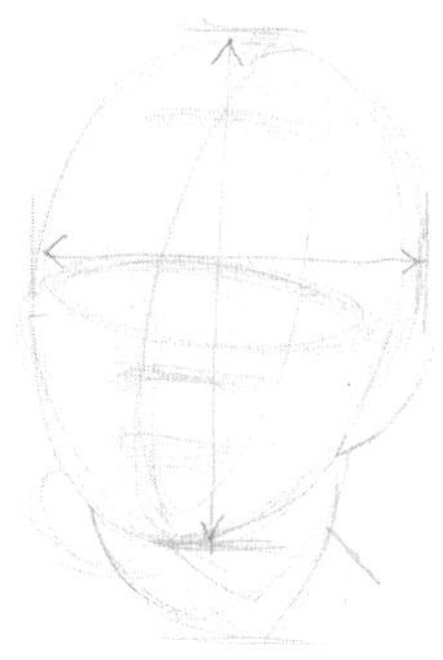

Step 1 *Overall shape and size*

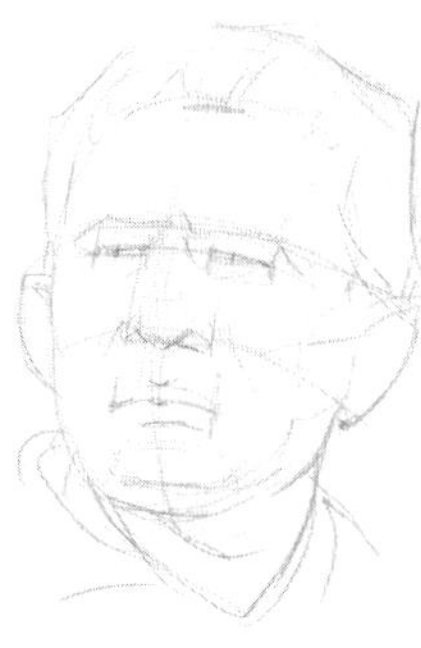

Step 2 *Proportions*

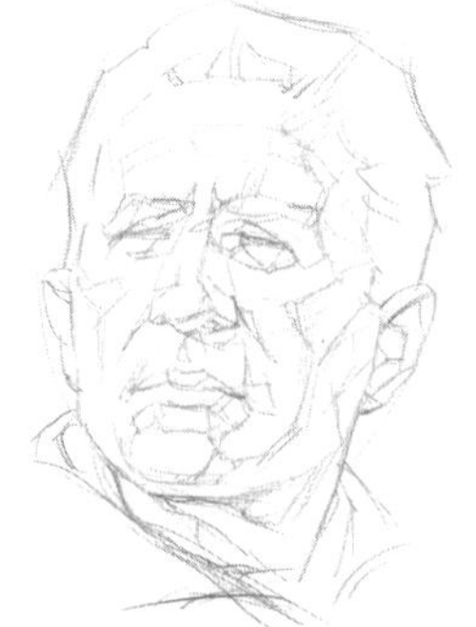

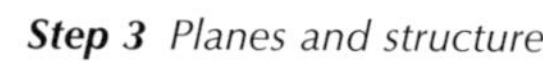

Step 3 *Planes and structure*

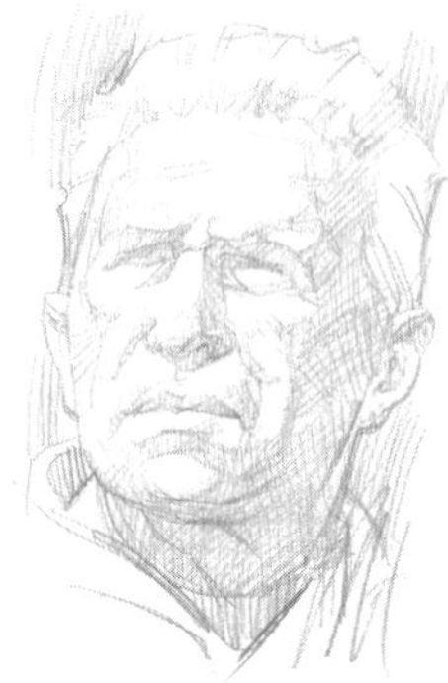

Step 4 *Tonal modulation*

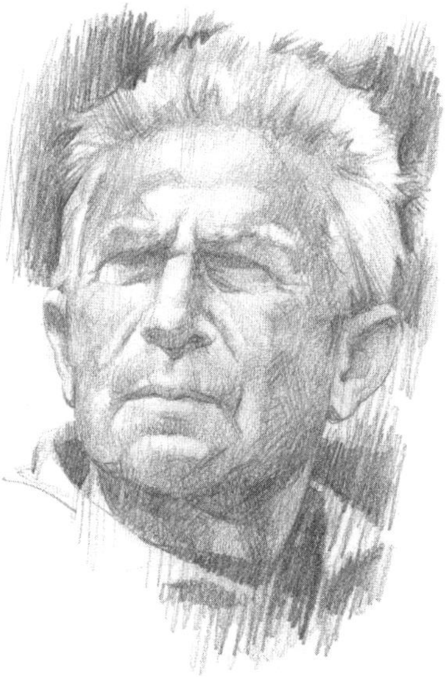

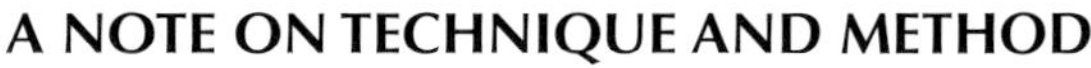

A NOTE ON TECHNIQUE AND METHOD

All the portraits on the following few pages were drawn using HB and B graphite on paper measuring 21 × 28cm (8¼ × 11in).

The tonal studies, which accompany the majority of the portraits, were drawn using a softer graphite – 4B and 6B – on paper measuring 15 × 21cm (6 × 8¼in).

The grid shown for each portrait can serve as an initial guide to reproduce the basic outlines of the head (after tracing it onto the drawing surface, at the desired size).

After the summary indication of the overall sizes, the next steps for producing the drawing involve controlling proportions, identifying the structural 'planes' and the modulation of *chiaroscuro* tones.

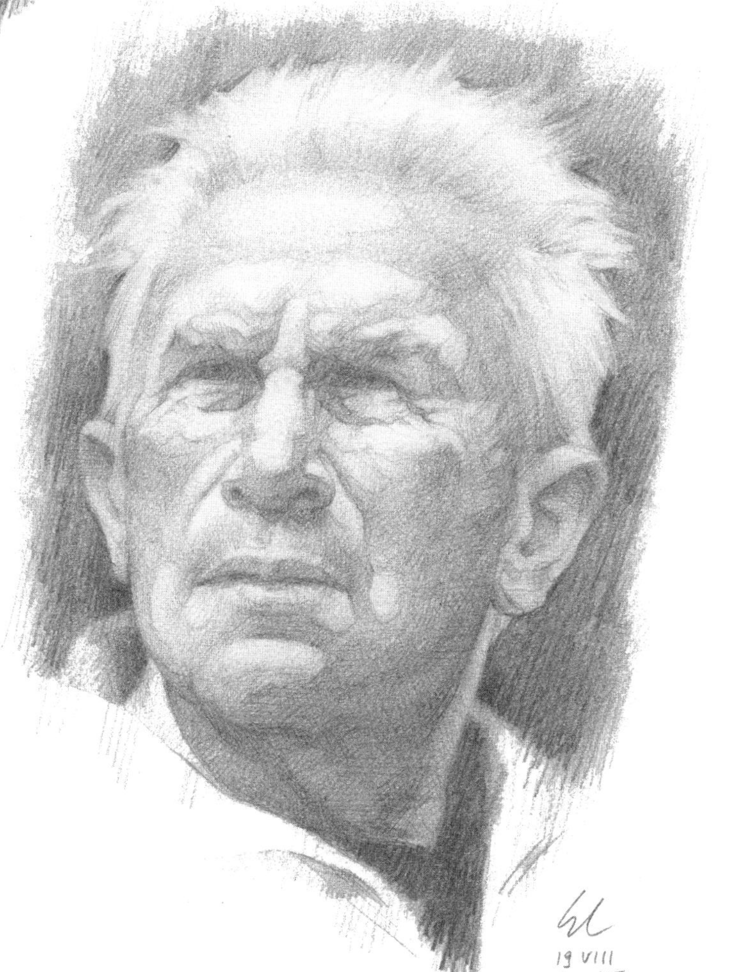

Tonal study

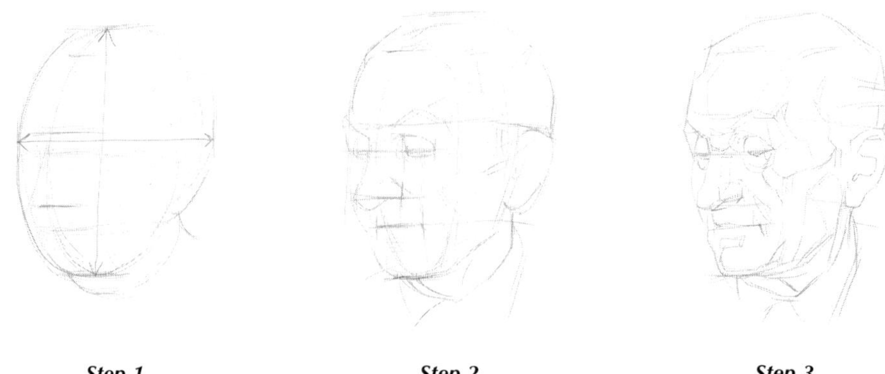

Step 1 ***Step 2*** ***Step 3***

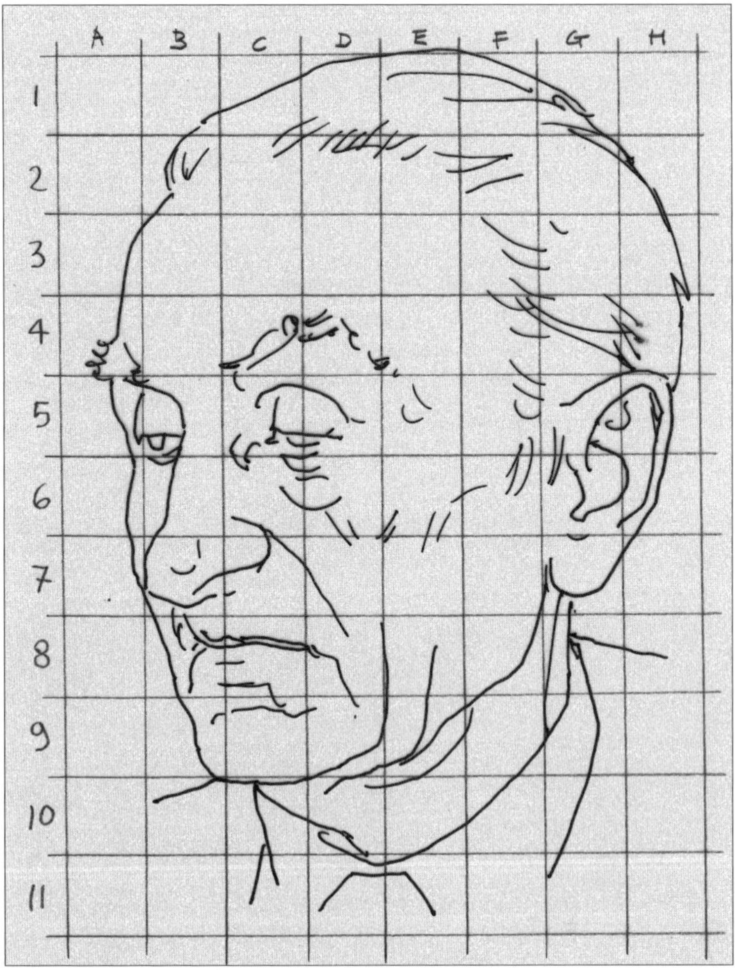

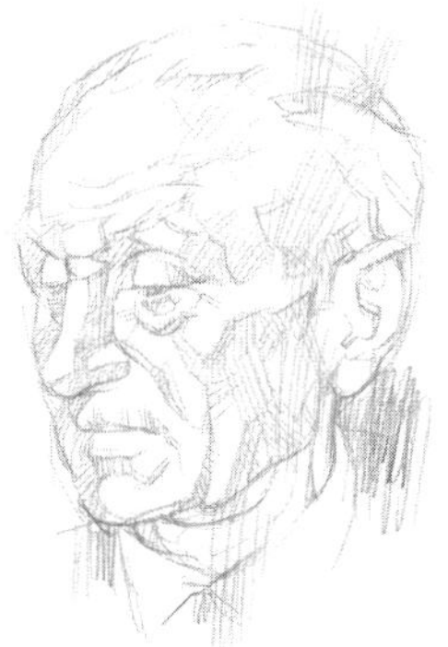

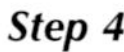

Step 4

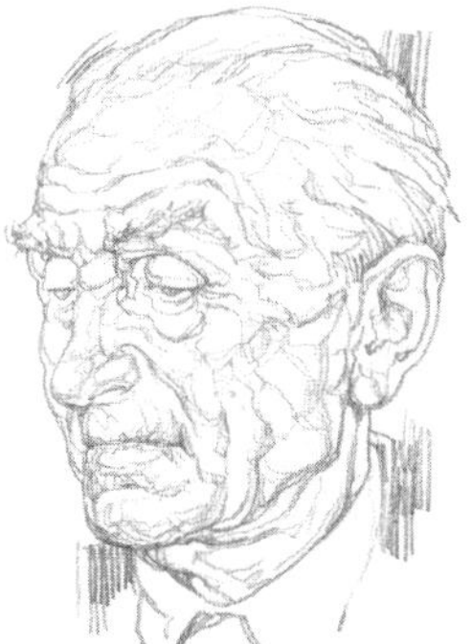

Tonal study

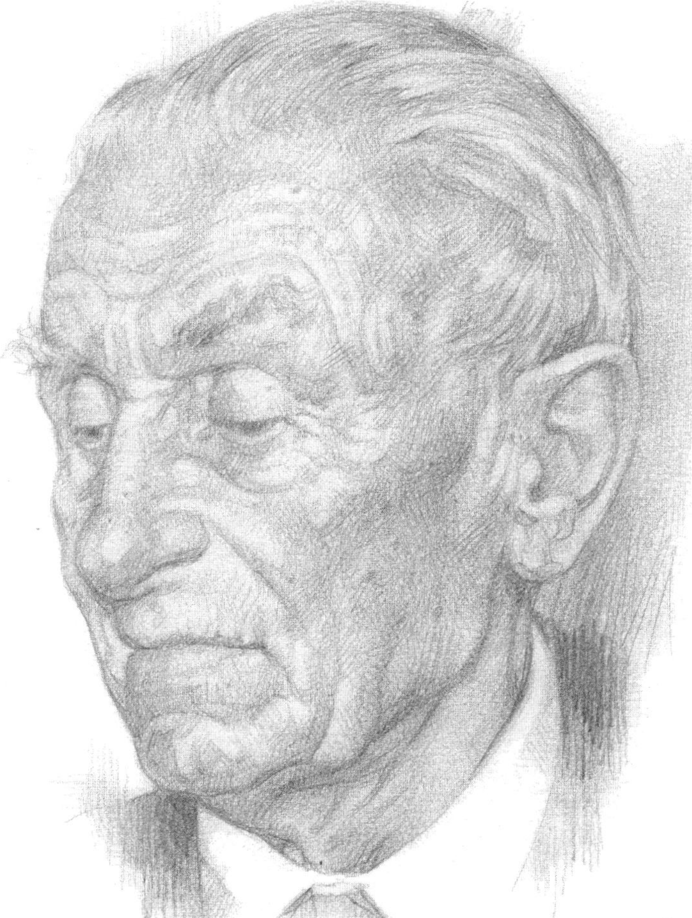

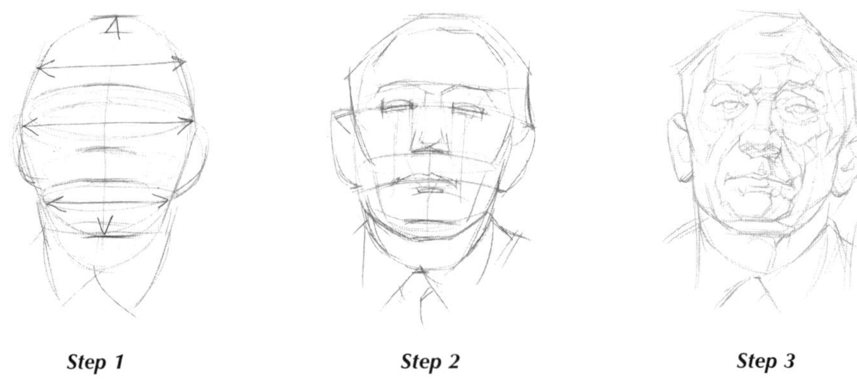

Step 1 *Step 2* *Step 3*

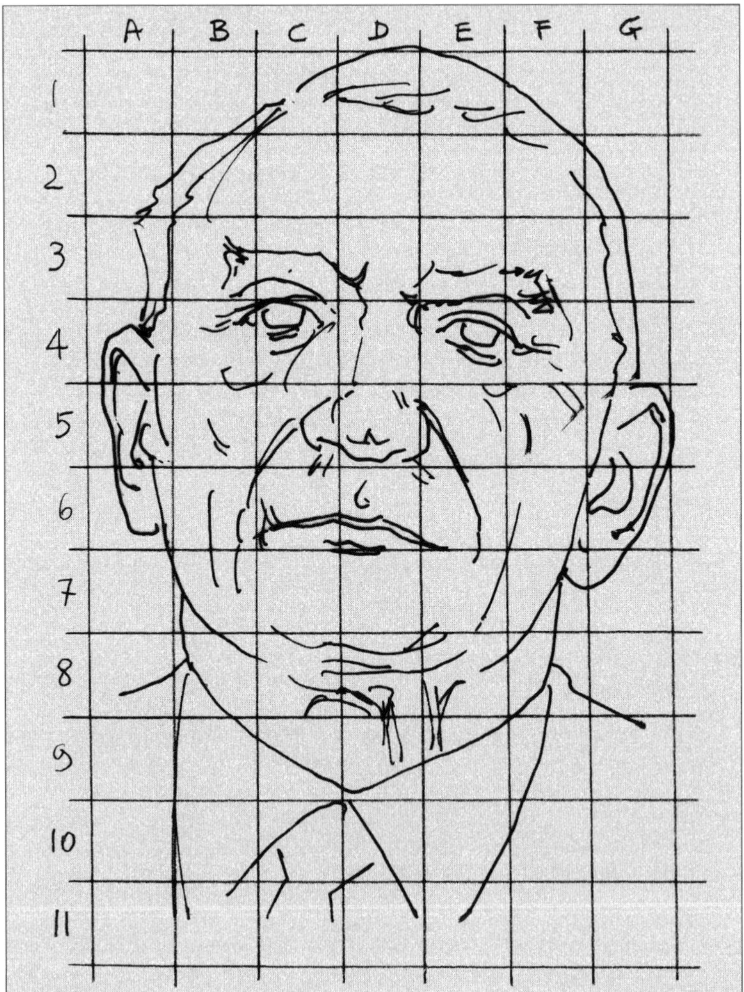

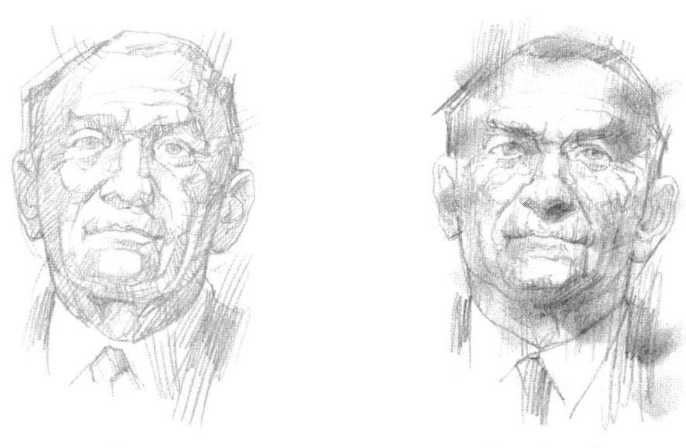

Step 4 *Tonal study*

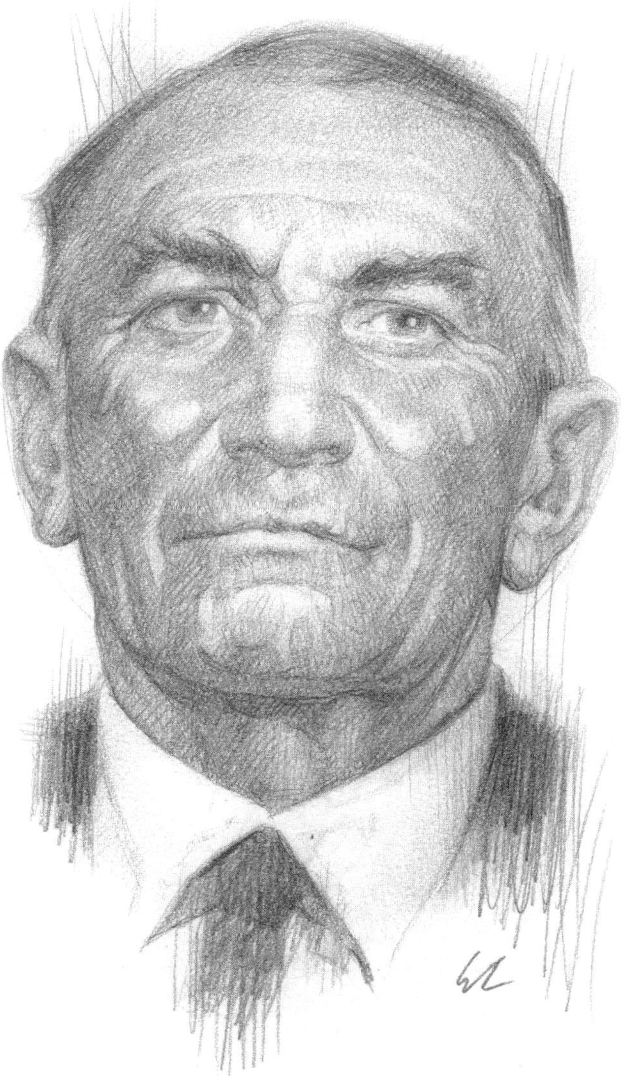

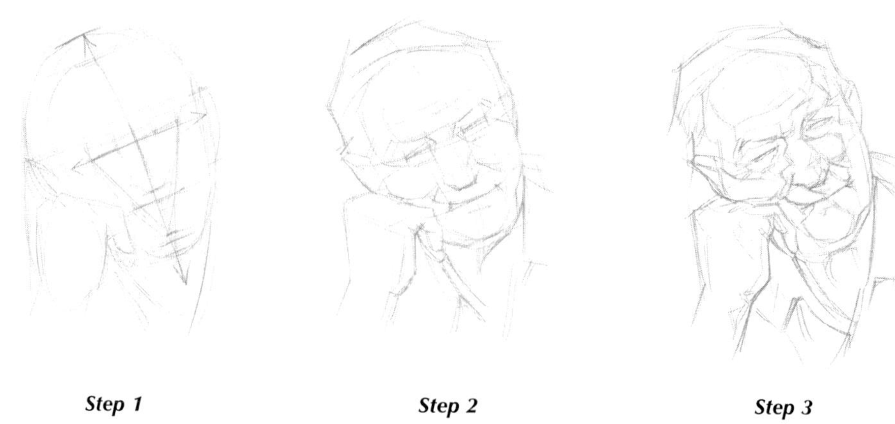

Step 1 *Step 2* *Step 3*

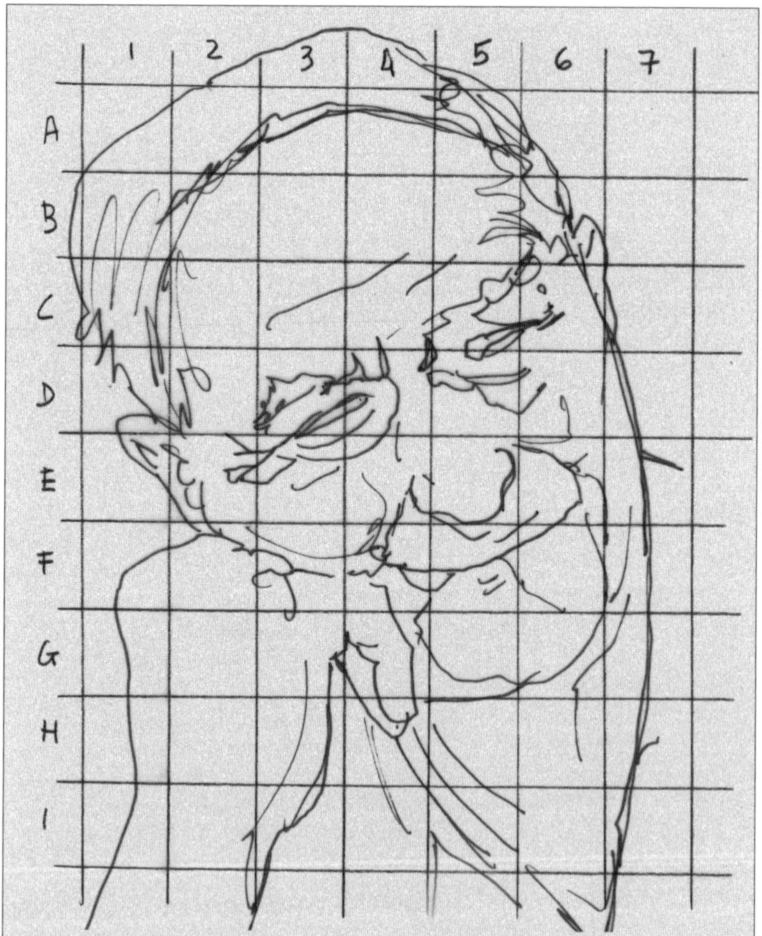

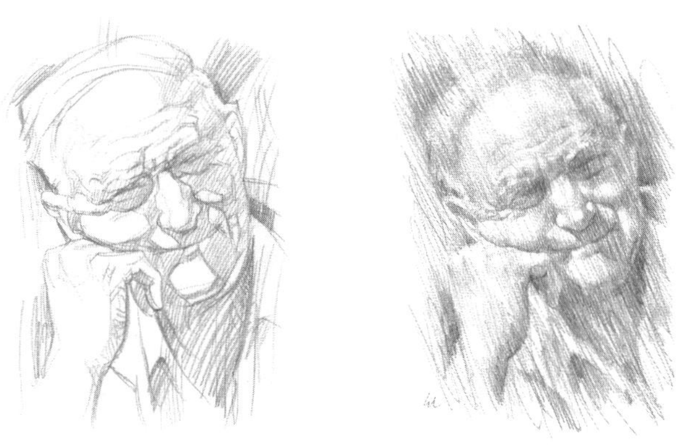

Step 4

Tonal study

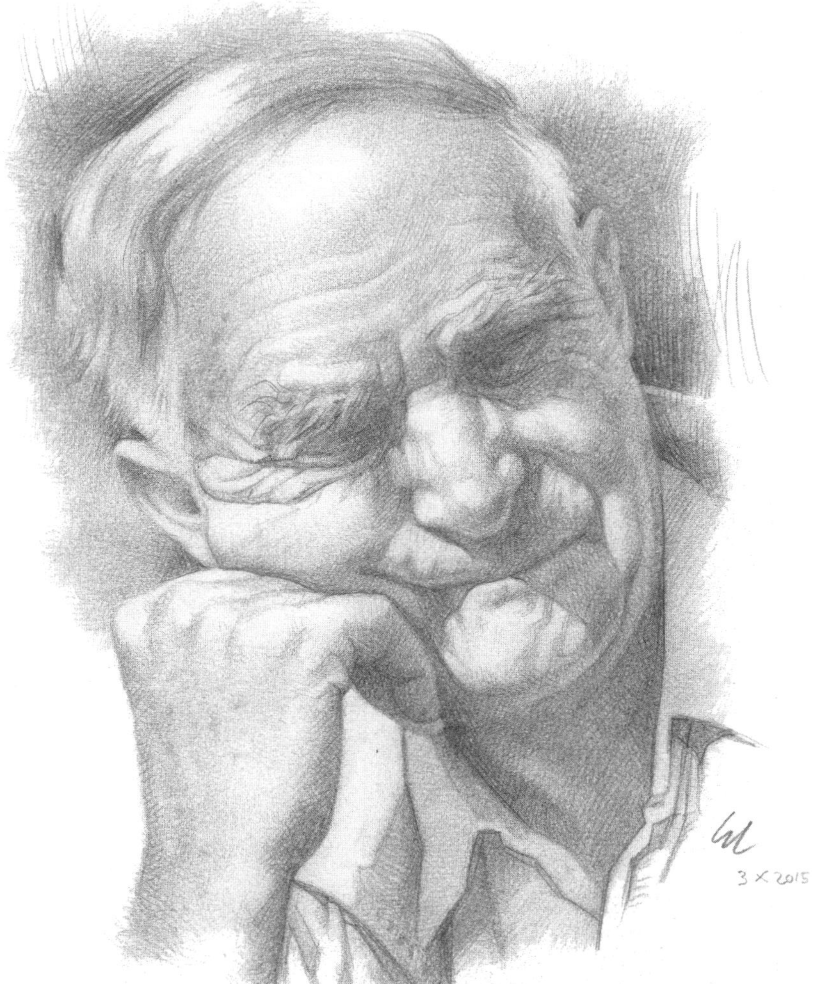

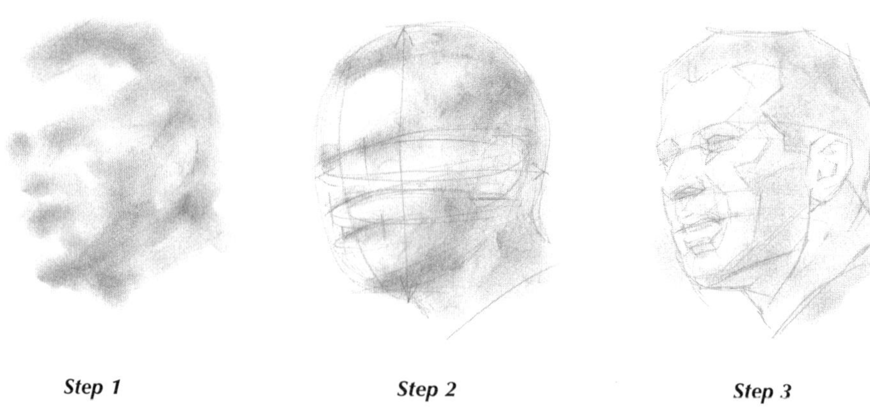

Step 1 *Step 2* *Step 3*

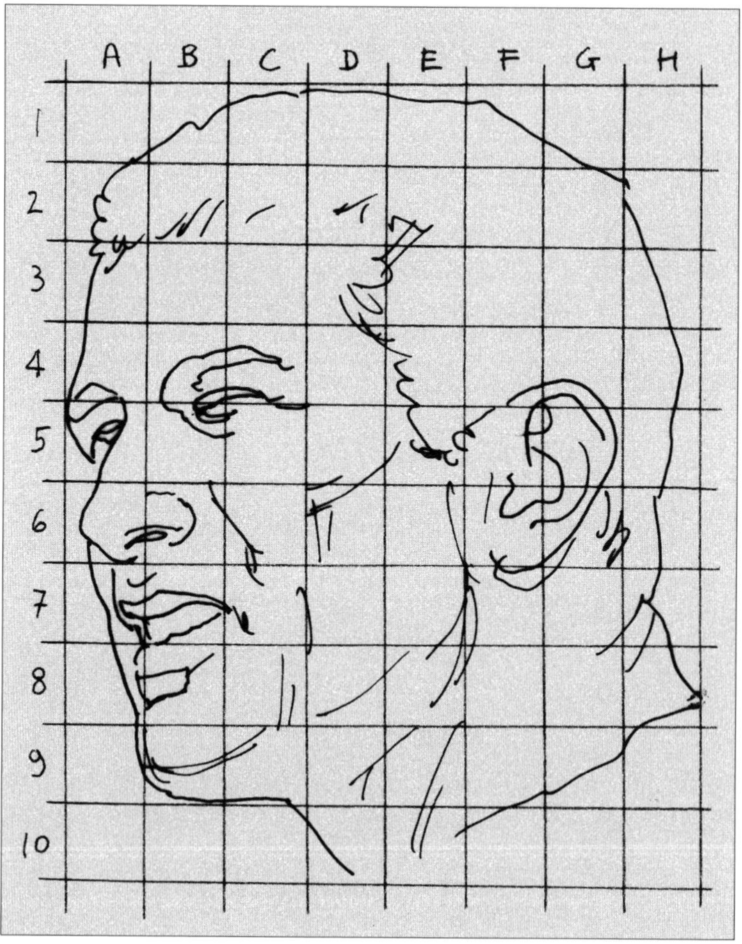

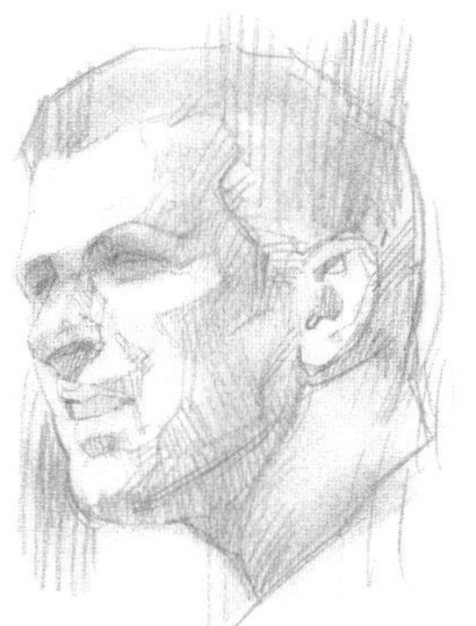

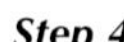

Step 4

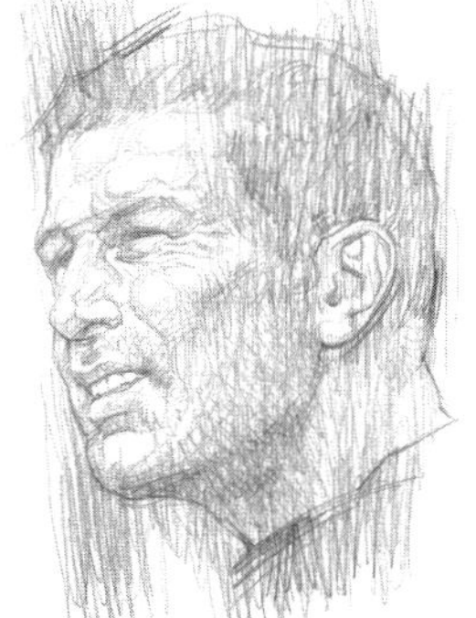

Tonal study

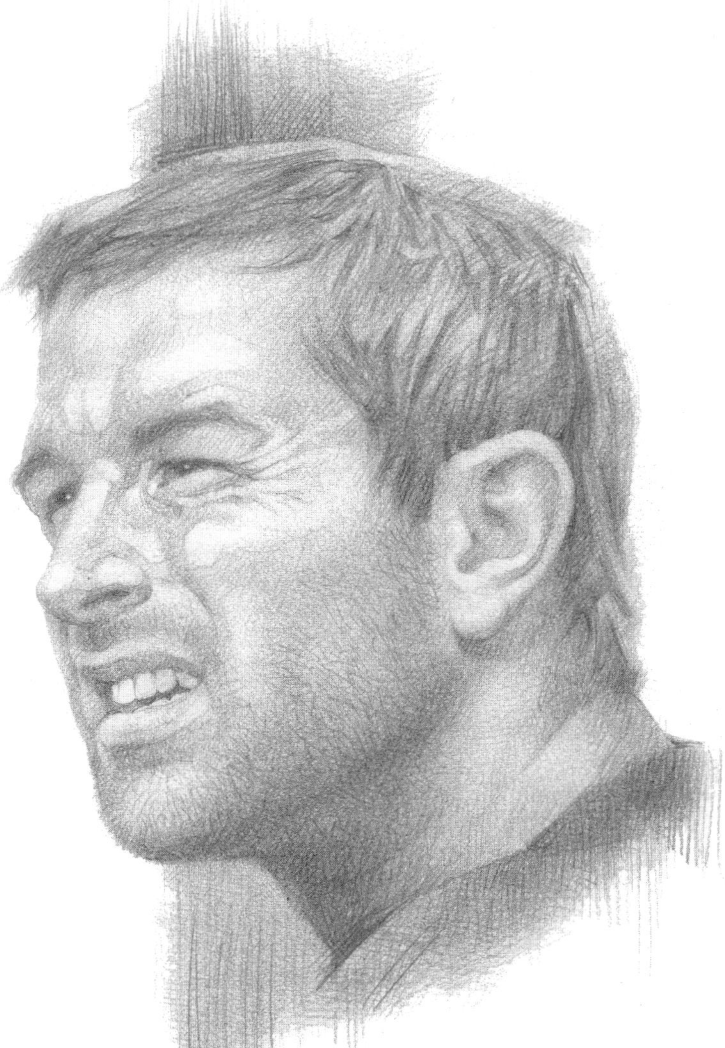

OTHER DRAWING MEDIA

There are many drawing media and there are countless styles in which they can be applied. On the opposite page I have chosen four of the most traditional and well-known media to portray the same face as that reproduced here in pencil, in order to allow for easy comparison.

While it is true that there are many computer programs that allow you to create amazing drawings directly onto digital tablets, simulating all the drawing and painting techniques, it is without doubt that the physical practice of drawing that offers the best guarantees for learning to observe and 'see', and above all to express the most authentic, emotional sensitivity.

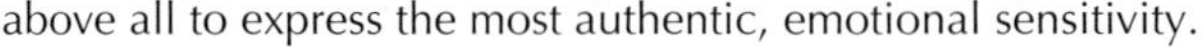

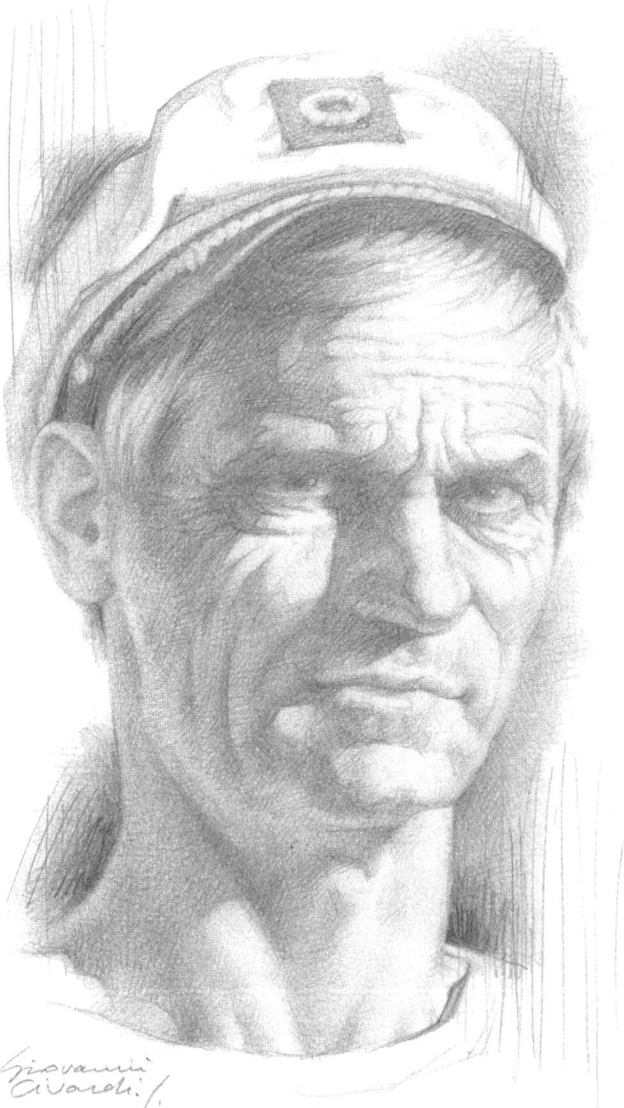

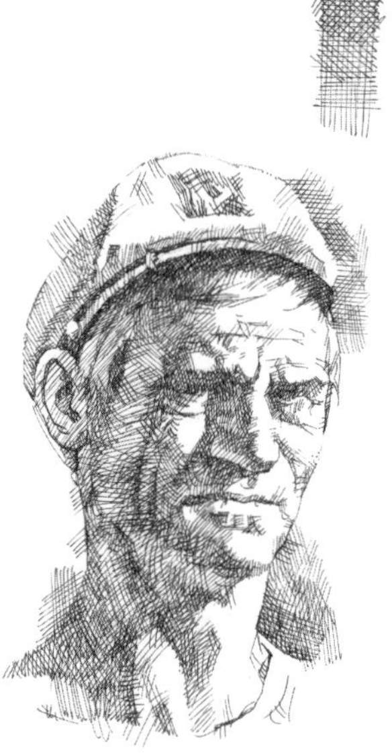

Pen and ink with regular lines
The lines are crossed and of various density to obtain the different gradations of tones. A technique derived from chalcographic etching (known as 'cut and counter-cut') is very effective, produced from parallel lines close to each other or crossing orthogonally or at various angles.

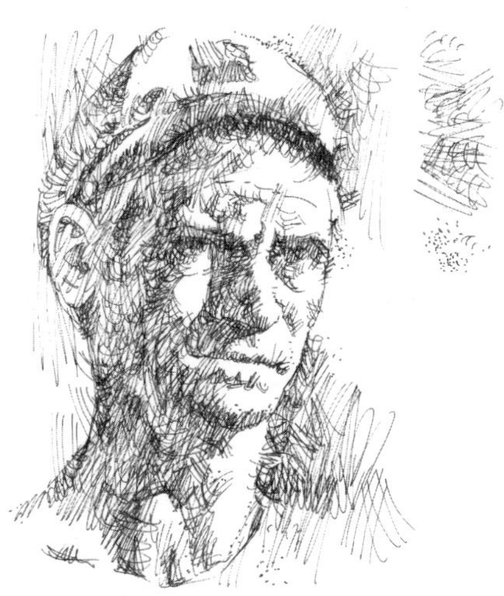

Pen and ink with free lines
The pen's lines in this case are thicker, further apart or cross freely. They appear to be highly irregular. However, the tonal values are gradually reached by making sure that the shadows are not too dense and that the lines, while varied and free, are not too random, thus causing confusion. A preliminary summary pencil drawing can be used as a guide and allows more confidence and spontaneity in the lines.

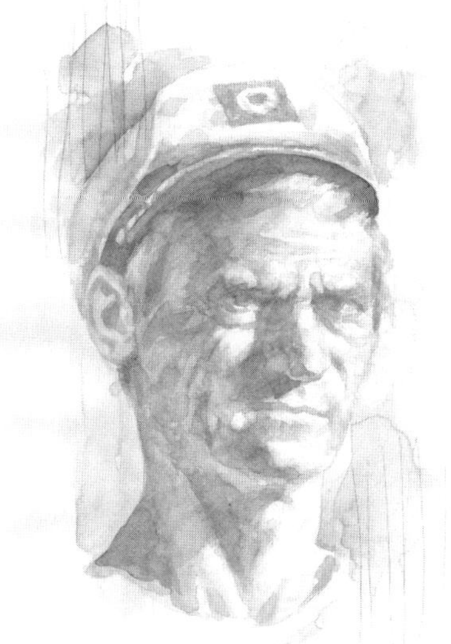

Monochrome watercolour
Using water-soluble graphite is a technique that lies midway between drawing and painting. It produces effects that are fairly well suited to portraits, especially of the sort of characterful face with which this volume is concerned.

Ink can be substituted for watercolour paint, and a very soft bristle brush used to apply it to the surface. An outline drawn with a pencil may help to provide greater consistency to the shapes: it can be left to show through the thin layers of paint, or even emphasized, in order to hint at spontaneity and structural consistency. The paper must be heavy enough to tolerate the moisture without cockling.

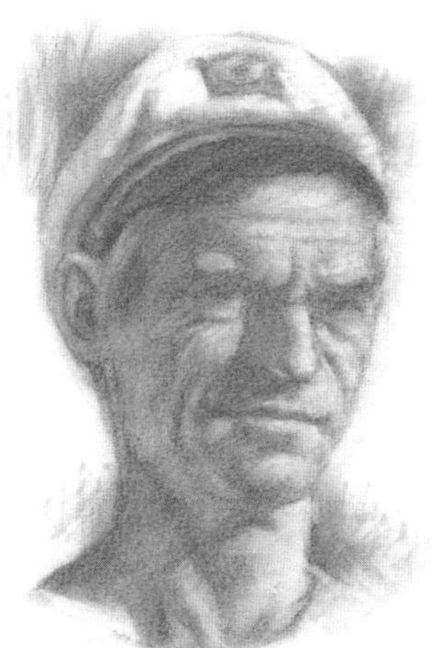

Compressed charcoal
Charcoal offers a wide range of *chiaroscuro* tones, from the softest to the most intense. It can be blended with the finger or a soft cloth, and can be erased or easily 'lightened'. There are various types, each with its own characteristics: for this study I used a brown coloured Conté pencil.

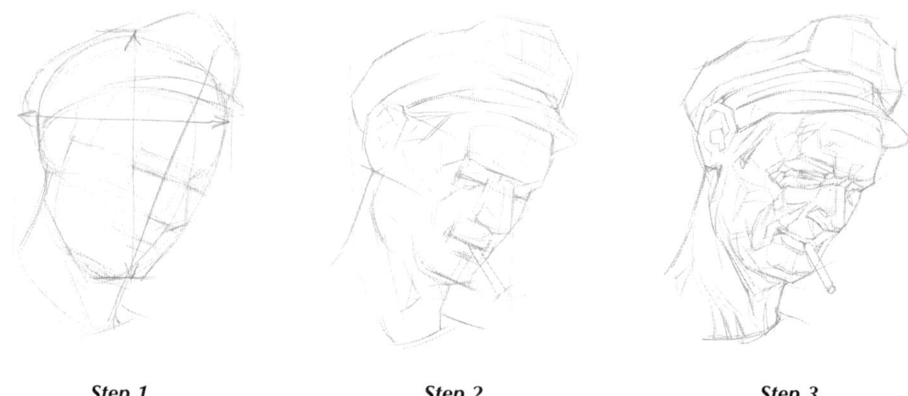

Step 1 *Step 2* *Step 3*

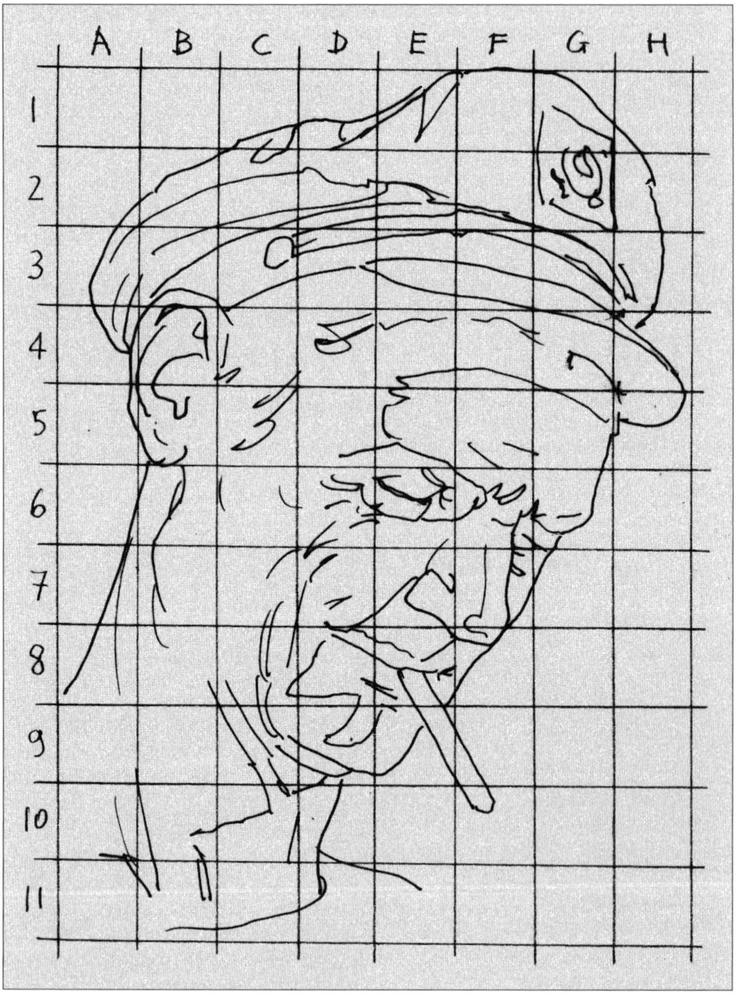

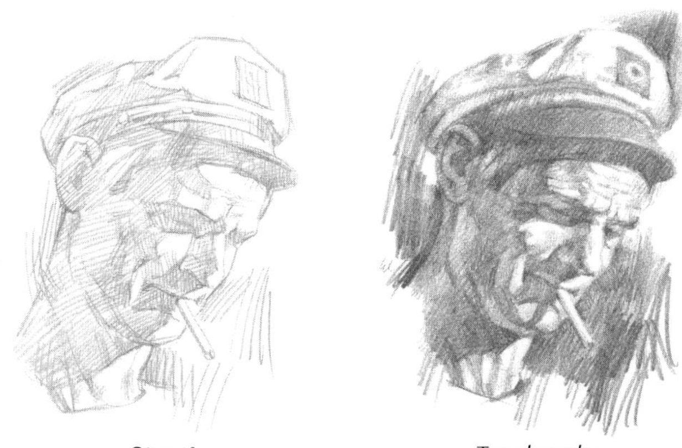

Step 4

Tonal study

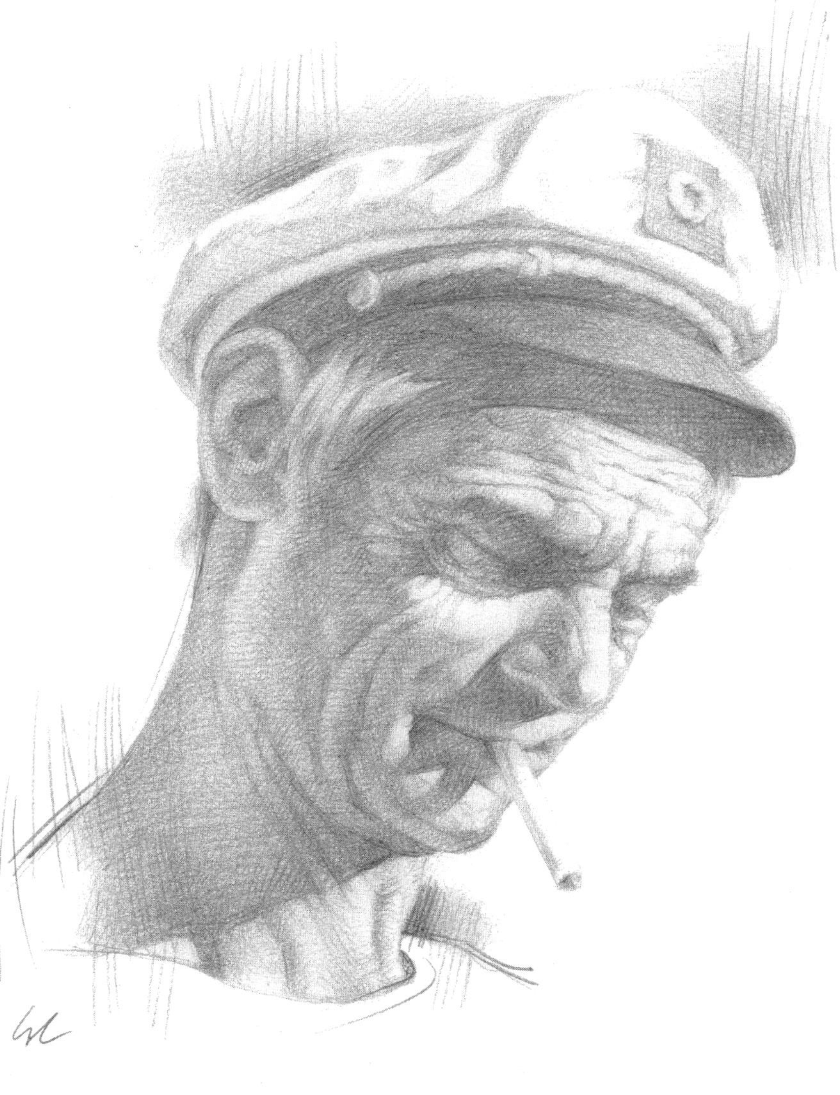

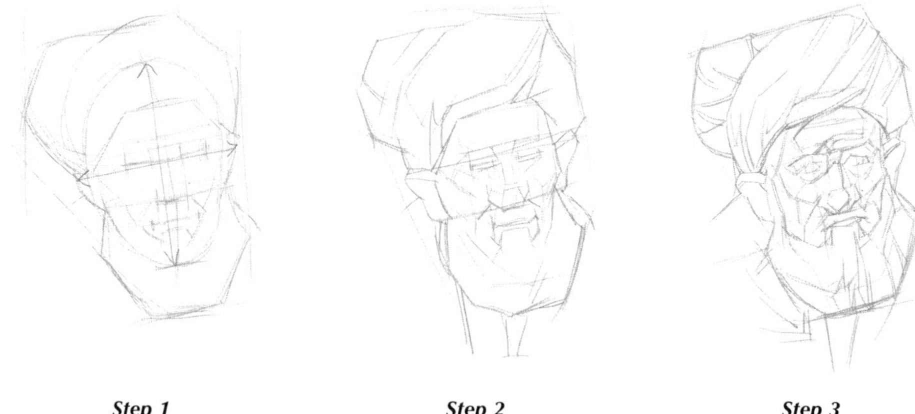

Step 1 *Step 2* *Step 3*

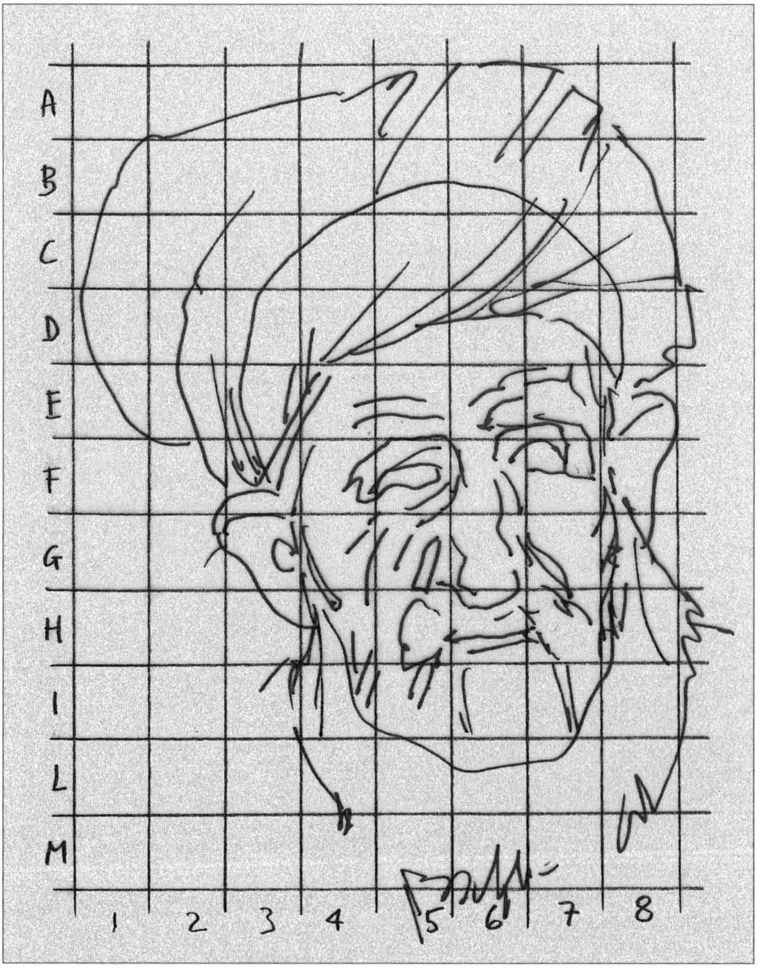

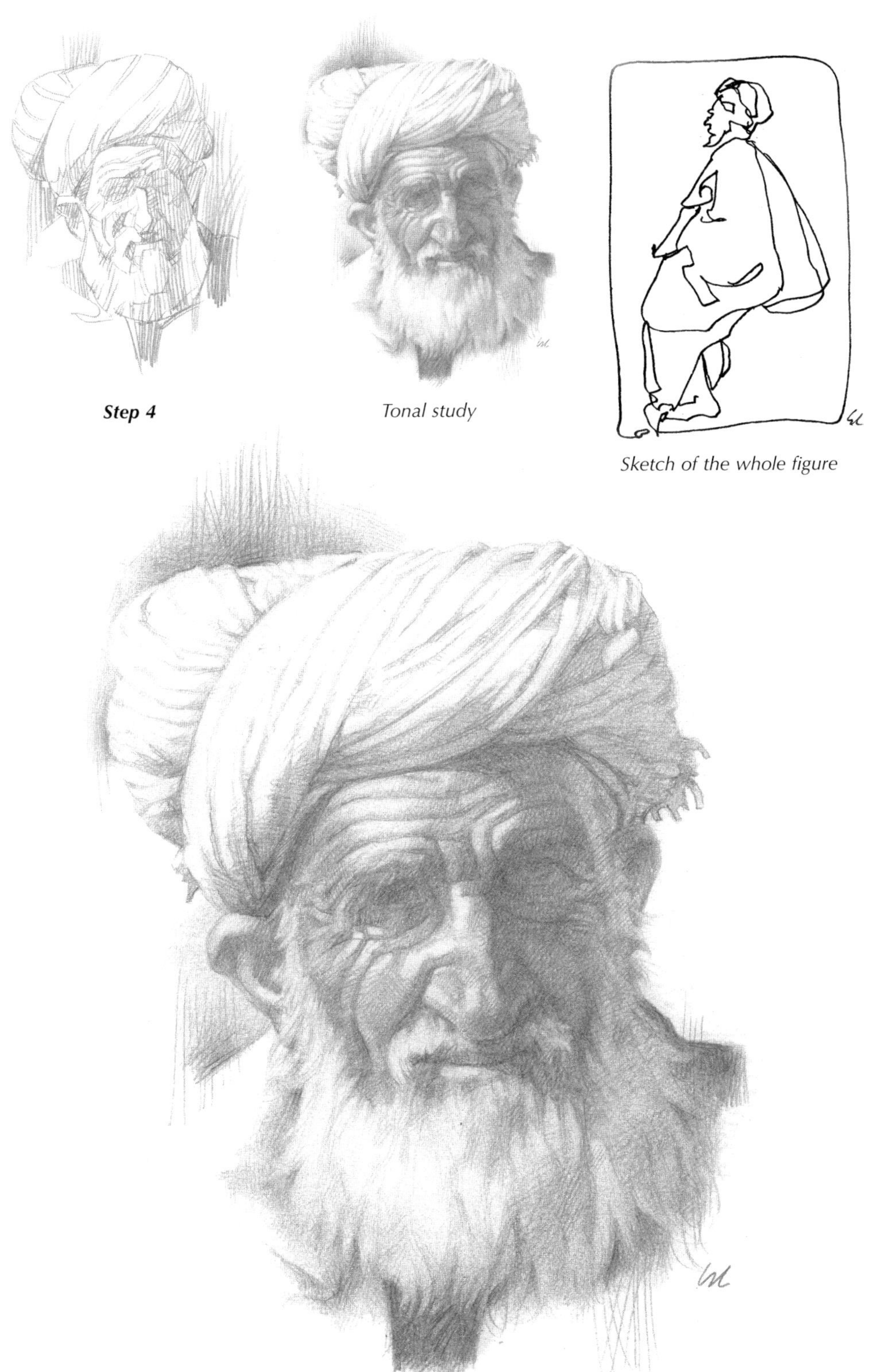

Step 4

Tonal study

Sketch of the whole figure

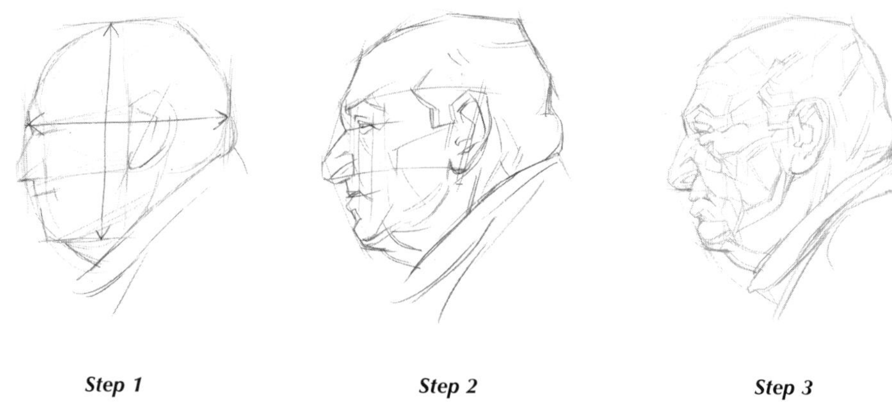

Step 1 *Step 2* *Step 3*

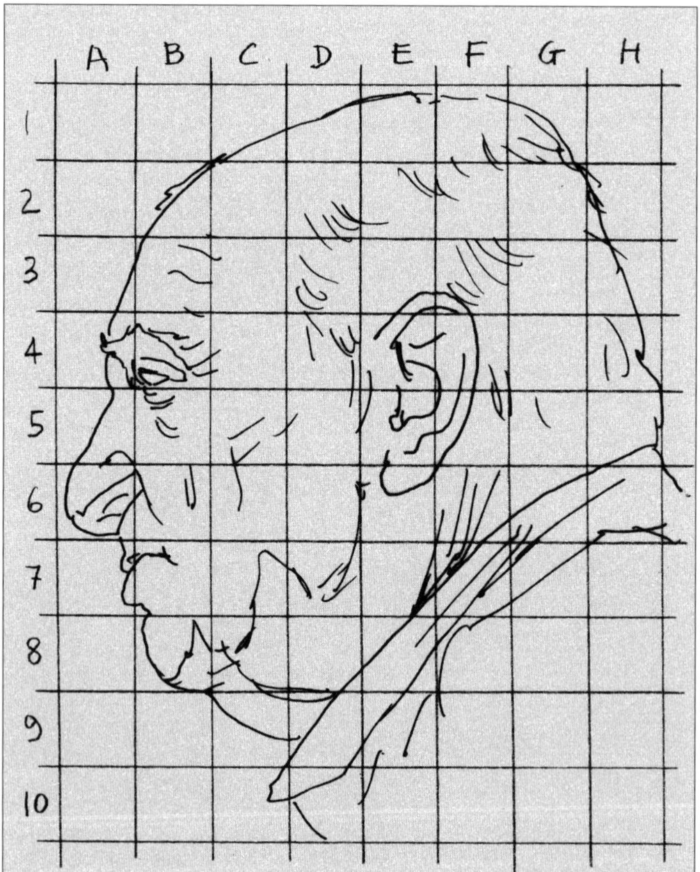

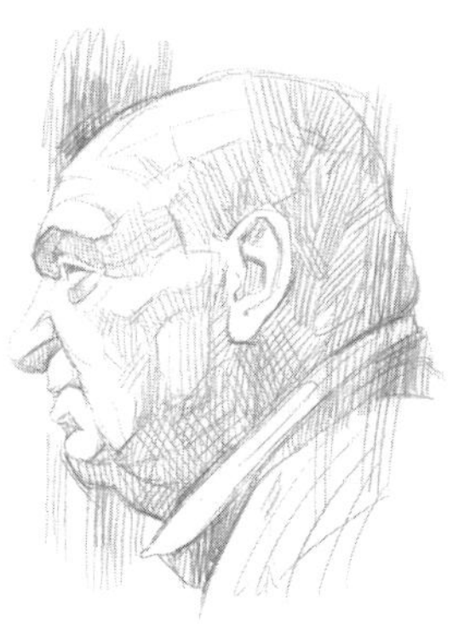

Step 4

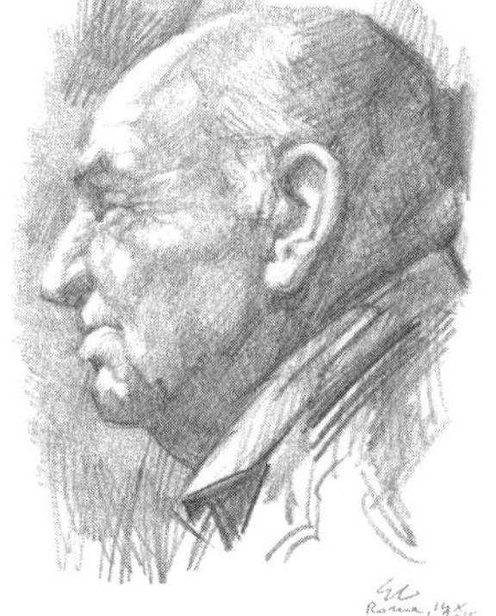

Tonal study

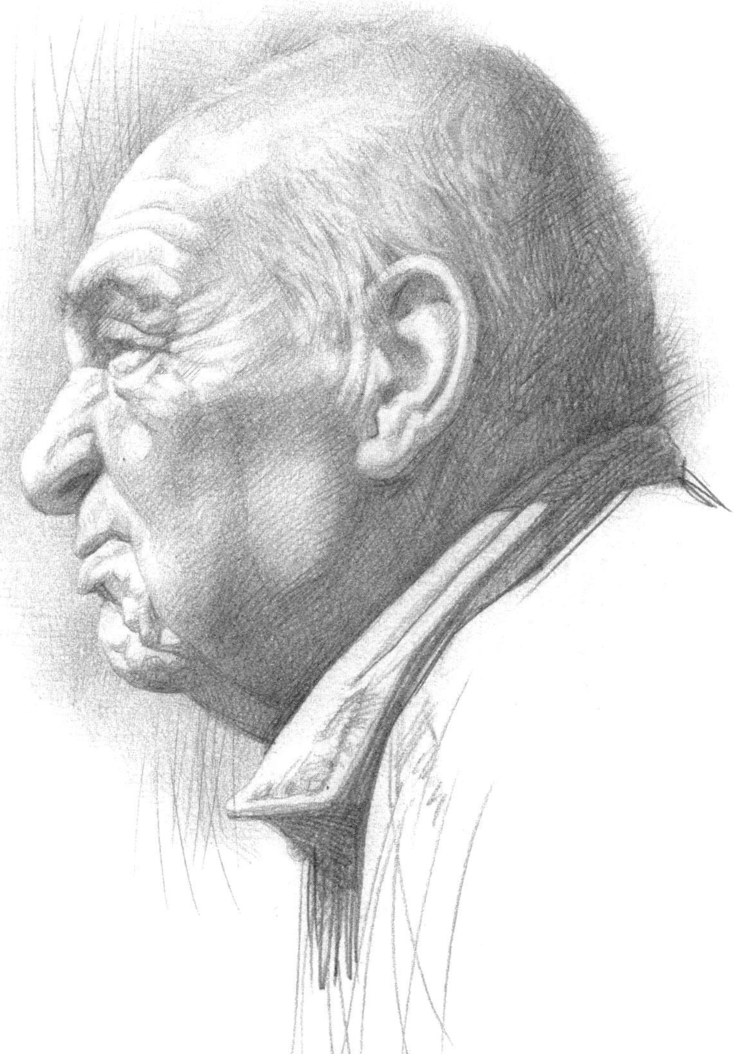

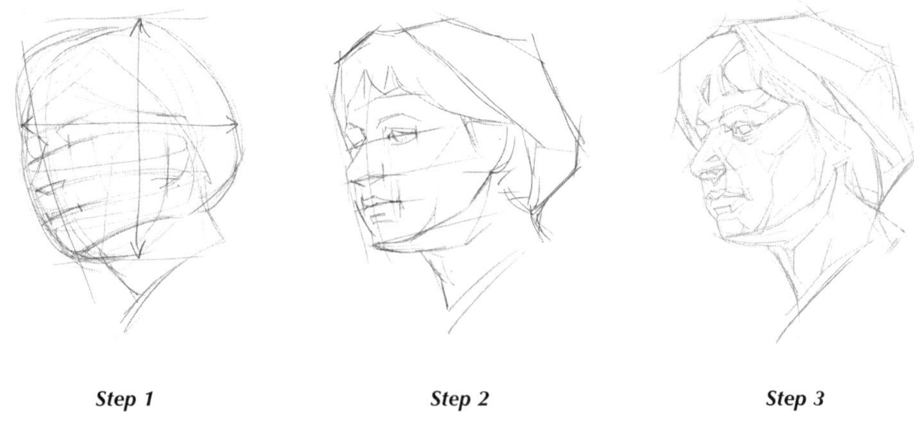

Step 1 *Step 2* *Step 3*

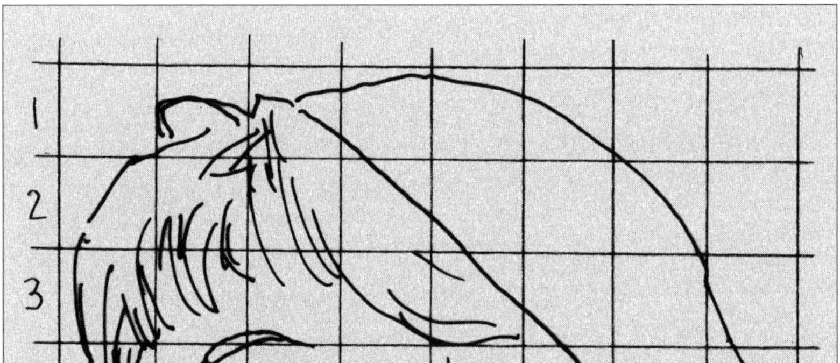

1 2 3 4 5 6 7 8

A B C D E F G H

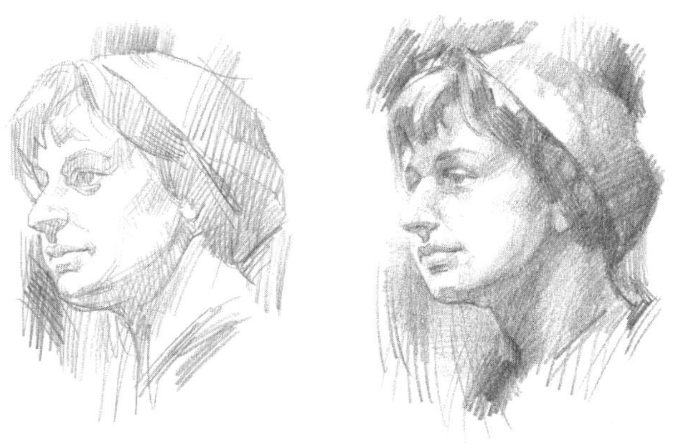

Step 4

Tonal study

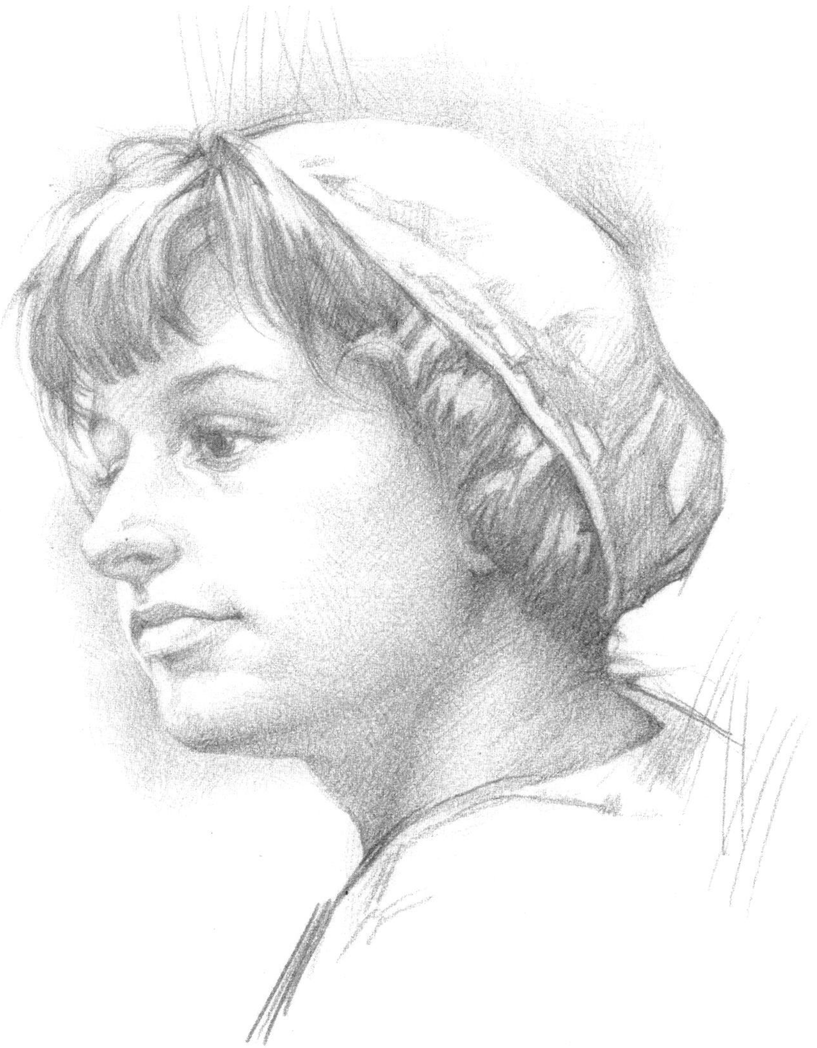

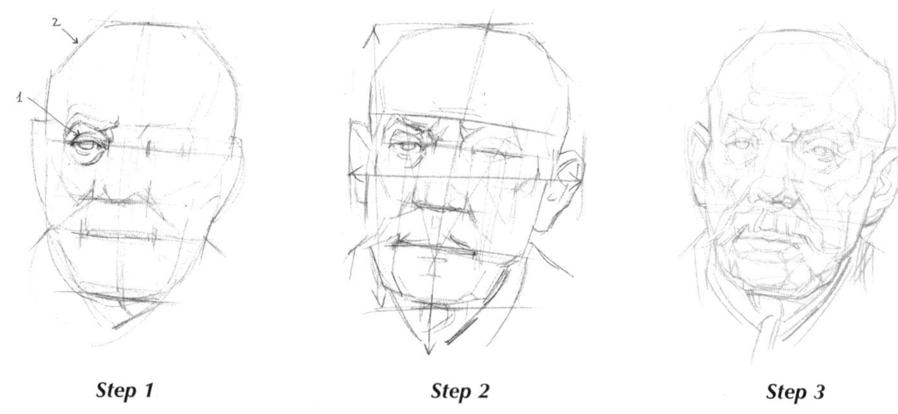

Step 1 *Step 2* *Step 3*

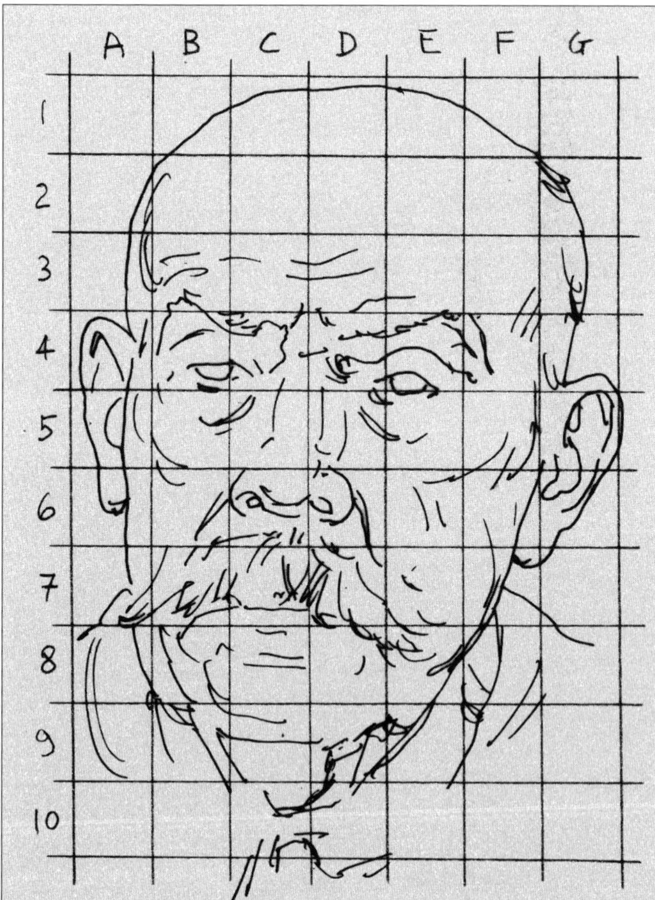

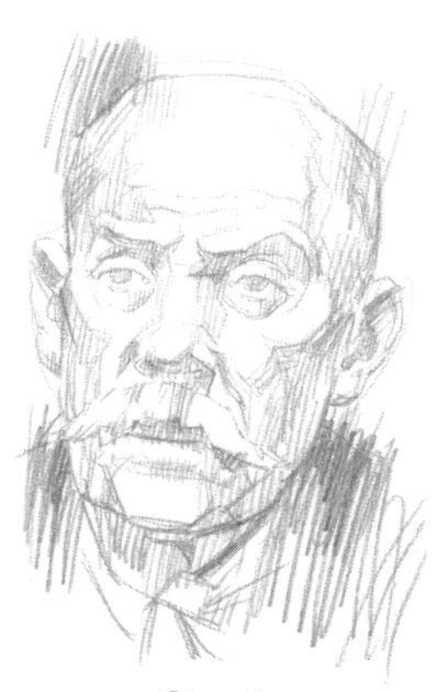

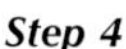

Step 4

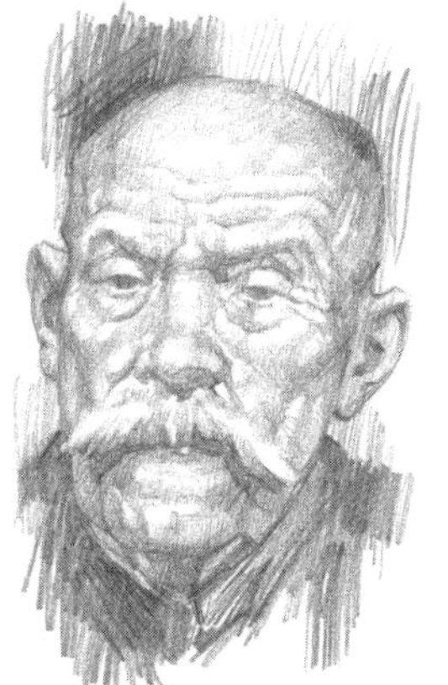

Tonal study

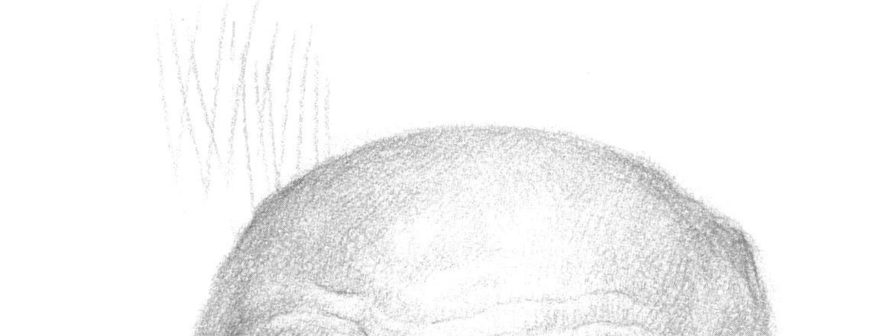

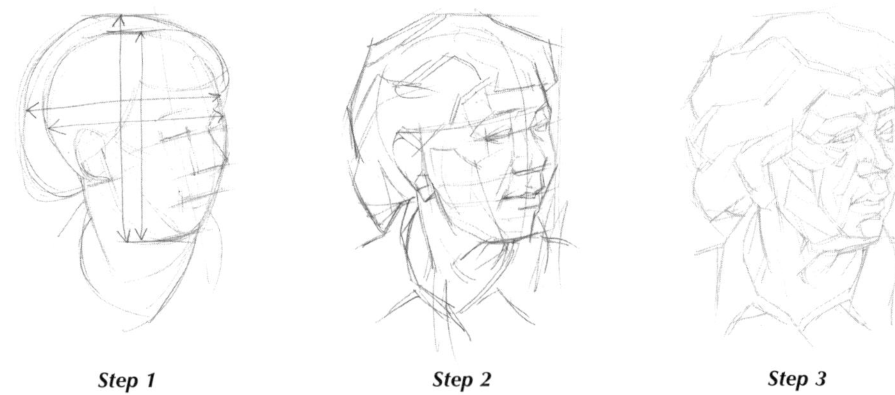

Step 1 *Step 2* *Step 3*

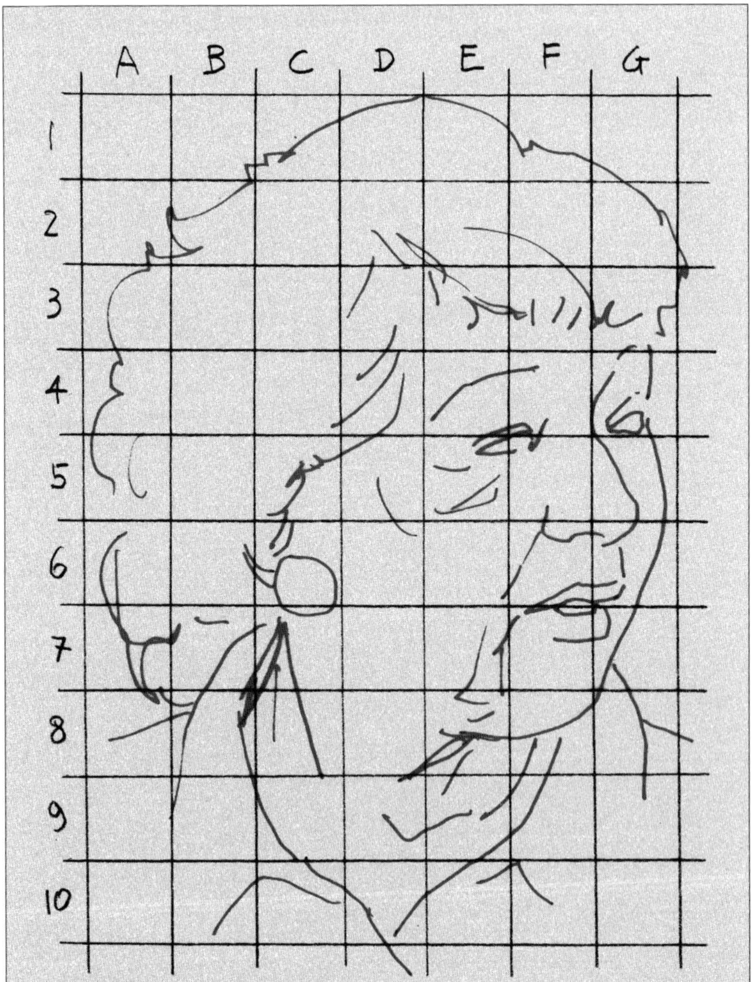

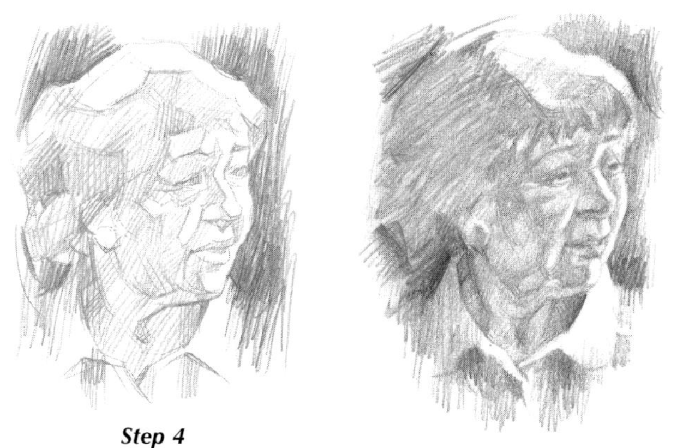

Step 4

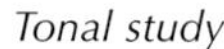

Tonal study

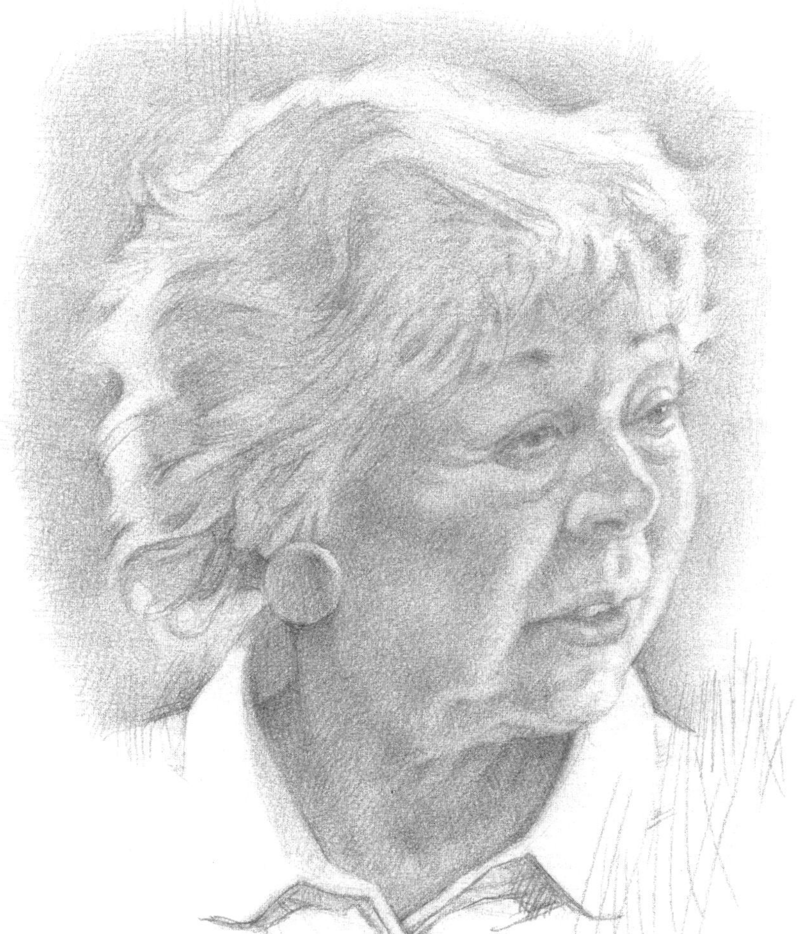

A useful exercise is to portray the same head using not just different techniques (as on pages 150–151), but also following different drawing procedures, to compare the results, as shown in the examples below.

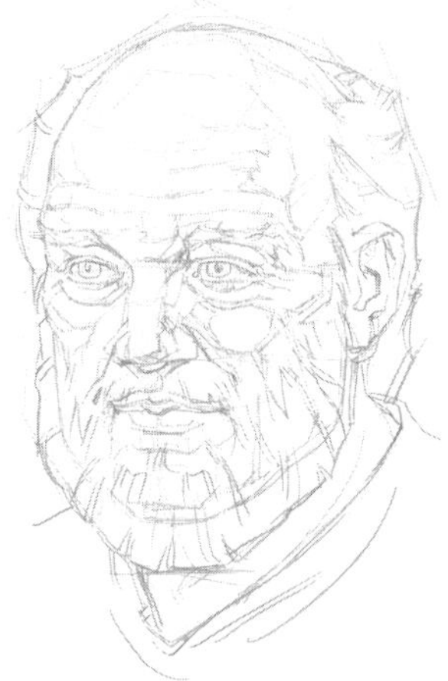

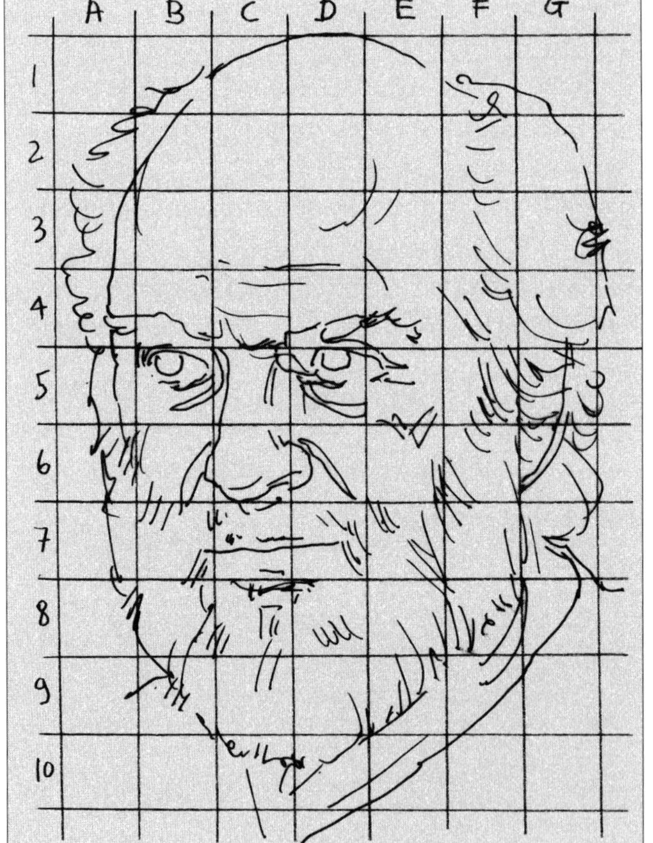

Here I traced the initial steps of a portrait drawing by following a structural procedure; that is, providing more emphasis on 'solid' elements that give volume and consistency to the head, pronouncing the shapes.

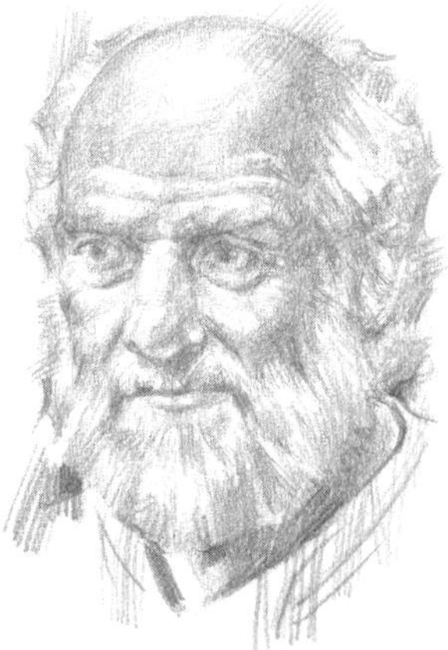

Here I have given preference to a procedure concentrated on tones of light and shade, that searches for the development of 'planes' described by the modulation in tone, while not neglecting the fidelity of the shapes.

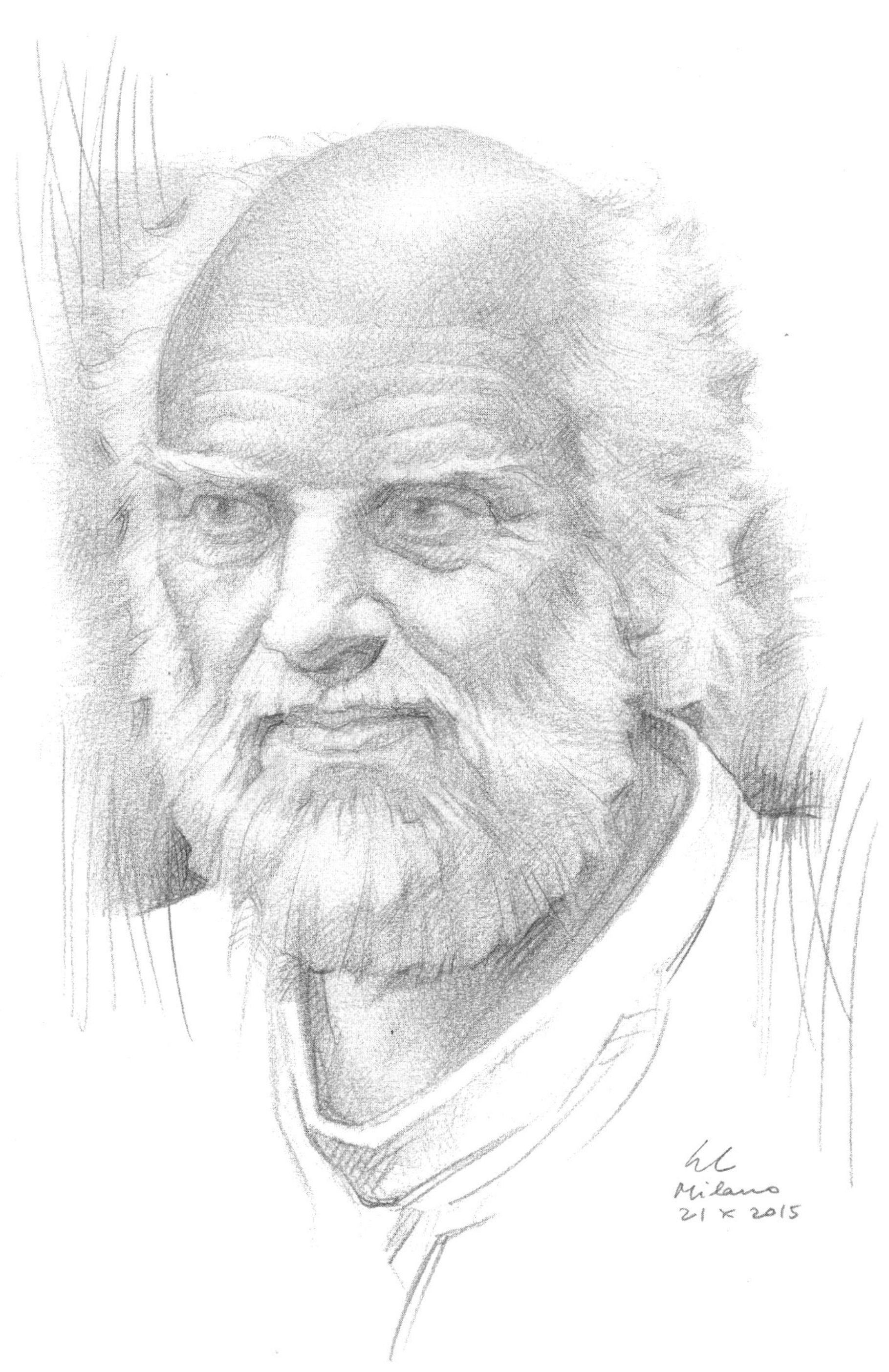
Milano
21 X 2015

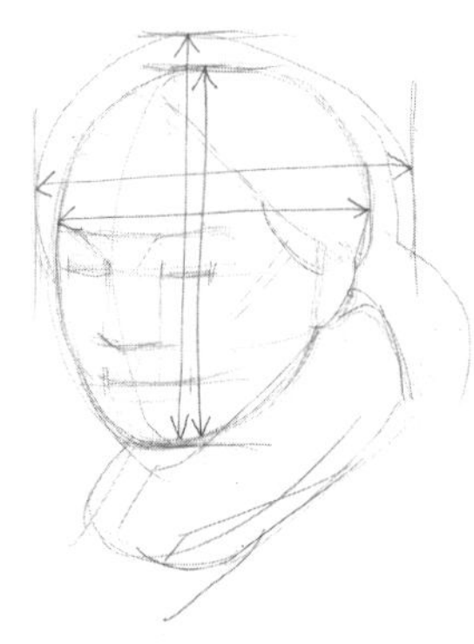

Step 1

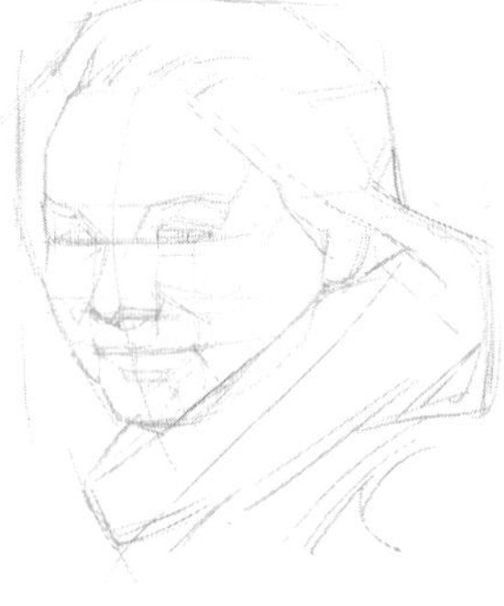

Step 2

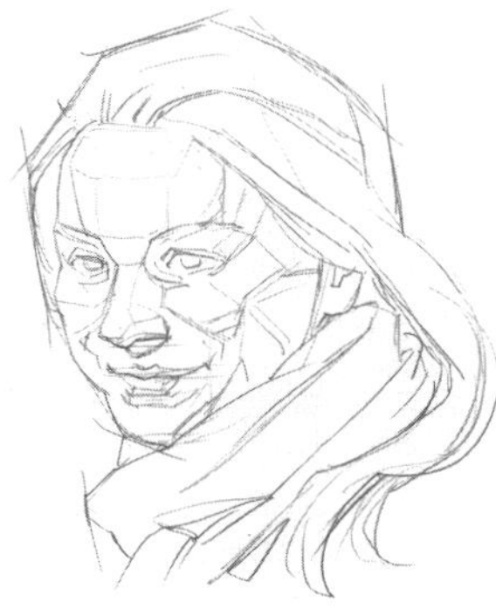

Step 3

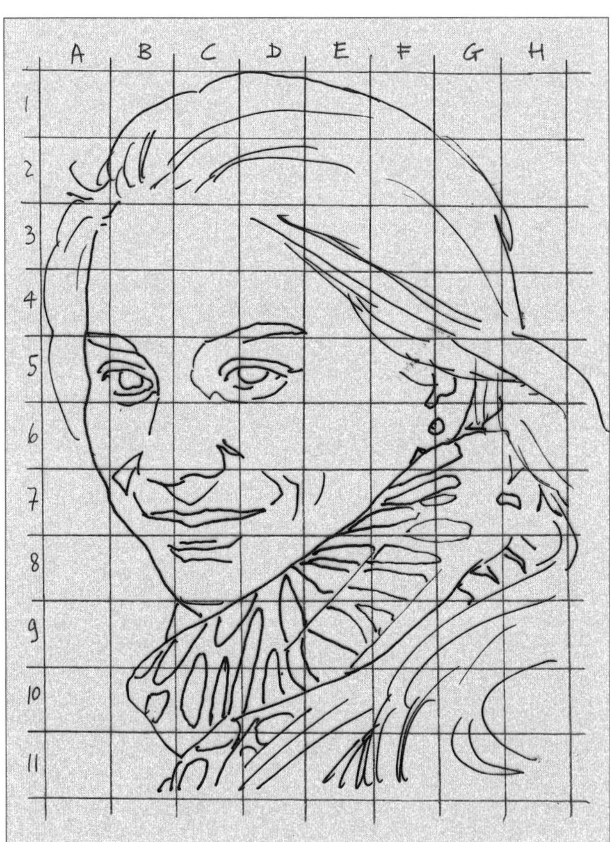

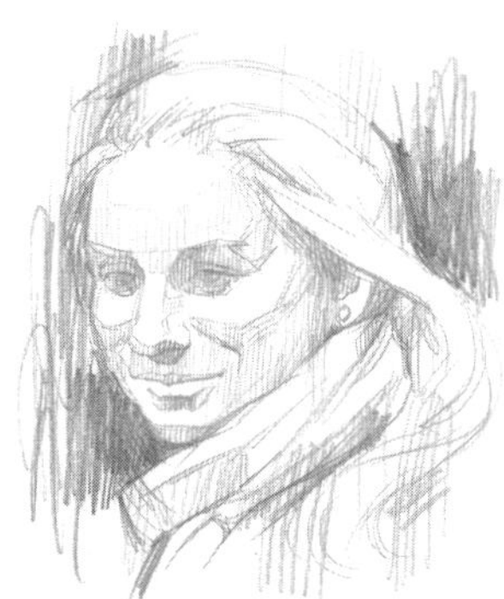

Step 4

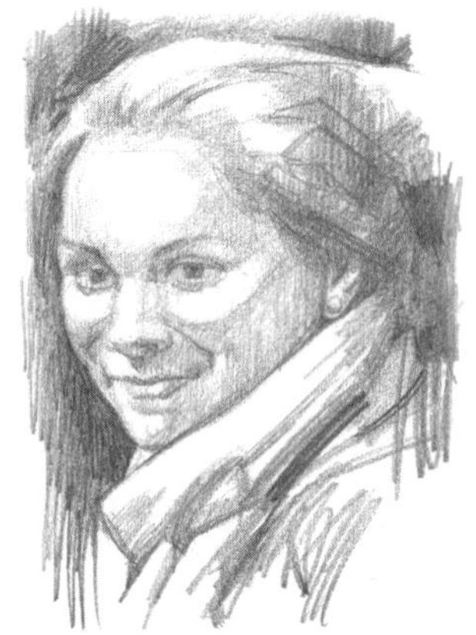

Tonal study

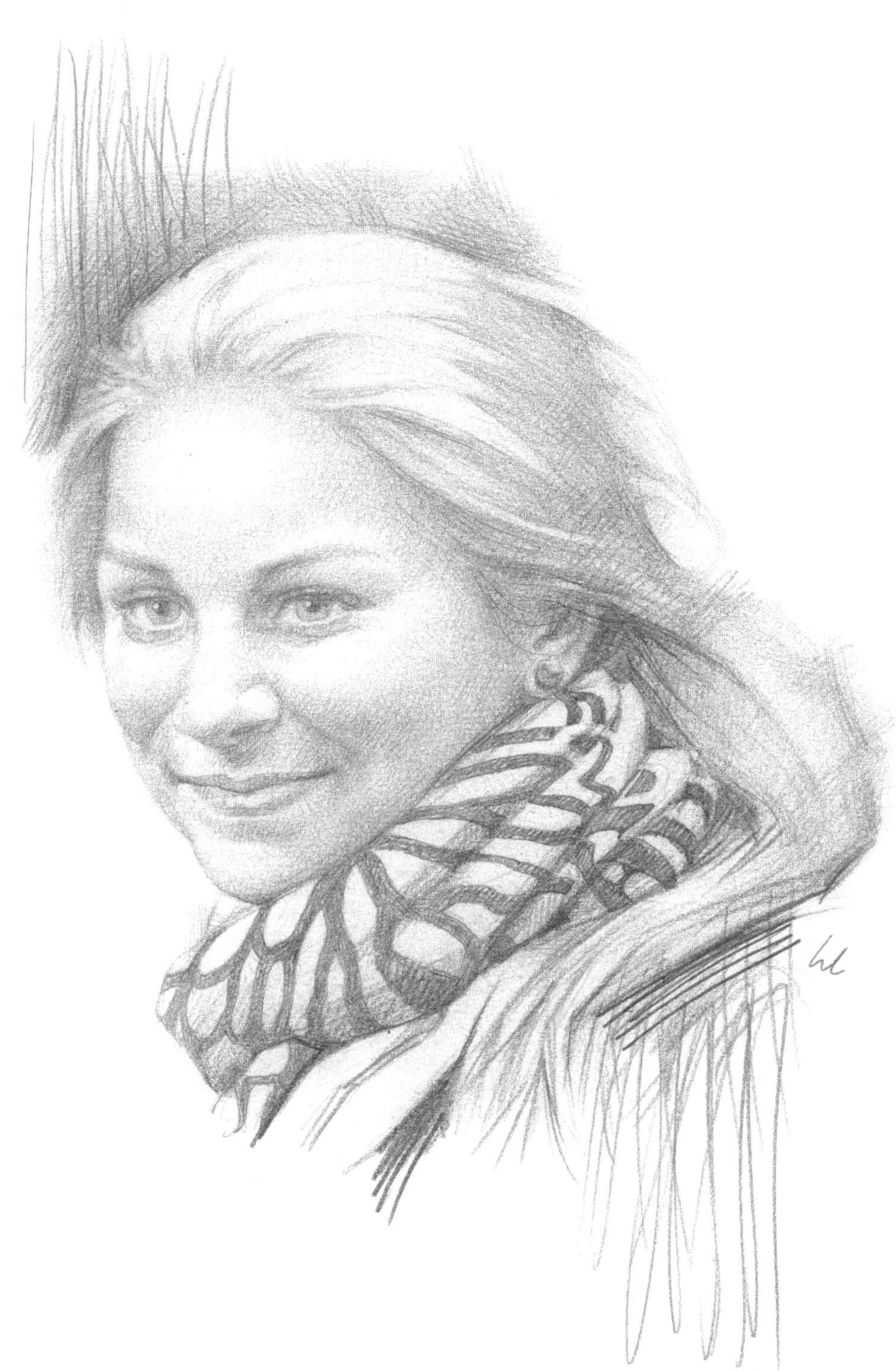

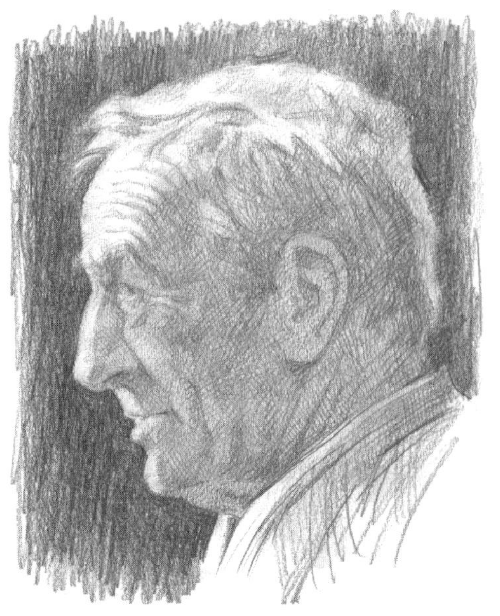

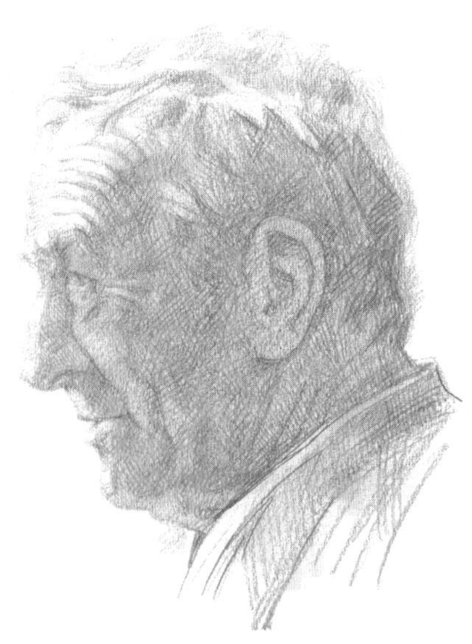

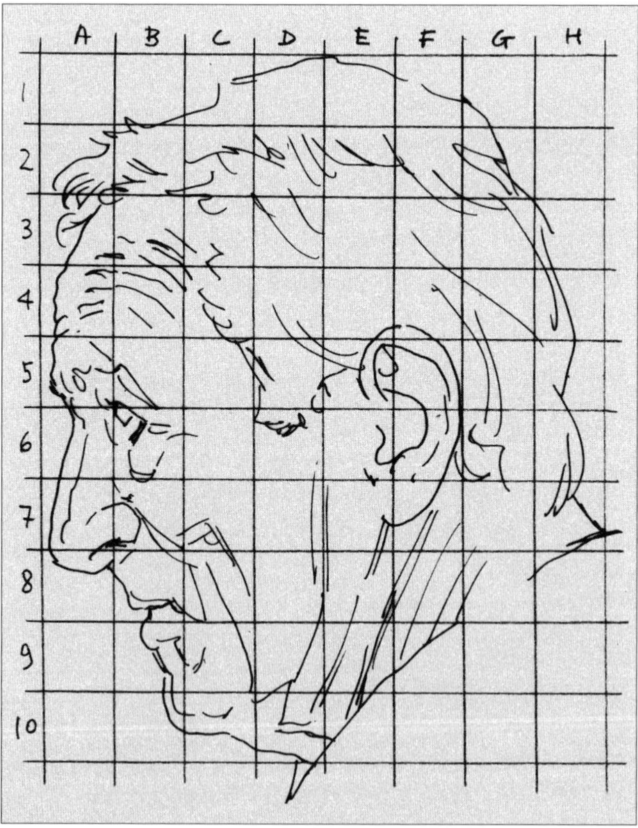

The face in the studies above uses the same tones of light and shade in both drawings, yet the result is rather different depending on whether the head is placed against a dark backdrop or a light one.

This effect is very important in portraiture. The very dark background lends apparent luminosity to the tones in the part of the face in shade, which, in contrast, appears to be quite light. The illuminated part of the profile seems to be even lighter. On the other hand, the white background makes the same shading tones seem rather dark, while the illuminated part of the face seems faded and lost in the surroundings.

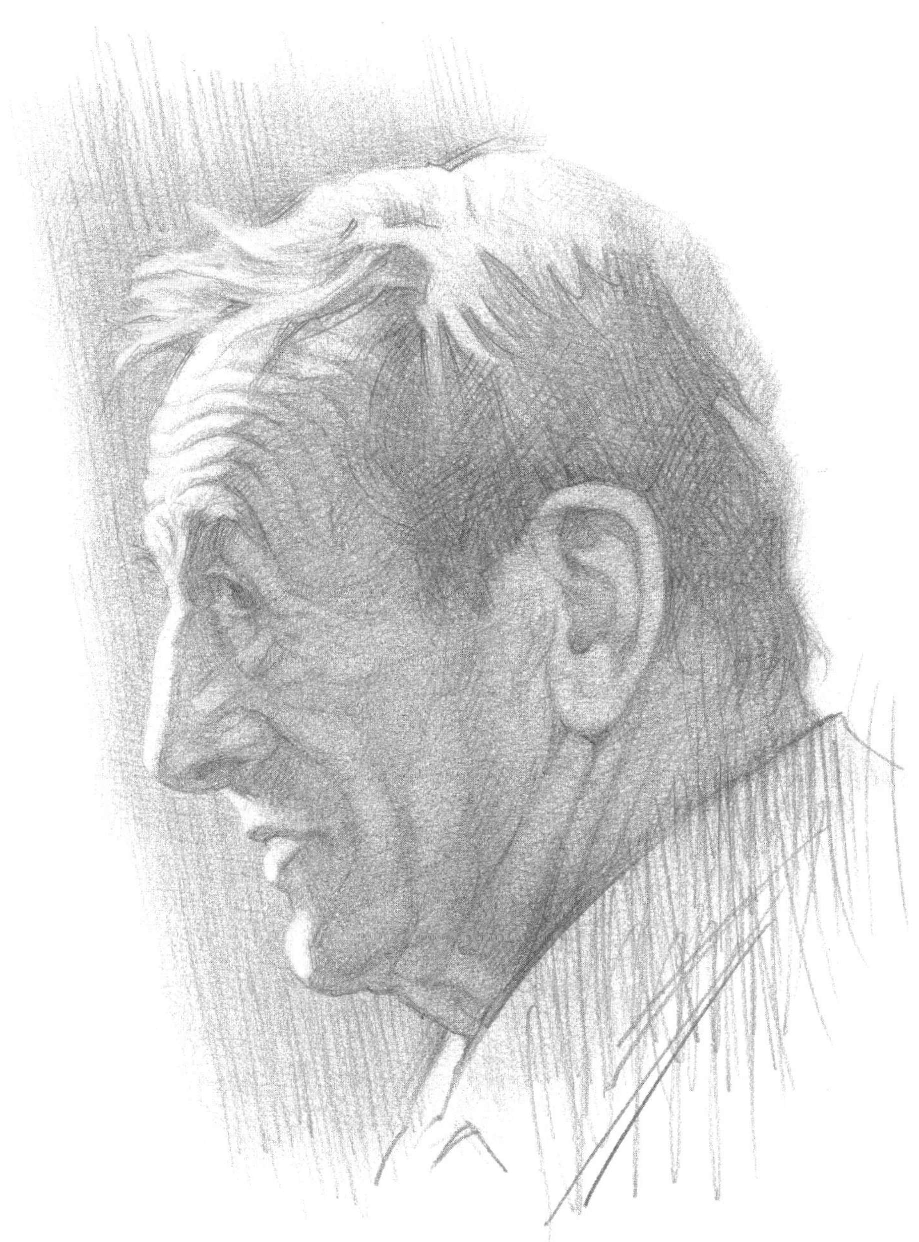

The drawing on this page, which is more elaborate than the two preceding studies, has lost a little simplicity and expressive spontaneity, but shows an improved, more balanced distribution of tonal hues that are mostly harmonized by a medium-intensity background.

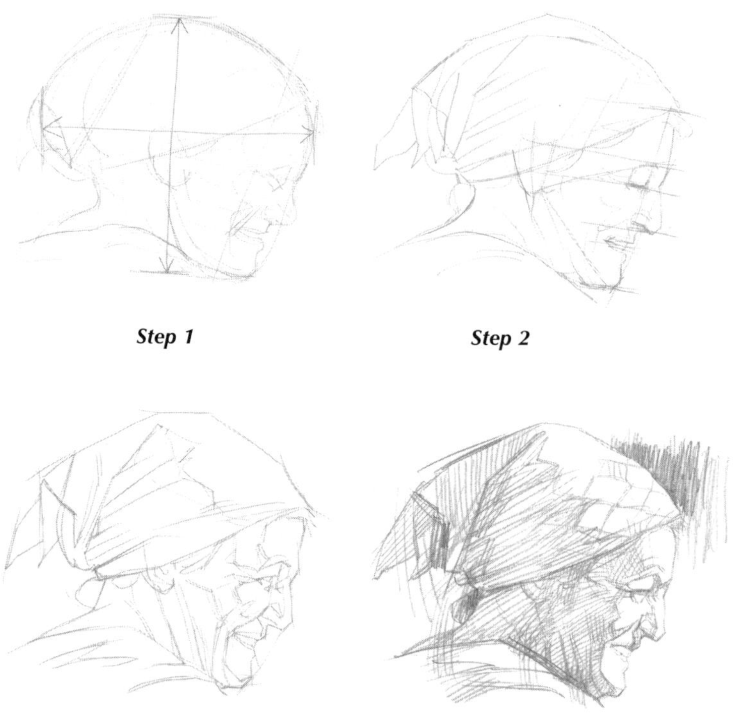

Step 1

Step 2

Step 3

Step 4

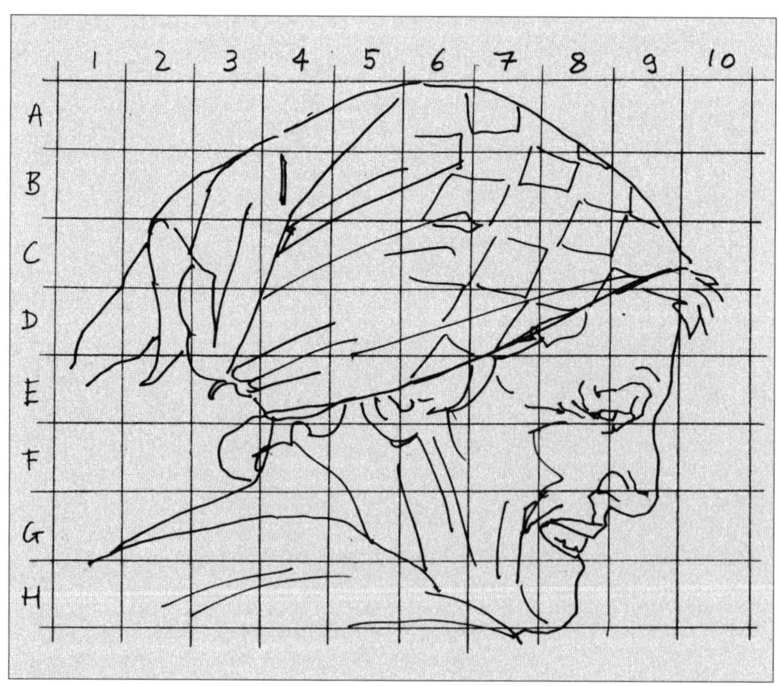

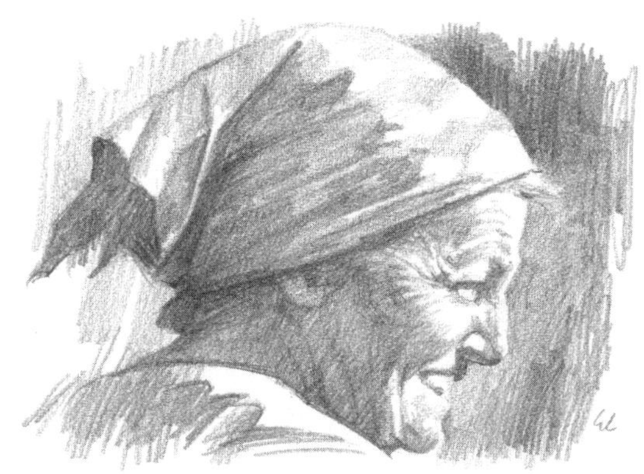

Tonal study

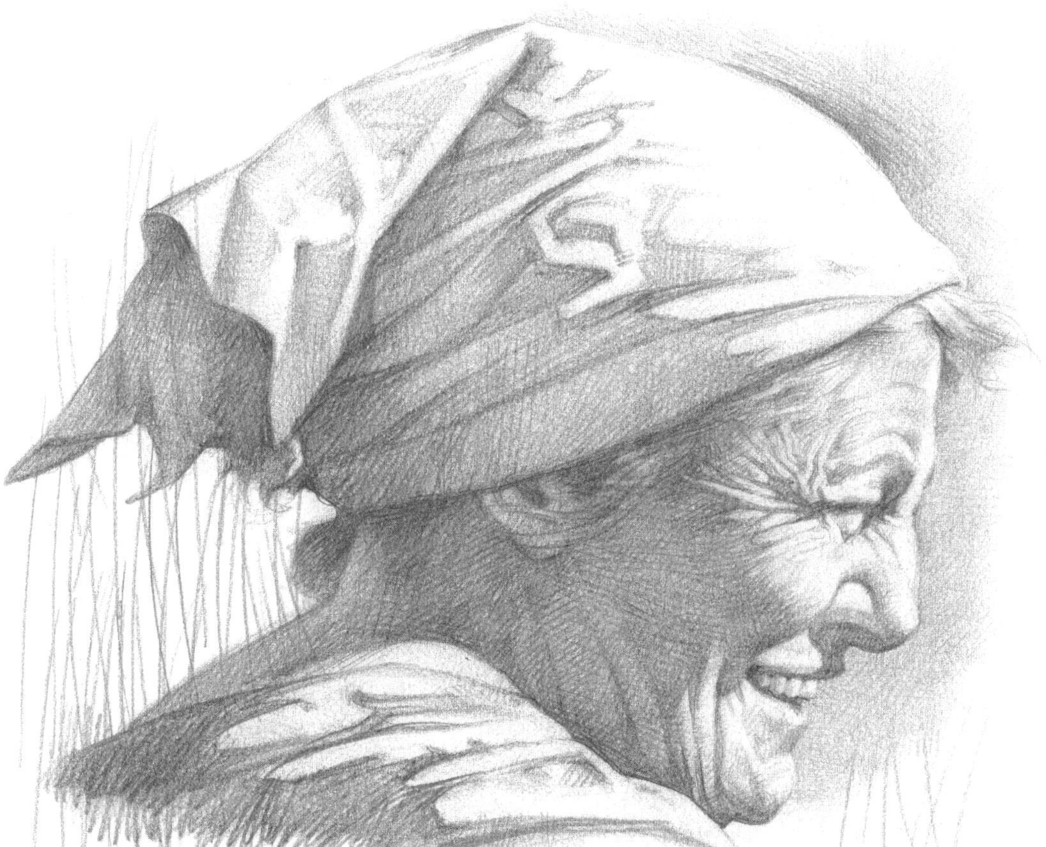

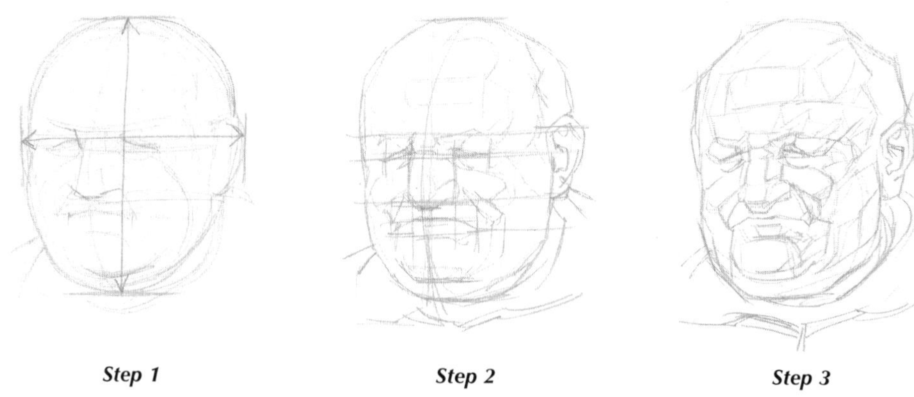

Step 1 *Step 2* *Step 3*

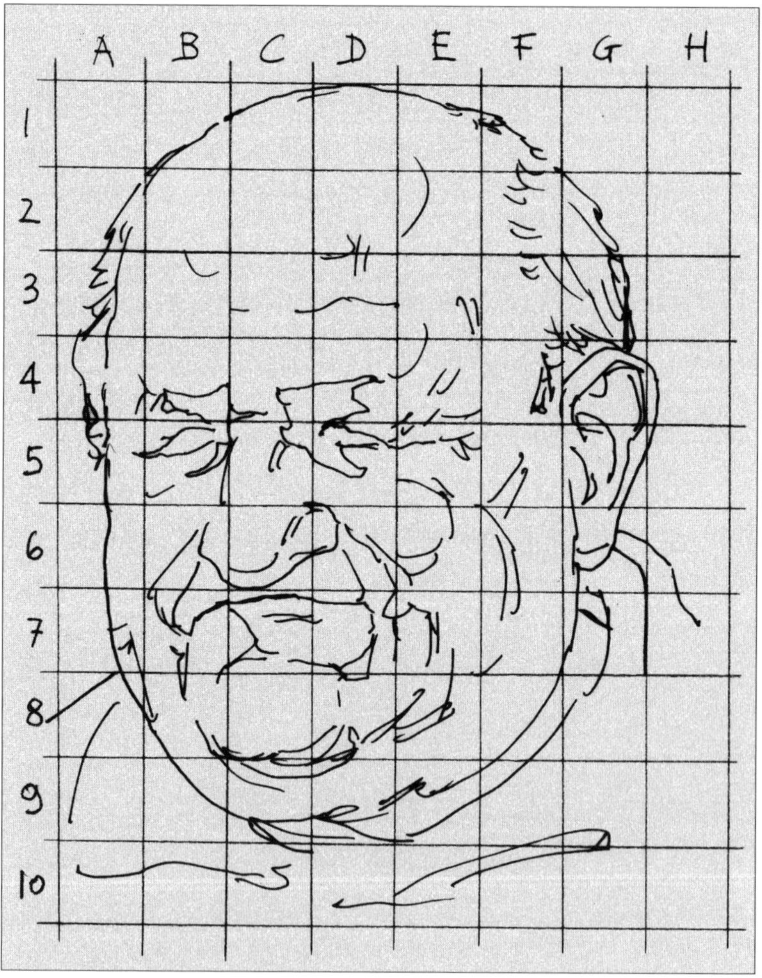

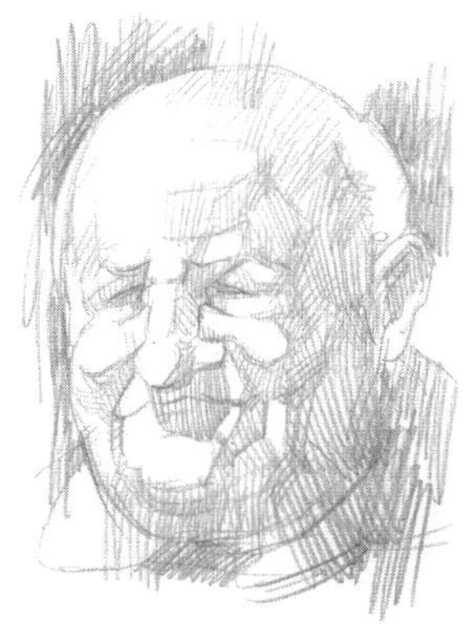

Step 4

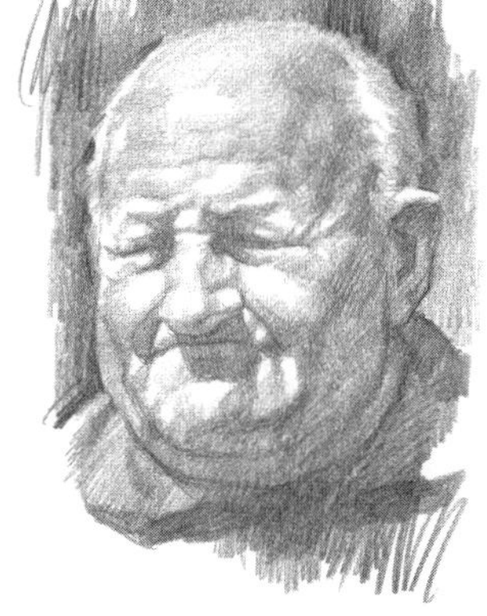

Tonal study

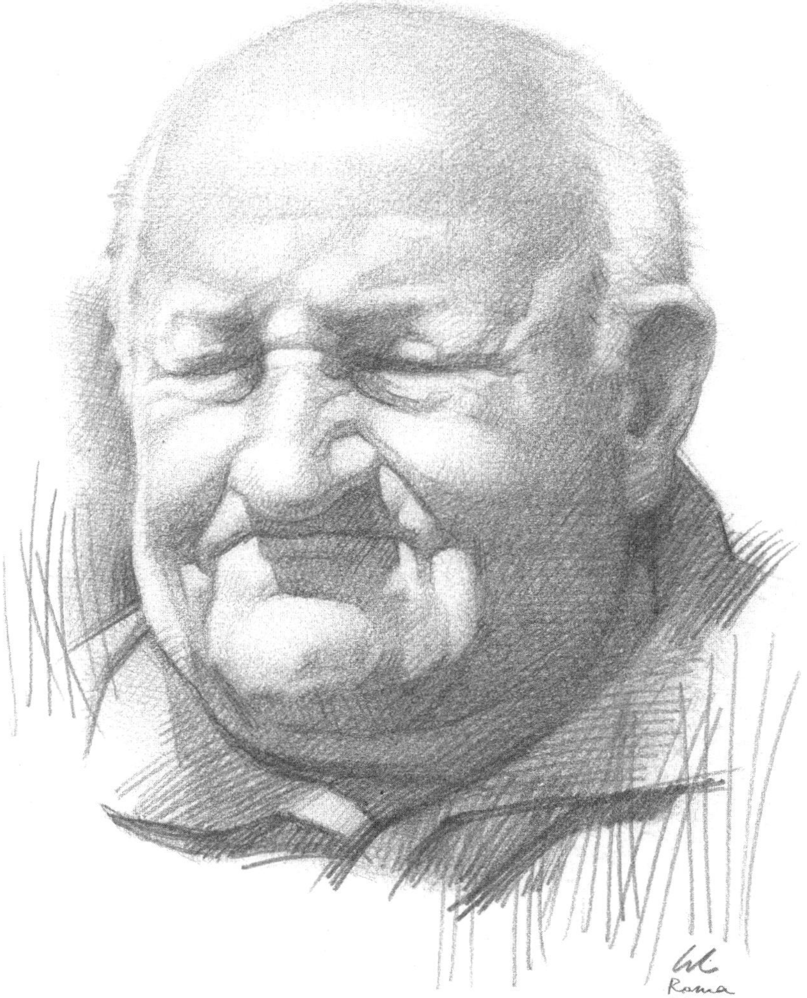

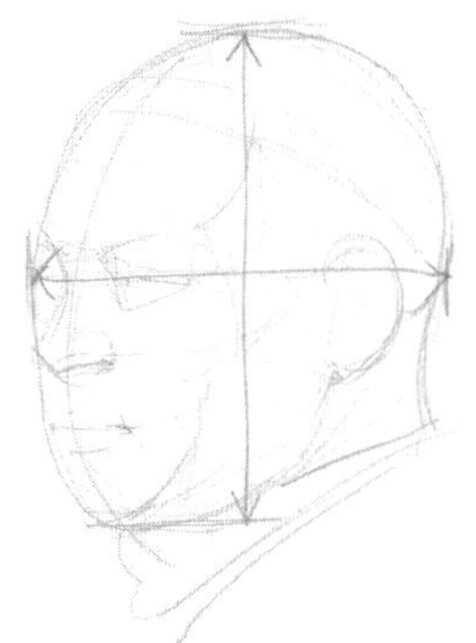

Step 1

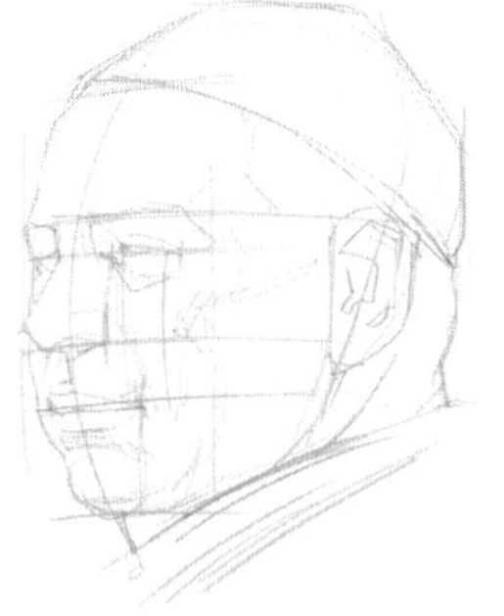

Step 2

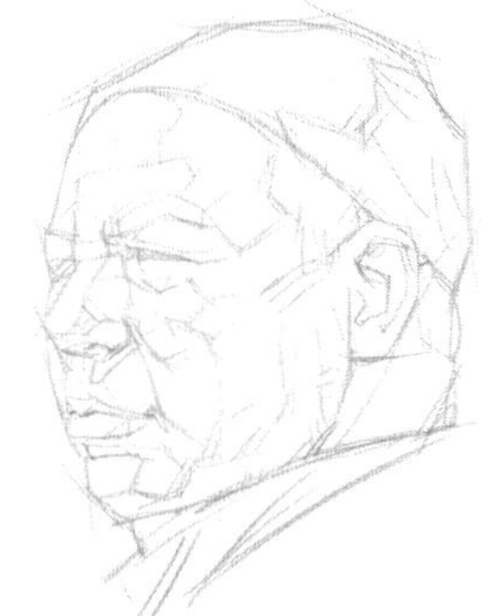

Step 3

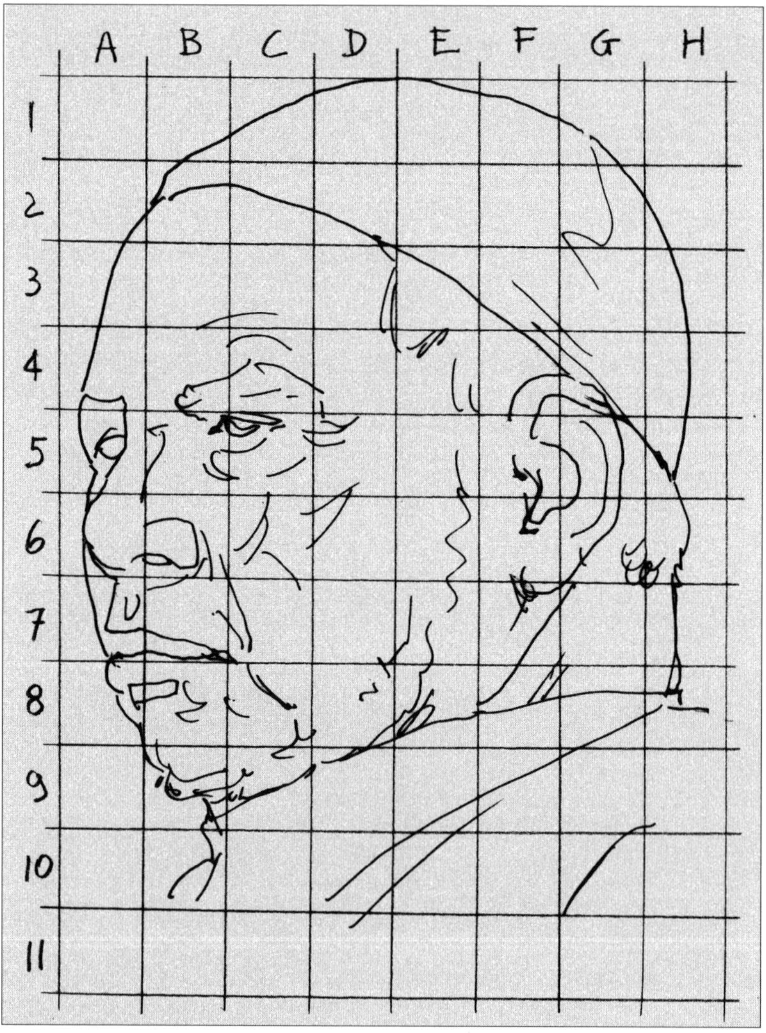

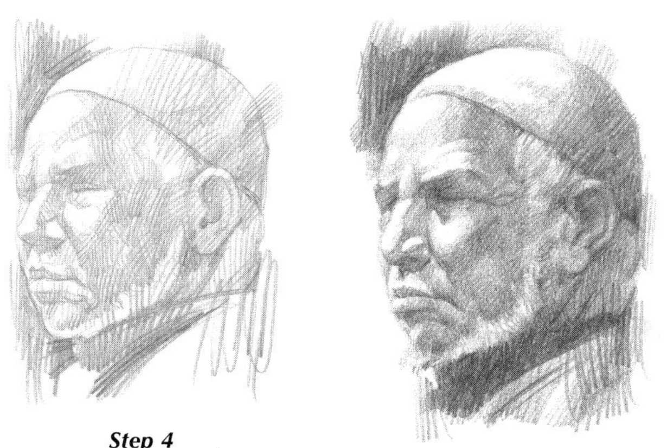

Tonal study

Step 4

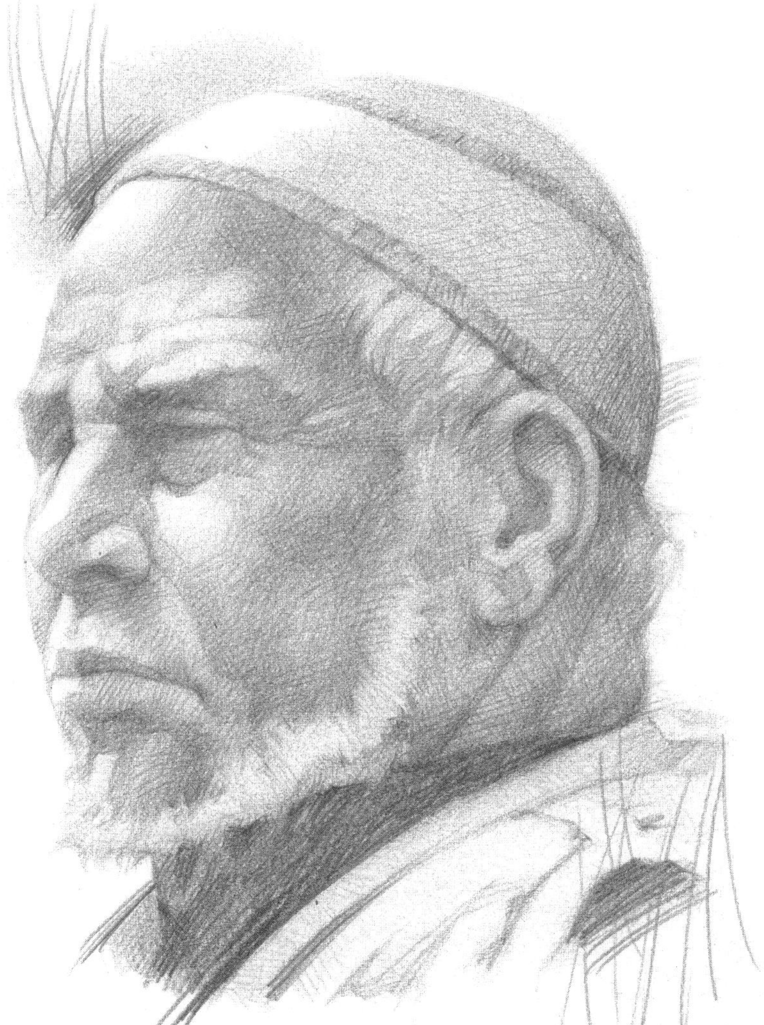

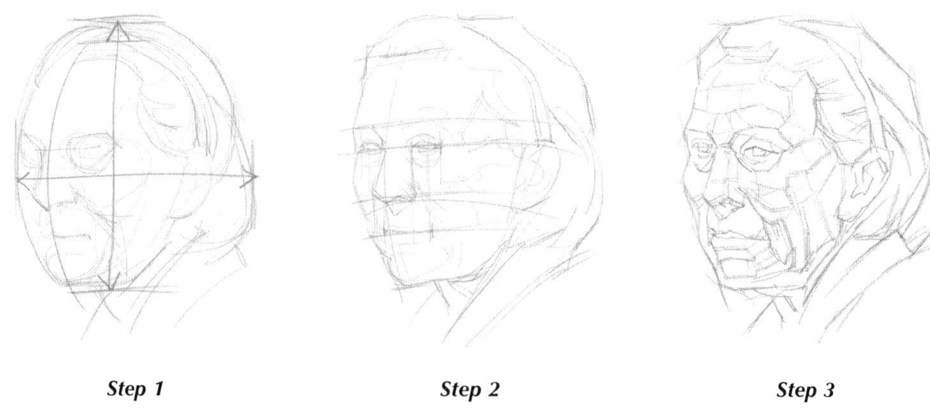

Step 1 *Step 2* *Step 3*

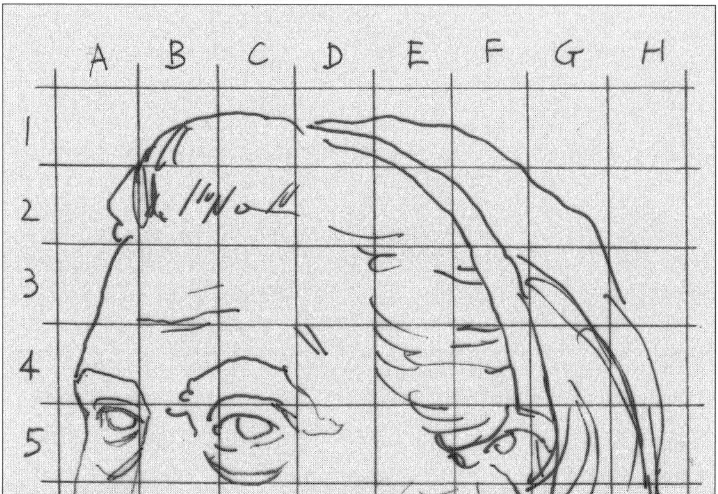

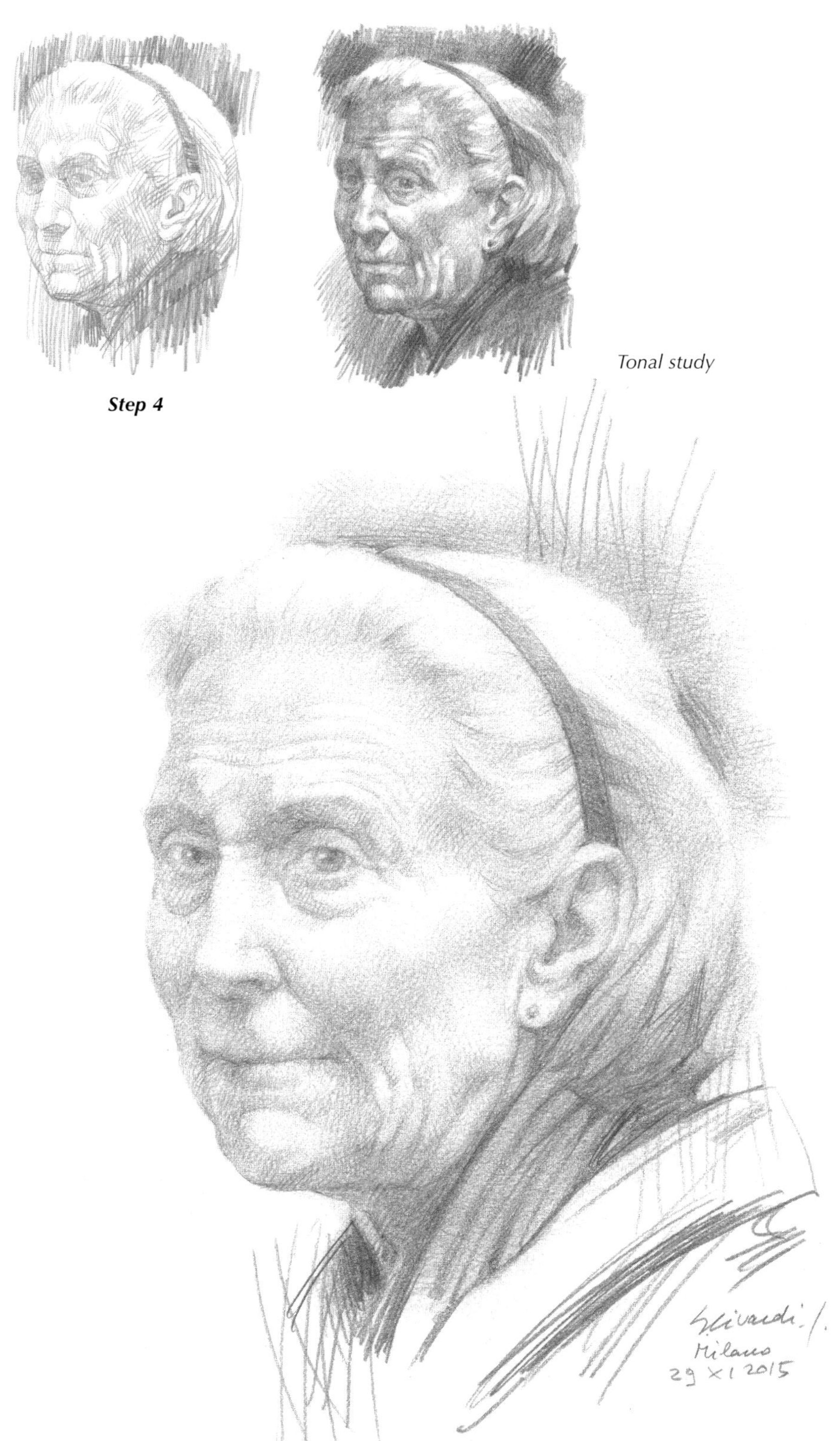

Step 4

Tonal study

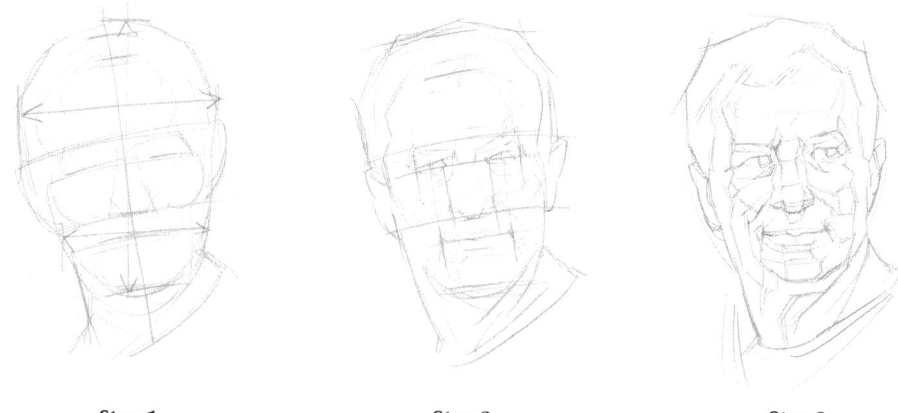

Step 1 ***Step 2*** ***Step 3***

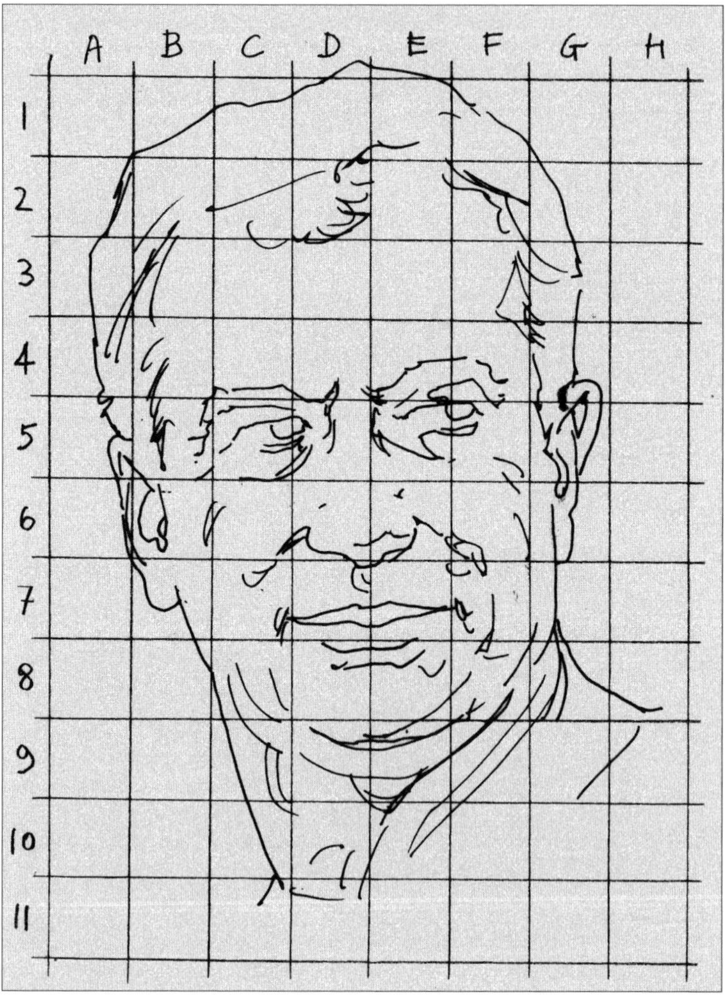

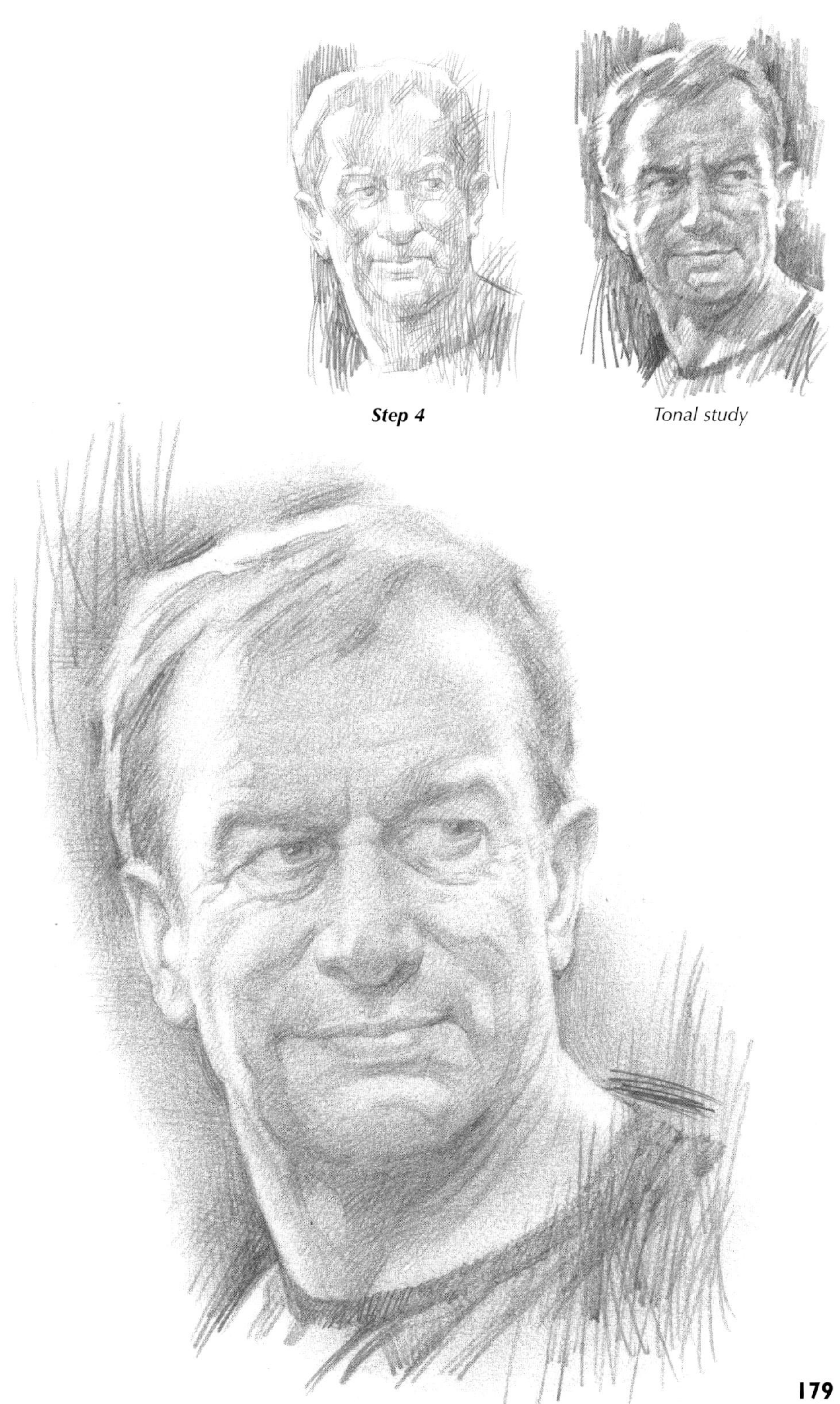

Step 4

Tonal study

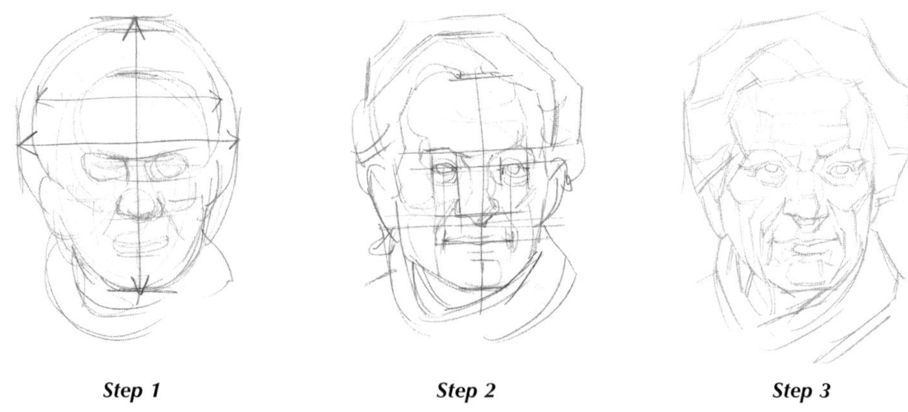

Step 1 *Step 2* *Step 3*

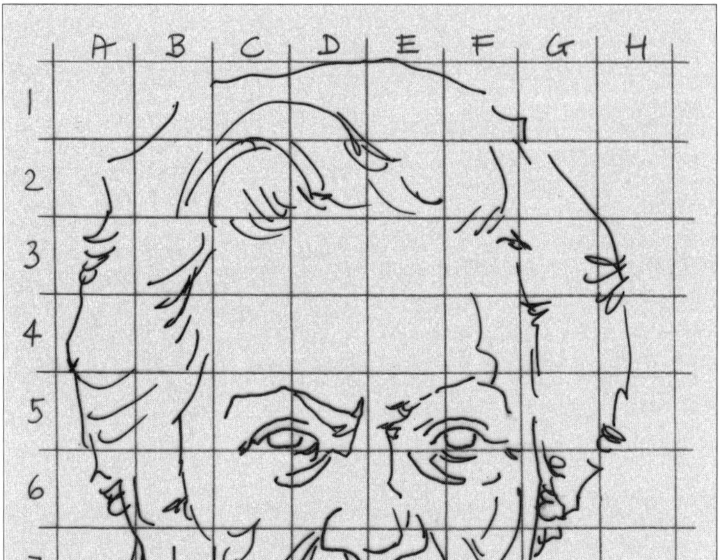

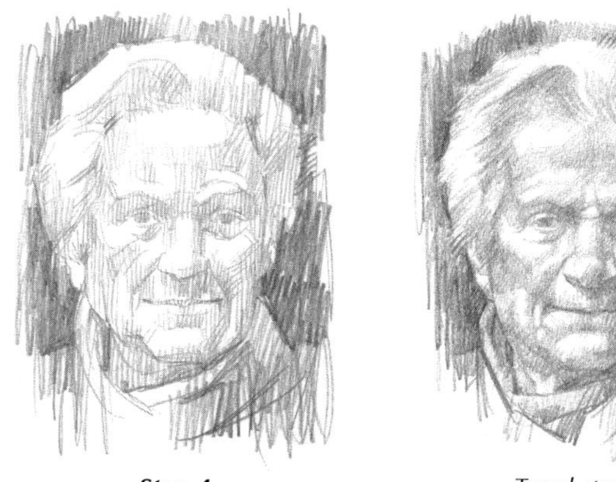

Step 4

Tonal study

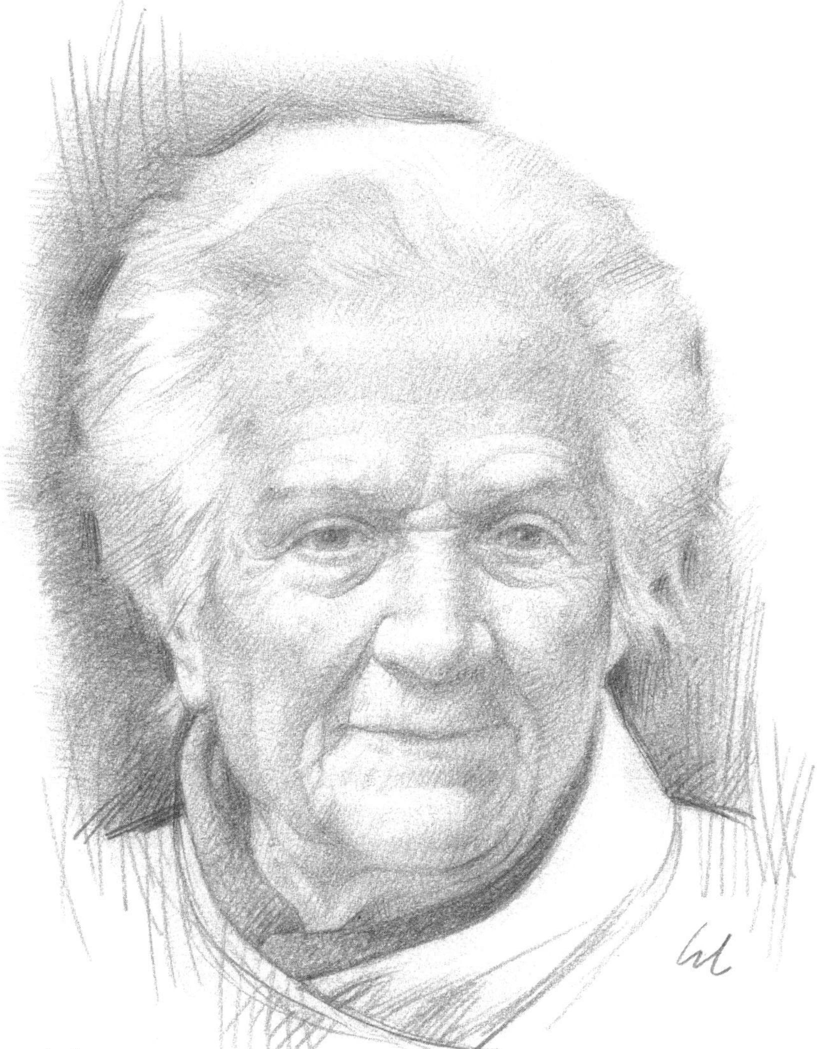

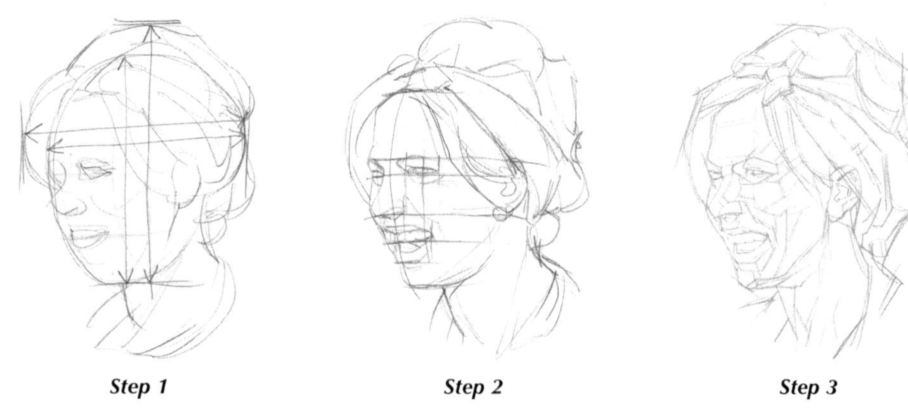

Step 1 **Step 2** **Step 3**

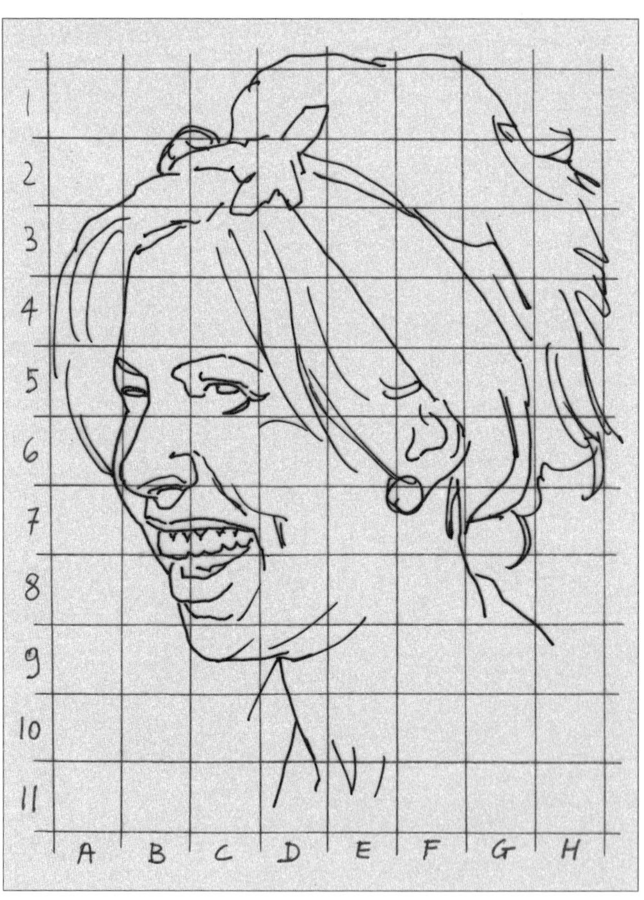

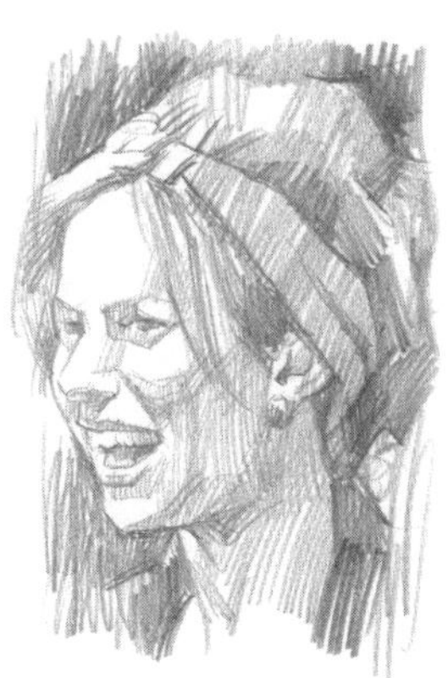

Step 4

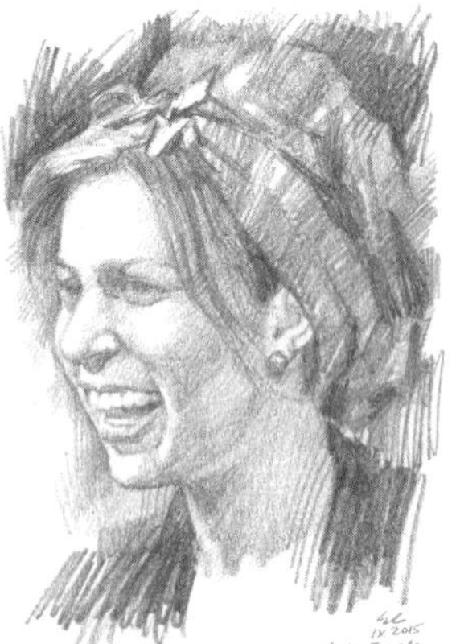

Tonal study

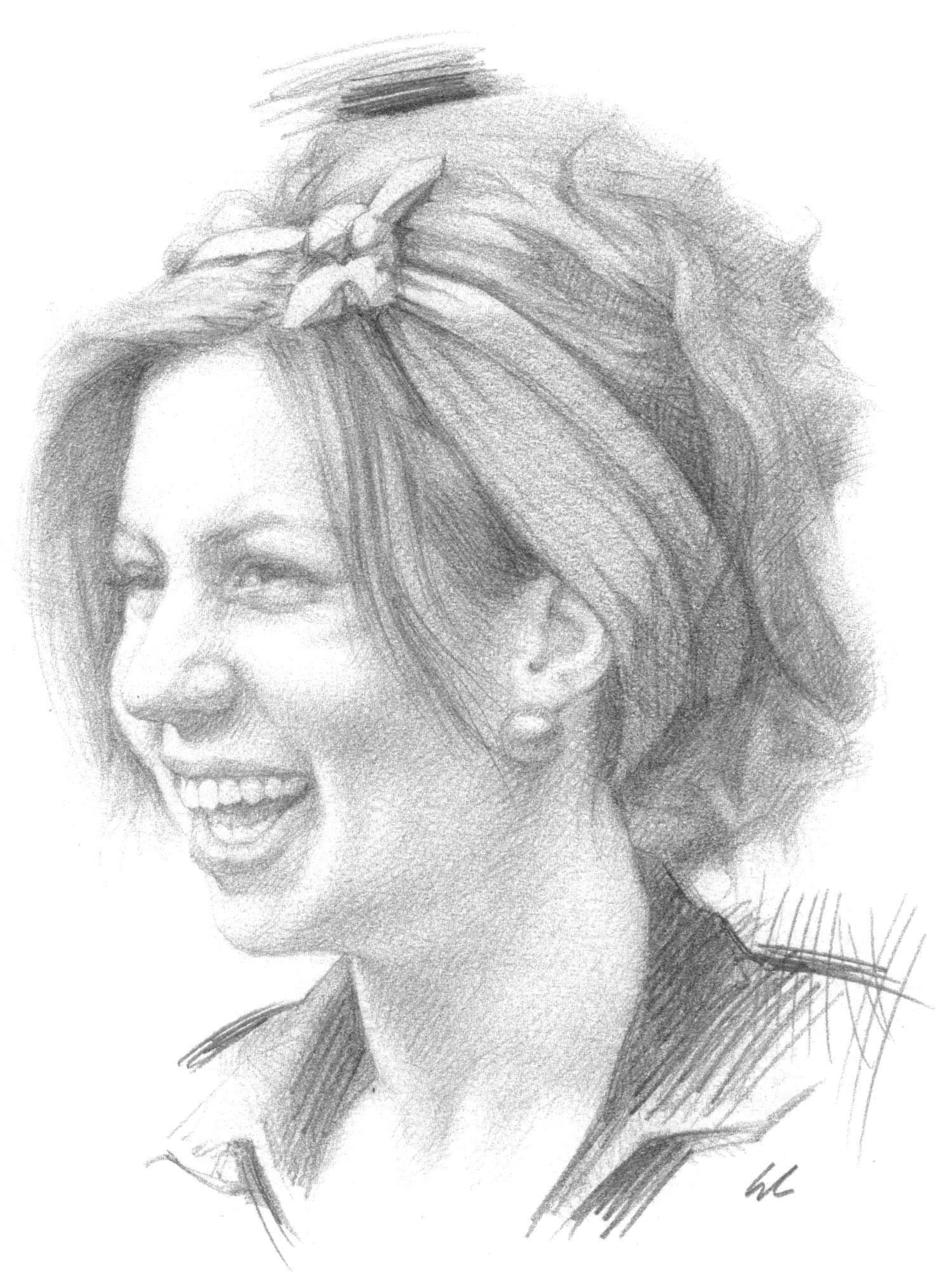

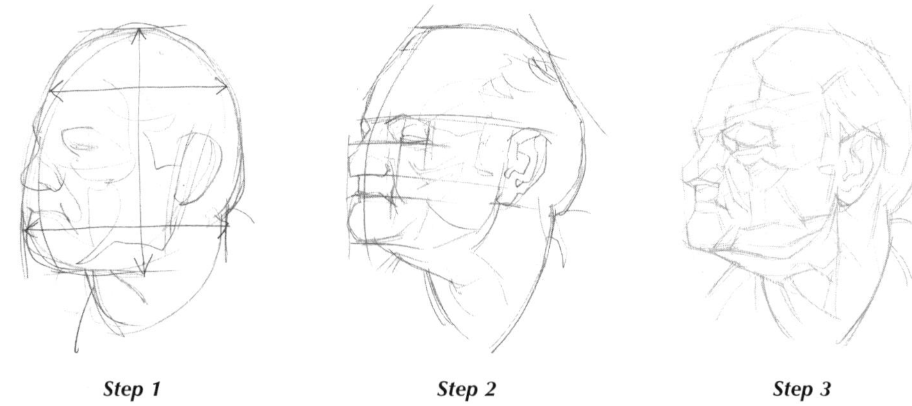

Step 1 *Step 2* *Step 3*

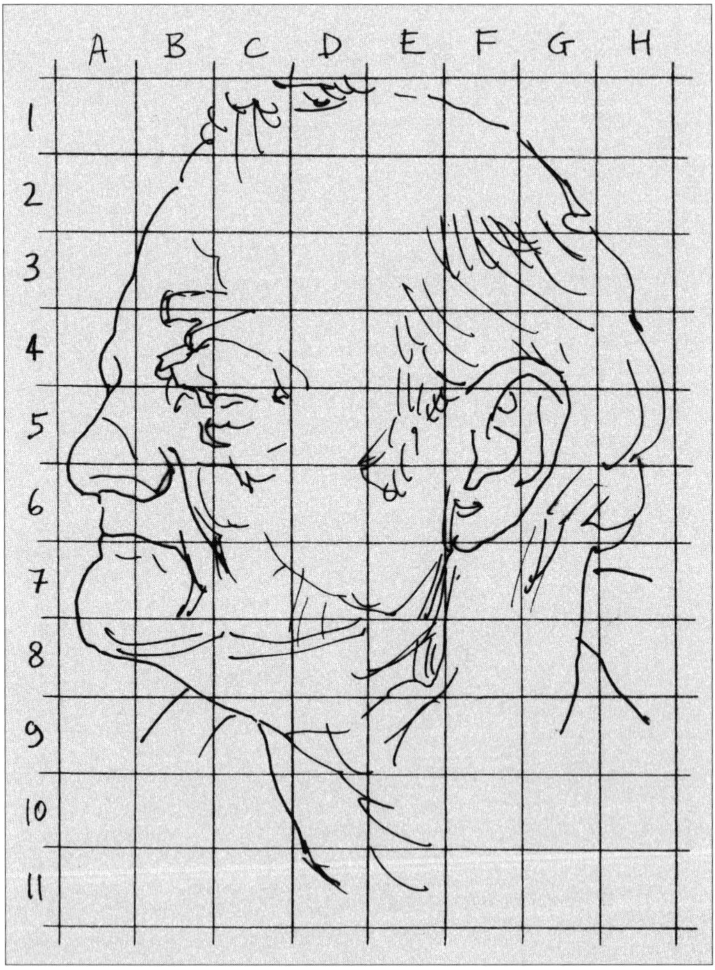

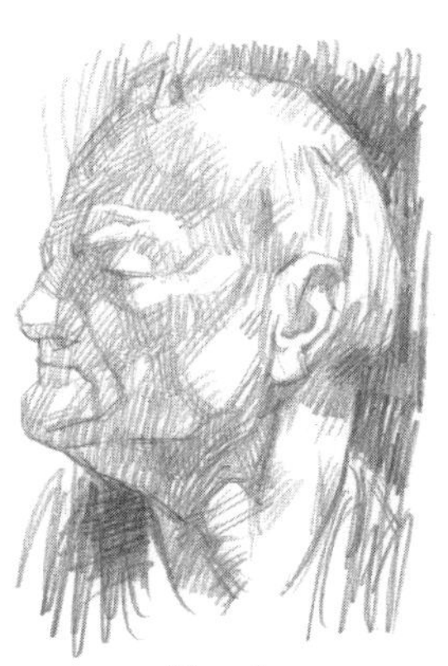

Step 4

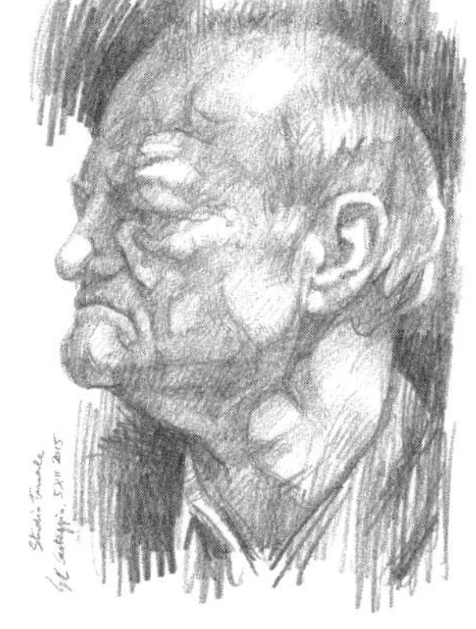

Tonal study

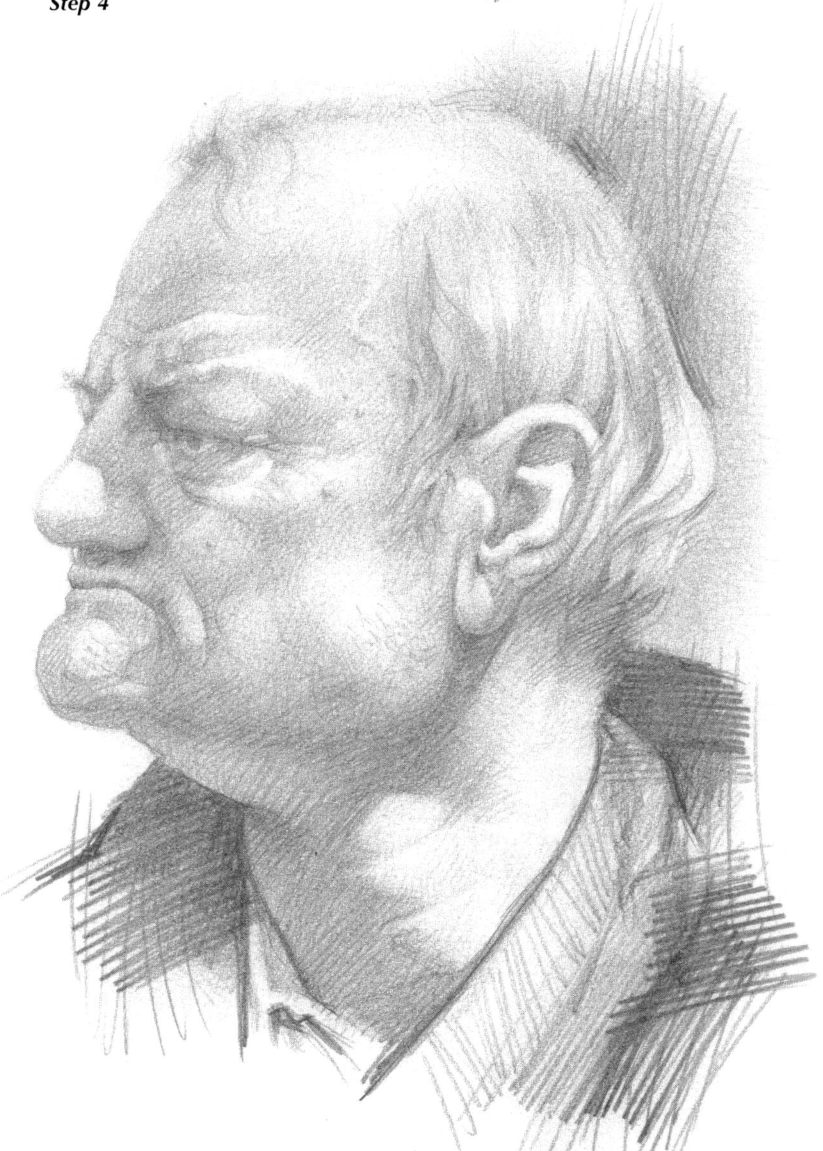

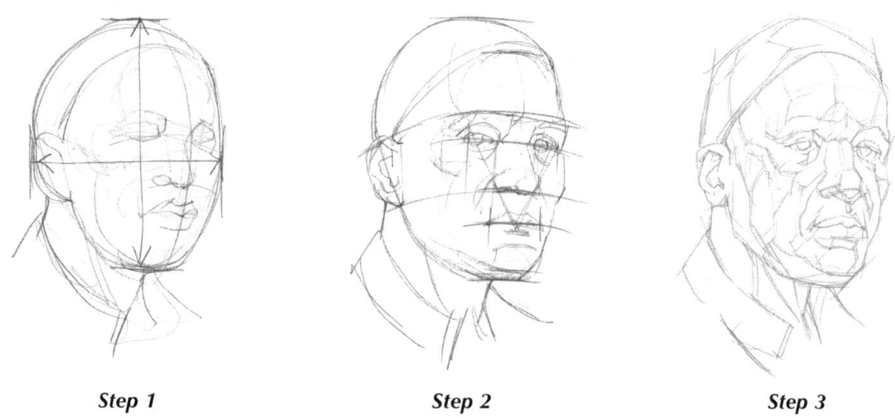

Step 1   *Step 2*   *Step 3*

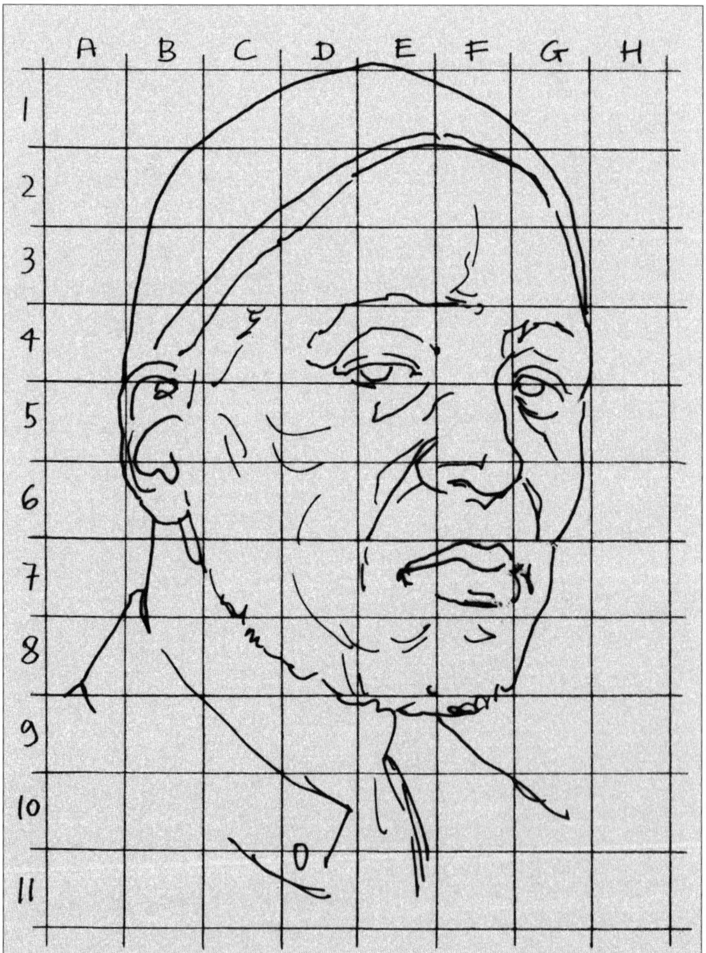

A B C D E F G H

1 2 3 4 5 6 7 8 9 10 11

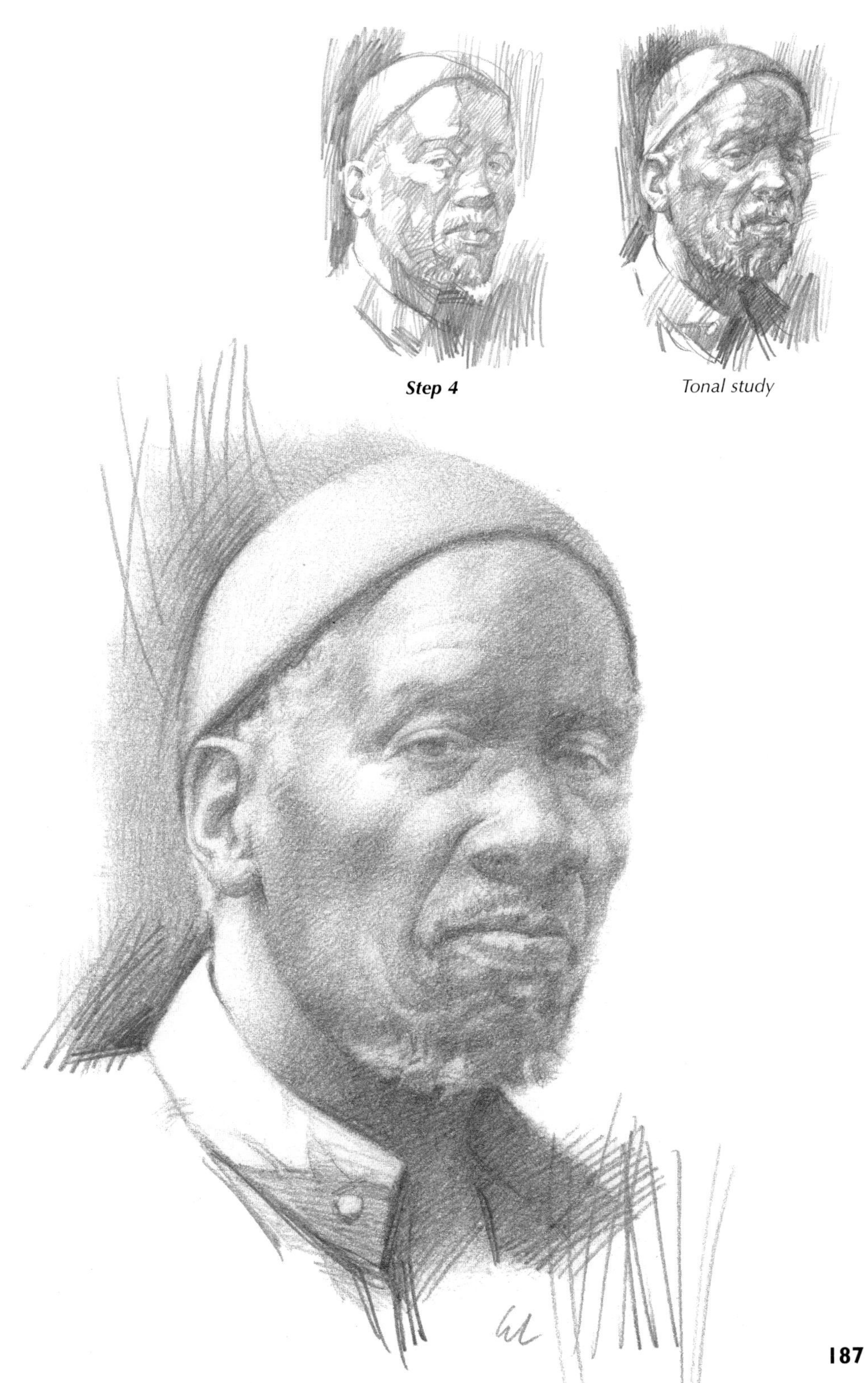

Step 4

Tonal study

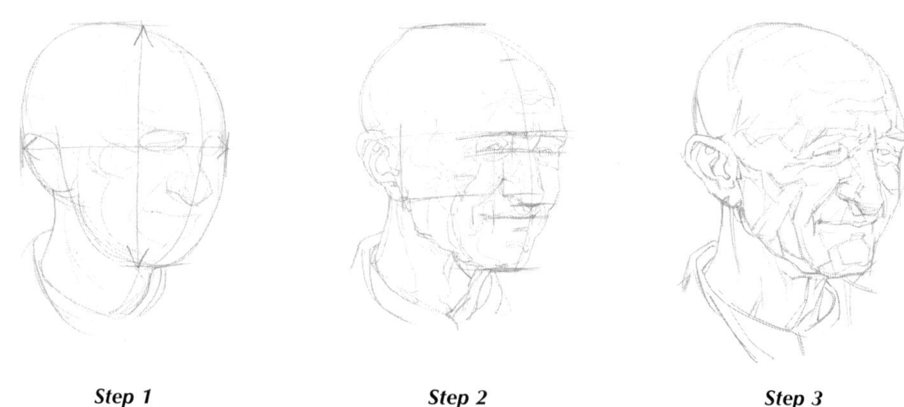

Step 1 *Step 2* *Step 3*

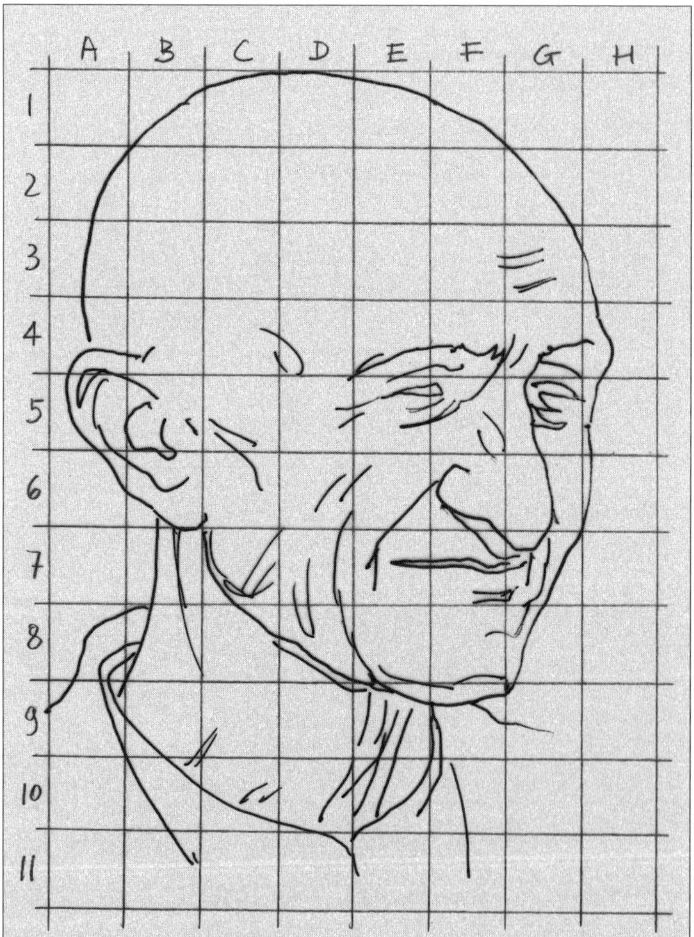

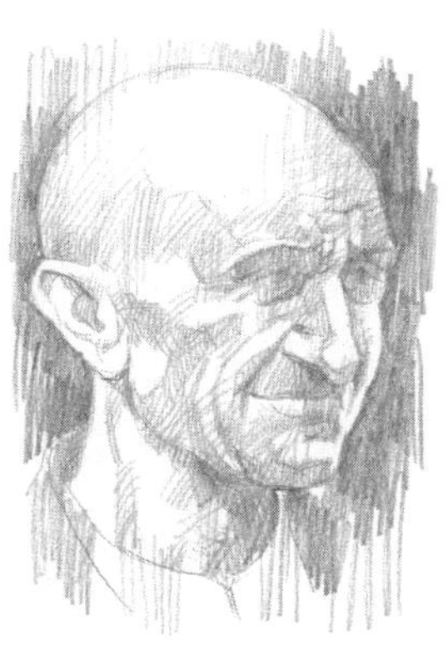

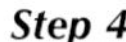

Step 4

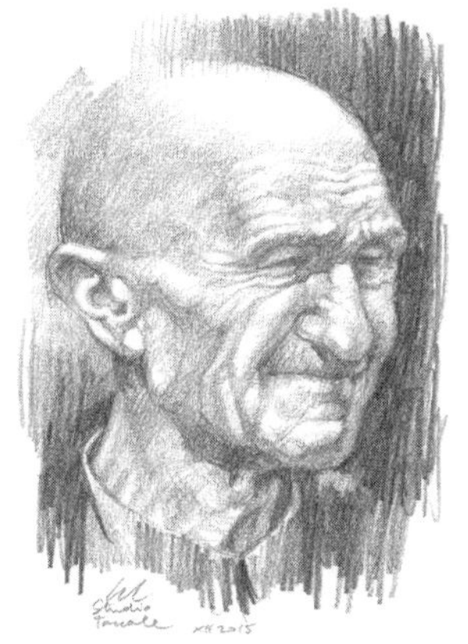

Tonal study

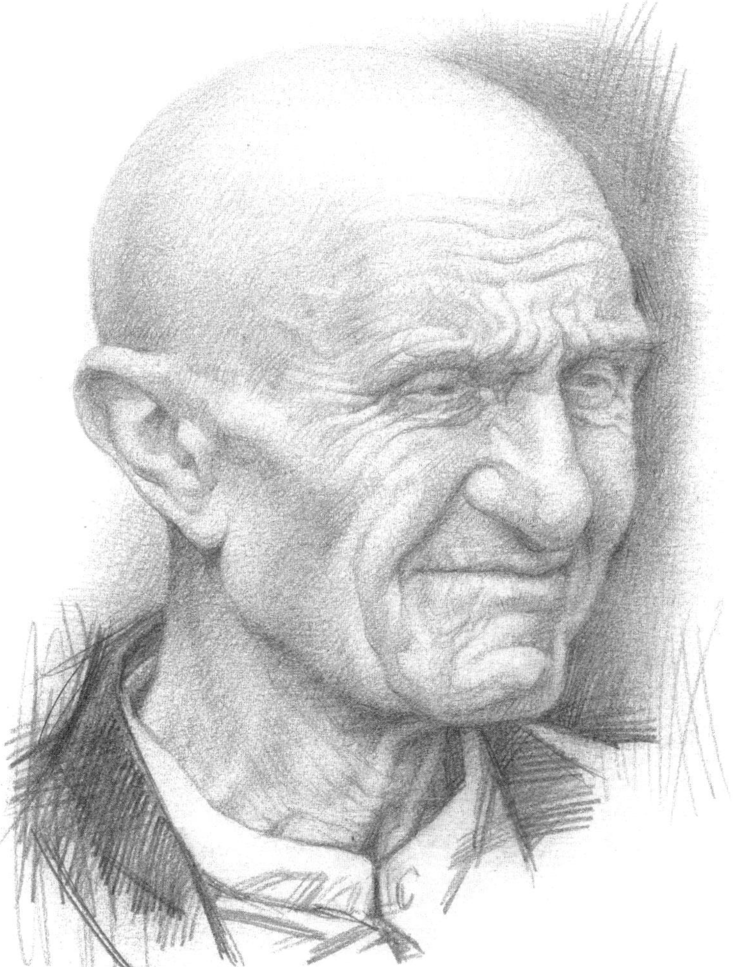

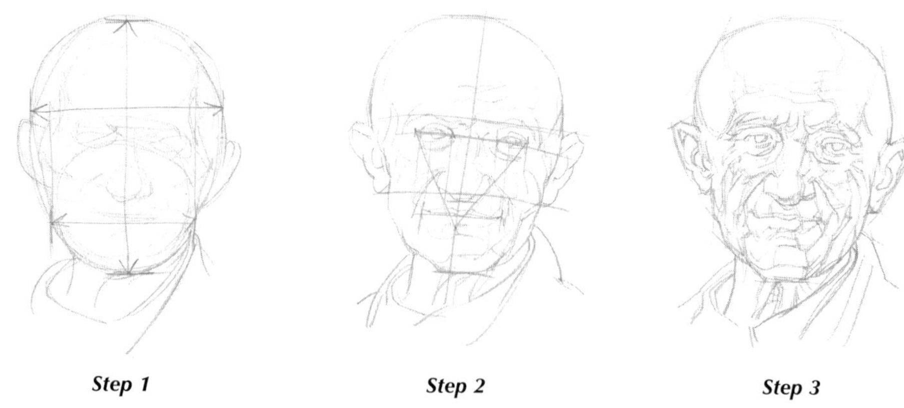

Step 1 *Step 2* *Step 3*

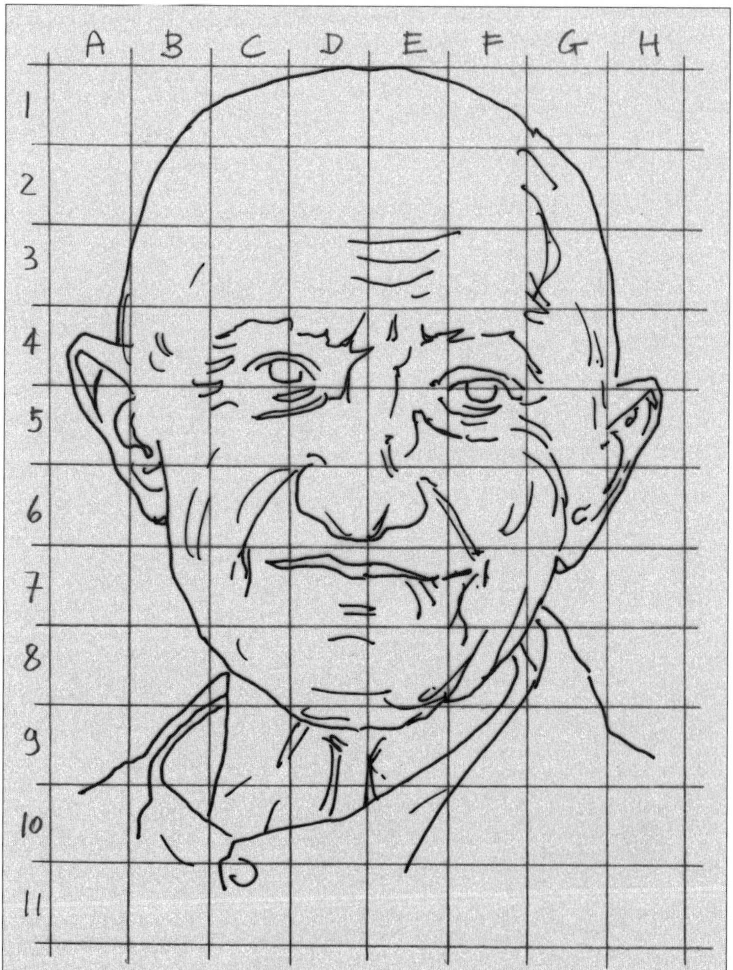

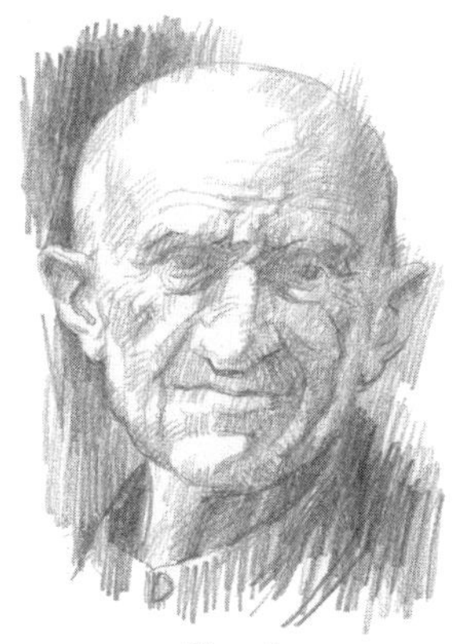
Step 4

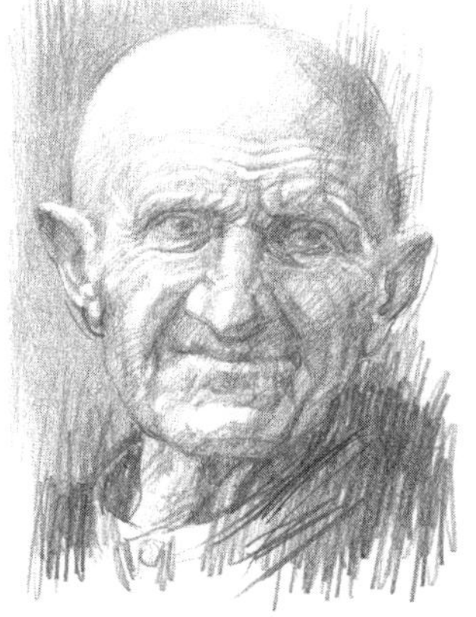
Tonal study

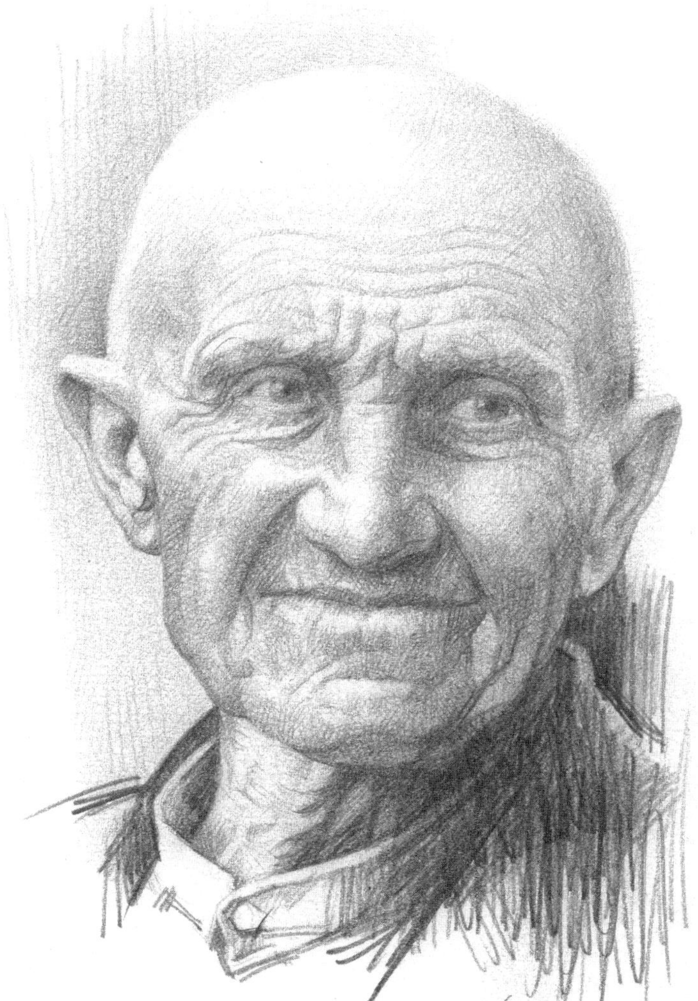

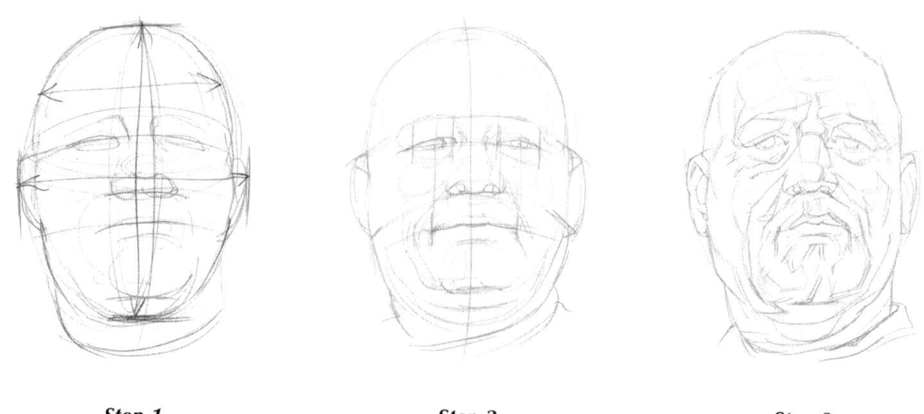

Step 1 *Step 2* *Step 3*

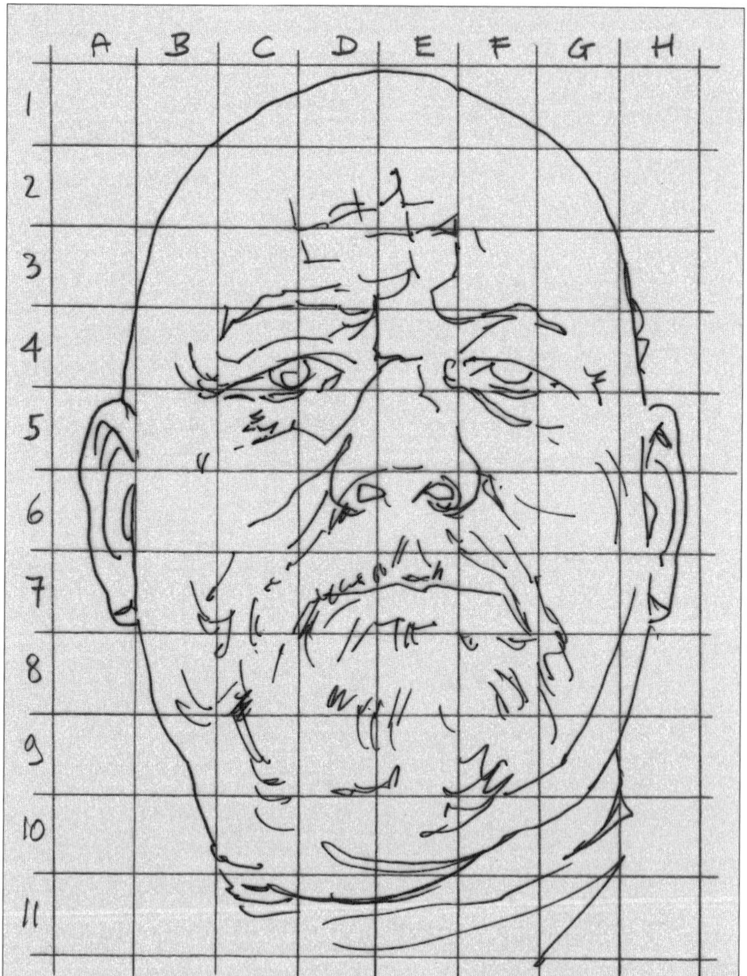

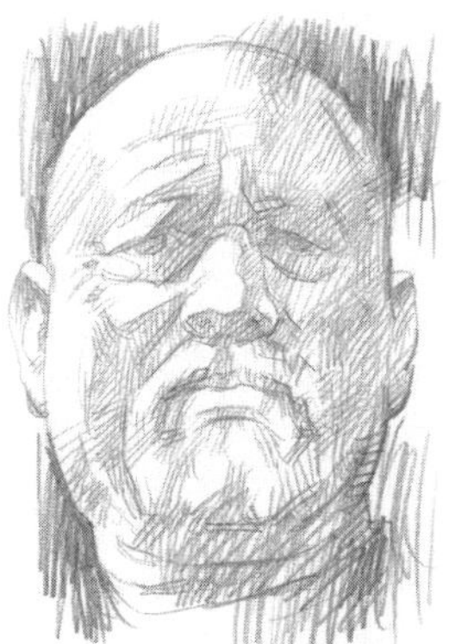

Step 4

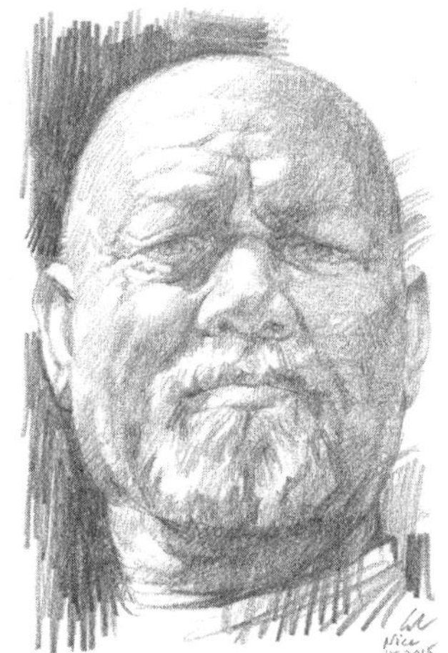

Tonal study

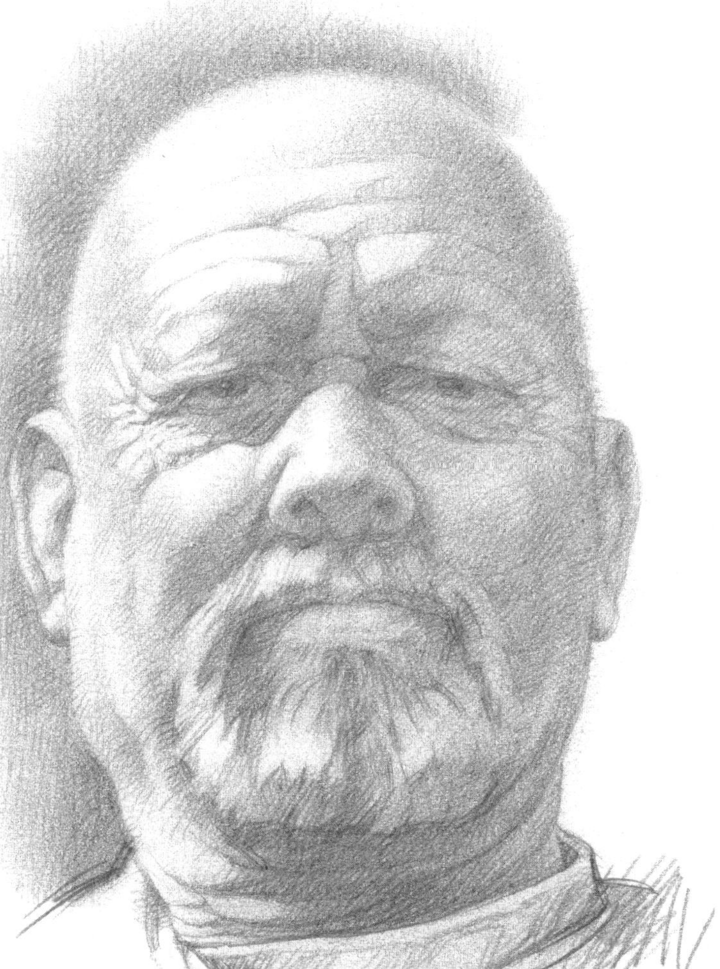

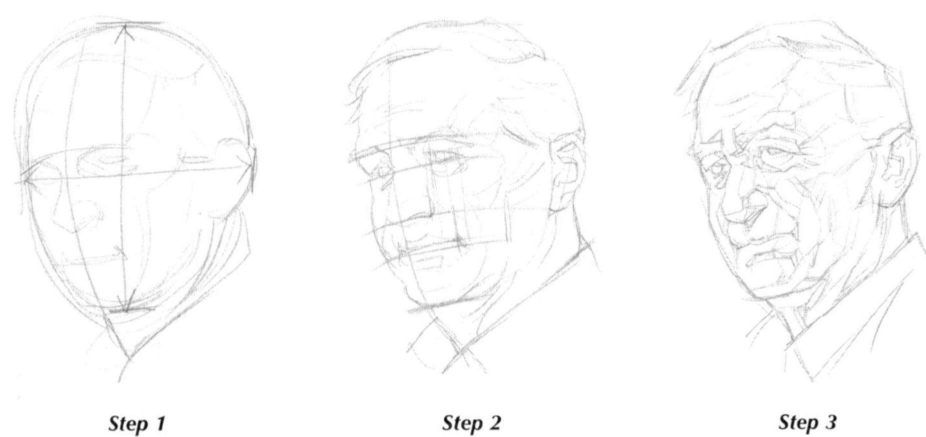

Step 1 *Step 2* *Step 3*

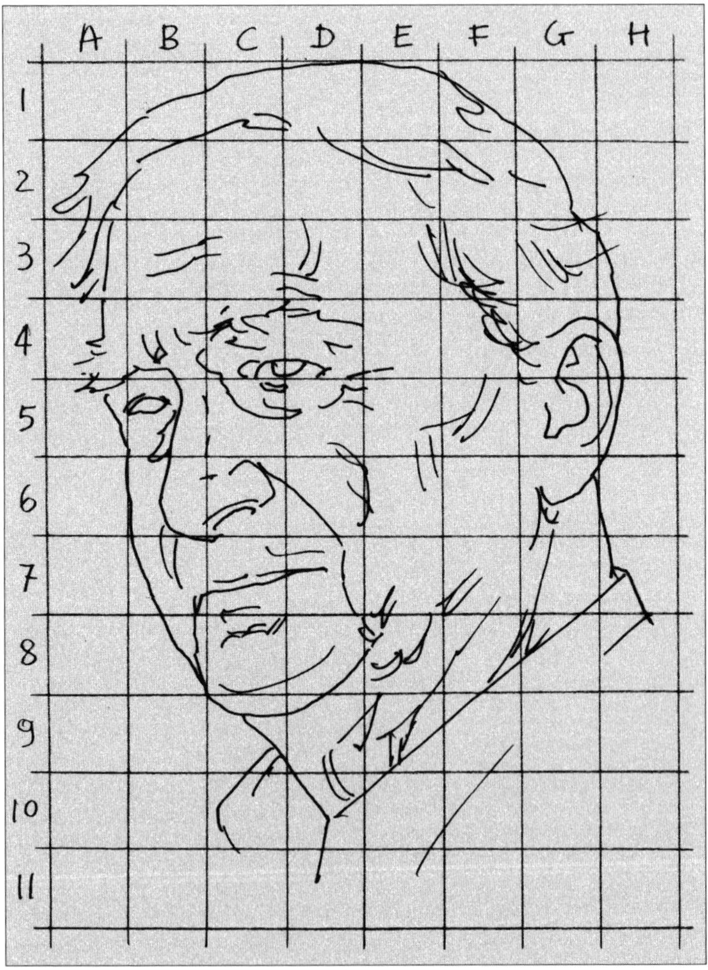

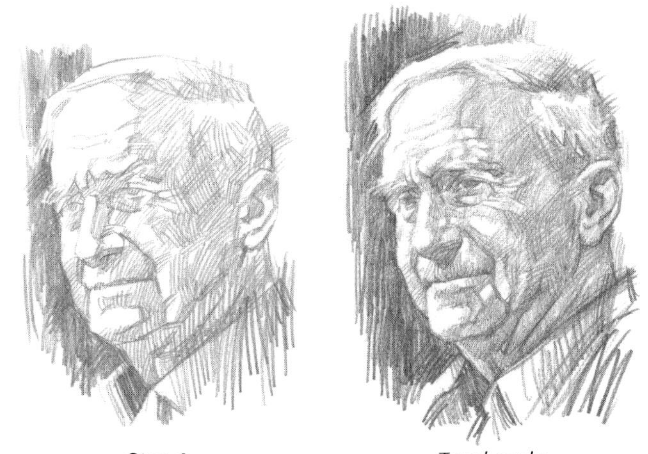

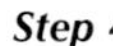

Step 4

Tonal study

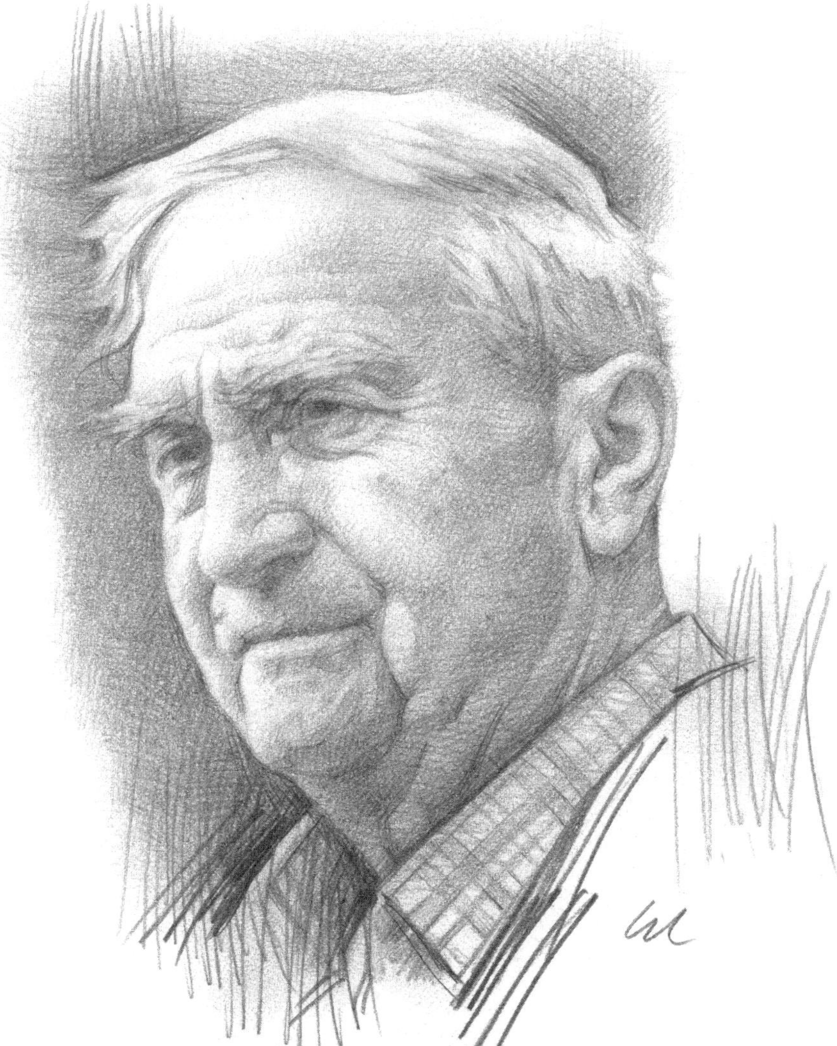

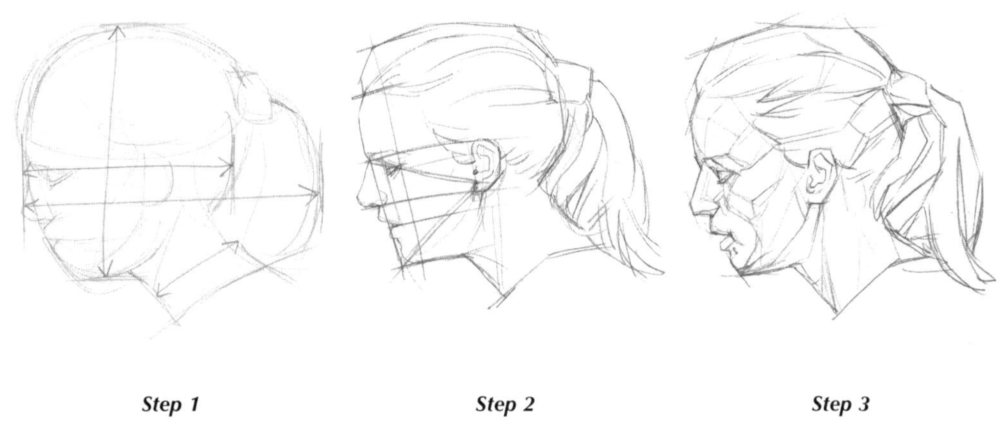

Step 1 *Step 2* *Step 3*

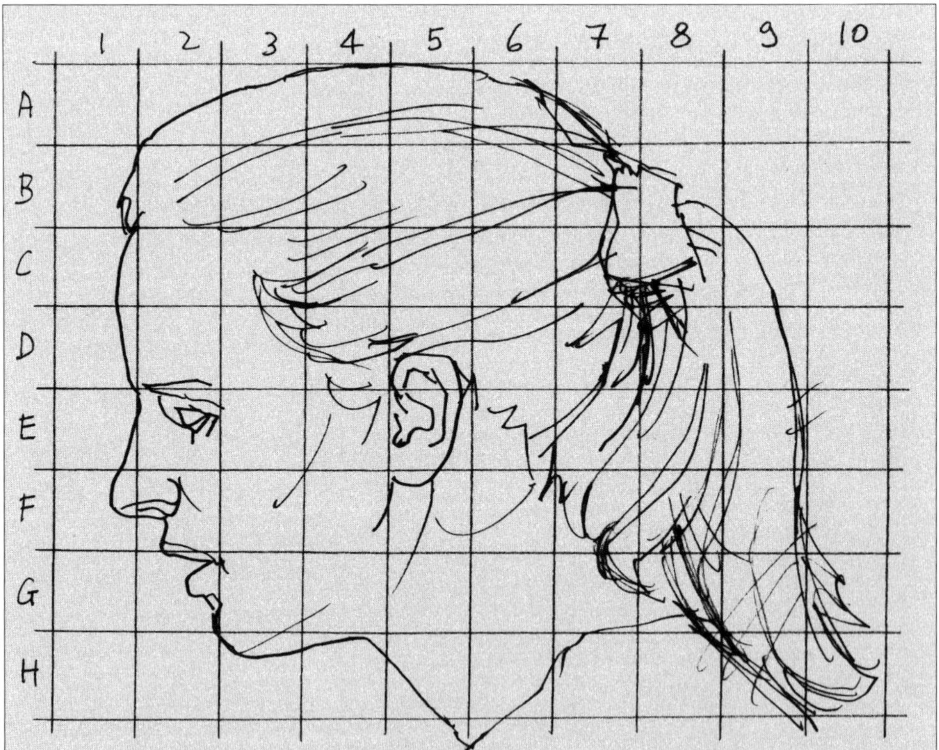

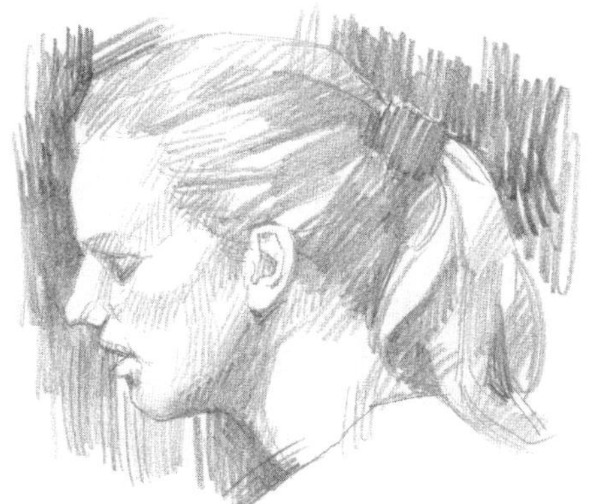

Step 4

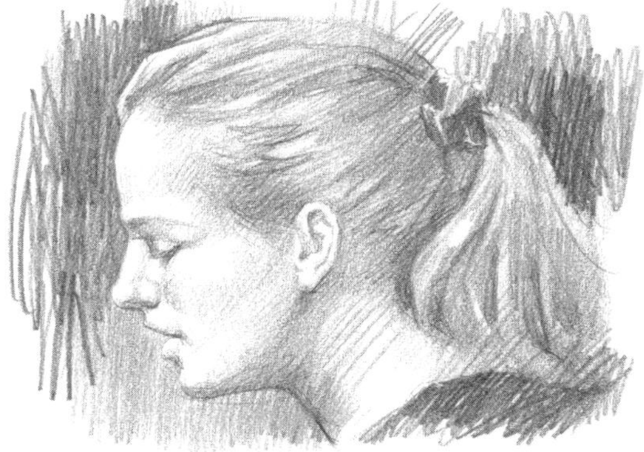

Tonal study

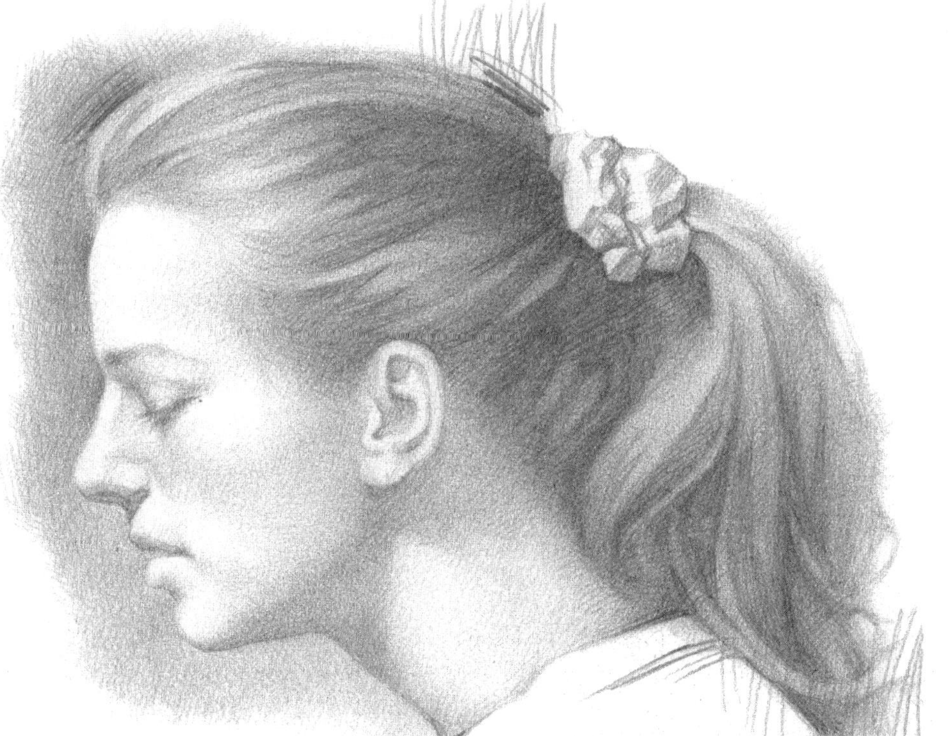

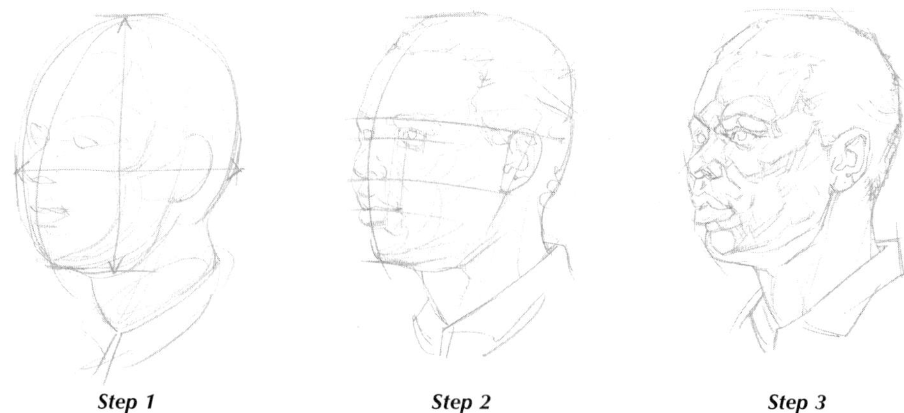

Step 1 *Step 2* *Step 3*

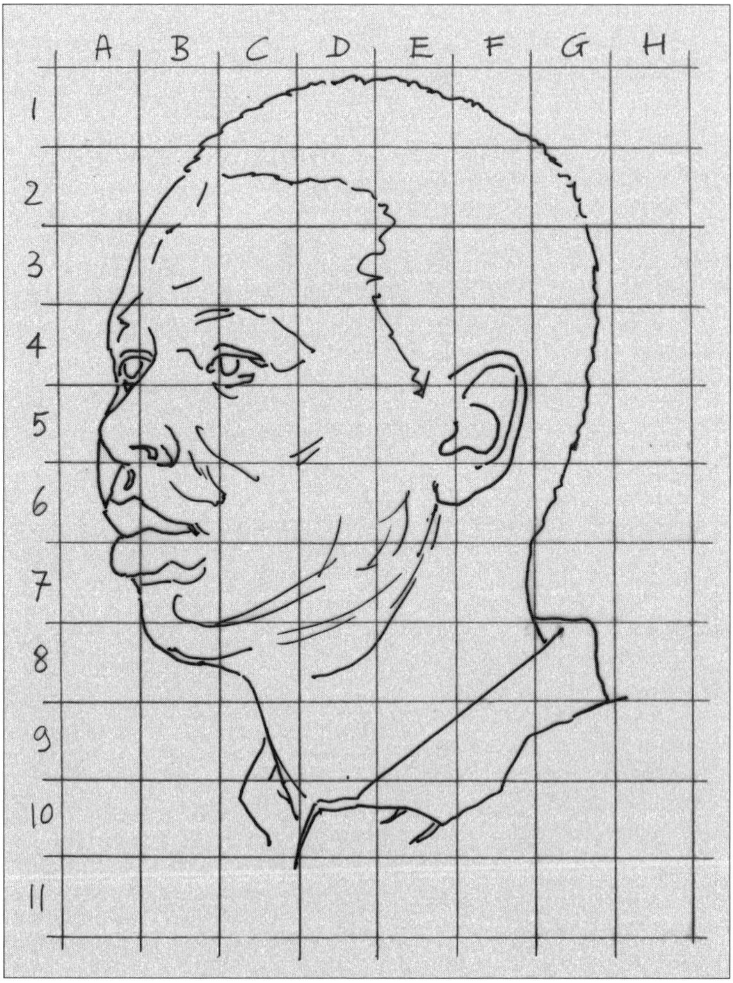

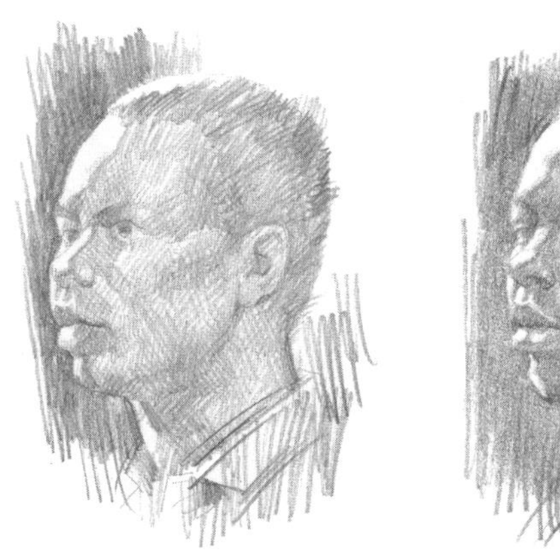

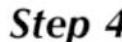

Step 4

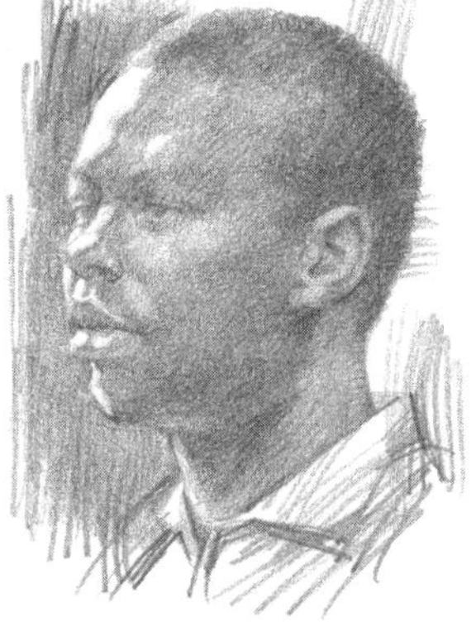

Tonal study

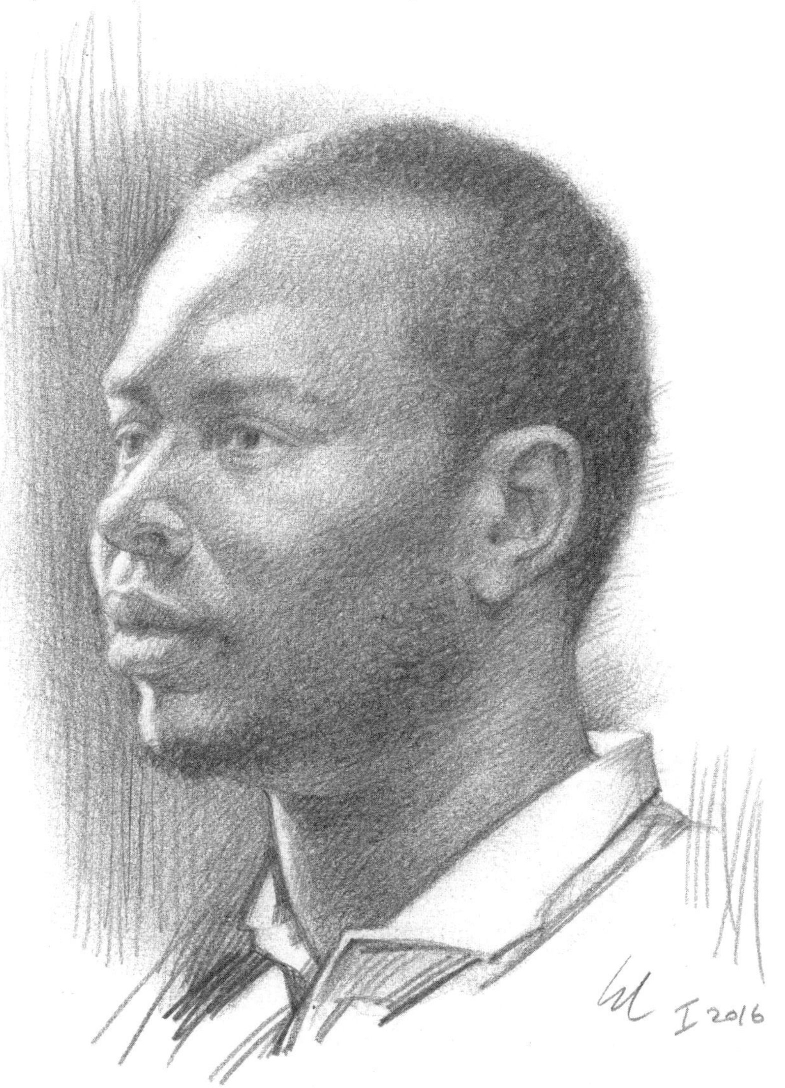

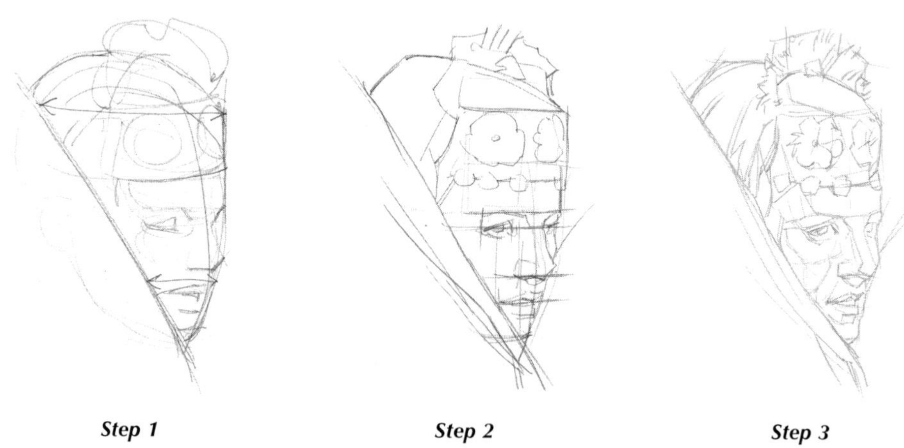

Step 1

Step 2

Step 3

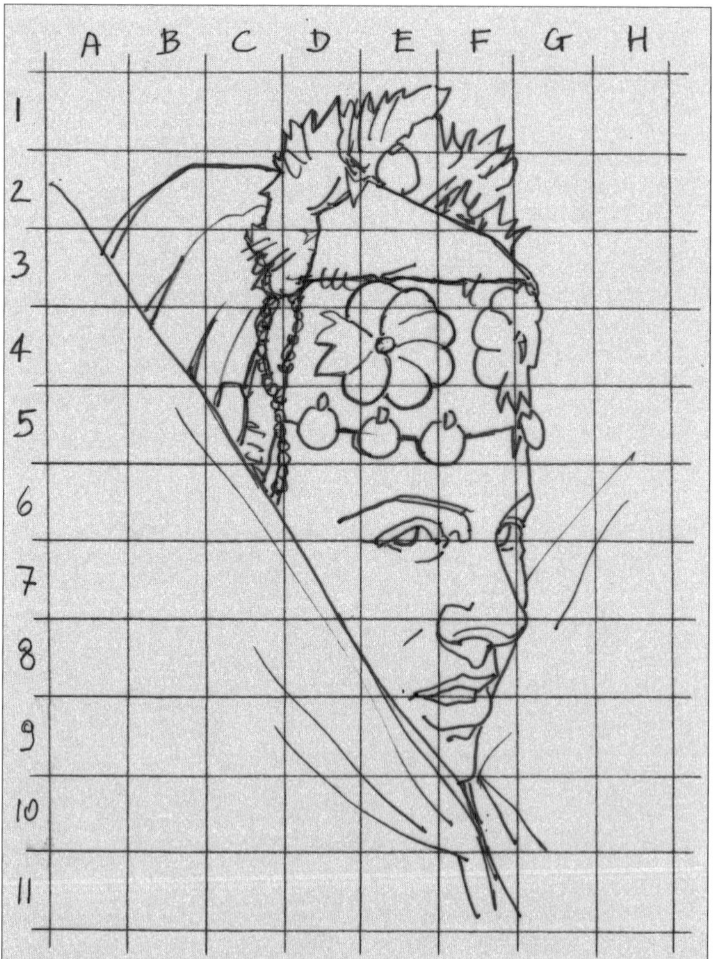

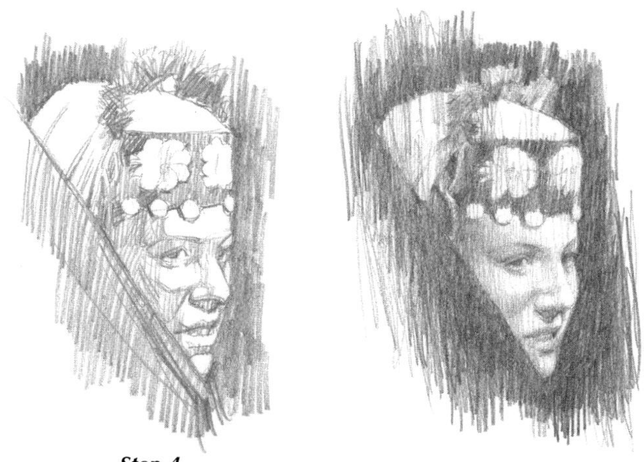

Step 4

Tonal study

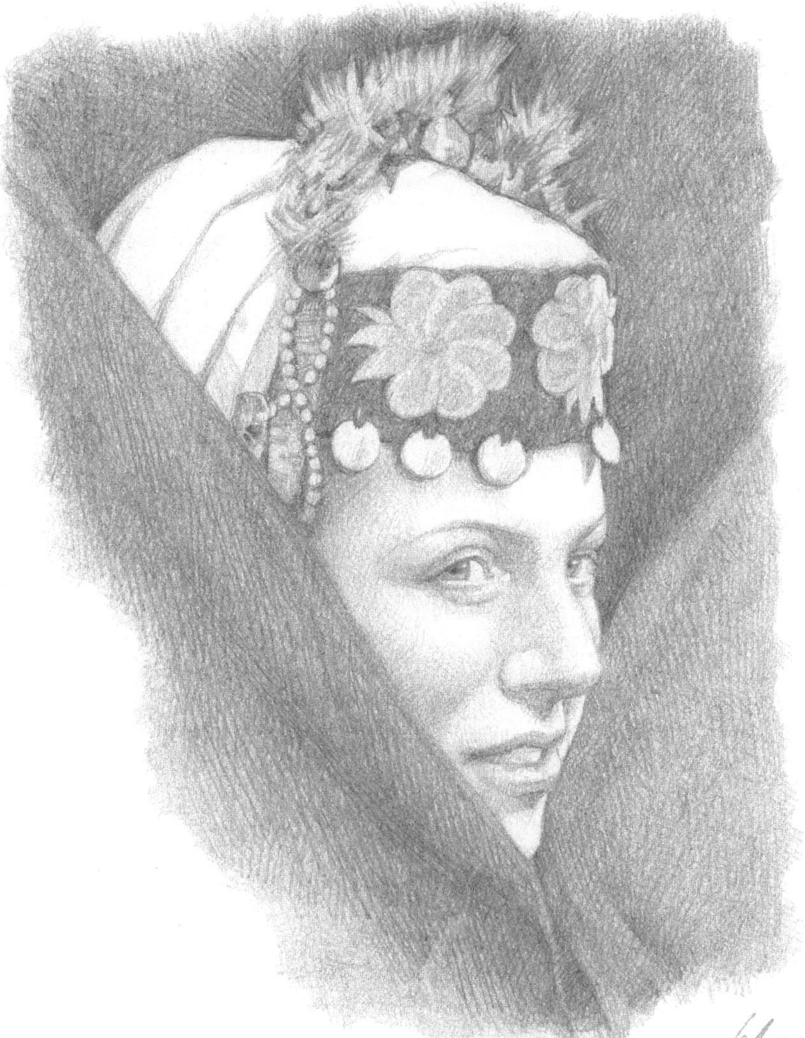

FINDING INSPIRATION

The face is the most important part of the body by which we recognize and identify a person, and it attracts us from early months of life as a fundamental visual element. In fact, some areas of the brain seem to be geared to immediately recognizing human faces and bodies; this is due to evolution, perhaps connected with the need to survive.

The tendency to perceive known shapes in vague, random patterns and therefore to see general likenesses of faces, heads and profiles emerge from chance associations of marks or spots is a universal one. The spots can be drips of colour, splashes of mud or ink, or simply accidental arrangements such as spots of rust or mould, cracks in walls, clouds, veins in stone and so forth. Such chance encounters have been seen by artists in both the East and the West throughout history, who often found beauty and inspiration in them for their most elaborate works. In these marks, everyone can see what their psychological state, existential experiences, subconscious visual culture or emotions allow them to see: frequently, what is 'seen' is connected to human or animal faces.

Concentrating on these random observations, or even looking for them deliberately, can be a good exercise for stimulating your visual imagination. Such subconscious suggestion, in a kind of free association, can lead to the most expressive, curious or grotesque faces, ones that are – almost by definition – characterful.

These pages show some images taken from the study notebook that I always keep with me: the richest source of attraction and stimulation are the cracks and veins in marble that can almost always be found in old churches and important buildings.

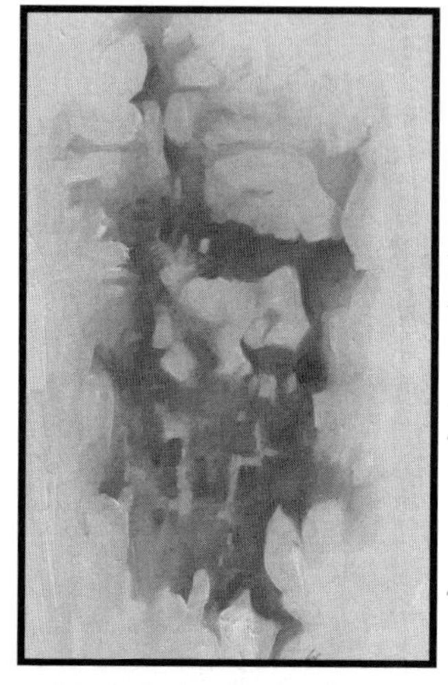

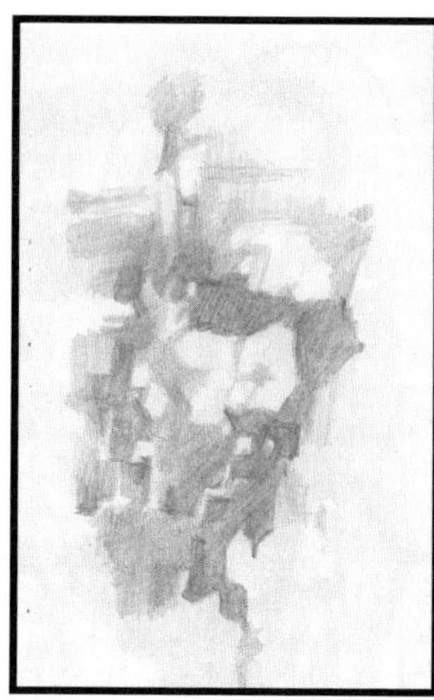

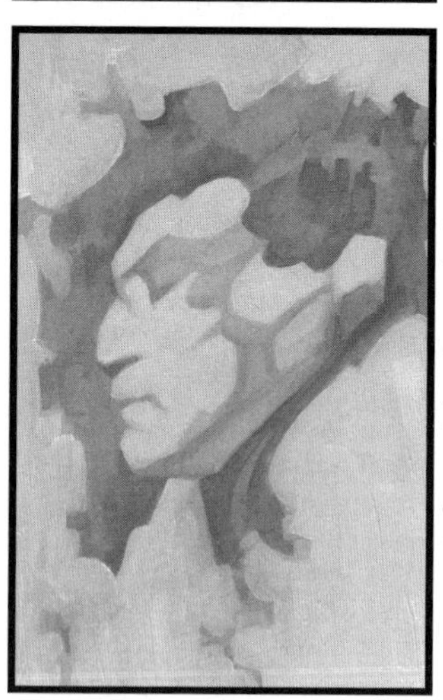

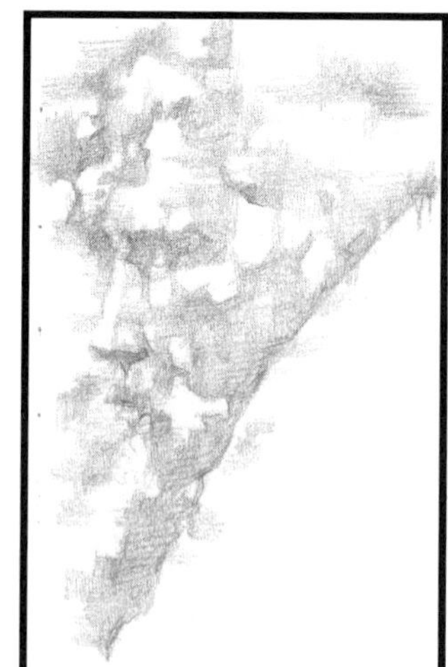

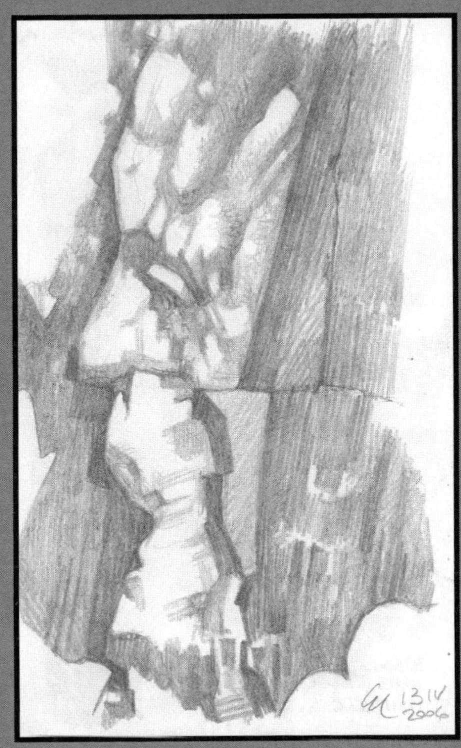
13 IV
2006
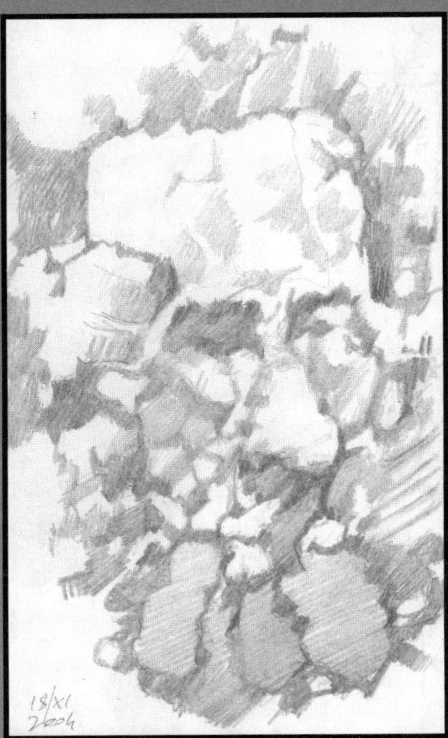
18/XI
2004
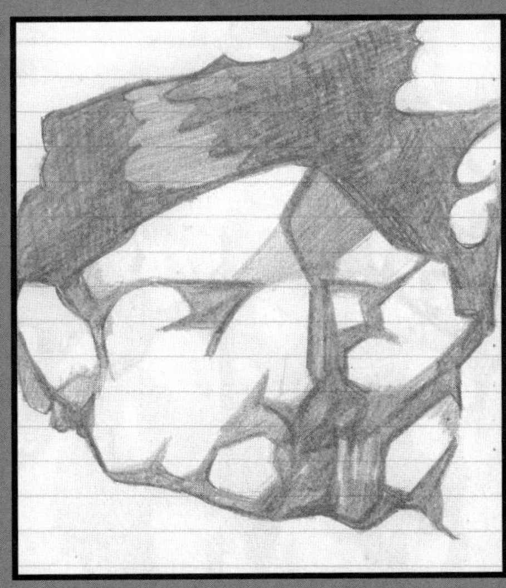
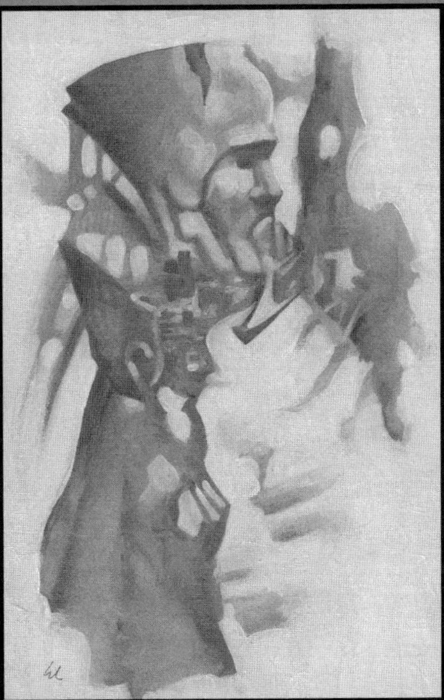

CHAPTER 3: DRAWING PORTRAITS OF BABIES AND CHILDREN

INTRODUCTION

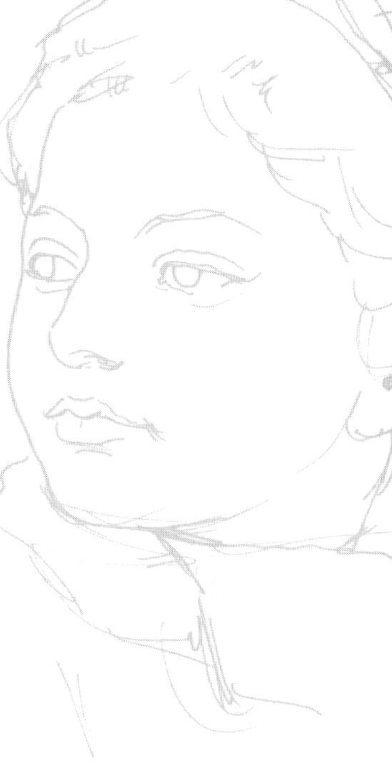

Children, like young animals, stimulate an instinctive sense of tenderness and protectiveness in adults, because of those typical features that characterize the head and face of the human infant: round head, big eyes, a small, rounded nose, chubby cheeks, small mouth and chin, curved forehead, soft, clear skin, and a tiny neck. It is no surprise that everyone loves children: there is, perhaps, no other period of a person's life when they are so often observed, photographed and drawn. In fact, drawing and painting children, especially in their earliest years, is almost a special branch of art. The painter, illustrator and sculptor are often called upon to include these subjects in their work.

When creating a child's 'portrait', the drawing (the quickest technique, compared to painting, and more in line with the freshness of youth and a child's tiny form) brings forth different problems to those posed by the individual adult. And yet, if the structure and proportions characteristic of each growing stage of the child's head are correctly understood and represented, the work is not impossibly difficult. When drawing children's faces, try to feel empathy for them and rely on the study of superficial shapes, rather than being dominated by the strict rules of 'structure' or by anatomical data, and avoid being drawn in and satisfied by the pleasure of a technical, analytical work to the point where you lose the aesthetic effect of spontaneous simplicity. Children's heads are such delicate forms that if an attempt is made to copy the more subtle and blended tones of *chiaroscuro* too accurately, the final result may be one of volumetric weakness.

In addition to being enjoyable, drawing children's faces can also become a rewarding source of income: many parents, grandparents and relatives still want and commission a portrait of their children to place alongside the several photographs (now stored on their laptop) so that they have a better, more affectionate and spontaneous souvenir of a moment during such a magical age.

'Who shows a child just as they are? Who sets it in its constellation and gives the measure of distance into its hand?'

Rainer Maria Rilke

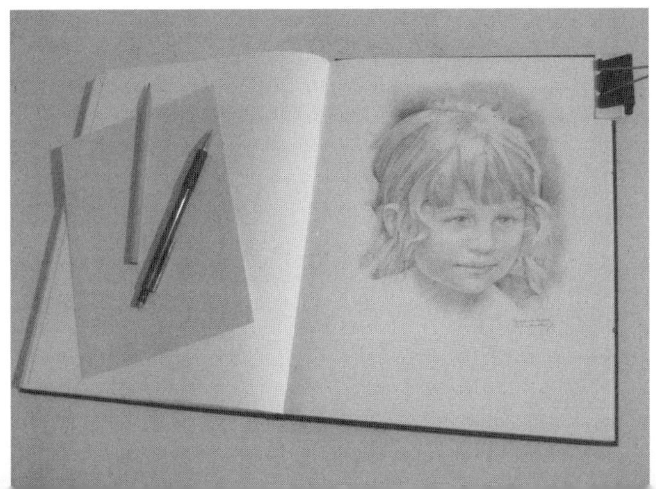

PRACTICAL CONSIDERATIONS

EQUIPMENT, SUPPORTS AND TECHNIQUES

The most common, simple traditional drawing techniques such as graphite, charcoal and coloured pencils are essential resources for drawing quick sketches from life, but are also suited to more elaborate drawings. If the small model stays still, on the other hand, or if drawn from a photograph, other techniques can be used, including painting techniques (pastels, watercolours, acrylic, oils and so on) that can explore the chromatic aspect of the model.

Children's portraits should be smaller than the natural size (about one-half to two-thirds) otherwise there is a risk of achieving an unpleasant effect of ageing the subject. Therefore, if only the head is drawn, the dimensions of the support must be about 40 × 50cm or 50 × 60cm (15¾ × 19¾in or 19¾ × 23½in).

In almost all cases, the aesthetic result of freshness so characteristic of a child's face is better if the additional elements surrounding the subject are omitted, leaving a predominantly neutral background, with a head only, with a slight hint of the neck, shoulders and clothes.

WHERE TO FIND SUBJECTS

Children are everywhere: it is easier to observe and gain the participation of children belonging to the artist's family, but also those of friends and acquaintances. Places where children gather (nurseries, primary schools, parks and gardens, beaches, etc.) are ideal for studying children's actions and their most typical, spontaneous expressions. However, in all cases (even if it is a portrait requested by the parents), it is necessary to strictly respect the need for privacy: before entering or stopping in gathering places, you must explain your purpose of action to the persons responsible for the security of the area, and ask their permission and help. Above all, do not directly approach the children that have attracted your artistic attention. In addition to common rules of clear conduct, there are cultural traditions and laws in many countries to protect young subjects and their image. There are customs and regulations that must be known, read and strictly adhered to.

Scientific or educational documentaries, television shows, newspapers or magazines (in particular the ones that include advertising images and concern themselves with health, wellness or fashion and so on) offer a large number of photographs of babies and young children. It would also be possible to take images of this type from the Internet, but as this is an extremely delicate subject, it is prudent and preferable to avoid this type of search. Drawings can only be made from published photographs for personal, private artistic practice and not for commercial use, as these sources are almost always subject to copyright.

HOW TO BEHAVE WITH CHILDREN (WHEN DRAWING OR PHOTOGRAPHING THEM)

Children are extremely sensitive and unpredictable. It is necessary to be empathic, spontaneous and loving with them. It is also helpful to have some idea about the typical behaviour of these early stages of development (favourite games and exploring the environment; expressions of desires, needs, feelings, tantrums and responses to stimuli; independence or reactions to strangers, etc.).

Formal portraits of children, such as ones done in the artist's studio and while posing in a conventional approach, were traditional in the past. They are now less frequent as more spontaneous poses are preferred in normal situations. Experience of live art work with young children can provide you with a few tips to adopt to reduce a child's lively movements. For example, plan for a member of the family to be present (parents, older brother or sister); place the children in an environment known to them, while they are busy with an activity or game; respect the children's characters and attention span, not letting them grow bored or disturbed by external stimulus (such as excessive lighting, noise or pets); plan short, discreet drawing sittings, while working at a distance and always maintaining the same level of sight. Children busy watching television often position their bodies in interesting and unusual ways, while their faces lose the expressions suited for a good drawing or portrait.

LIGHTING AND *CHIAROSCURO*

The delicacy of the forms of a baby's face requires lighting to be diffused, simple and not too intense, and from an almost frontal or slightly oblique position. Natural light is better than artificial light, which must however be quite soft, as babies tend to squint and pull funny faces in reaction to the sun.

The shadows on their faces should not be too dark or large: the points where the shadows are denser are usually the corners of the lips or nostrils, but without the intensity of the darkness in the pupils or even irises.

Sometimes a rear or side source of lighting produces a good effect if it is additional and associated with the main front lighting: it is an expressive trick used in photography, and an aesthetic element applied to formal portraits, even for very young children, as long as the multiple light sources do not interfere with each other or cancel out the natural volume of the form.

MANNER AND EXPRESSIONS

Although they are an attractive artistic subject, small children are not easy models as they never stay still for the necessary time to draw them and they cannot be asked to pose. Extemporary sketches give good results, however, due to their immediacy and ability to capture the essence of the subject: for this reason, they should never be corrected or 'completed' afterwards. The task is perhaps easier with babies: using the times between their frequent feeding, when they are resting or asleep, it is possible to draw them relatively calmly.

A baby's gaze is attractive if directed at the observer, but usually attitudes, expressions or spontaneous, random glimpses that only photographs can capture and fully describe are more appealing, adding to the memory of having seen it directly.

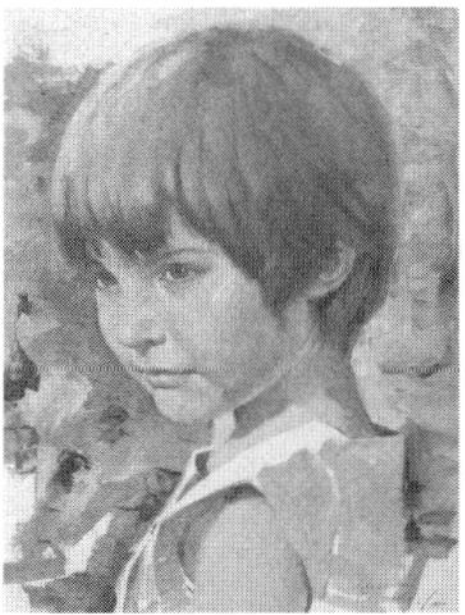

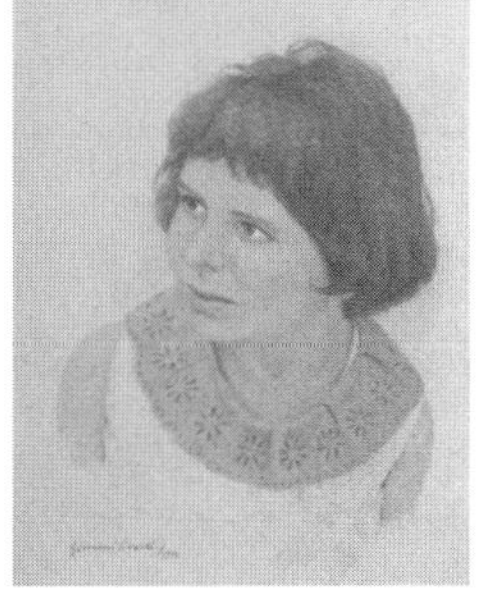

WHAT TO OBSERVE AND HOW TO OBSERVE IT

In the first two years of life (and, above all, in babies), it is very difficult to distinguish a boy from a girl by looking at the face only. Some hints of the typical different characteristics can be seen in the face regarding for example the height or width of the cheekbones and nose.

When portraying children, the artist must consider the structure, the shape of the head and the proportions of the face, rather than the actual anatomic structure that underlies these elements: the skull is always essential for defining the almost spherical shape of the whole head and the limits of the face, but the muscles are still soft and deep and hidden by fat pads, so that they do not in any way influence the surface. All in all, when drawing children's faces, it is better to be guided by human, aesthetic sensitivity than by rigid structure and anatomical directions.

When drawing, it is important to suggest the actual and apparent age of the child. Precise ratios of proportion between the main elements of the face like eyes, nose and chin, their correct position and the delicate play of light and shade, avoiding shadows and colours that are too intense, features that are too lively, tonal planes that are too clearly articulated, will help to achieve this.

The sequence for observing the model is reflected in the sequence of executive phases of the drawing, inspired by the face (see pages 218–223): 1) evaluate the overall shape and main proportions; 2) trace the vertical median line and the horizontal line (which indicates the level of the orbital arches: all the other facial elements are located below this line); 3) divide the face (the lower-half of the overall shape of the head) into four sections using equidistant horizontal lines of equal height, indicating the level on which our facial features are located (eyes, nostrils, lips, chin); 4) place the ear; 5) evaluate the volumetric structure and the tonal shades that reveal it; 6) create the light and shade, with slightly graduated tones – when tracing shadows and shaping forms (using a pencil, pen or brush) it is sometimes advisable to follow the curves of the forms, as well as suggest their volume with delicate, blended tones.

ANATOMICAL NOTIONS AND PROPORTIONS

In a baby, the skull bones have some spaces between them that have not yet ossified, the fontanelles. These are spaces where the cranial sutures join, and are filled by cartilage. There are six main fontanelles: two medial, anterior and posterior; two anterior lateral and two posterior lateral. The skull is fairly plastic at birth and any deformations resulting from labour are reversible in a short space of time.

The full development of the skull is evidenced by the continuous changes in ratio between the volume and the height of the two parts as a person grows; for example, at birth, the ratio between the face and the braincase is about 1:8; at five years of age, 1:5; as an adult, 1:2. The disproportion is due to the greater, faster growth of the neurocranium after birth: approaching six years of age, it is almost 90% of the size of that of an adult. Meanwhile, the cranium becomes more regularly curved, as the parietal prominences that are so accentuated in early infancy become much less pronounced. The facial skeleton remains small in proportion, however, as it is related to the development of oral and nasal cavities, the tongue, and the appearance of teeth. A baby's jawbone is very small and delicate, comprising two separate halves that join together during the first year of life.

In children the face seems to be set back in relation to the front part of the braincase, but during puberty it is gradually pushed outwards by the development of the sensory organs contained within it, of the cranial base and the jaw. In the last years of childhood (about eleven to twelve years of age), the face develops more rapidly than the neurocranium, until it achieves the physical appearance of adulthood.

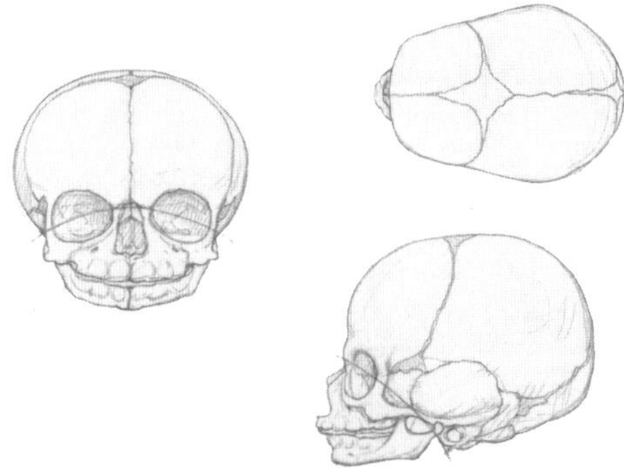

An infant's skull in a frontal, lateral and overhead projection. The curved line shows the conventional border between the facial skeleton and the braincase and highlights the difference in proportion, height and volume.

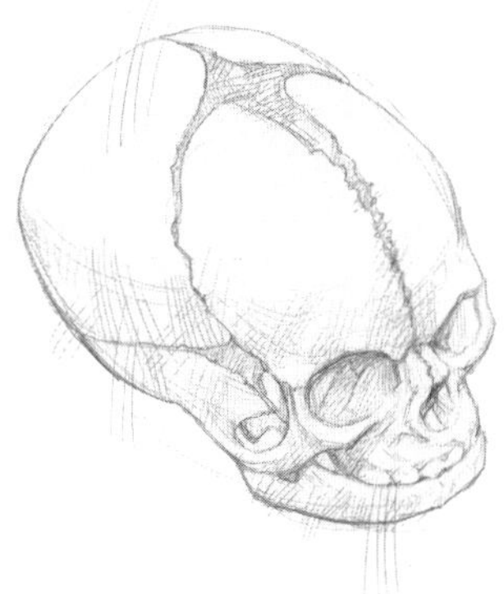

Oblique projection of a baby's skull. The clearest, largest fontanelle is the anterior medial one (bregmatic), which can be felt in the early months of a baby's life, underneath the skin.

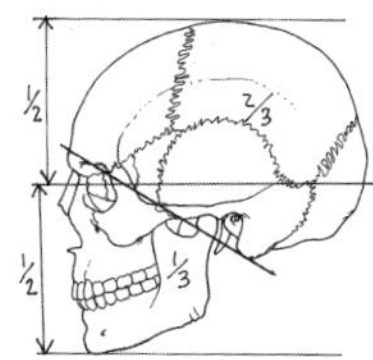

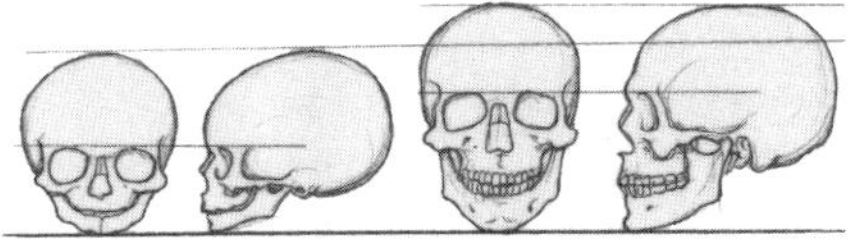

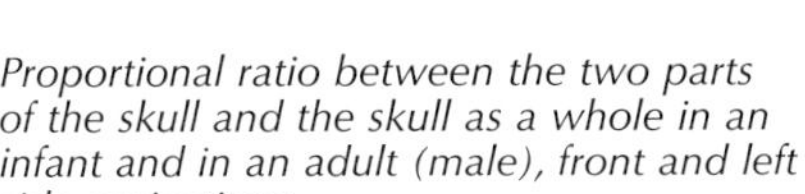

Proportional ratio between the two parts of the skull and the skull as a whole in an infant and in an adult (male), front and left side projections.

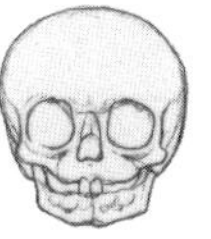

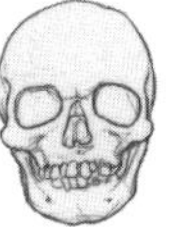

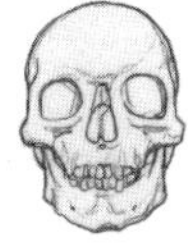

Conformation of the skull at various ages: nine months; nine to ten years; adult.

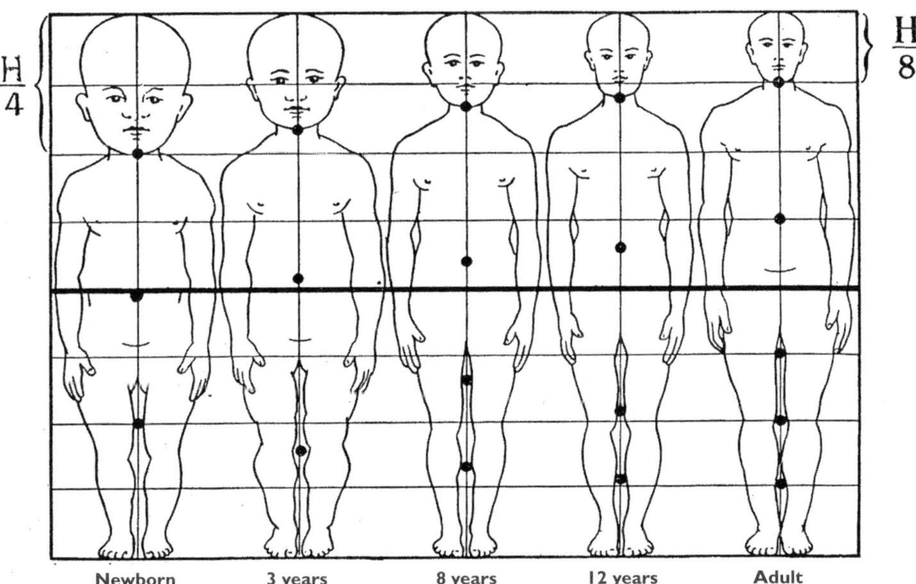

Diagram by H. Stratz showing the development and proportions of the body and head during various stages of growth. At birth, the height of the head corresponds to one quarter of the length of the entire body, while in an adult, it is about one-eighth of the height. The proportions of a baby's body change rapidly, with phases of varying intensity, up to the beginning of adolescence (about fifteen to seventeen years of age), and then occur more slowly, confirming some differences between males and females.

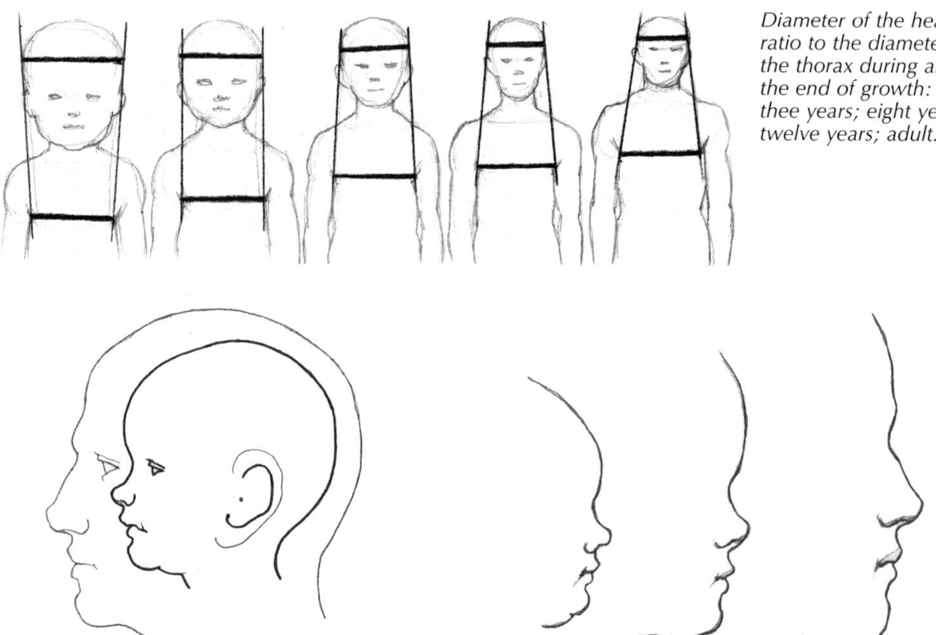

Diameter of the head in ratio to the diameter of the thorax during and at the end of growth: baby; thee years; eight years; twelve years; adult.

Comparison between the head's profile and volume in a young child (about two years old) and in an adult.

Line of the facial profile at different ages: early months; six years; twenty years.

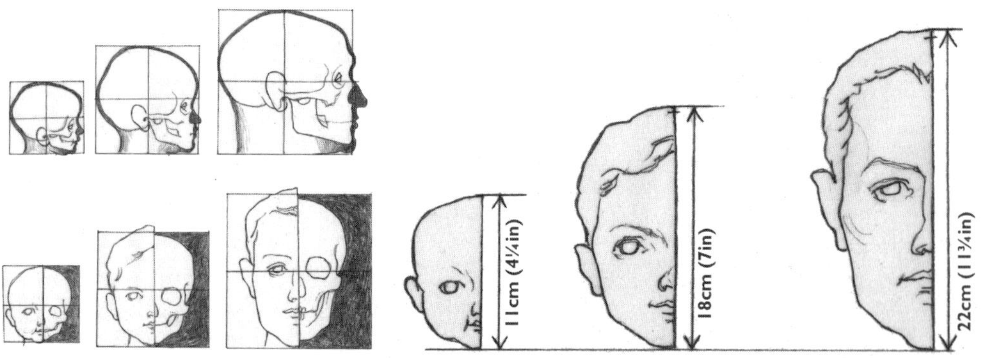

Infant; six years; adult. Ratios of proportion and thickness between the bone structure and the external forms (provided by 'soft tissue'). In an infant, the maximum length (frontal-occipital) of the head is about 11cm (4¼in). The maximum width (biparietal diameter) is about 9cm (3½in).

Average height of the head at different ages: infant; six years; adult.

PROPORTIONS

A child's face is not a miniature version of an adult's: the proportions and characteristics are typical and very different. When drawing a child's face (especially at an early age and up to adolescence), it is necessary to consider the elements, shapes and their ratios, both common and fundamental. Some of these can be demonstrated by drawing the head (from the front and from the side) within a square frame: the eyes and ears are located below or just inside the horizontal median line that divides the height of the head into two halves: the face is smaller than the head; the nape of the neck juts out and the neck is small, slim and short; the outer ear seems larger than the other facial features; the bridge of the nose is concave while the tip points upwards; eyelashes are long while eyebrows are thin and sparse; the upper lip sticks out more than the lower lip; the chin is small and not a sharp shape; cheeks are full and rounded; and the iris is almost the same diameter as an adult's and is fully exposed, seeming large compared to the space between the upper and lower eyelids (the palpebral fissure). The following diagrams by A. Loomis show the average proportions of the head, from the front and in profile, that can be found in the early years.

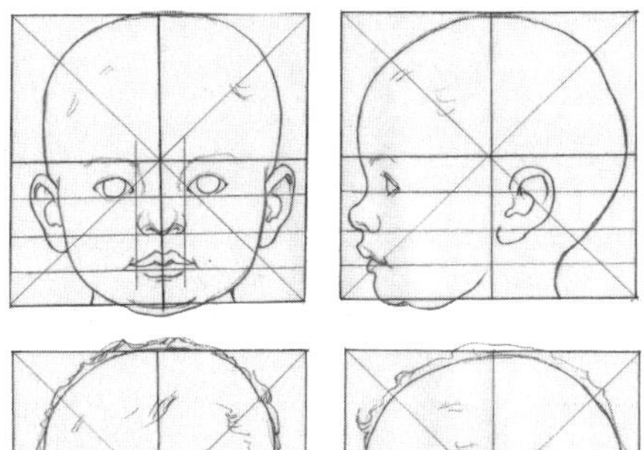

At approx. **one year**: *the eyes and ears are below the horizontal median line; the jaw is short, low and rounded with a wide angle; the forehead is convex and jutting; the bridge of the nose is concave; the chin is small and cheeks are chubby; eyebrows are very thin, hair is fine and sparse; the nape of the neck is prominent and the neck is thin and short; the eyes appear large and wide apart.*

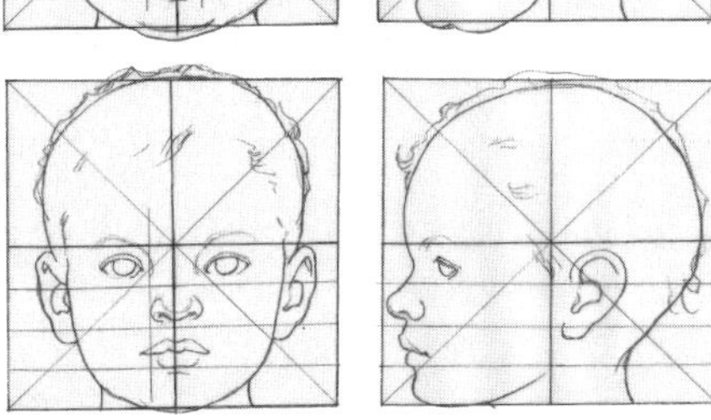

At approx. **two to three years**: *the level of the eyes and ears rises a little towards the horizontal axis, but never reaches it, indicating a change in ratio between the volumes of the face and the neurocranium; the forehead is convex but less prominent; the upper and lower jawbones grow in size and length to make room for deciduous teeth; the nose is less concave; the upper lip juts out less and the chin is more defined; the hair is thicker and more abundant.*

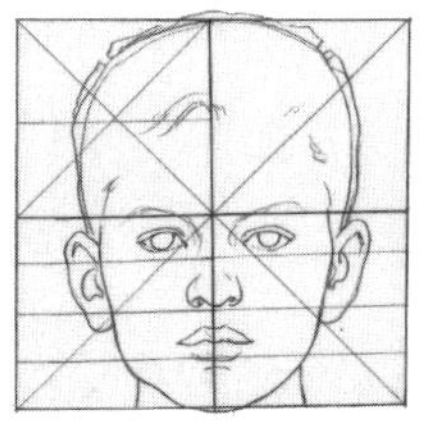

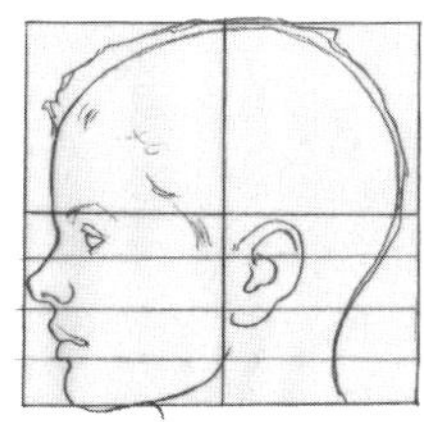

At approx. **six to seven years**: *in the early years of life, it is rather difficult to distinguish the distinctive traits between males and females from only the face. Even the bone structure only has some aspects of dimorphism that then develop in adults, such as the angle of the jawbone and the shape and thickness of the orbital areas. The differentiation in facial features and proportions mainly occurs during puberty, but around six or seven years of age, some characteristics common to both sexes can still be seen.*

MORPHOLOGY OF A CHILD

Drawing eyes, nose, lips, etc. in their exact position and in profile with the chin and forehead is much more important than a mere attention to detail in order to effectively render the child's likeness and age. Growing up, our faces become longer and are more similar to those of an adult, changing the proportions that are typical of all children in the early stages of growth.

Sometimes it may be wise to emphasize the forms of the face a little (but not the ratios, and without tending towards a caricature) in order to characterize age or expression in a better way. The jaw and chin are not developed much and the lower part of the face is therefore very short, creating a strong contrast with the width of the forehead, the fullness of the cheeks, the jutting out lips and the thin neck.

A child's skin is very thin and smooth, with a light covering of hair. A child's skin at birth will be paler than it will become in adulthood. Varying degrees of pigmentation gradually appear in the early months of life; many white-skinned children (Caucasoid), in particular those with blonde or red hair, often have small, slightly darker marks on their skin (freckles), which must be portrayed in the drawing with due caution and only very lightly.

Ratio between bone structure and external shape of the head (at approx. one year of age)

The soft tissues, such as the muscles, subcutaneous layers and skin, form the layer (of varying thickness, depending on the regions) that covers the entire skull and provides the external shape to the head, giving the individual's physiognomic traits of the face. In a small child the layer is extremely thin over most of the head, due to the small size of the masticatory and mimicry muscles, but the layer is rather thick over the cheeks, owing to the presence of well-developed fat deposits called buccal fat pads. Sometimes, surface veins can be seen through extremely fine skin especially on the forehead and temples.

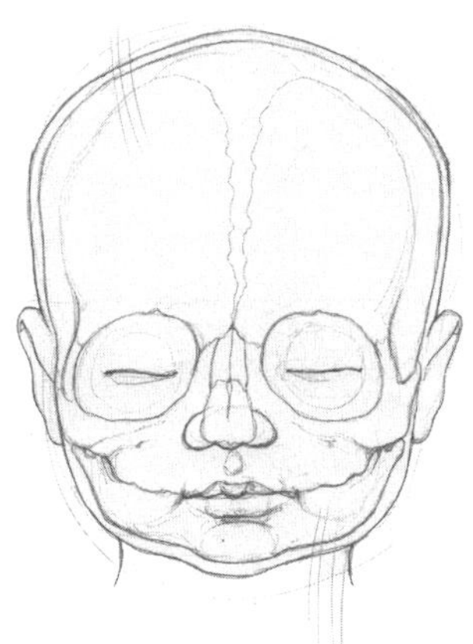

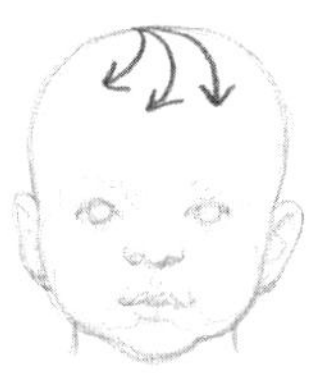

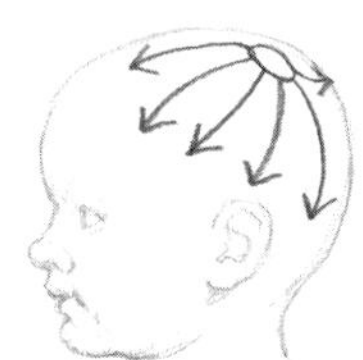

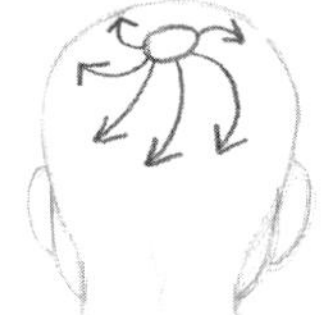

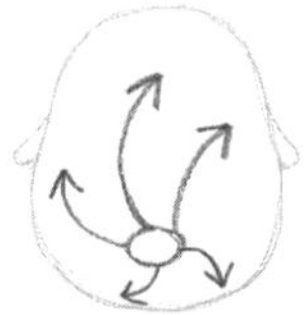

Direction of hair growth

At birth, hair can be sparse or thick, very fair or dark, but quite fine, soft and smooth. In later months, hair becomes stronger, thicker, longer and with a more defined colour. It grows from a central vortex placed at the top of the skull and extends in several directions, as shown in the diagram, usually from left to right. The hairline, so characteristic in adulthood, only develops gradually as a child on the forehead and temples.

Hair is a very important physical feature when sketching children's faces and expressions. Sometimes their hair is tidy, styled and cut according to what current fashion dictates, or tied in plaits or ponytails, but it can often also be dishevelled by the wind and ruffled by play.

The shape of hair can vary from smooth to wavy to frizzy. Natural colour also varies, from very fair (blonde) to very dark (black) or of an intermediate colour (such as chestnut brown or reddish). For each colour, lighting causes areas of shadow and reflections in the hair. When drawing a child's hair it is necessary to consider how soft it is, whether it is thick or fine, wavy, straight or curly, and its overall volume, which is subject to the effect of lighting. Hair must not be drawn as individual strands using a number of lines, but drawn to represent the main mass of hair: a few odd, thin lines are enough to hint at lighter sections, or the way it is arranged and in which direction. After identifying the 'local tone', that is, the predominant colour of the child's hair, draw in the darkest areas first, adding then the mid-tone areas, and finally the lighter, reflected areas. Of course, it would be possible to sketch this sequence in reverse, but the result would be less effective. Building tones in order of intensity is enough to suggest the lighter or darker colours present in a child's hair.

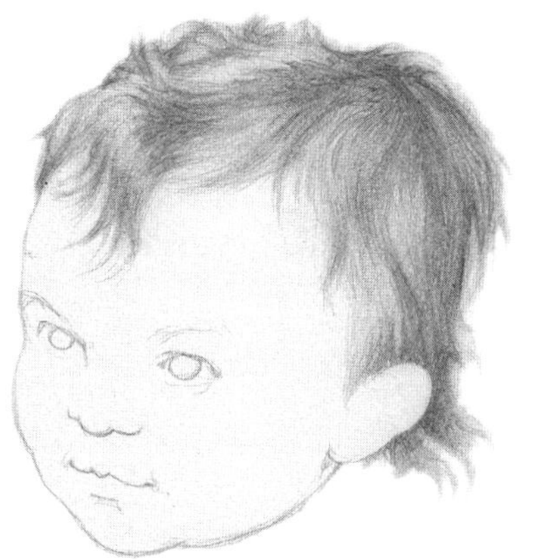

Light-coloured hair

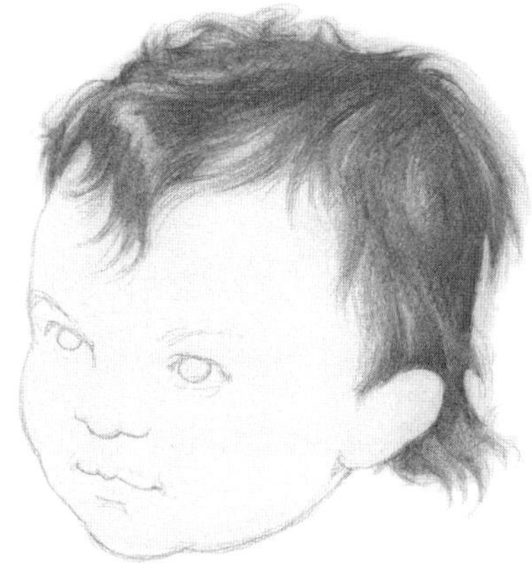

Dark-coloured hair

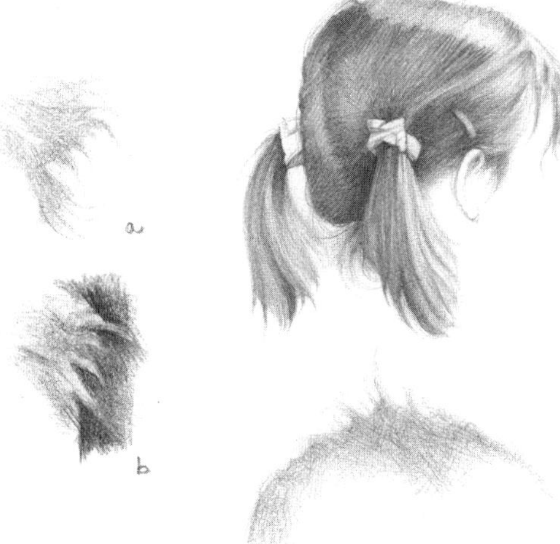

Parents of very young children (but only while they remain young…) enjoy choosing fun, unusual hairstyles for them, which are sometimes traditional or extremely ingenious. One useful trick to suggest softness is to provide contrast to the outline of the hair by making it less defined in a some areas, with a few stray hairs standing out against a dark background (b) or vice versa (a).

FACIAL FEATURES

THE OUTER EAR

In children, the outer ear is very similar in aspect to that of an adult (see pages 50–51) but is more rounded, with an axis slightly tilted backwards and jutting out to varying degrees. Especially in the early months of life, the ear appears larger than other elements of the face and in relation to the head itself. In accordance with the smaller scale of the skull, the ear is in a lower position on the skull, corresponding to the outer ear canal on the temporal bone, next to the mandible joint.

Drawing the outer ear must be accurate but not detailed excessively, as it is a feature of lesser importance when compared with the eyes and lips – two characteristics to which one should give the most attention.

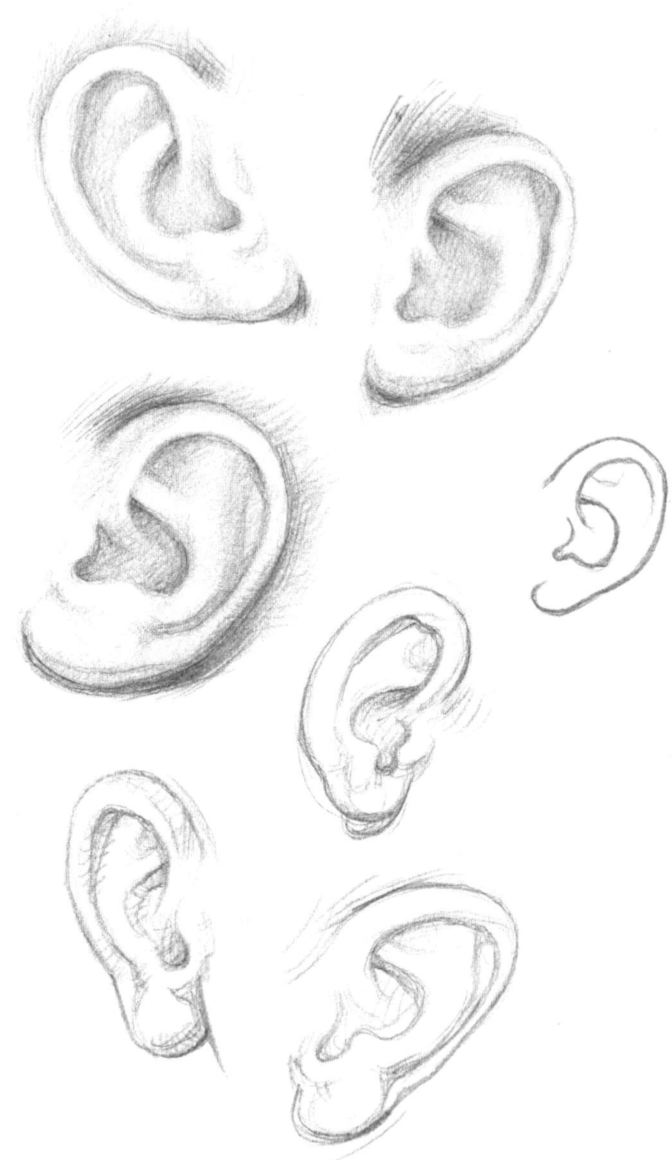

THE NOSE

In very small children, the nasal bones and cartilage are not yet developed: the bridge is not sharp and is close to the plane of the face; the nose is concave and the tip aimed upwards, making it seem short. The concave bridge is accentuated by the convexity of the forehead, which has a very characteristic form in early years, in both genders and various ethnicities. During childhood and adolescence, as a result of the growth of the facial skeleton, the nose becomes longer, more defined at the bridge and wider at the nostrils. When drawing the nose (in a face of any age, but especially in children), it is advisable not to place too much emphasis on light and shade: it is sufficient to indicate its position exactly, together with volume and delicately suggest (i.e. without clear lines or intense shading) the rounded, soft forms of the tip and nostrils.

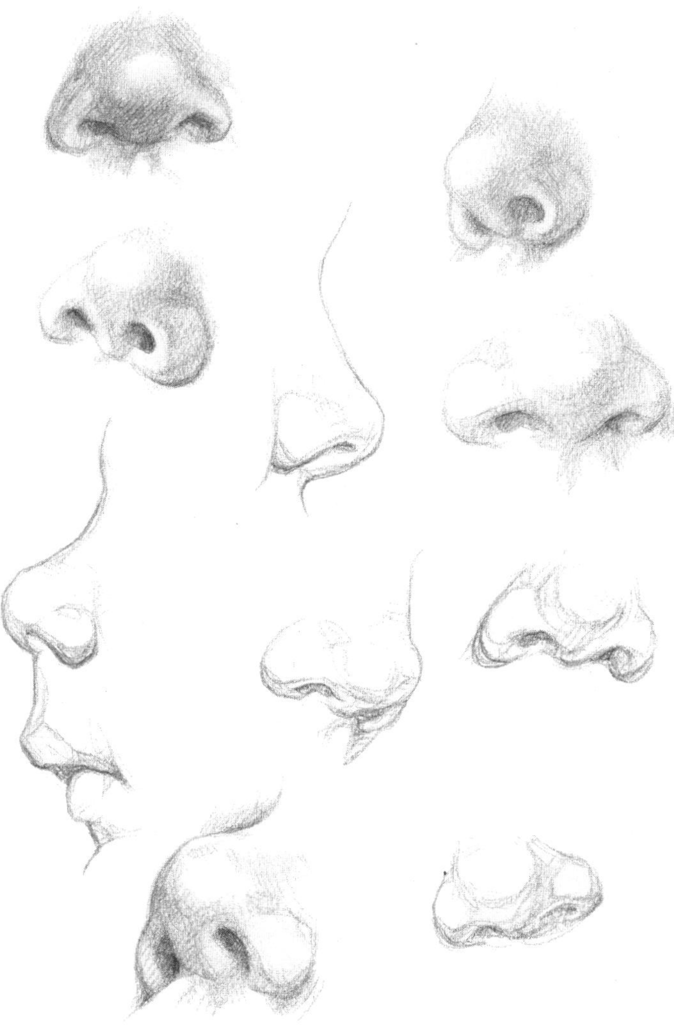

THE EYES

At birth, the eyeball is not yet at full size but, in ratio, the iris and cornea already have a diameter that is close to that of an adult. (approx. 12–13mm (½in). This makes a child's eyes look very large and noticeable, an effect accentuated even more so because the iris is emphasized by the small palpebral fissure and the reduced size of the face. When a child's eyes are fully open, the upper eyelid is barely visible, while the inner joining of the lids contain the small pink formation called the caruncle. At birth, irises are almost always a pale colour (blue-grey or blue) as they do not contain the final pigment. In the early months, the sclerotic coat (the white part of the eye that can only be seen in small parts at the side of the iris) is greyish in colour, influenced by the dark tone of the underlying retina. A newborn baby's eyes protrude a little compared to the orbital plane and are further apart than they will be at a later date. The exact position of the eyes in a drawing of a child's face is very important, as the level of proportion (see page 211) is characteristic: varying in relation to the different phases of growth, it alone clearly indicates the child's or adolescent's age. The eyelids are thin, fringed with long lashes. Eyebrows are sparse and thin, especially in the early years of life: they gradually become thicker, darker and more arched.

Children of central and east Asian decent also have a characteristic shape of their upper lid that describes an almond-shaped eye. This fold is in the skin and extends from the root of the nose and covers the upper lid and inner corner of the eye. In young children, this fold can sometimes be accentuated as a vertical flap (epicanthic fold) that covers the medial angle of the eye and the lacrimal caruncle: it is usually a temporary shape, which diminishes in later years.

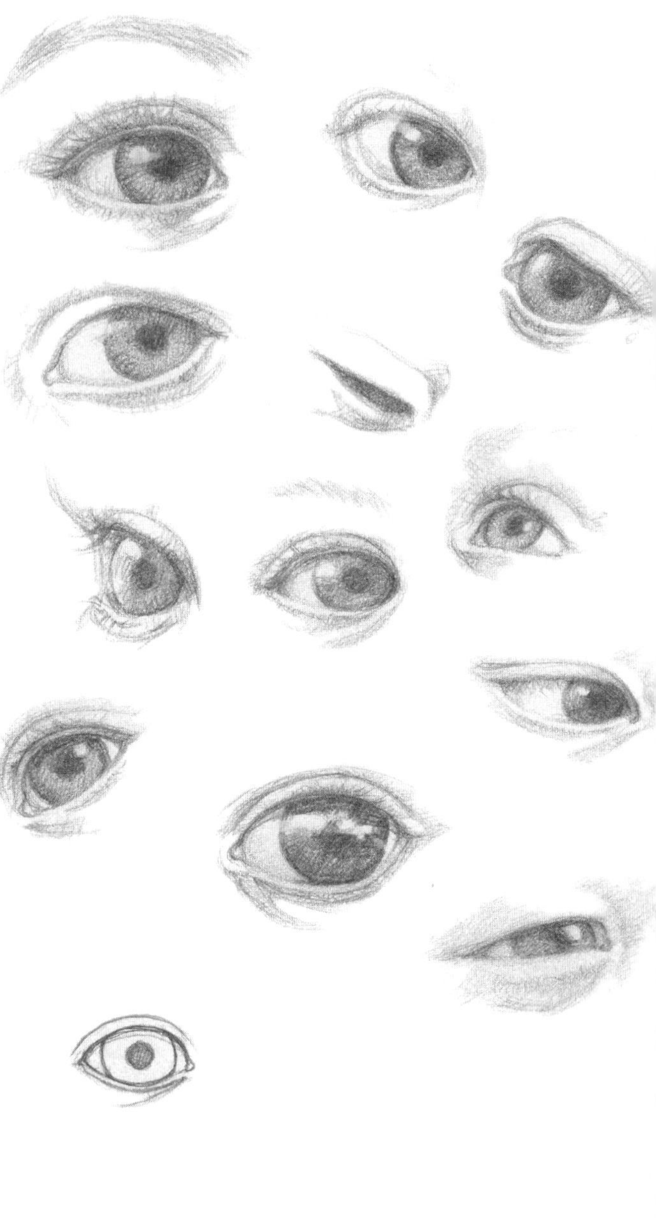

THE LIPS

Lips are extremely flexible and expressive and, depending on a child's age, allow you to see the tongue or teeth – primary or permanent – depending on number and position (for example: towards eight months the two lower central incisors appear; at one year, the four upper incisors appear; at about eighteen months, the other two lower incisors; at around two years, canines and remaining teeth). In very small children, the two lips are especially soft and delicate, and are different in shape to one other: the upper lip is bigger in volume and juts outwards – especially in the centre – more than the lower lip, which is less defined and sometimes only outlined by the shadow formed in the groove below it. As children's cheeks are full and rounded, the corners (junctions) of the mouth are distinct and deep, while the small chin recedes into the face in comparison with the lips. If seen from the front, they have an almost triangular shape, but it is possible to distinguish lines and depressions on each lip, which are much more distinctive on the upper one (there are three parts: a central relief and two flatter parts to the side) and more blurred on the lower one (where there are two weakly convex areas separated by a central, shallow depression). These grooves flatten when spread into a smile, or are accentuated when the mouth puckers up when sulking. The infant often keeps his lips open so they are almost always wetted with saliva, and for this reason often seem shiny and reflective.

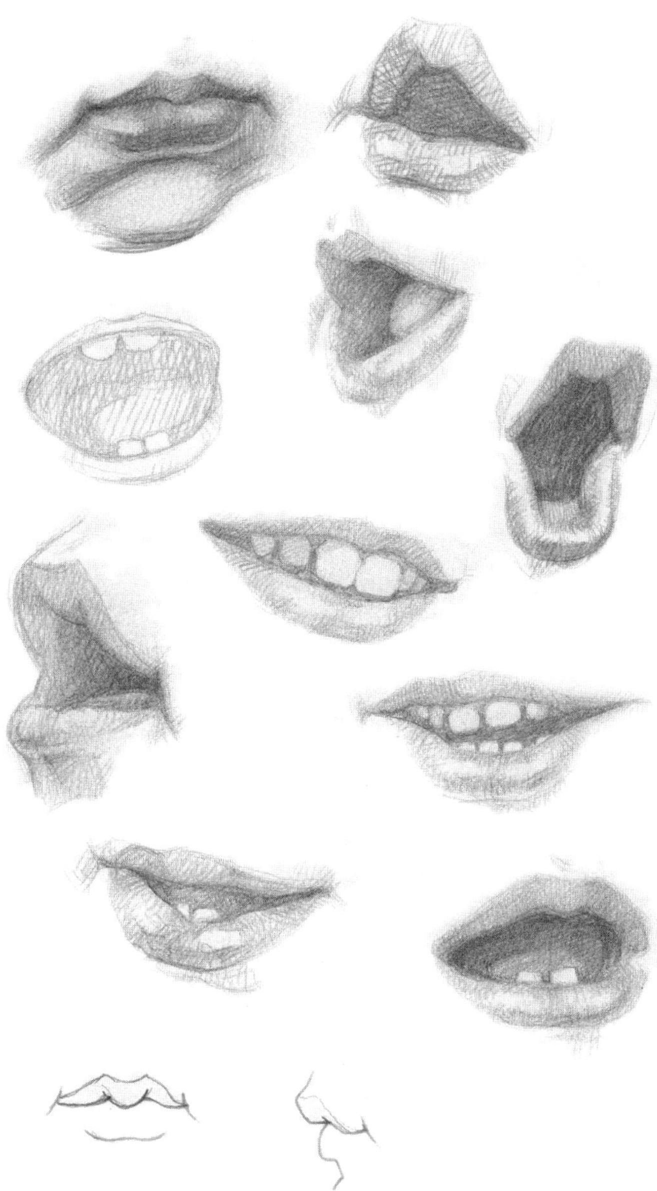

DRAWING METHODS

When drawing children's faces, do not obsess over the details too much: it is much more important and effective to capture the child's attitude and expression, and also facial proportions, form and lighting. These elements alone are sufficient for achieving an authentic and faithful likeness of a 'portrait'.

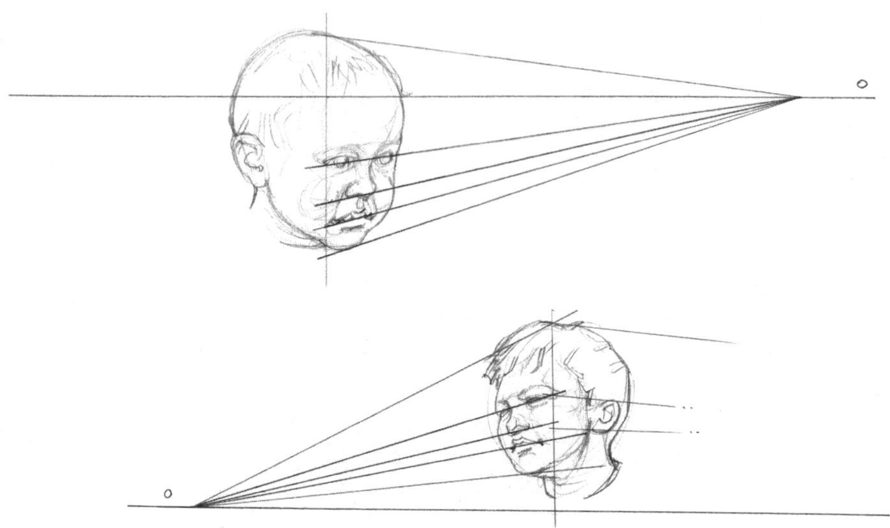

PERSPECTIVE

Perspective is a drawing method used to represent depth and spatial relationships on a two-dimensional surface. Therefore, in order to be correctly portrayed, the head must be drawn so as to take the principles of oblique line perspective into consideration. The head can be imagined as if it were placed in a cube, where the edges will touch the areas of the face that jut out most. In this way, it becomes easier to put the main physical features 'into perspective' with some approximation, helping to gauge the right levels and distance between features, and ensure they are consistent with the curved surface on which they lie. A child's head is very small, but rules of perspective are still applicable – although the result is less visible than that on an adult's head, which is wider, more sharply outlined and with a solid structure.

TRADITIONAL METHODS: GENERIC SEQUENCES TO BE FOLLOWED

There are several ways to proceed in drawing, depending on each artist's preference and needs. At the start, it is wise to experiment and compare in order to decide which technique suits your style and ability.

This page shows the most simple, intuitive and 'academic' method; on the next page are another two line drawings, similar in result, but rather different in the way of conceiving and perceiving the image. For example, **Method A** is deductive, starting from general to detail, and views the head as an overall volume on which details of the face are then introduced; **Method B** (inductive, from detail to general) is based on the choice of a significant physiognomic trait (eye, nose, etc.) from which one then proceeds, determining its ratio between it and other features, and coordinating them so as to gradually build the overall shape.

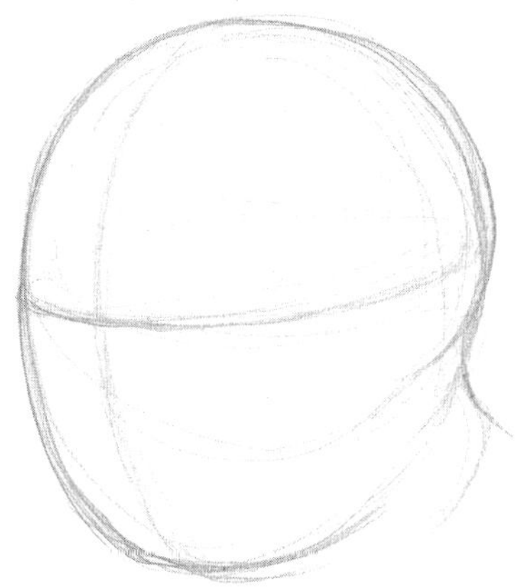

Step 1 *Outline of the overall shape of the head, its chosen dimensions ('bulk'), the level of the eyebrows (curved line) and the median line of the face.*

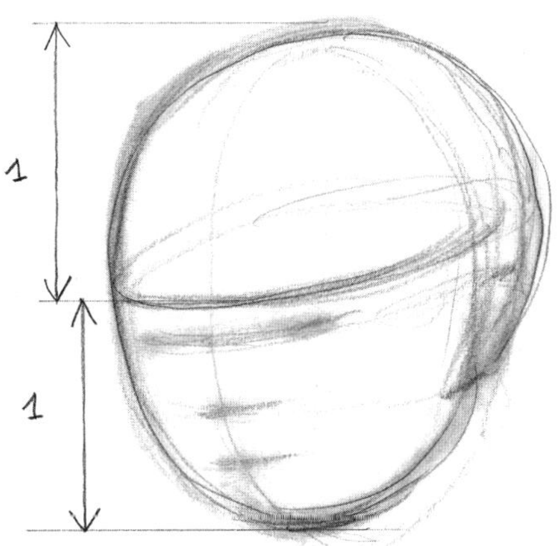

Step 2 *The levels on which the eyes, nose, lips and ears sit are defined.*

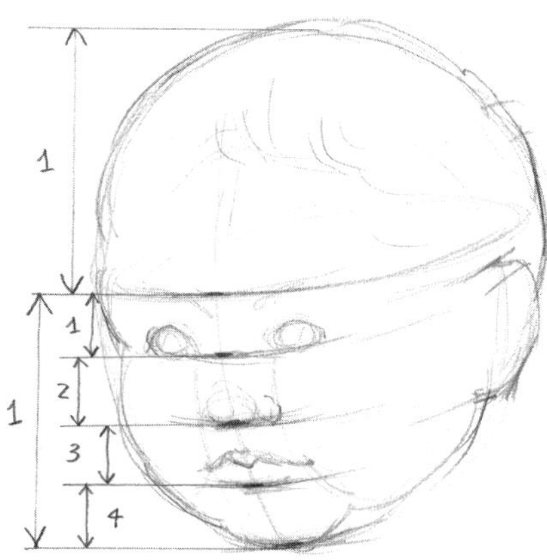

Step 3 *Definition of proportions and distances between the levels of facial elements.*

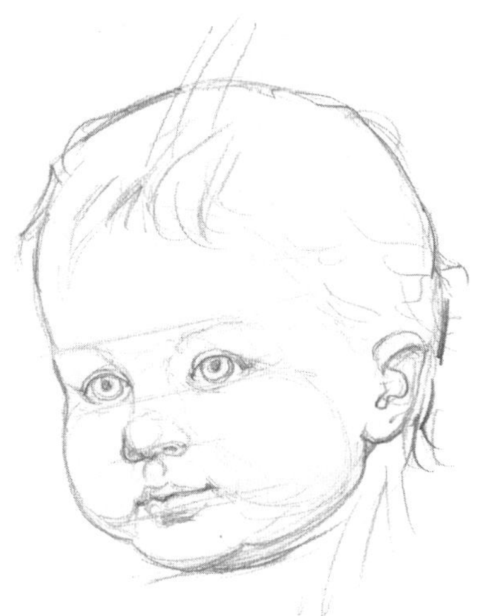

Step 4 *Elaboration of the forms and light and shade.*

METHOD A (DESCRIBED ON THE PREVIOUS PAGE)

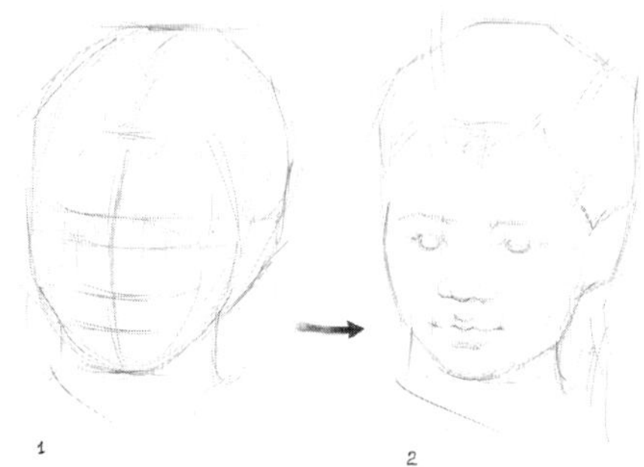

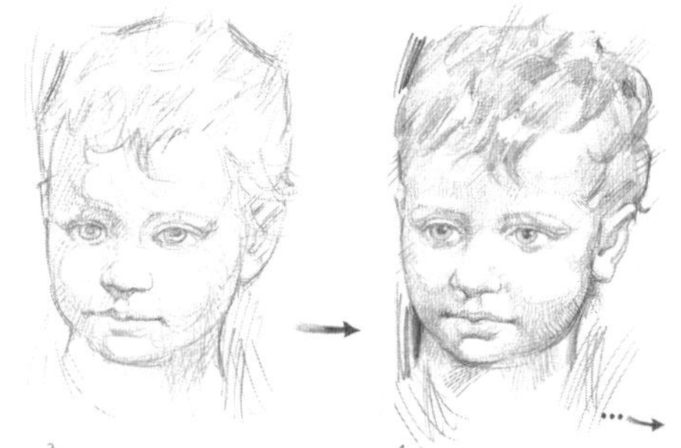

Step 1 *Outline of the overall shape of the head, its chosen dimensions ('bulk'), the level of the eyebrows (curved line) and the median line of the face.*

Step 2 *Sketch of the overall shape of the head and details of the hairline, eyebrows, eyes, nose and mouth.*

Step 3 *Shapes and elements of the face defined through simple line drawing.*

Step 4 *Elaboration of the tones.*

METHOD B (DESCRIBED ON THE PREVIOUS PAGE)

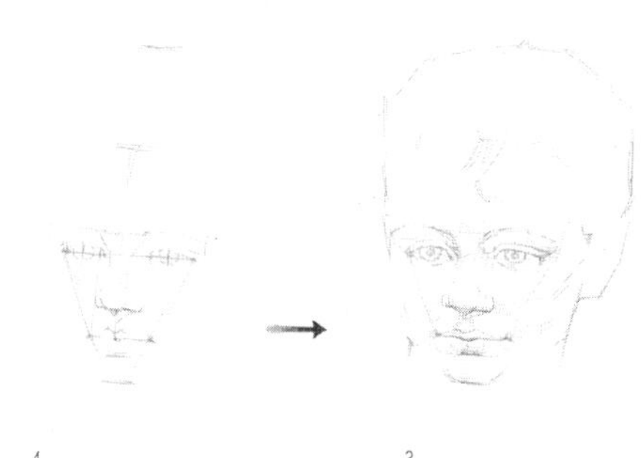

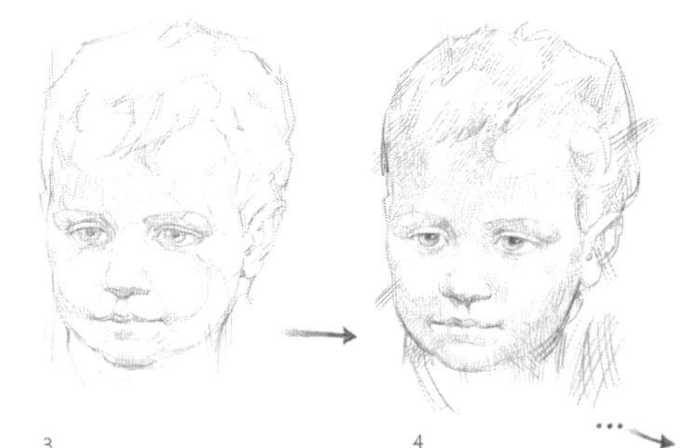

Step 1 *Choice of a facial feature and structure of the facial triangle (eyes, nose, lips).*

Step 2 *Evaluation of ratios between chosen feature and contiguous elements.*

Step 3 *Definition of the whole head through simple lines.*

Step 4 *Elaboration of the forms and tones.*

Another, more 'painterly' way of drawing places less emphasis on the linear style (at least on a conceptual level) and favours the 'tonal' one: more importance is given to the light and shade appearing on the head – known as 'mass drawing' – than to its structural lines. From the early stages of drawing, tone and lighting – or *chiaroscuro* – take precedence over the outlines of the face, and the volume of the whole head, or of each physiognomic trait, emerges from the contrast and accordance of tones. Using suitable tools (charcoal, ink wash, soft graphite, etc.) you can experiment with this method as you practise the more linear style (following both a deductive and an inductive path), as the correctness of proportions and the right positioning of features are essential in any method adopted, especially when drawing very young children.

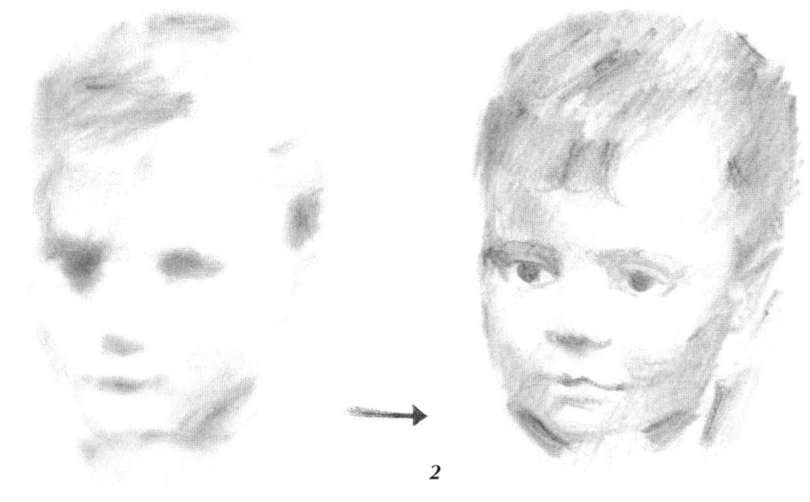

1

2

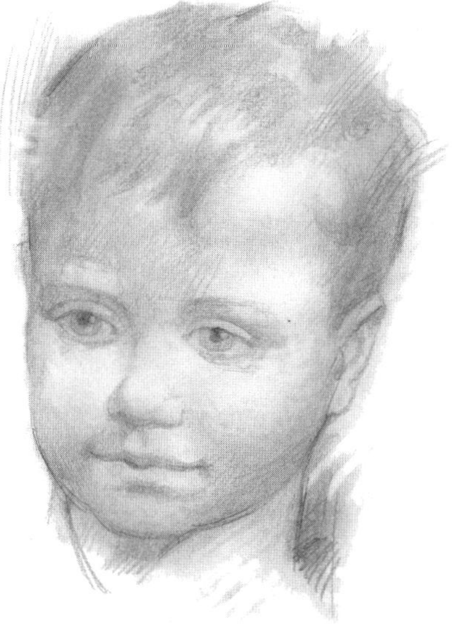

3

Step 1 *Indication of the darker tonal areas, enough to suggest the position and size of the physiognomic traits and the volume of the head.*

Step 2 *Definition of the initial tones and introduction of intermediate tones (the white of the paper represents the tone of the most highlighted areas).*

Step 3 *Elaboration of tonal values and introduction of small details, accents of shade and light, and so on.*

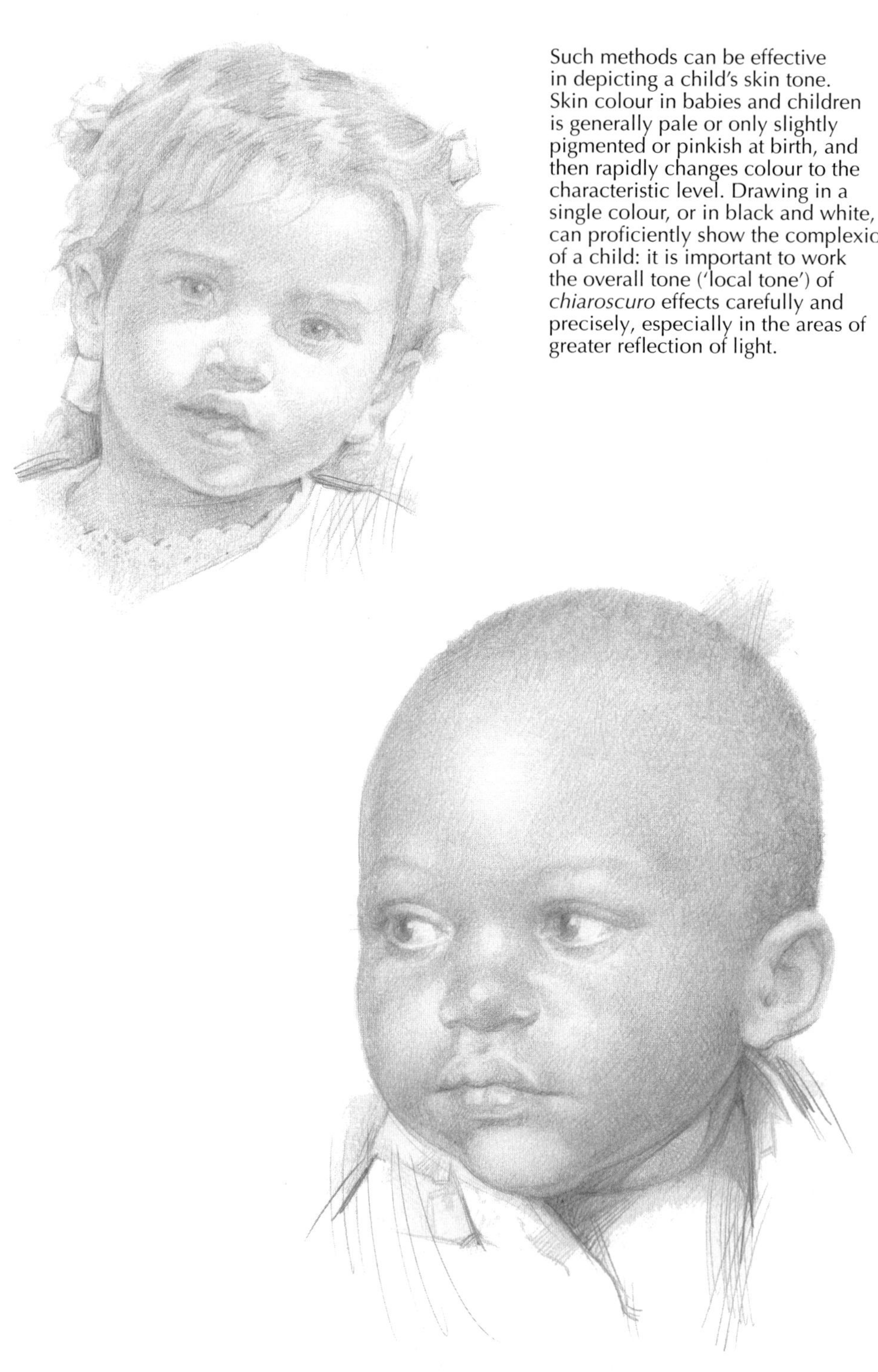

Such methods can be effective in depicting a child's skin tone. Skin colour in babies and children is generally pale or only slightly pigmented or pinkish at birth, and then rapidly changes colour to the characteristic level. Drawing in a single colour, or in black and white, can proficiently show the complexion of a child: it is important to work the overall tone ('local tone') of *chiaroscuro* effects carefully and precisely, especially in the areas of greater reflection of light.

Little ones are fascinating to observe and sketch. It is not always easy to portray children in a busy environment, however, either through drawing or photography: it is often wise to just observe them from a distance, attempt a few quick sketches and capture a few aspects of their features and expressions.

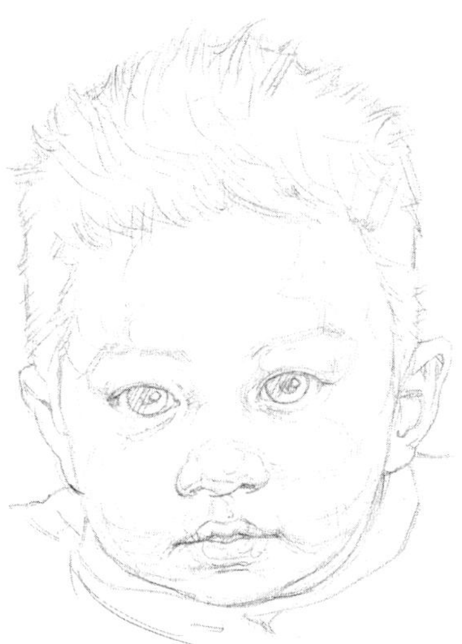

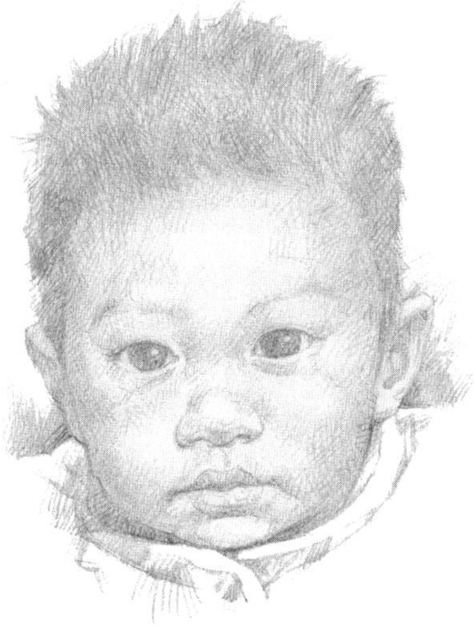

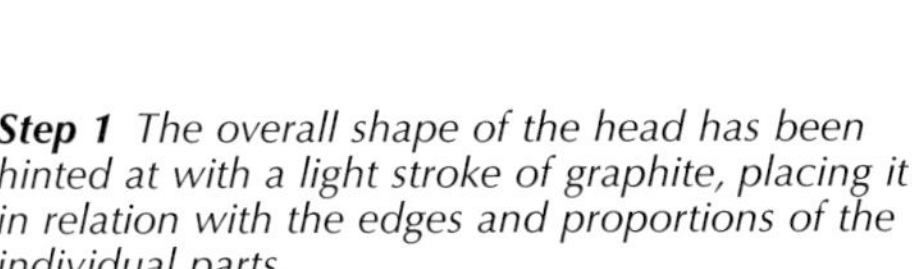

Step 1 *The overall shape of the head has been hinted at with a light stroke of graphite, placing it in relation with the edges and proportions of the individual parts.*

Step 2 *Gradual modulation of light and shade, beginning with the light tones and then proceeding with the more intense shade and accents on the darker tones.*

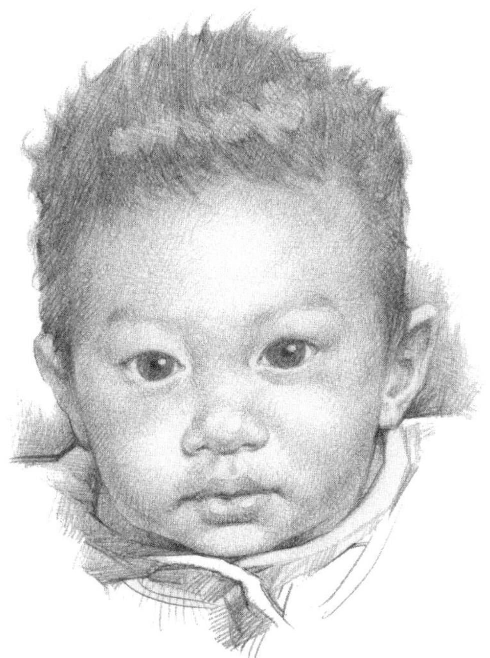

DRAWING TECHNIQUES

The faces of babies and young children have delicate, rounded features that blend into each other harmoniously. It is therefore an important decision to use a graphic technique and expressive style to portray them that is suited to rendering these characteristics effectively. The baby's delicate forms tempt one towards an accurate, softly blended drawing, but this is a tendency that should be controlled carefully, to avoid a sentimental portrayal. Although it may be difficult to capture the articulation of tonal 'planes' on a baby's face, and it is advisable to reduce the intensity and size of shades, it is wise however to adopt a style that combines a mixture of forms with a moderate vigour in drawing. Some of the most commonly used drawing techniques in childhood portraiture are mentioned in this section (up to page 227): a comparison between the characteristics peculiar to each of them and an examination of the relative results of expression will help you to choose the one most in keeping with your temperament and style, and to the features of the small model.

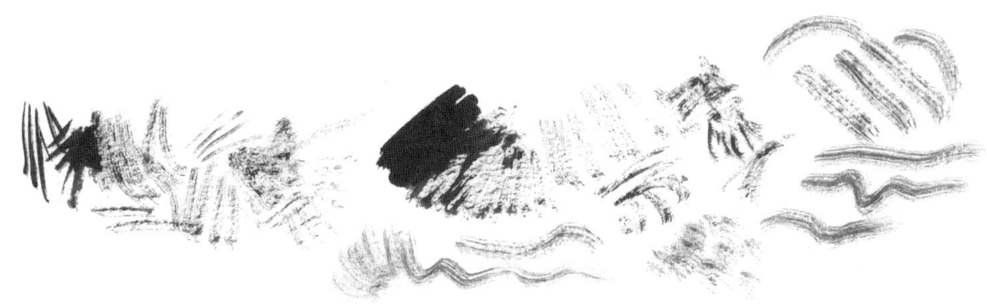

DRY BRUSH

See page 13.

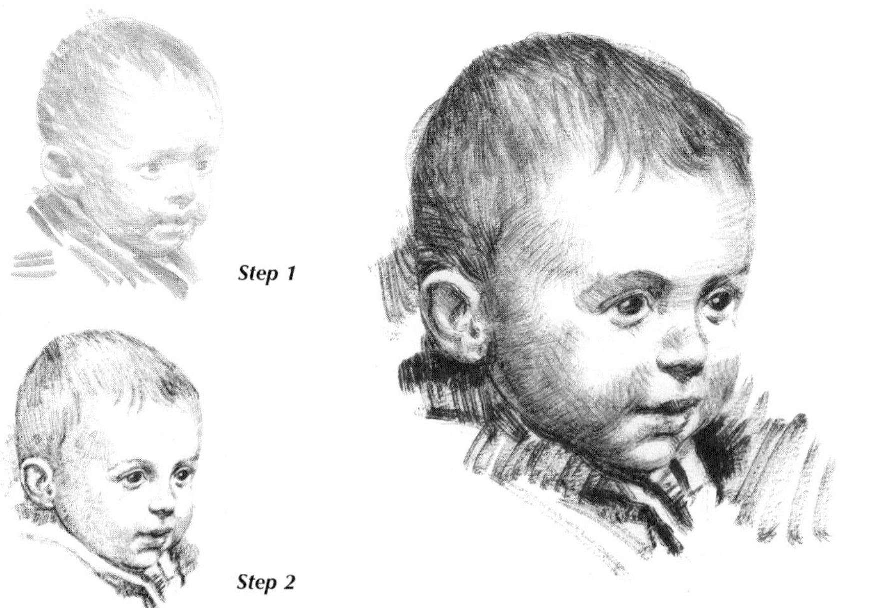

Step 1

Step 2

PEN AND INK

Lines that are closer or wider apart, and crossed over each other with varying intensity, depicting the main tones (beginning from the lighter ones and proceeding with the varying intensity of *chiaroscuro*) must be applied confidently, but also lightly and with caution in order to reproduce the delicate forms and convexity of the child's face.

A drawing is normally traced first with a pencil to plan the direction of the lines, how thick they need to be, and to be sure the proportions are correct. If, however, the drawing is done directly in pen with no initial pencil sketch (right), a more immediate, spontaneous effect is achieved that is lively and expressive; on the other hand it also introduces some difficulties – technical (lines cannot be erased, there is a risk of ink marks) and psychological (fear of making a mistake, uncertainty in defining proportions, etc.) – though all can be overcome by hard, continuous practice.

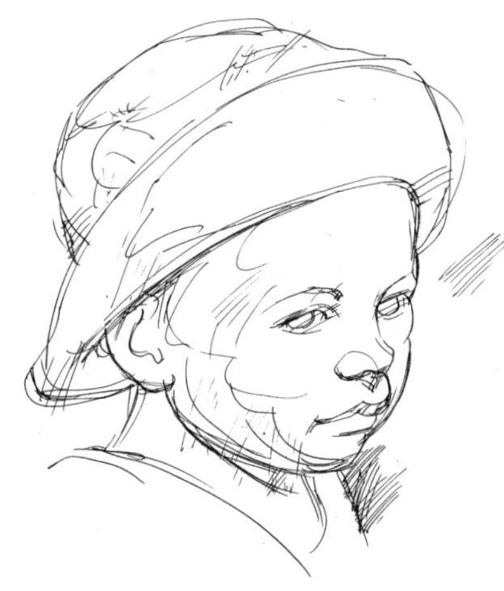

Drawing with no preparation, directly using pen.

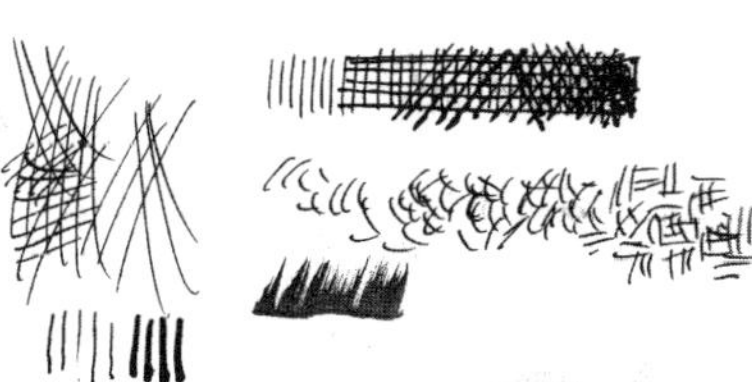

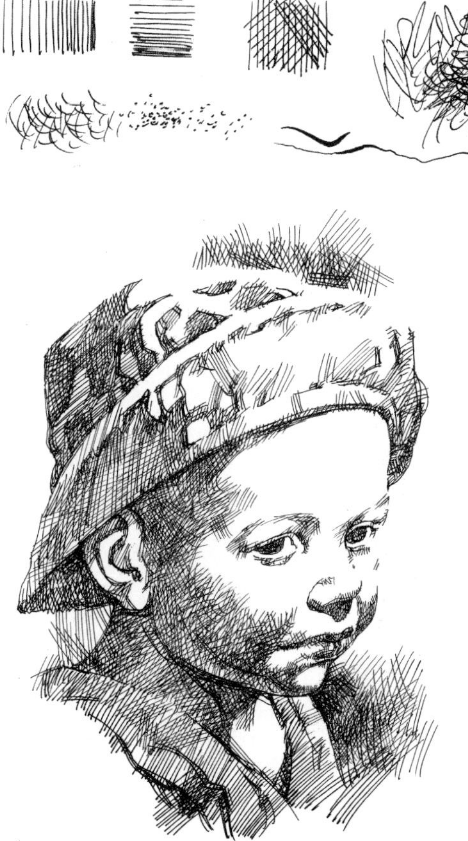

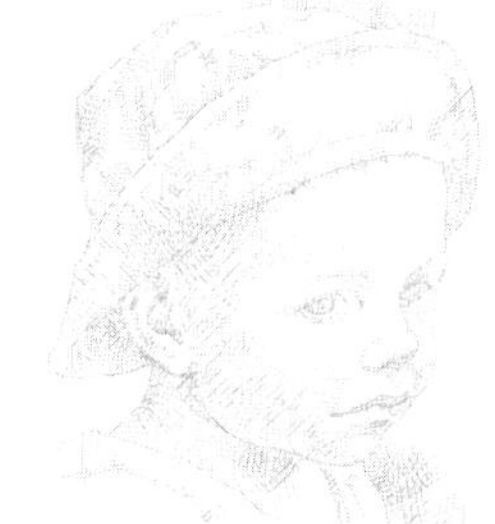

Step 1 *Pencil guide drawing*

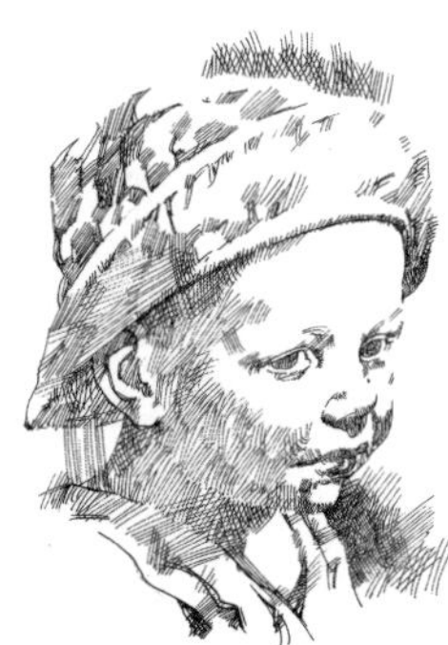

Step 2

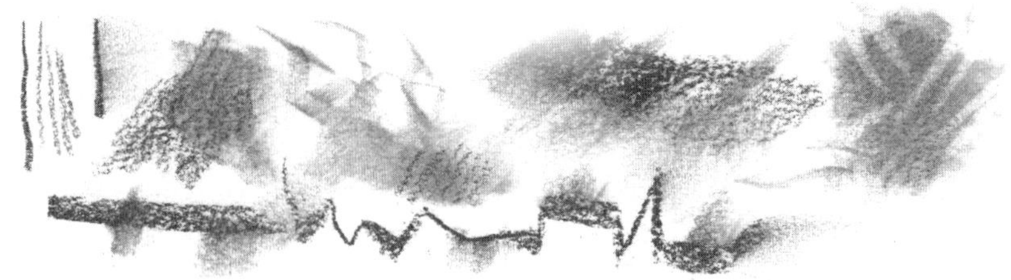

CHARCOAL AND SANGUINE

Charcoal (carbonized wood or compressed dust) is very malleable and allows you to get very nuanced shades of grey or deep black. Sanguine has similar properties, but with brown or reddish colours. The gradations of the colours, as with all 'dry' techniques (pastels, chalks, etc.) are attained by blending the intense lines with the finger (or a cloth, brush, or blending stump) or by 'lightening' them using a soft rubber. Charcoal is not very stable and is dusty by nature, and it is therefore better to reduce any flaking in the finished drawing by fixing it with a specific protective liquid.

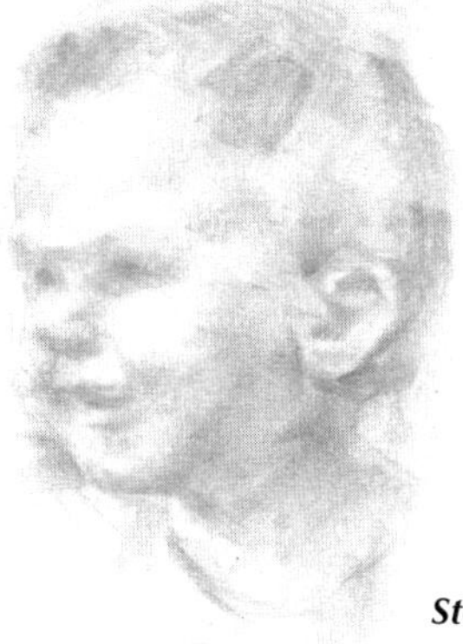

Step 1

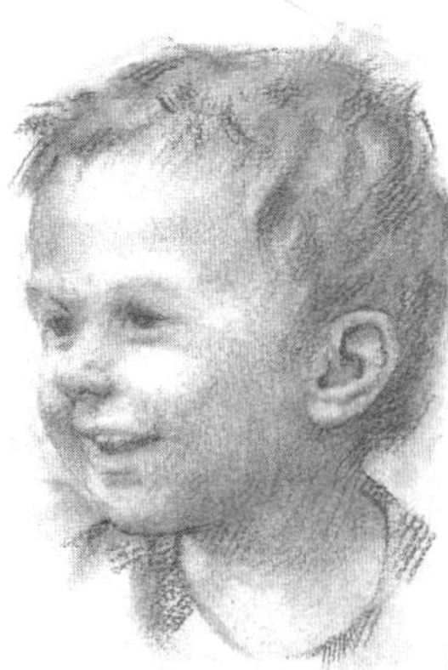

Step 2

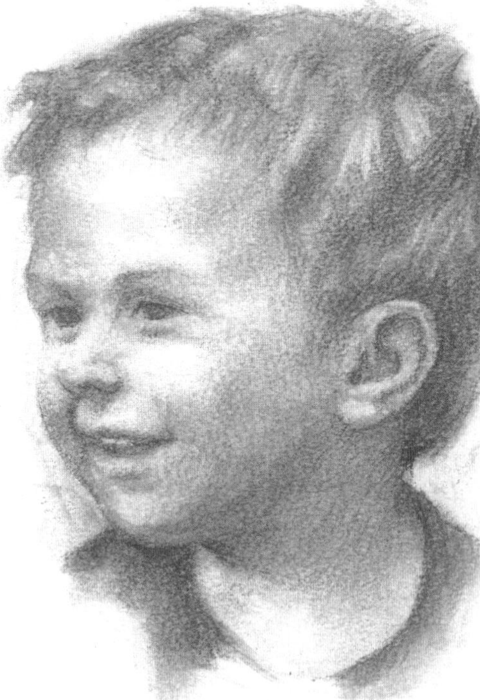

SOFT GRAPHITE

Graphite is one of the most simple, versatile tools available to artists for any kind of drawing and for any expressive style. Graphite is made in various degrees of hardness and is available in cylindrical shapes of varying diameter, from the thinnest (pencil, propelling pencil, etc.) to the thicker variety, which can be held without the need for any support, and which are usually in softer grades (such as 6B and 9B). Soft graphite allows you to draw wide, dark lines that can easily be blended using the fingers. Unlike medium and hard graphite (HB, H, etc.), that are suited to small, clear, detailed drawings, the softer 'greasy' ones are more suited to drawings that are less rich in detail, but much larger, spontaneous and vigorous, while keeping the subtly changing shapes of children's faces. The best effects with soft graphite are attained on rough paper, where the lines spread and become more blurred.

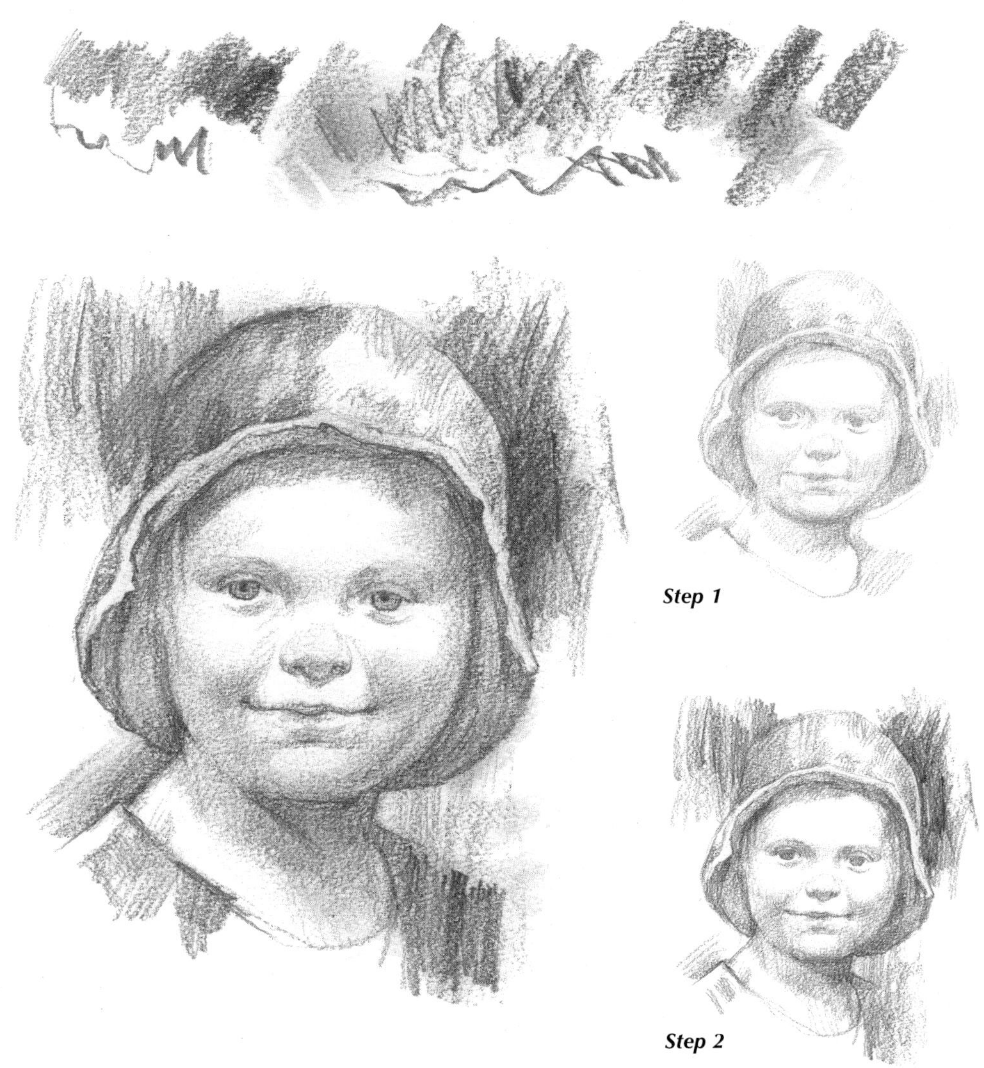

Step 1

Step 2

A GALLERY OF FACES

In this large section (up to page 341), I am going to show you a range of study drawings of children's faces, of varying age, gender and expressions. They were all created with graphite on paper:[1] 'black and white', so typical of most graphic techniques, is also an intitial and aesthetic choice as it adds intensity and effectiveness to shapes. My intention is for these drawings to stimulate the habit of drawing from observation, and suggests how to proceed and analyze the model. This is why I have adopted here a realistic, descriptive style, but certainly (as it is only one possible starting point) each artist needs to develop their own distinctive style.

I have already mentioned (see page 16) the difficulties in getting children to 'pose' (younger ones may move around constantly, while older children pull unsuitable expressions): almost all the drawings shown here come from a very quick, preliminary sketch taken from a live model, and from a number of documentation photographs taken almost at random and 'by surprise'. These indeed are essential for providing greater consistency to the detailed study and, in my case, to succeed in slightly, but consistently, altering the facial features a little in order to reduce the actual likeness with respect to the principles of confidentiality.

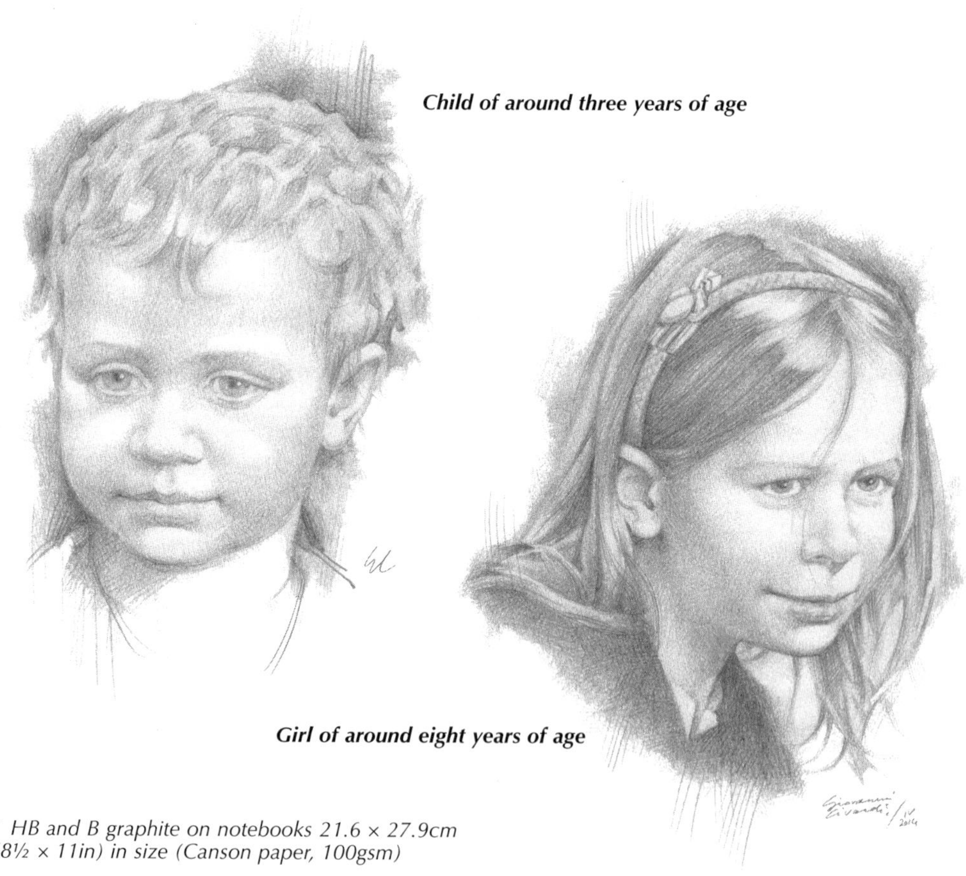

Child of around three years of age

Girl of around eight years of age

[1] HB and B graphite on notebooks 21.6 × 27.9cm (8½ × 11in) in size (Canson paper, 100gsm)

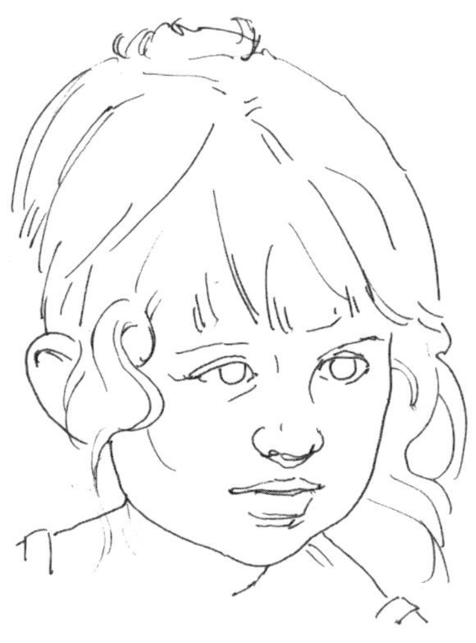

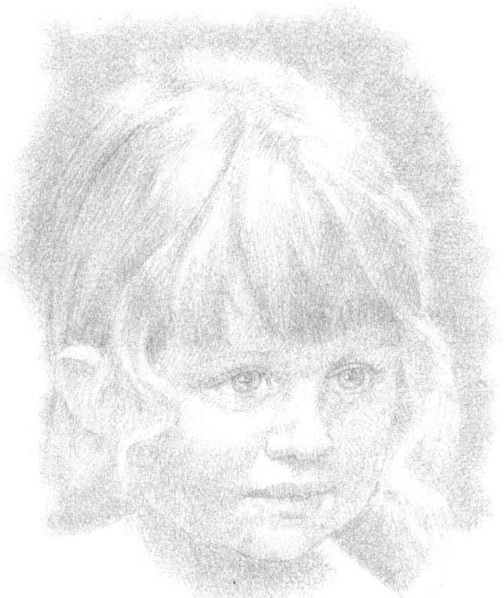

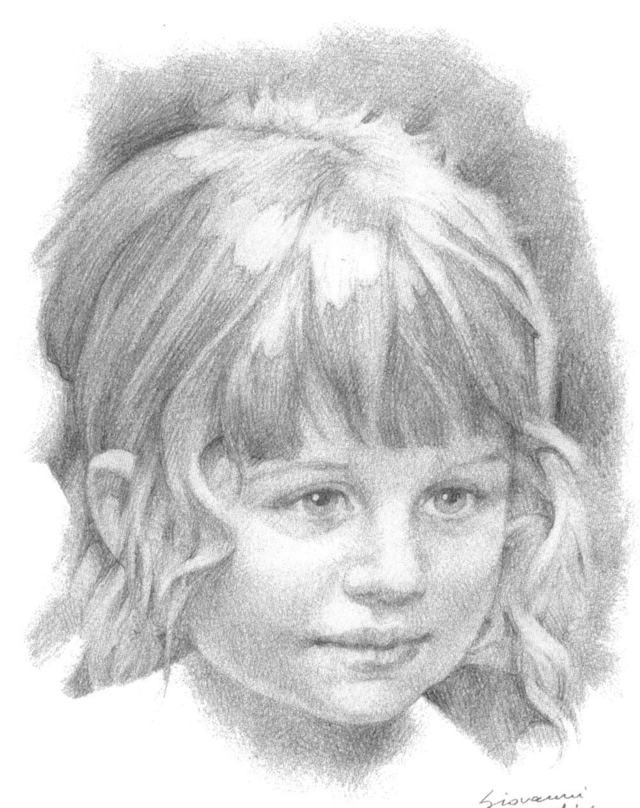

Child of around three years of age

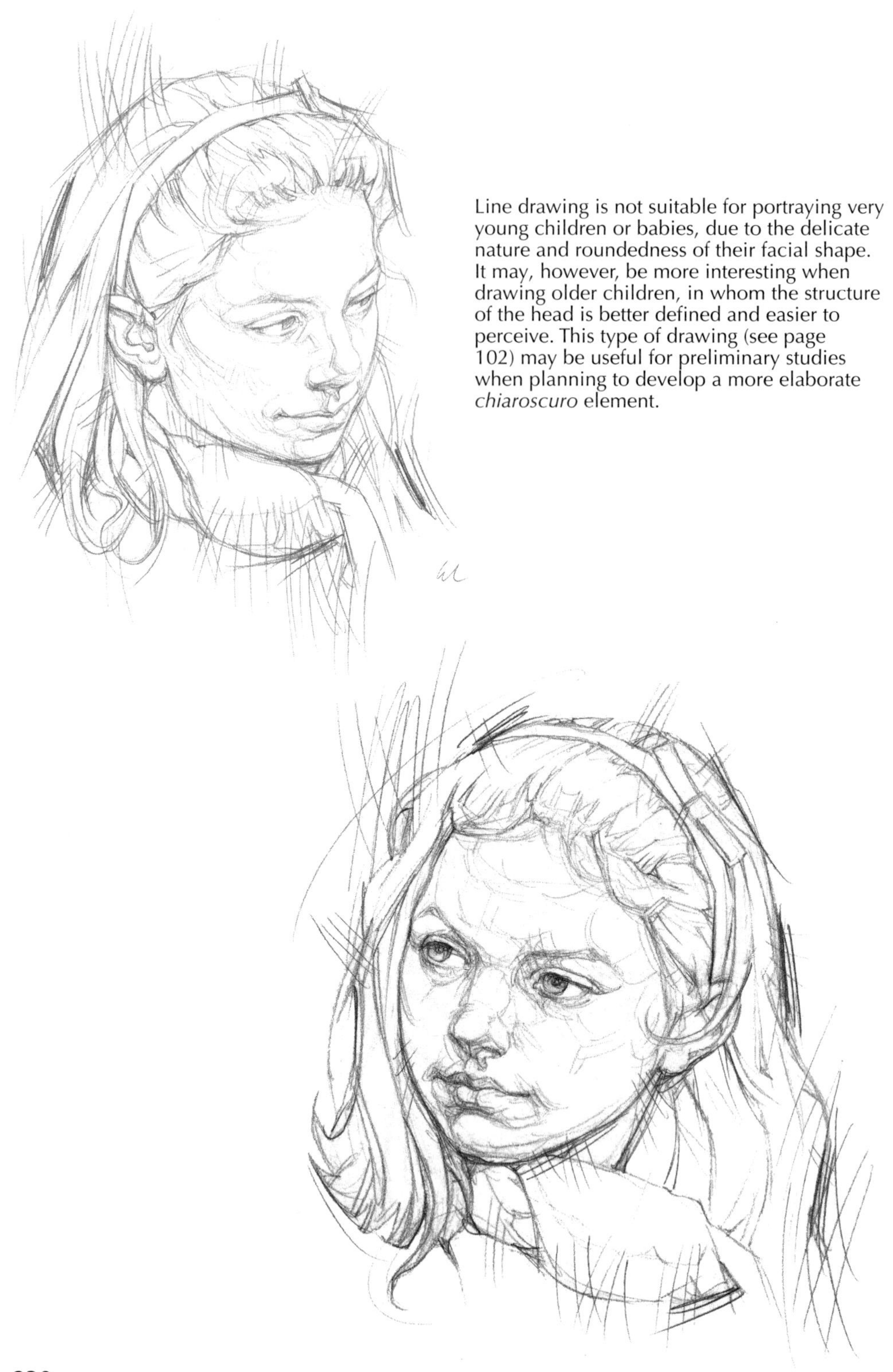

Line drawing is not suitable for portraying very young children or babies, due to the delicate nature and roundedness of their facial shape. It may, however, be more interesting when drawing older children, in whom the structure of the head is better defined and easier to perceive. This type of drawing (see page 102) may be useful for preliminary studies when planning to develop a more elaborate *chiaroscuro* element.

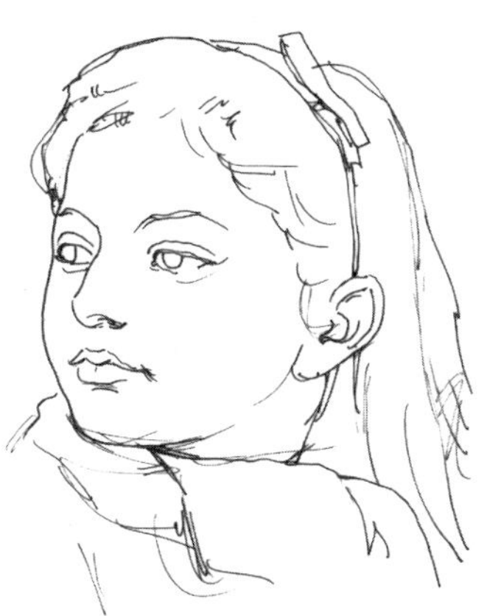

Girl of about 10 years of age

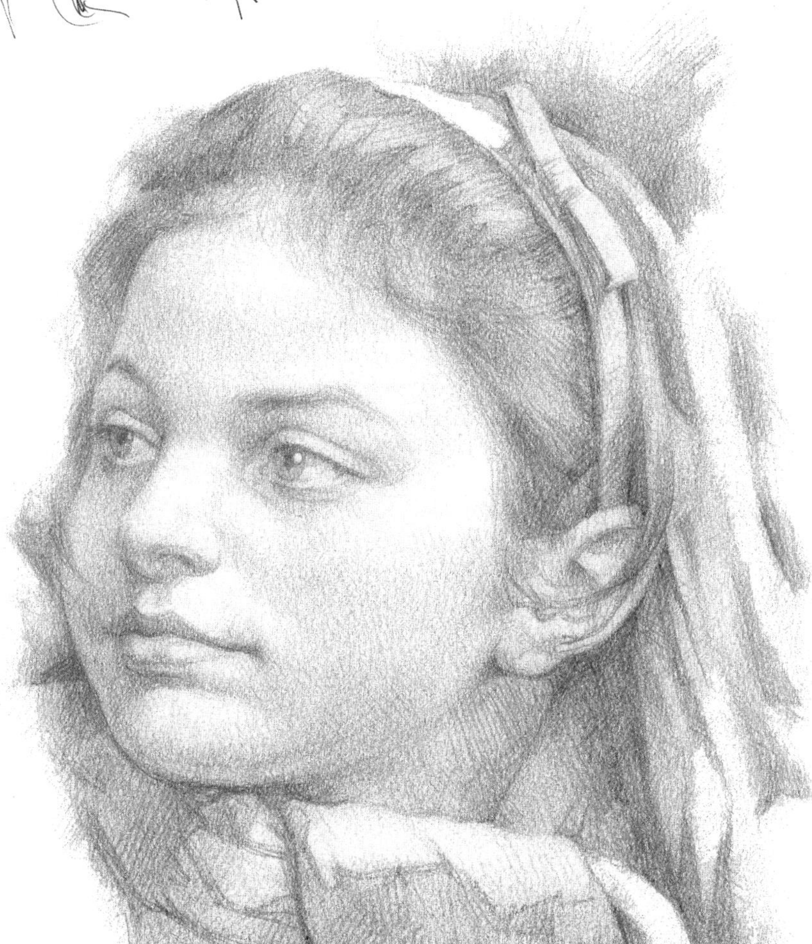

Alongside many of the portraits that appear on the pages in this section, I have also chosen to show the outline of the head, drawn directly in pen, in order to have an immediate idea of the compositional effect and the set of physiognomic traits. I have only depicted some essential elements in these quick, schematic drawings, just enough to characterize a child's expression and attitude, and the head's proportions and structure. If seen as an initial exercise of observation, my intention with this type of schema may serve as an initial sketch for a drawing to be embellished with a more complex technique; or for a painting – just enlarge the sketch using the grid technique (see pages 138–139 and pages 264–266) or make a photocopy of a suitable size.

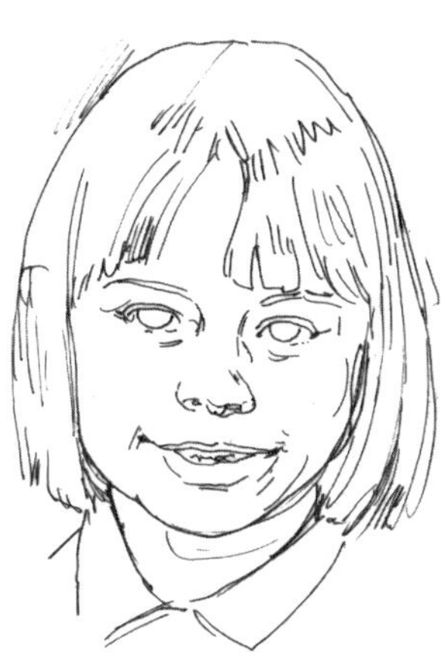

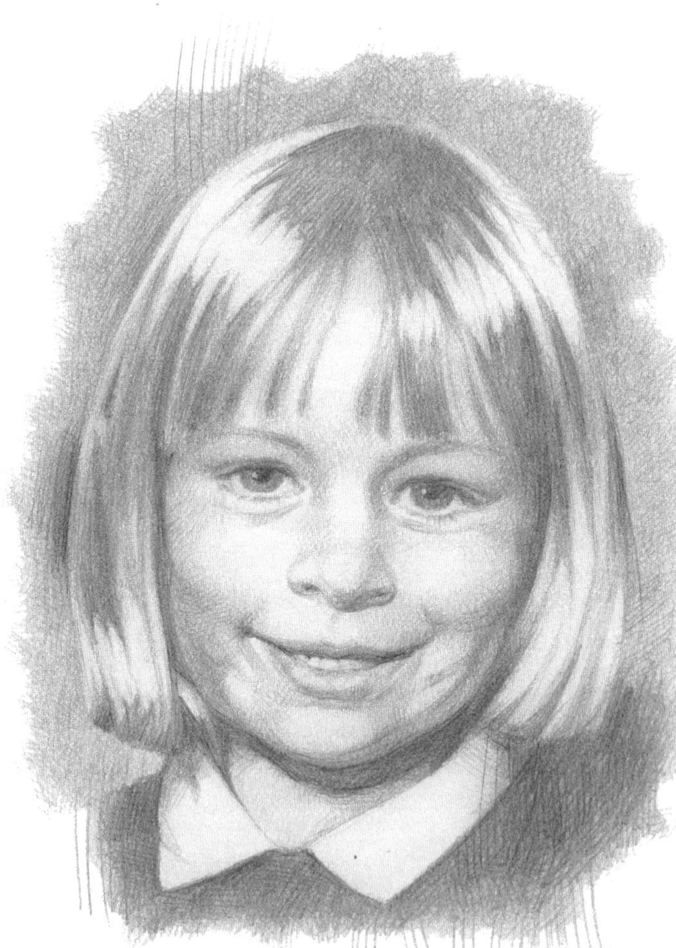

Girl of about six years of age

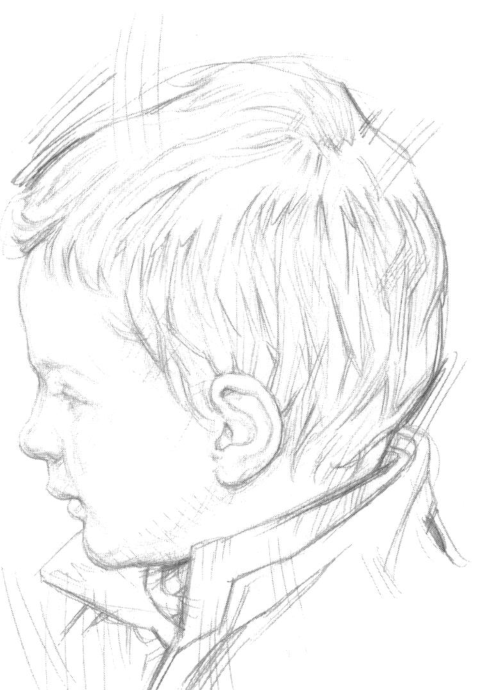

The characteristics that make young children's faces so typical and attractive can be seen in the profile: the protruding upper lip, the concavity of the bridge of the child's nose and the roundness of the tip, the convex forehead and the length of their eyelashes.

A young skull and face tend to show some characteristics of a child's ethnic group, but remain only just hinted at and ambiguous until adolescence. For example, prognathism (i.e. prominent jaw bones) is not commonly seen in early years. Foreheads have two symmetrical convexities; the frontal crest has only have one central convexity in children, which contributes to accentuating the typical prominence in a child's profile.

If seen from above, the shape of the head (which corresponds almost exactly to the skull) differs according to population: long (dolichocephalic) typically seen in children of African origin; short (brachycephalic) in those of Asian descent; intermediate (mesocephalic) in those of European origin.

Boy of about three years of age

Up until three or four months of age, a baby's neck is weak and is not able to fully support its head, which is very large in relation to the rest of its body. Up until about the age of two, a child's neck remains very short, with fine circular folds around it that make it look as if the head has been 'rested' on the child's shoulders. In later years of childhood, the neck is still delicate and thin, although it gradually becomes longer.

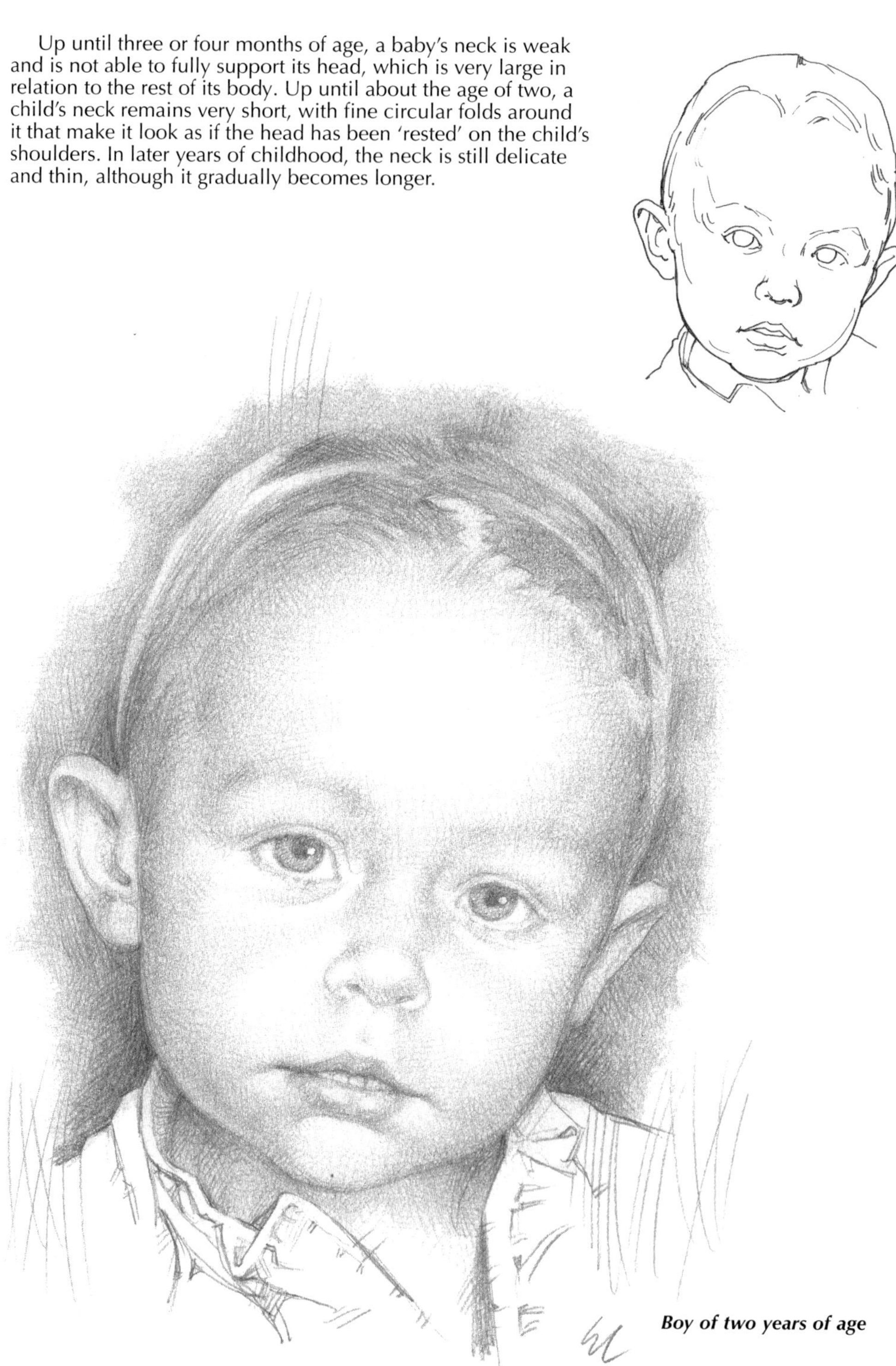

Boy of two years of age

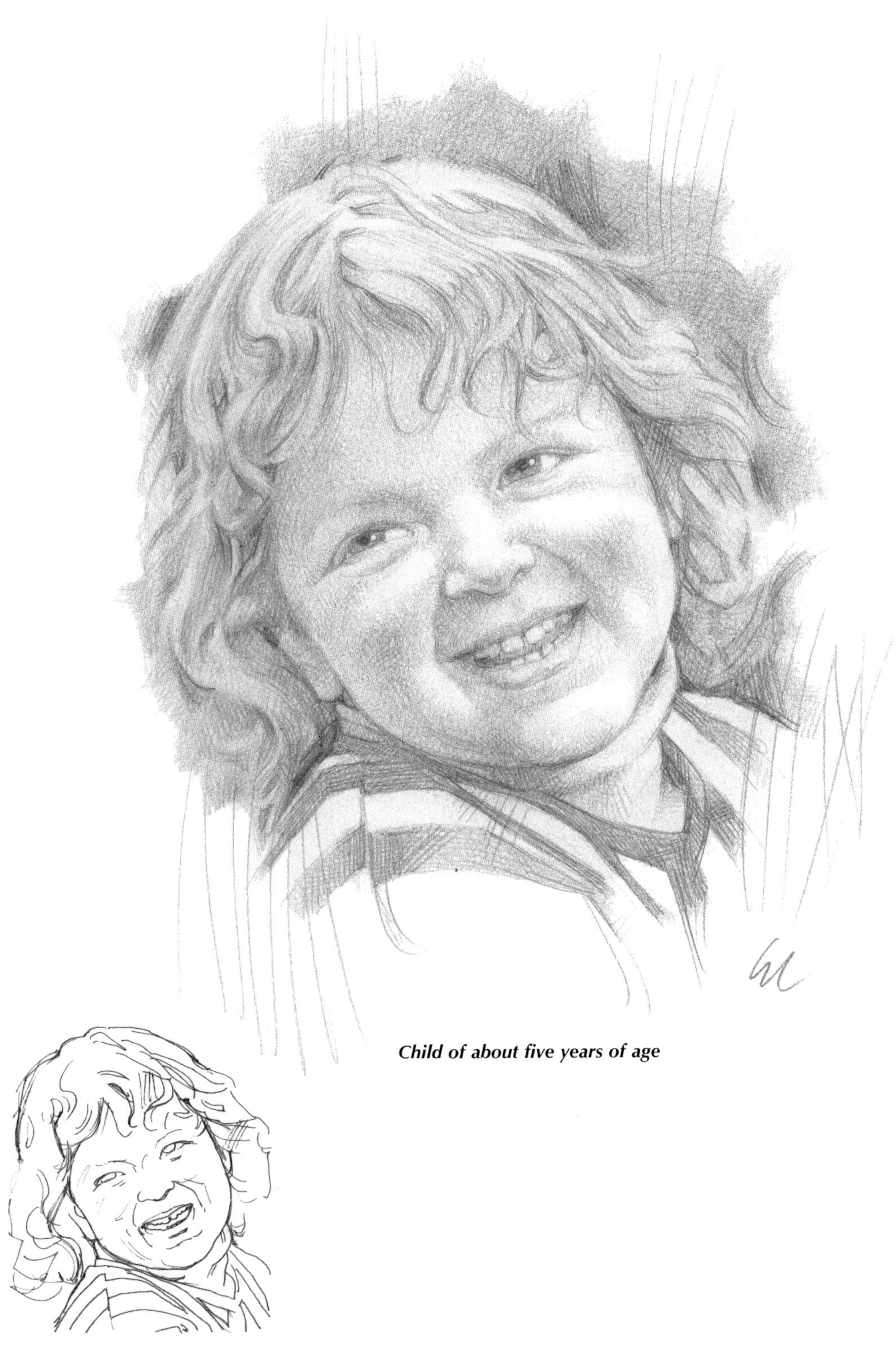

Child of about five years of age

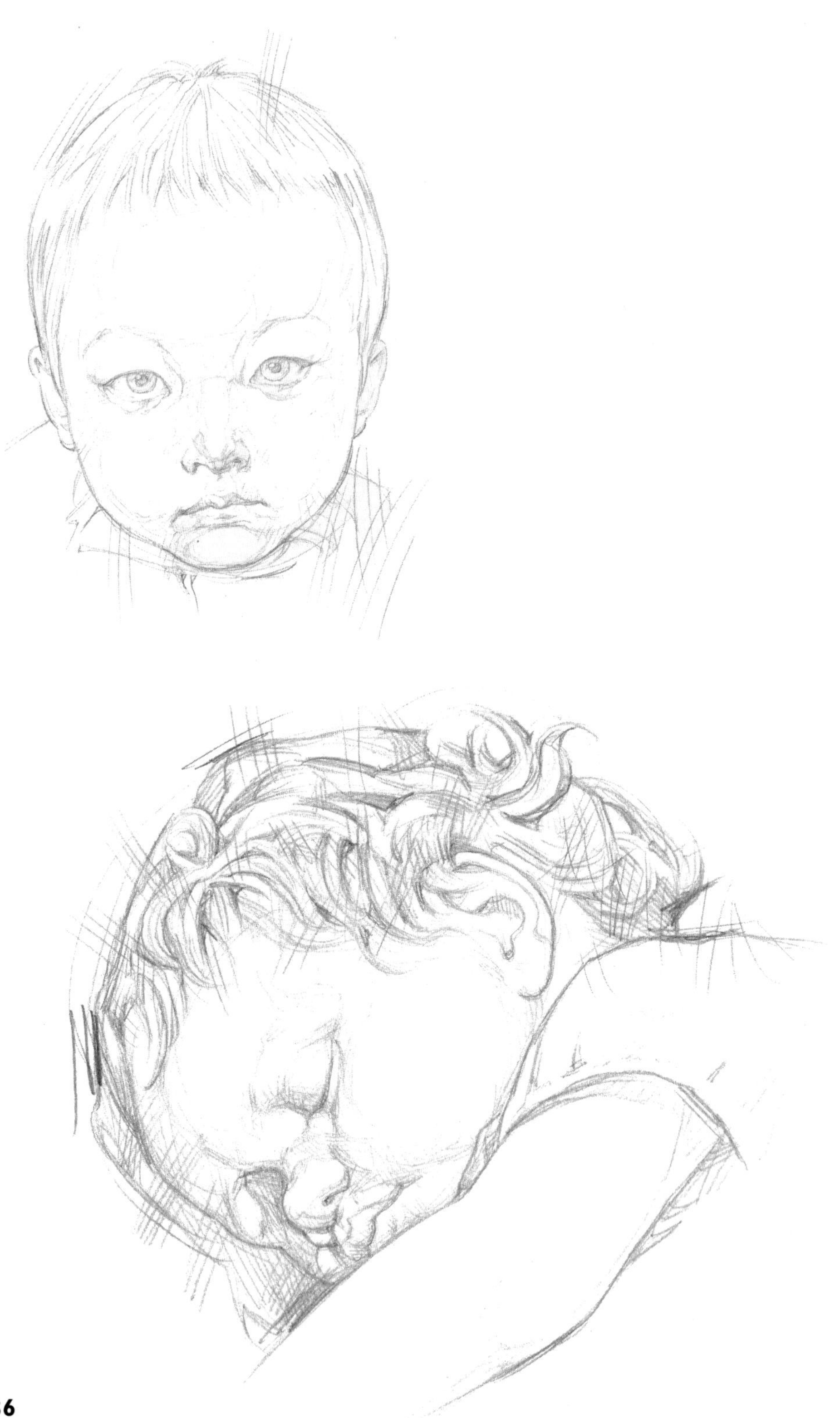

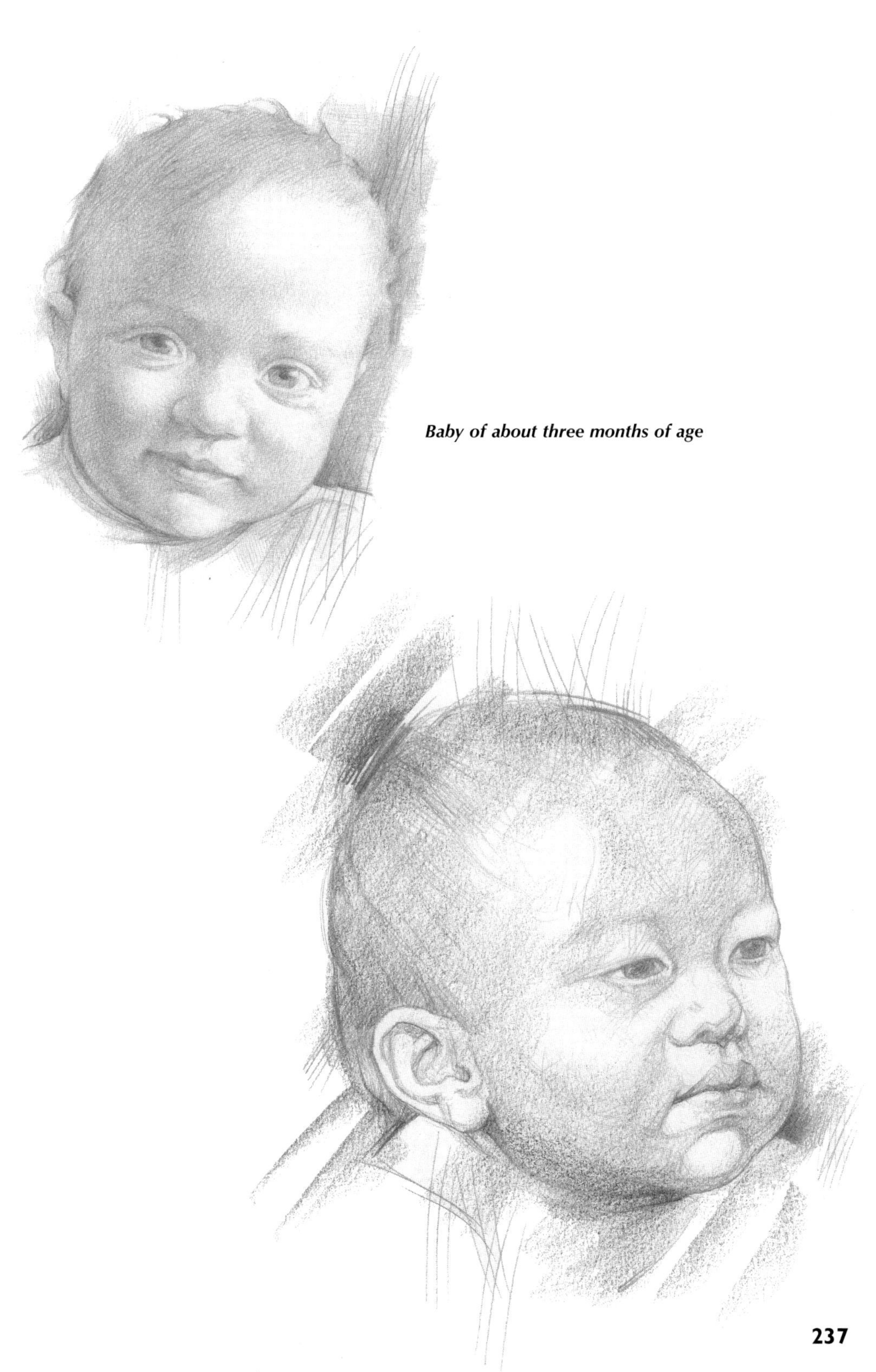

Baby of about three months of age

When smiling, the base of the nose widens a little and the nostrils appear dilated and wider apart. However, in drawings, it is advisable not to emphasize this tendency; indeed, it should be more hinted at than described, using rather light strokes and without shading that is too intense or sharp.

In addition the lips widen and relax when smiling, almost always leaving the front teeth (milk teeth or permanent ones) visible in the position and number dictated by the relative growing phase. After about six years, the permanent upper-central incisors appear rather large in relation to the size of the face and, not uncommonly, a little apart from each other, leaving a gap (diastema) which gives an appearance of geniality.

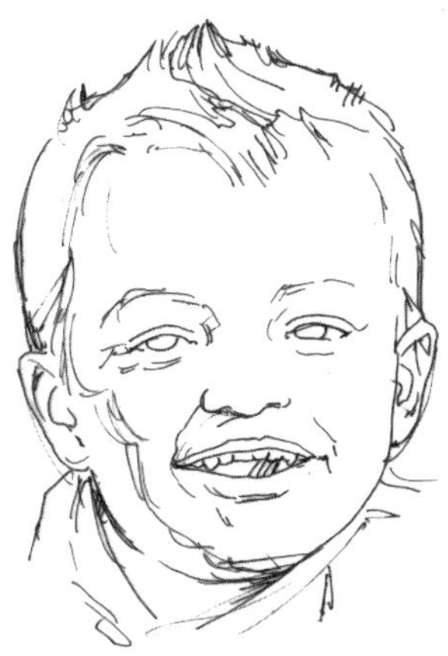

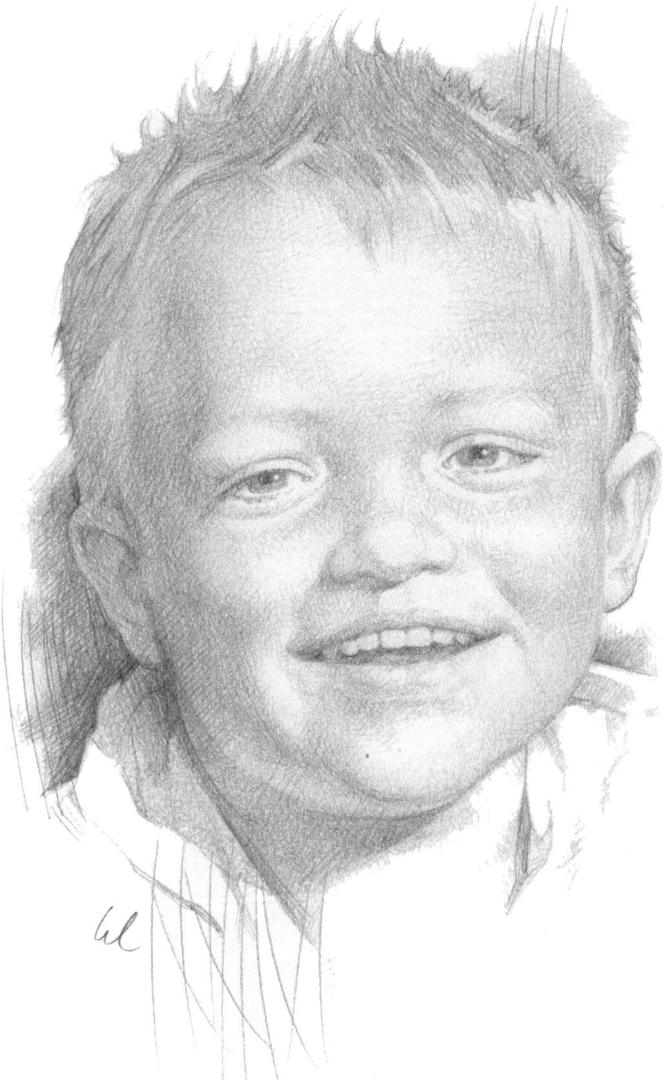

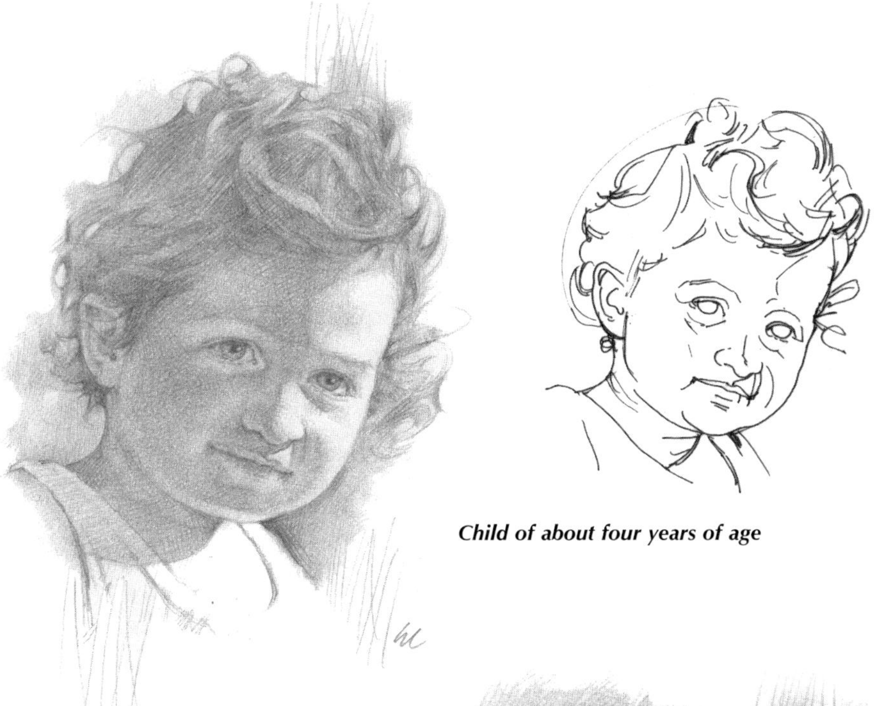

Child of about four years of age

Child of about six years of age

From the age of about five to seven years, milk teeth are gradually replaced by permanent ones. The sequence is similar to that of the appearance of the milk teeth: for example, the first to be replaced with permanent teeth are the lower central incisors, followed by all the upper incisors. A child's smile often reveals 'windows' – temporary gum spaces during the replacement period.

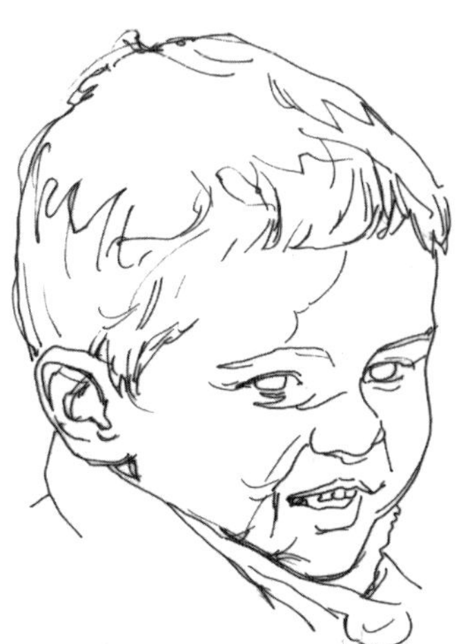

Child of about four years of age

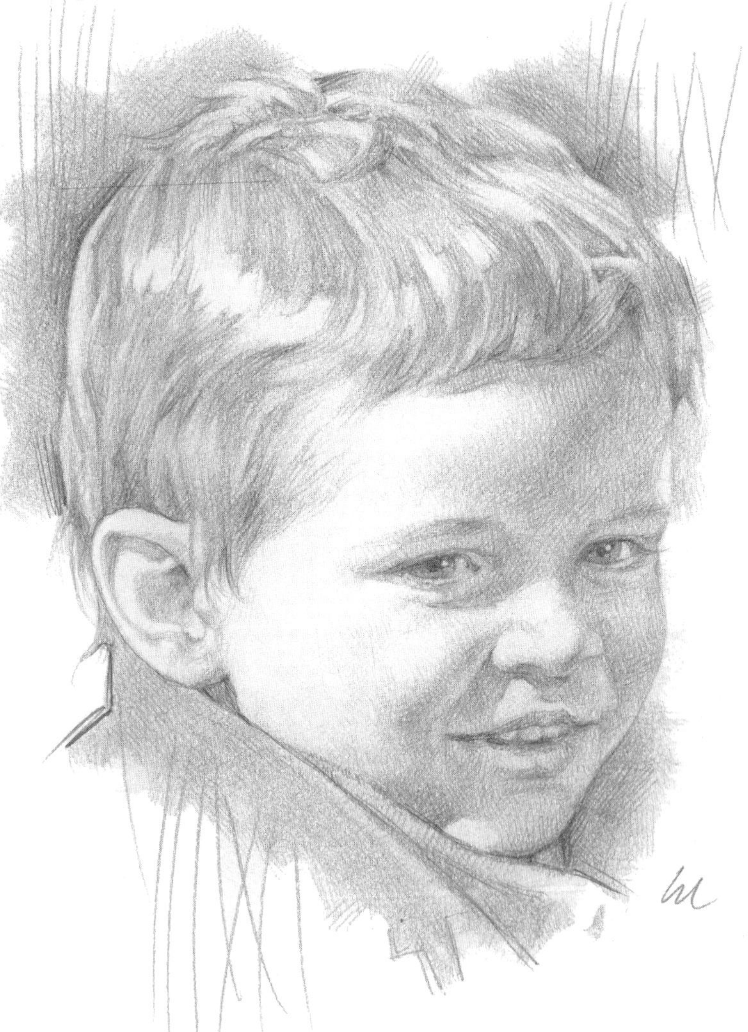

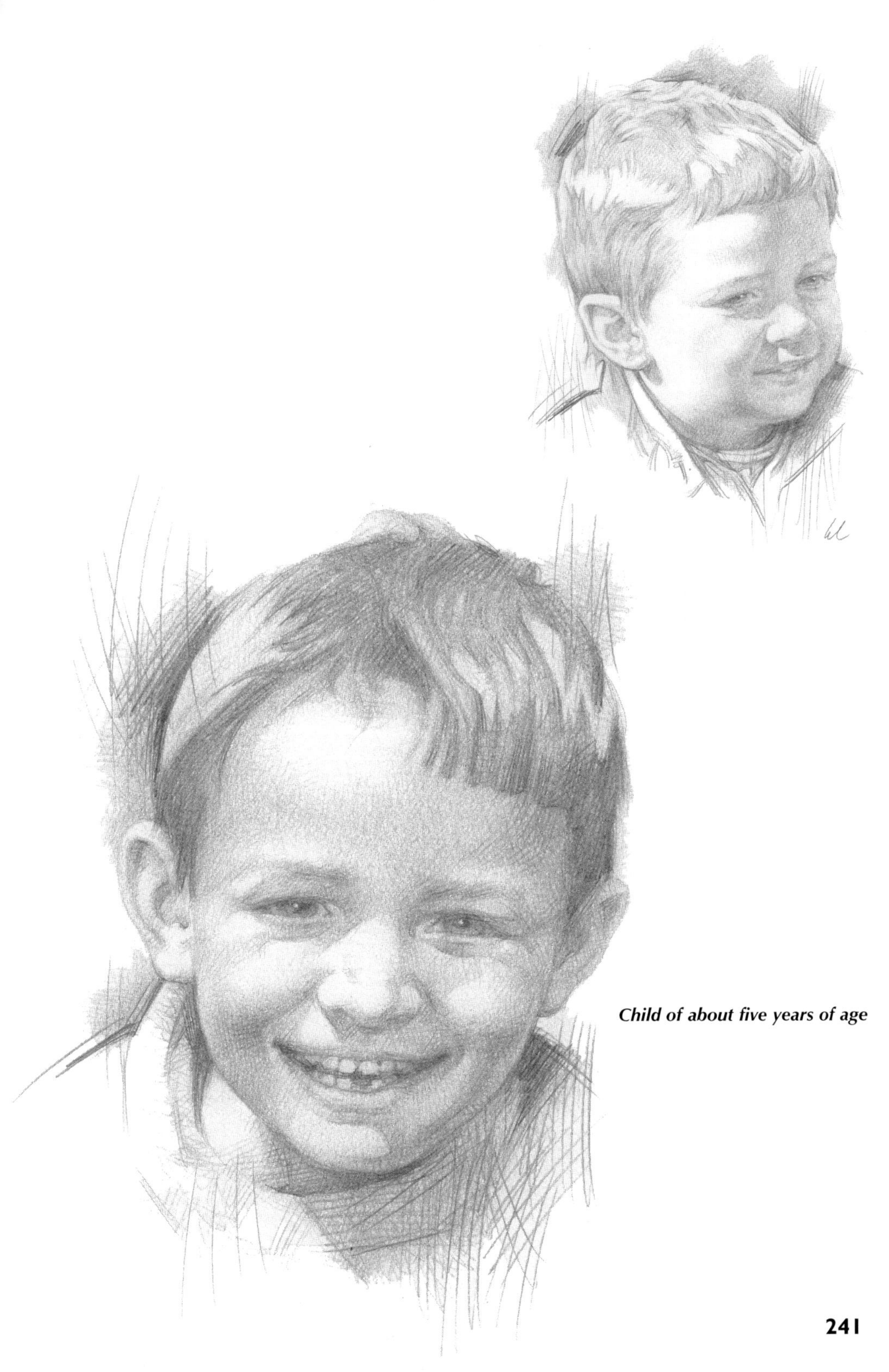

Child of about five years of age

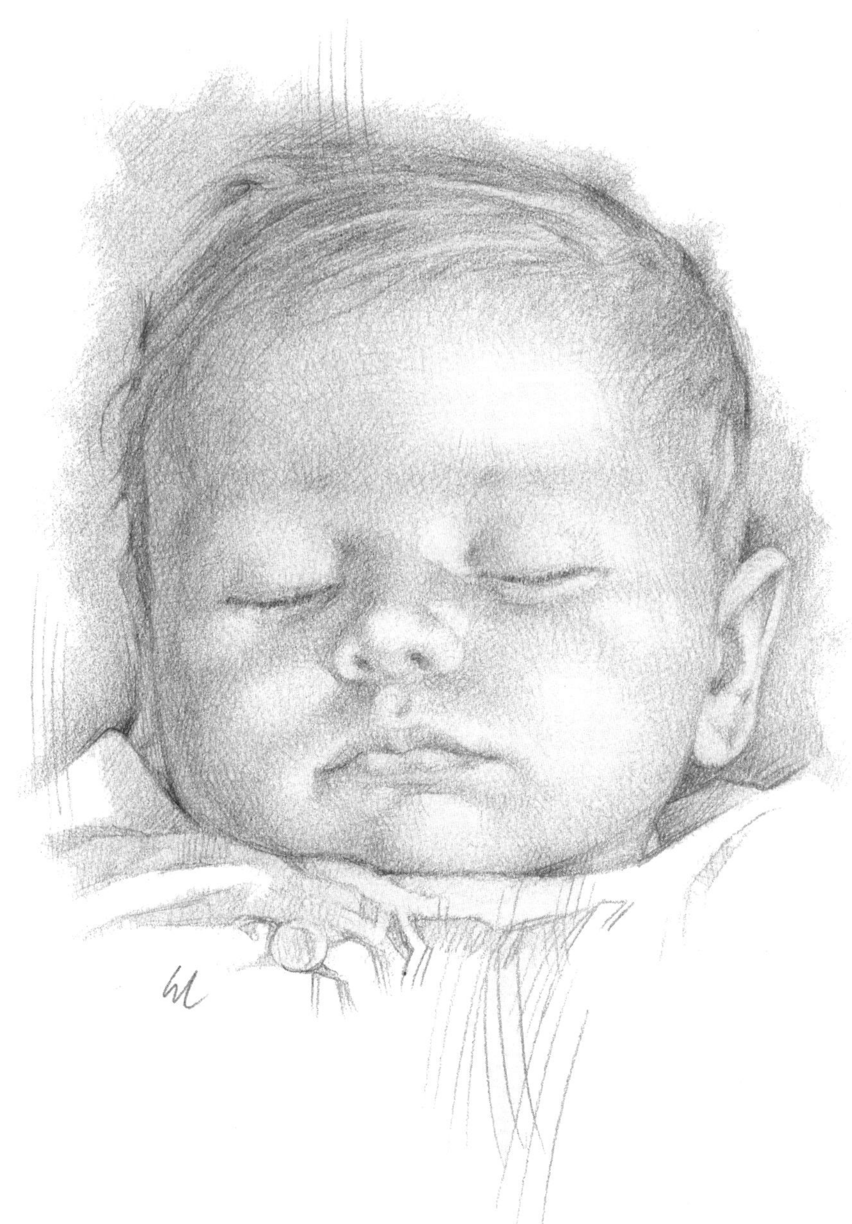

In the early years of life, babies sleep for long periods of time: the expression they assume is extremely endearing, although quite monotonous. However, these moments are perhaps the only ones when they are still long enough to produce an accurate life drawing. The nasolabial groove, which is easy to see in an adult, is totally absent in a baby, as the passage from the upper lip to the convex cheek is very gradual and soft in both volume and blending of tones.

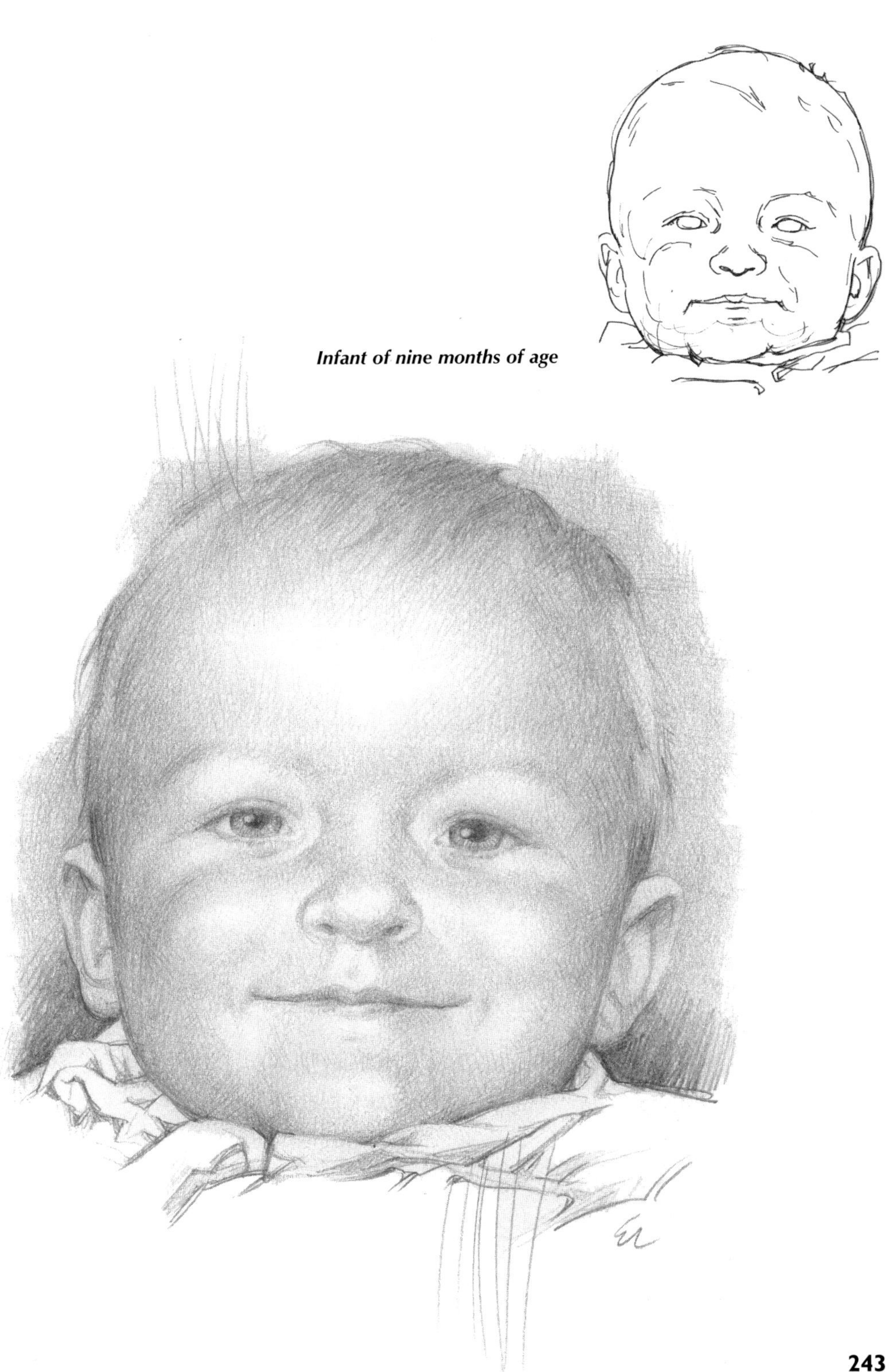

Infant of nine months of age

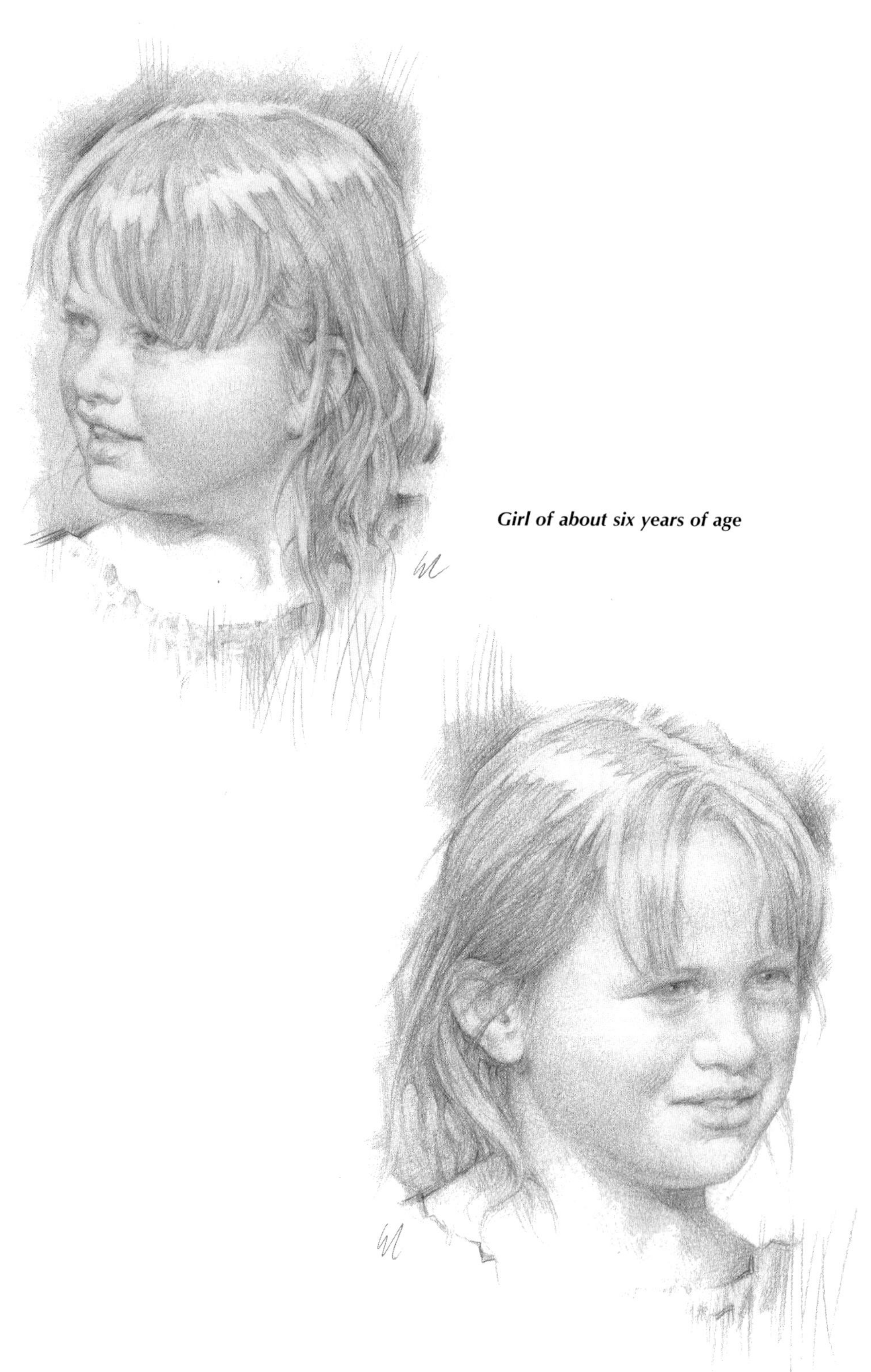

Girl of about six years of age

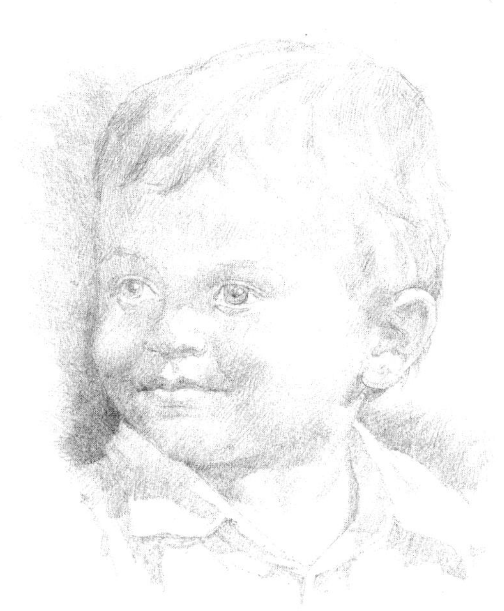

Child about three years of age

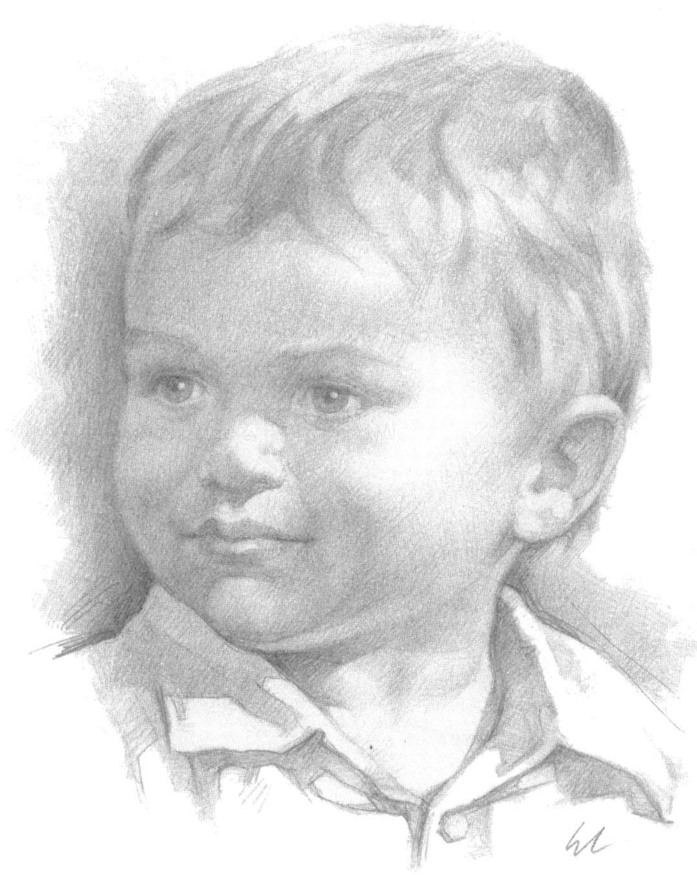

A child's facial features and the shape of the head and neck, in the early years of life, provide only a subtle indication of some of the typical characteristics of populations that are found in the adults.

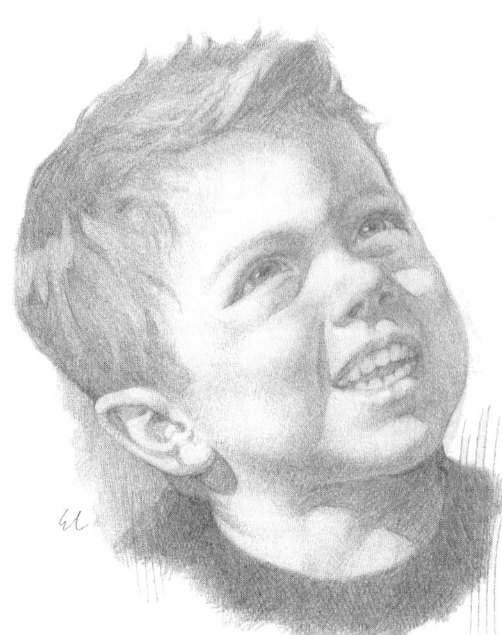

Boy of about four years of age

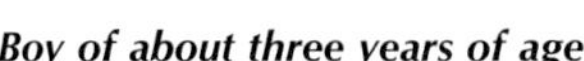

Boy of about three years of age

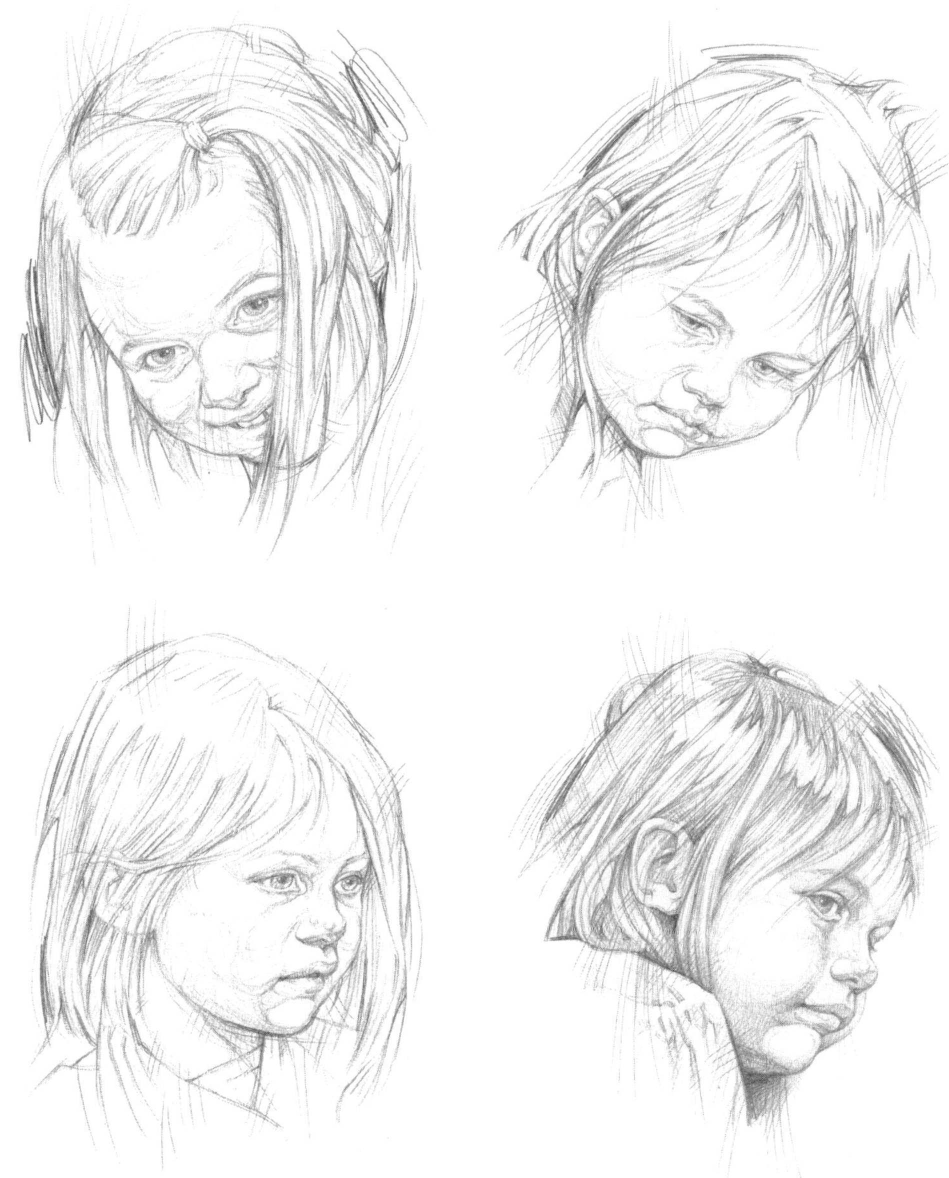

If the young subject (perhaps an adolescent) is a member of the artist's family, or is in any case in the environmental and social conditions to be observed calmly and quietly, it is a good idea to take advantage of the circumstances and draw some sketches from life in sequence, in varying degrees of detail. Line drawings are suitable in these cases as they allow precision, clarity of marks and are quick to complete, while allowing an effective examination of proportions.

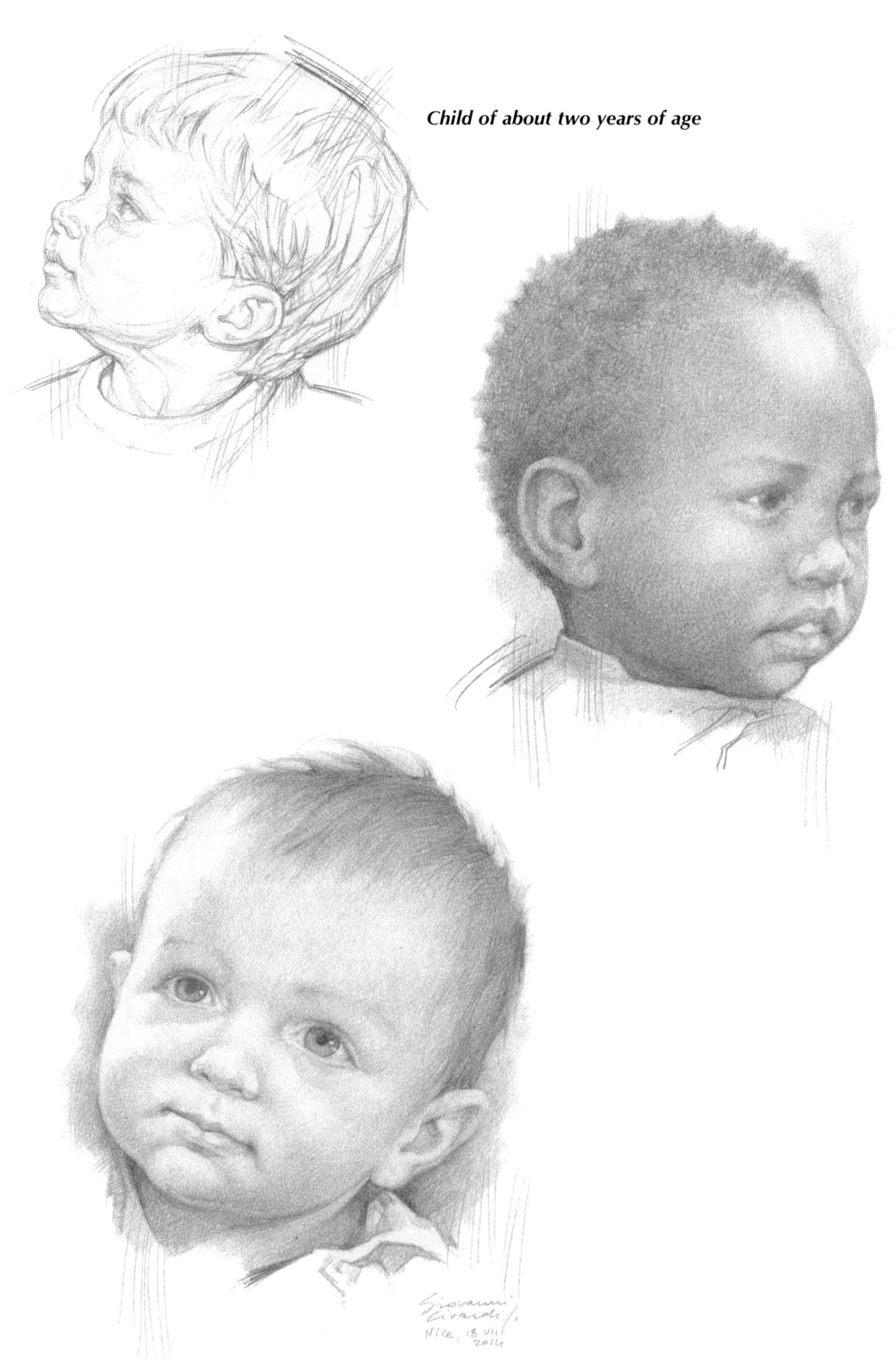

Child of about two years of age

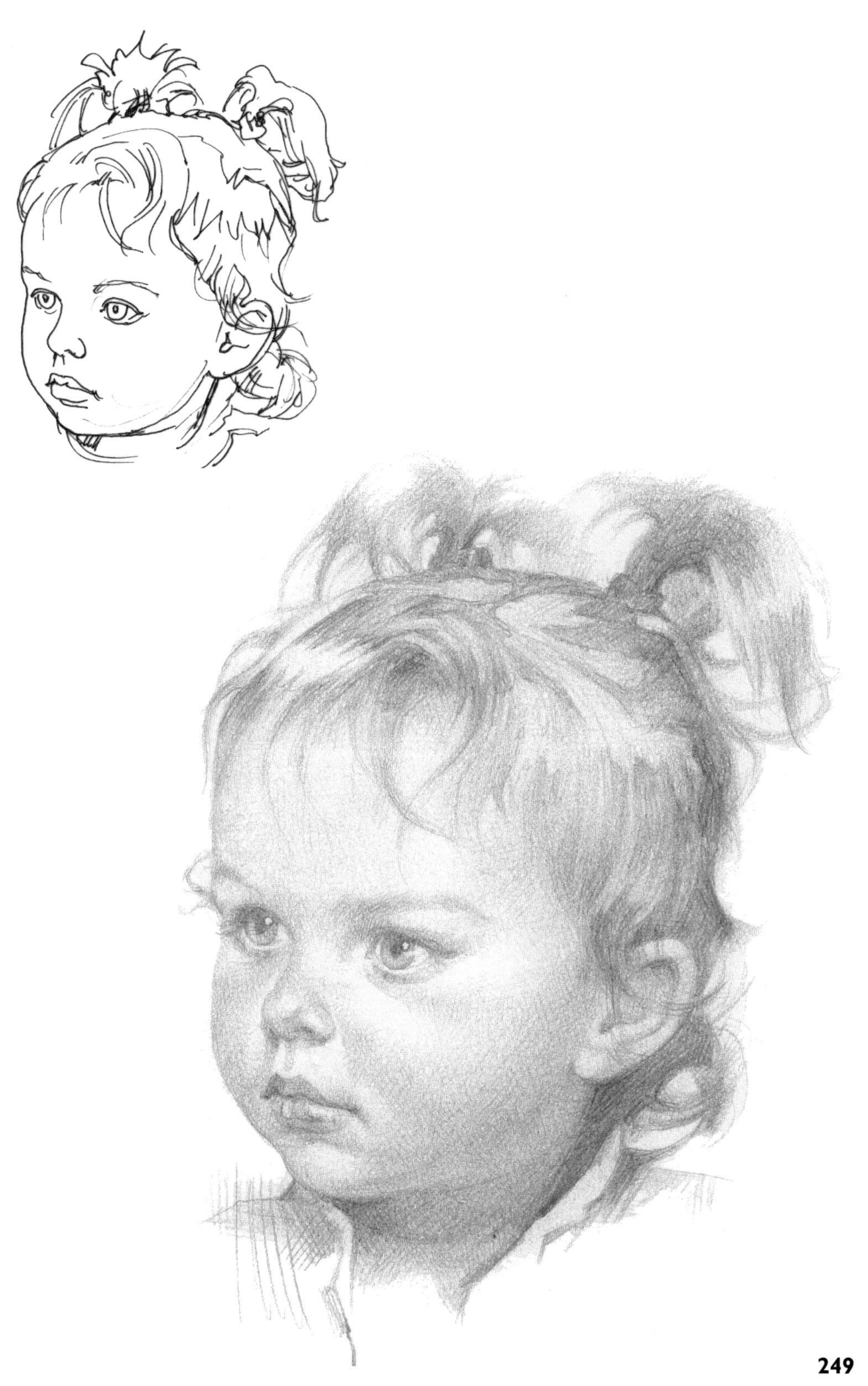

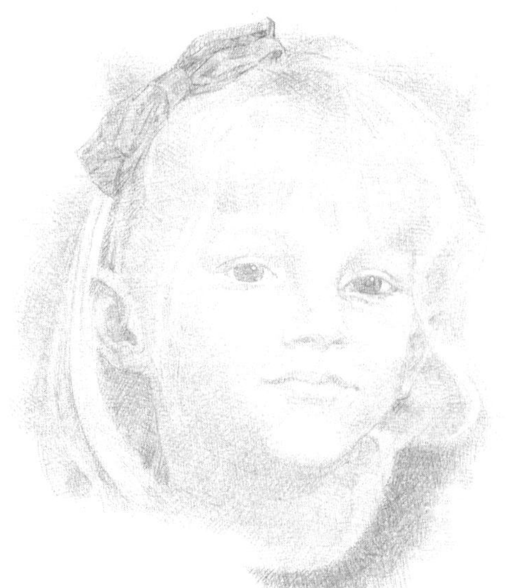

A drawing based predominantly on tonal variations (see pages 220–221) can be created in several ways, for example by adding the final tonal values almost immediately (a procedure similar to the painting technique known as '*alla prima*') or by proceeding with gradations from light to dark, which I chose to do in this drawing. In the initial phase, the tones are very light, almost indistinct, but in the more detailed phase, they reach an intensity that is suited to portraying the soft volume of a young face.

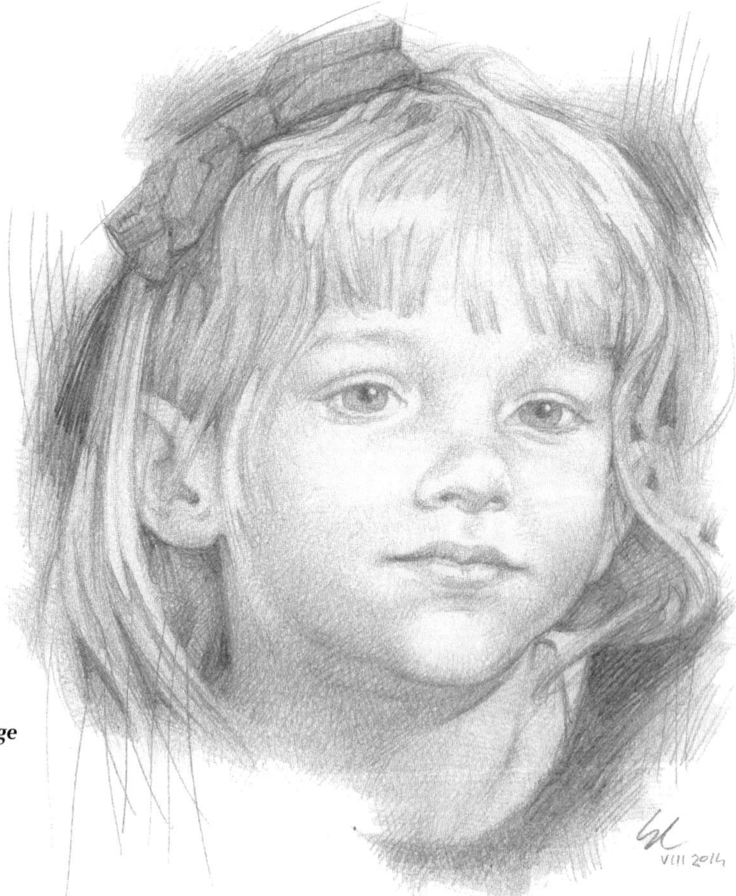

Girl of five years of age

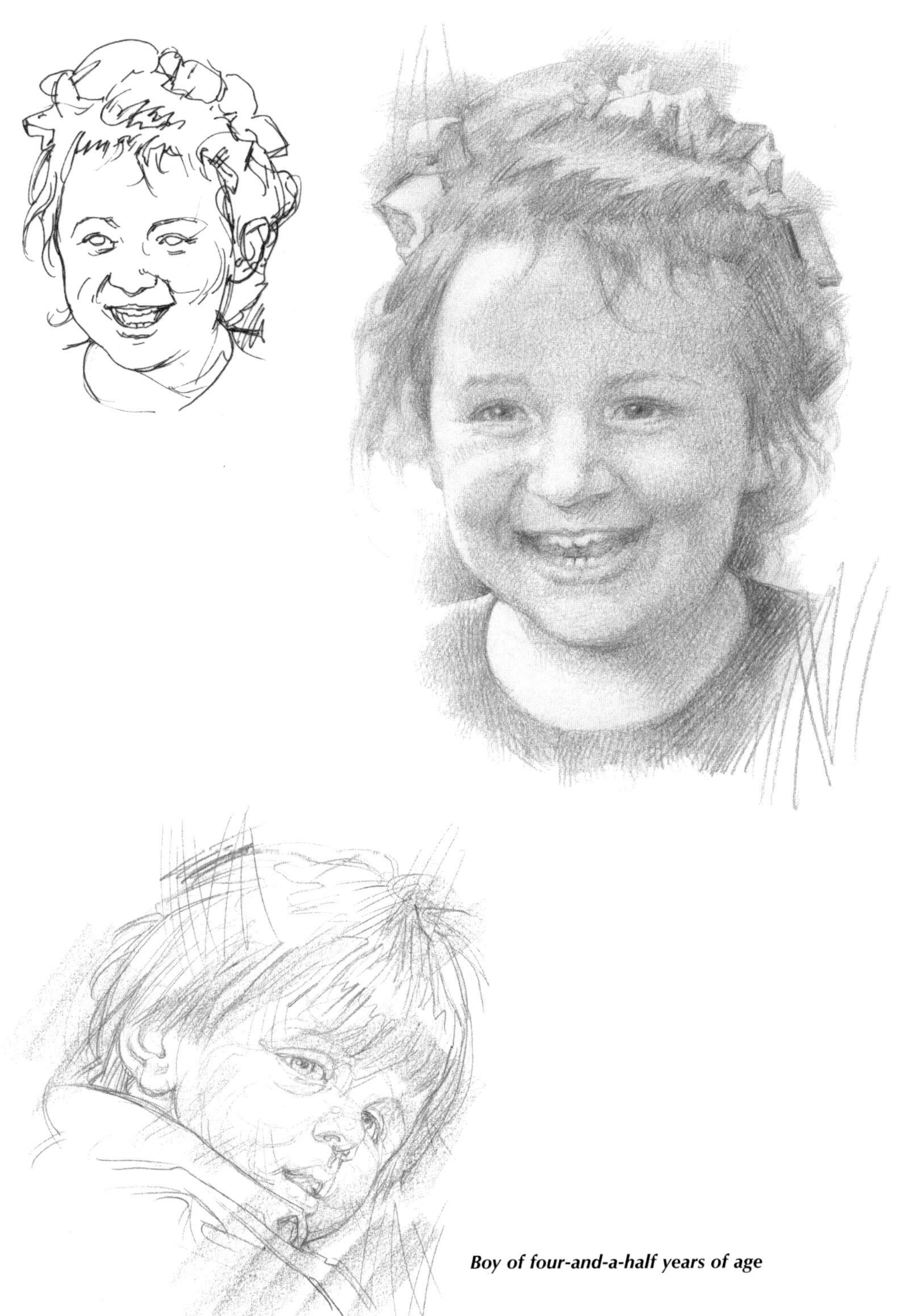

Boy of four-and-a-half years of age

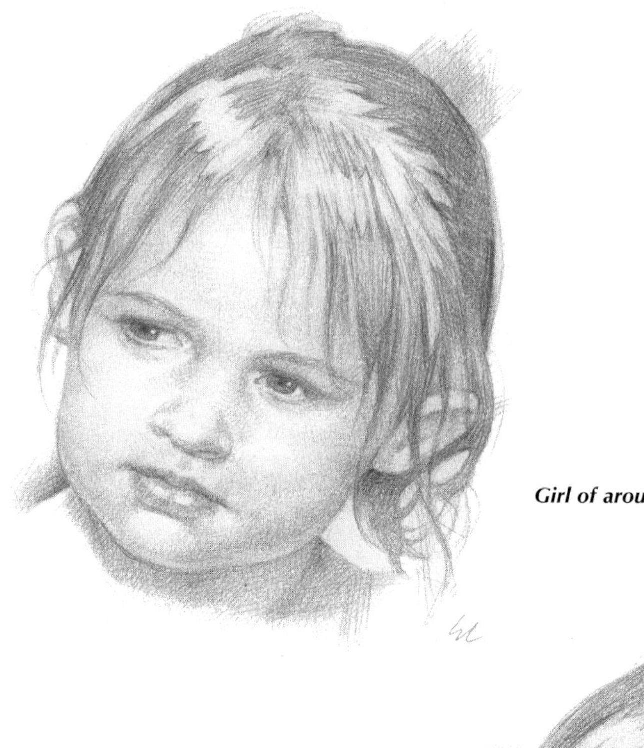

Girl of around four years of age

Photography is essential for capturing changing expressions in children. These are rapid and fleeting, such that they prevent any drawing being done from life: it is necessary to observe them, fix them in the 'visual' memory and be lucky enough to photograph them at significant moments.

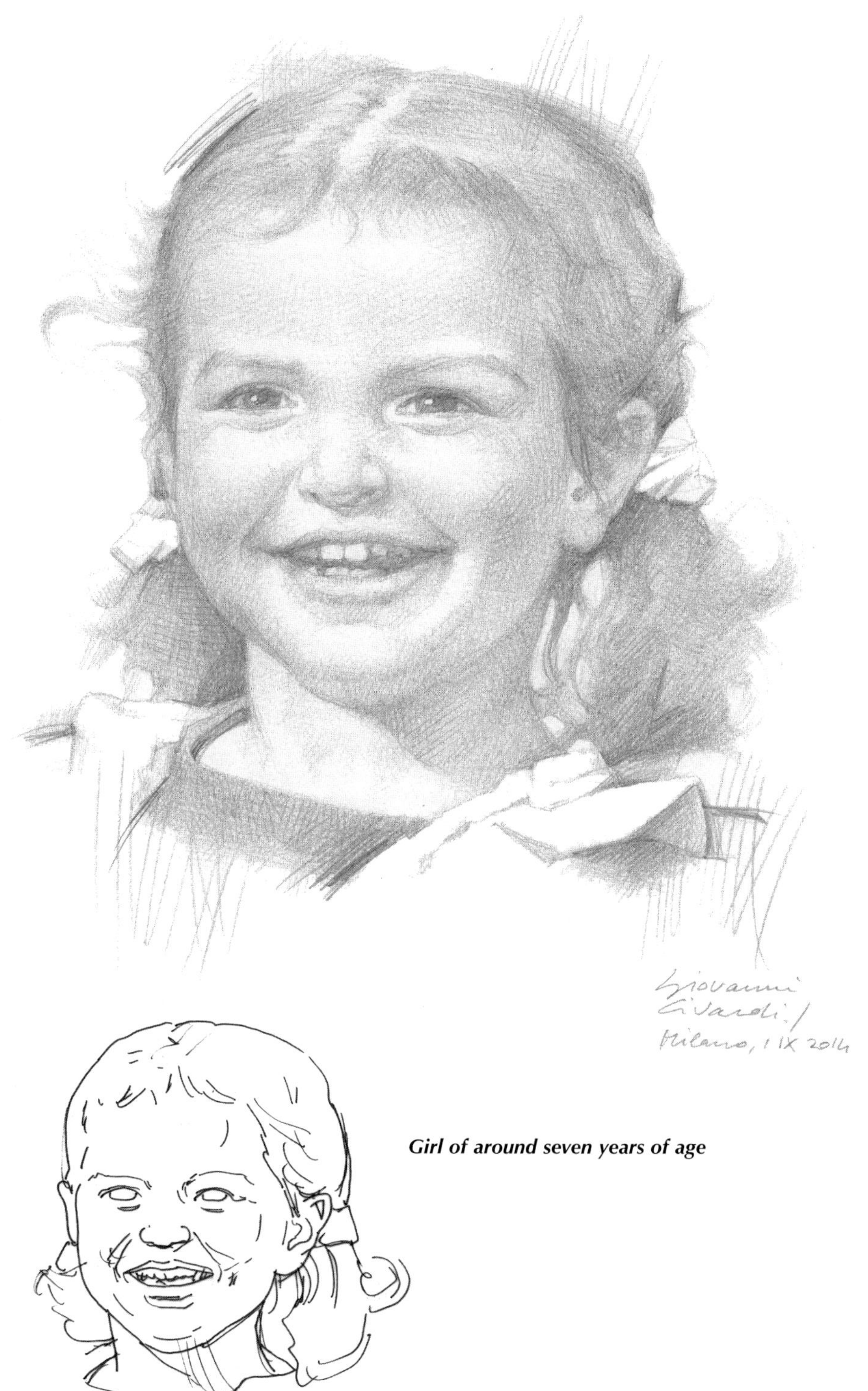

Girl of around seven years of age

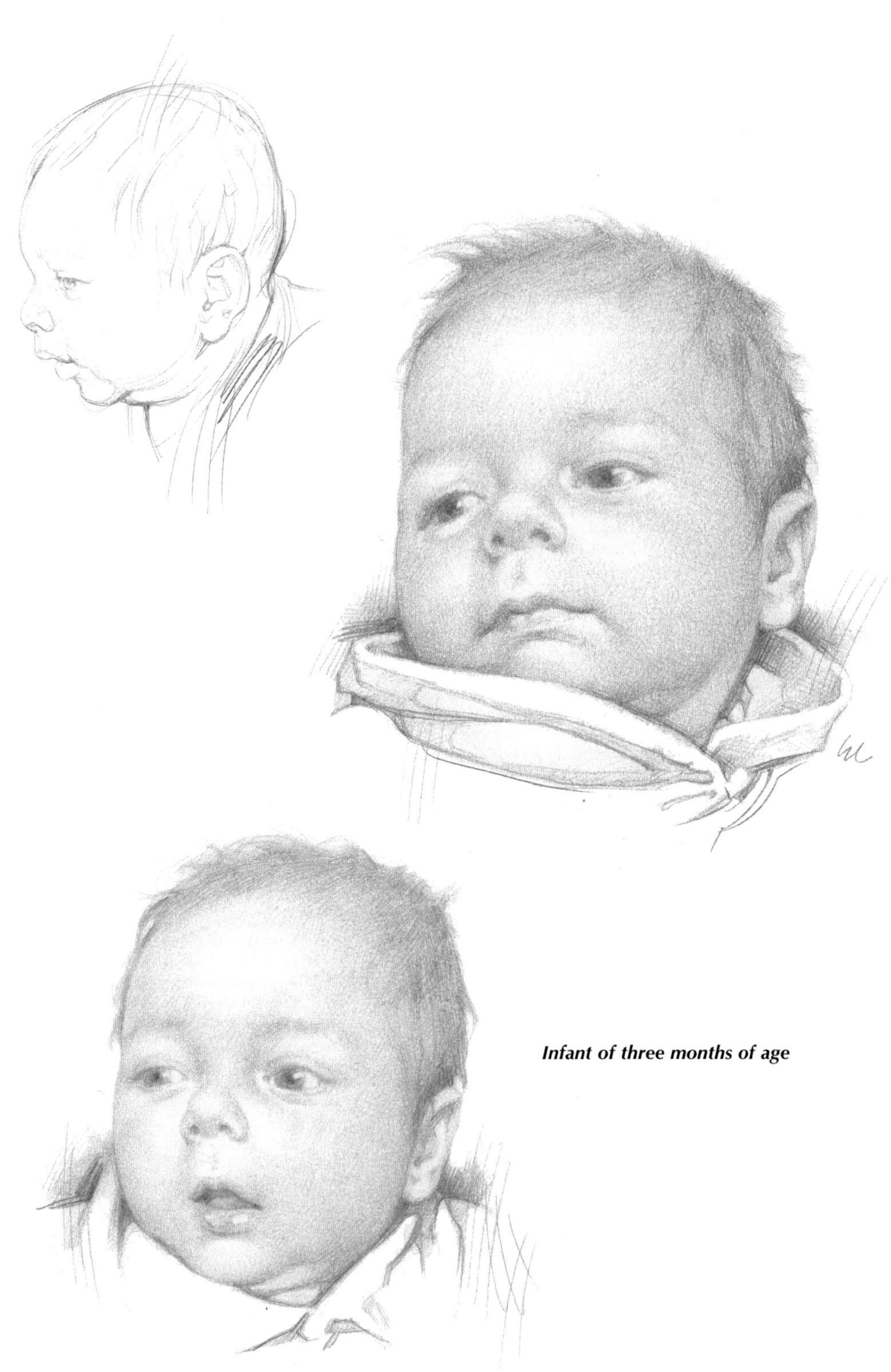

Infant of three months of age

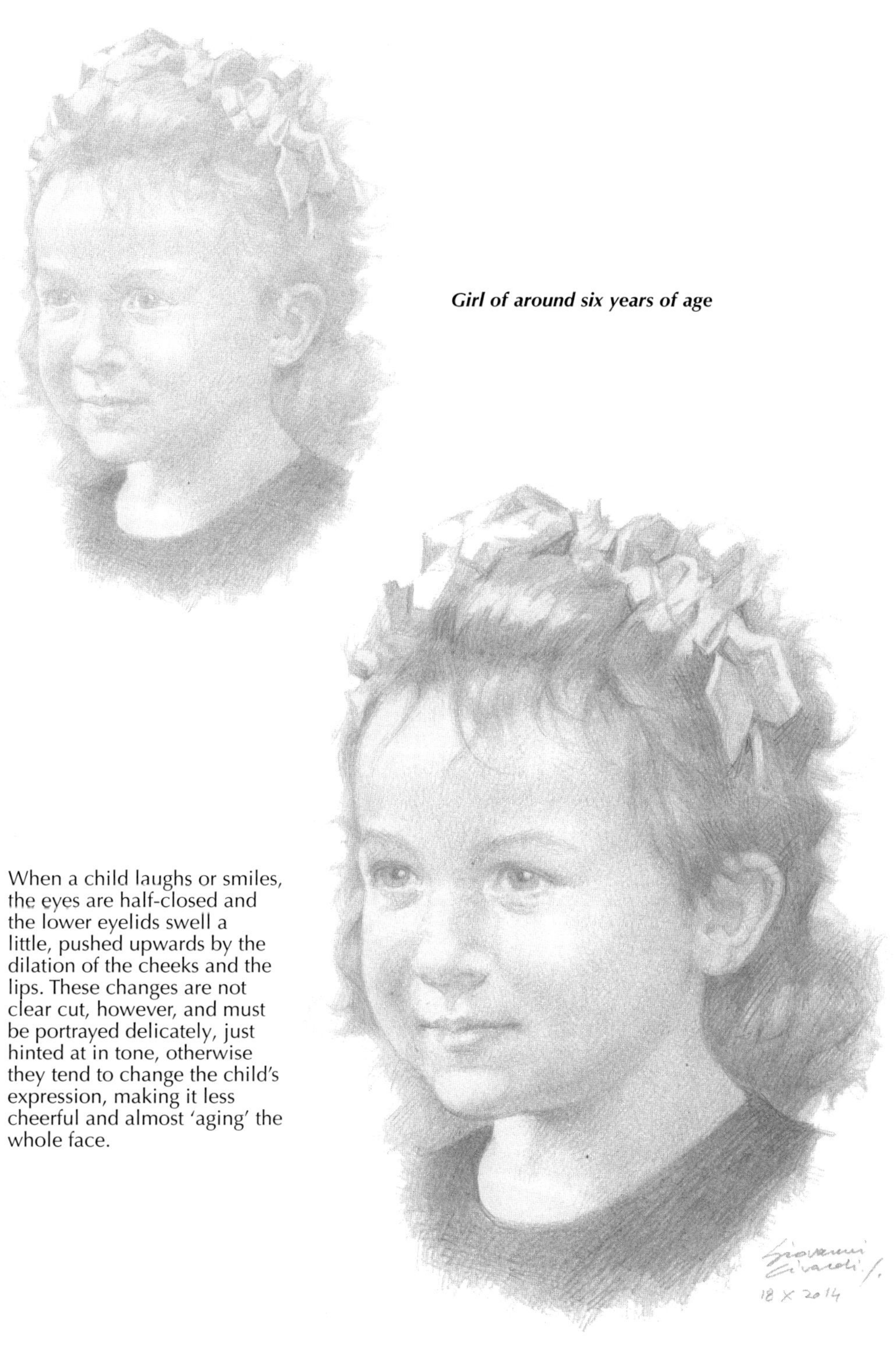

Girl of around six years of age

When a child laughs or smiles, the eyes are half-closed and the lower eyelids swell a little, pushed upwards by the dilation of the cheeks and the lips. These changes are not clear cut, however, and must be portrayed delicately, just hinted at in tone, otherwise they tend to change the child's expression, making it less cheerful and almost 'aging' the whole face.

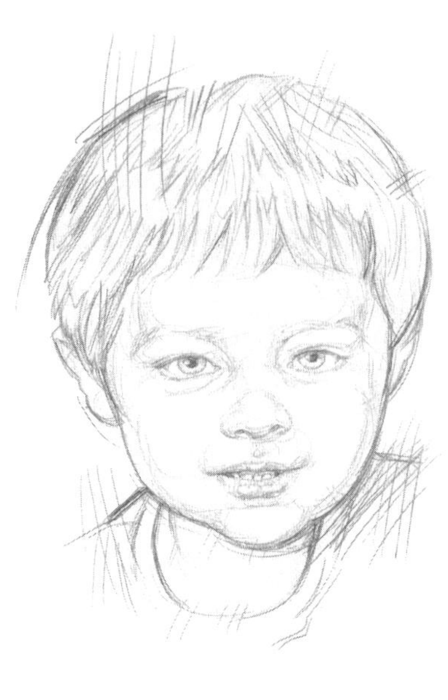

Child of three years of age

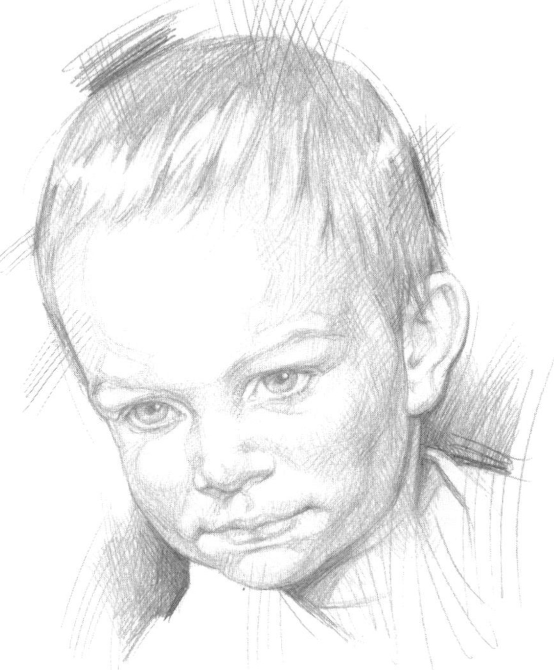

Child of three years of age

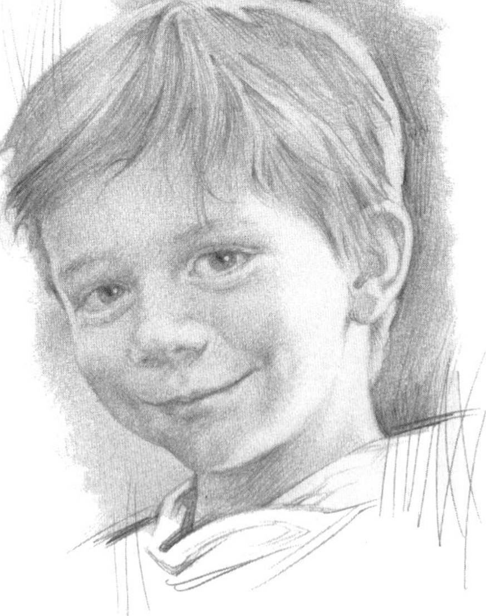

Boy of three-and-a-half years of age

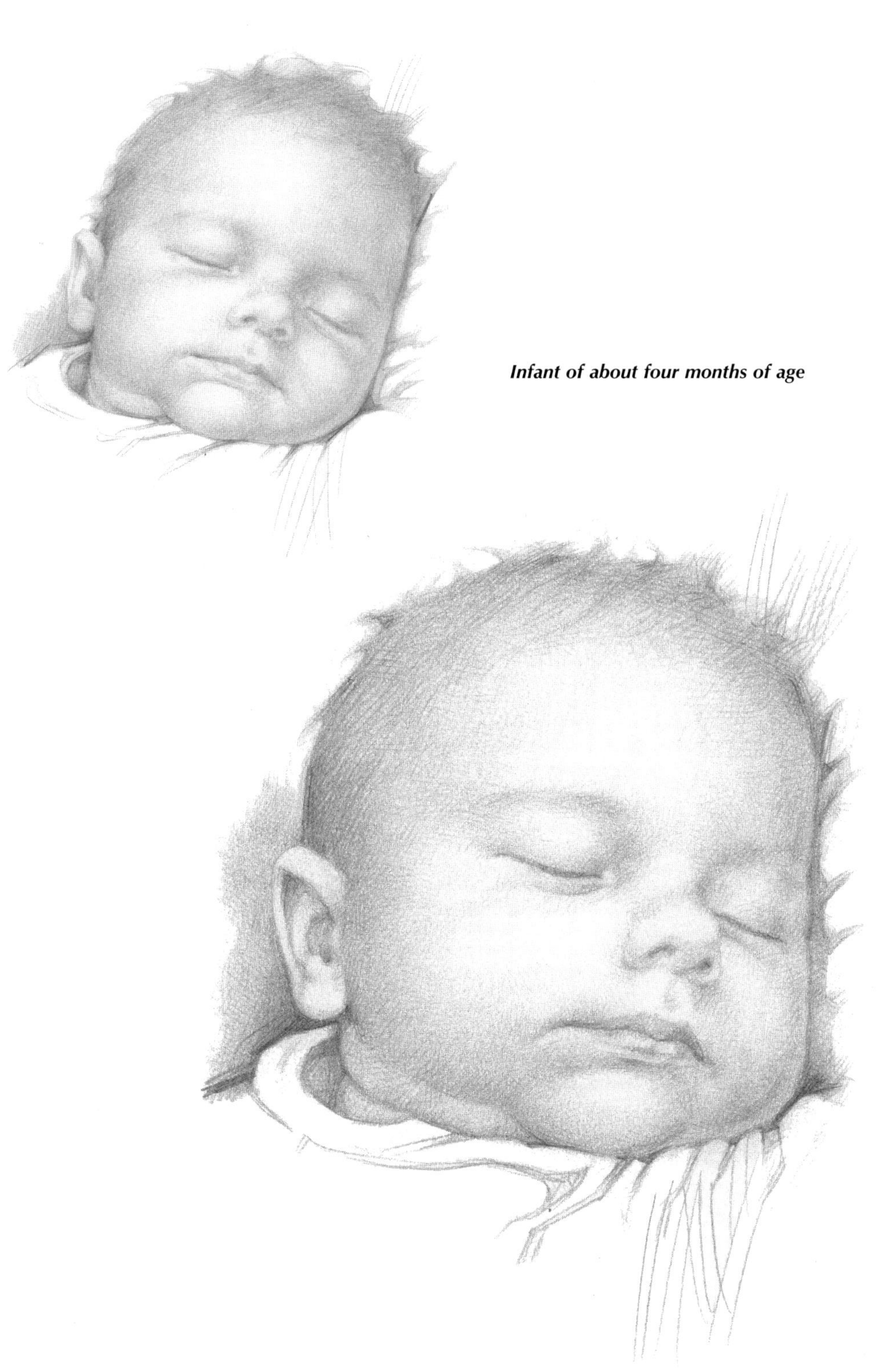

Infant of about four months of age

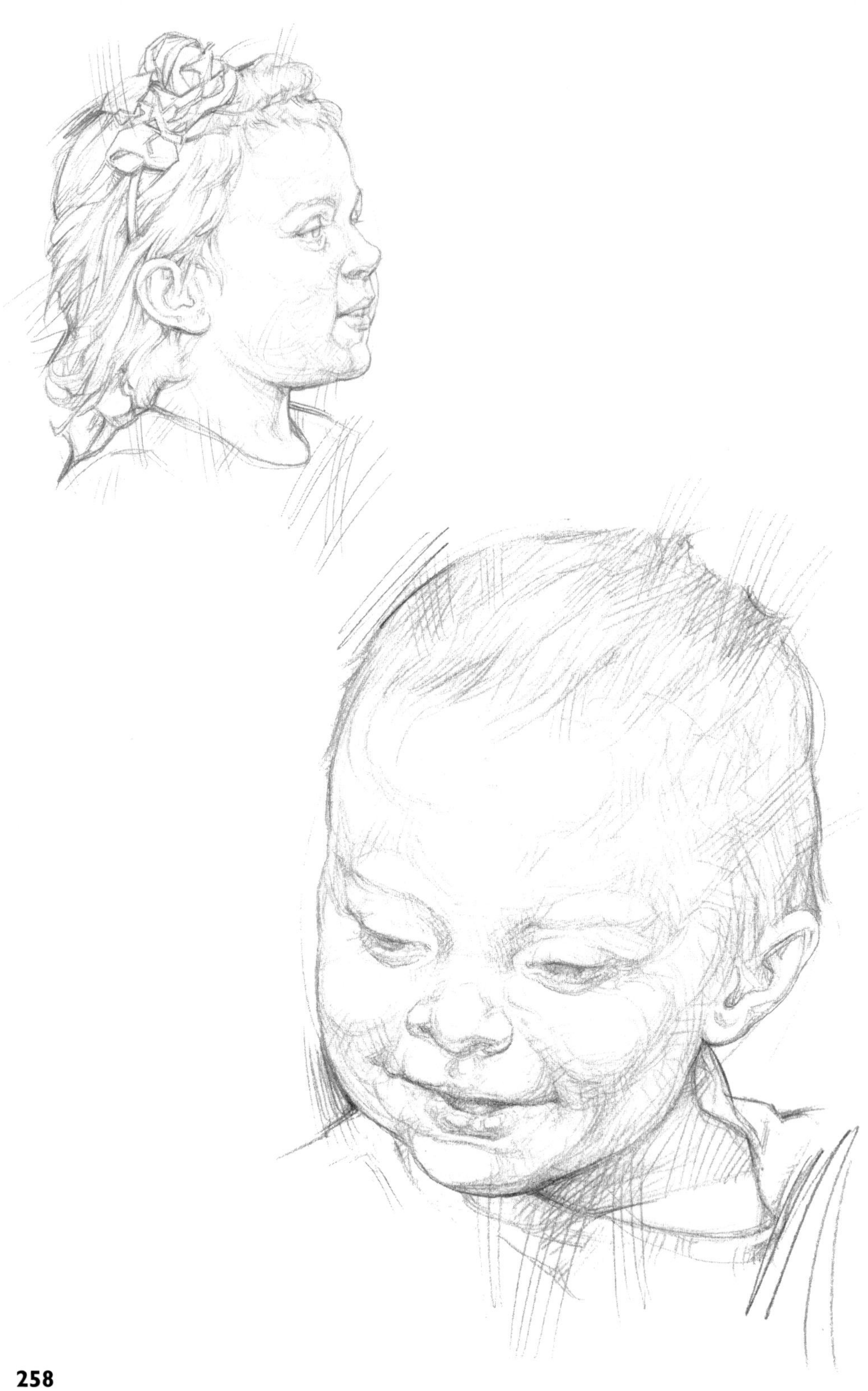

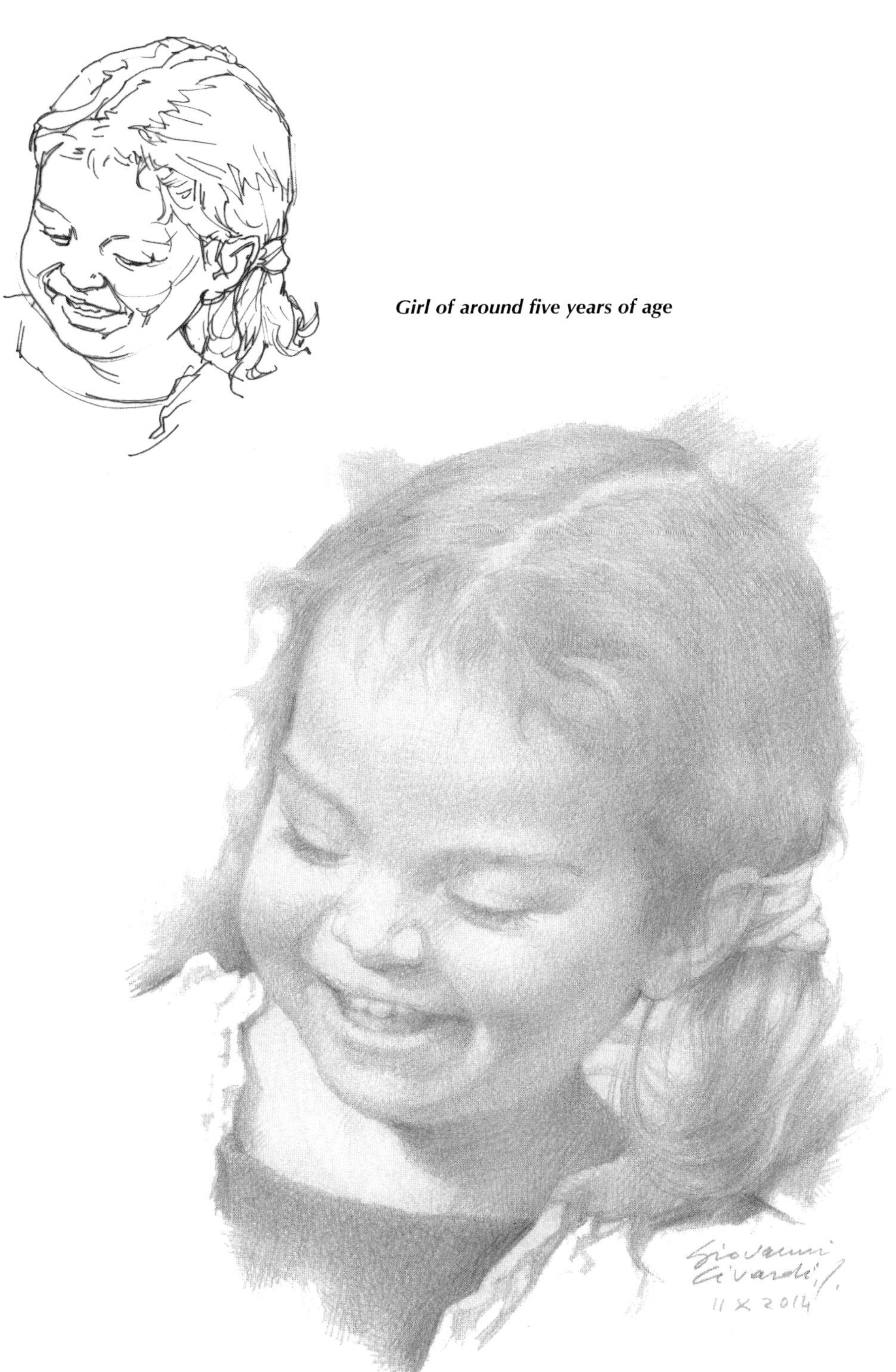

Girl of around five years of age

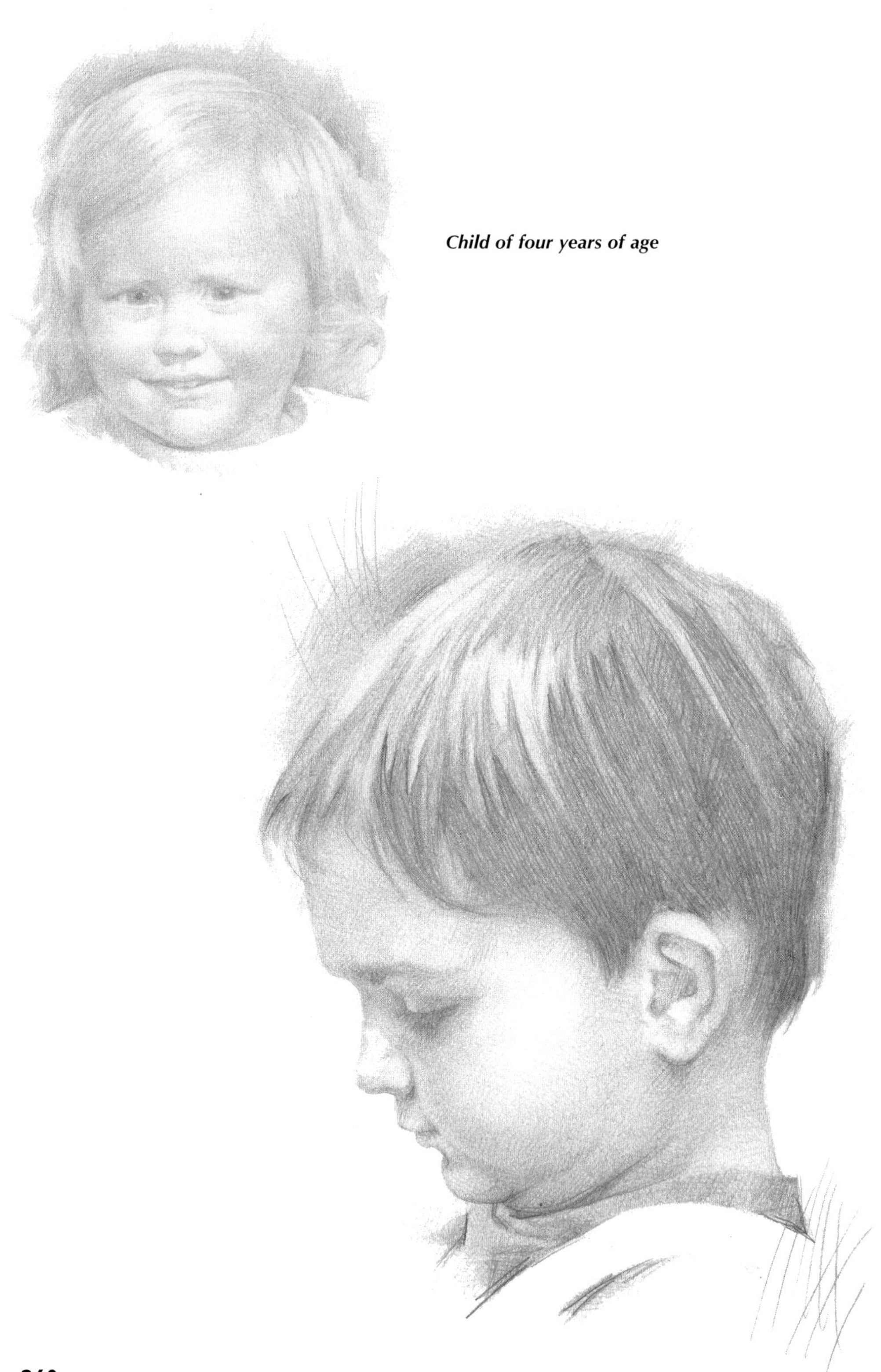

Child of four years of age

FROM THE FAMILY ALBUM

It is usually not difficult to find family photographs in any home. They are perhaps collected in a dusty, well-cared for album, or gathered together in no particular order in envelopes or boxes that have been relegated to a corner of the attic. In recent years, documentation of family life has been entrusted to the various forms of digital technology, to be consulted on a computer screen or television but, until a few years ago, photographs printed on paper, especially in black and white, were the norm and often of rather exceptional quality. In fact, only the most important life events, holidays or new births deserved a photo, to preserve the memory.

These photographs evoke emotions, due to their 'ancient' appearance, with studied lighting and pose, 'professional' in their aesthetic aspect. It is therefore enjoyable (and a little nostalgic) to pick out a few family features in the children's or other young faces from our old photographs: parents, grandparents, playmates, a few ancestors or even ourselves. In many cases, it is possible to go back several decades with these images. They may also be more recent, but still 'dated' in their outward fashions. In this way we can discover interesting and curious physical features, expressions, attitudes, hairstyles and clothes, from the past: all aesthetic stimuli that can make the portraiture of children even more exciting.

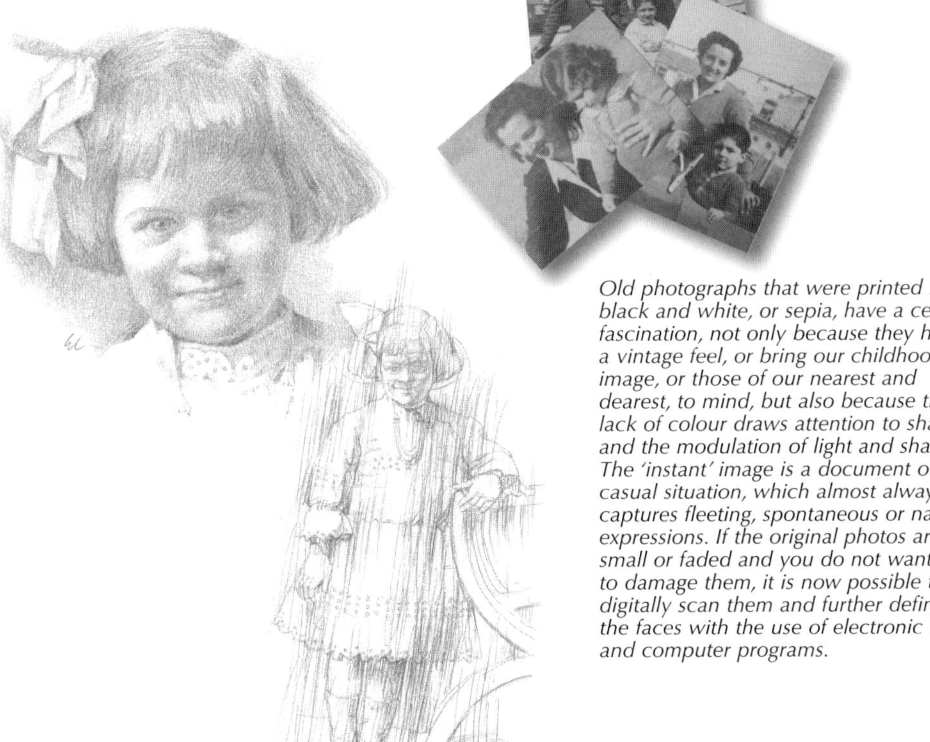

Old photographs that were printed in black and white, or sepia, have a certain fascination, not only because they have a vintage feel, or bring our childhood image, or those of our nearest and dearest, to mind, but also because the lack of colour draws attention to shape and the modulation of light and shade. The 'instant' image is a document of a casual situation, which almost always captures fleeting, spontaneous or naïve expressions. If the original photos are small or faded and you do not want to damage them, it is now possible to digitally scan them and further define the faces with the use of electronic tools and computer programs.

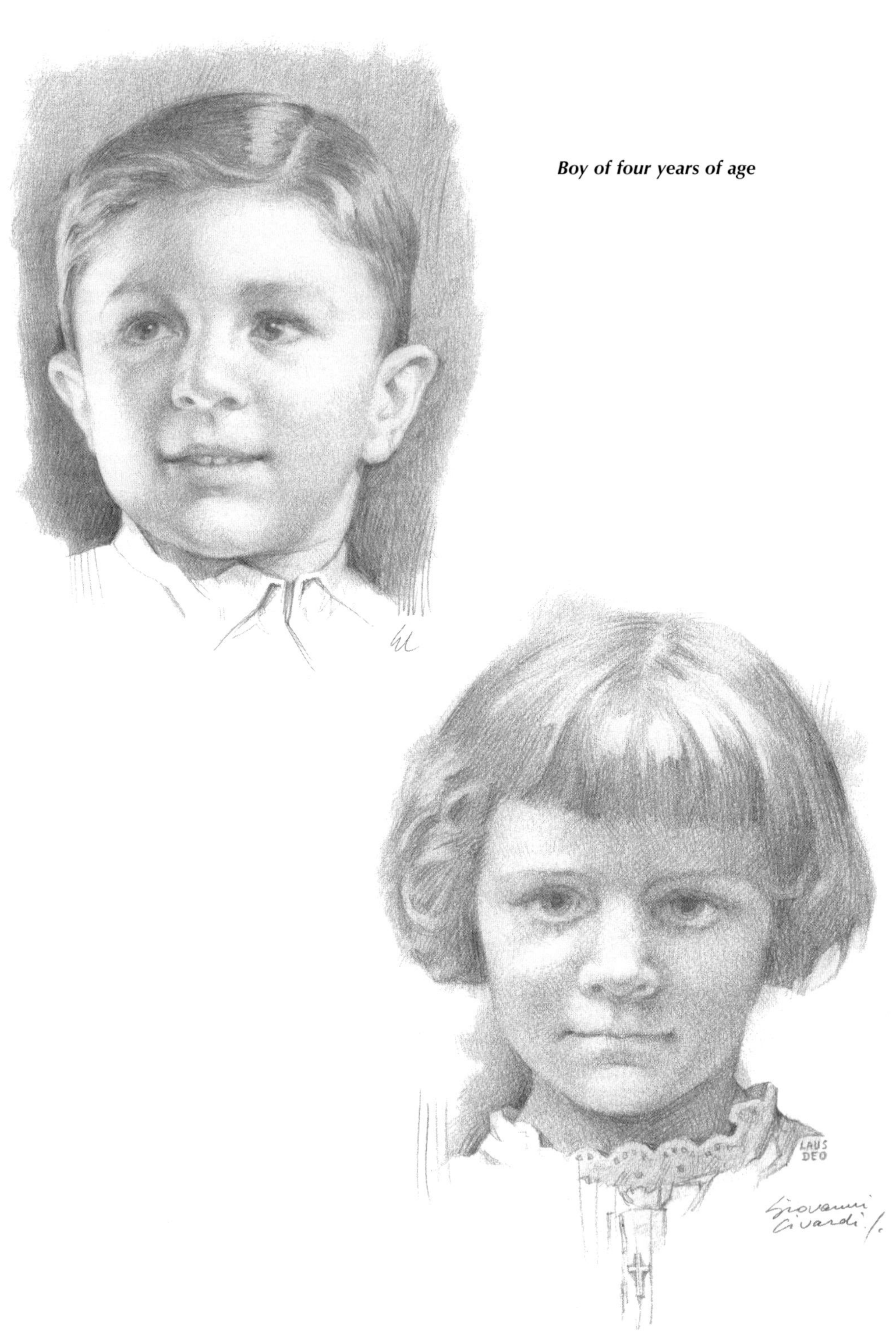

Boy of four years of age

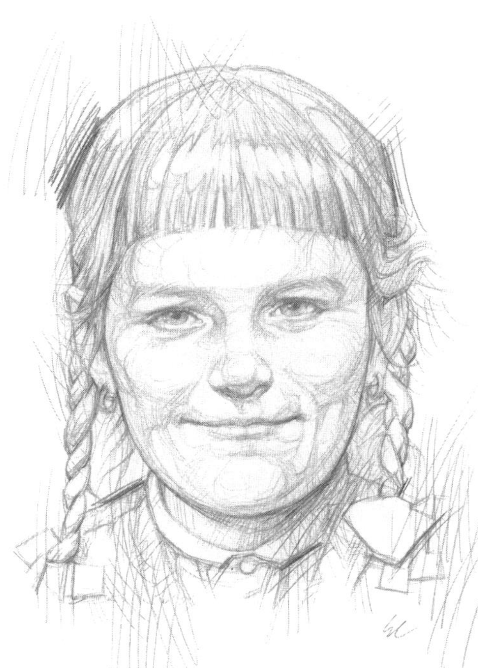

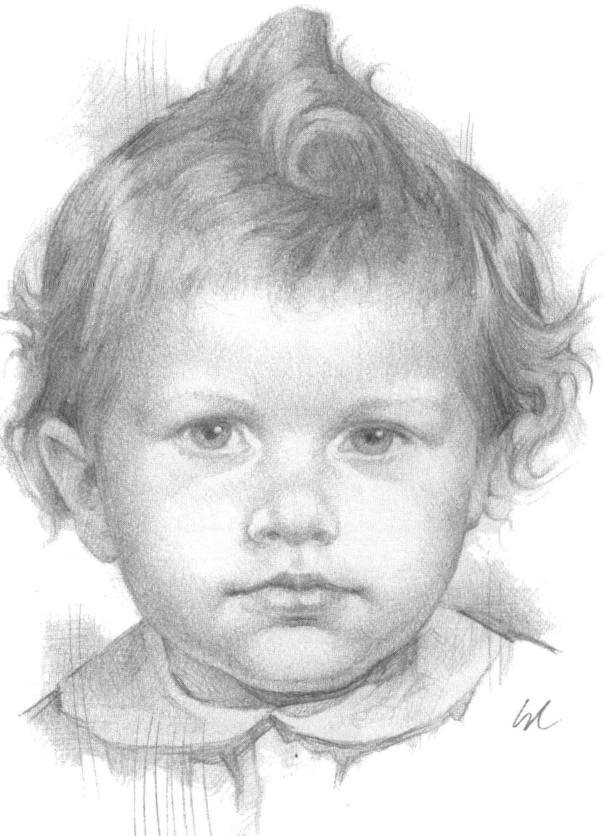

The photographs that I used as a source of inspiration and as documentation for drawing the child portraits shown on these pages are easily 'datable' to certain eras and cultures, like almost all images in which human figures and their surrounding environment appear. They are black and white photographs that date back to the beginning and the middle of the last century, and although we are only examining the faces, they portray clothes and hairstyles that were fashionable in that period.

DRAWING PORTRAITS OF BABIES AND CHILDREN USING GRIDS

The principle on which this book is based is an extremely old and simple one, and can be summarized best by looking to some reflections of the art historian Ernst Gombrich (1909–2001) on an artist's training (for example, in his book *Art and Illusion*).

In Medieval and Renaissance art studios (and after that, in the academies) there was a belief that art was 'conceptual', in the sense that it was necessary first to learn, in theory and practice, how to draw the structural outline of an object – including human beings – before the artist was allowed to use a living individual as a model.

Many model sketchbooks could be found in the studios too. These were collections of drawings – produced by the Masters, or reproduced from their best works – that pupils had to copy as practice and to build up a useful collection of pictures for conceptualizing and executing commissions.

Many manual and mechanical procedures have been developed to exactly reproduce an image. Some allow the artist to retain the original dimensions, others to alter them proportionally in order to enlarge or reduce the resulting image. The most common procedures include photocopying; photograph printing; distance projection (with an episcope, for opaque images, or using a projector for translucent images); tracing (using tracing paper or a lightbox); and digital computer processing. These methods all aid the artist's practical and preparatory work, but they also undoubtedly slow learning and the skill of interpretation. It is therefore better to resort to an older, simpler, more intuitive method – that of drawing a grid or mesh, which can be used for portraying complex forms from a live model and for reproducing a flat image on the same or a different scale. In both cases, it means placing a grid of squares between the artist's eye and the image he or she intends to portray. The images with which Albrecht Dürer (1471–1528) describes this procedure are well-known.

To work in a fixed position from life, a physical frame can be used: a wooden square onto which thin threads have been fixed horizontally and vertically to form a grid. The number of threads can be chosen at will to alter the number of squares. After tracing a similar grid onto your paper or other working surface, it is simple to outline the details of what you see in each corresponding square.

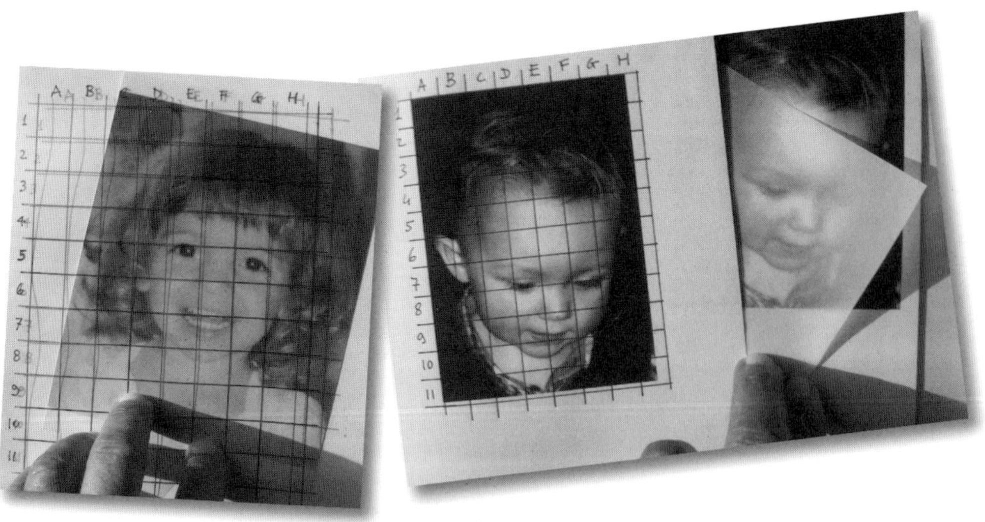

To reproduce a flat image such as a photograph or drawing, the grid can be drawn either directly or indirectly on the image itself or copied onto the sheet, using the methods shown below.

The grid used by artists to copy drawings is inspired by, and is similar to, the one used in Ancient Egyptian art to calculate the proportions of figures and find the position of their anatomical parts. However, in this case, the grid was used to create a drawing in an established style, or to give instructions for such an image to be drawn accurately, while today it is used to reproduce a pre-existing image.

Although the procedure has been applied by many artists from various eras (David, Degas, Ingres, Boldini and Klimt, amongst others), it is obvious that the use of a grid to reproduce an image is simply a mechanical expedient to aid the work. It must not be allowed to lower the artist's vital capacity for observation, understanding and interpretation, nor to let the direct gesture of the drawing itself 'waste away' or prevent other developments in personal style. We can therefore say that it is not a 'method' for learning to draw, or to avoid the difficulty of assessing proportions, but is rather an aid for an artist's first steps, making him or her reflect and study the subject more closely. On the other hand, almost all modern conceptions of art shun the rigid 'academic' training of an artist and shy away from (or totally reject) traditional procedures and methods, aiming more at the development of a pure skill.

To increase or reduce the area of an image, photograph, or a sheet of paper, draw a diagonal line and choose the new size.

To translate an image faithfully and easily, when increasing or reducing the size, use a square 'grid' (a set of horizontal and vertical lines in any case) drawn lightly on the reference image (photograph, drawing or even in one's surroundings) and on the sheet being drawn on. In order to avoid damaging the image that is being altered, do it on a photocopy of the image or overlay it with tracing paper. Creating the grid must be intuitive: the interval between the horizontal and vertical lines is usually constant and chosen according to the enlargement measurements and the degree of precision with which you wish to transfer the reference image details.

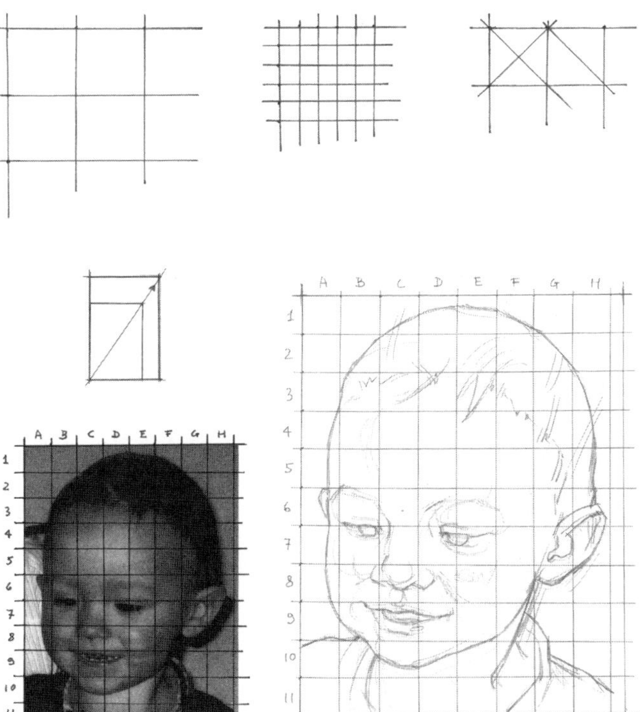

PROPORTIONS AND PROCEDURE

As discussed on pages 210–211, the proportions of a child's head are very different from those of an adult: the face is lower in relation to the cranium; additionally, the hair is much finer and the eyes appear very big. A child's head is more rounded overall, and both front and side projections can be set in a square.

The page opposite contains a schematic drawing of the sequence usually followed when enlarging an image using the grid method, with reference to a photograph or another drawing (steps A–F). If we exclude the 'mechanical' enlarging phase, the procedure as shown in the lower part of the drawing (steps 1–4) is similar to the one that is usually used intuitively when working directly from a live model.

A – *Model; from life.*

B – *Photograph of the model; preferably black and white, printed on paper.*

C – *Grid; with the spacing between the lines dependent on the degree of precision desired. The closer together the lines are, the finer the grid will be, and the greater the precision. In order to avoid damaging the photograph, a grid can be traced on a photocopy or a transparent acetate sheet placed over the image (see page 264 for an example), and fixed firmly to the paper. Be aware of possible distortions of perspective that will be accentuated through enlarging.*

D – *Trace the grid onto your drawing surface (paper, canvas or other support) with the same number of squares but with the lines further apart, corresponding to the increase in size desired. Draw the lines lightly using a sharp pencil so that they can be erased easily afterwards. Write in corresponding numbers and letters to aid identification of the specific squares. Avoid technical expedients to enlarge or reduce the subject.*

E – *Trace the features from the corresponding squares on the photograph onto the drawing surface.*

F – *Once you have drawn the summary features of the subject, erase the grid.*

DRAWING DIRECTLY

With practice, you will be able to use a grid with fewer squares (or abandon it completely) and draw directly. You can simply follow the intuitive procedure below, based on descriptive representation, which applies equally to drawings made from live models and those from photographs

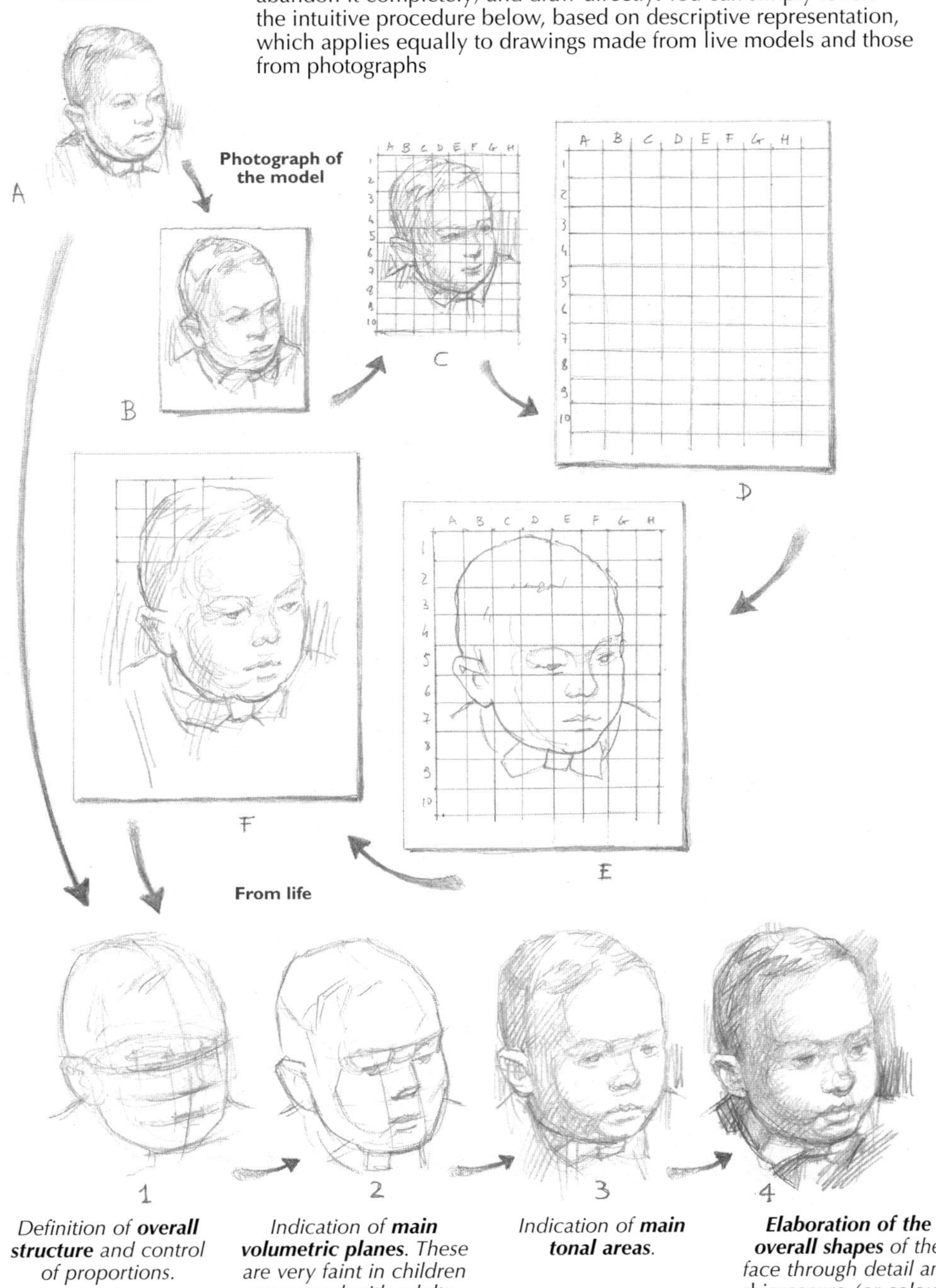

*Definition of **overall structure** and control of proportions.*

*Indication of **main volumetric planes**. These are very faint in children compared with adults, so these planes must not be accentuated.*

*Indication of **main tonal areas**.*

***Elaboration of the overall shapes** of the face through detail and chiaroscuro (or colour).*

PORTRAIT STUDIES

The following drawings have been chosen to give ideas and opportunity for practice, in order to be able to observe and study the proportions and shapes of children's and babies' faces. The rather neutral style that I have used to create them is a reflection of this purpose. The picture on which the grid is placed is taken back to the most simple, basic lines that are useful for immediately grasping the overall shape and position of each detail.

The grid is usually traced onto the image to be reproduced (whether a photograph or another drawing), but here I preferred to trace only the summary features, just enough to begin the subsequent elaboration.

You can use the grid that accompanies each portrait and continue to reproduce the finished drawing exactly as it appears, or you can try altering the dimensions and drawing or painting techniques. You can also try using colour on the work or applying different, more personal expressive styles.

I have used a variety of drawing techniques, both traditional and more innovative, for these portraits. Some techniques lend themselves well to portraying the soft, delicate shapes of children's faces; others, especially if particularly elaborate or time-consuming, are less suitable for reflecting the spontaneous characteristics of a pose and the simplicity of the execution.

Once you have acquired the skills of assessing proportions and the ability to trace shapes and handle tone through *chiaroscuro*, I advise that you set aside the grid and attempt a direct evaluation of the proportions and facial features, in order to achieve the most personal portrait.

All the portraits in this section were drawn using HB and B graphite pencils on paper measuring 21 × 28cm (8¼ × 11in). It is necessary to check the proportional ratios and volumetric consistency before elaborating – to the degree of definition that you wish to create, and consistent with the style you have chosen – the shading tones, and the details of the face and background.

The three initial phases – size, structure and shadows – summarized opposite, are more valuable when drawing the young model directly from life, but are also applicable when using a grid to trace the basic lines. They refer mainly to the conceptual steps that are always useful for analyzing the shapes of a face and reproducing them effectively.

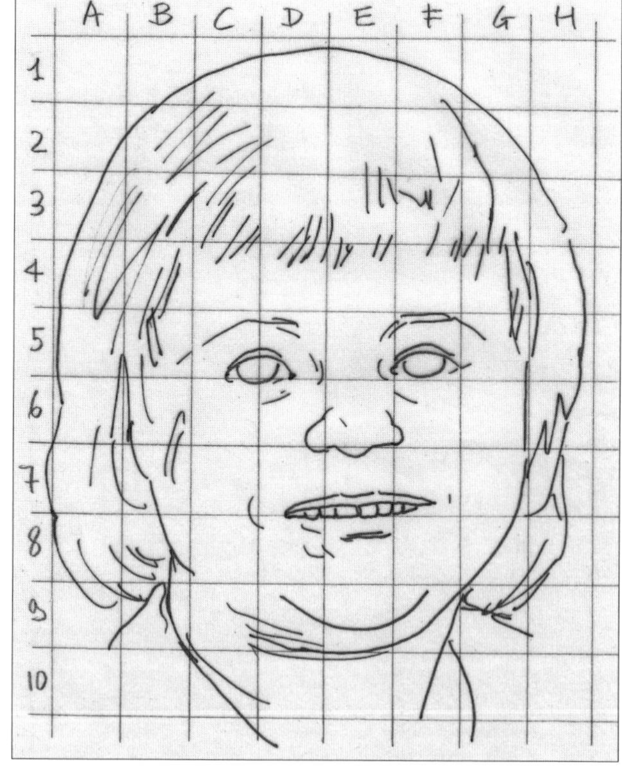

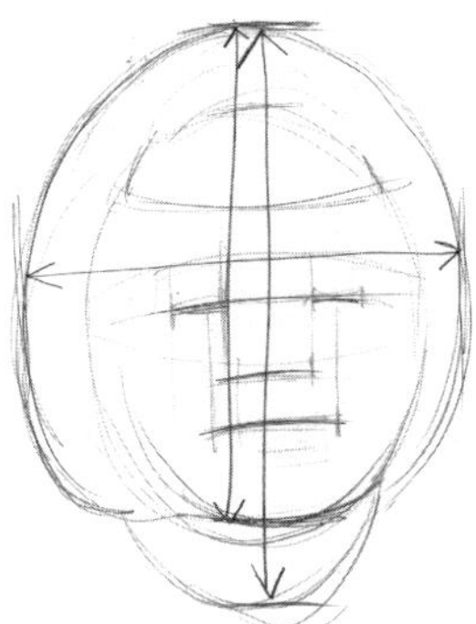
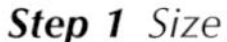

Step 1 *Size*

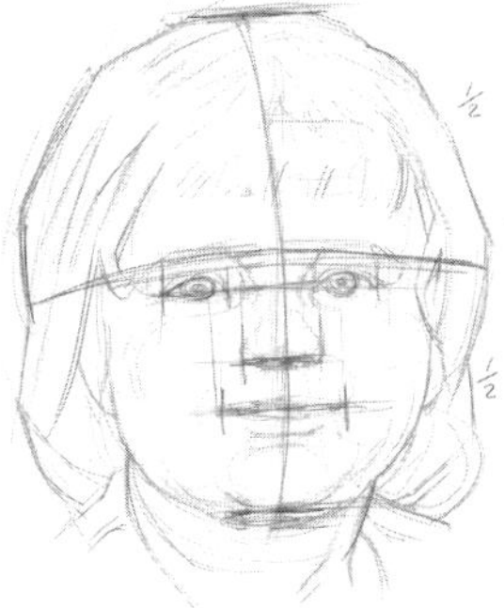

Step 2 *Structure*

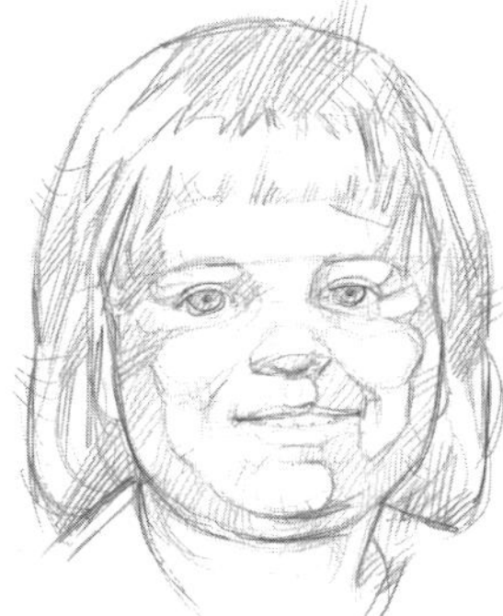

Step 3 *Shadows*

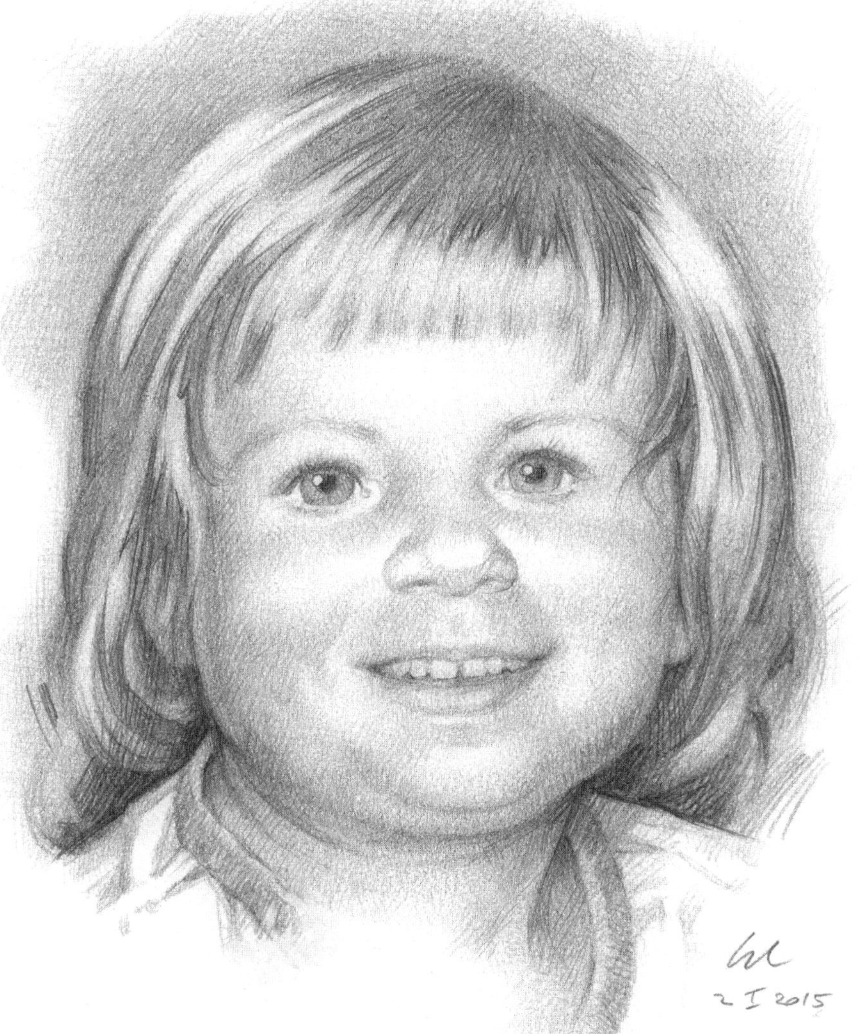

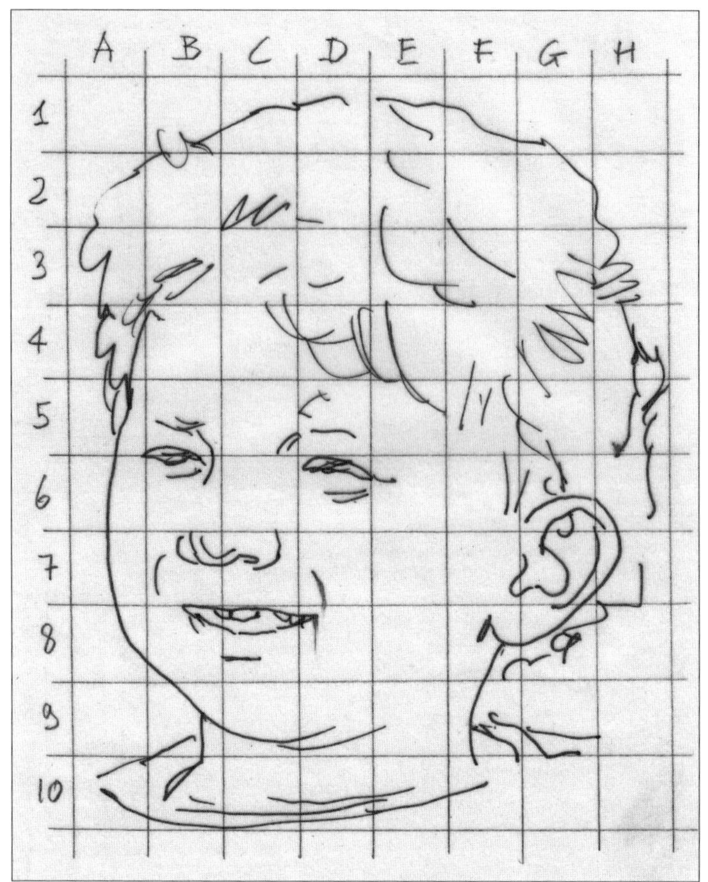

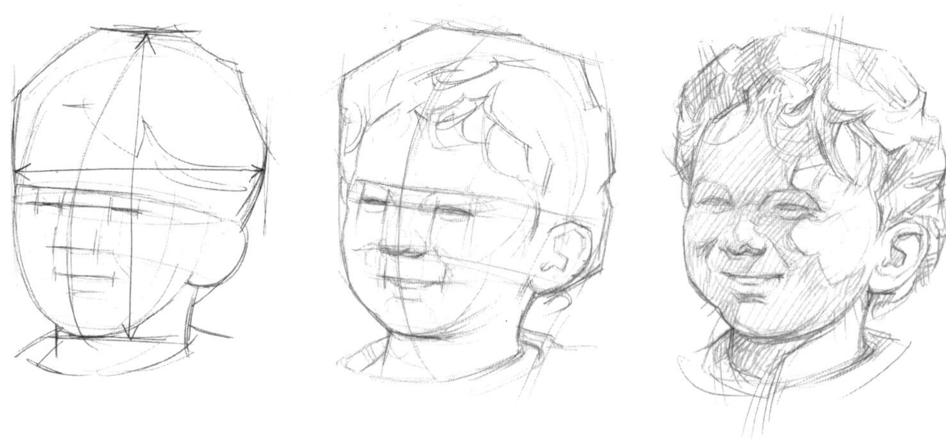

Step 1 *Size* **Step 2** *Structure* **Step 3** *Shadows*

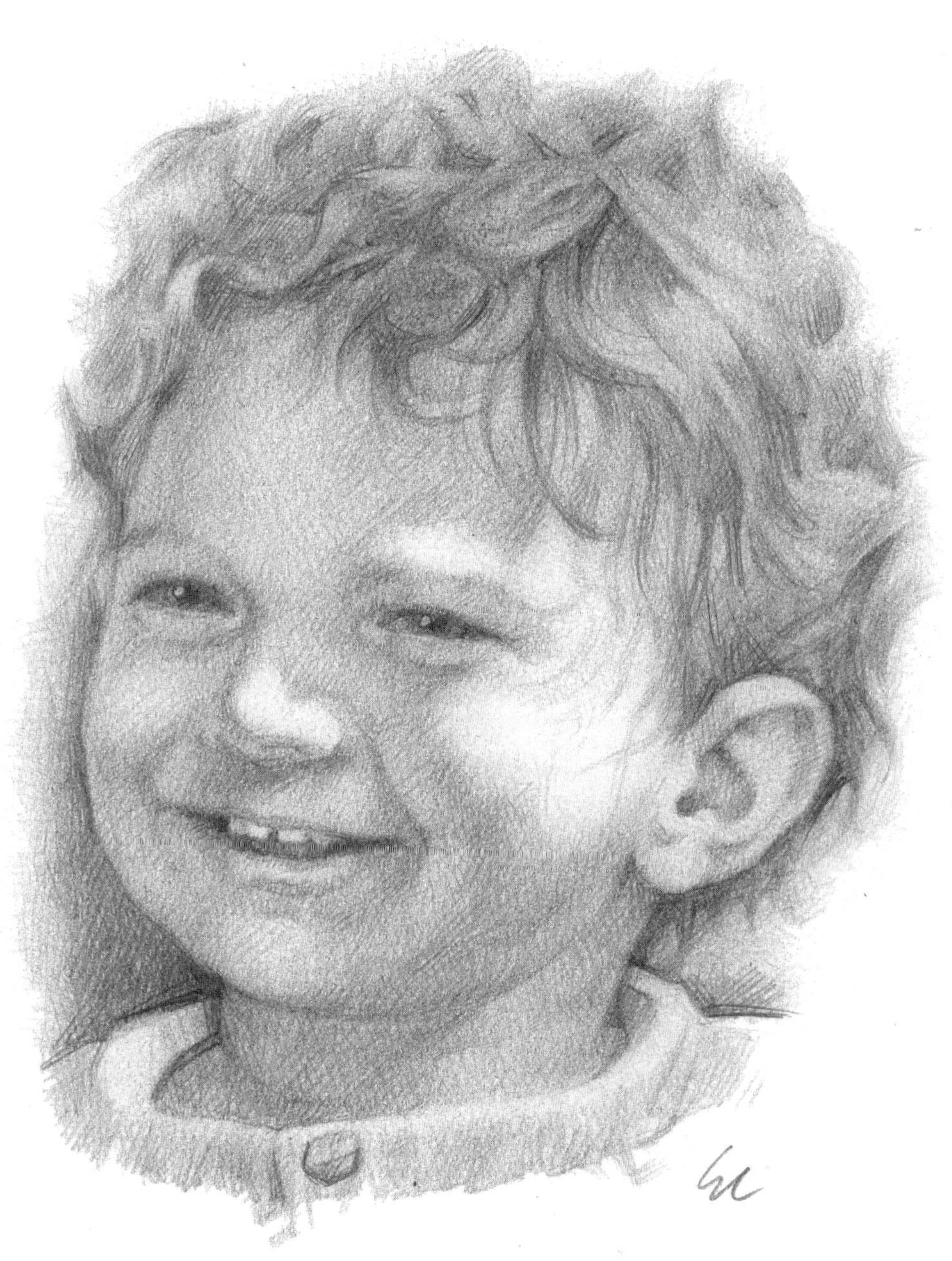

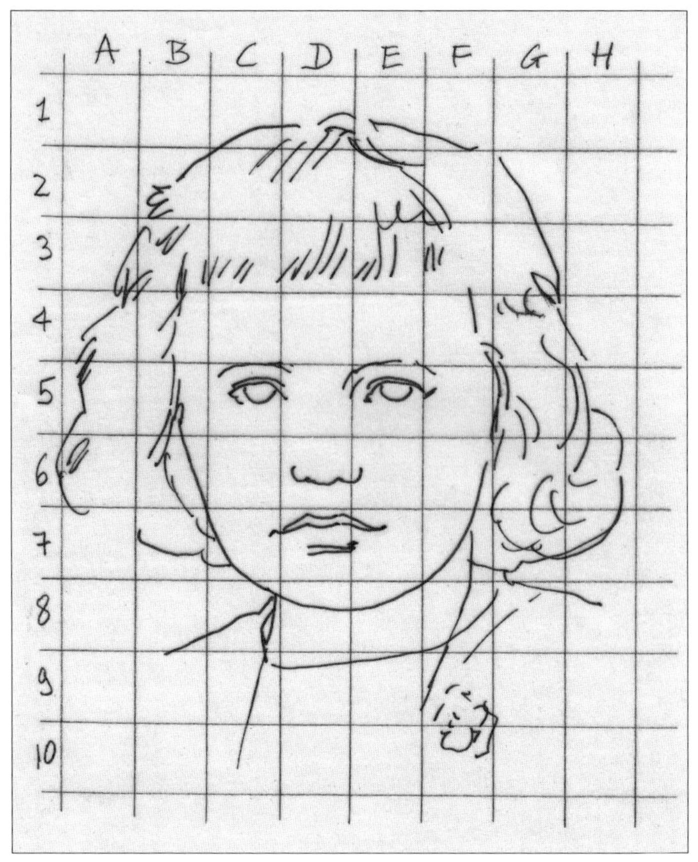

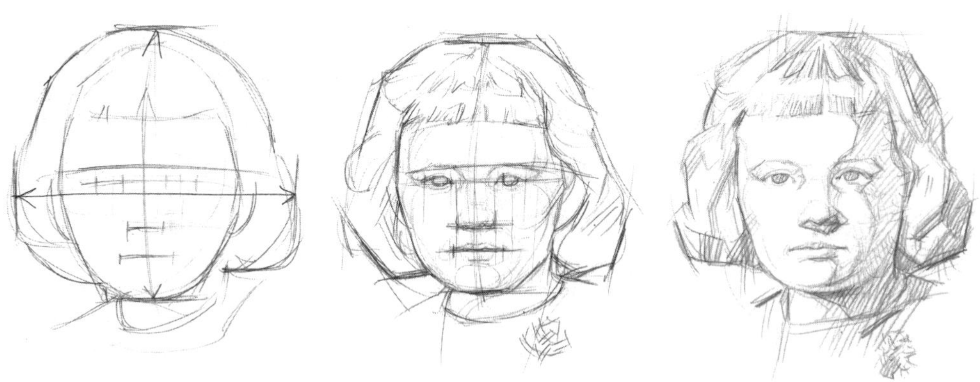

Step 1 *Size* **Step 2** *Structure* **Step 3** *Shadows*

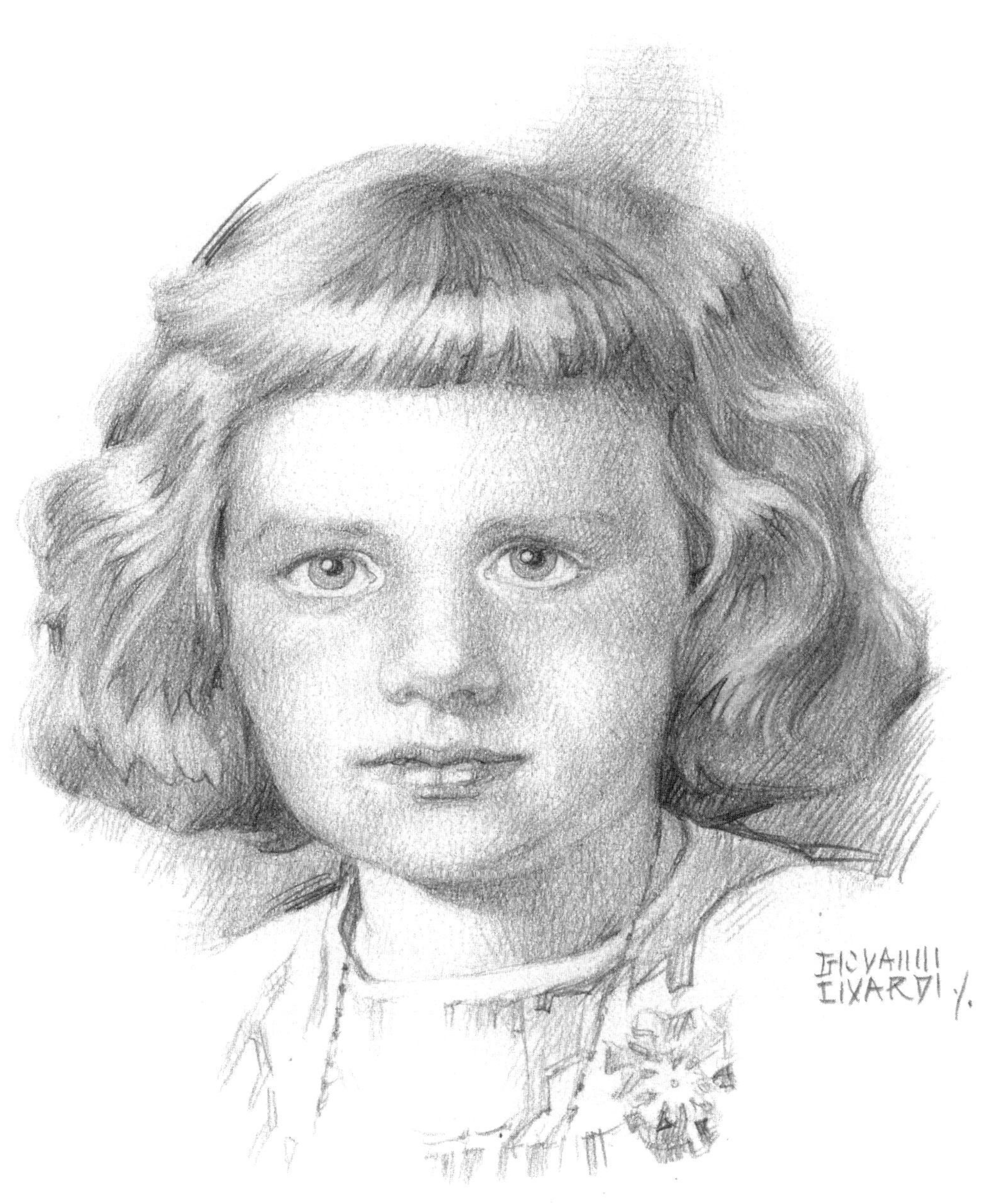
GIOVANNI
CIVARDI

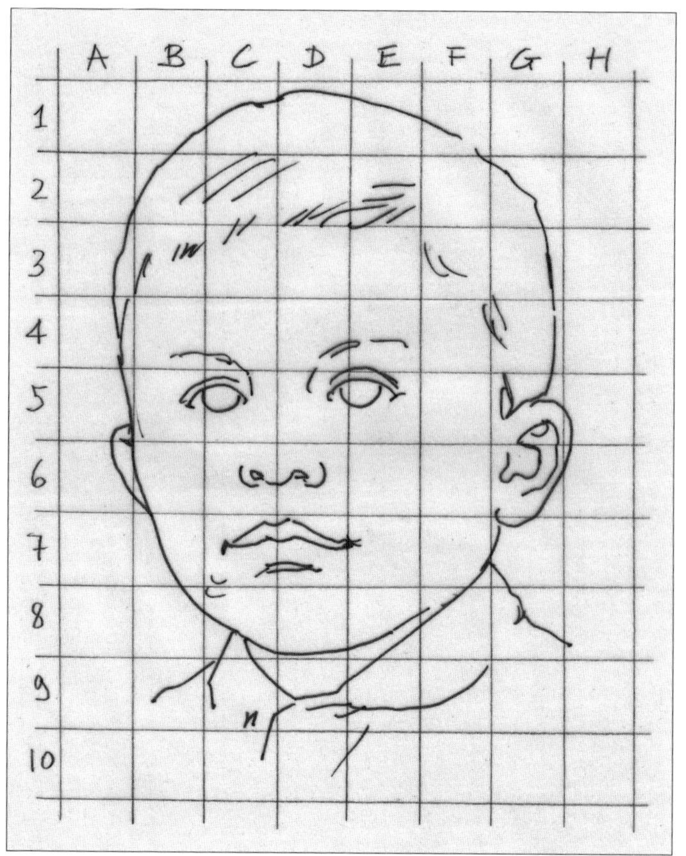

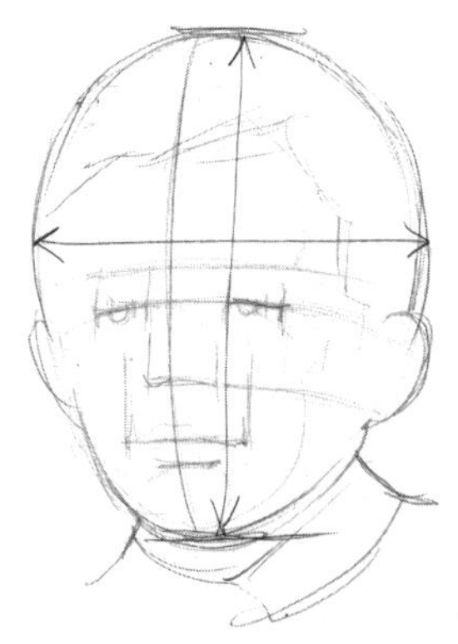

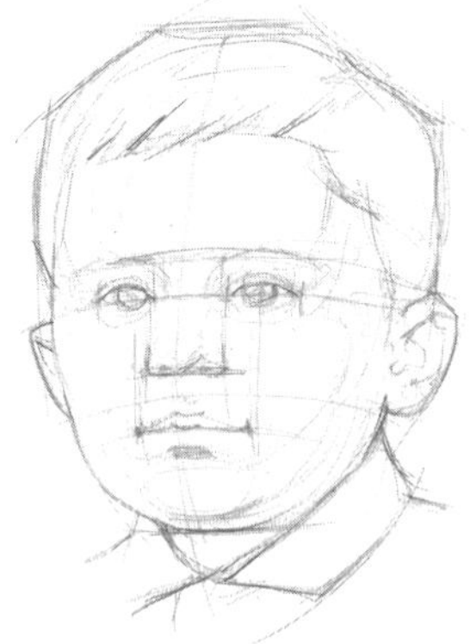

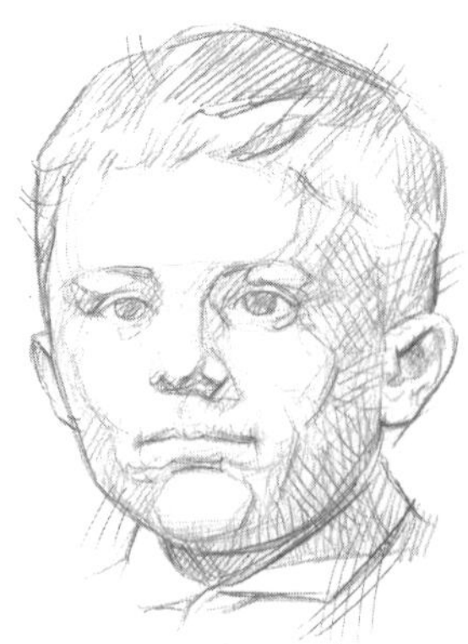

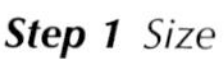

Step 1 *Size* ***Step 2*** *Structure* ***Step 3*** *Shadows*

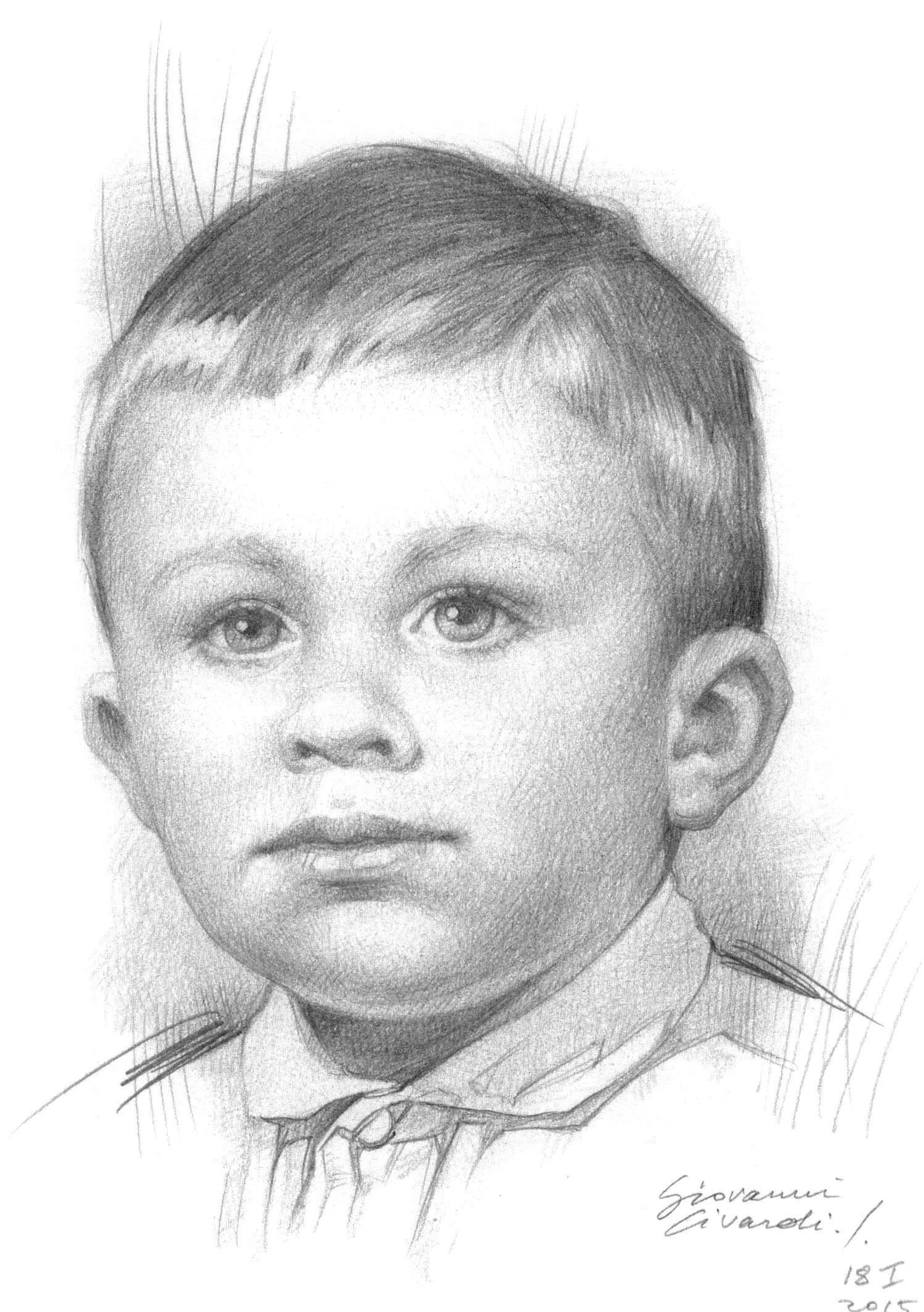
Giovanni
Civardi.
18 I
2015

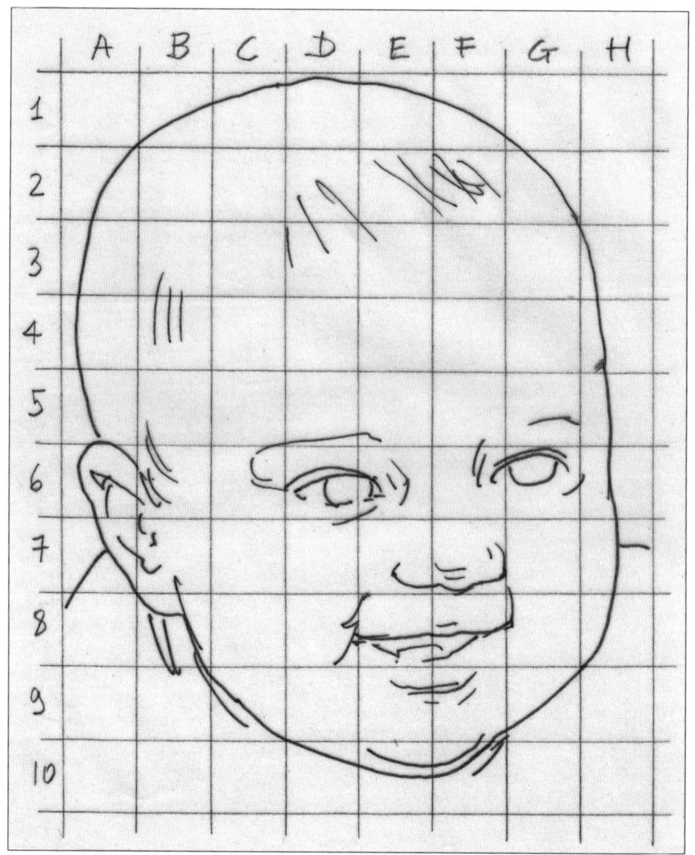

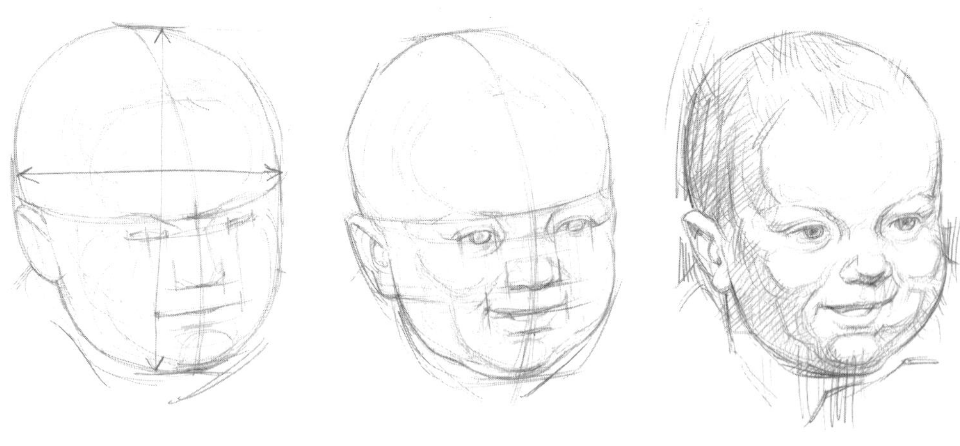

Step 1 *Size*

Step 2 *Structure*

Step 3 *Shadows*

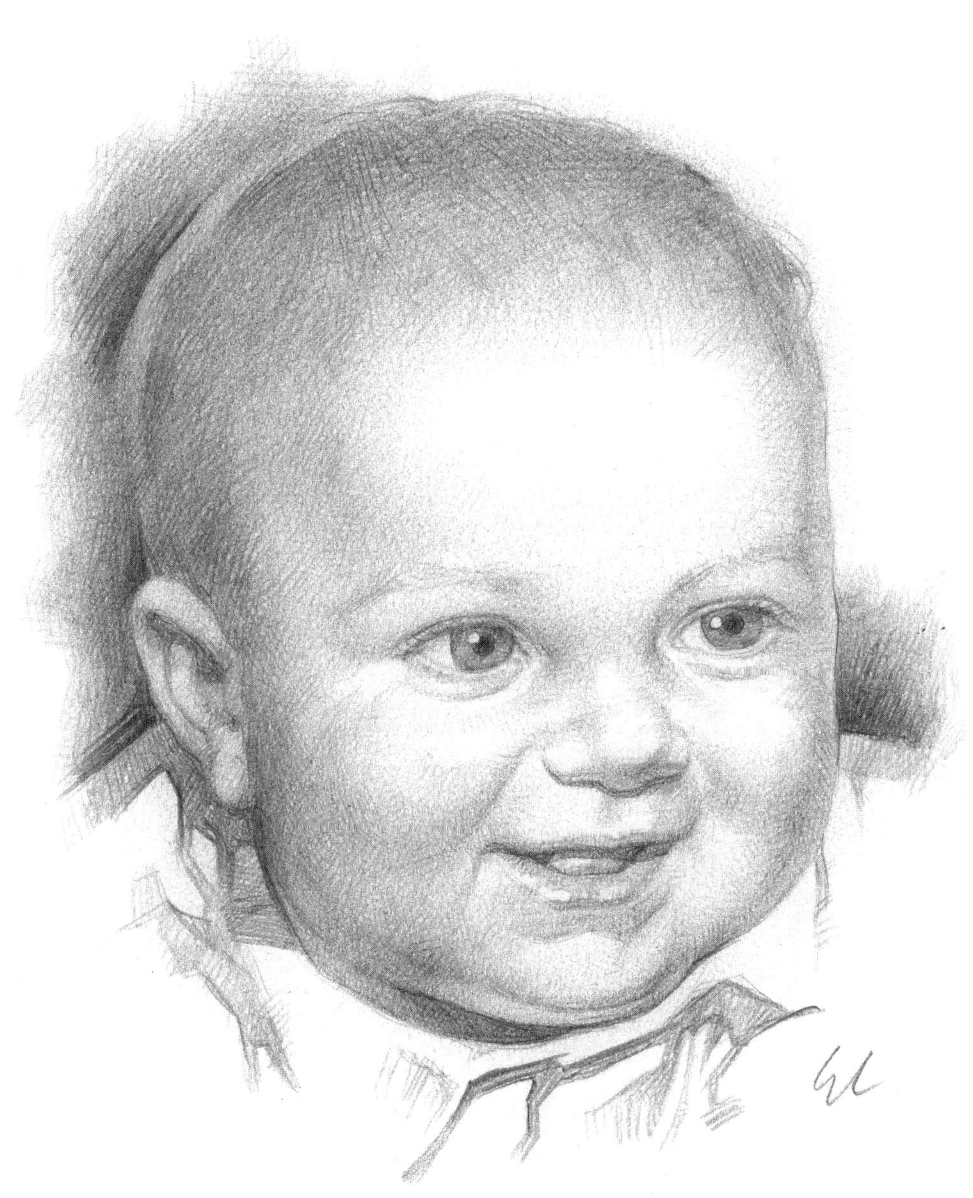

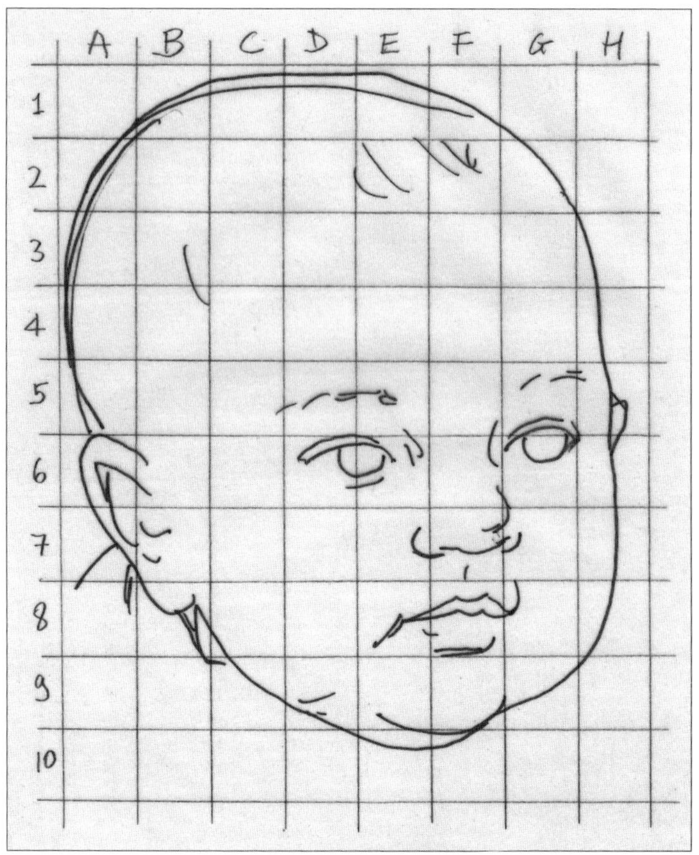

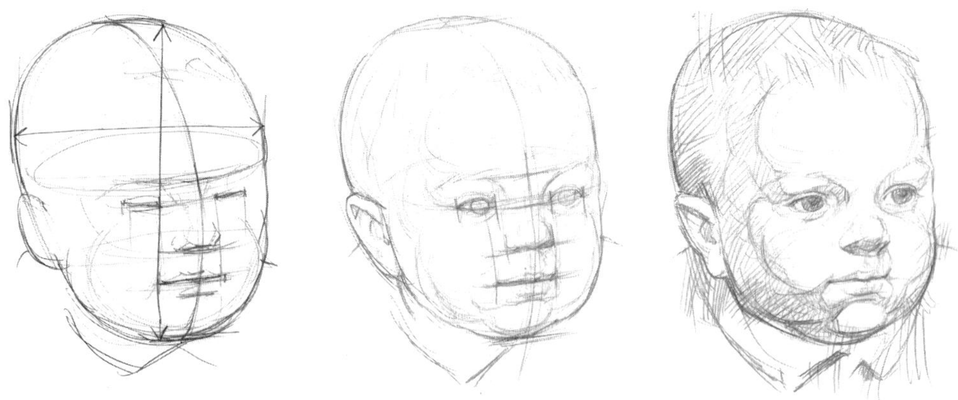

Step 1 *Size* **Step 2** *Structure* **Step 3** *Shadows*

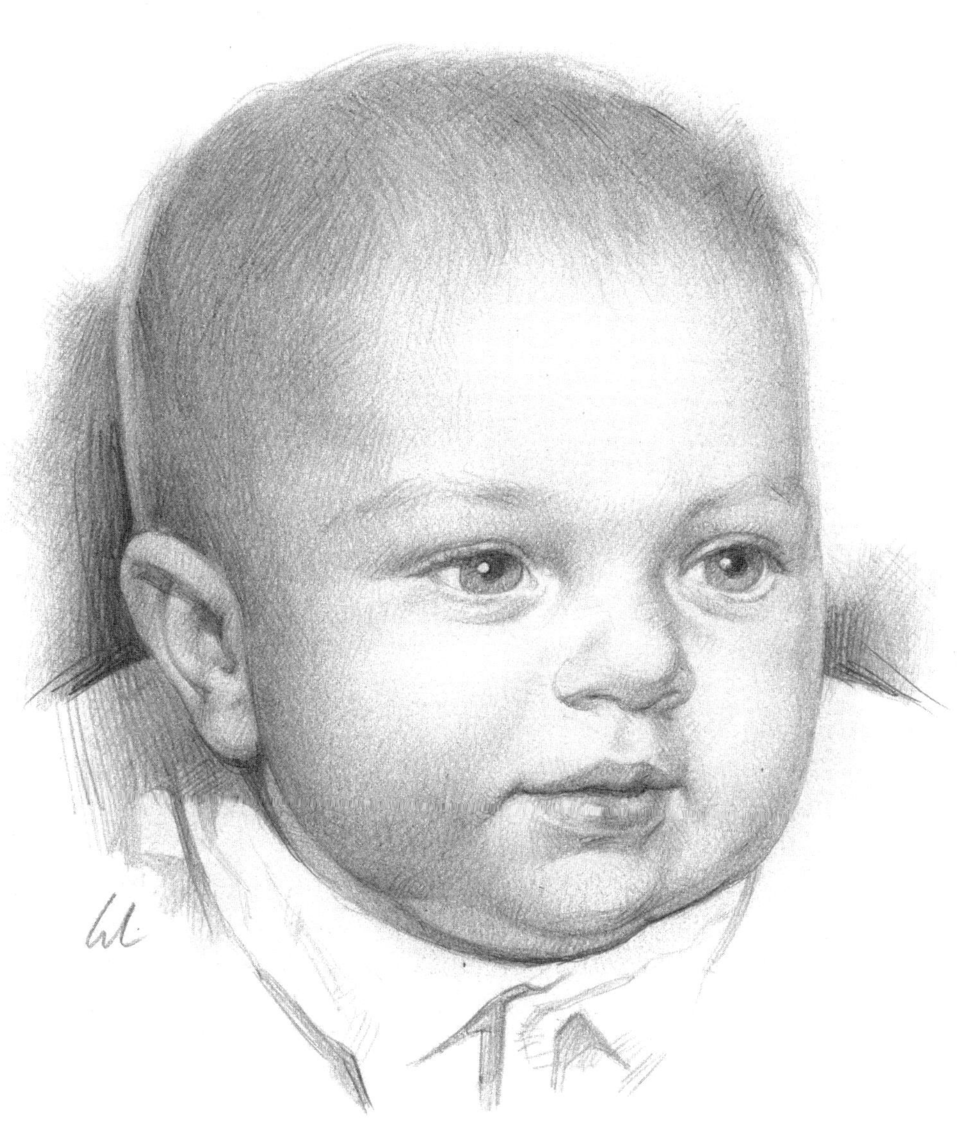

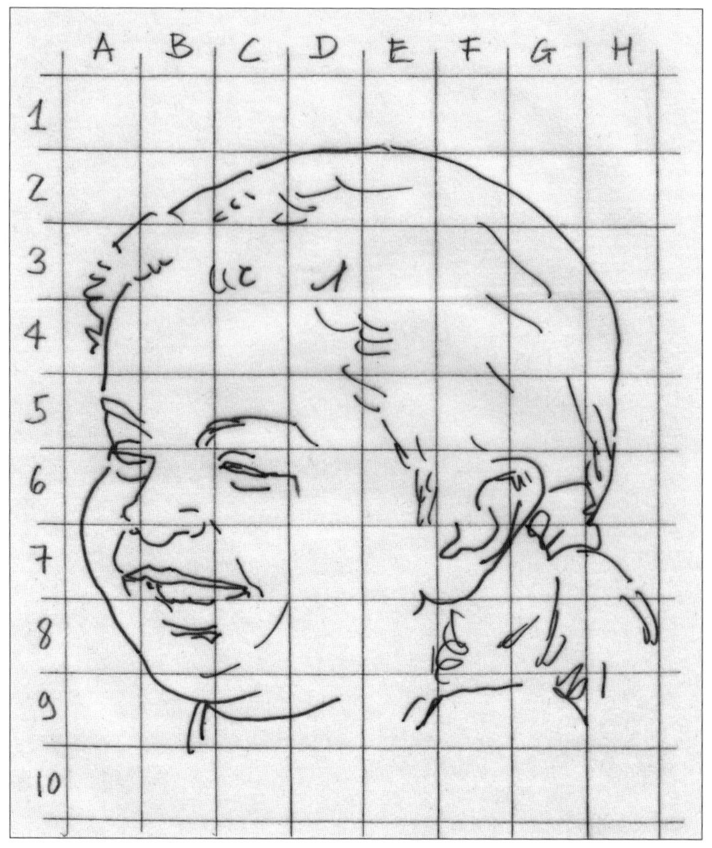

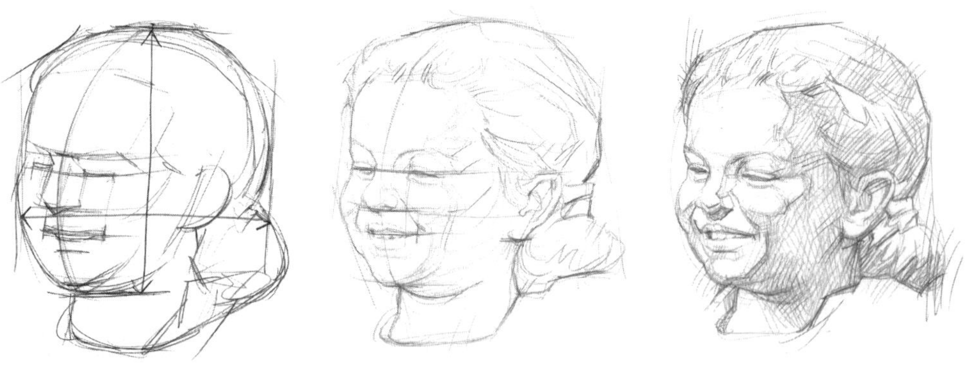

Step 1 *Size*

Step 2 *Structure*

Step 3 *Shadows*

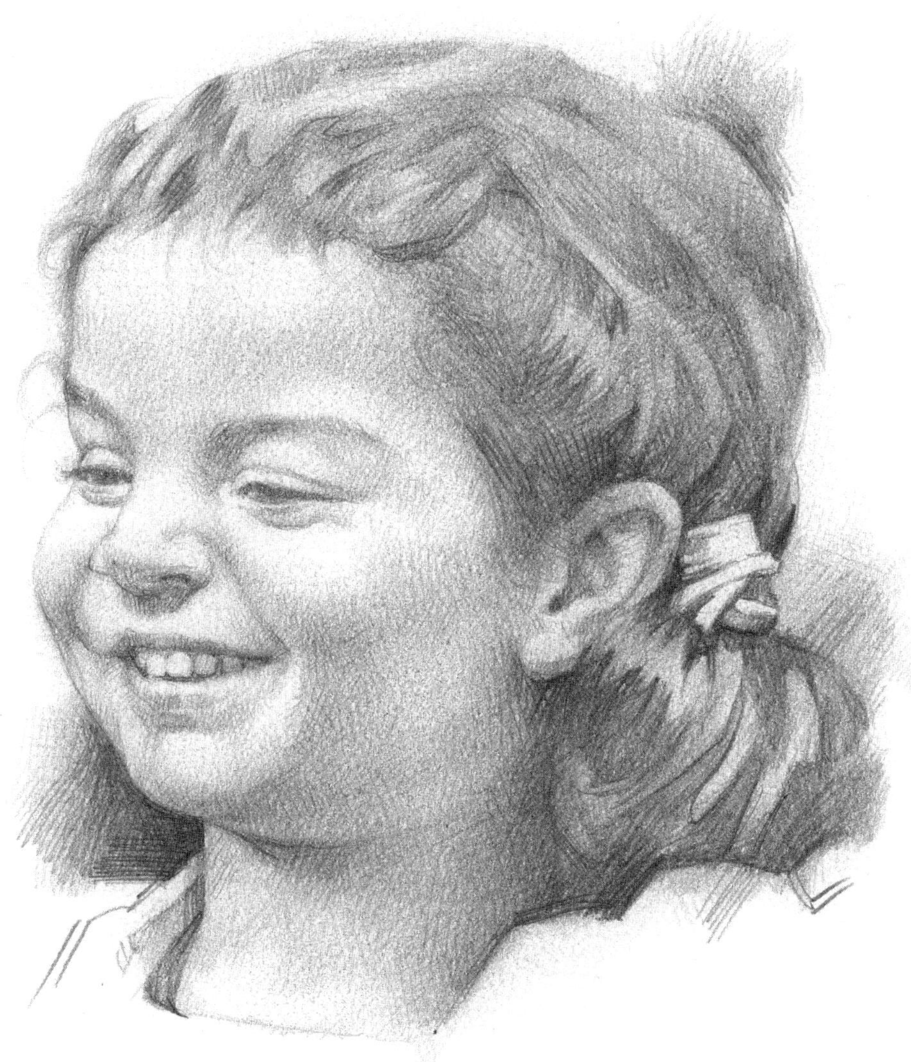

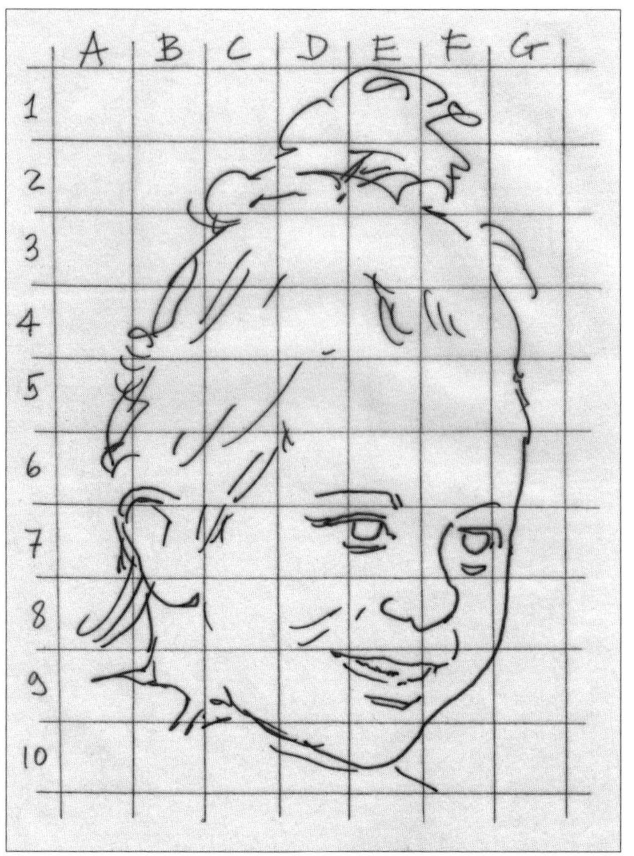

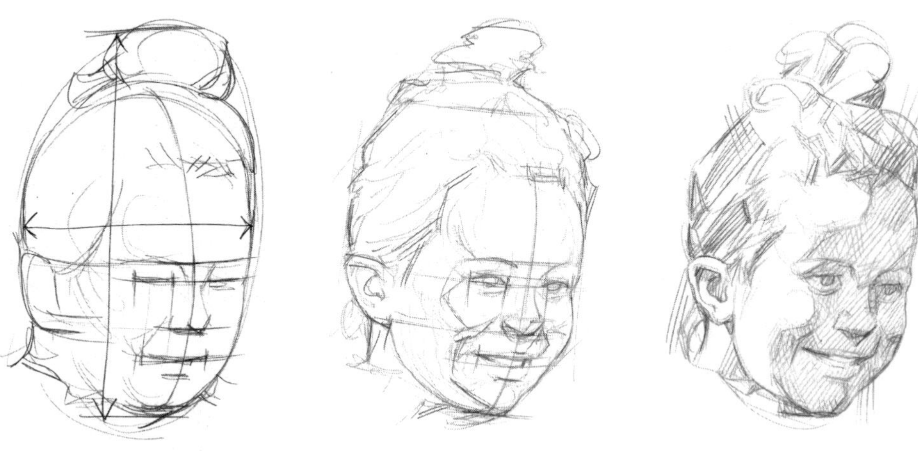

Step 1 *Size* ***Step 2*** *Structure* ***Step 3*** *Shadows*

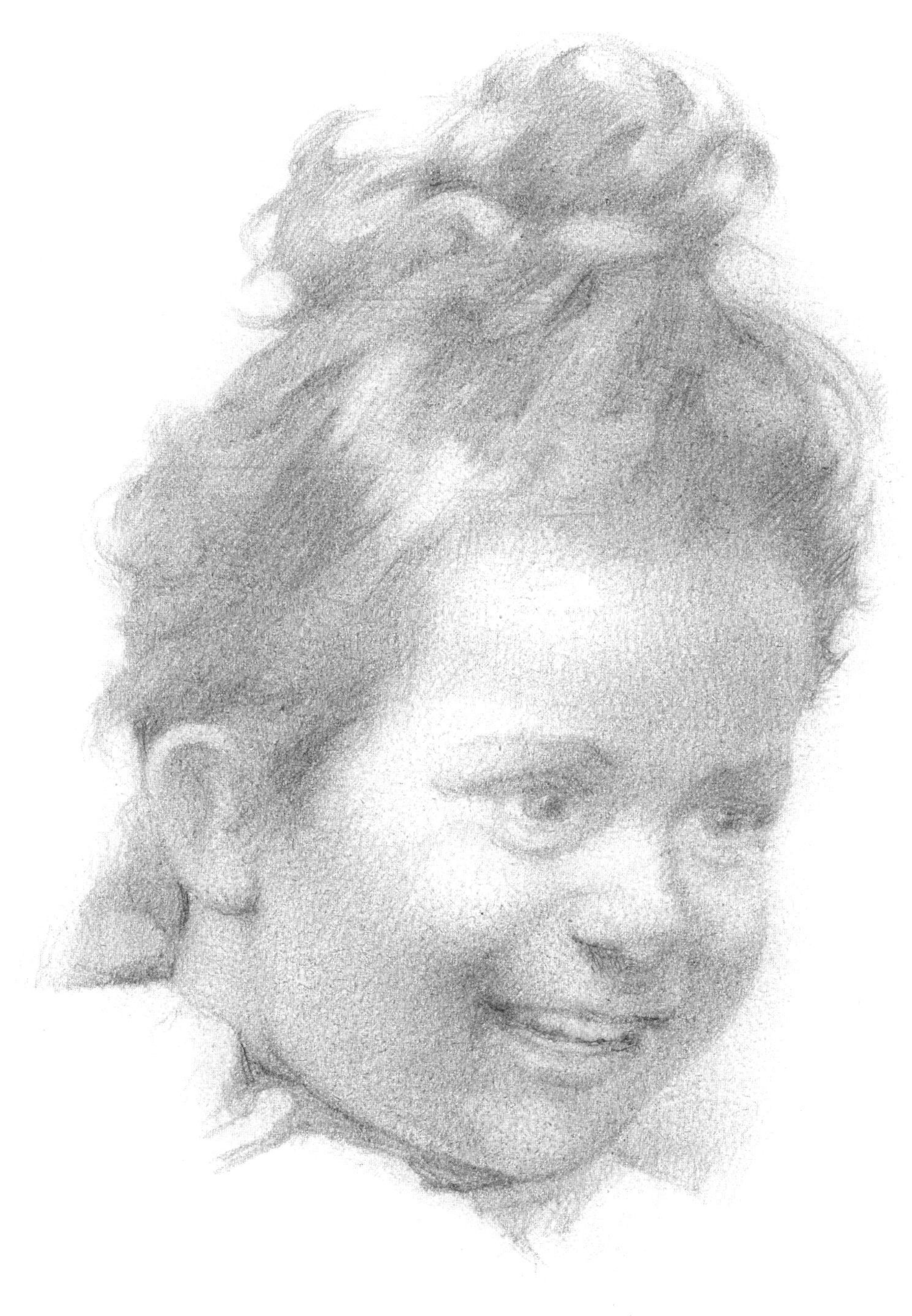

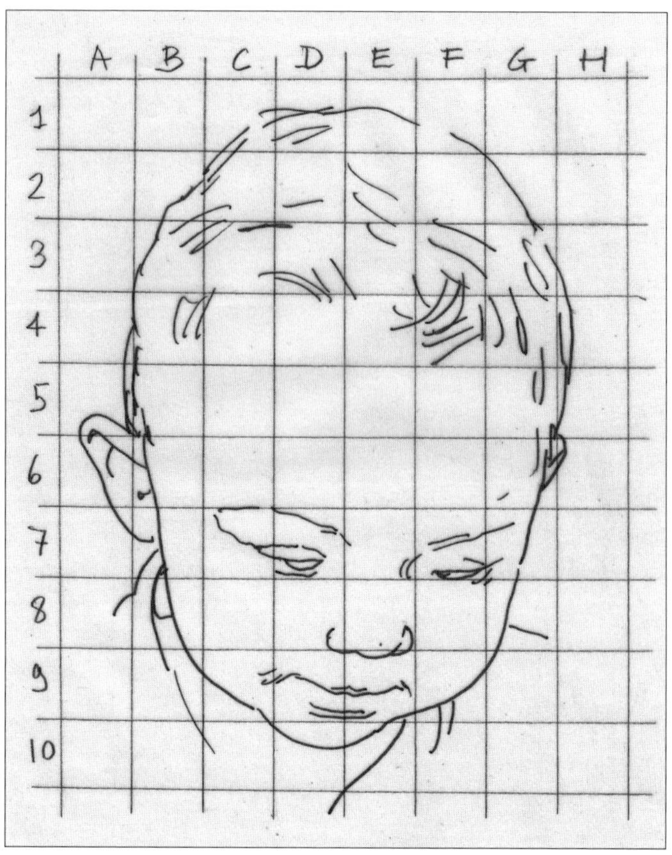

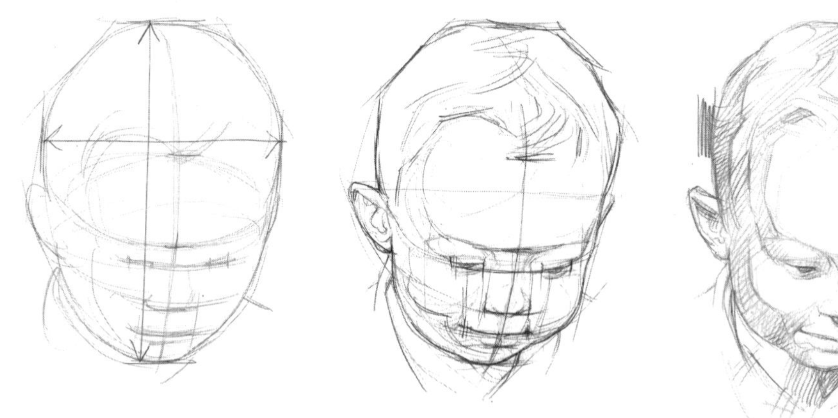

Step 1 *Size* **Step 2** *Structure* **Step 3** *Shadows*

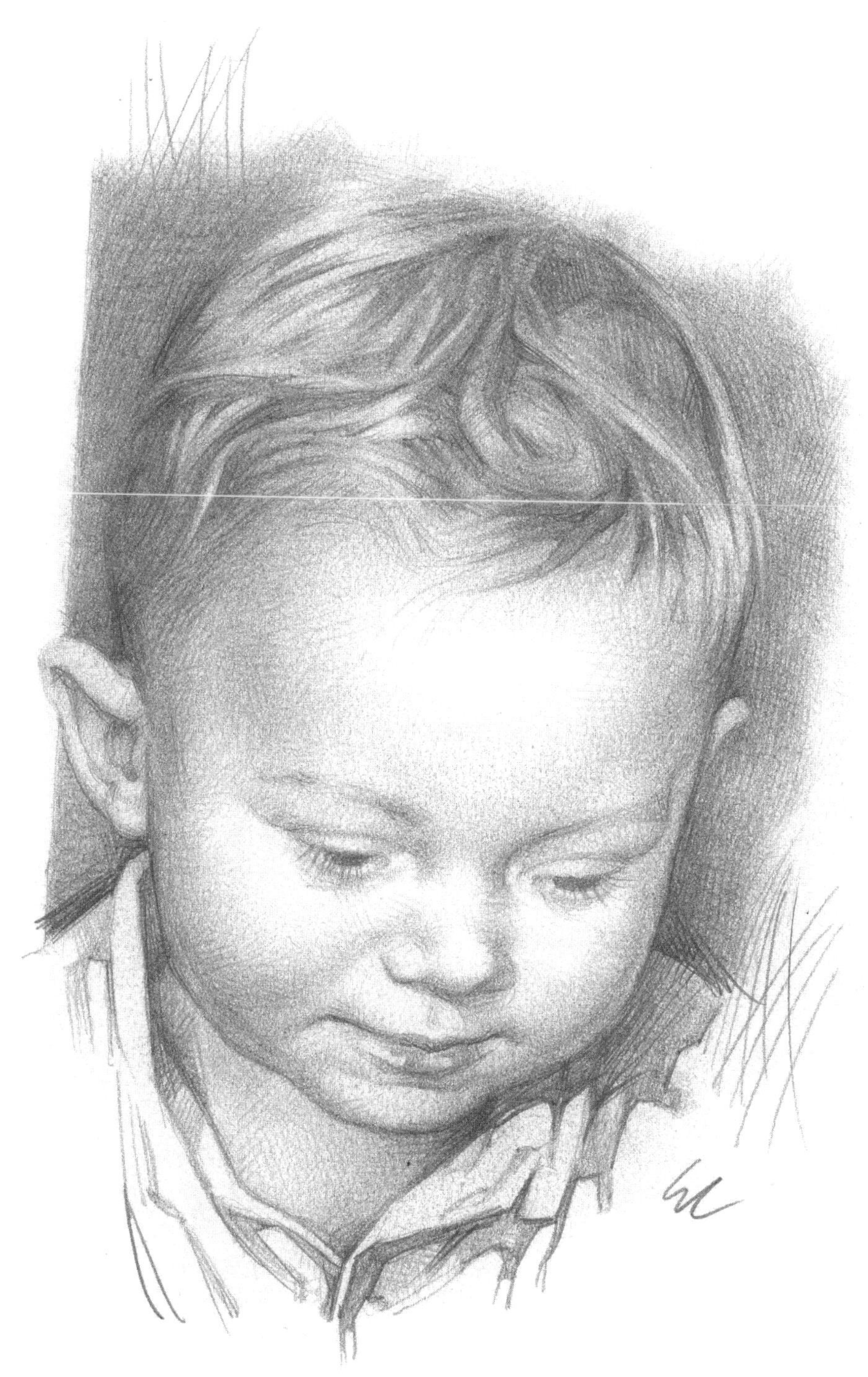

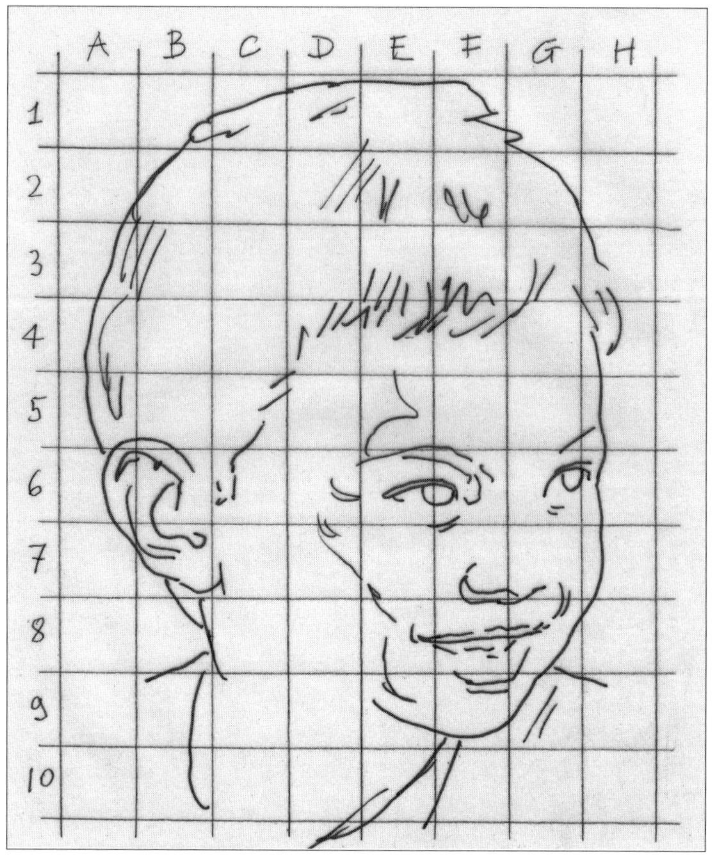

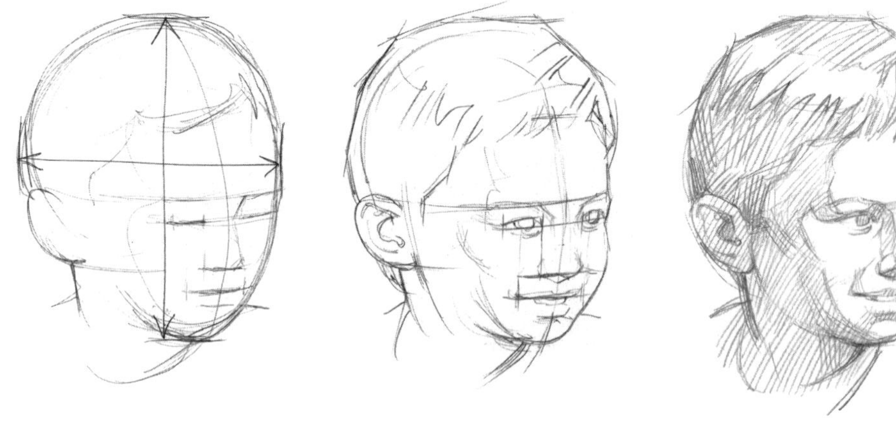

Step 1 *Size*

Step 2 *Structure*

Step 3 *Shadows*

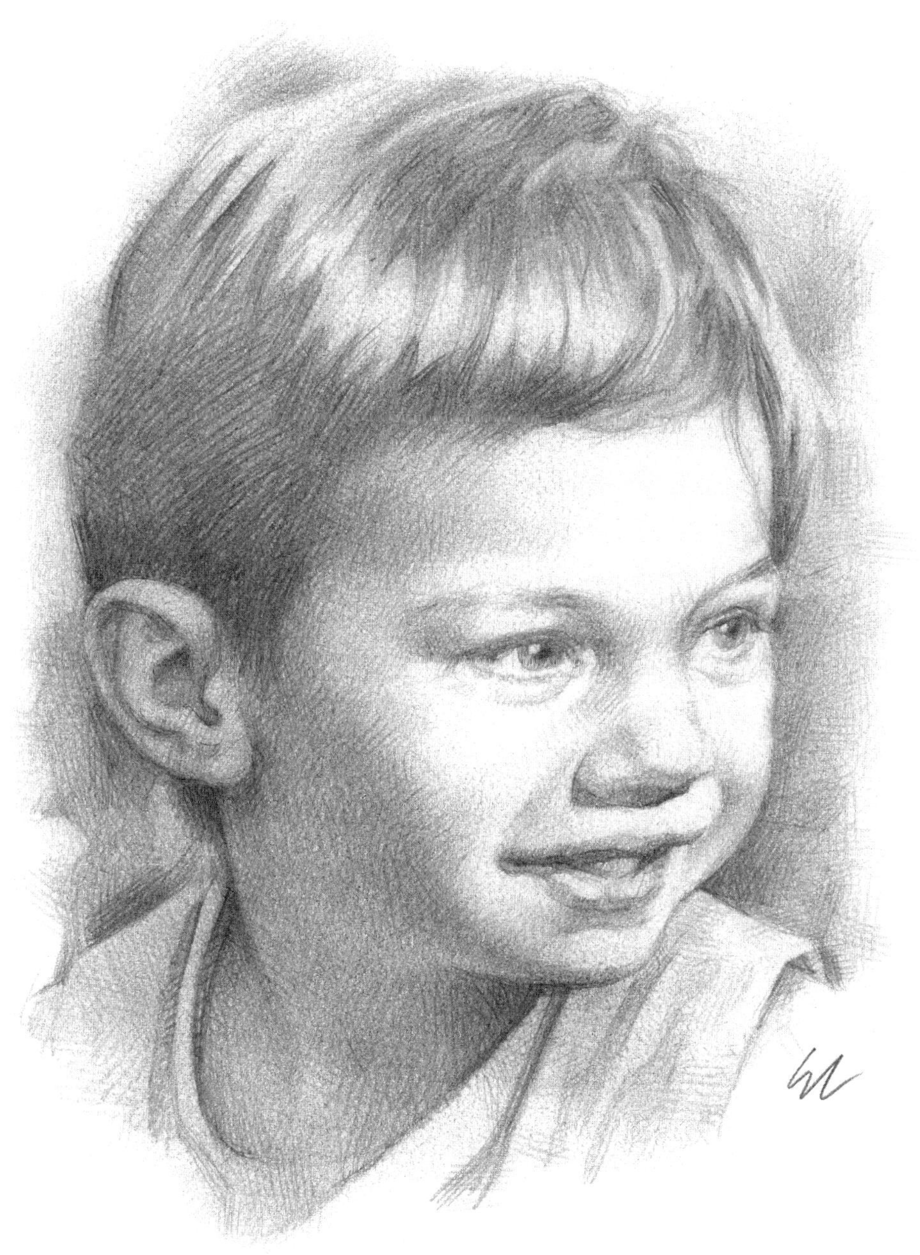

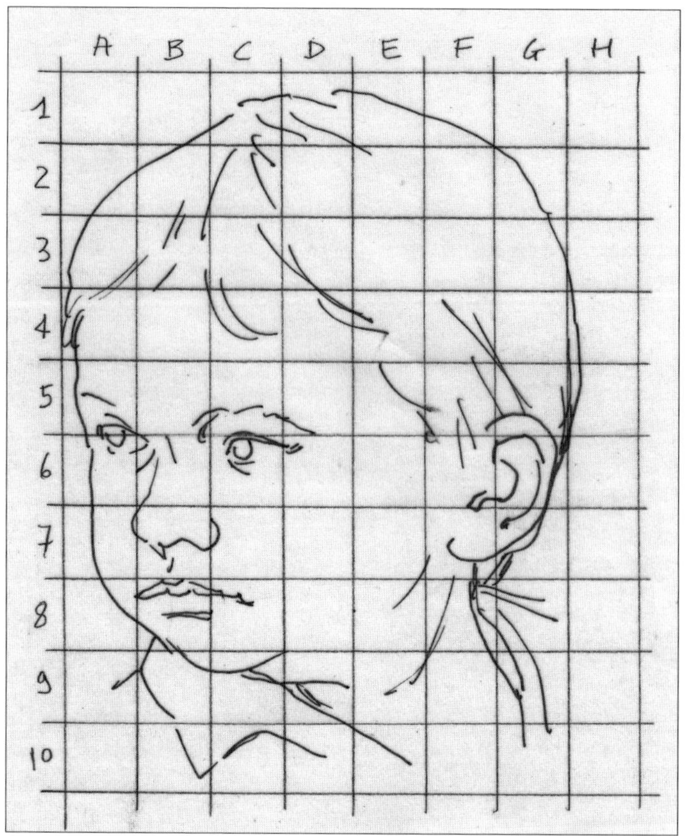

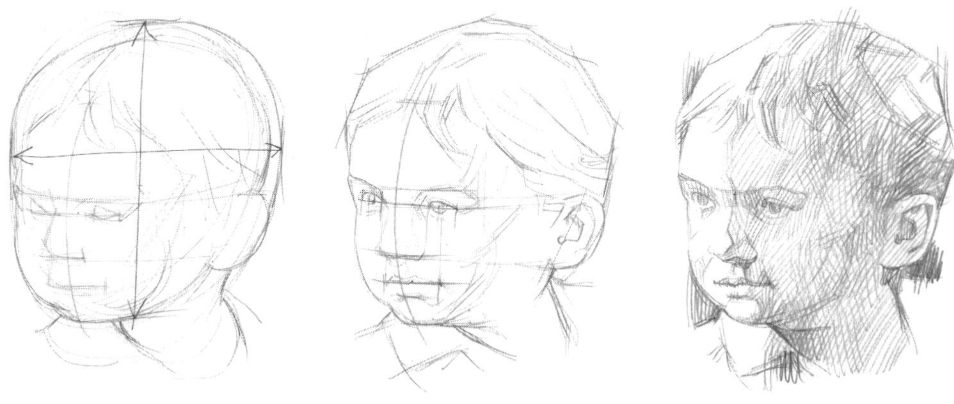

Step 1 *Size* **Step 2** *Structure* **Step 3** *Shadows*

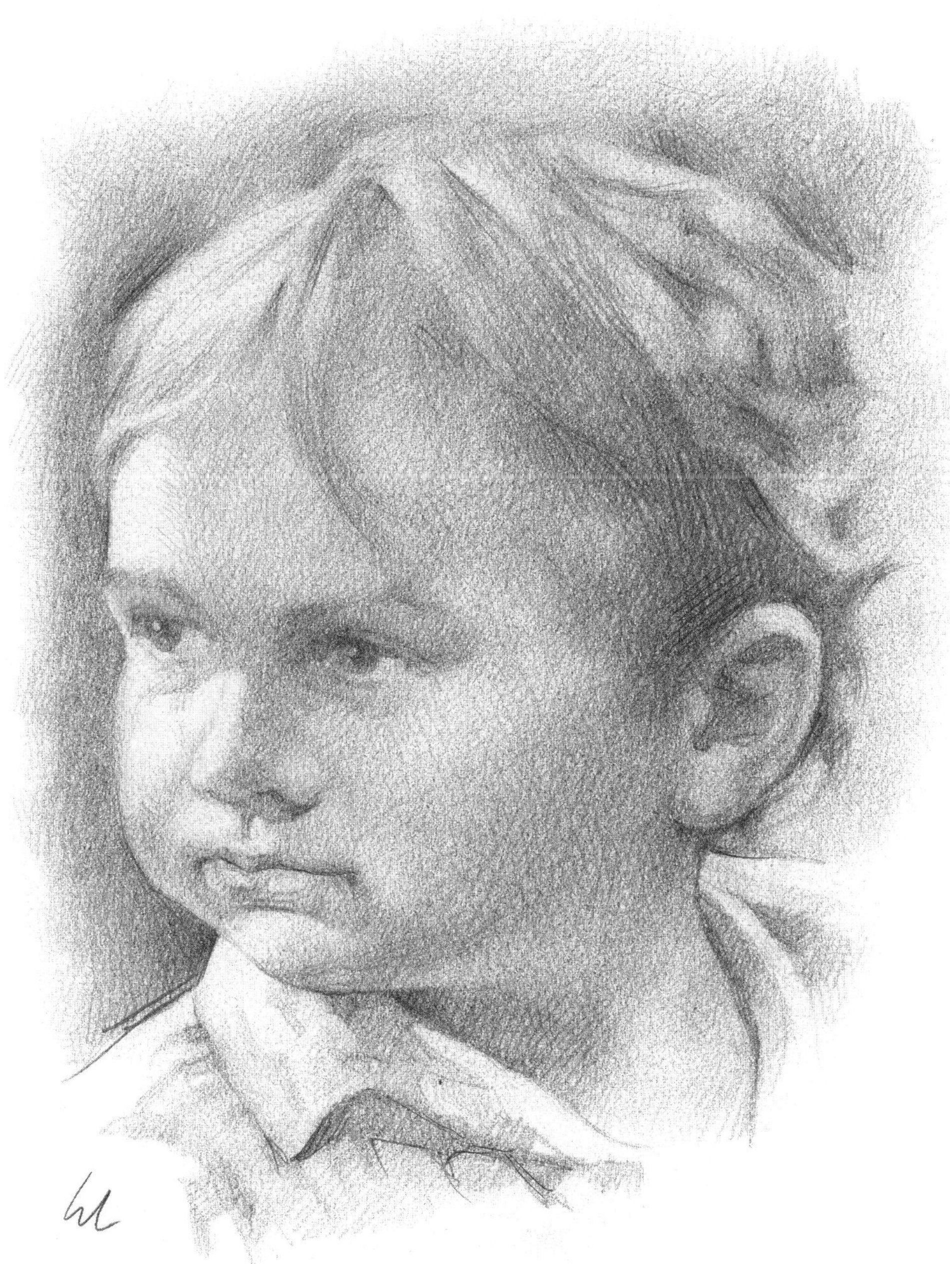

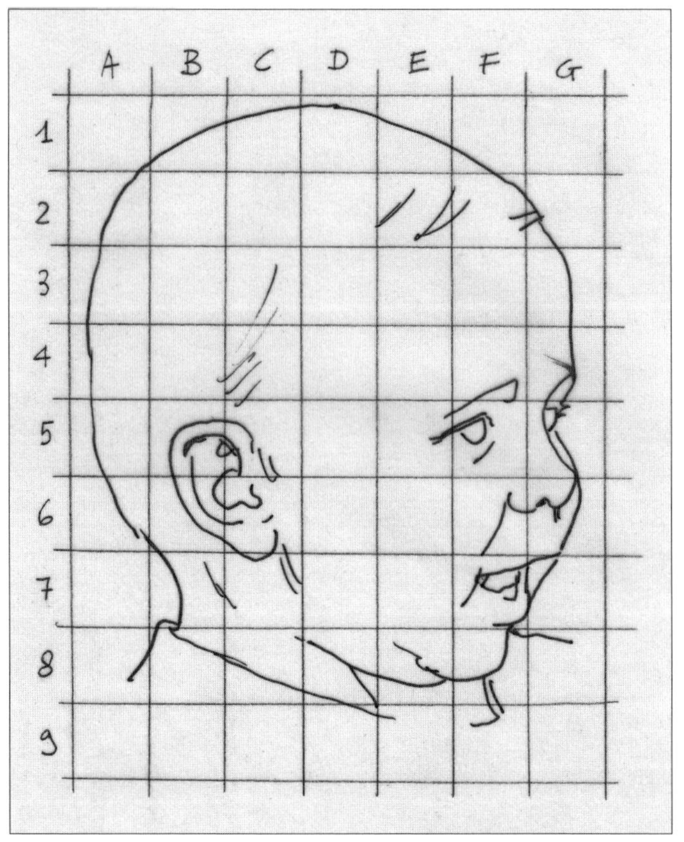

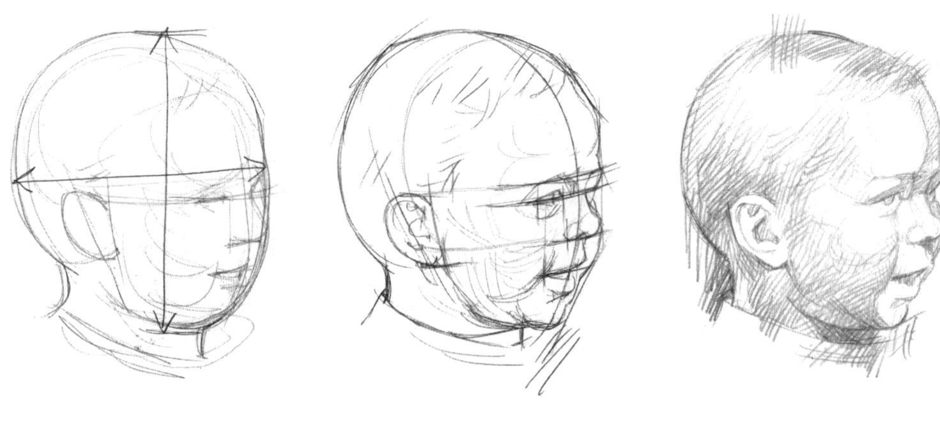

Step 1 *Size*   ***Step 2*** *Structure*   ***Step 3*** *Shadows*

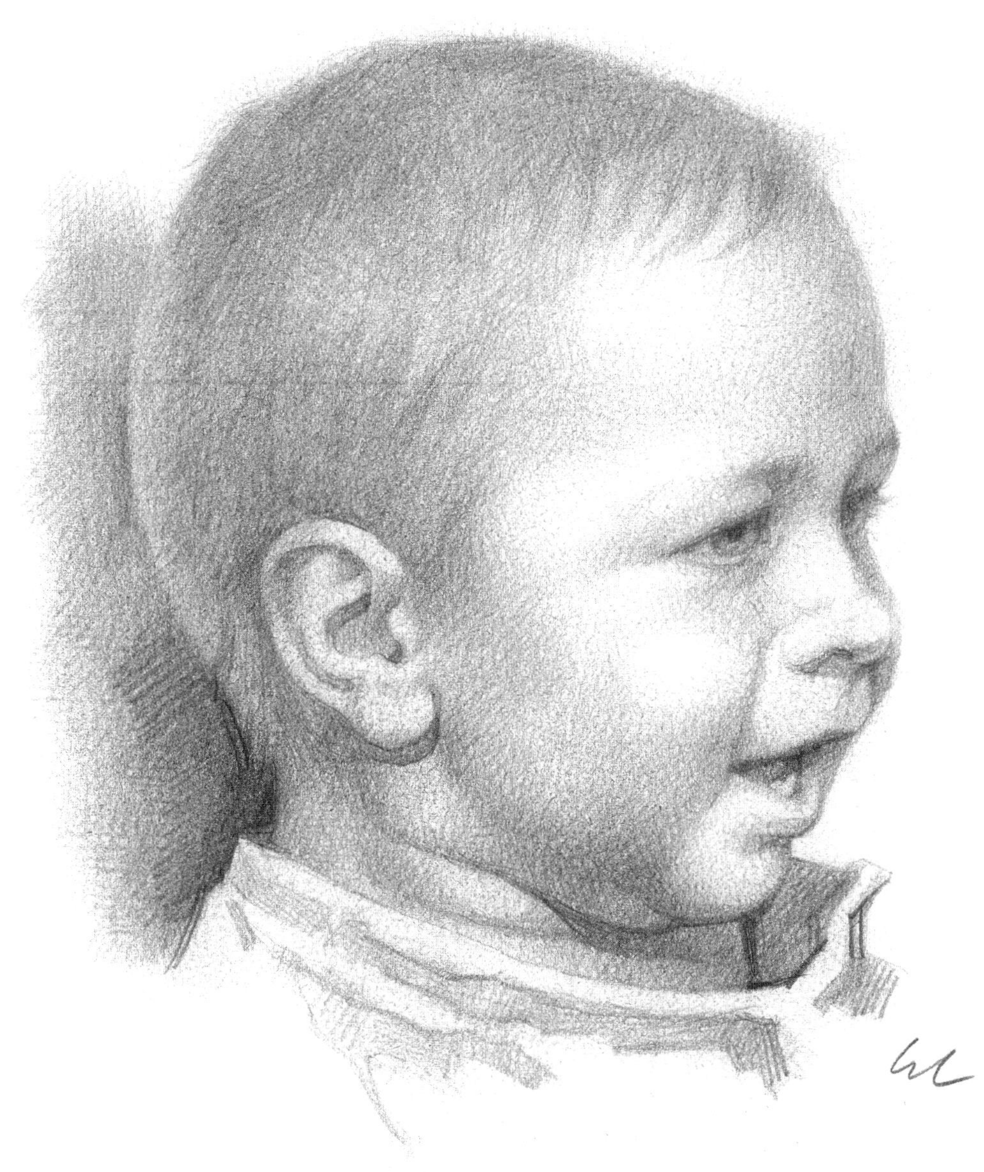

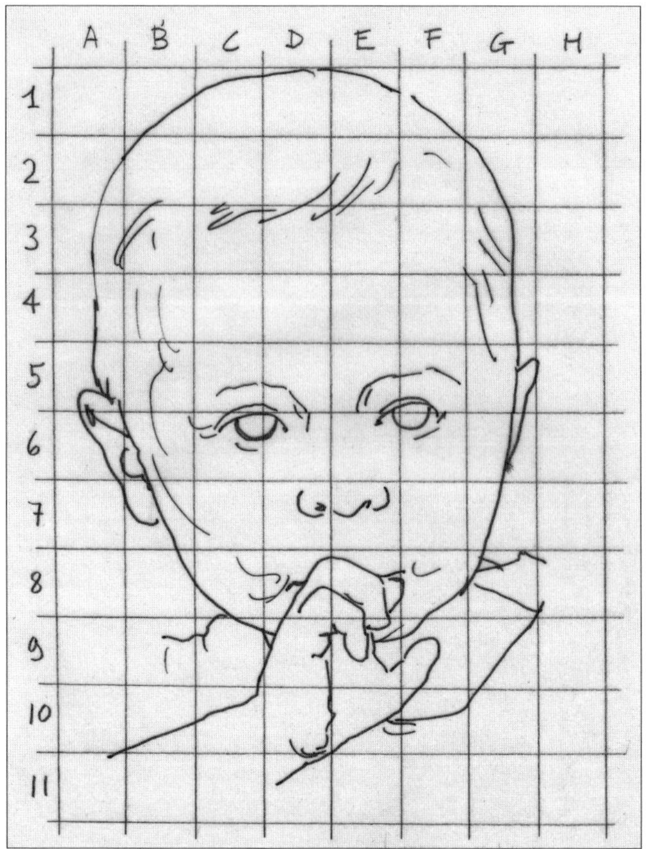

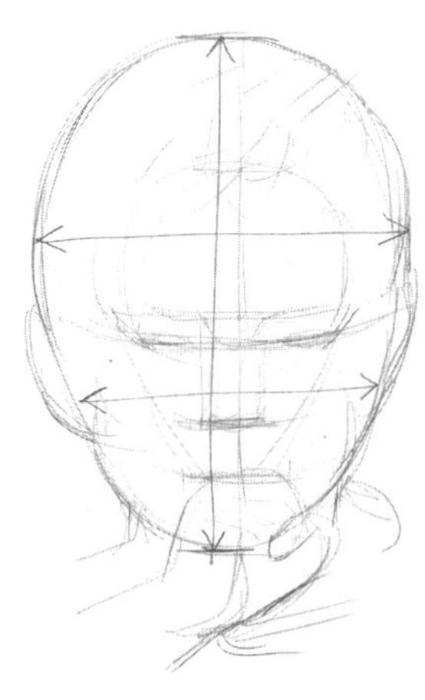

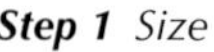

Step 1 *Size*

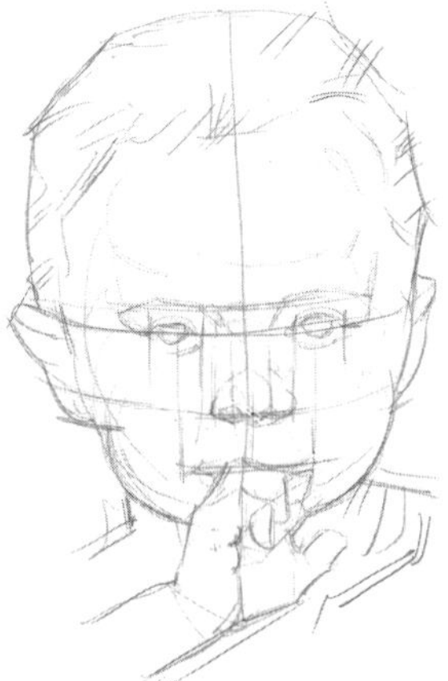

Step 2 *Structure*

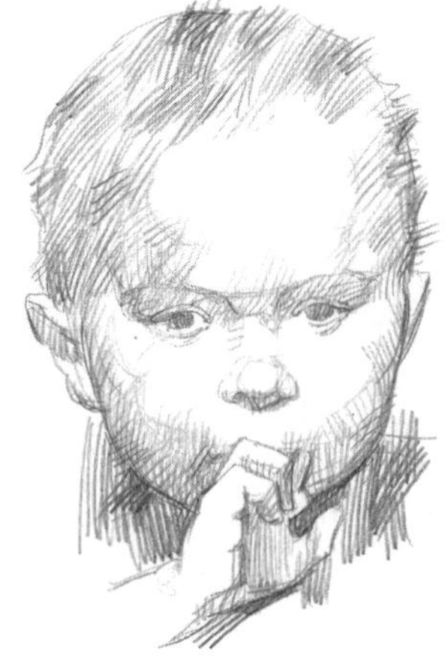

Step 3 *Shadows*

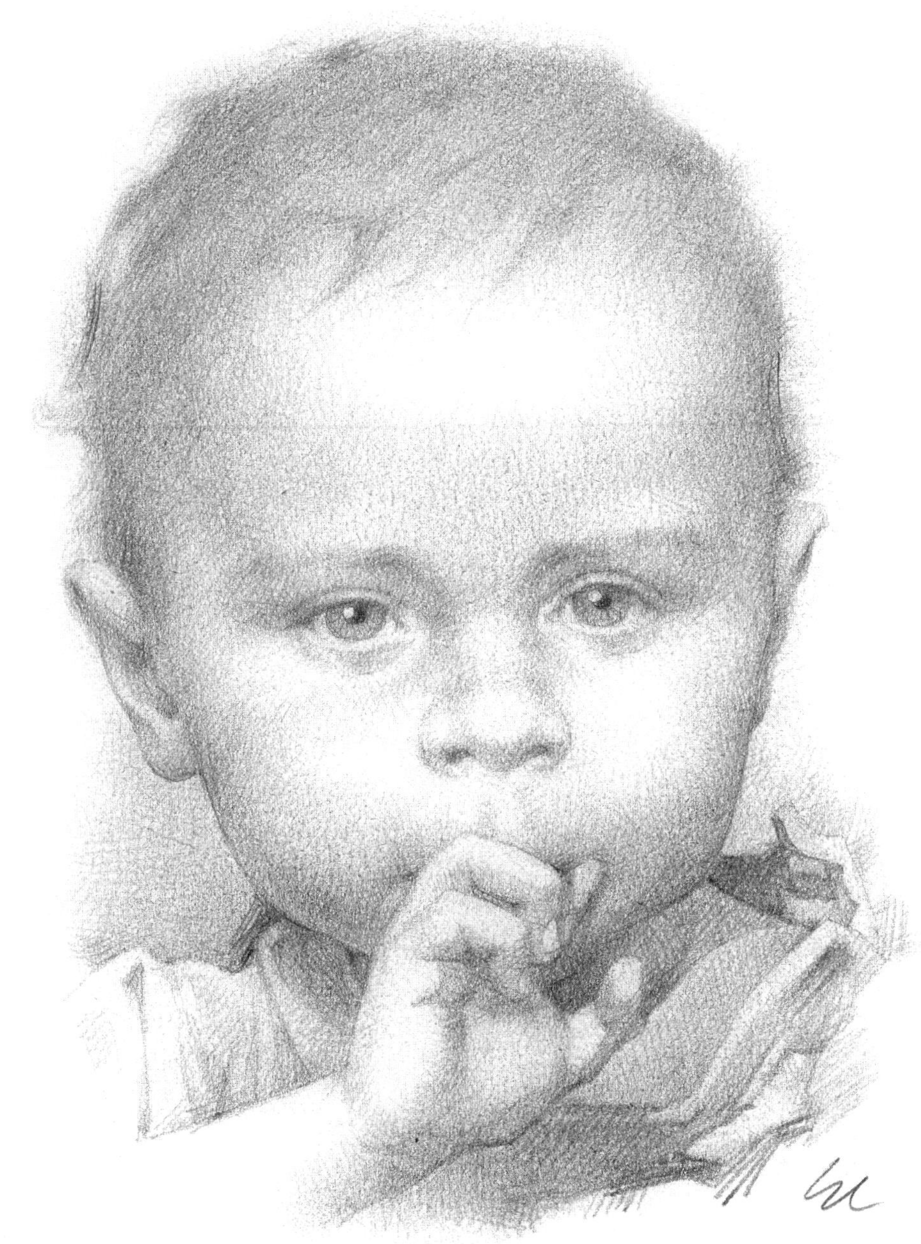

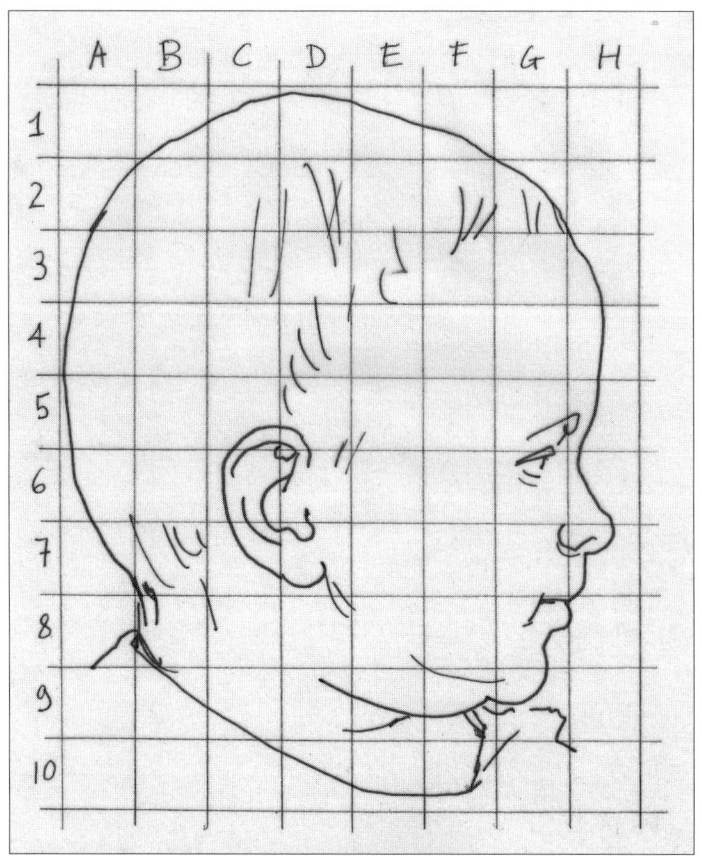

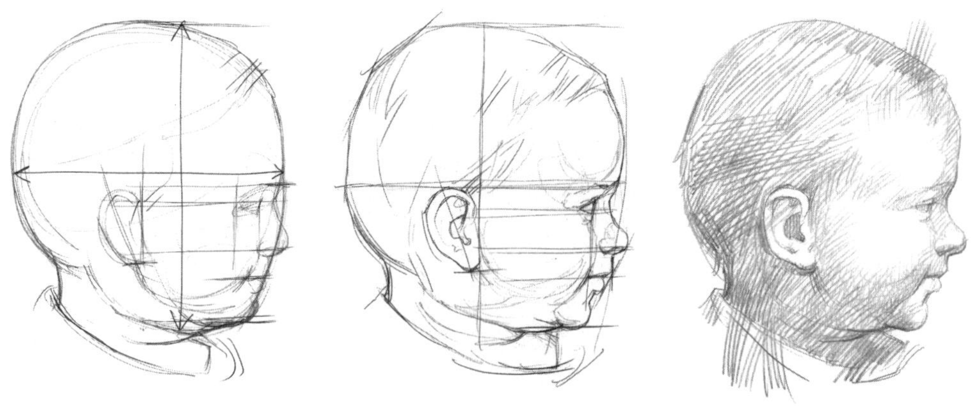

Step 1 *Size* ***Step 2*** *Structure* ***Step 3*** *Shadows*

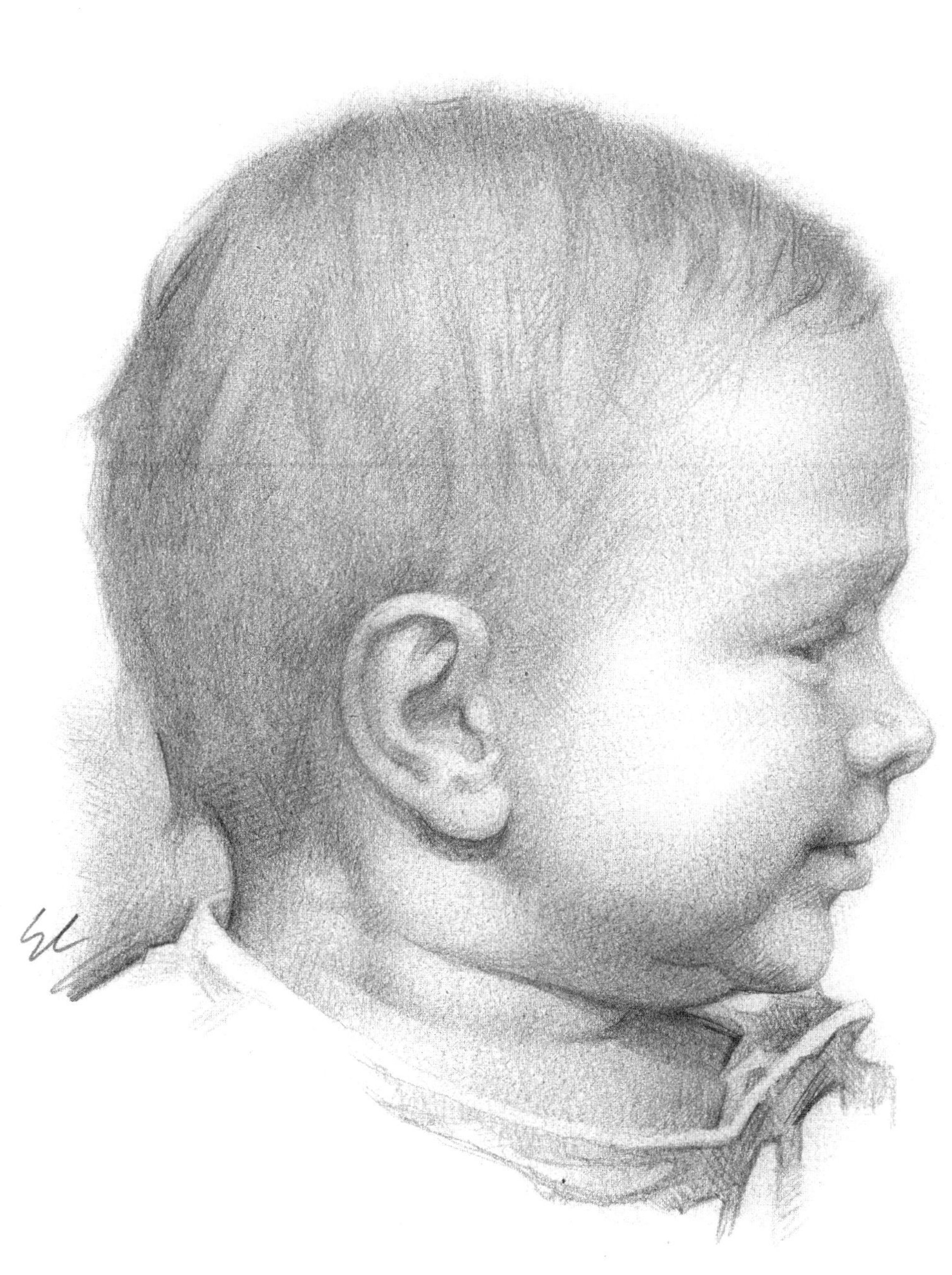

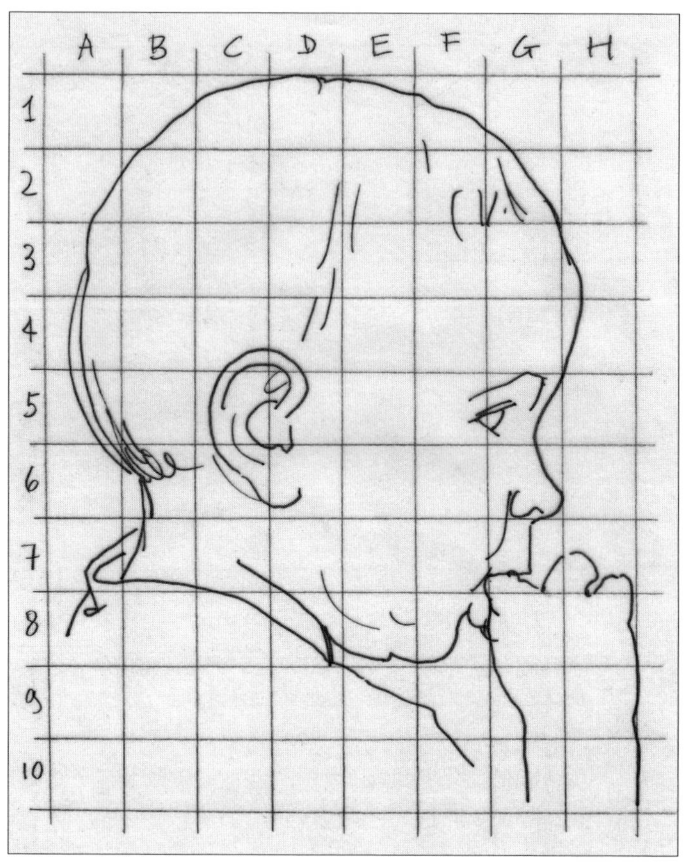

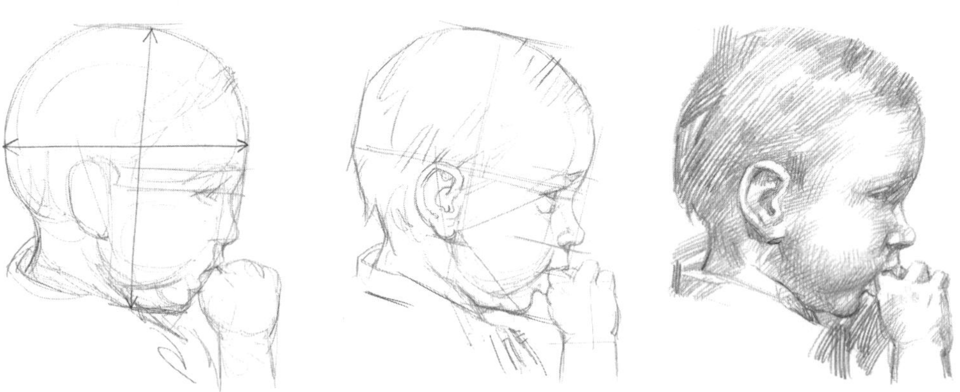

Step 1 *Size*

Step 2 *Structure*

Step 3 *Shadows*

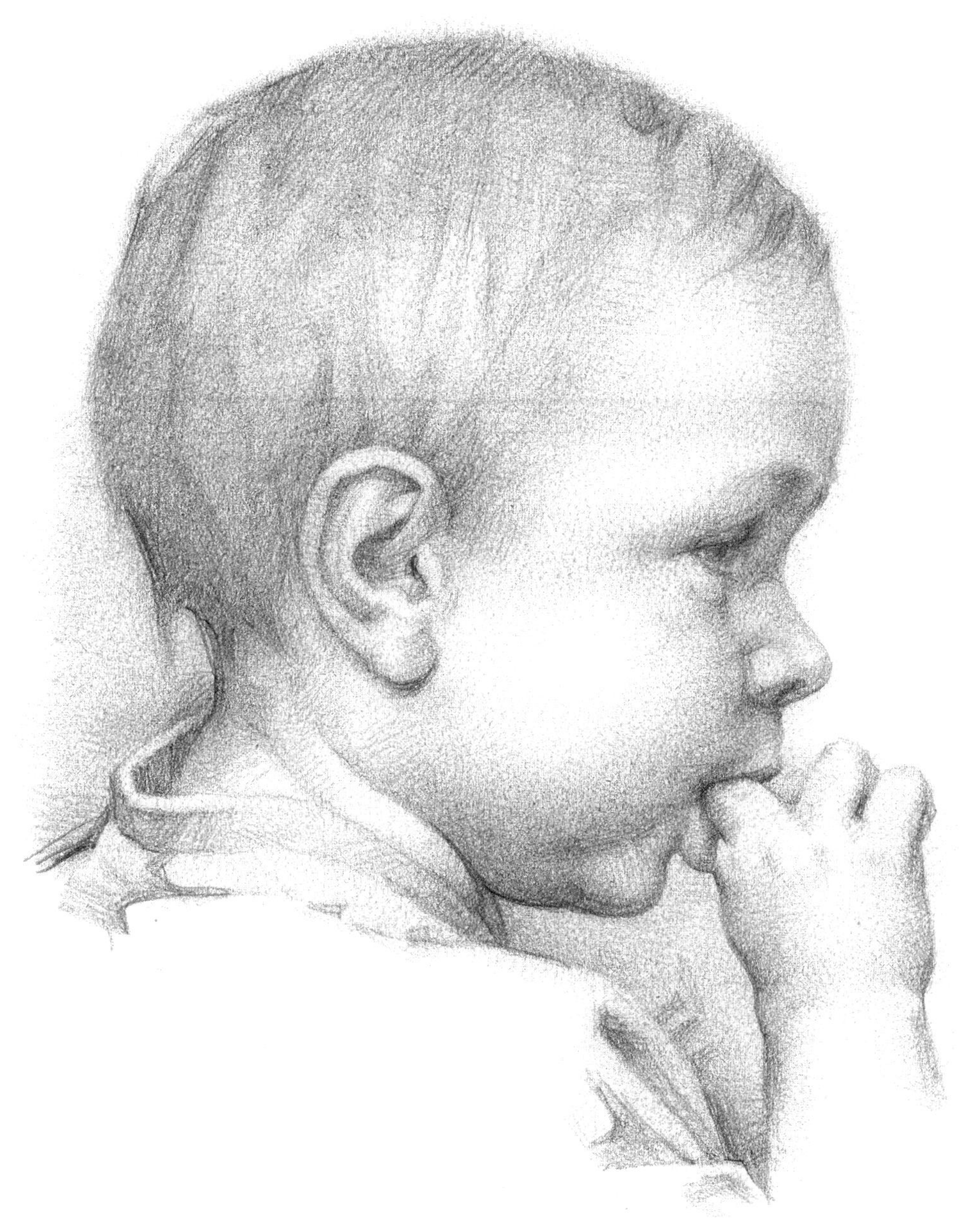

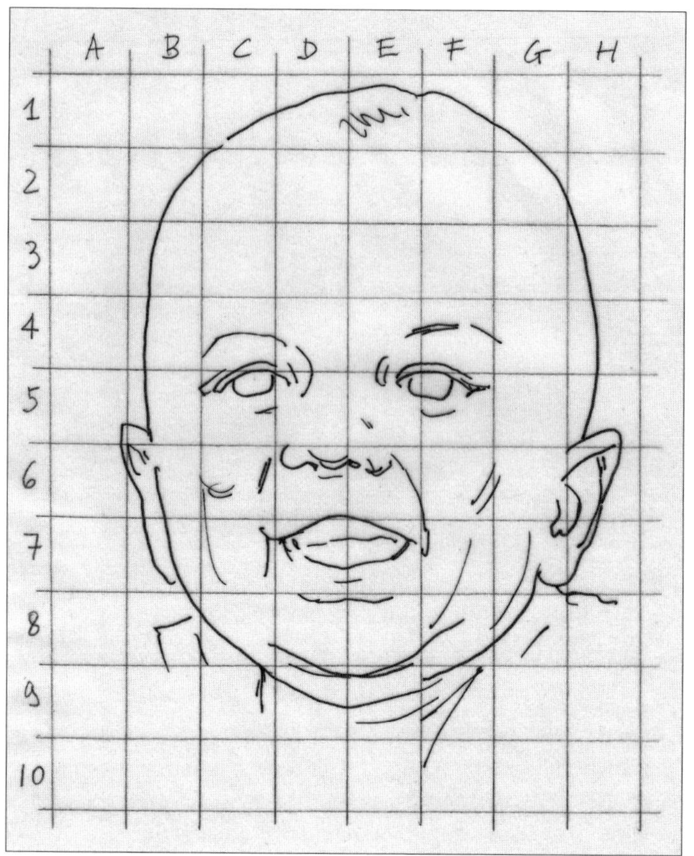

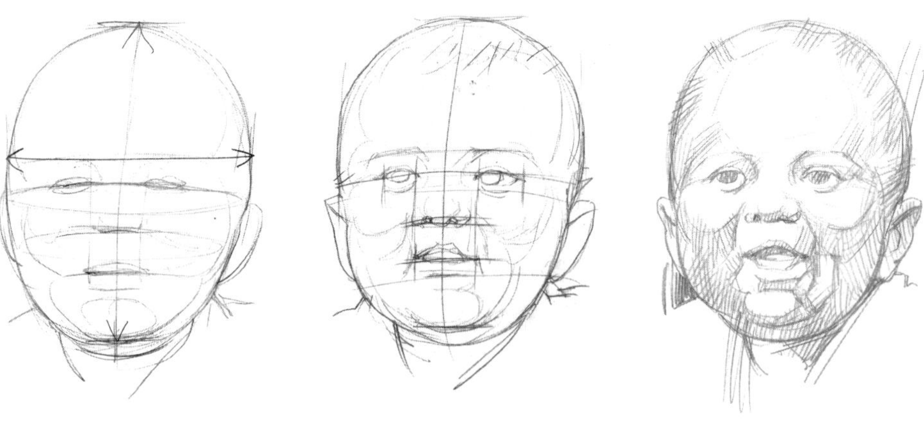

Step 1 *Size* **Step 2** *Structure* **Step 3** *Shadows*

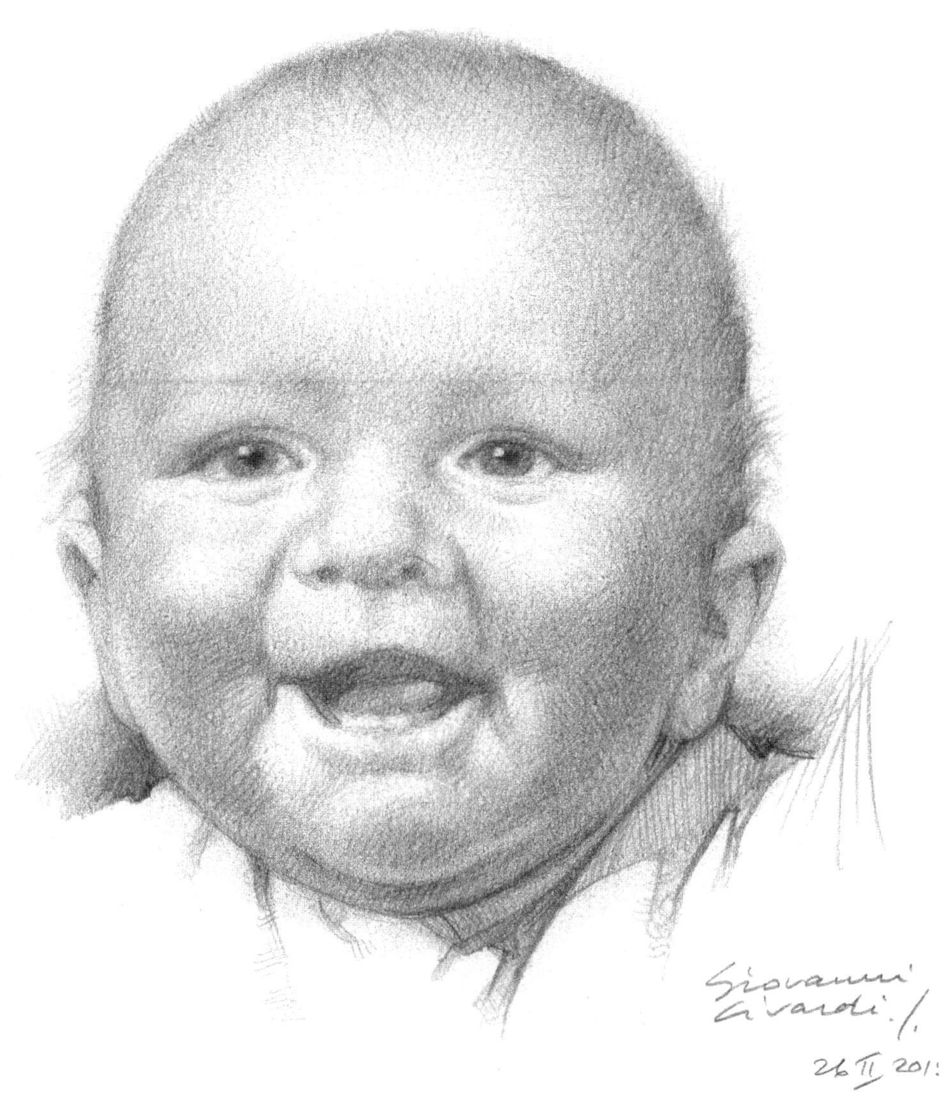
Giovanni
Civardi
26 II 201

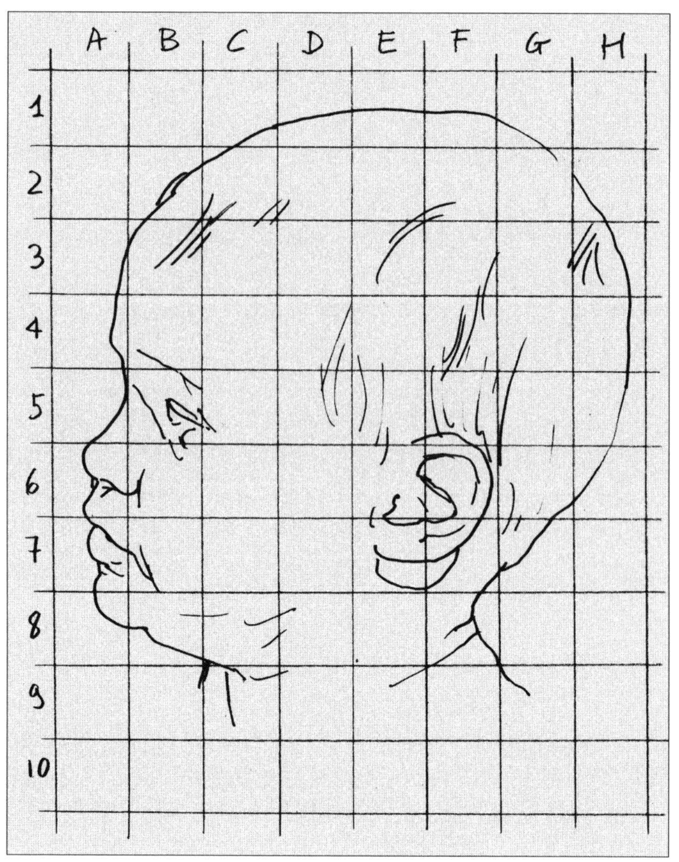

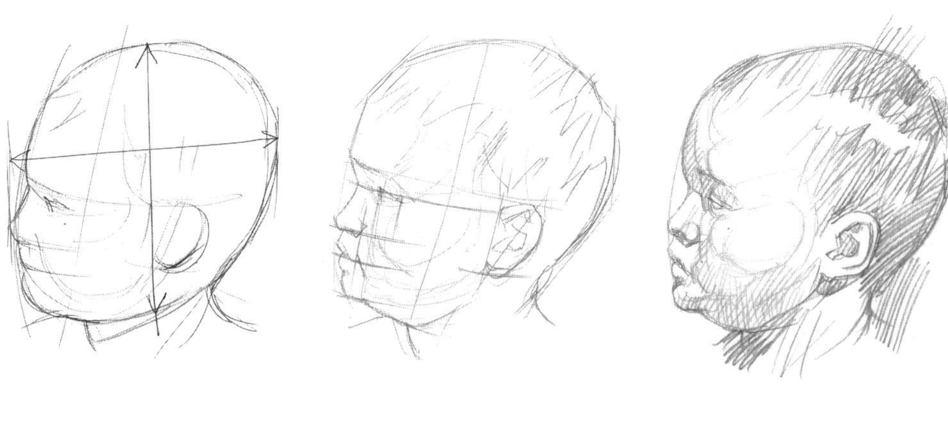

Step 1 *Size*

Step 2 *Structure*

Step 3 *Shadows*

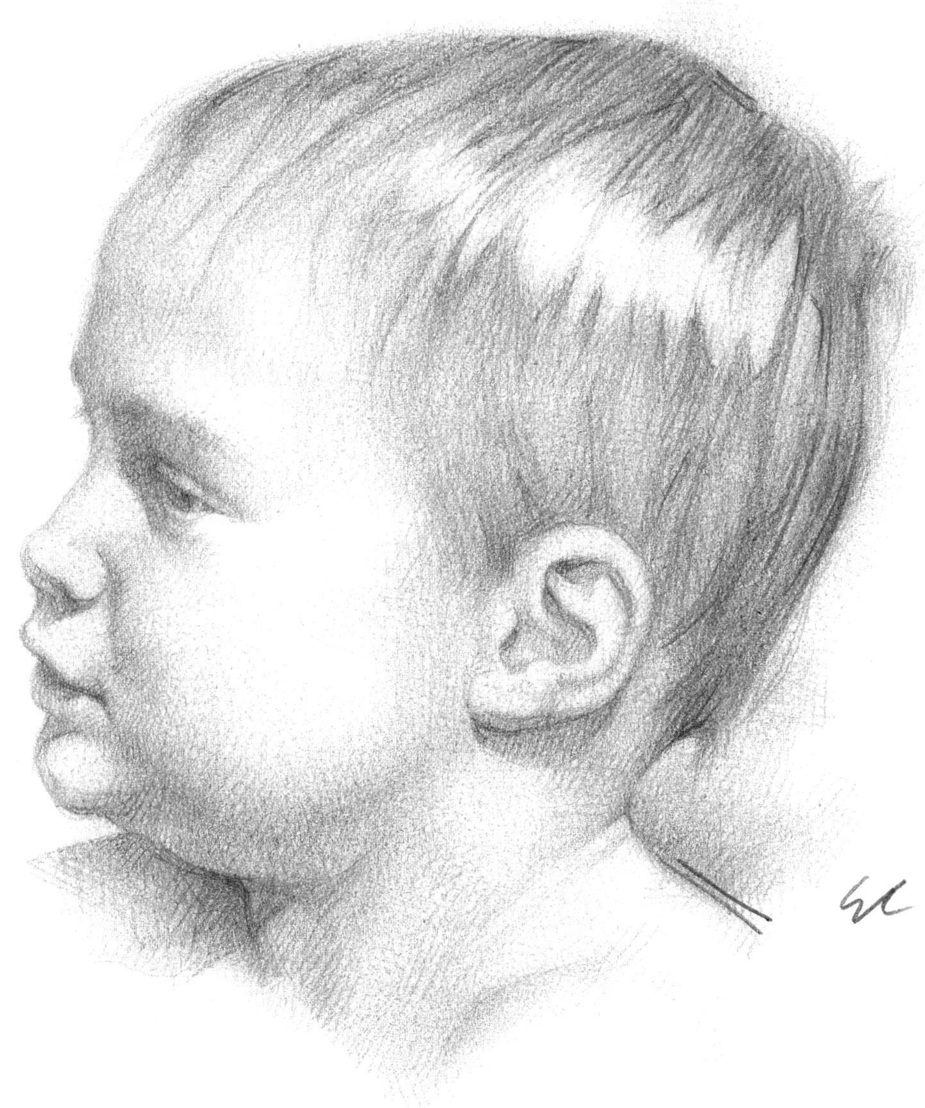

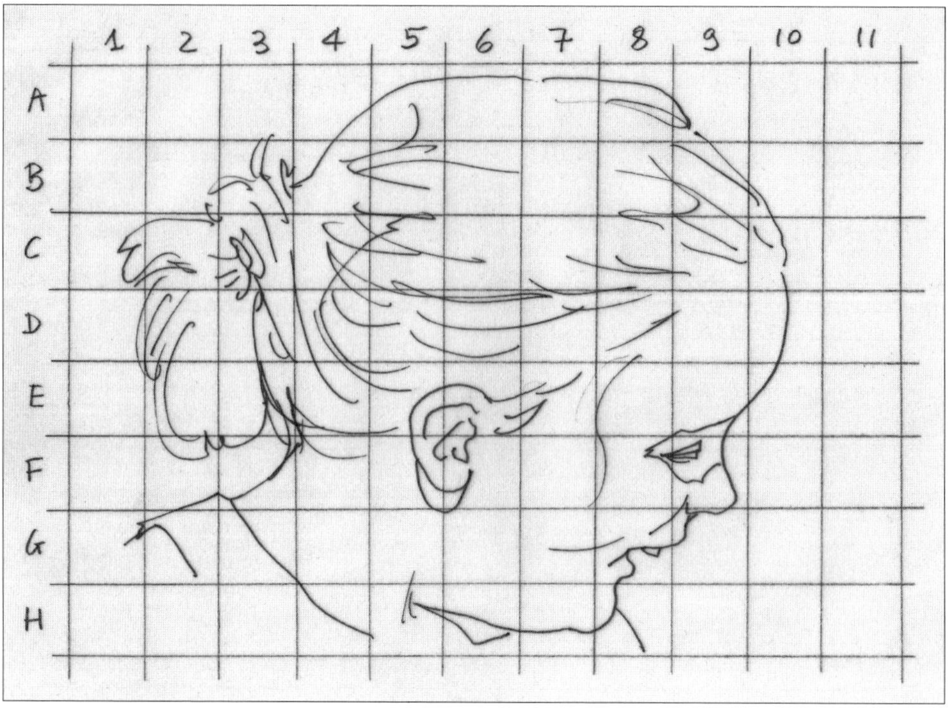

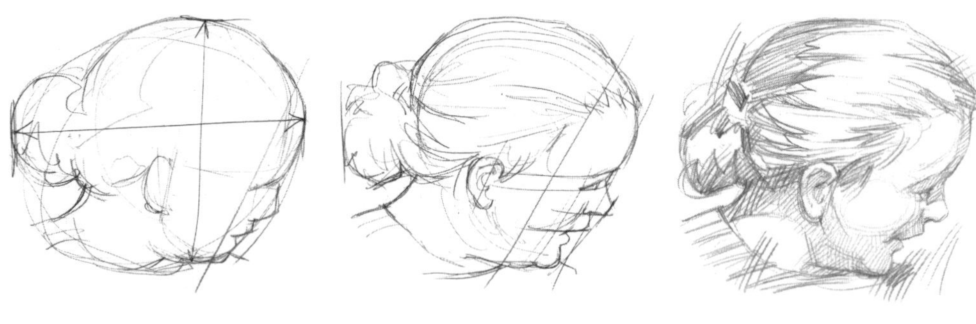

Step 1 *Size* ***Step 2*** *Structure* ***Step 3*** *Shadows*

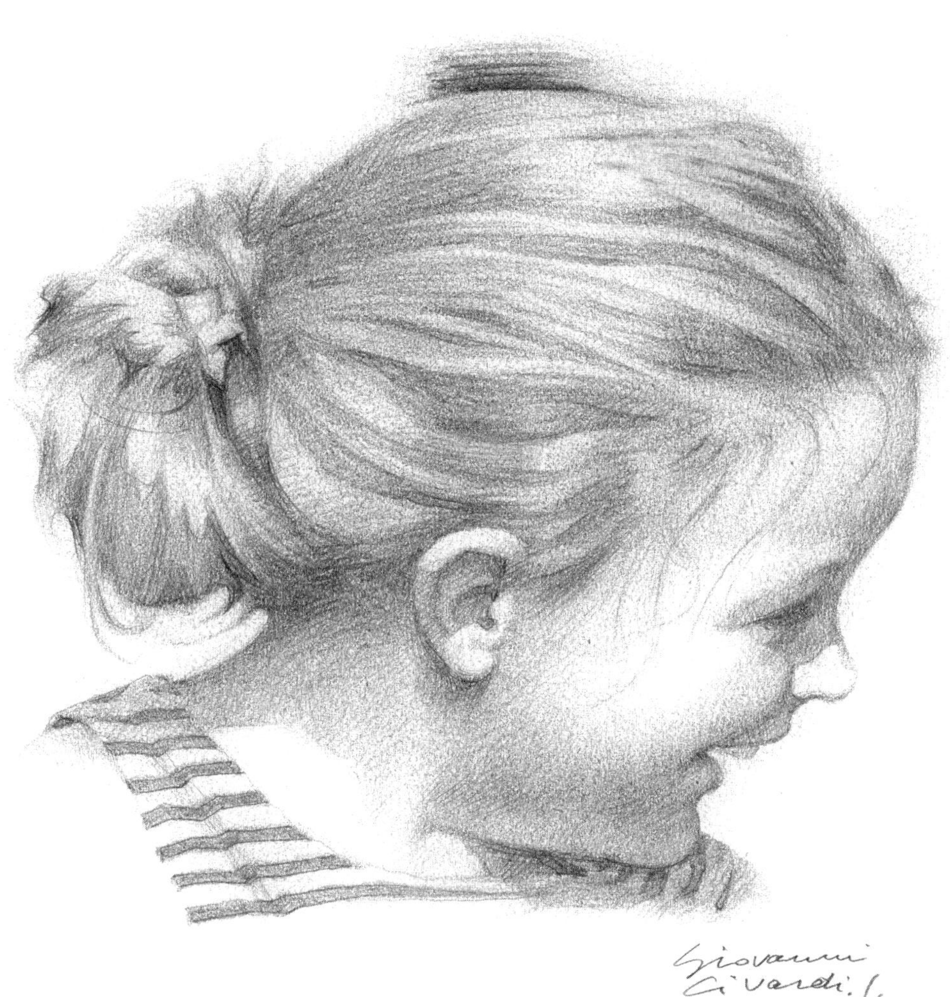
Giovanni
Civardi f.

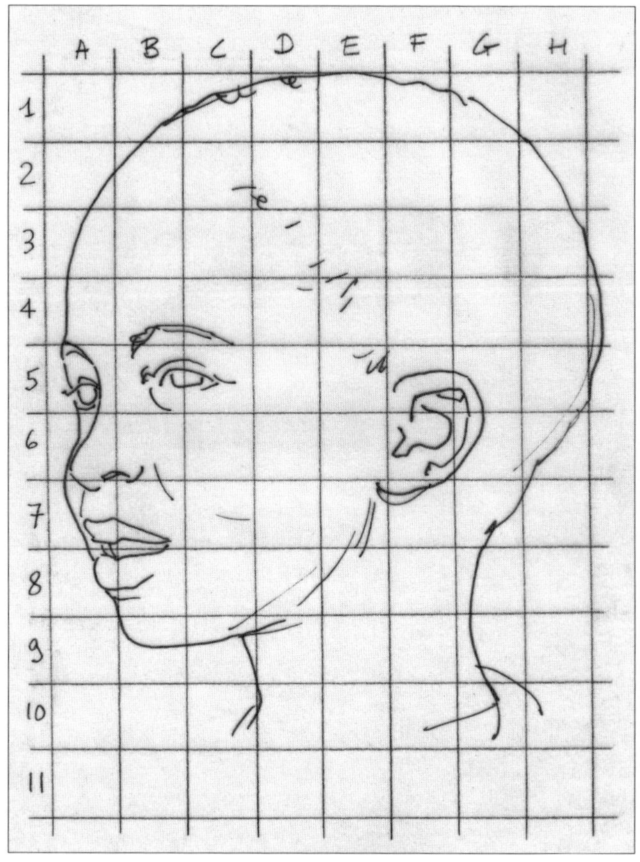

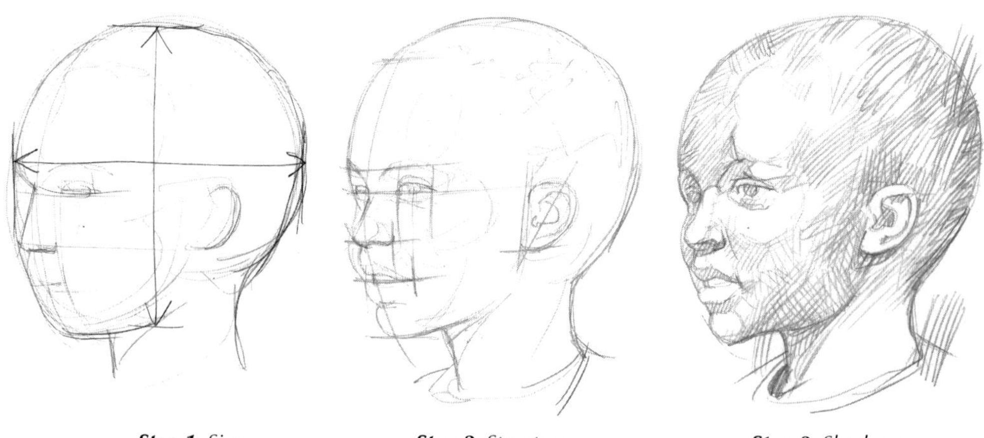

Step 1 *Size* **Step 2** *Structure* **Step 3** *Shadows*

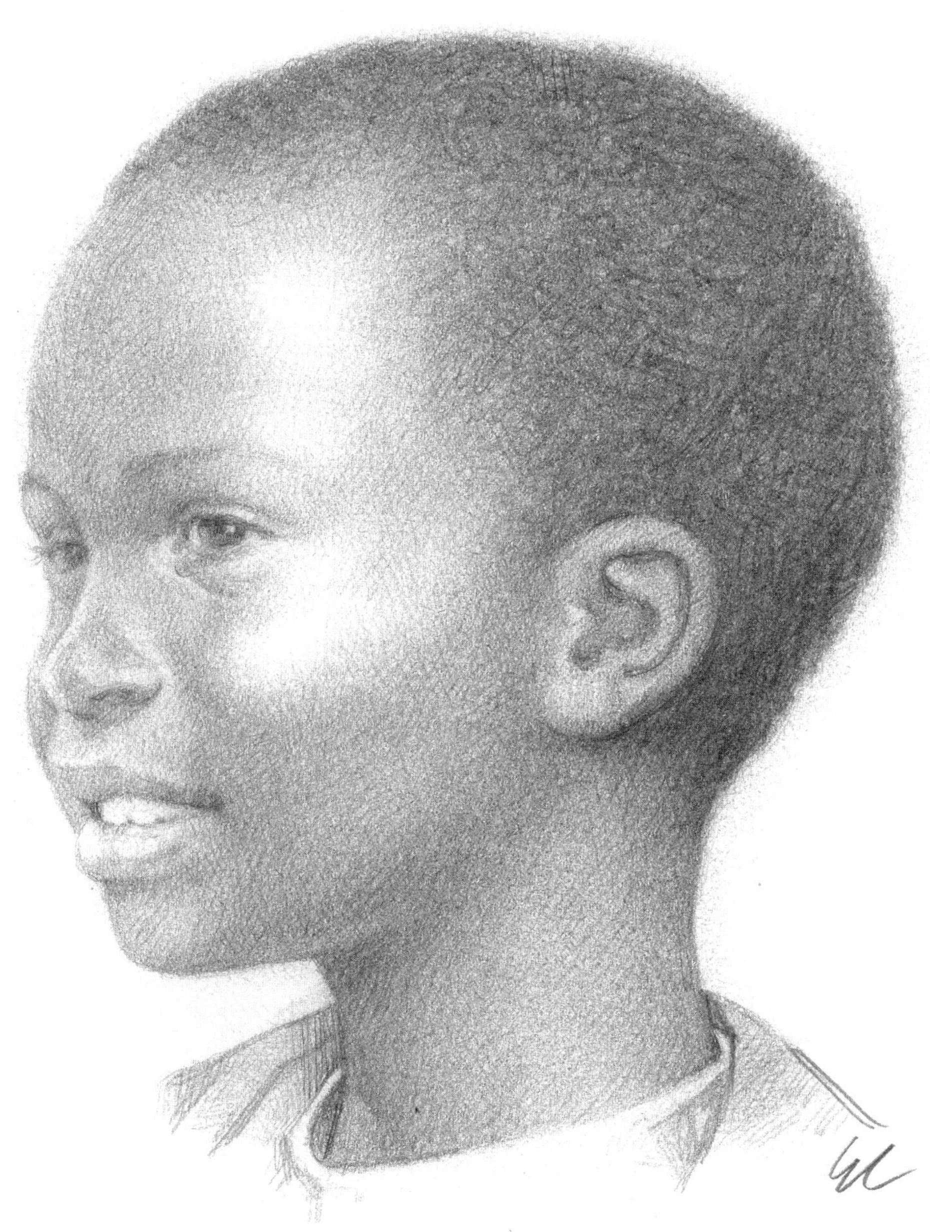

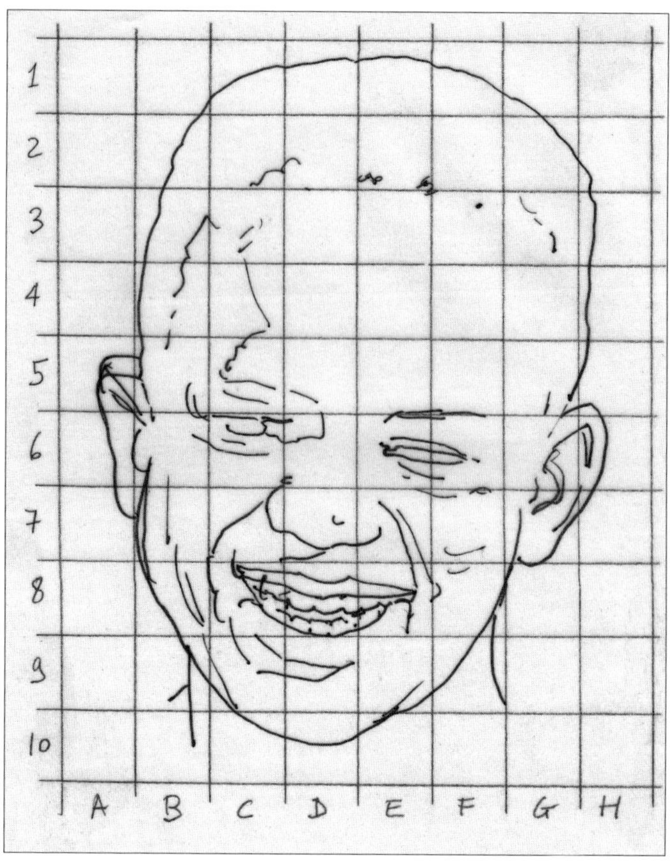

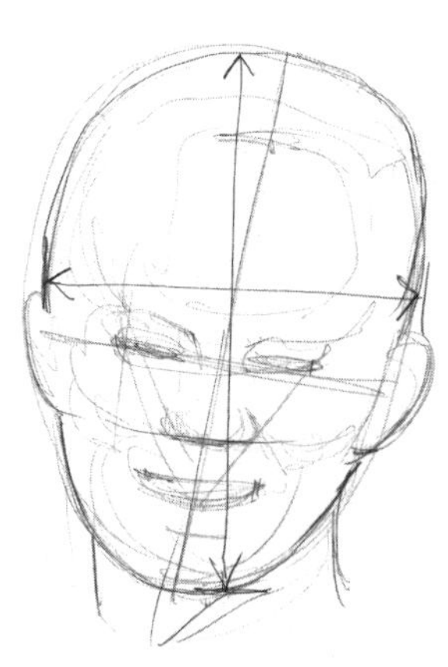

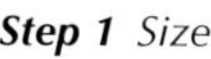

Step 1 *Size*

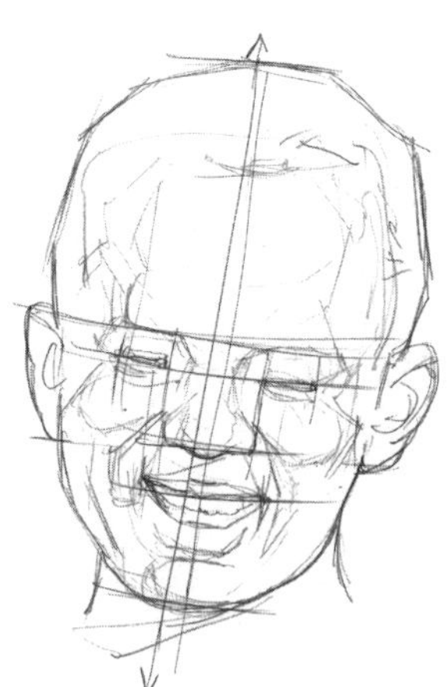

Step 2 *Structure*

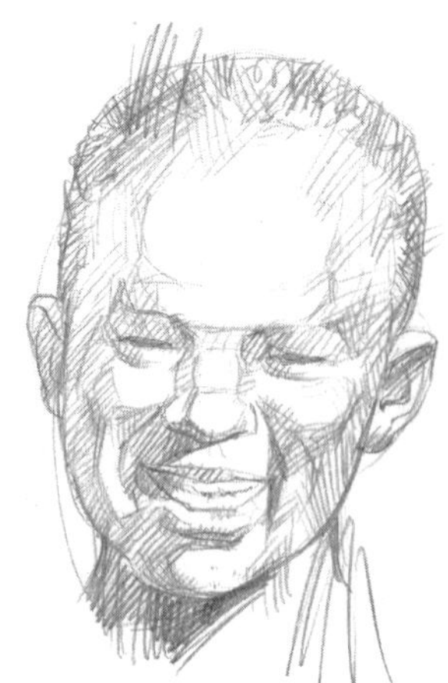

Step 3 *Shadows*

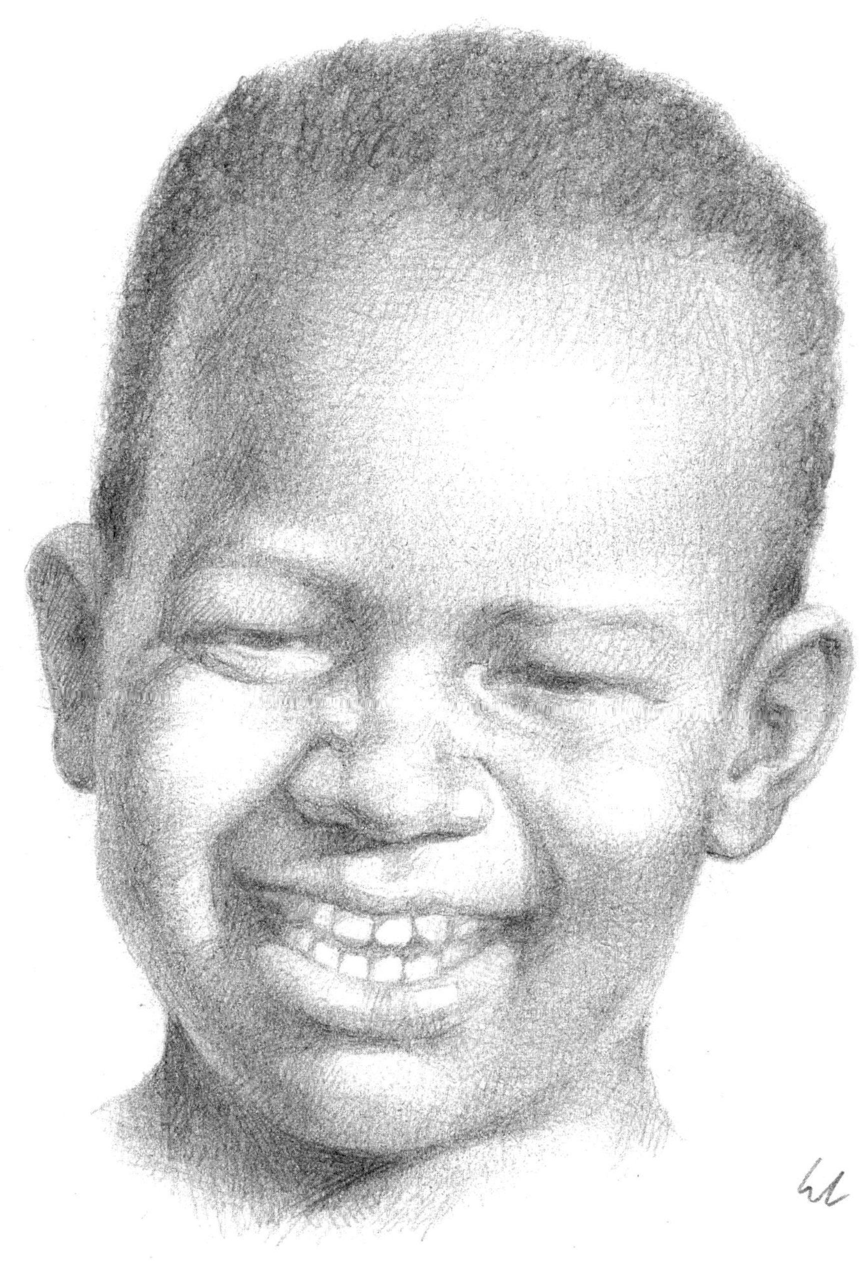

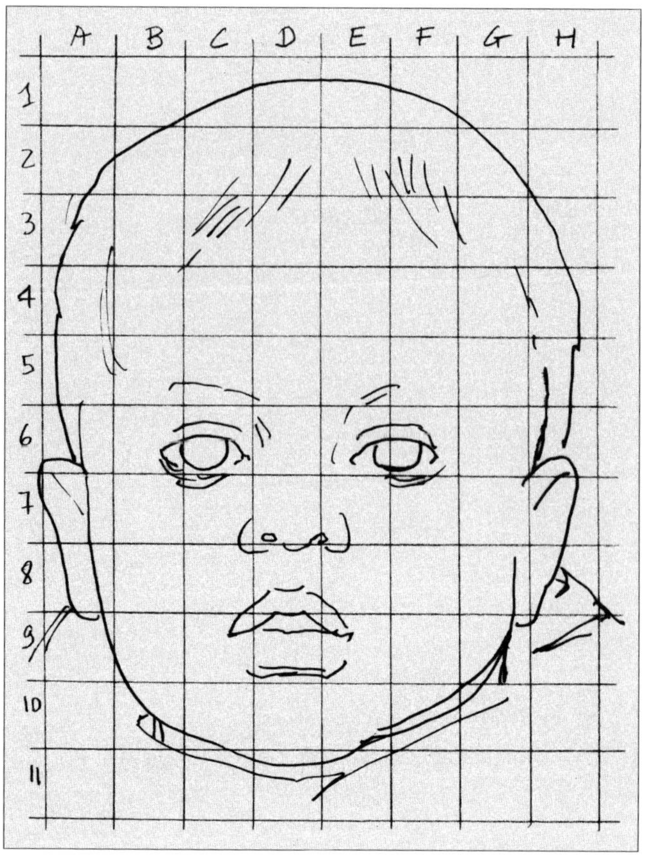

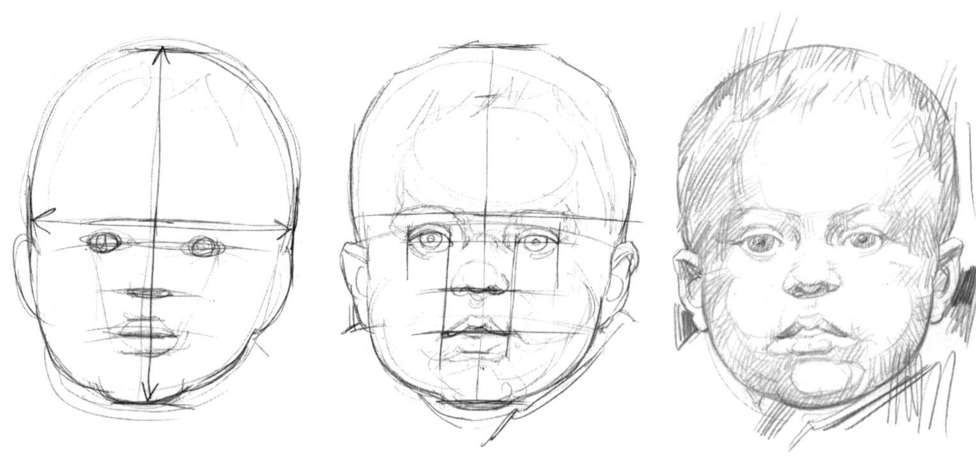

Step 1 *Size* **Step 2** *Structure* **Step 3** *Shadows*

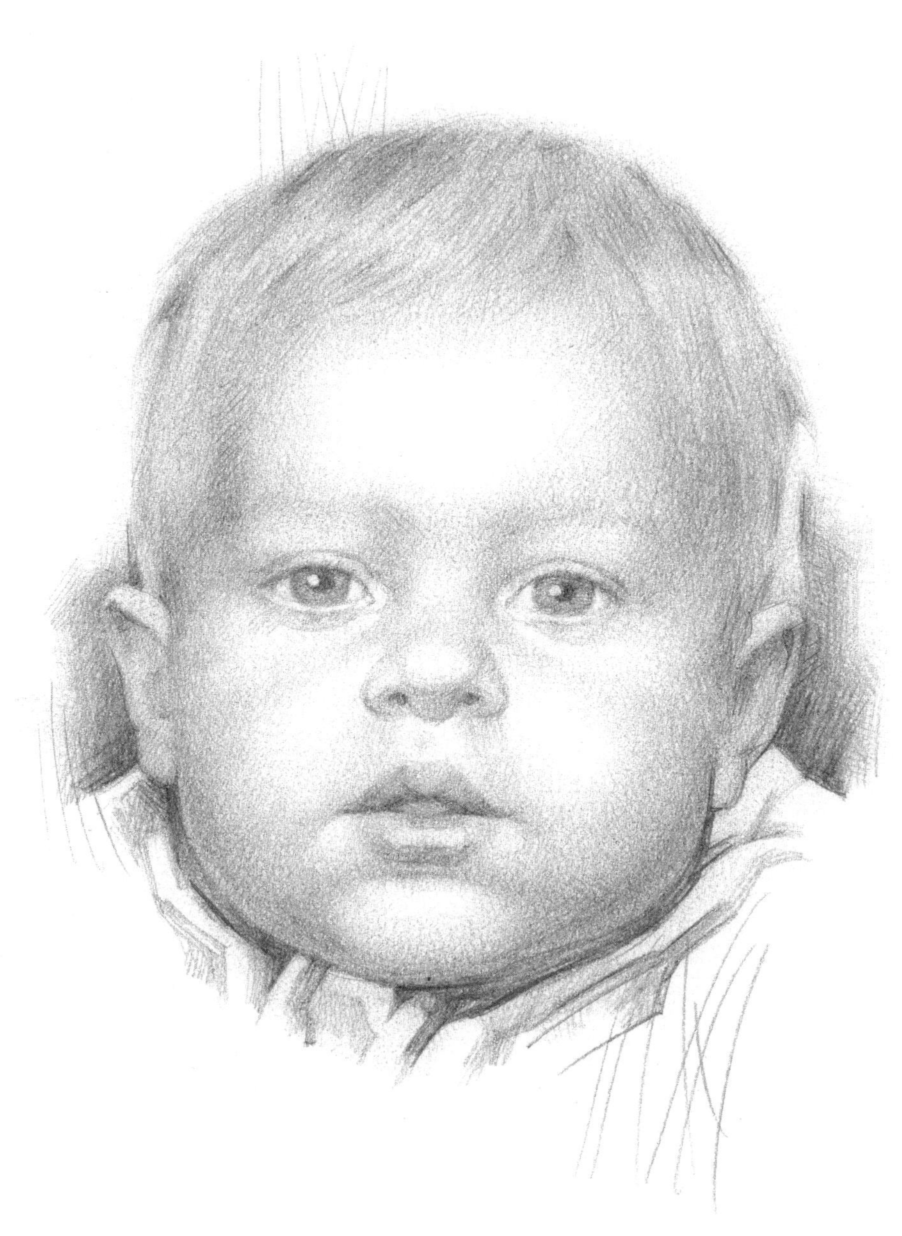

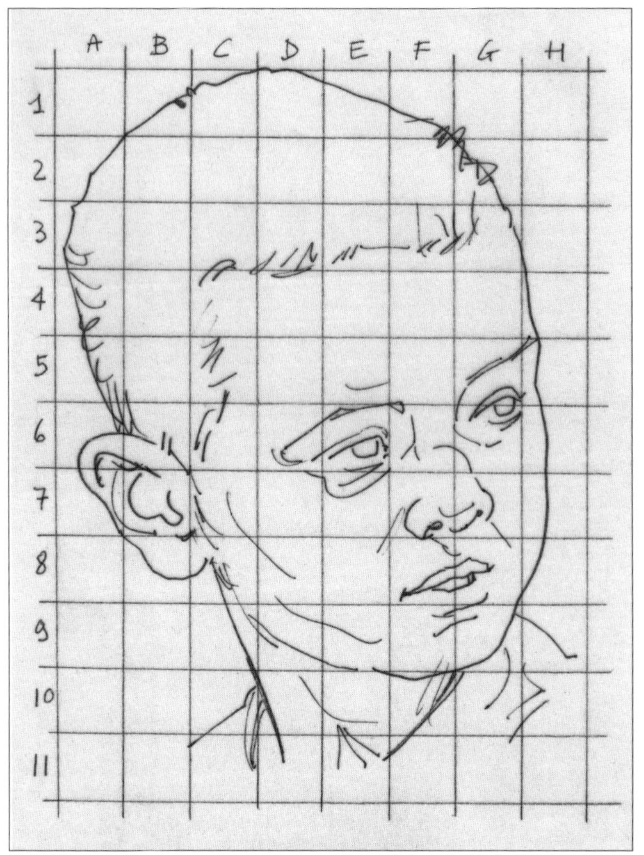

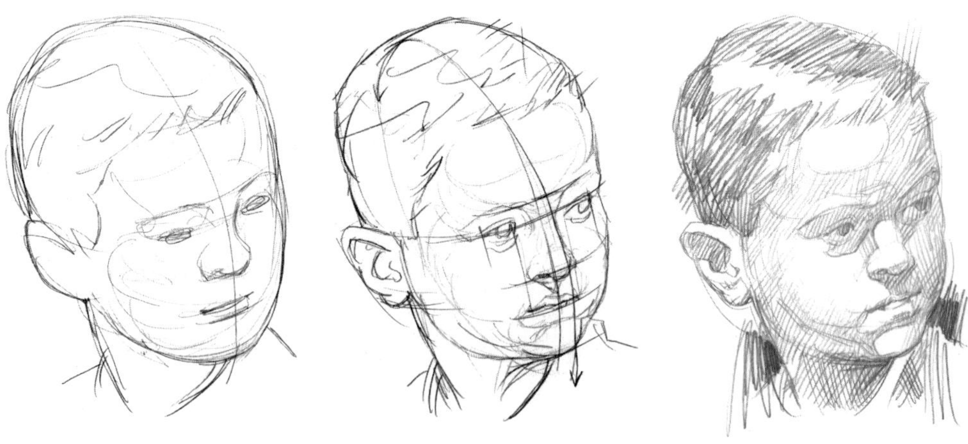

Step 1 *Size*

Step 2 *Structure*

Step 3 *Shadows*

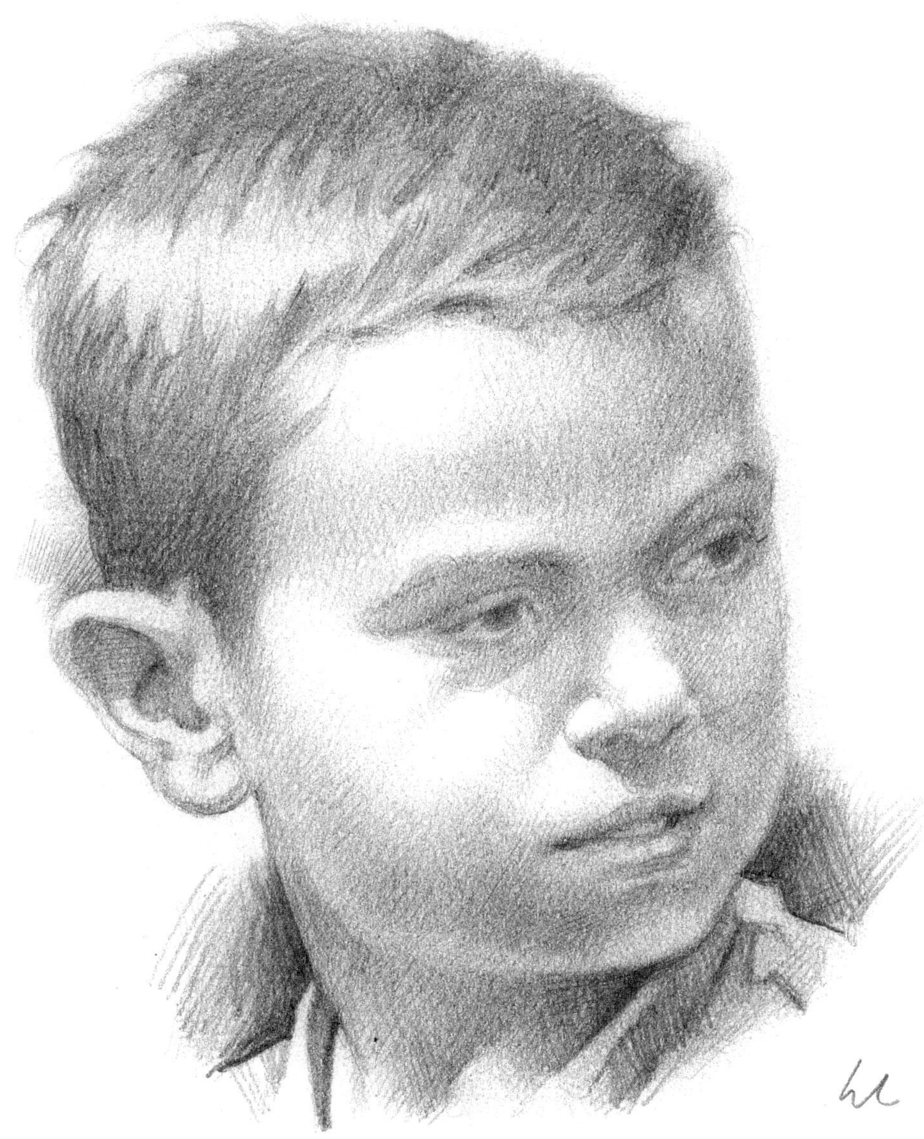

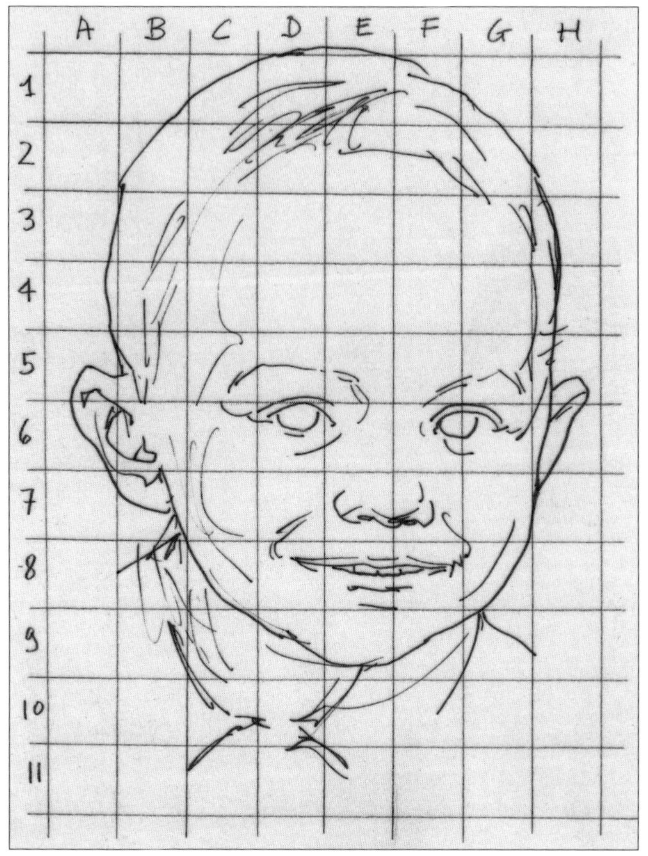

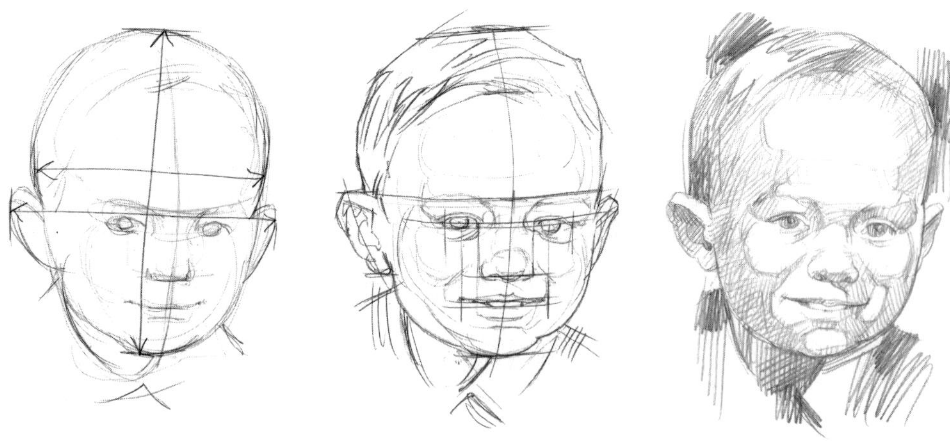

Step 1 *Size*

Step 2 *Structure*

Step 3 *Shadows*

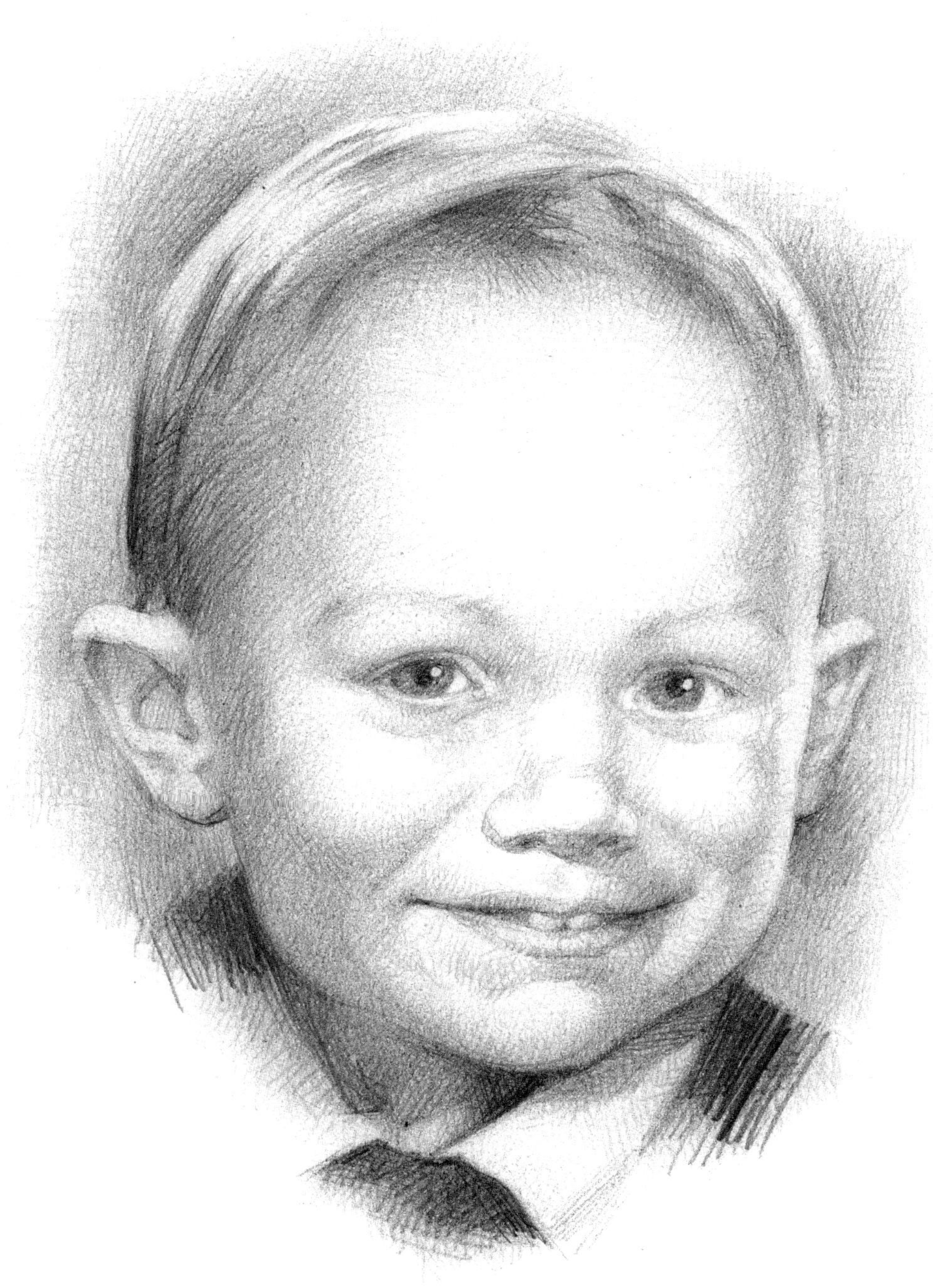

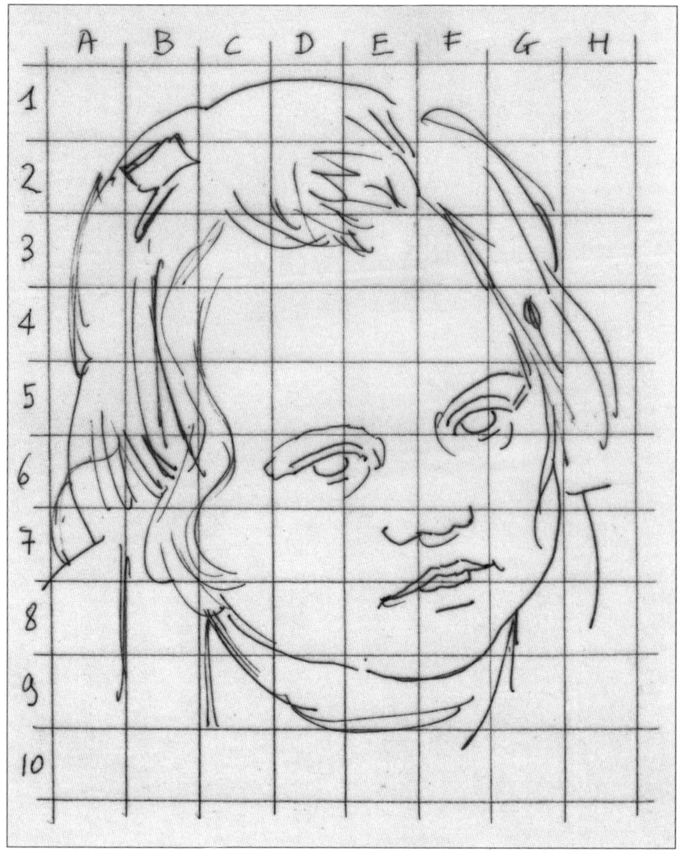

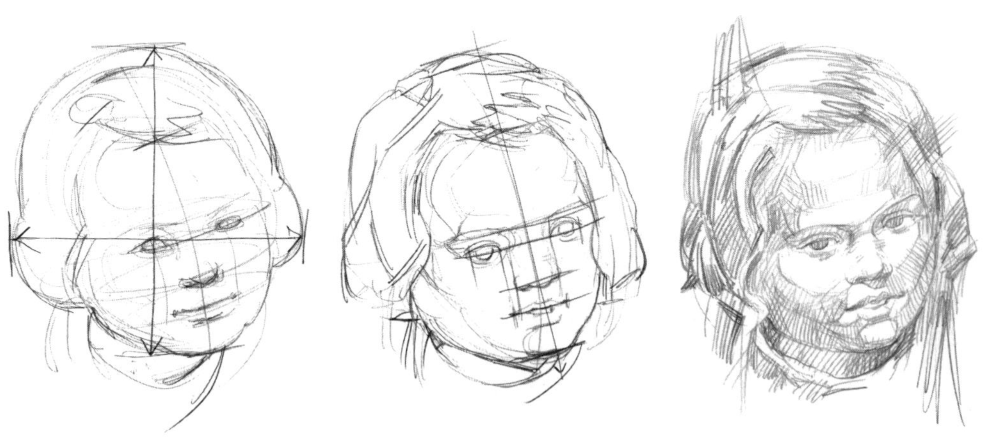

Step 1 *Size*

Step 2 *Structure*

Step 3 *Shadows*

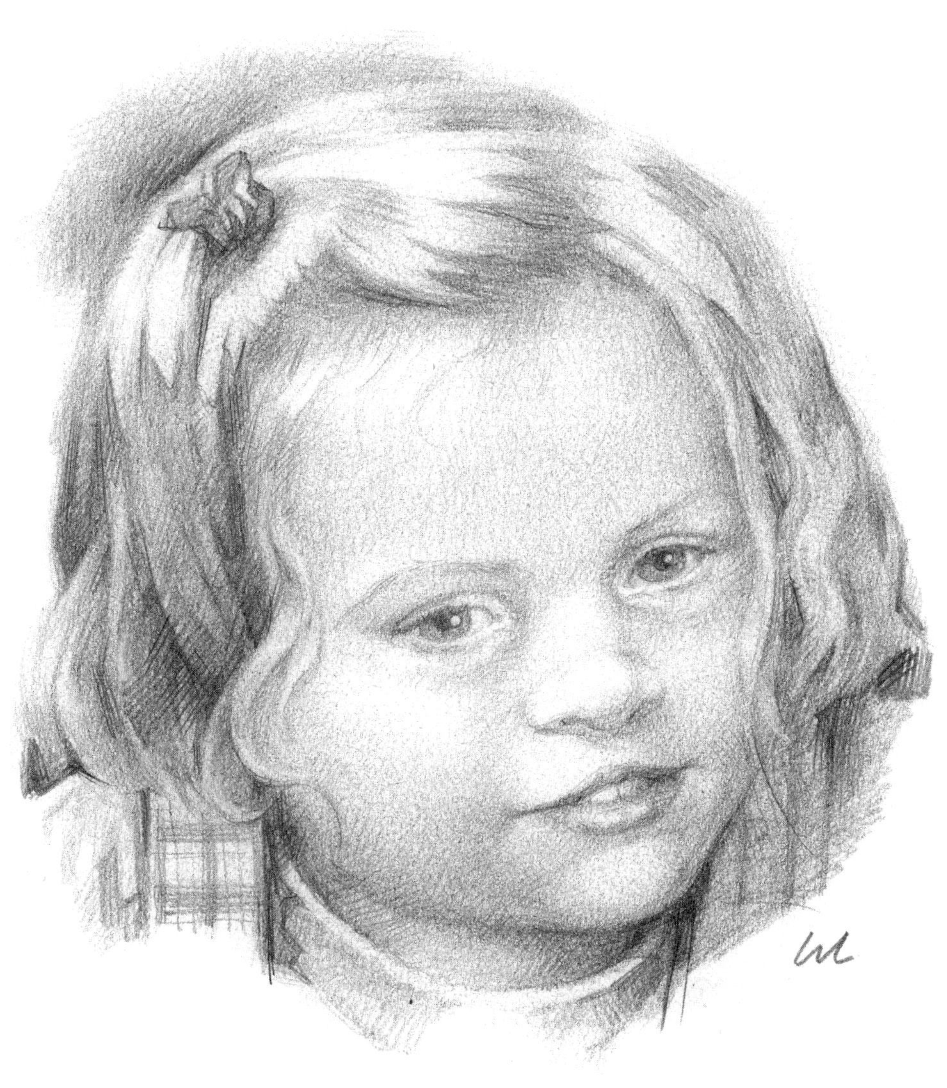

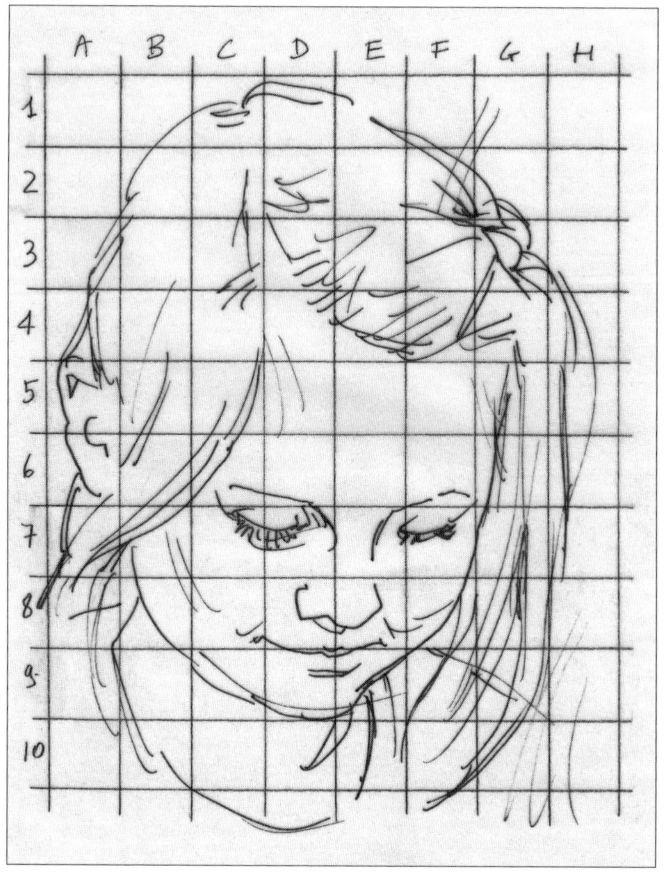

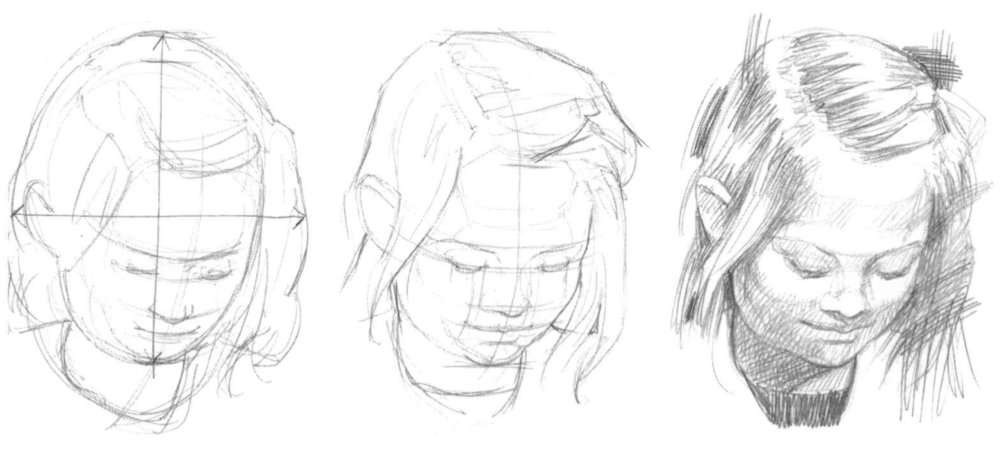

Step 1 *Size* **Step 2** *Structure* **Step 3** *Shadows*

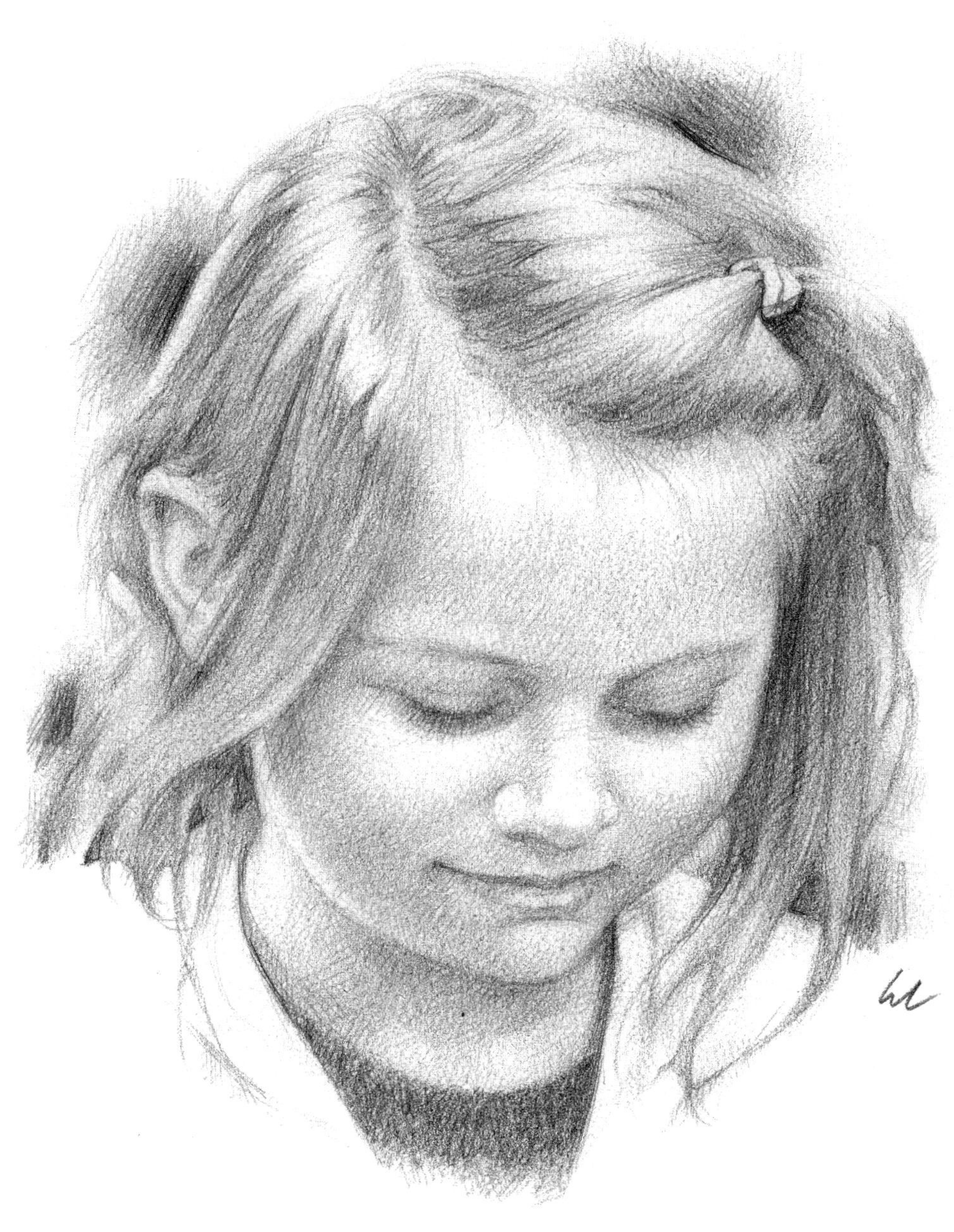

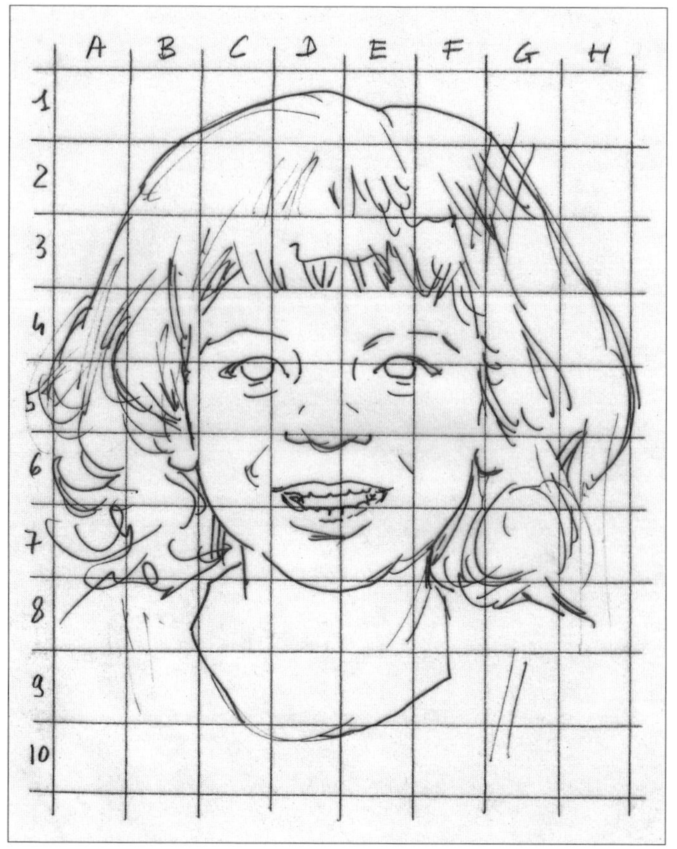

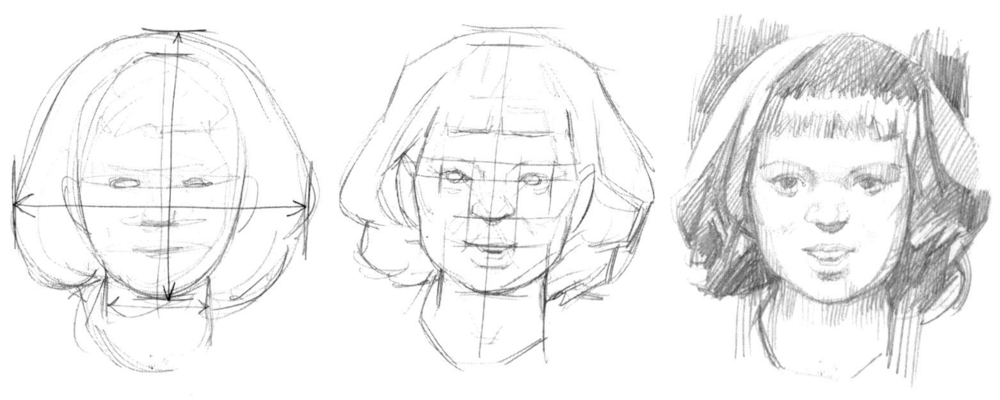

Step 1 *Size* ***Step 2*** *Structure* ***Step 3*** *Shadows*

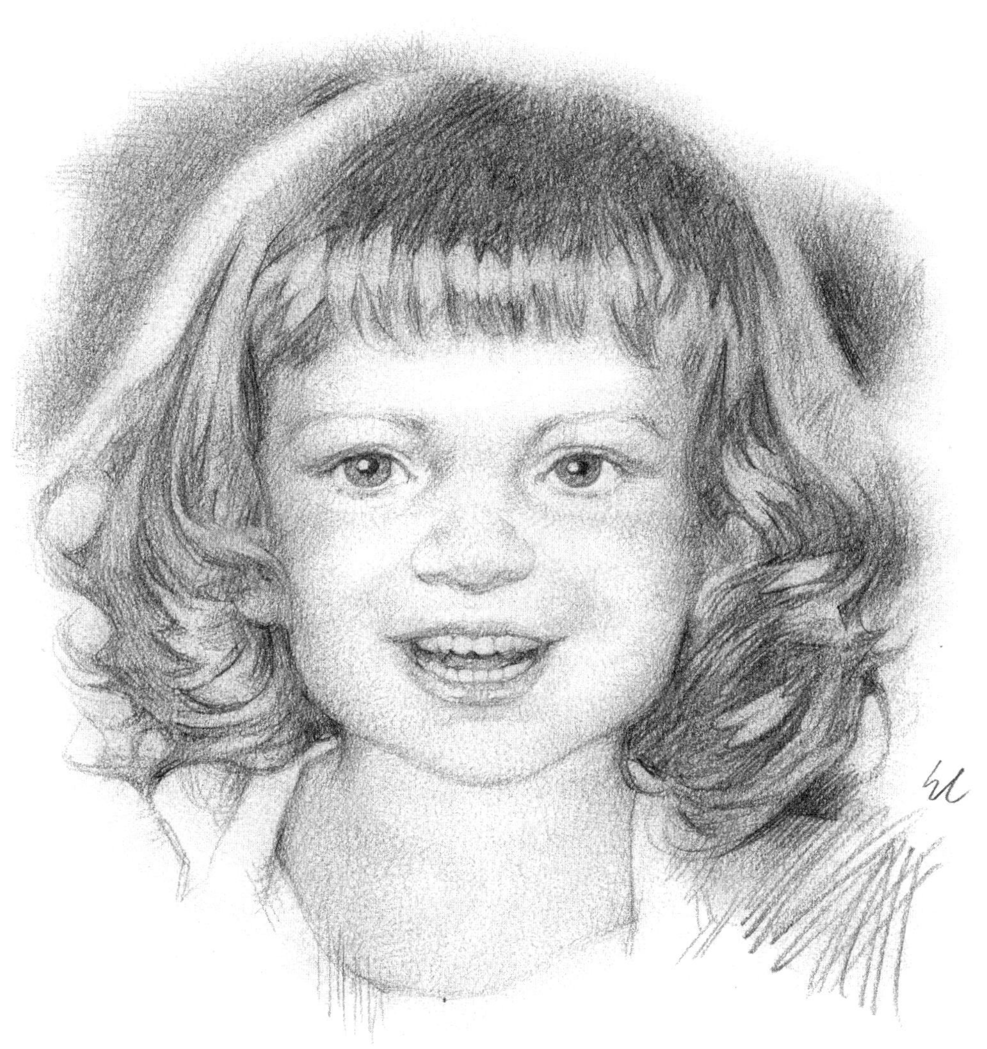

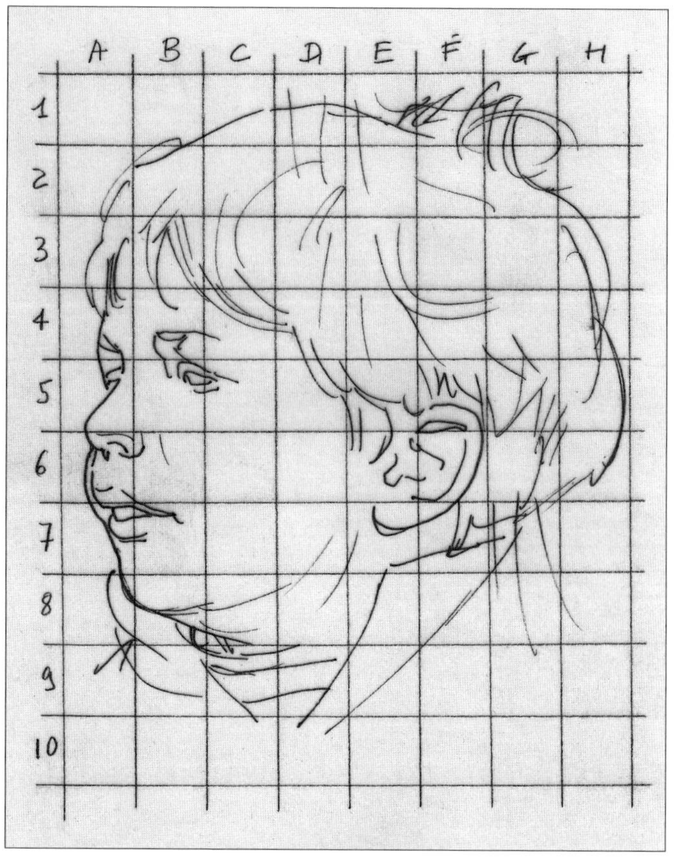

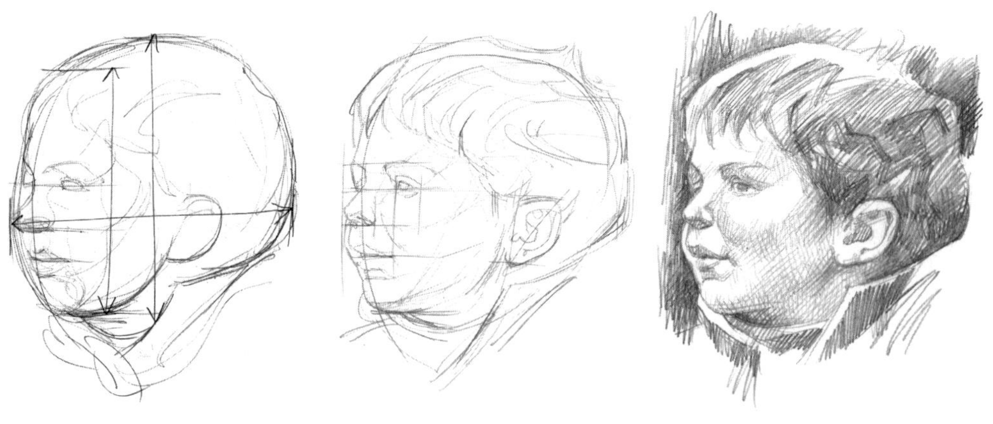

Step 1 *Size*

Step 2 *Structure*

Step 3 *Shadows*

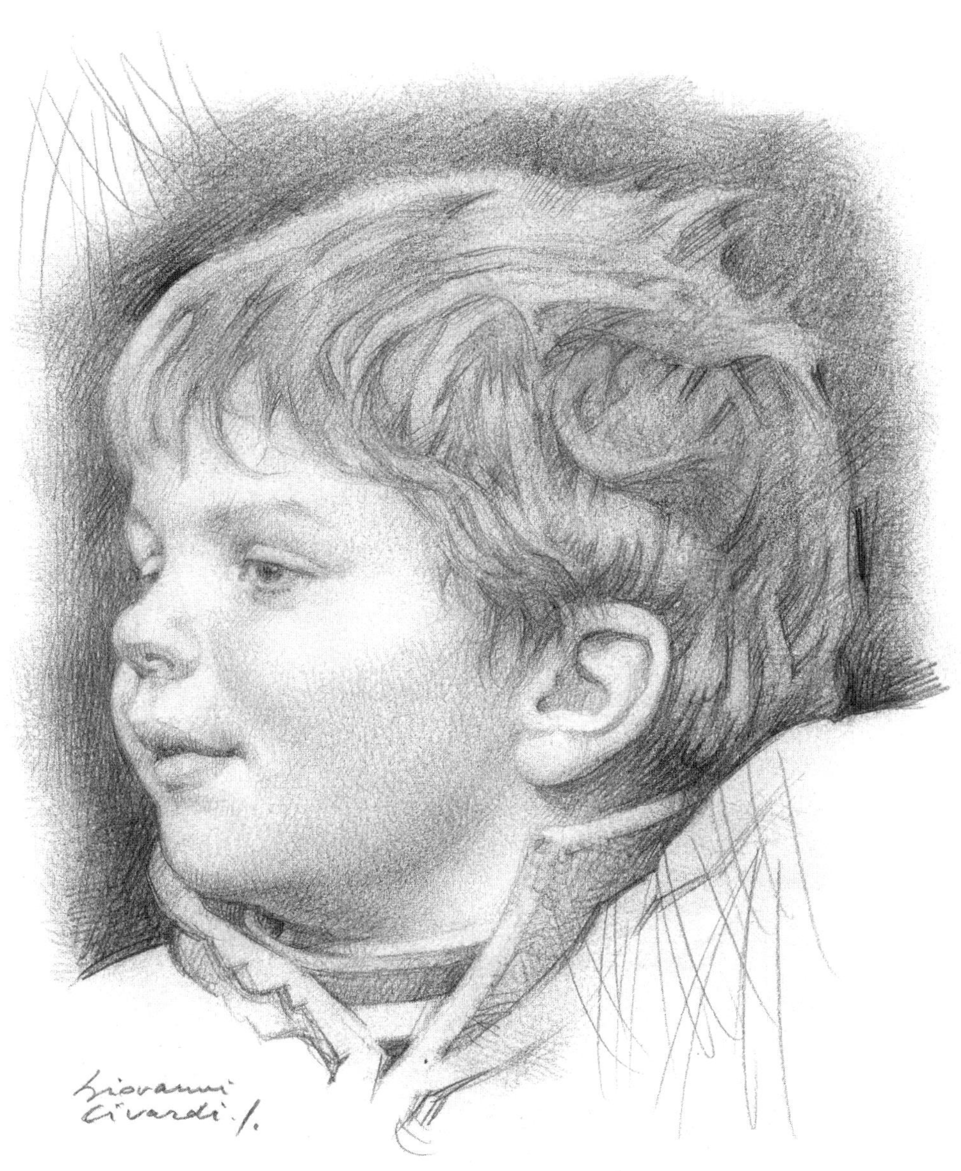
Giovanni
Civardi

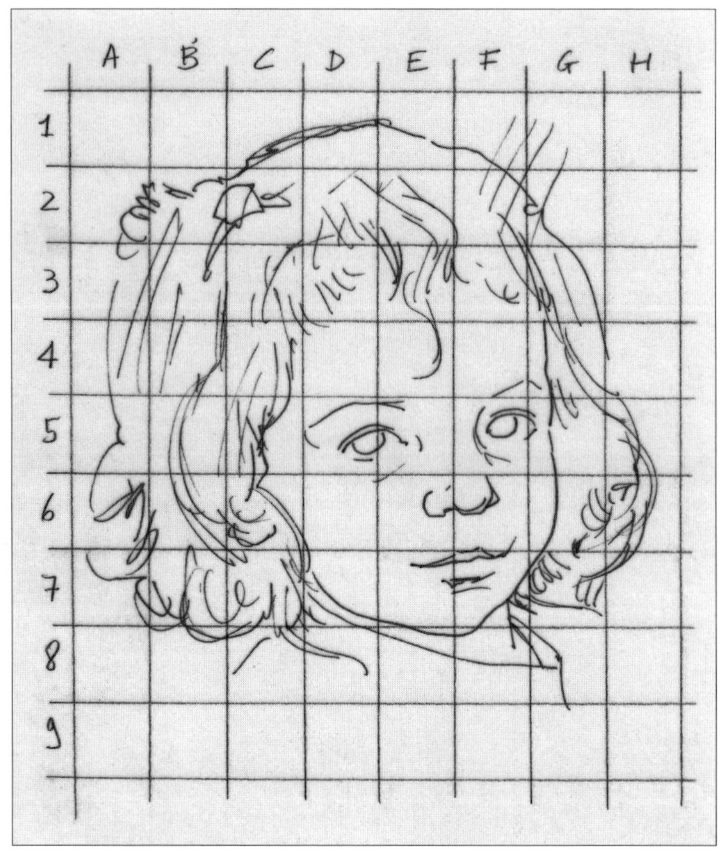

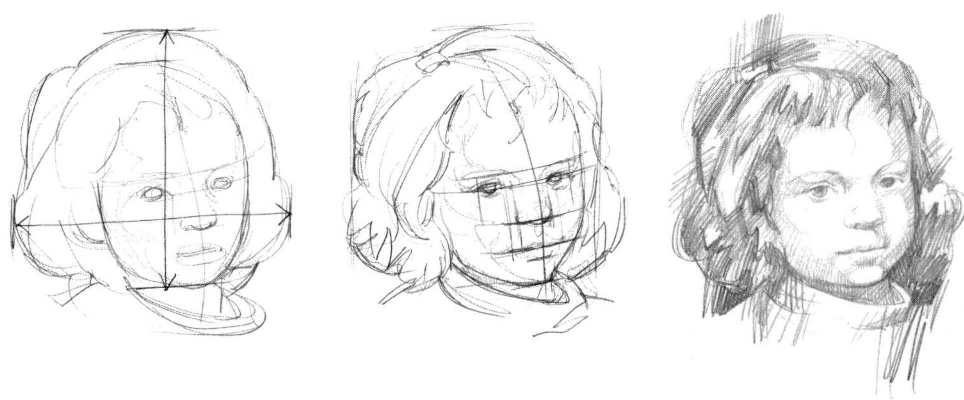

Step 1 *Size* **Step 2** *Structure* **Step 3** *Shadows*

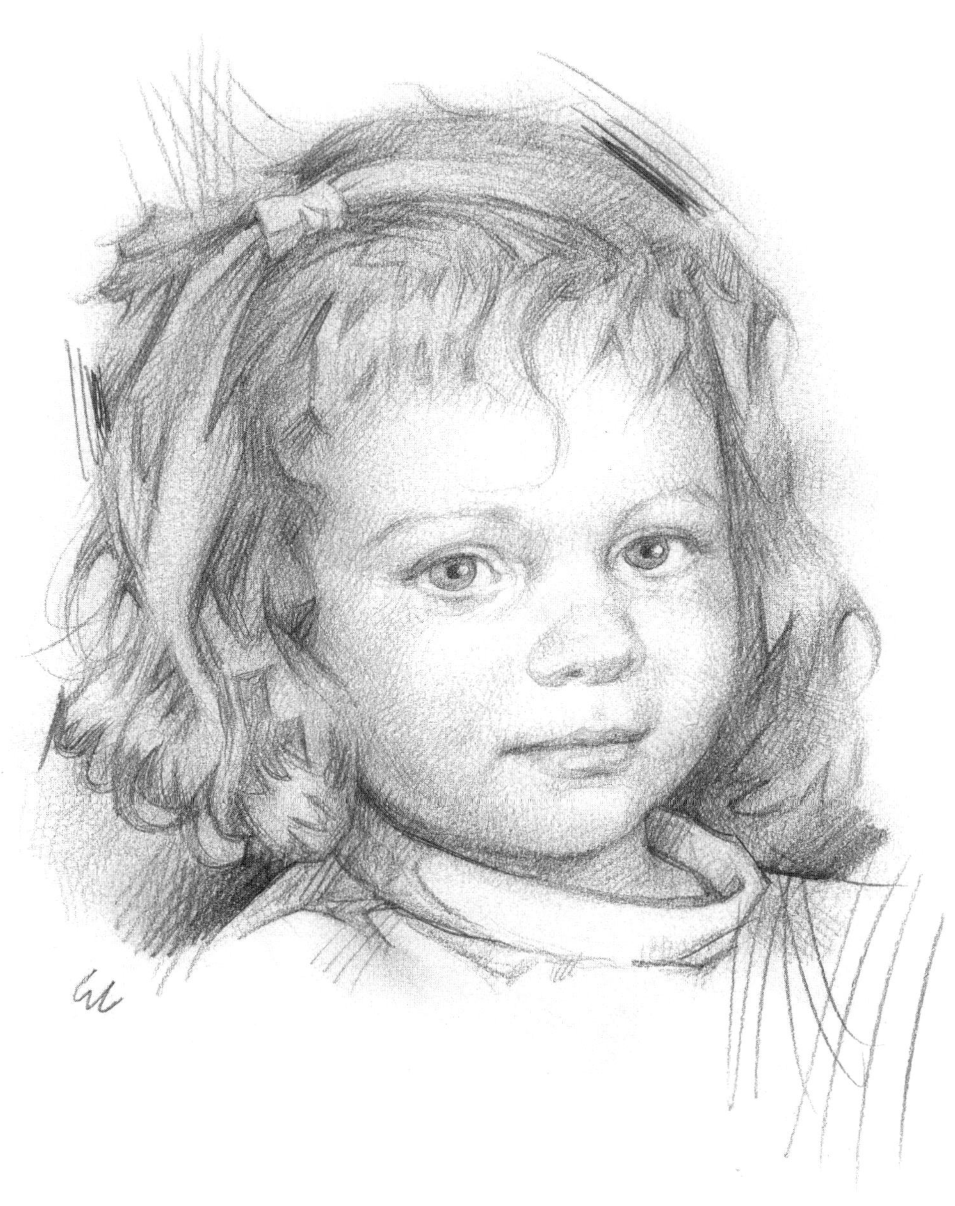

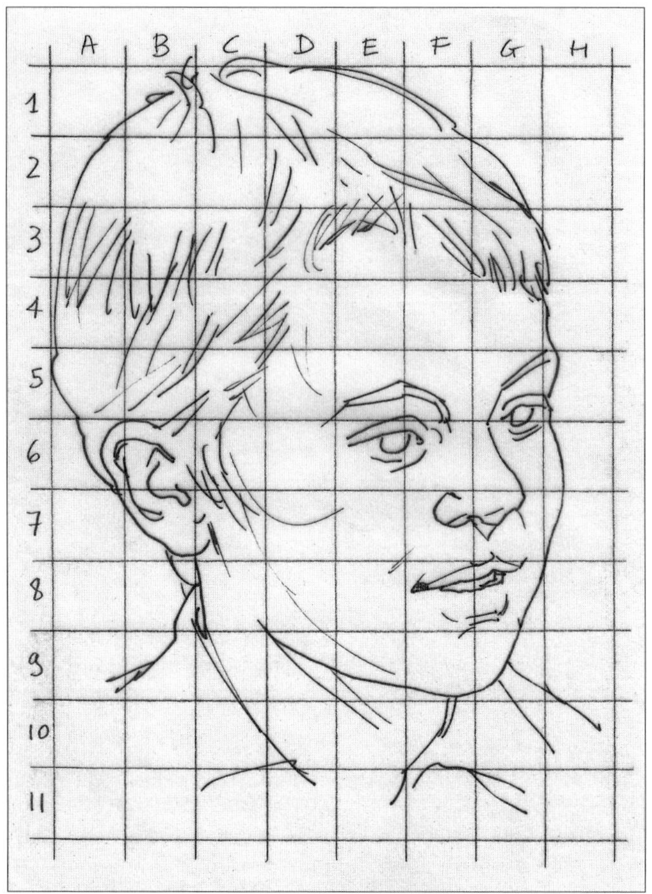

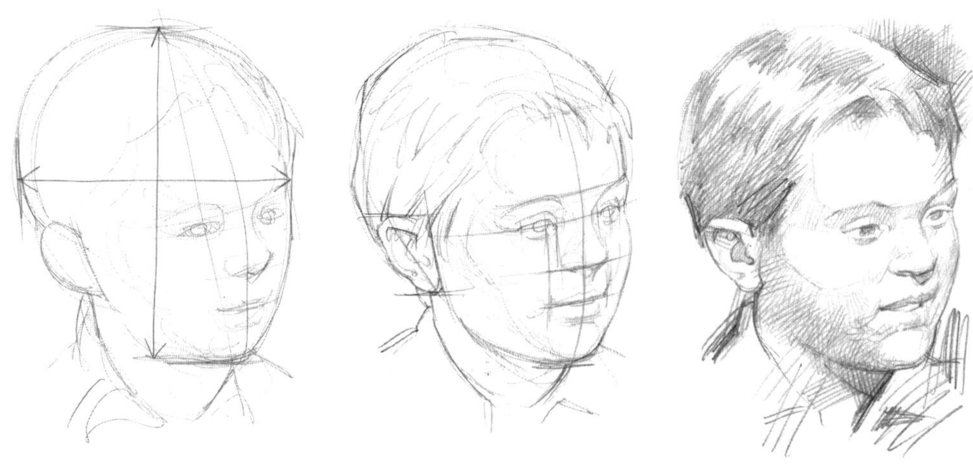

Step 1 *Size* ***Step 2*** *Structure* ***Step 3*** *Shadows*

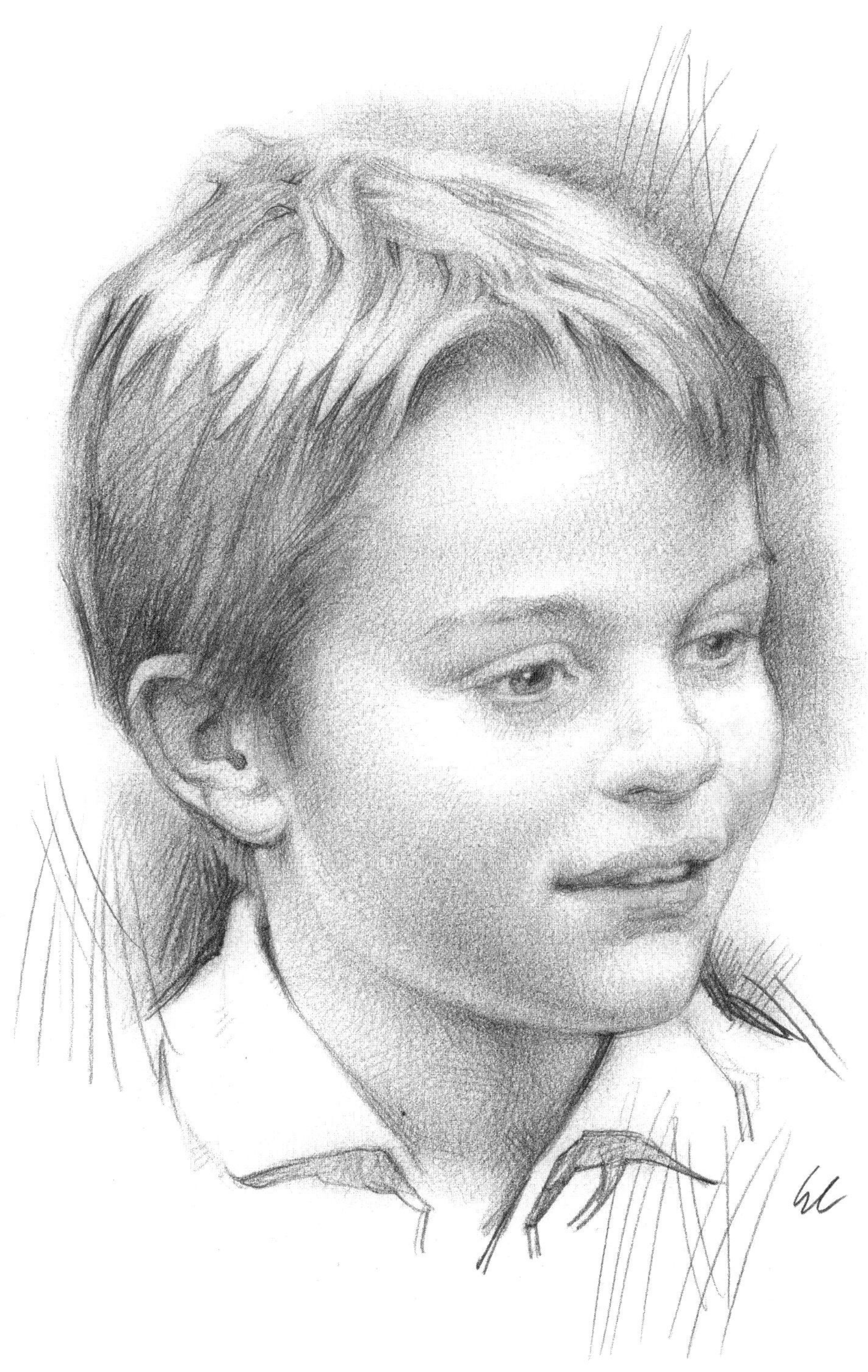

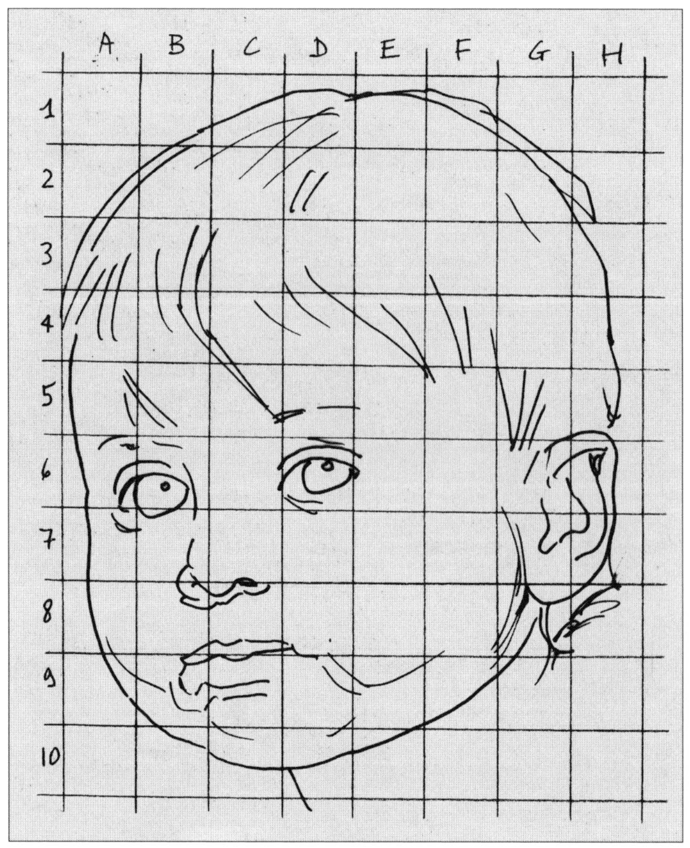

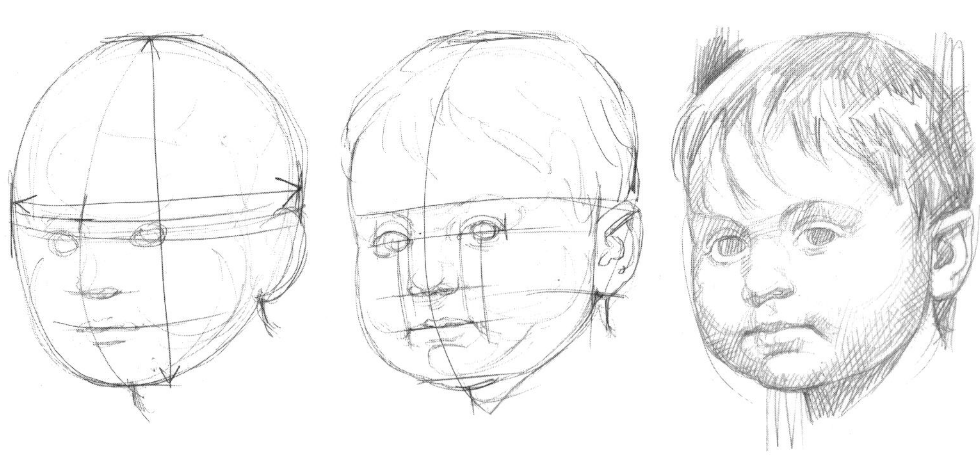

Step 1 *Size* **Step 2** *Structure* **Step 3** *Shadows*

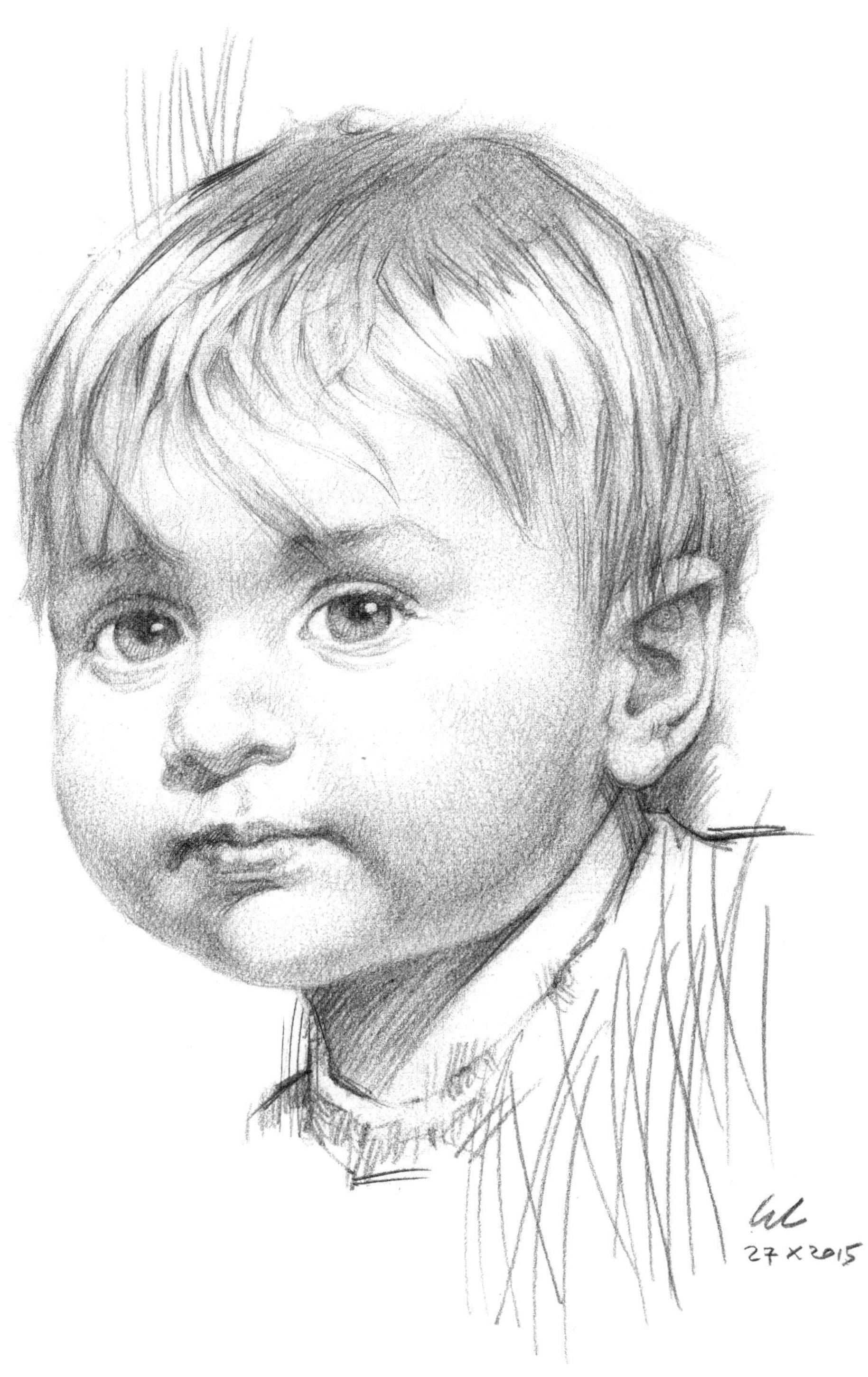
27 X 2015

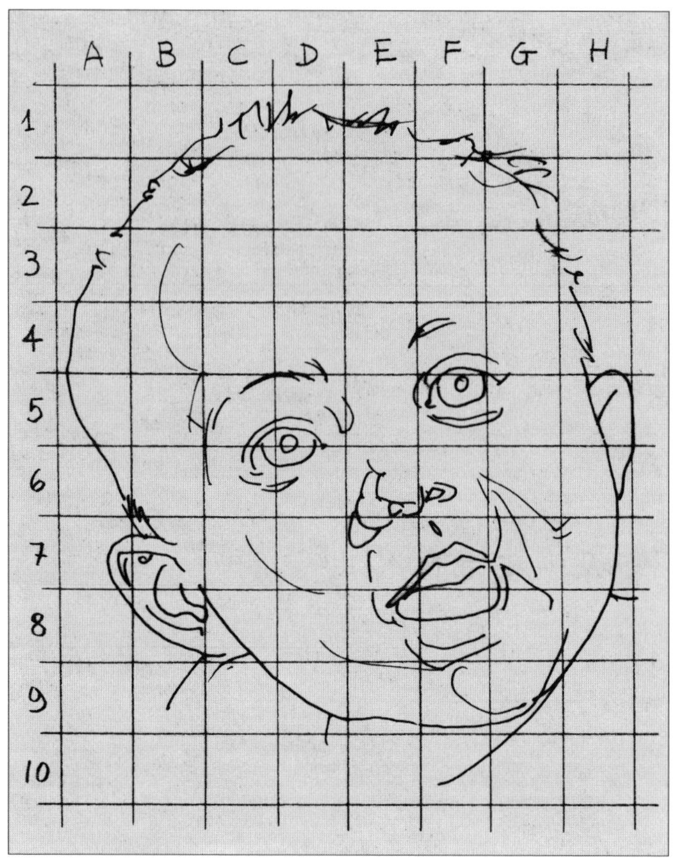

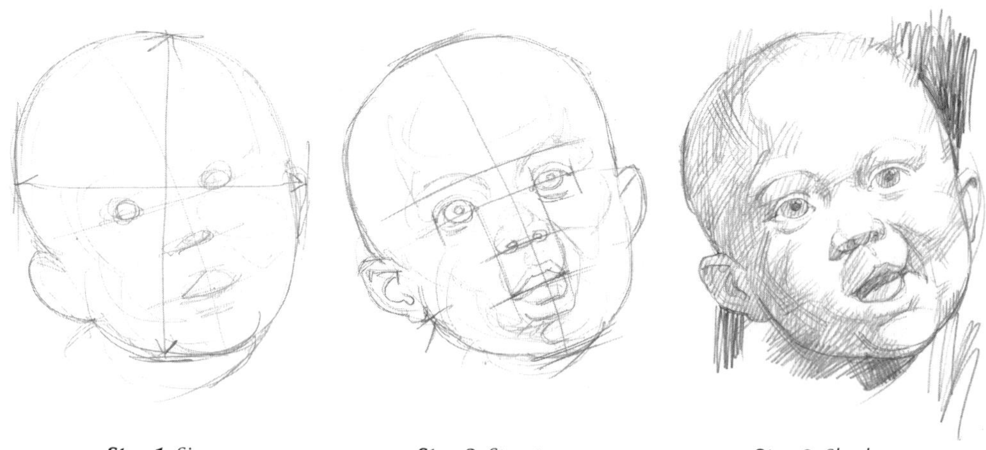

Step 1 *Size*　　***Step 2*** *Structure*　　***Step 3*** *Shadows*

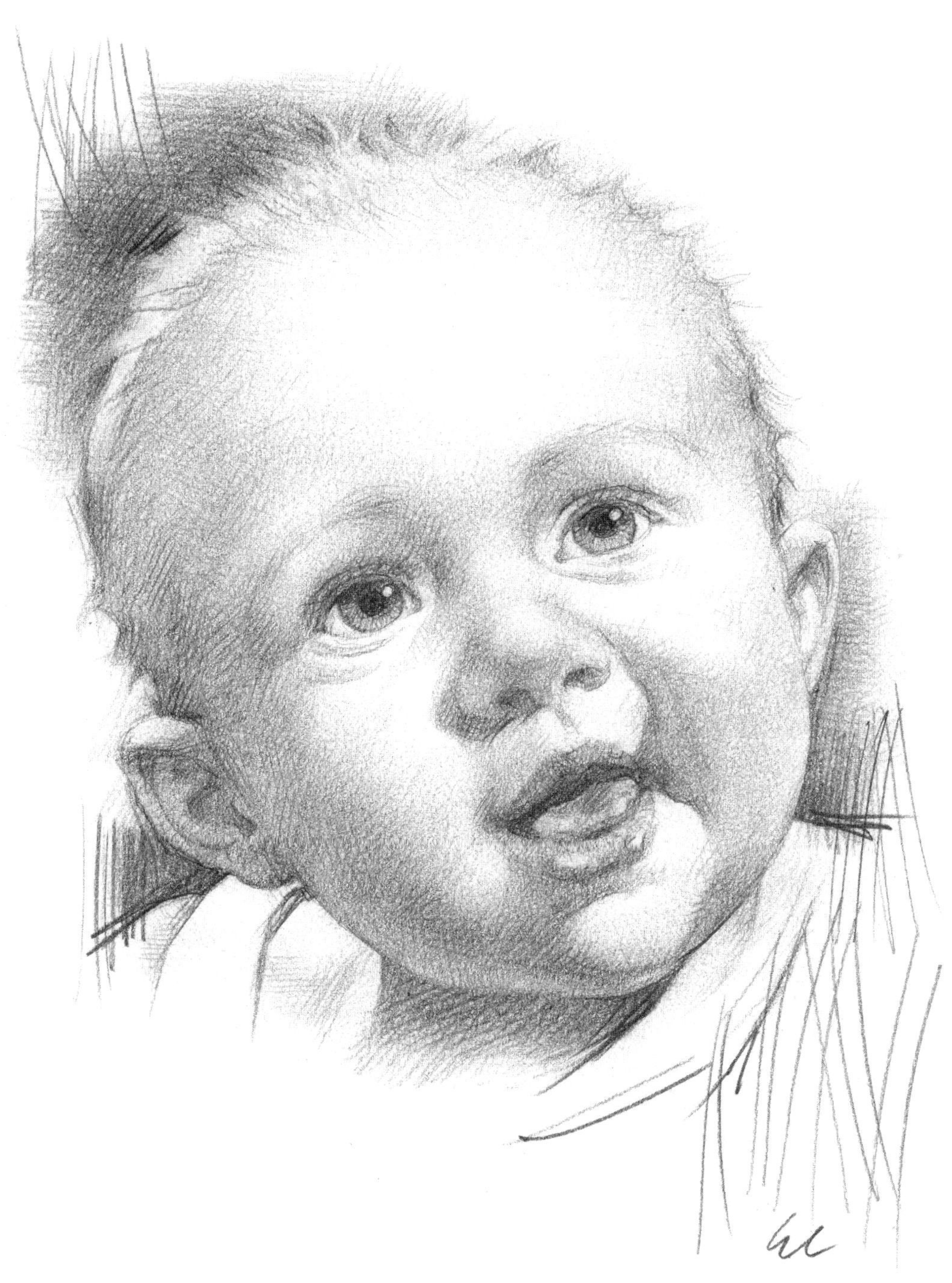

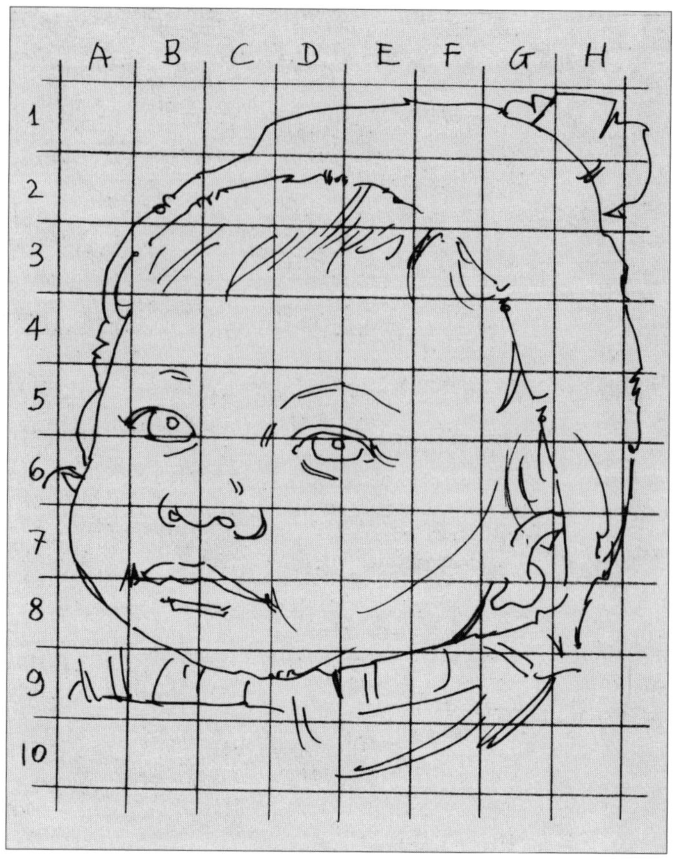

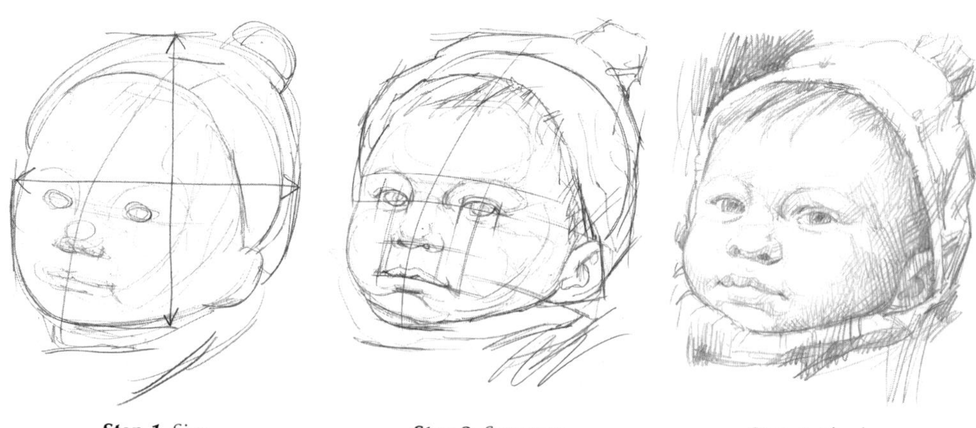

Step 1 *Size*

Step 2 *Structure*

Step 3 *Shadows*

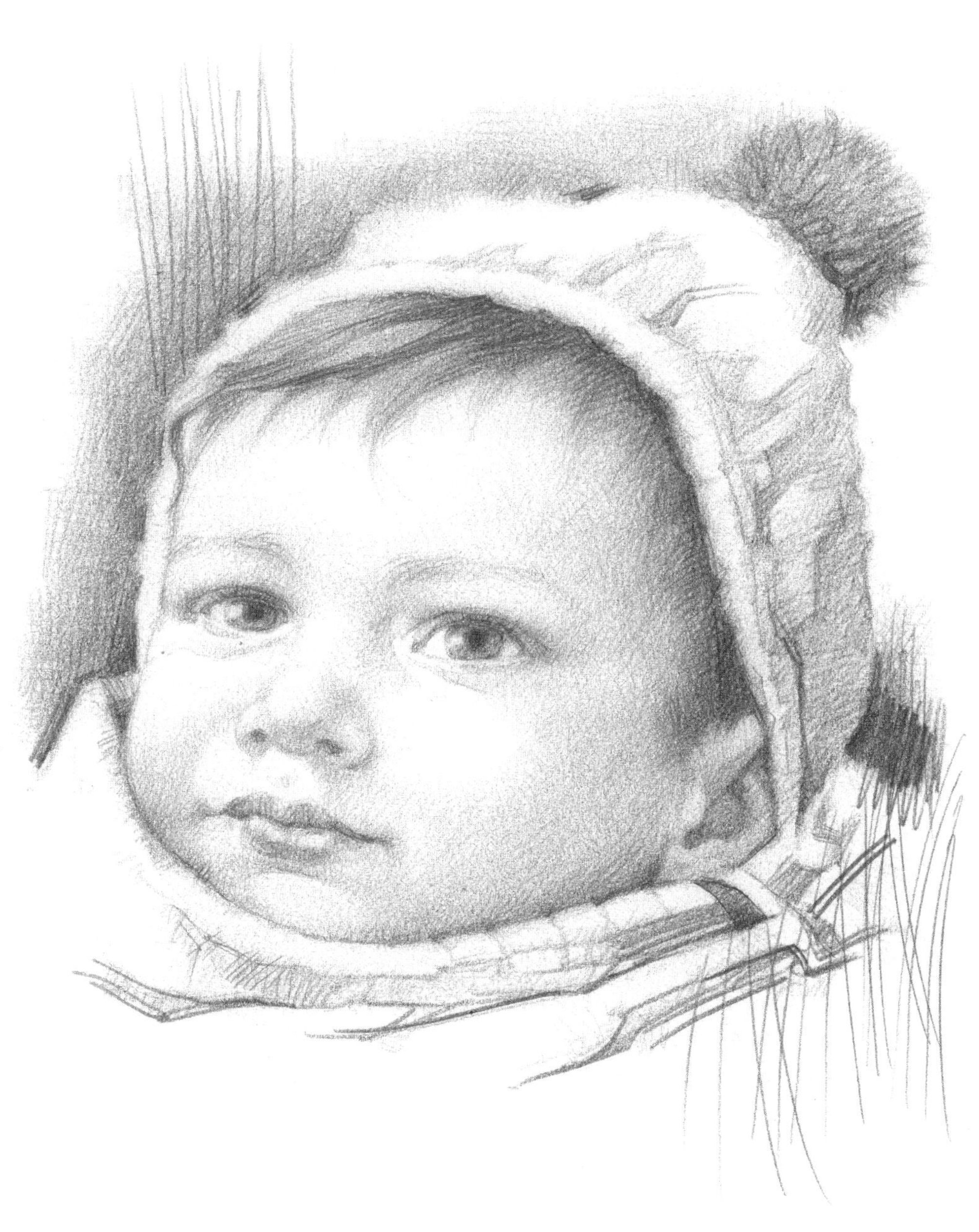

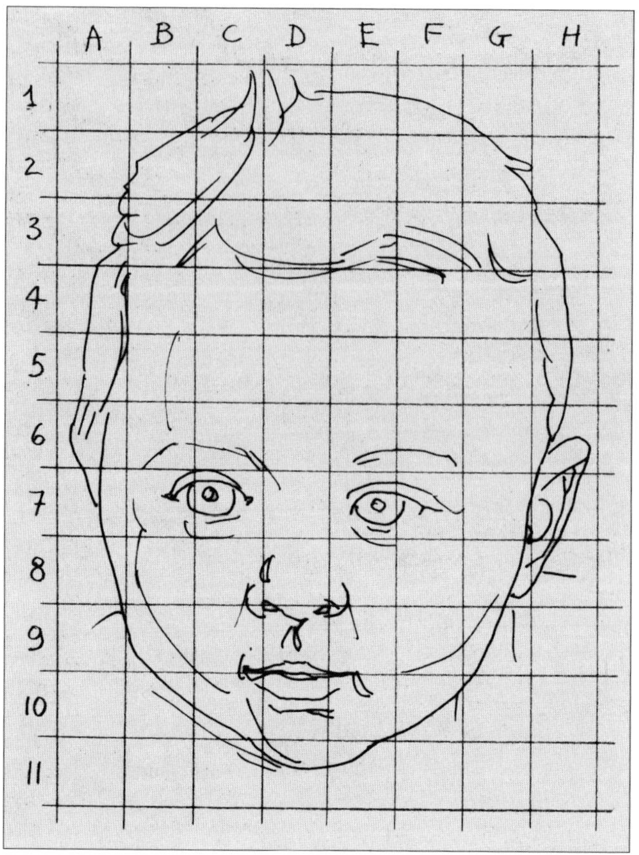

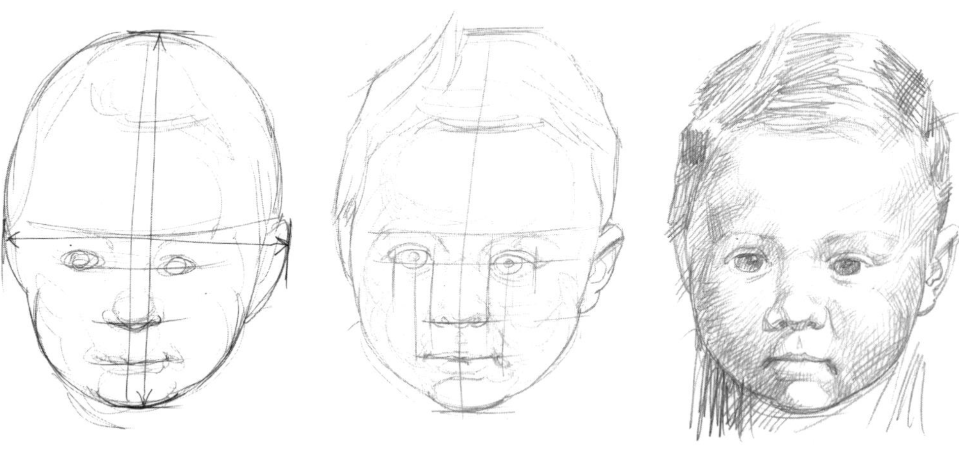

Step 1 *Size* **Step 2** *Structure* **Step 3** *Shadows*

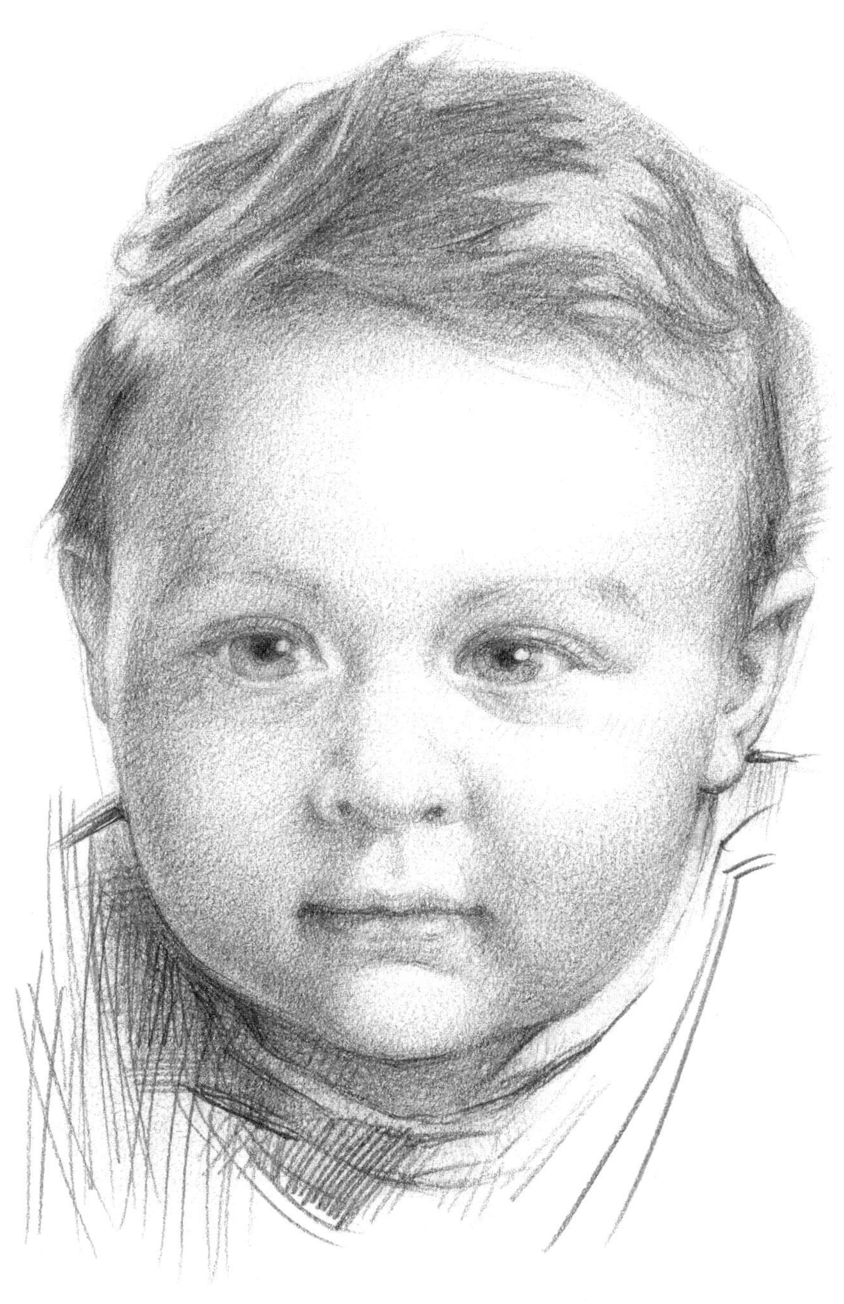

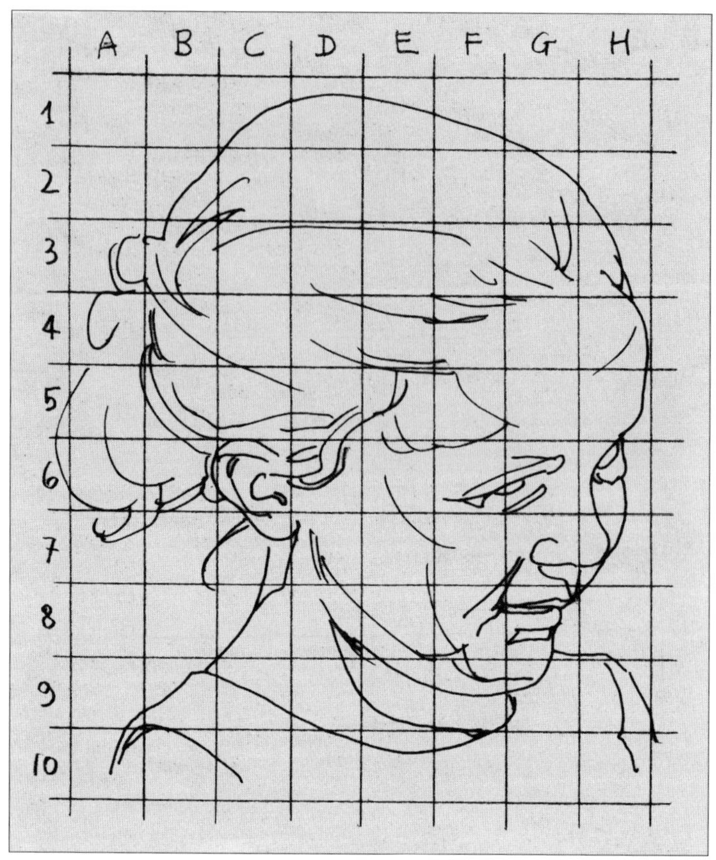

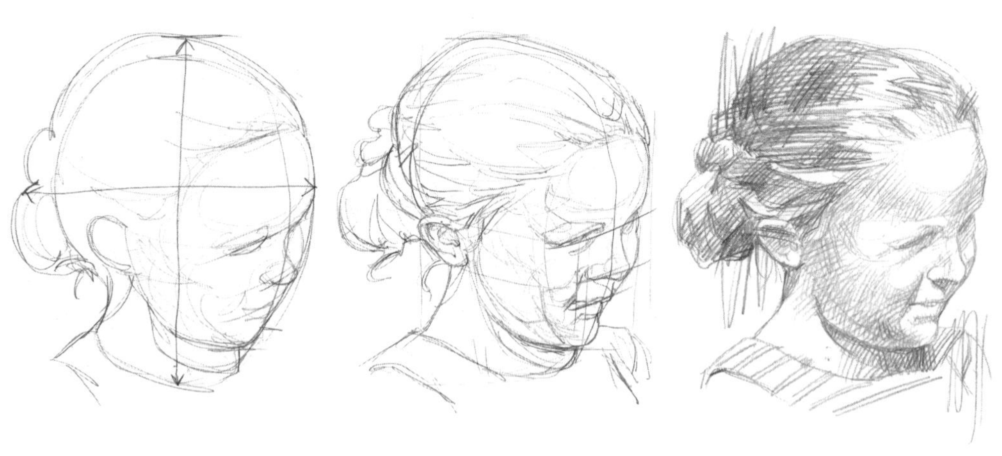

Step 1 *Size*　　**Step 2** *Structure*　　**Step 3** *Shadows*

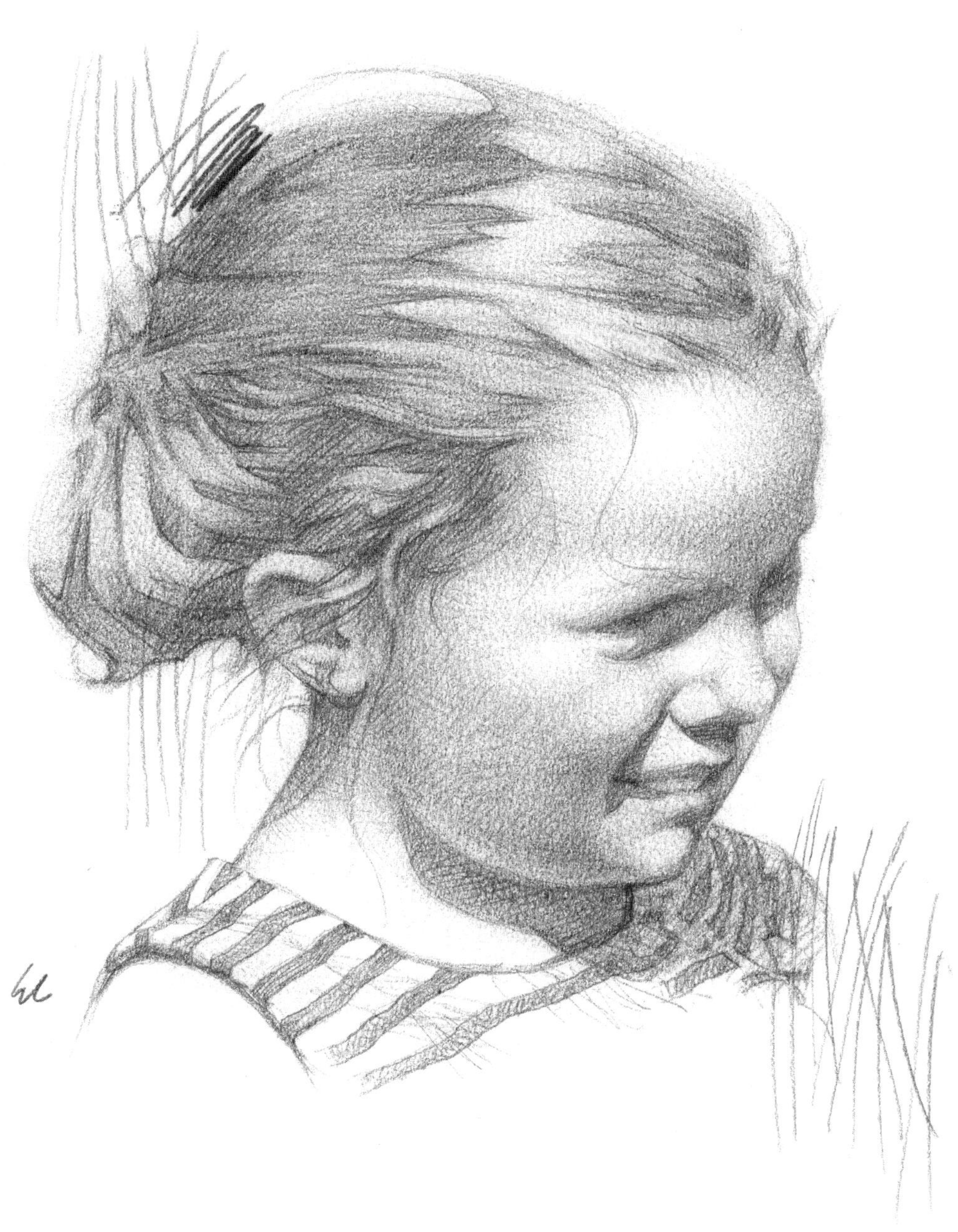

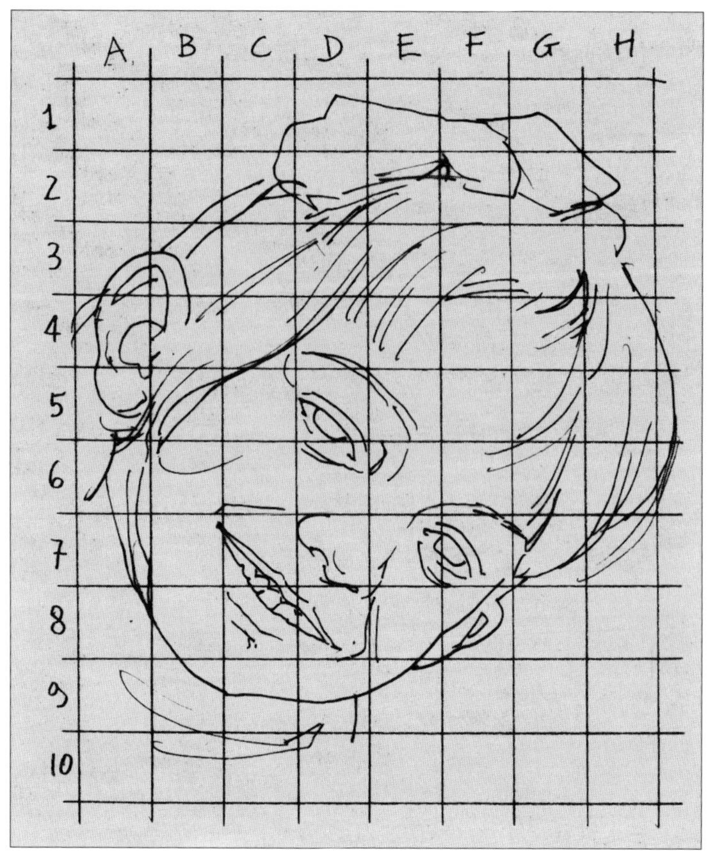

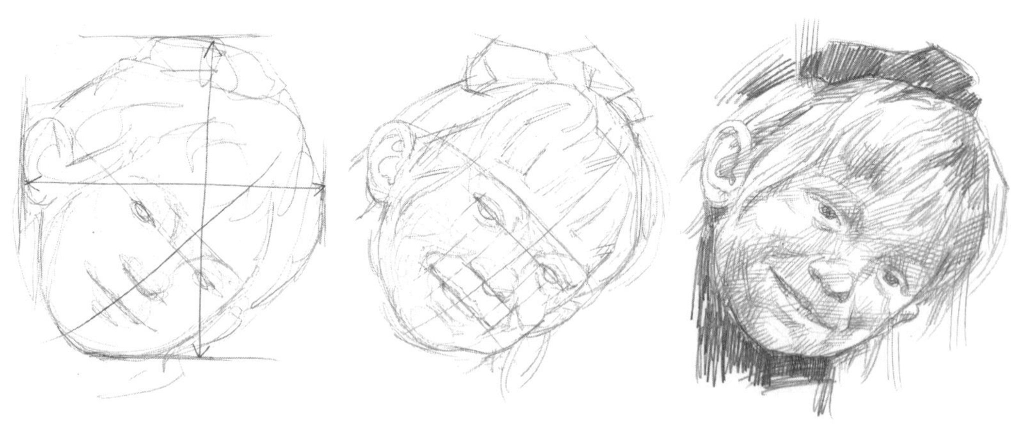

Step 1 *Size* **Step 2** *Structure* **Step 3** *Shadows*

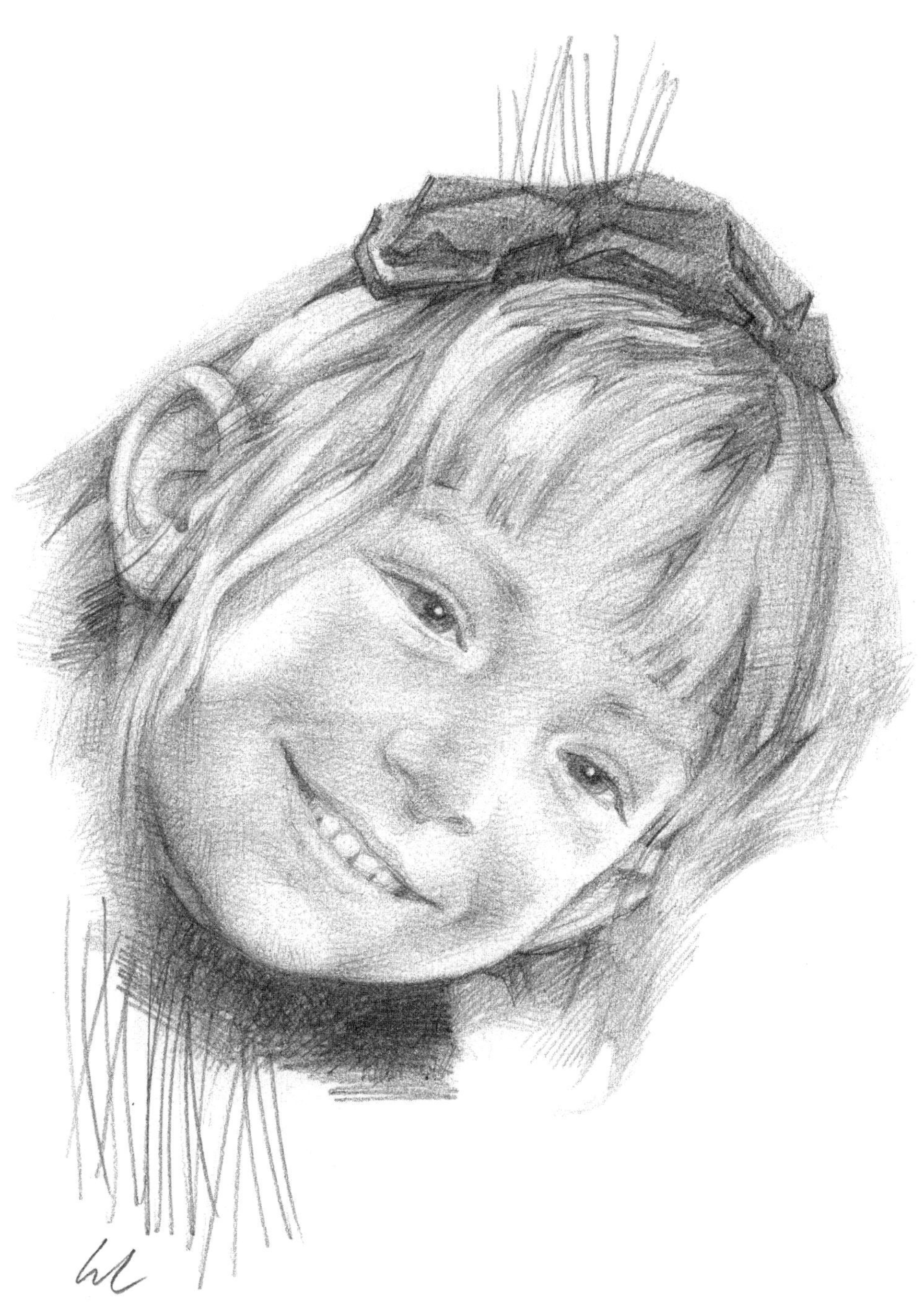

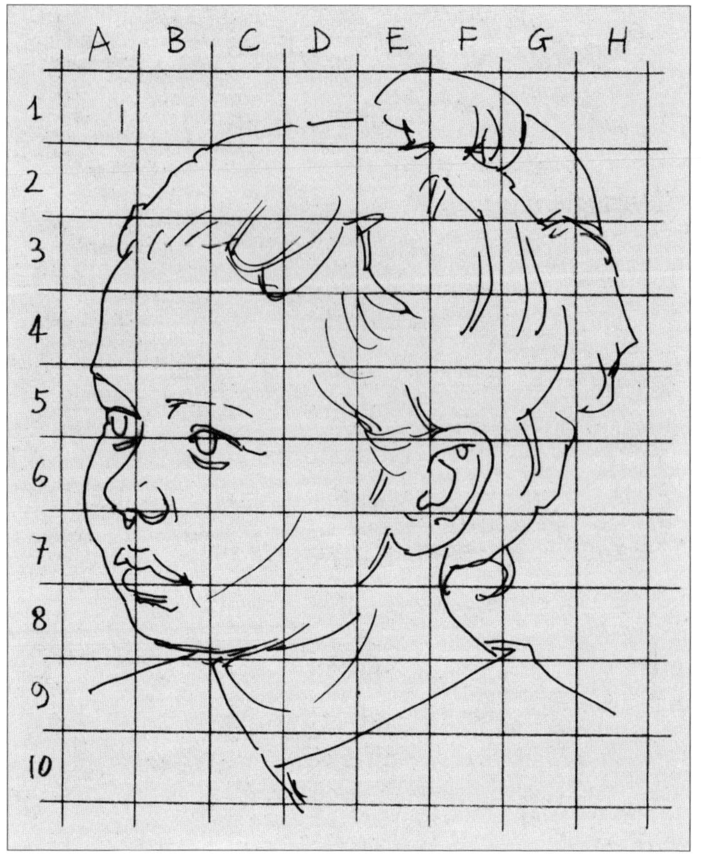

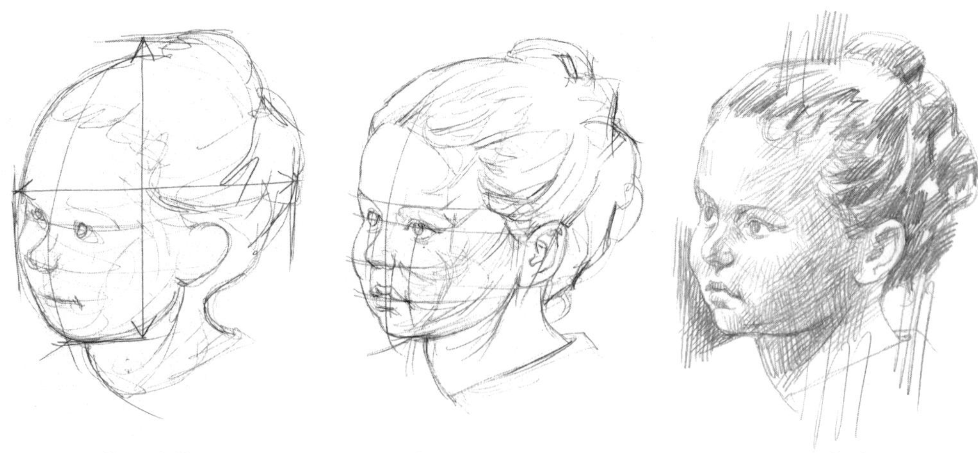

Step 1 *Size*

Step 2 *Structure*

Step 3 *Shadows*

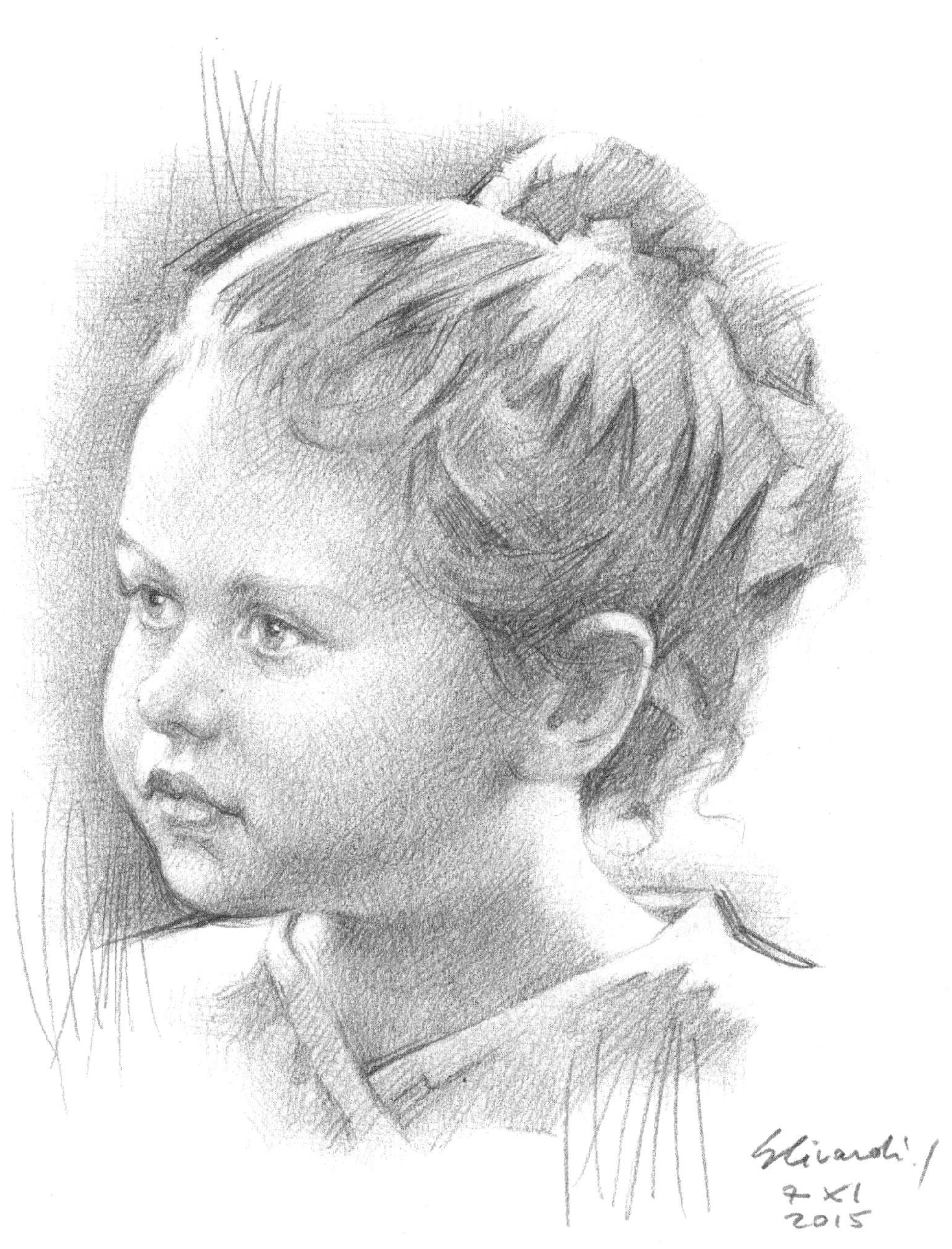
7 XI
2015

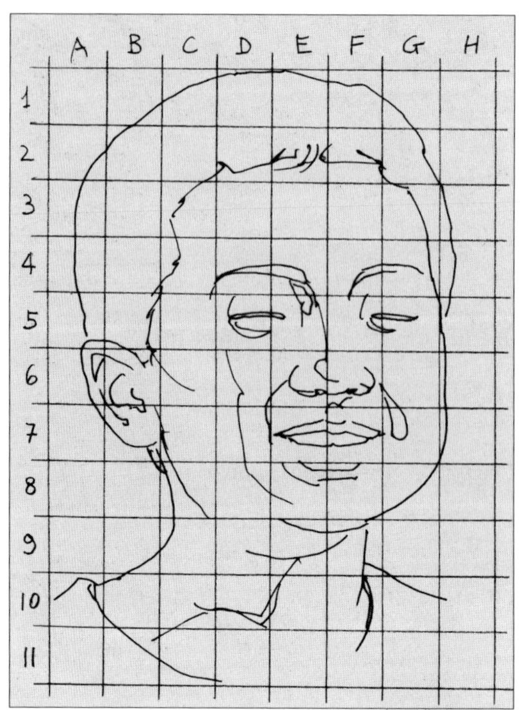
A B C D E F G H
1
2
3
4
5
6
7
8
9
10
11

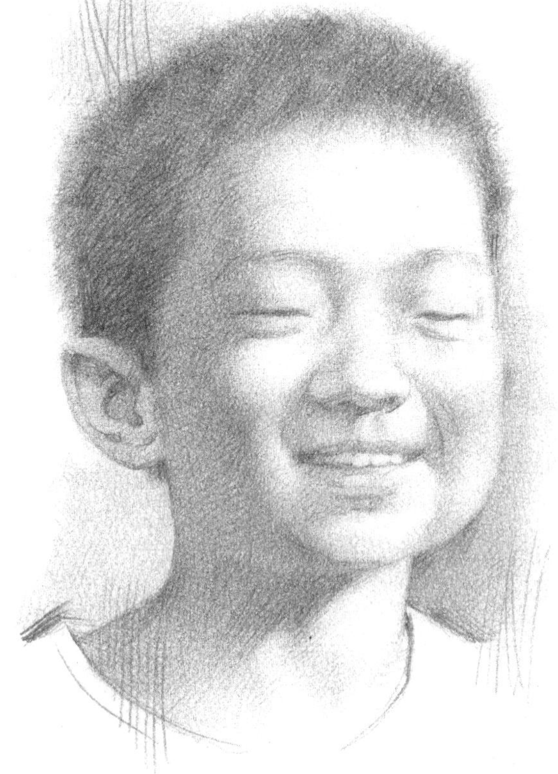

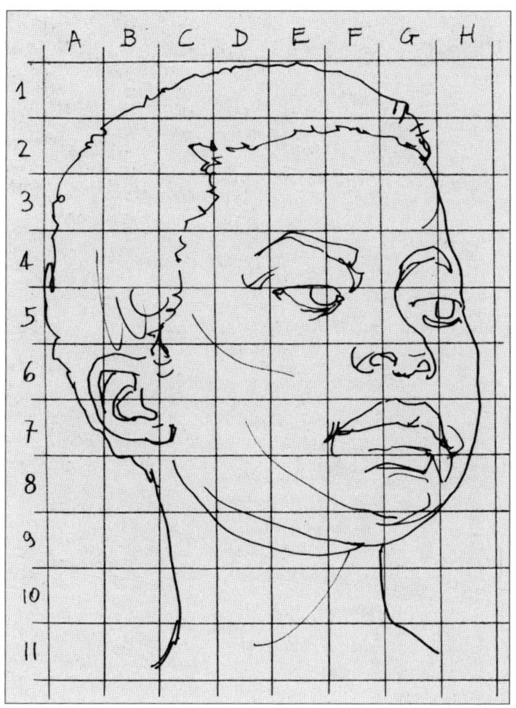
A B C D E F G H
1
2
3
4
5
6
7
8
9
10
11

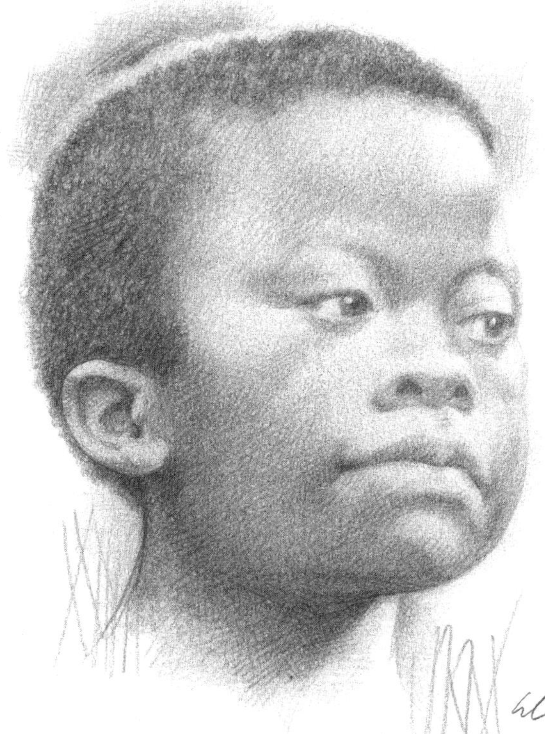

CHAPTER 4: SKETCHING FACES AND FIGURES

INTRODUCTION

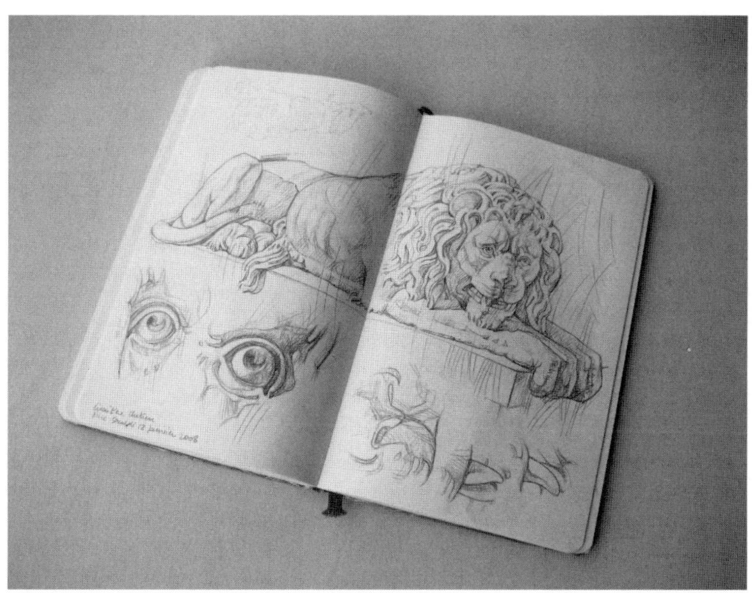

Drawing the human form is one of the richest and most complete experiences an artist can have. But whether you wish to draw the entire body or just the face, the fullness of this experience is only achieved by hard work and application. The usual approach to learning about the figure is through life study: studying the anatomical form of a living model. Alongside this method – which has provided the foundation of artistic training for many centuries – there is also the possibility of branching out from our academic study of models to include models who have been volunteered by life, so to speak: people we find everywhere around us in the streets and in public places; people, in short, in all their different shapes and sizes, and with their multitude of body postures, gestures, moods and expressions. To be able to carry out this kind of supplementary study it is important to develop a constant habit – *nulla die sine linea* (not a day without a line), as the ancient maxim puts it – of making rapid drawings or sketches from life depicting people going about their daily lives.

As a rule, a sketchbook is not intended for public display. It is both intimate and personal, which is why it allows the artist to experience things in a completely free, spontaneous and exploratory way. Knowledge of how to portray strangers who have been caught in all kinds of attitudes and circumstances is important for an artist's technical training and for the growth of his or her critical abilities. Indeed, perseverance in the practice of sketching will result in the refining of an artist's gifts of observation and interpretation and it will lead to an ability to see deeply; it will help in making choices that are rapid, confident, essential and concise. This is because the ability to draw people, with all their many subtle differences of face, figure and gesture, stance, movement and so on, derives, above all, from careful and thoughtful observation combined with an indispensible knowledge of anatomy and proportion and this is then transformed through the artist's personal interpretation.

GETTING STARTED

It is more than likely that you make a sketch to get down the initial germ of an idea for a figurative work. However you go about it, your sketch will result from the careful observation of an object or situation, rendered by means of a few essential and meaningful strokes.

- Get into the habit of always carrying a pencil and small sketchbook with you – the kind that will easily slip into a bag or pocket so that it is always on hand when something attracts your attention or stimulates your interest. There can be many reasons for stopping to make a sketch, apart from the simple desire to keep your hand and eye in constant practice. You may wish to gather and note down important information, or analyze a complex structure or, perhaps most importantly, keep your eye well trained in perceiving proportions, relationships and forms correctly. Then there is the motive of acquiring the ability to observe and select essential features, coordinating your observation, your judgement and the movements of your hand in graphic form.
- Do not worry about the aesthetic result of the sketch. It is no more than a simple piece of note taking, a private and personal visual record that is unlikely to be put on show for others to see. You should be more concerned with preserving the freshness and immediacy of the impression on the paper – never go back to a sketch to add finishing touches.
- Do not attempt to get everything down on paper that you see in a figure. Given the limited amount of time at your disposal and the temporary nature of the pose, you should concentrate on what is essential, or what you consider to be so. Therefore, once you have fixed the general lines of a figure's overall stance, or the attitude of a face, you should either do the same again (circumstances permitting), by analyzing the subject from a different angle, or investigate the structure of individual aspects in greater detail.

Sketching people in real environments, when the subjects are not posing for you intentionally and may be completely unaware that they are being observed and portrayed, might appear very difficult and even 'paralyzing'. But there is no real reason for faint-heartedness or feeling daunted at the prospect of working in public – hardly anyone will notice what you are doing anyway. Diligence will certainly bring you many rewards, building up your confidence and improving your artistic abilities. Finding emotional and technical solutions to the obstacles that prevent you from carrying out a fully finished drawing will hone your abilities to explore and summarize, making your style of expression more personal.

There are almost unlimited opportunities for sketching faces and figures from life, whether outdoors or inside your home, and they offer the widest possible choice of forms, characters and poses. People are found just about everywhere, but, in order to exploit these opportunities fully, it is desirable to find a comfortable vantage point from which you can easily observe the people around you without being disturbed. Ideal places could be, for example, restaurants, parks, beaches, public transport systems or museums. These are places where people slow down their pace of life or relax a little. Models and poses keep on changing, but there is still enough time to portray them after a quick and profitable few seconds of observation. If the person you are drawing changes their position, do not worry; you can start another sketch from scratch in the expectation that they will – probably – reassume their original pose, or a similar one, after a while.

Portraying a figure in movement is a truly difficult task. It is, however, one that should not be overlooked as it instils the habit of capturing the flow of the limbs, the direction of movement and the bodily attitudes that initiate and aid them. A great deal of attention is required for observing people and learning how to use your memory to reconstruct the basic sequences of movements. Try to anticipate the next phase of a given movement – many human actions (walking, running and dancing, for example) consist of repeated cycles and this makes it possible to reassemble their dynamic sequence from memory, concentrating your attention every now and then on an individual phase. In this respect, photography may sometimes prove useful, even indispensible at times, but photographs should of course be treated solely as a source of valuable information and not just as images to be reproduced uncritically. It is also worthwhile concentrating on some of the practical aspects of the depiction process: to draw the movements you see without worrying too much about what your drawing looks like or how scientifically accurate it is; to simplify the forms and to seek out the lines of direction that best express the feeling and direction of motion; to work with full and concise, summary pencil strokes; to concentrate on the flow-lines and on the body's main axes; to try to suggest the figure's forms rather than define them and to avoid reproducing 'known' details (details that you know are there but that are impossible to perceive at a glance) at the expense of the overall form. Sketching entails the need to work in an unfinished, but not sloppy, way.

As sketching is, by definition, performed quickly, succinctly and in 'real time', it is difficult to break down the sketching process into distinct successive stages of execution. Nonetheless, you have to start somewhere when you make your marks on the paper:

a If you are dealing, for example, with the whole figure (whether clothed or naked), you could begin with a quick, light line to mark out the space that the figure will occupy on the page of your sketchpad (maximum height, maximum width, and so on). This could be followed by hinting at the main divisions of the body (head, torso, limbs) and their proportional relationships to each other. You could finish by defining the most important profiles, the areas of shade and details that cannot be omitted.

b It is possible to follow a similar sequence when drawing just the head, moving from the general elements to the specifics, or, once you have worked out the overall space it will take up on the page, you could then move on to defining the dimensions and the form of an important detail (an eye, the nose, etc.). Move from this to constructing the entire head and the relationships of each part to another, moving from specifics to the general elements.

The choice of which of these two approaches to adopt will depend on the artist's attitude and preferences, but also on the position in which they find the subject they intend to sketch.

If you feel too intimidated by the idea of sketching people from life, you may be able to prepare yourself psychologically and improve your confidence by drawing statues and sculptures in museums or monuments in public places (see pages 382–400). Nevertheless, once you have acquired experience through drawing in museums, try to move straight on to sketching figures from life.

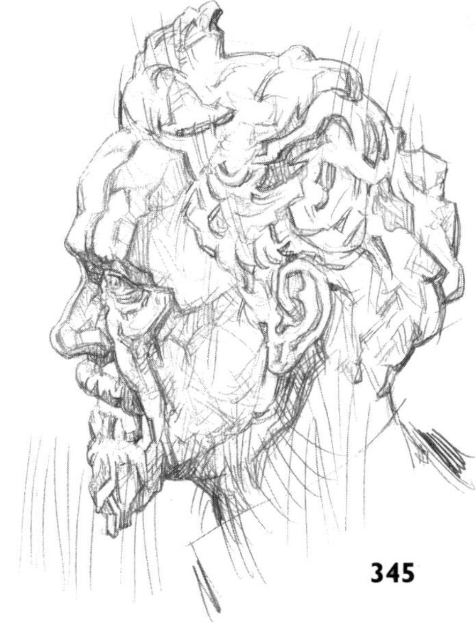

A REPERTOIRE OF FACES

When making life drawings of the heads or faces of people you do not know – even when sketching them quickly – it is important to remember that we must respect the privacy of people who have not given their consent to be used as models. Of course, this is not a full portrait that you are drawing, just a study of structure or of expression. Nonetheless, if the drawing is well executed, a resemblance will be captured and this may be against the wishes of the person concerned, should it so happen that the sketch is later shown in public. Make your intentions known to the person concerned and ask for their consent, in the light of possible subsequent developments. Having done so, you can work with greater peace of mind. In most cases, however, you will be busy contending with the extremely mobile nature of people's expressions and the way that heads can move so quickly; learning to work, in other words, in the full knowledge that the sketch you are making may have to be interrupted at any moment and at any stage of development.

For these reasons, try to choose situations in which you can reasonably expect at least a few moments of relative stillness (in restaurants, waiting rooms, parks, etc.), and learn to get the essential features down on paper quickly, keeping them constantly updated in your mind so that you are able to complete the sketch even after the model has walked away. If you have the time, and the opportunity presents itself, draw the head from different viewpoints and, if possible, analyze some of its details. I sketched the man shown opposite, top, during a visit to an art exhibition while he was engrossed in studying a sculpture. The men in uniform were drawn at an historic commemoration. Such occasions make excellent opportunities to find people dressed up in picturesque, antique military uniforms. The participants often have a real air about them of being 'perfectly posed', as if they are just waiting for sketchers and photographers to come along.

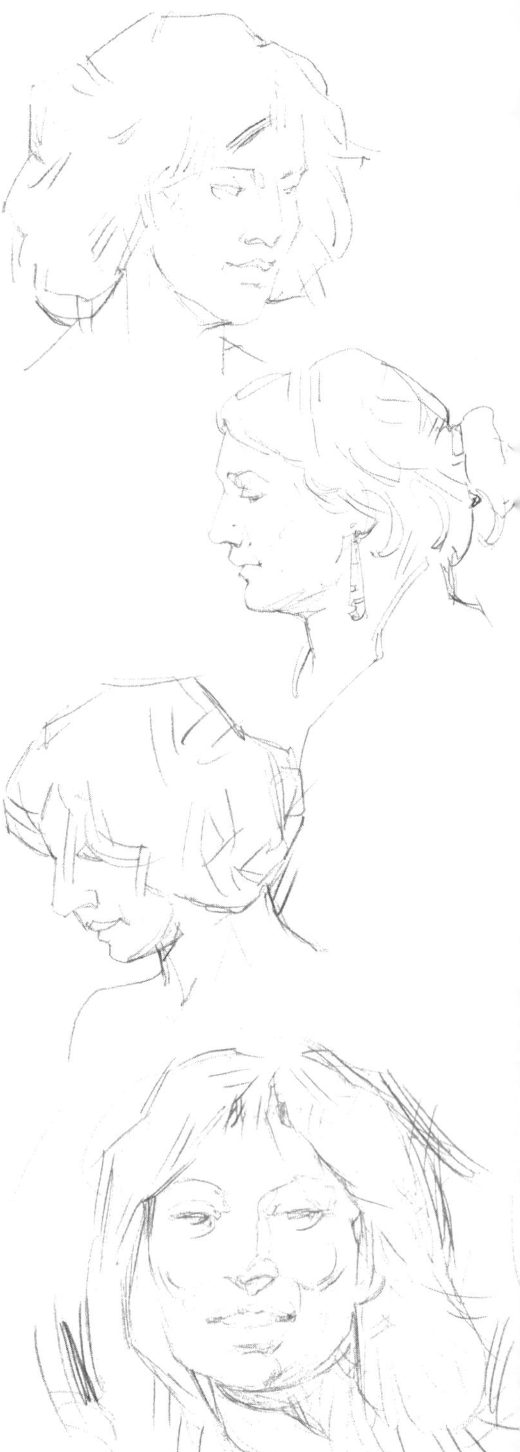

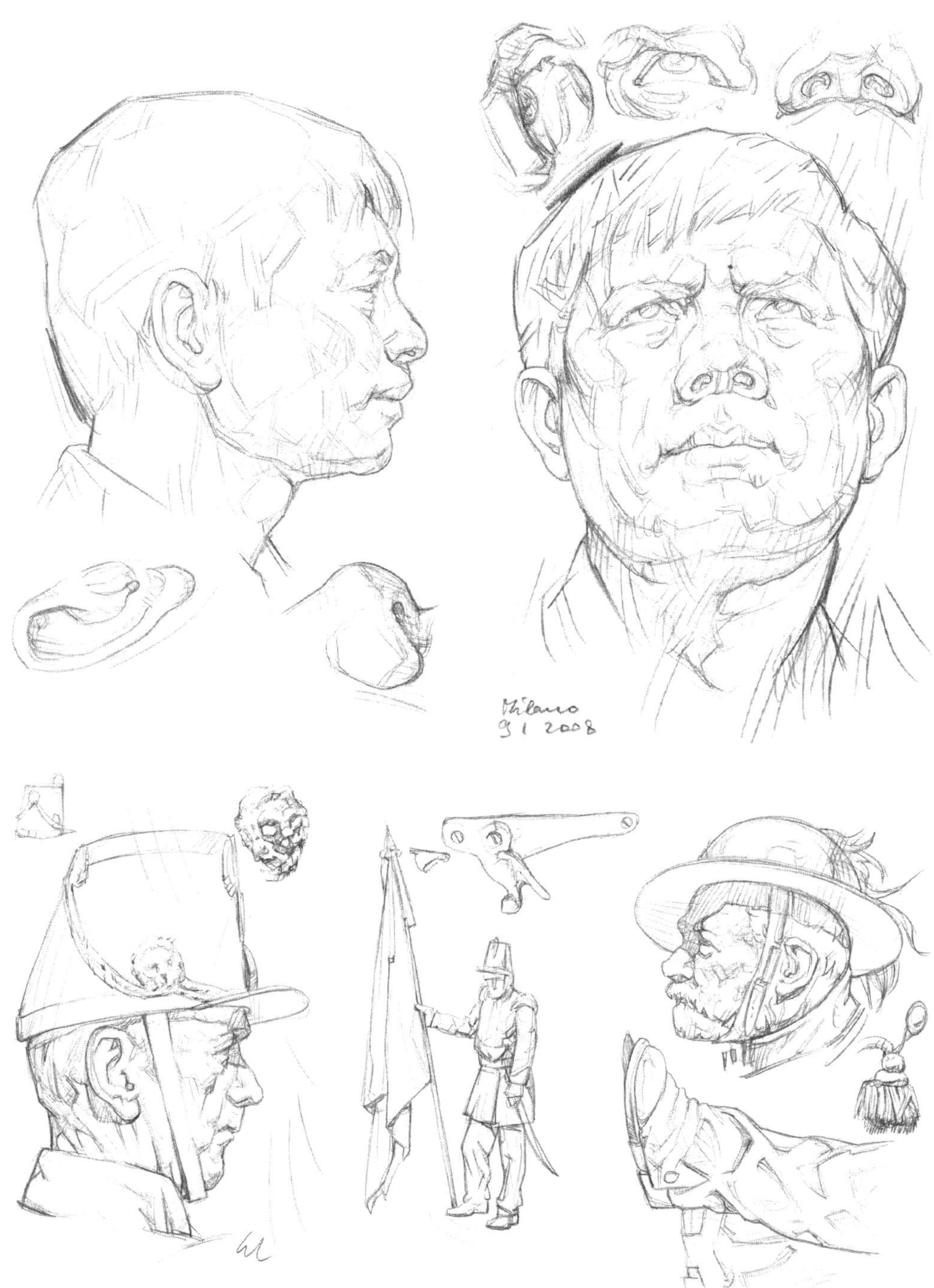
Milano
9 1 2008

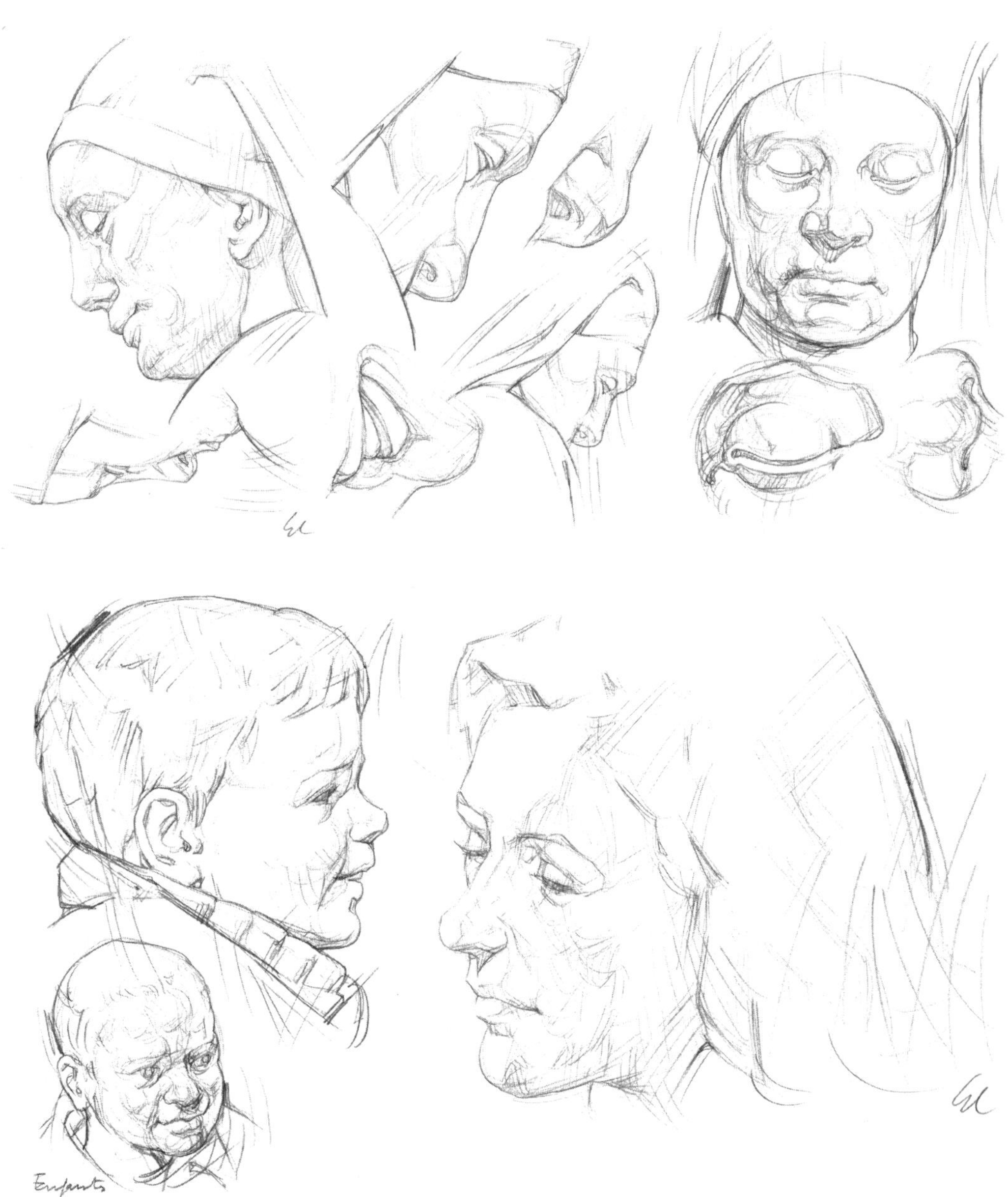

The nurse (top left) was so focused on her task of applying a dressing that she appeared almost immobilized and statue-like. This provided me with a rare opportunity to make an unhurried study of her face and of some of its more interesting details. Children, by contrast, are terrifically full of life and can only be sketched in a summary and impressionistic way, working largely from memory. Photographs may seem to offer a solution to this problem, but using them results in drawings in which immediacy is subdued when compared with those done 'in the field' (see page 358).

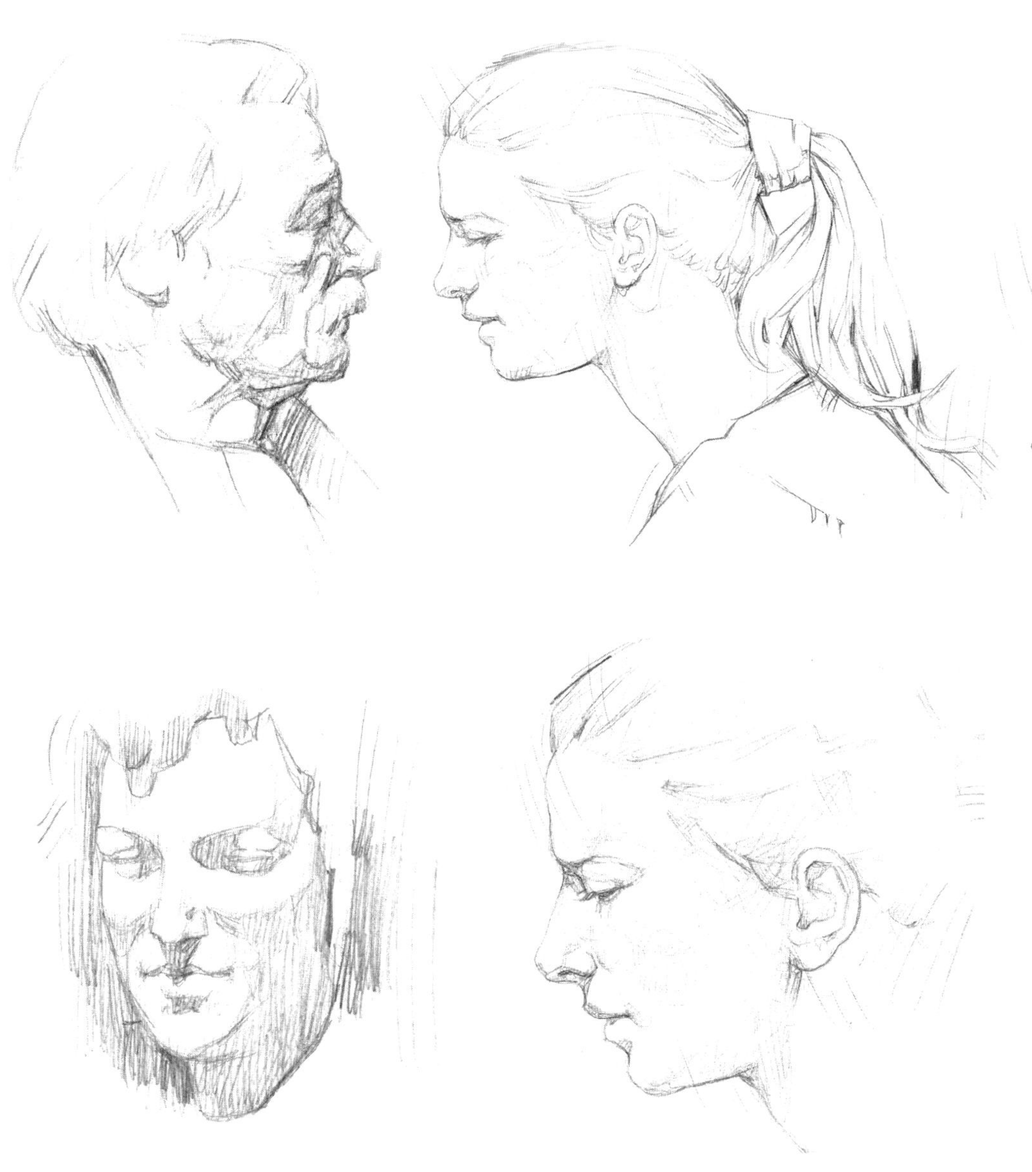

The technical process of sketching becomes almost automatic and is dictated by the amount of time available – or, to be exact, the amount of time allowed to you by your model. The first marks on the paper are basically light, exploratory lines, mapping out the dimensions and composition. A further opportunity for investigation will allow you to briefly introduce tonal modulation.

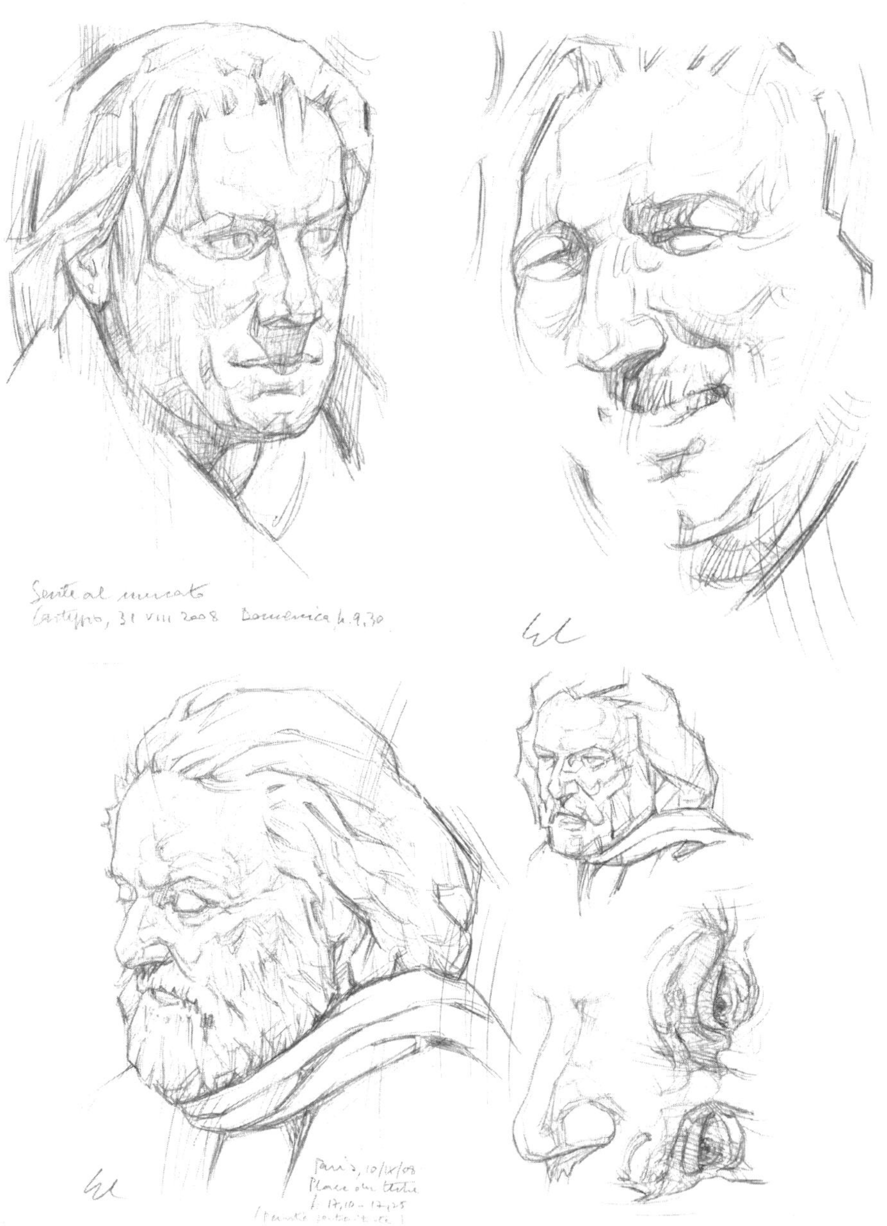

The faces you see reproduced on this and the following pages (to page 357) were drawn during recent stays in Paris. The *Place du Tertre*, in Montmartre, is an ideal spot for sketching figures, but it is an especially good source of faces as it is constantly visited by a great number of people who wander through the alleyways, stopping in front of the street artists who set up their easels in the square each day. These artists themselves make ideal subjects, but a lot of the tourists also sit for on-the-spot portraits, which enabled me to make my own sketches of them, positioning myself beside or behind the shoulder of the actual portraitist.

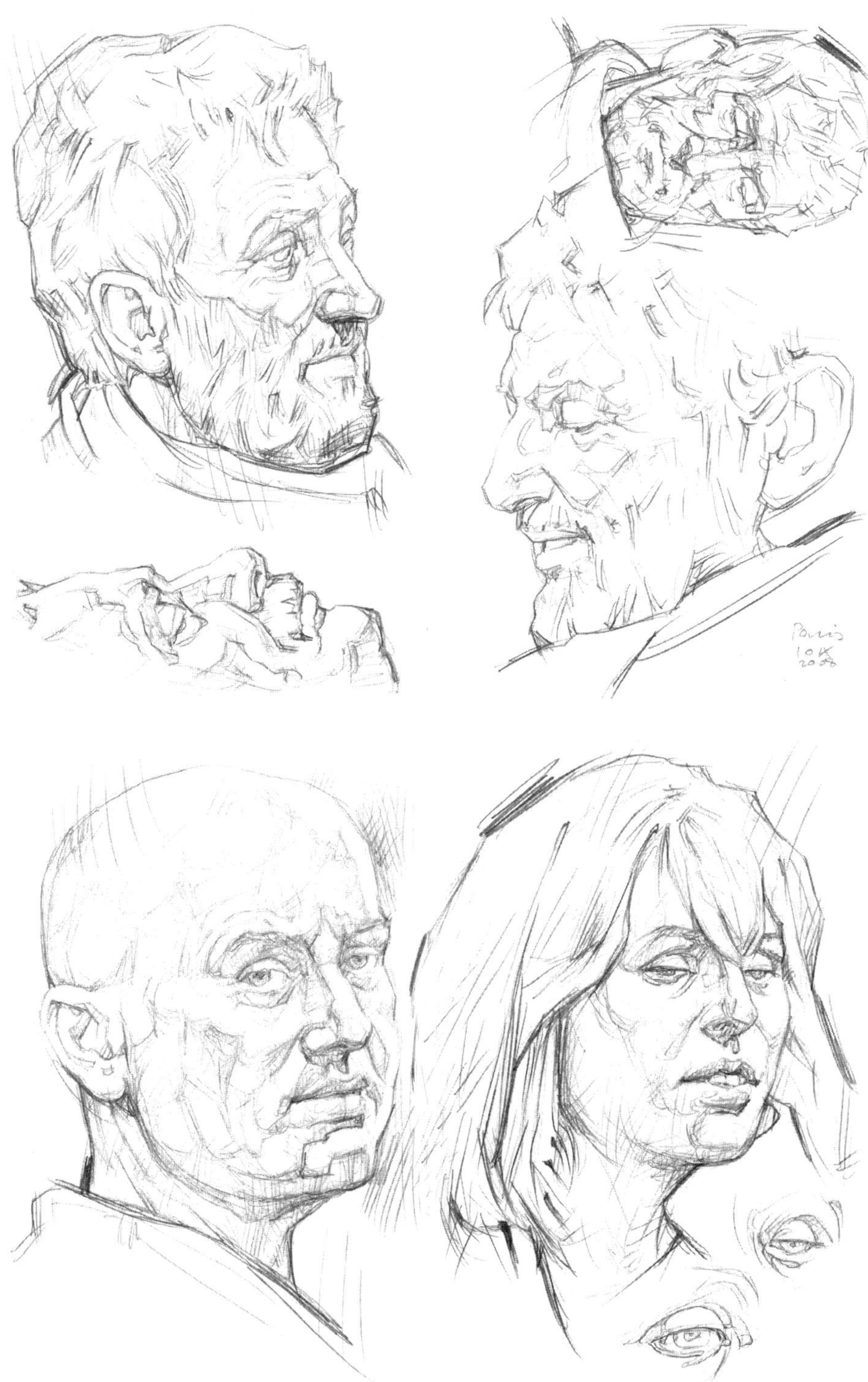

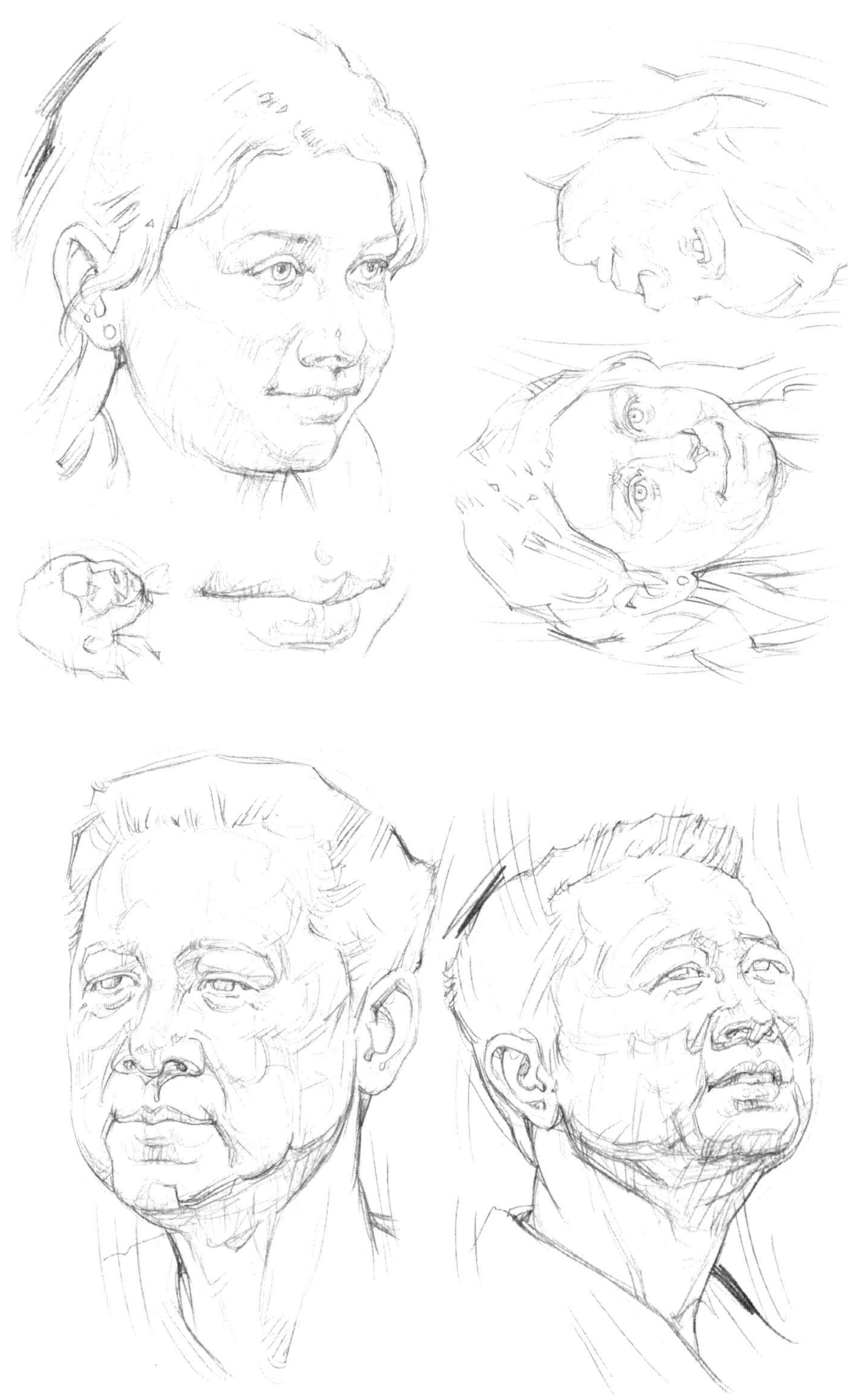

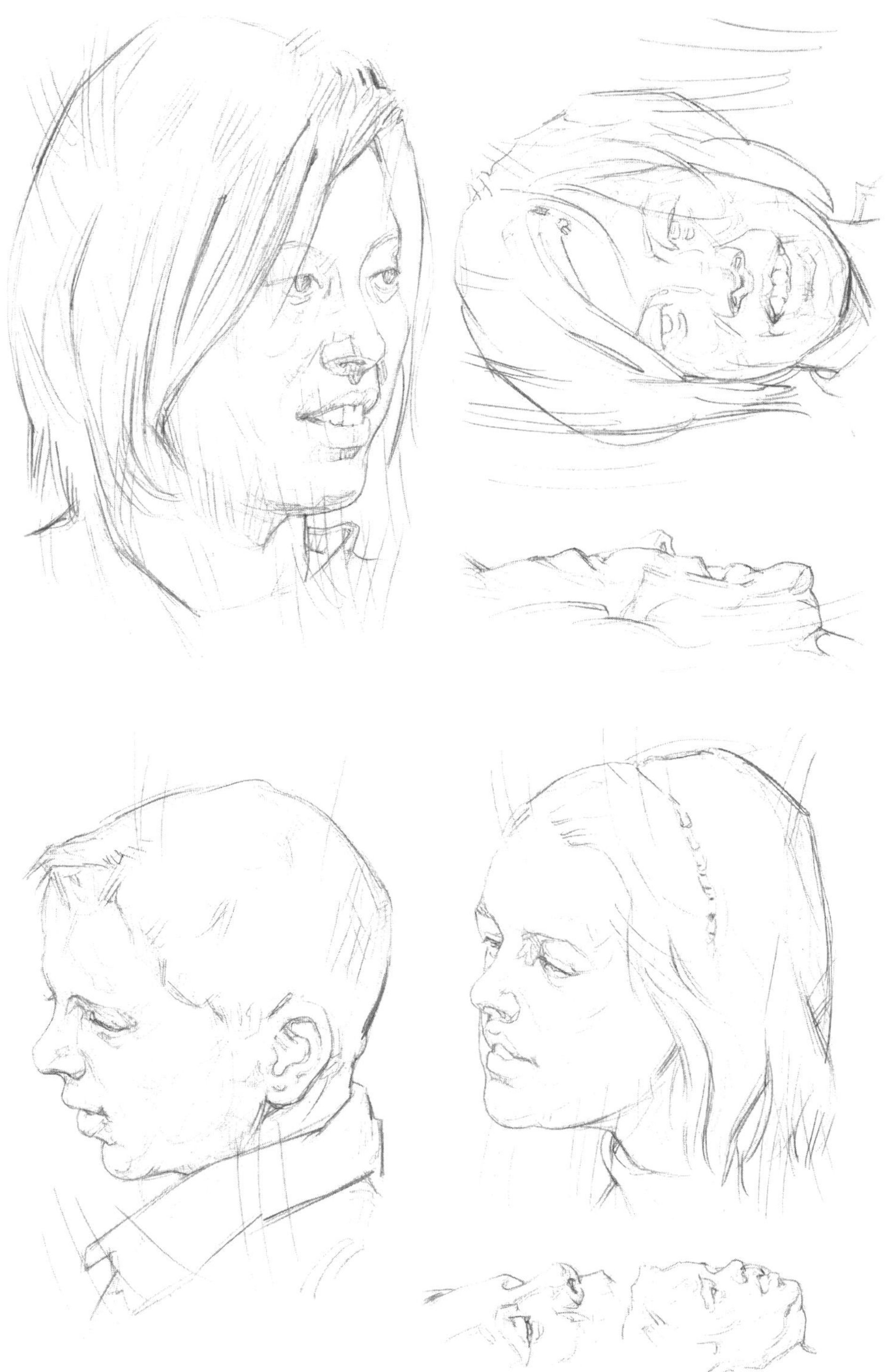

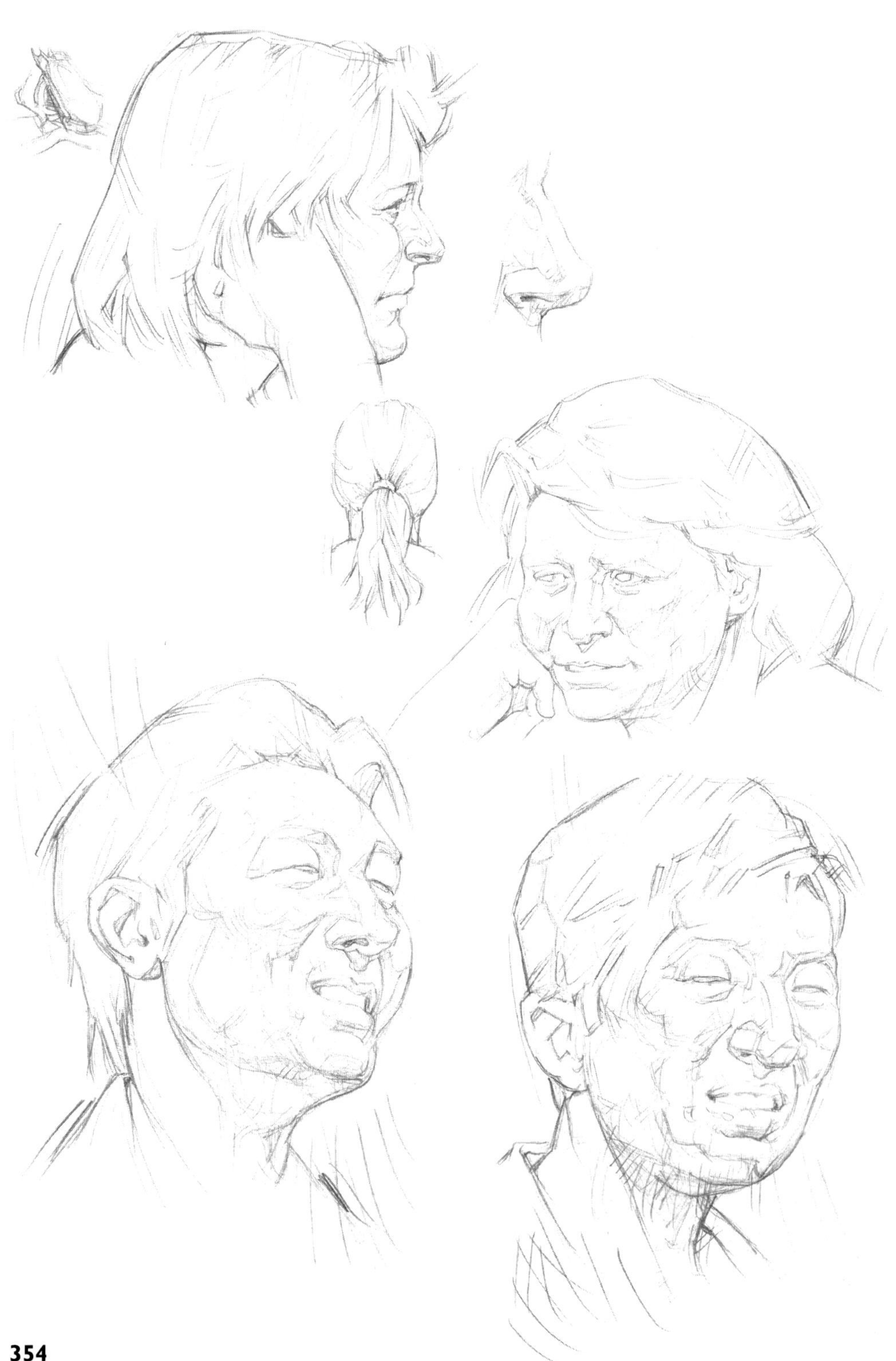

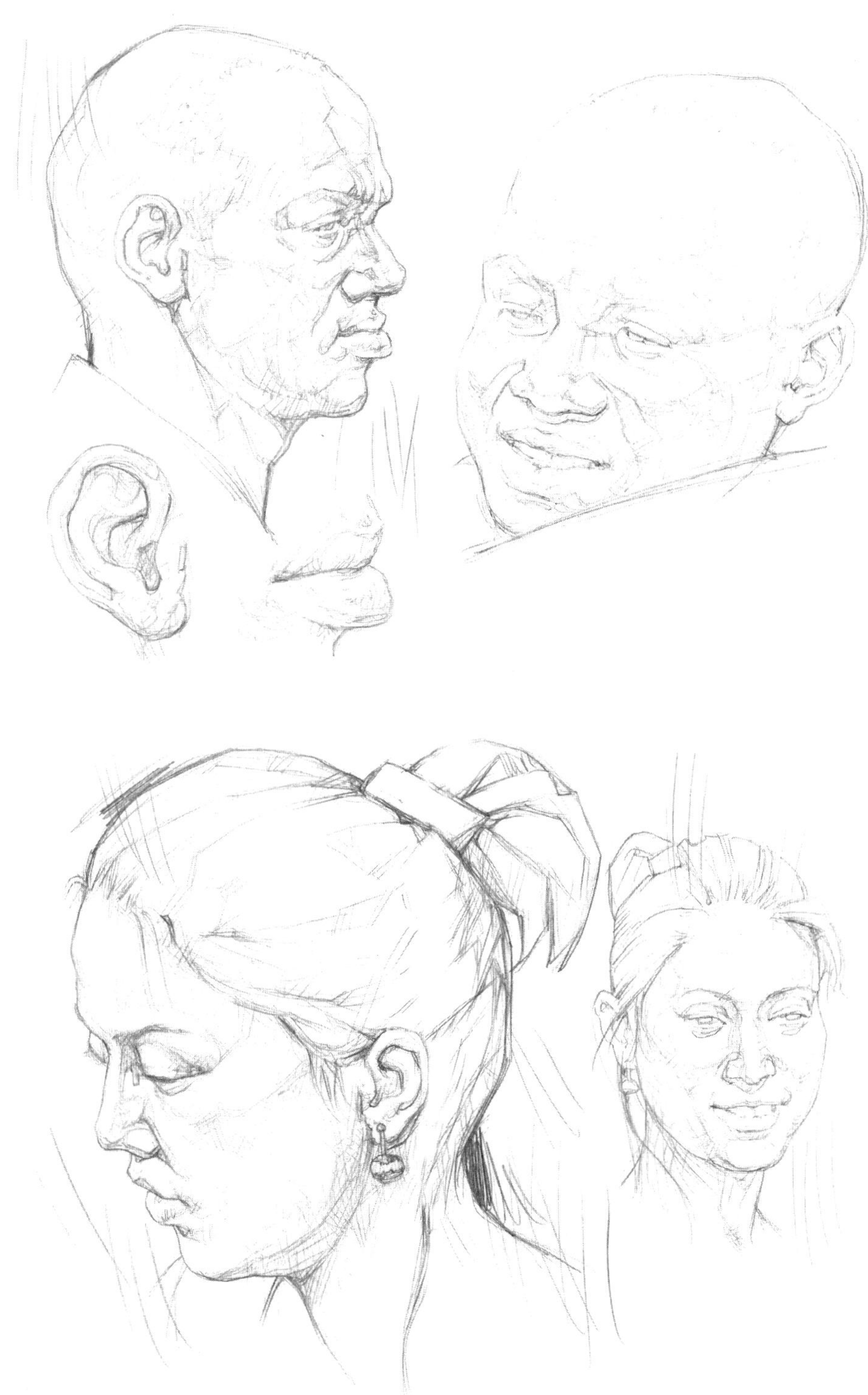

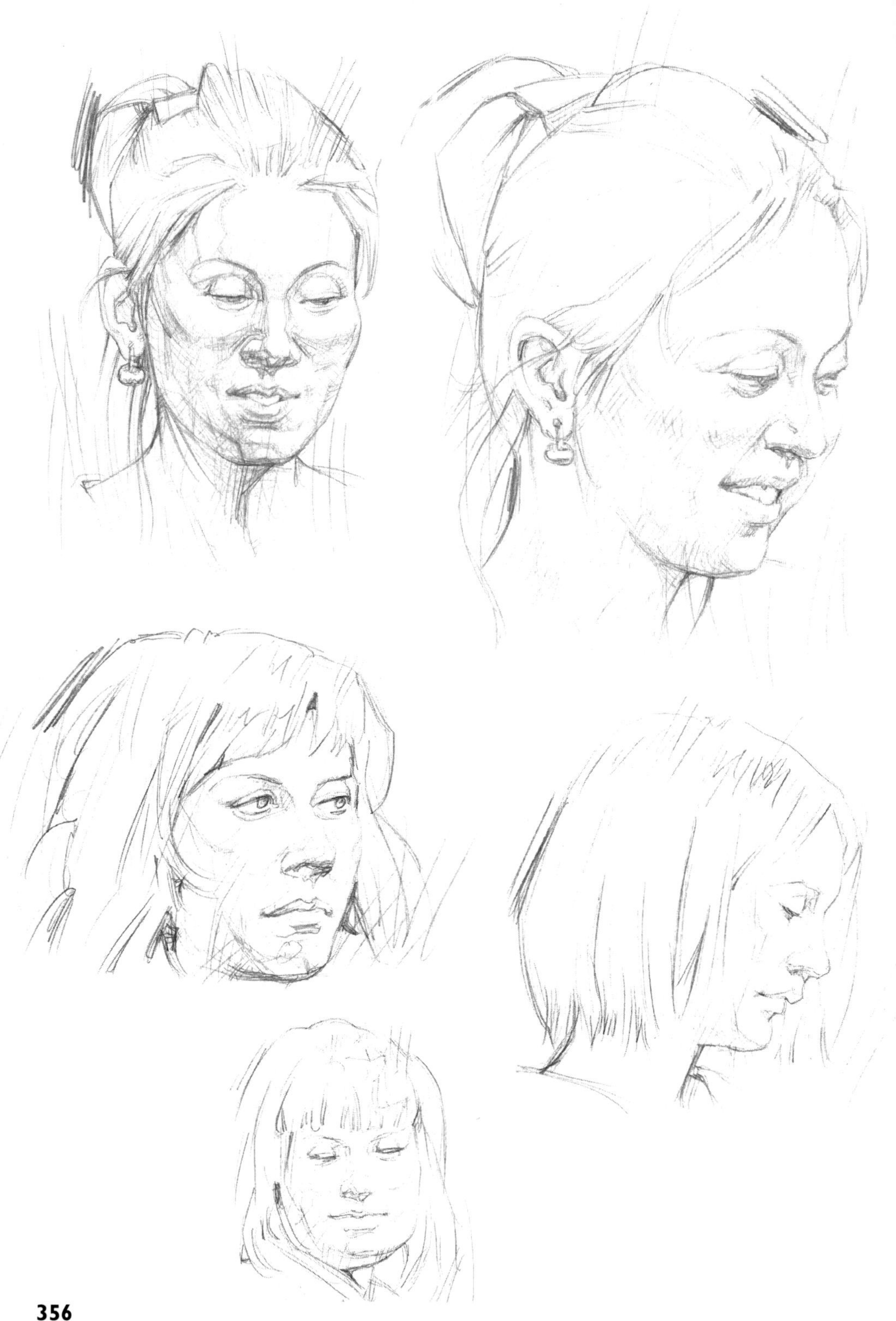

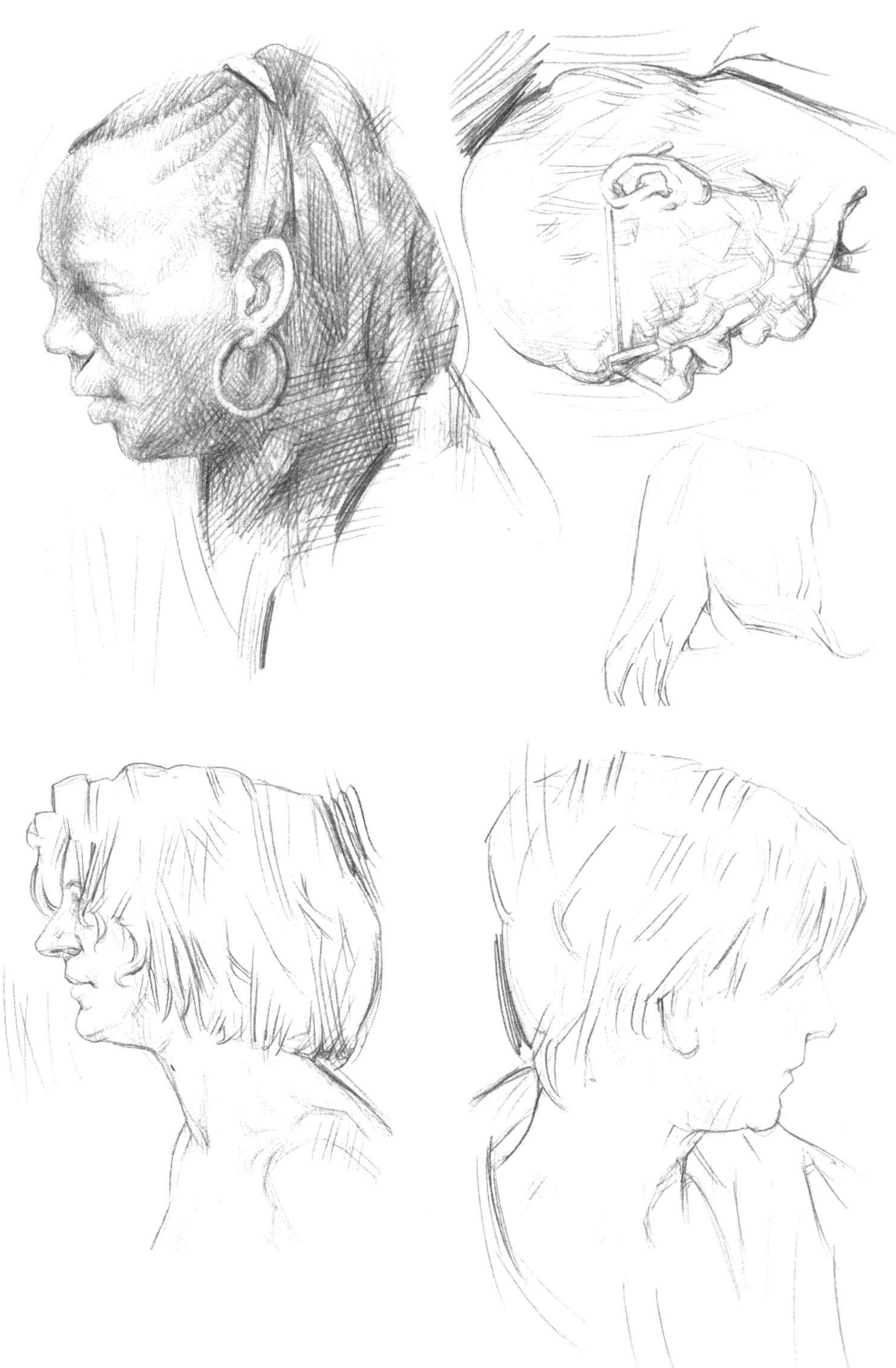

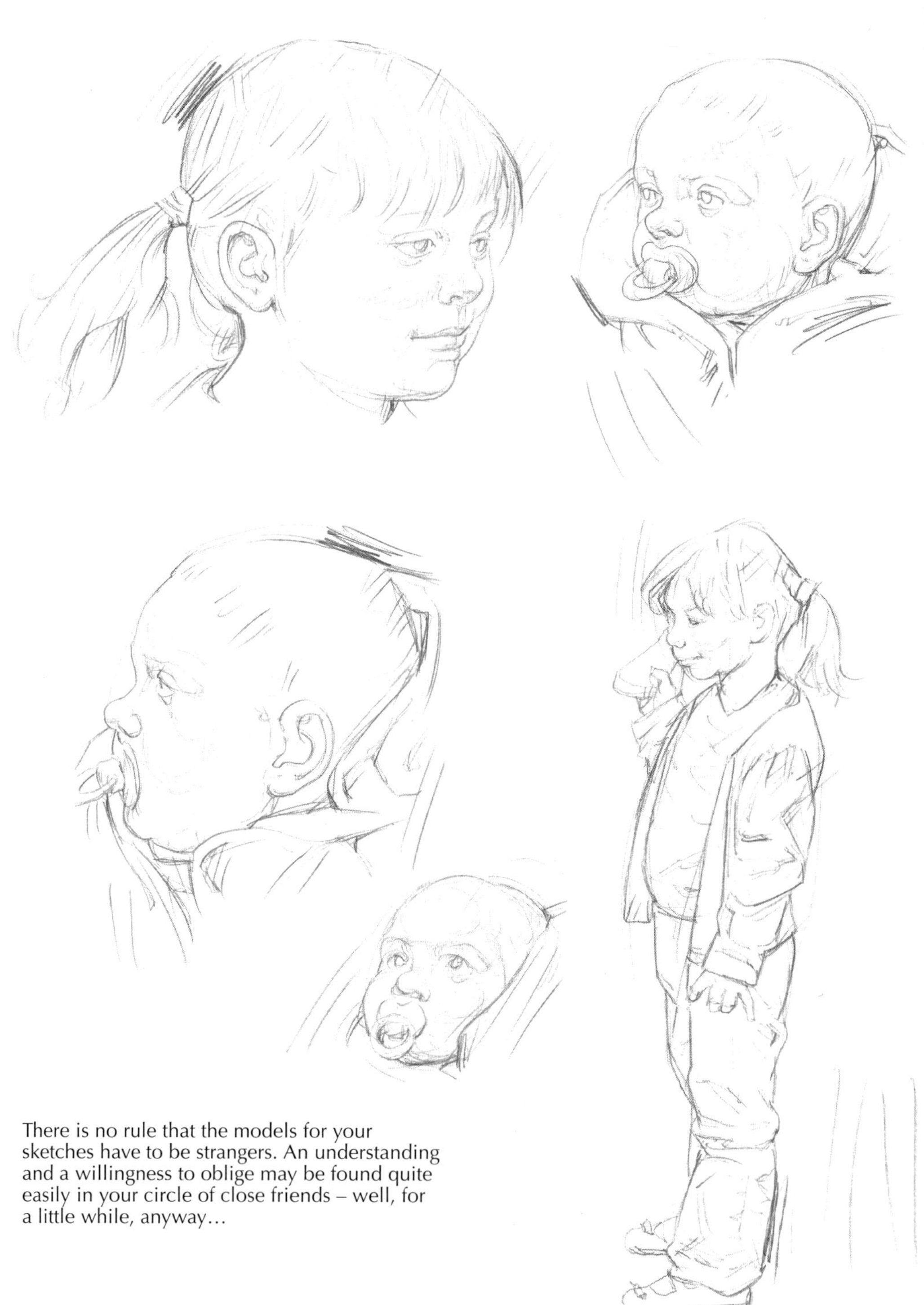

There is no rule that the models for your sketches have to be strangers. An understanding and a willingness to oblige may be found quite easily in your circle of close friends – well, for a little while, anyway…

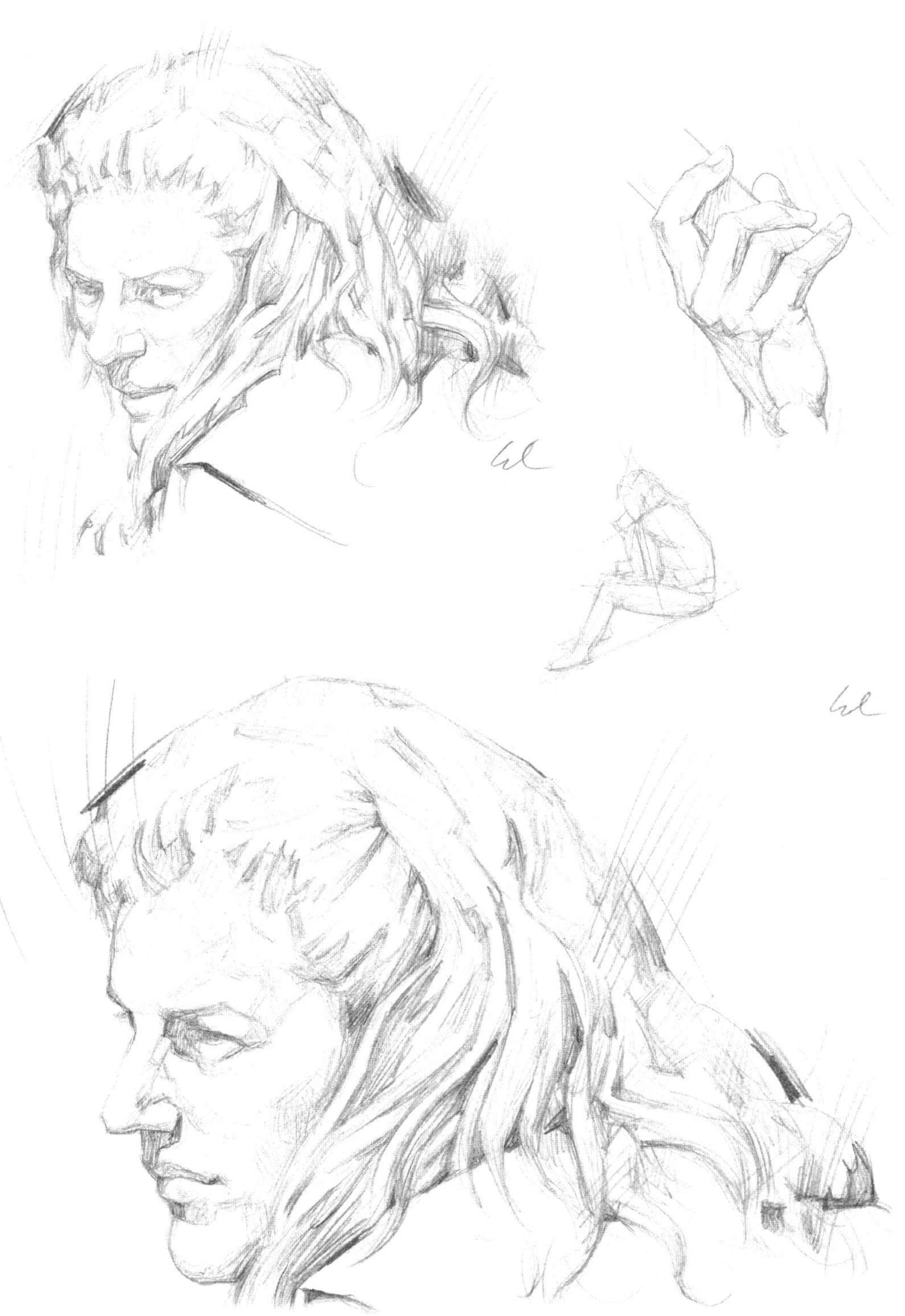

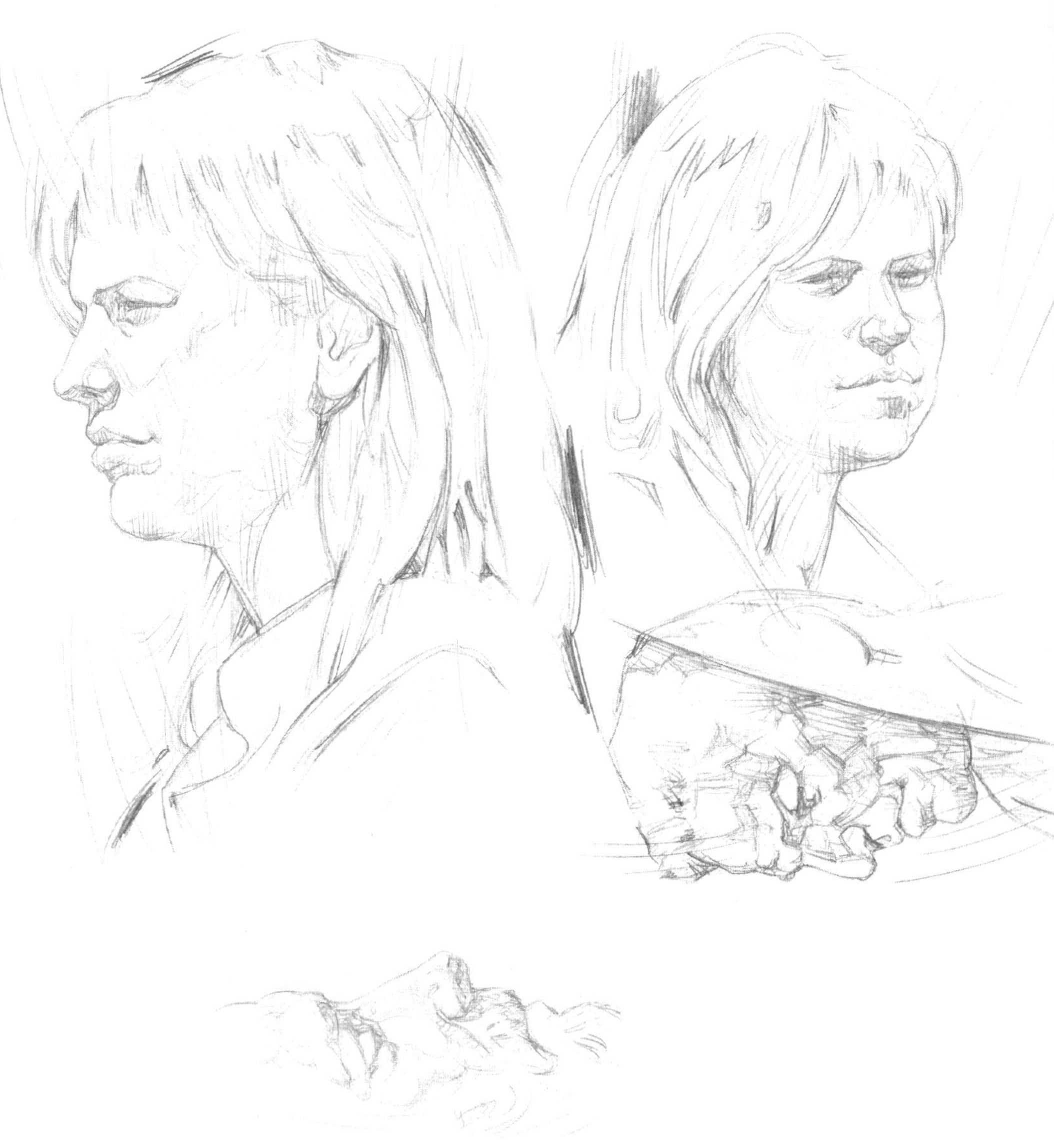

These subjects were sketched in Milan's *Giardini Pubblici* (a large park in the centre of Milan). The spring sun encourages people to laze for a while in such places. They are also full of children running about and playing, but it is much easier (using a little stealth) to draw the people charged with looking after the children. They move about far less and their attentive gazes give rise to interesting expressions and stances.

Unfortunately, even in such peaceful environments, opportunities to develop drawings further are rare, and you have to content yourself with sketches made up of just a few lines or areas of shading. Frequently practising sketching will quickly give you confidence in picking out just the essential elements.

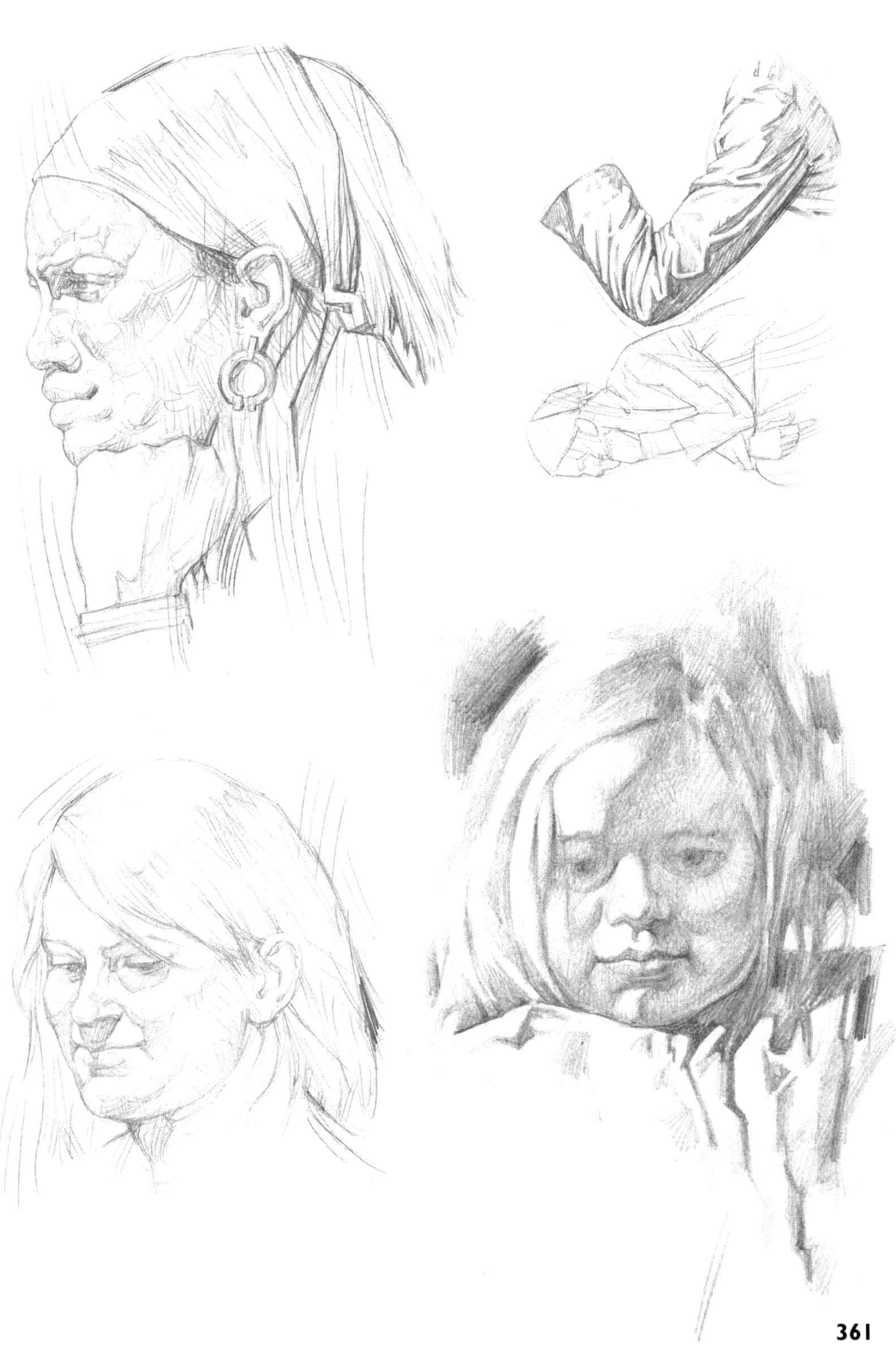

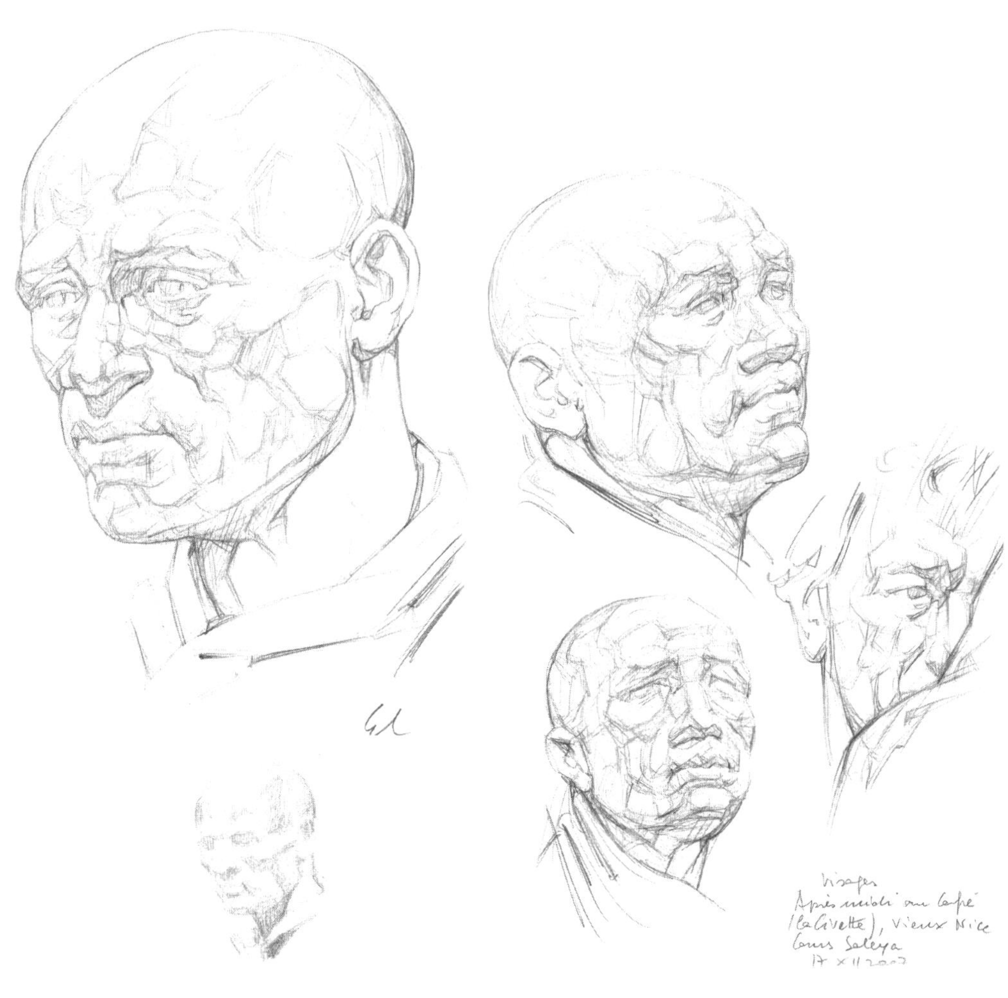

These drawings show how the outcome of your sketch is determined by the amount of time your unwitting model grants you. On this page you can see a sketch of a head that I was able to bring to a sufficient level of elaboration: I managed, at least, to outline and investigate the modelled surface of the skeletal structure, the play of the musculature and also to indicate the areas of shade belonging to each muscle. At this point, the 'model' was seated at a café table and concentrating on reading a newspaper. Opposite, the same person (top) started assuming ever more fleeting positions until I could do little more than jot down structure-line layouts of the overall form of his head.

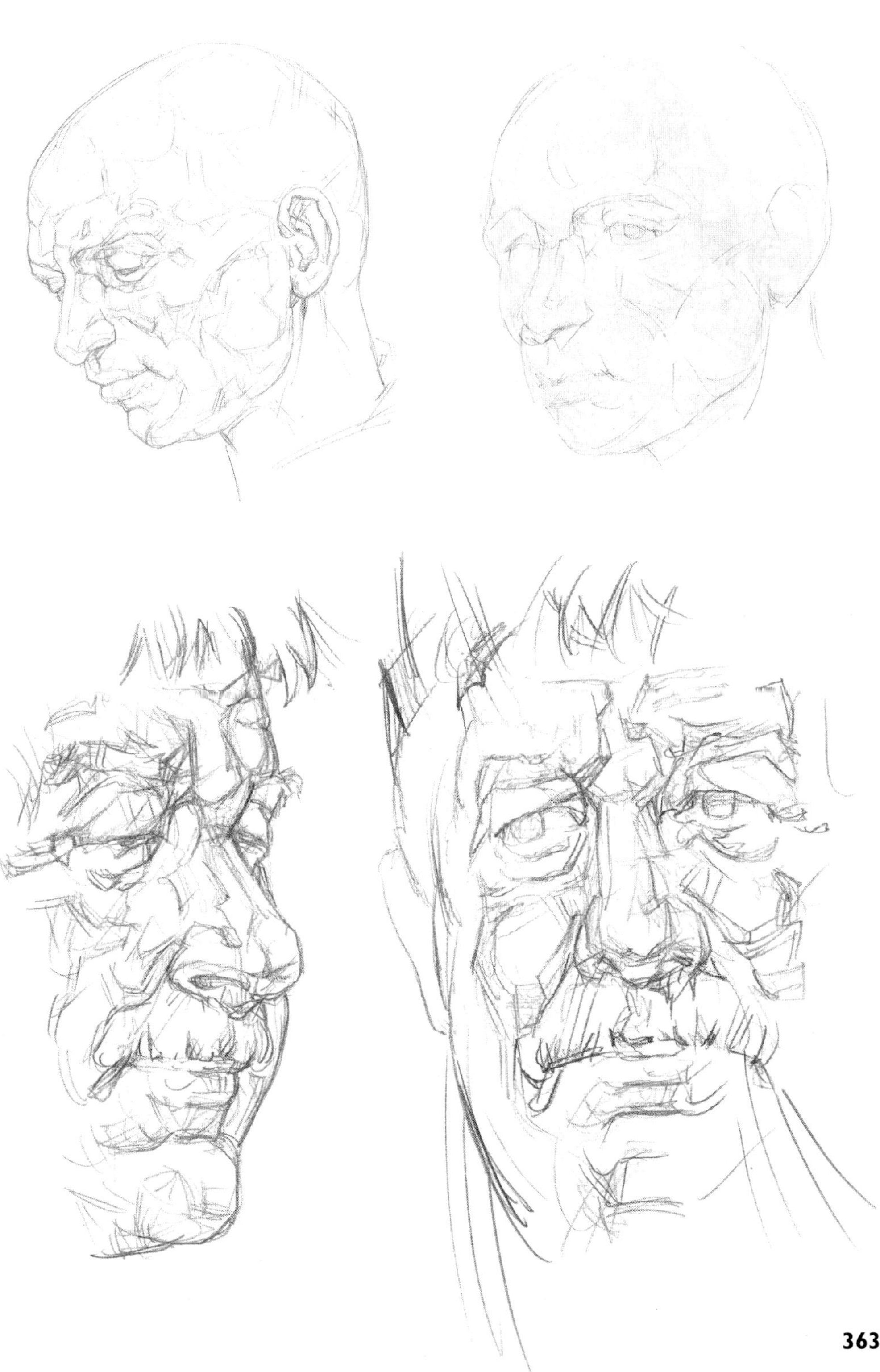

A REPERTOIRE OF FIGURES

Sketching figures is more difficult than sketching faces and yet, at the same time, it is noticeably simpler. The difficulty is due to the structural complexity of the figure as a whole (added to which, figures are almost invariably covered by clothing) and to the larger scope of bodily movements. It is simpler because of the way posture can be read immediately and because of the way that points of interest are scattered about (we are interested not just in the face, but in the torso, the limbs, the folds in the clothing, etc.), which means we do not need to analyze individual details quite so closely. Many of the more appealing body positions that seem most suited for sketching are over too quickly for them to be noted down directly in real time, even with a few strokes. Rather than falling back on the use of photography, the problem can be solved by stepping up your concentration levels and frequency of practice, as well as by making greater use of your visual memory. Constant practice will, in a short while, bring proficiency in the skill of summarizing the gist of what you see and depicting it effectively. When a position is held by your 'model' for longer, you may have enough time to make a fairly elaborate sketch, which, with luck, may be repeated from different viewpoints.

The sketches reproduced in this section were made at different times and in different places (on the street, in museums, on the beach, etc.) and under the most varied conditions. These circumstances are, I hope, evident in the sketches themselves. I have arranged them in assorted groups without any commentary, simply so that they may convey some idea of the wide range of opportunities that exist for observation and the variety of results that can be achieved.

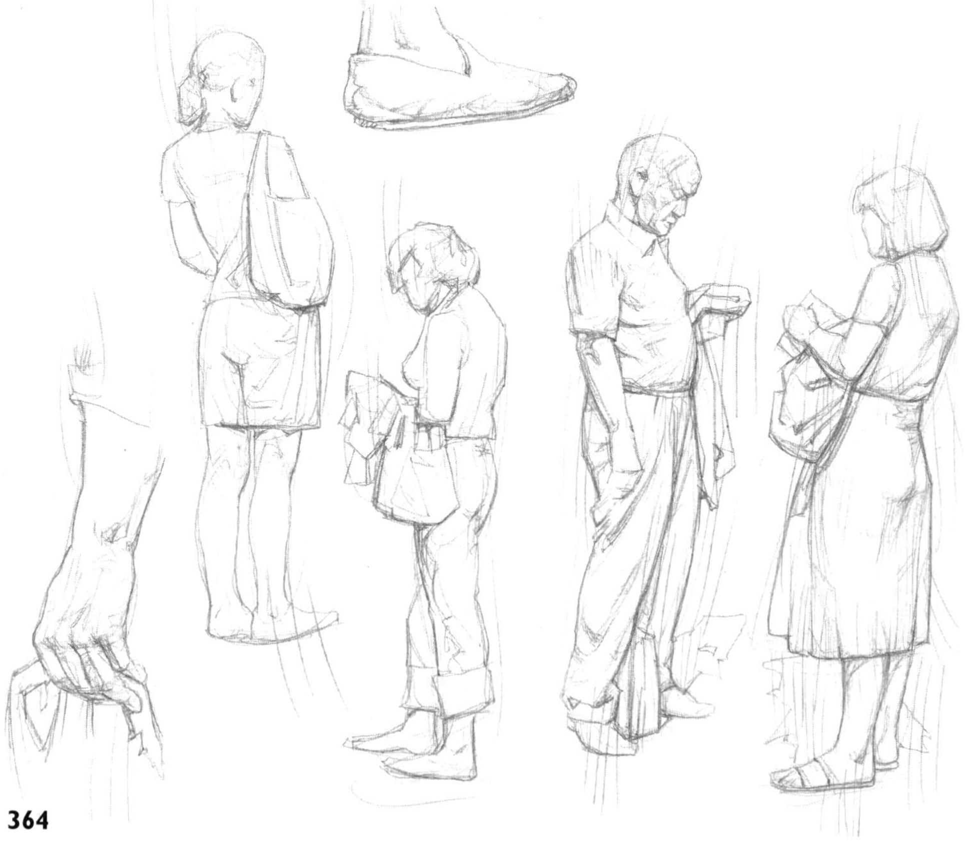

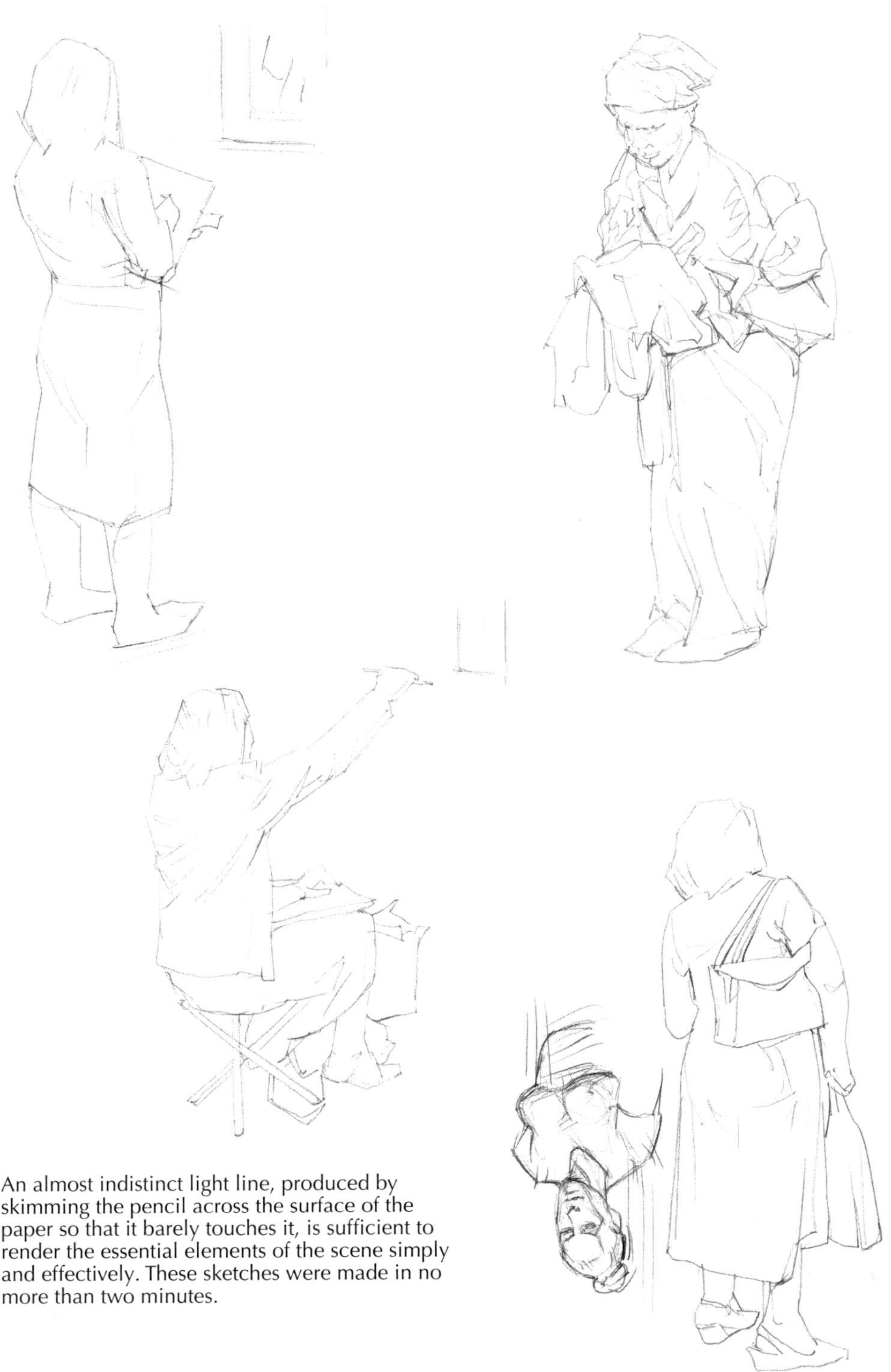

An almost indistinct light line, produced by skimming the pencil across the surface of the paper so that it barely touches it, is sufficient to render the essential elements of the scene simply and effectively. These sketches were made in no more than two minutes.

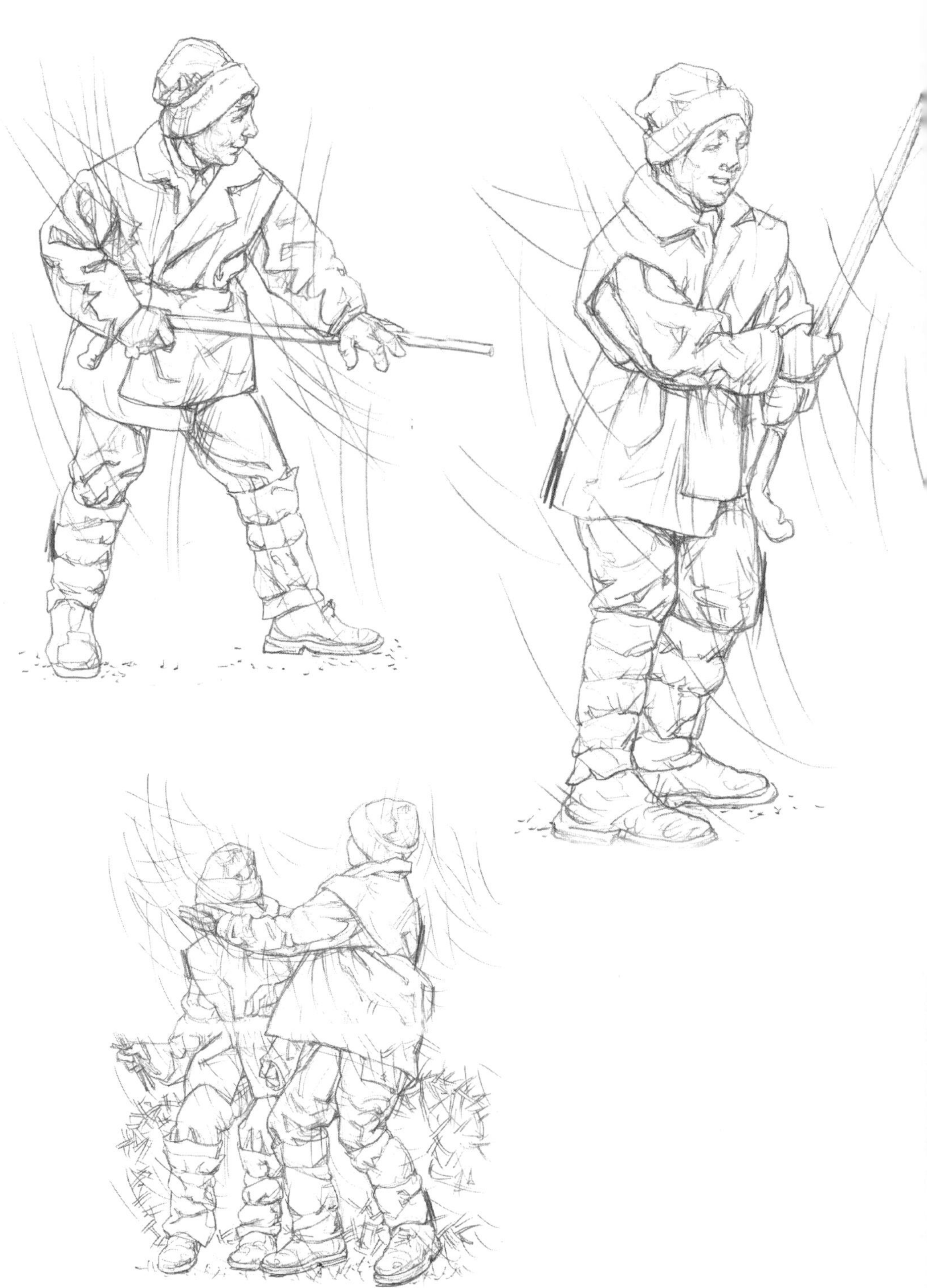

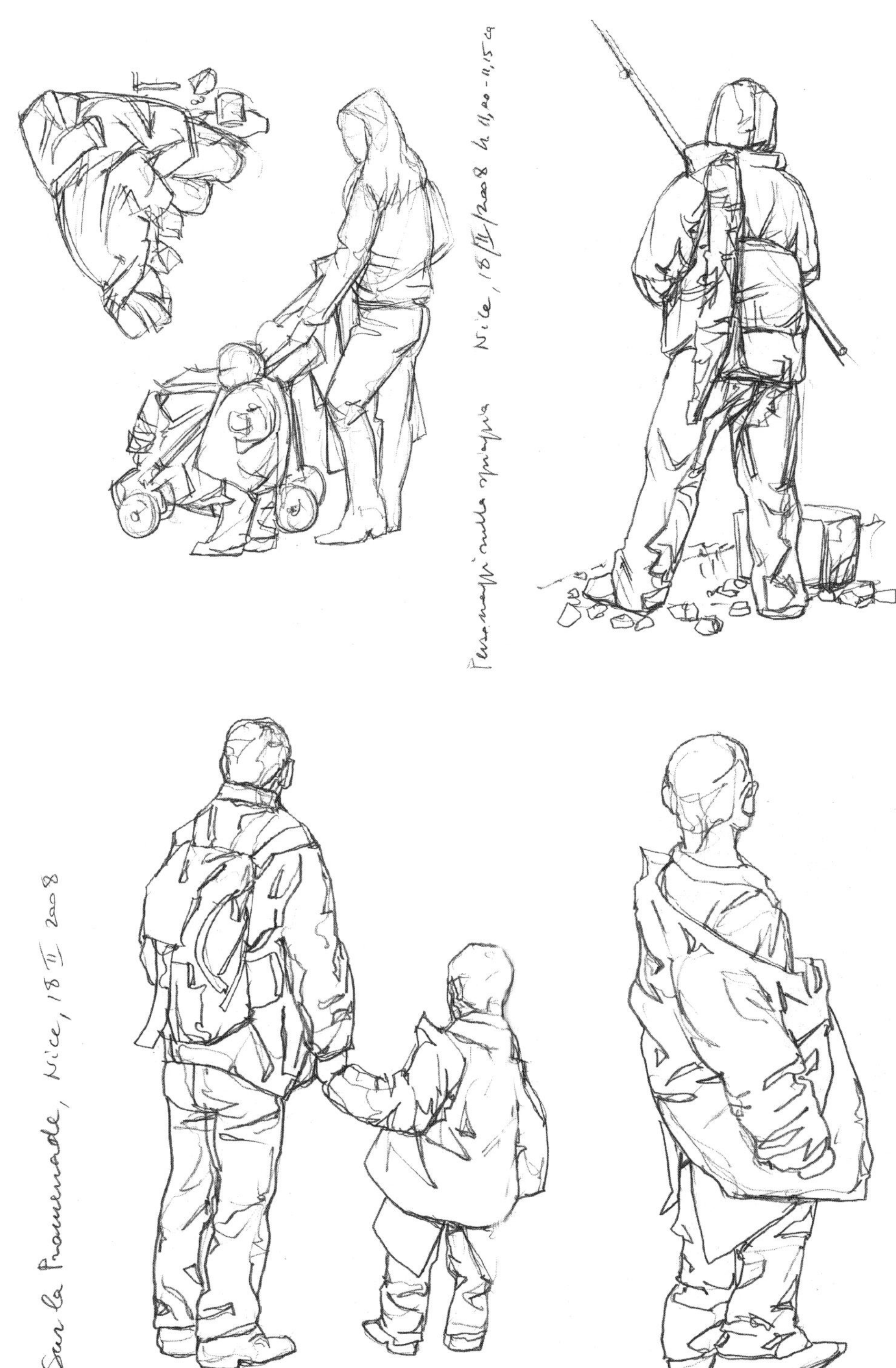
Personaggi sulla spiaggia Nice, 18/II/2008 h. 11,00-11,15 ca
Sur la Promenade, Nice, 18 II 2008

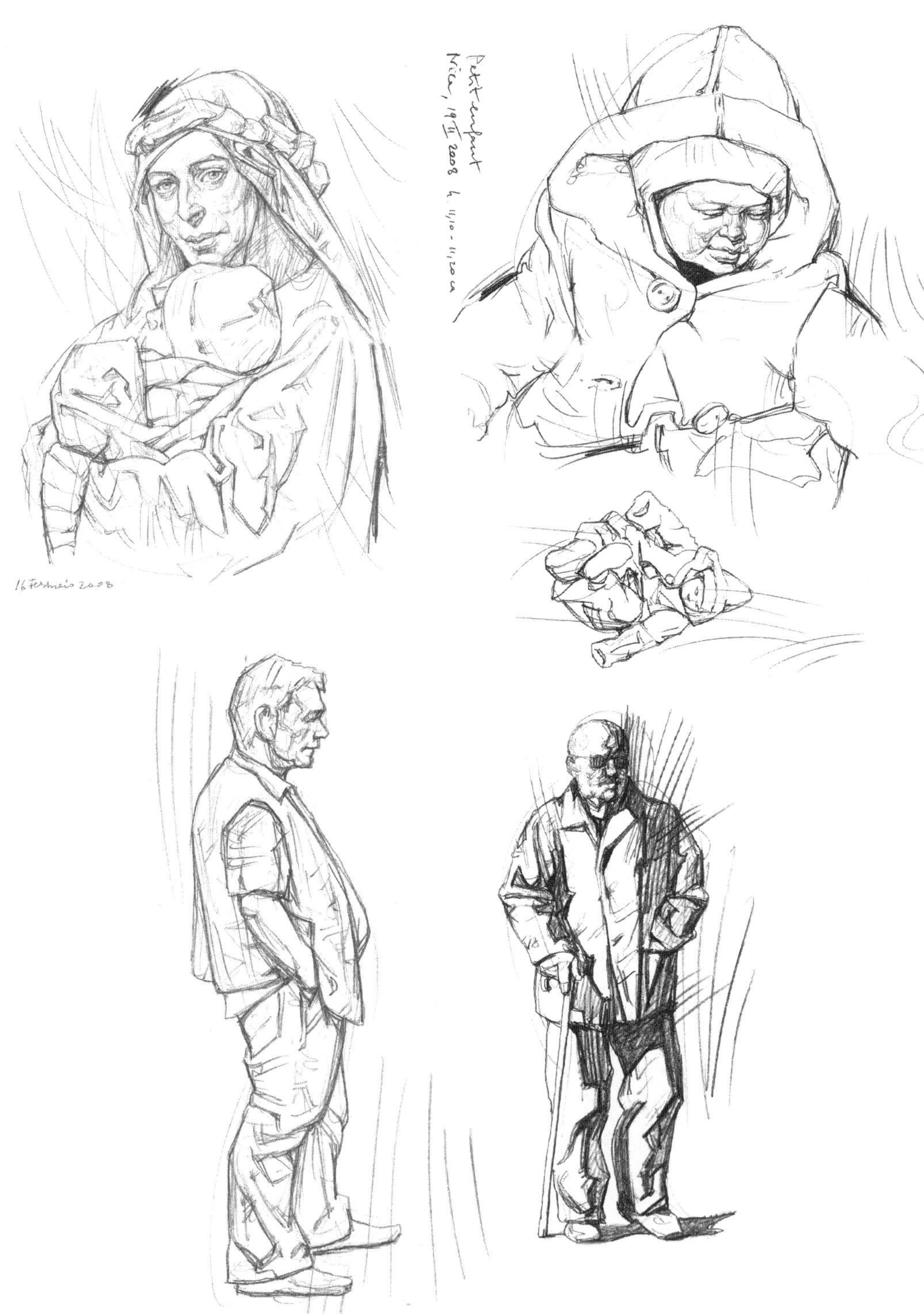
Petit enfant
Nica, 19 II 2008 h. 11,10 - 11,20 ca
16 Febbraio 2008

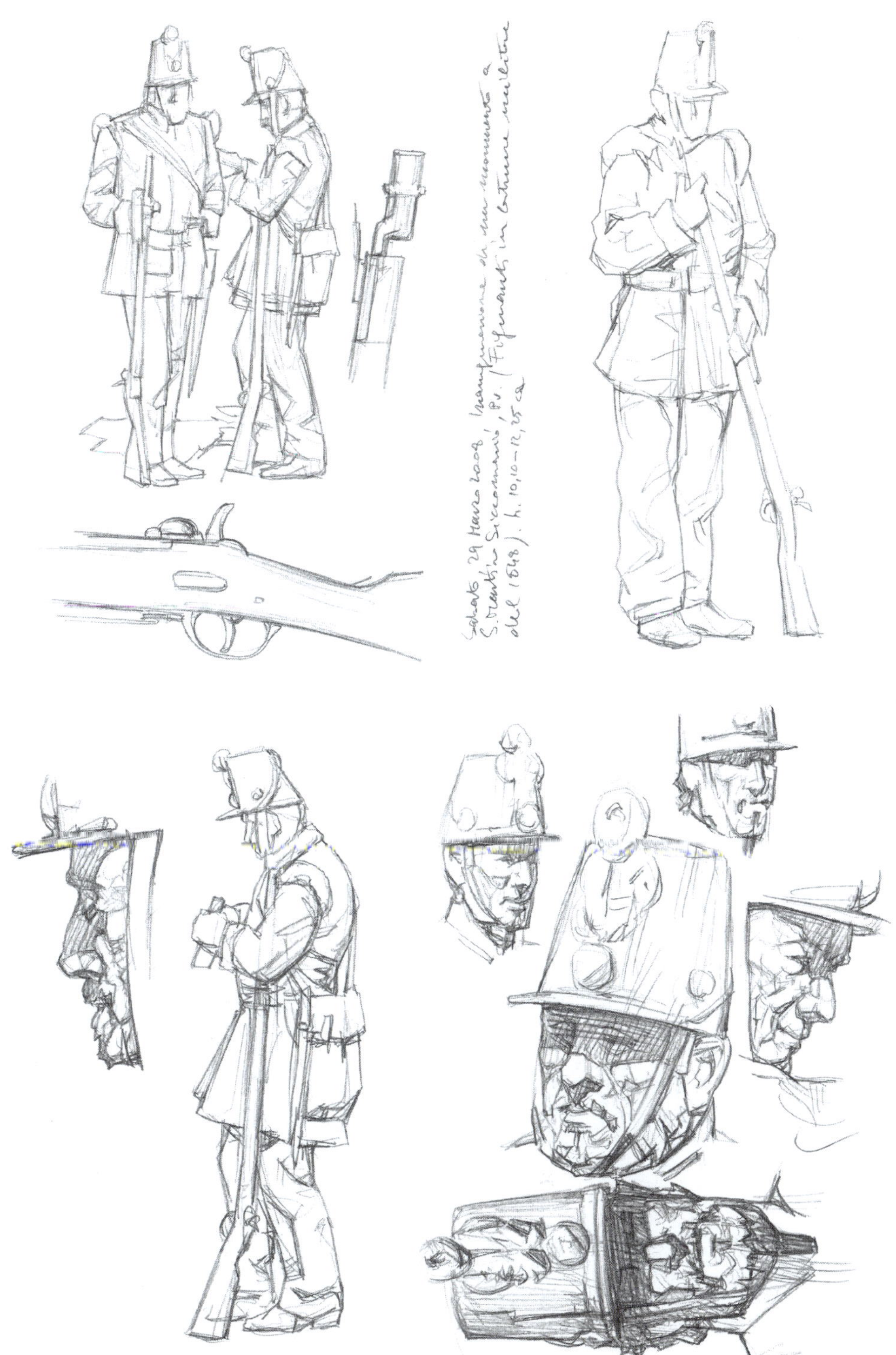
Sabato 29 Marzo 2008, Manifestazione di una rievocazione a
S. Martino Siccomario, Pv. (Figuranti in costume militare
del 1848). h. 10,10–12,25 ca

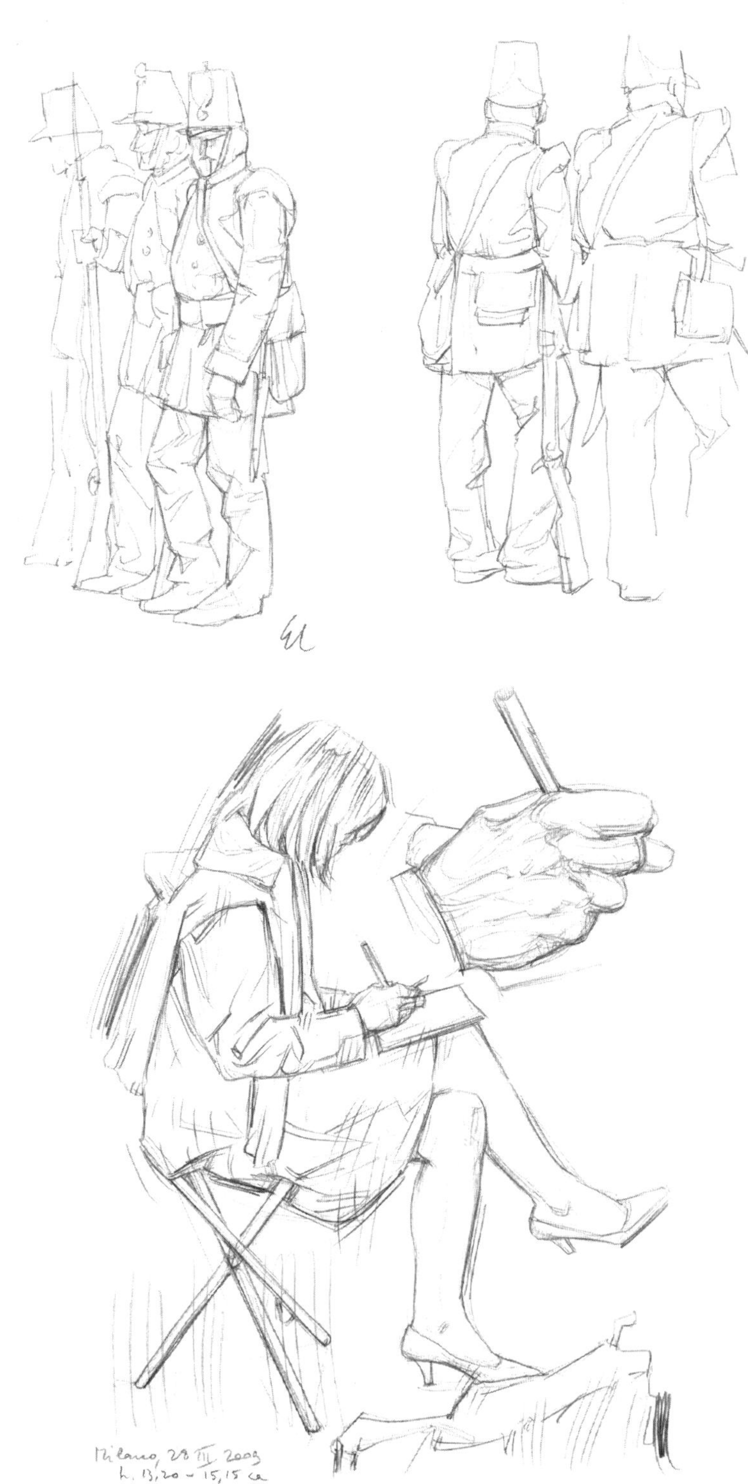

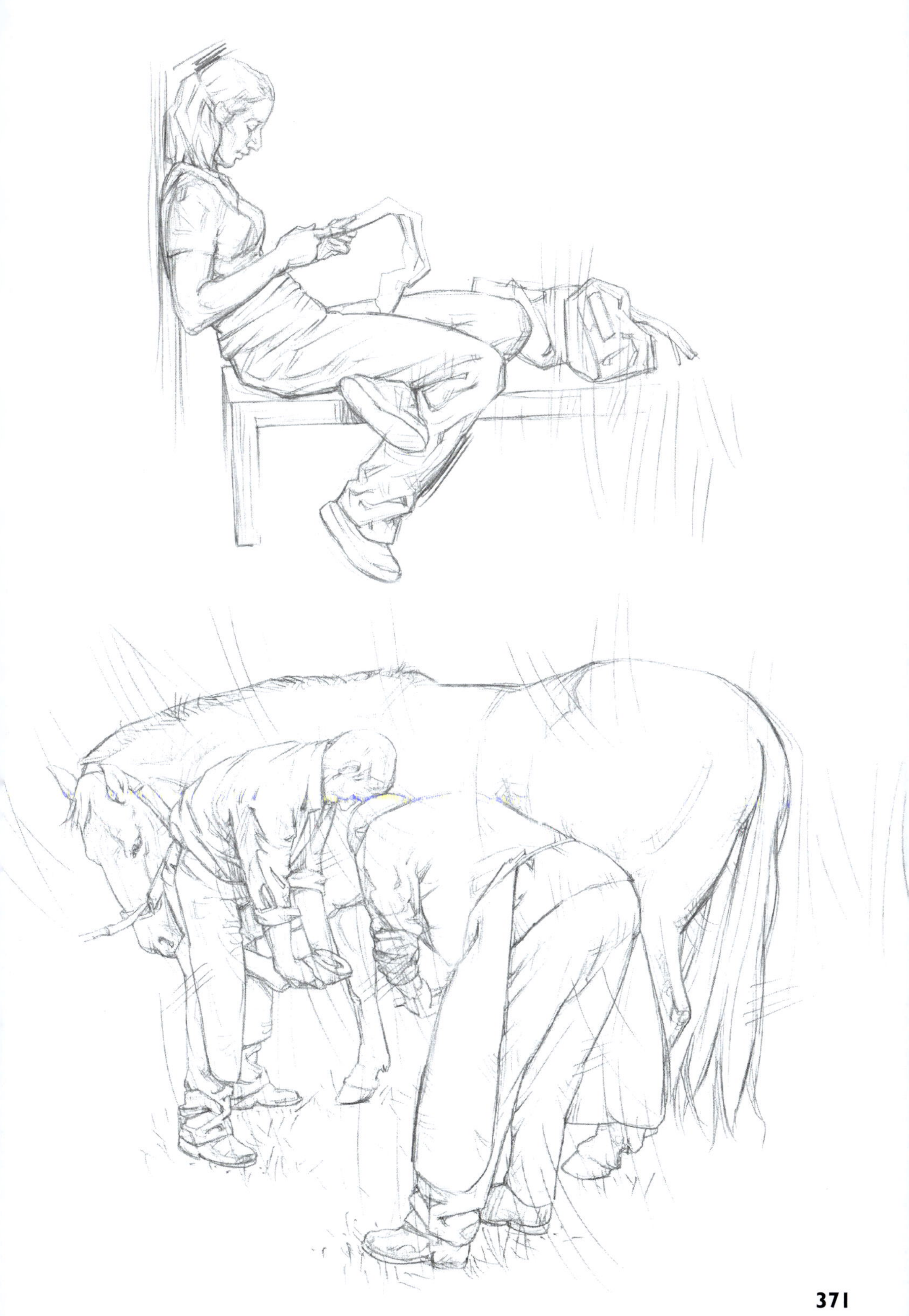

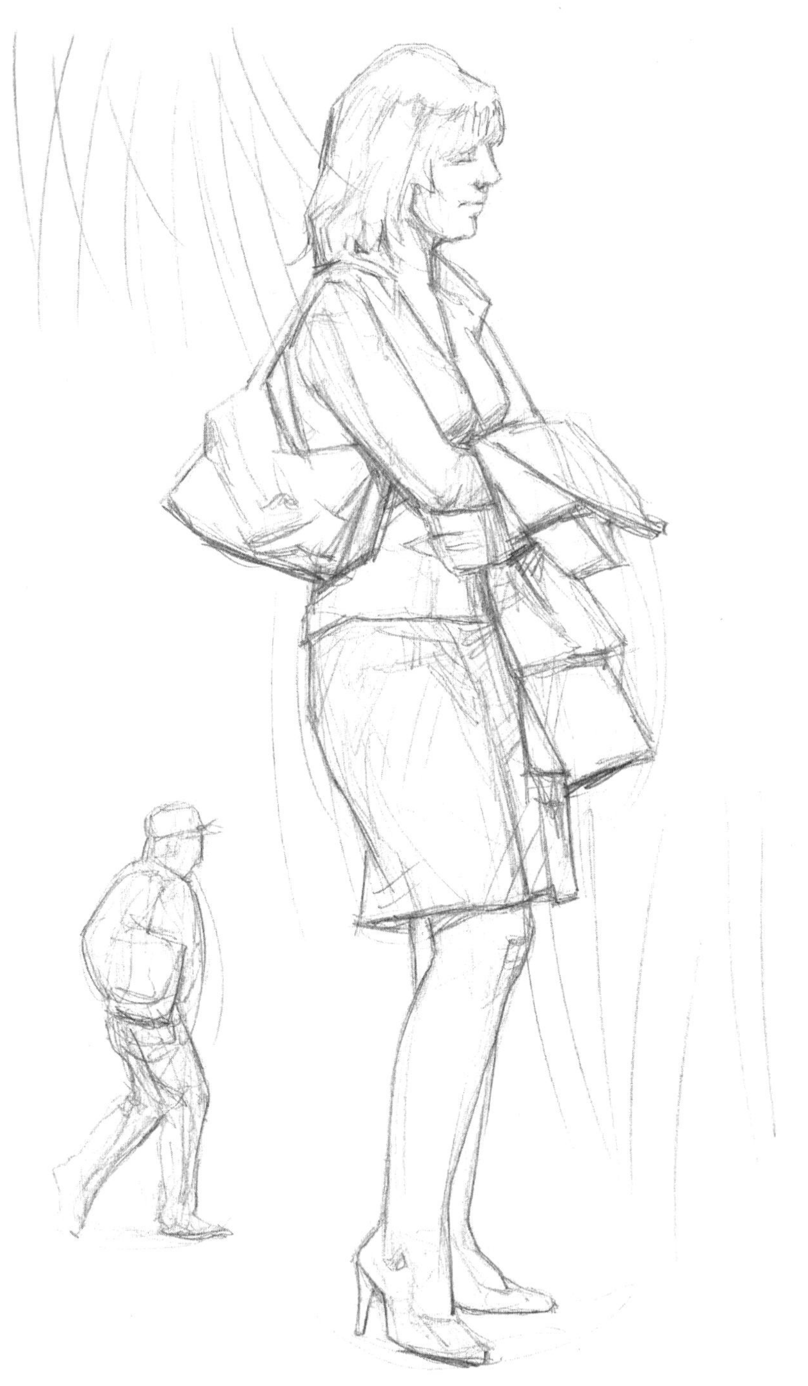

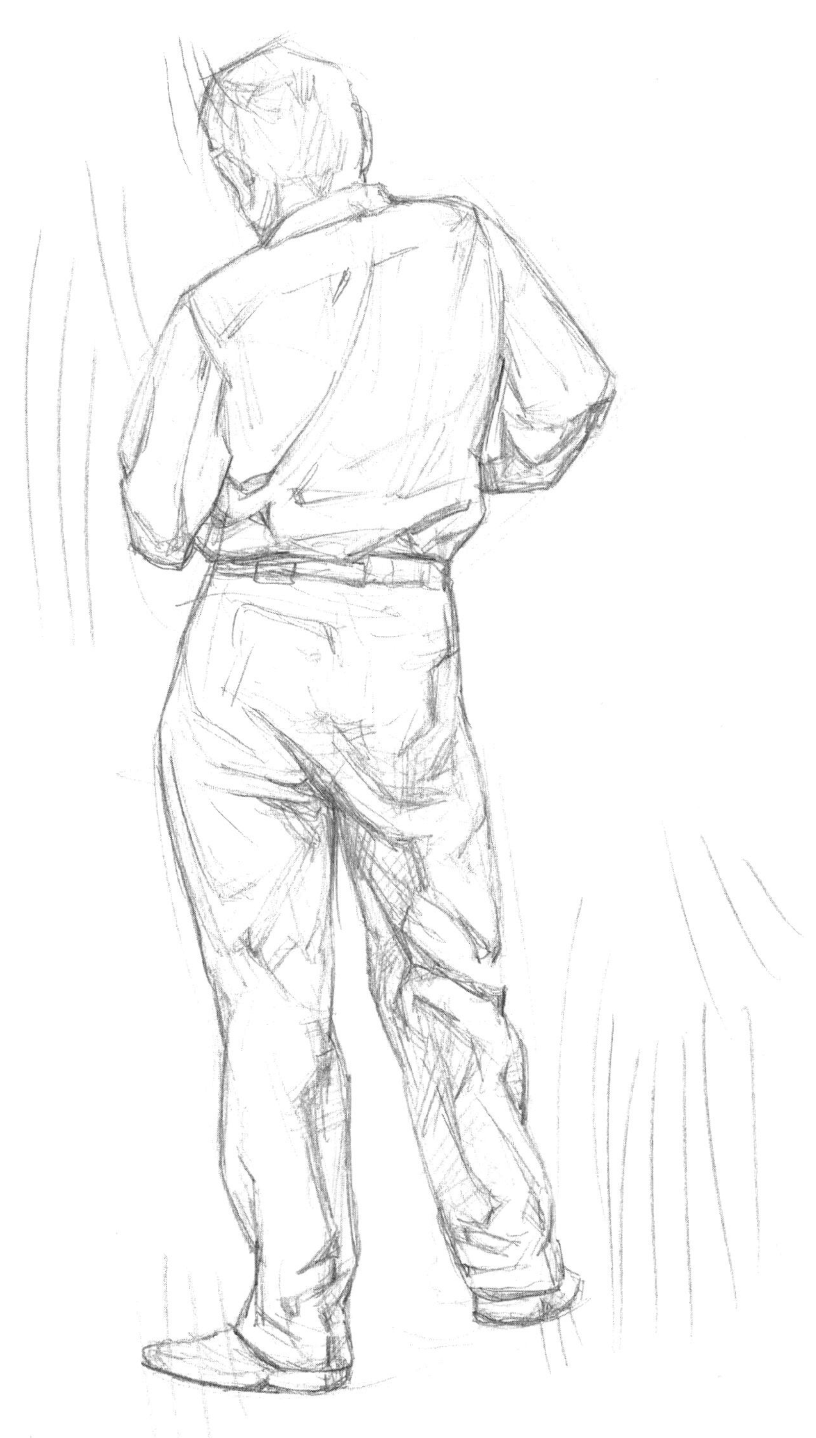

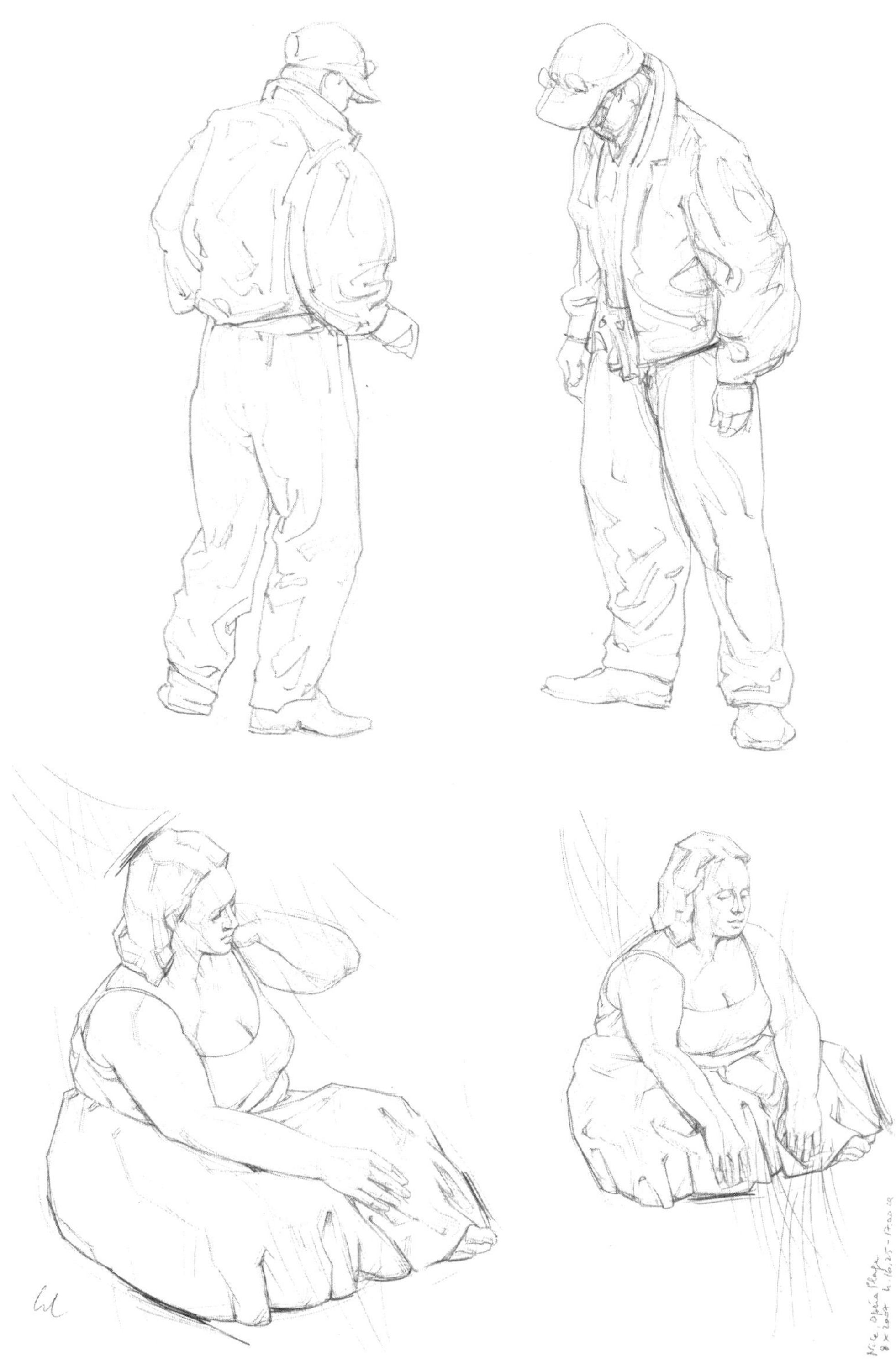

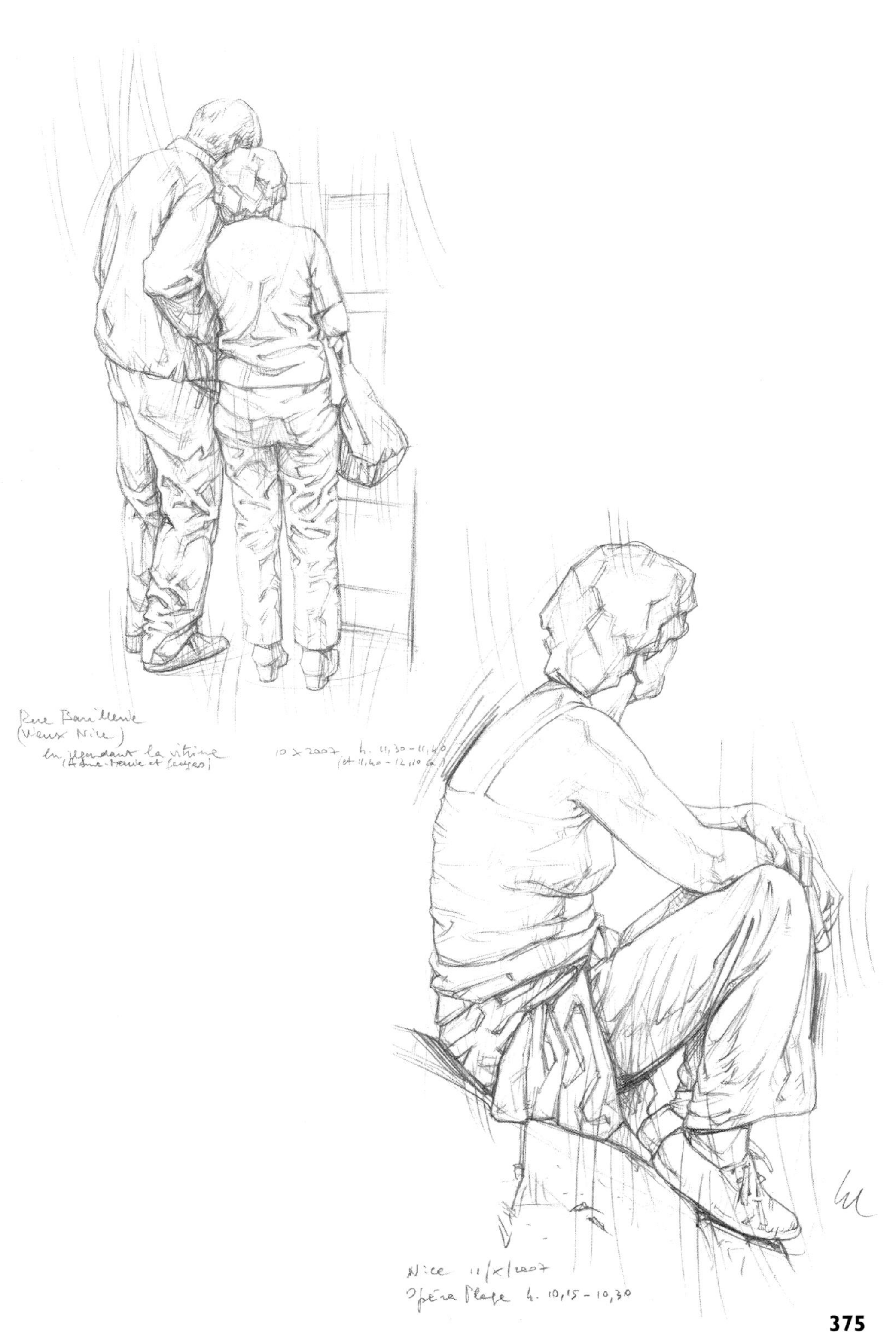
Rue Barillerie
(Vieux Nice)
en regardant la vitrine
10 X 2007 h. 11,30 – 11,40
Nice 11/X/2007
Opéra Plage h. 10,15 – 10,30

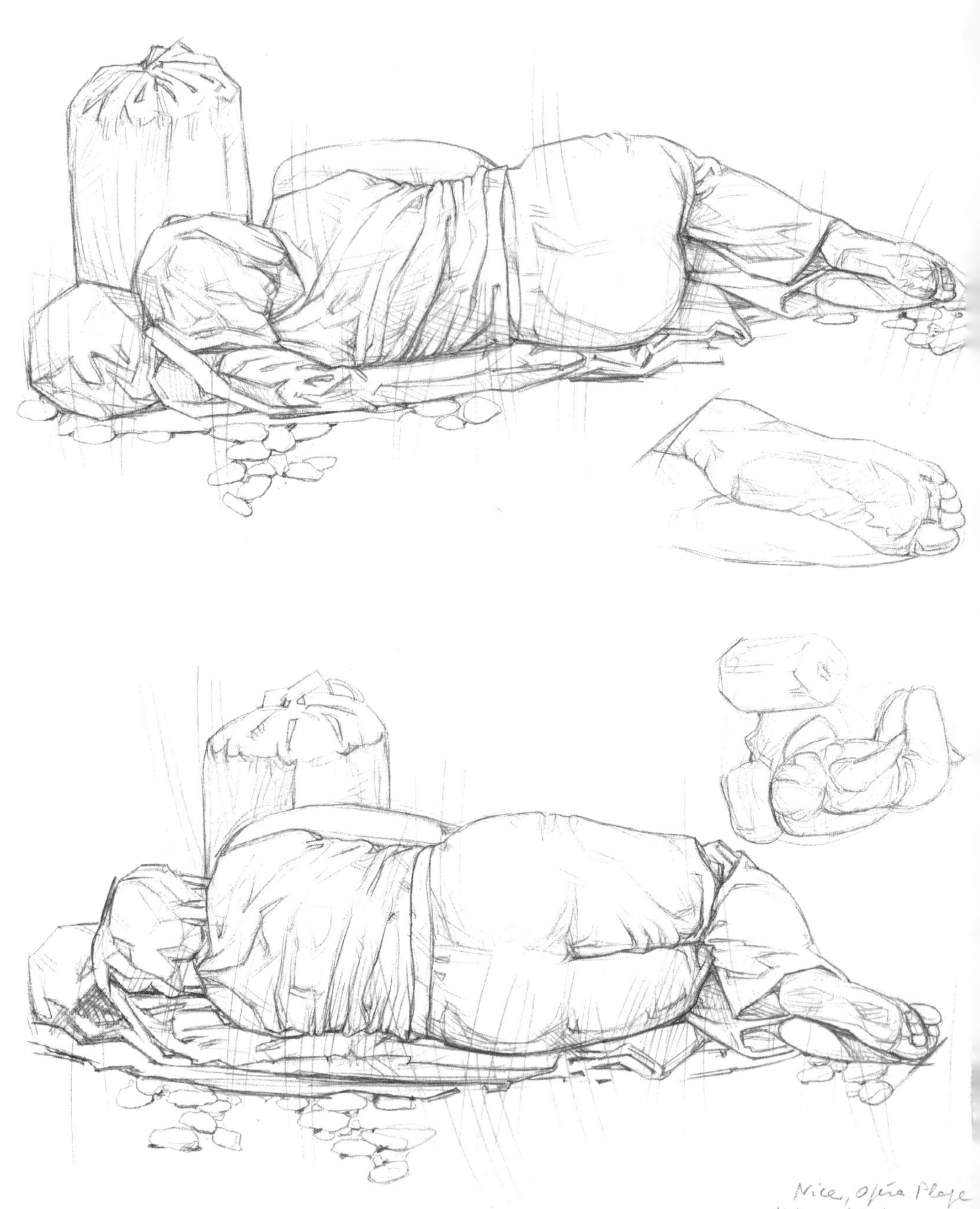
Nice, Opéra Plage
10 x h. 11,10 - 11,50

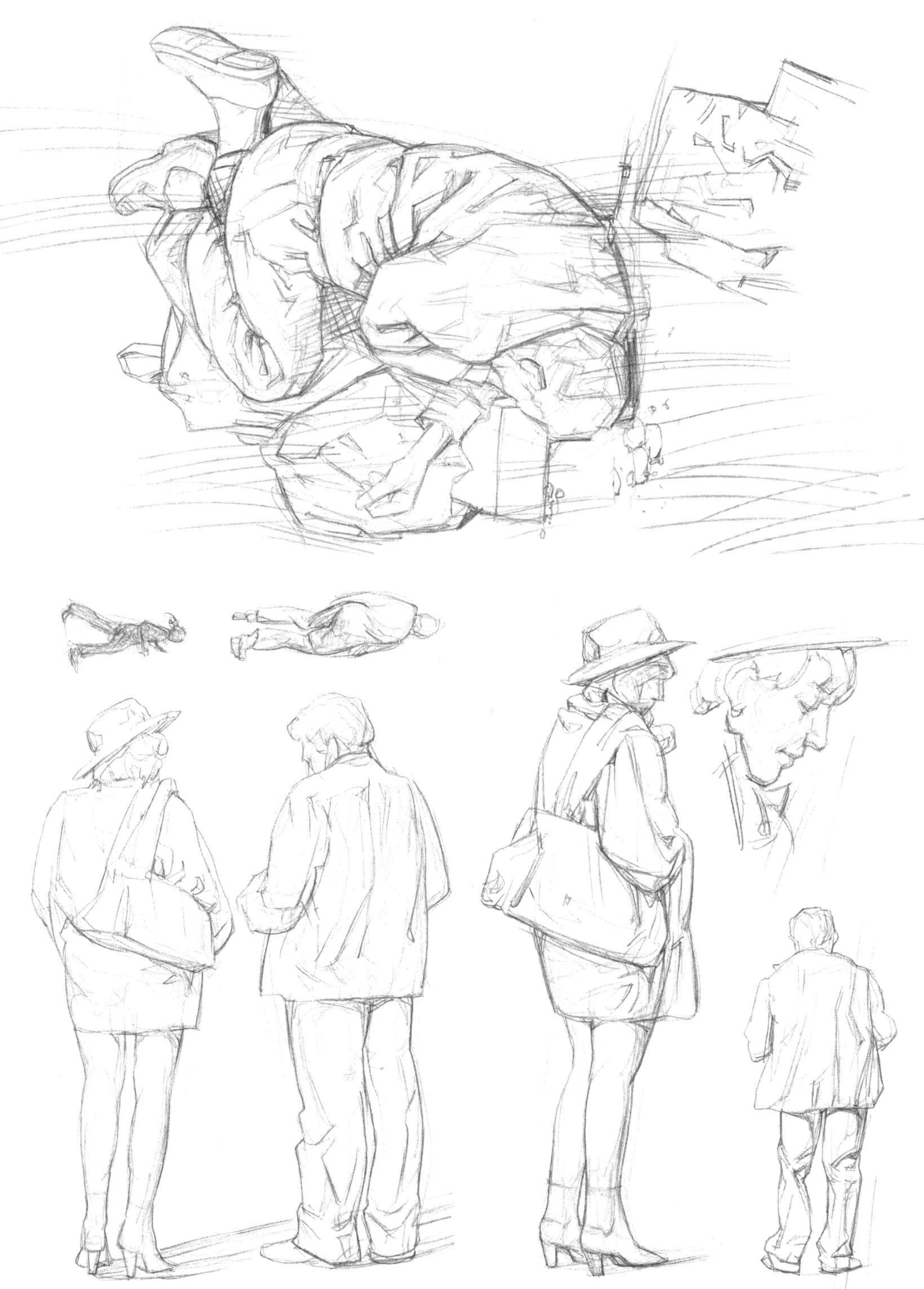

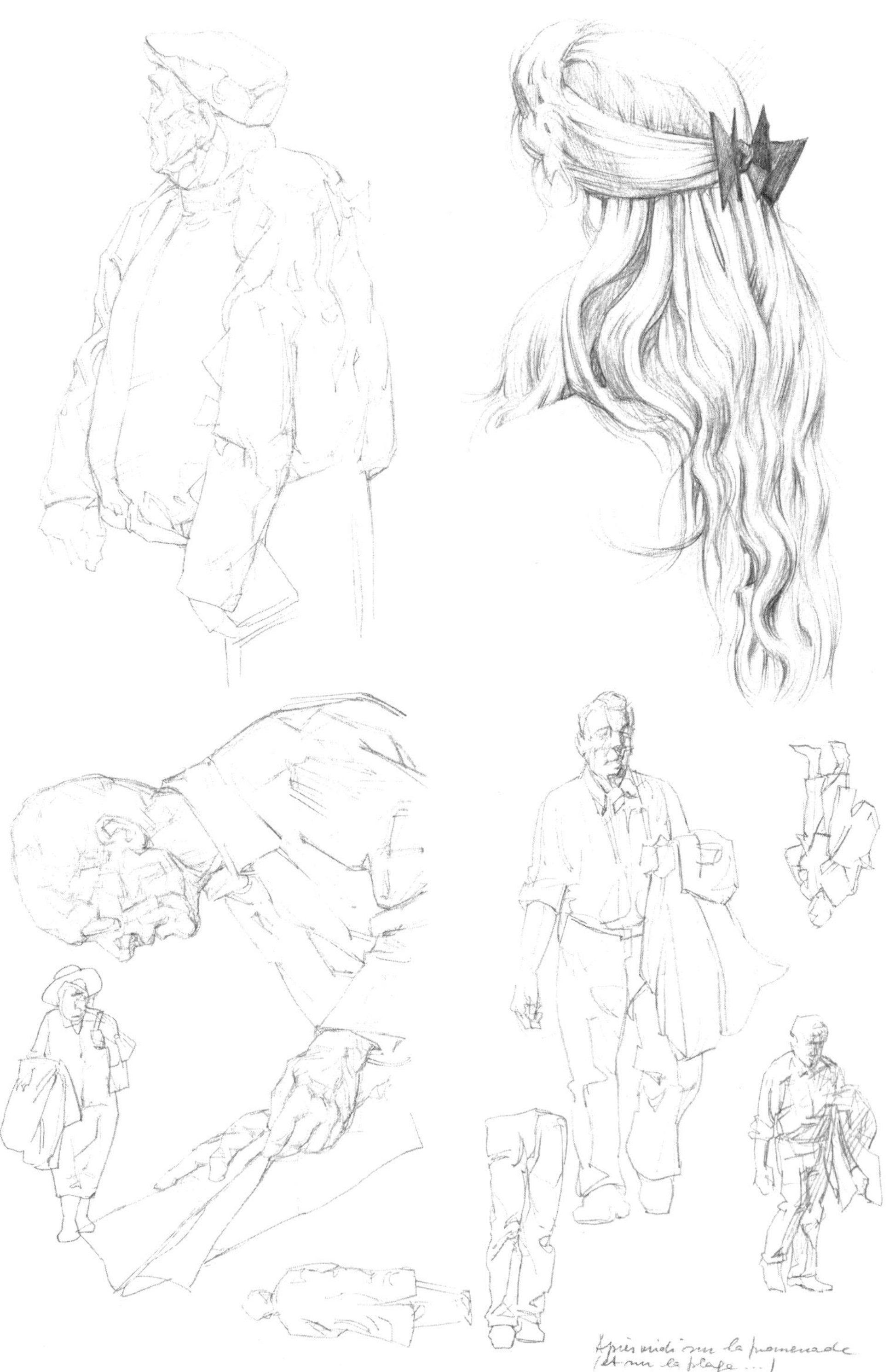
Après-midi sur la promenade
(et sur la plage ...)

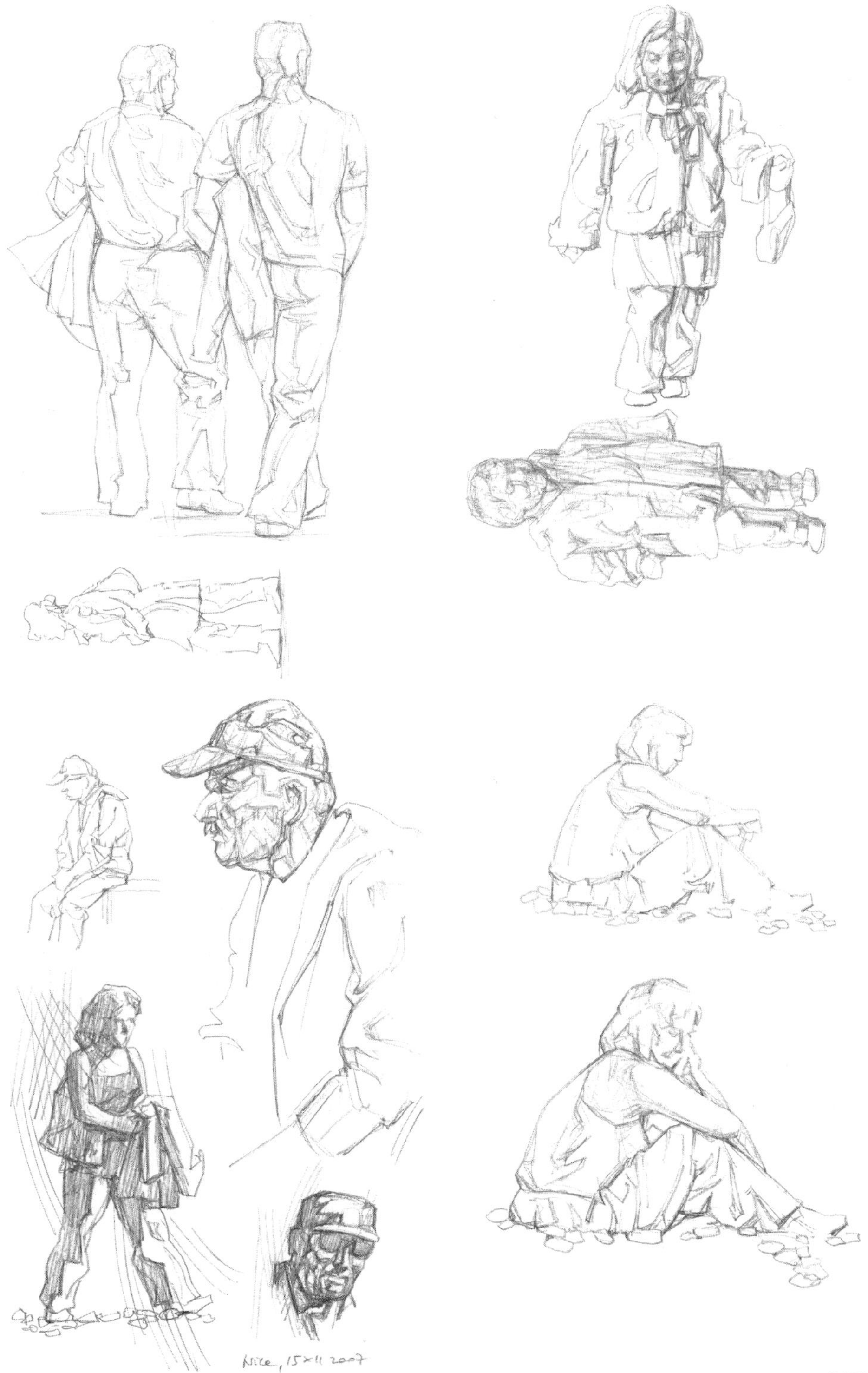
Nice, 15 XII 2007

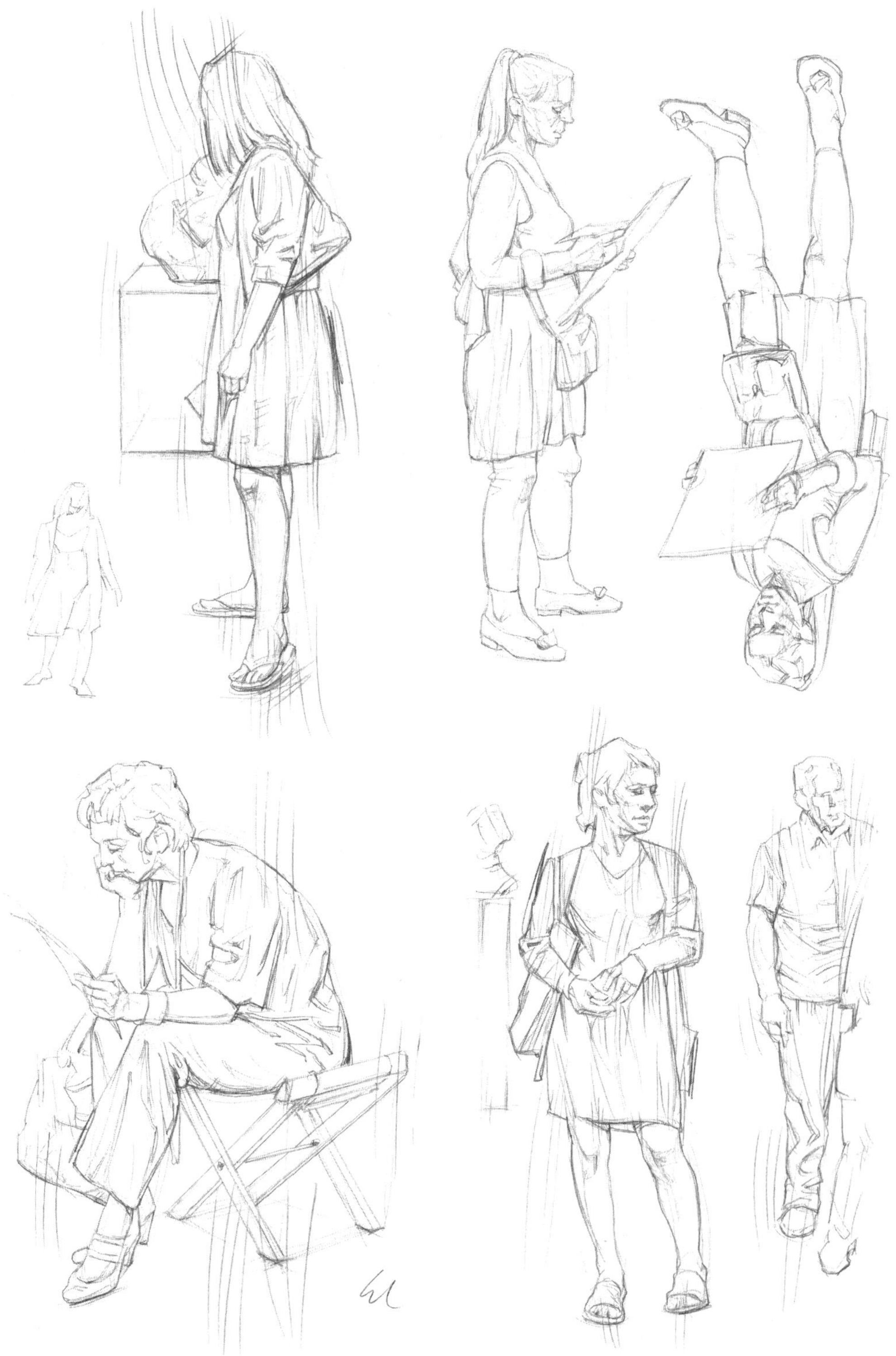

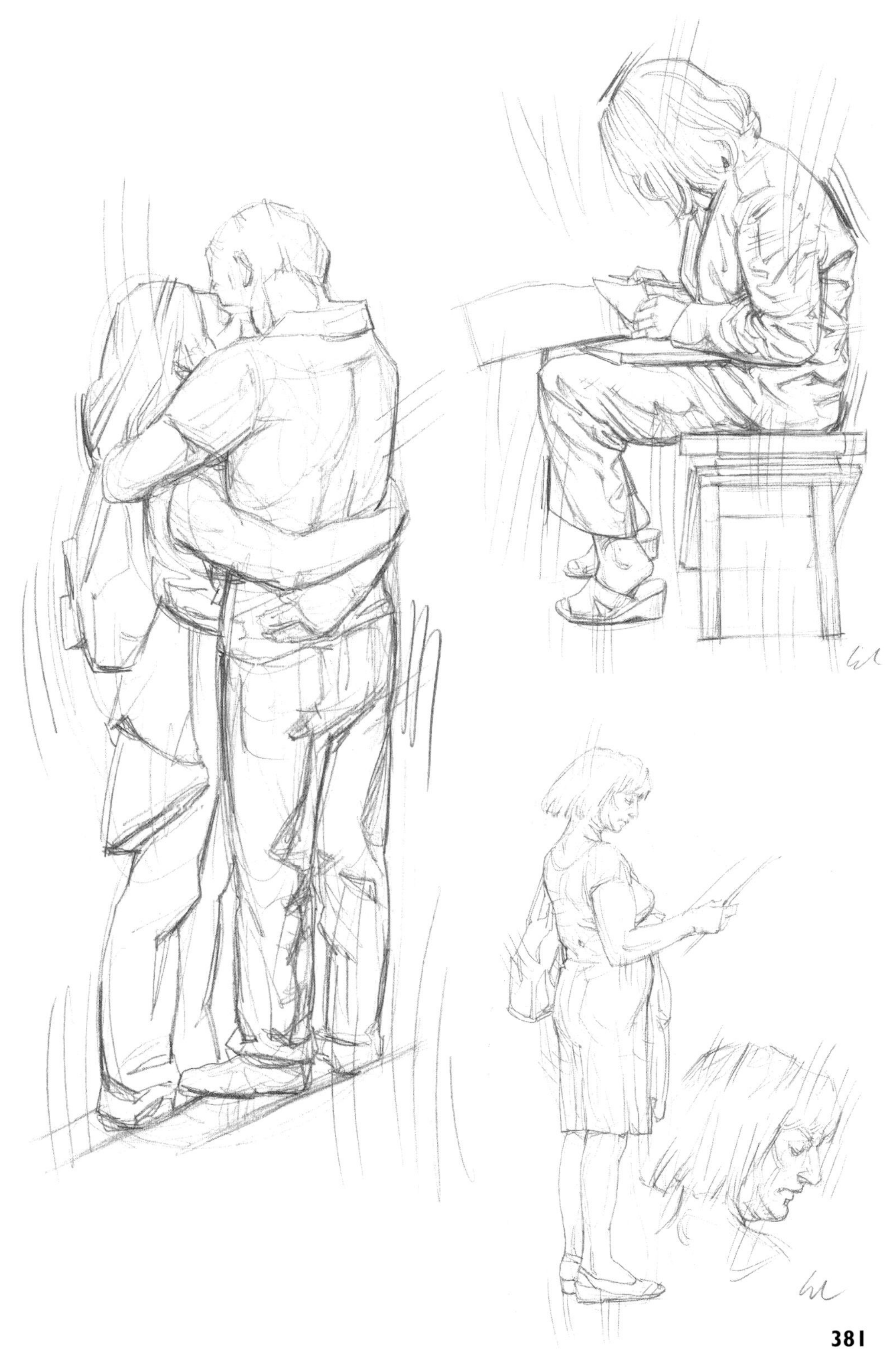

DRAWING STATUES: SCULPTURES FROM THE MUSÉE RODIN, PARIS

I have already laid out some of the reasons why you might choose to begin by drawing sculptures before moving on to tackle sketches from life (see pages 344–345). It is obvious that a 'model' that stays still permits you to work calmly, attentively and comfortably. In addition, a sketch from life involves greater inherent risks (for example of not being able to finish, failure, being interrupted, etc.), than the carefully thought-out and prolonged study of an immobile subject. In fact, this is why the constant practice of sketching is so important. The training it provides will enable you to make split-second, precise observations; it helps you to understand what you see and grasp the gist of a scene quickly; it develops sureness of hand, an eye for composition and draughtmanship.

In common with many other artists, my aesthetic preferences have led me to choose the Rodin Museum as a place for my personal training. The statues of this great sculptor offer unique and fascinating opportunities for analysis of anatomy, composition and proportion, and for observation of surface modulation. Furthermore, in this museum the statues are well placed and well lit (some of them have been positioned in an adjacent garden), and they may be studied with ease from various distances and viewpoints.

The practice of drawing from works of art is a very profitable one for acquiring technical training and mastery of your craft, as well as for refining your artistic and critical sensibilities.

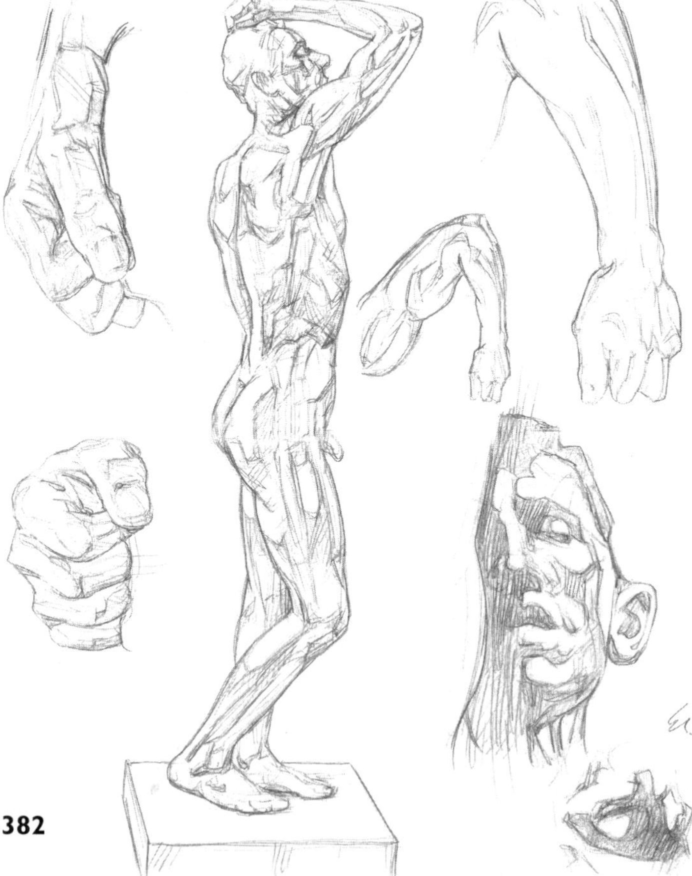

The Age of Bronze (1876)
Bronze, 181cm (71in) high

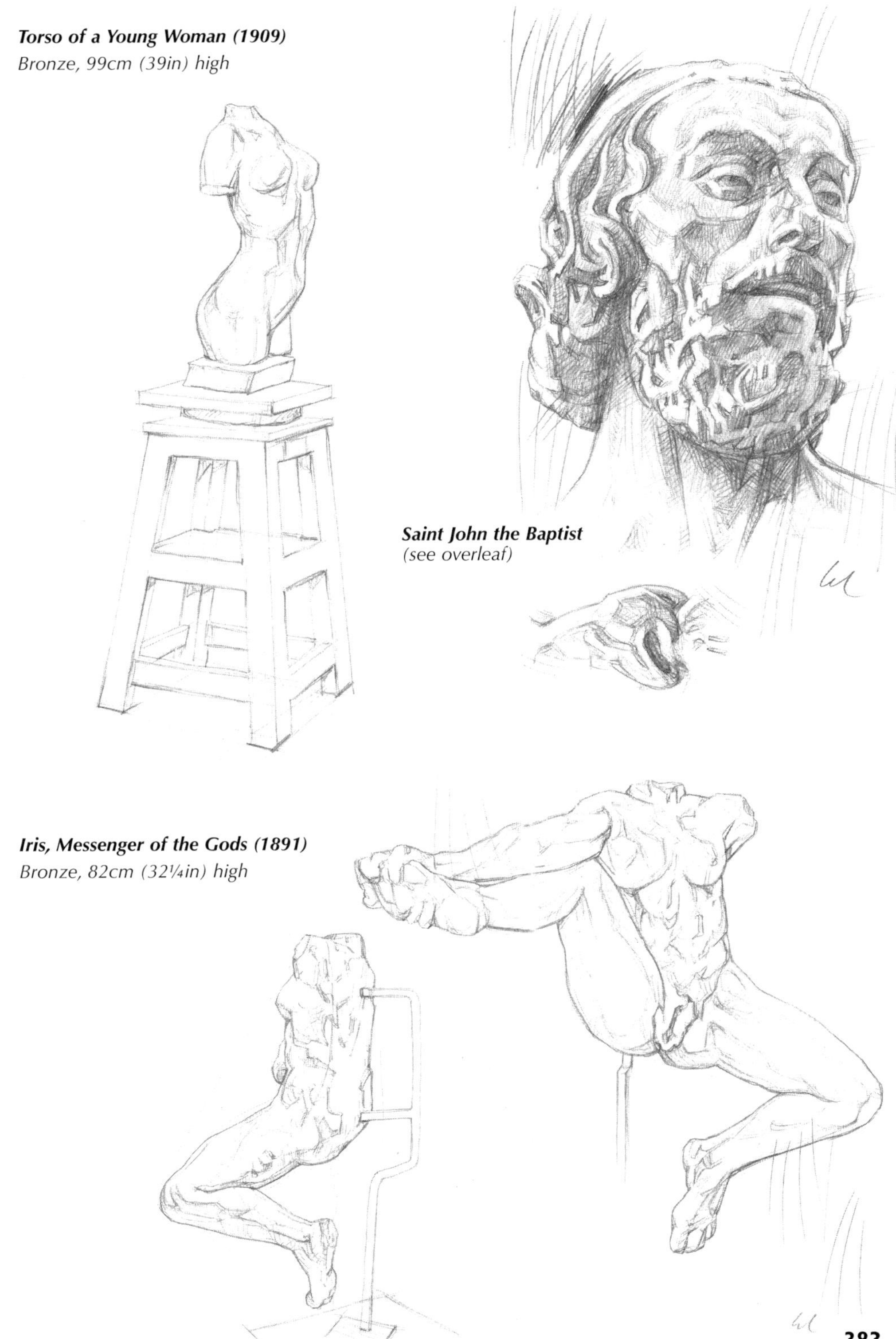

Torso of a Young Woman (1909)
Bronze, 99cm (39in) high

Saint John the Baptist
(see overleaf)

Iris, Messenger of the Gods (1891)
Bronze, 82cm (32¼in) high

Saint John the Baptist (1879)

Bronze, 200cm (78¾in) high

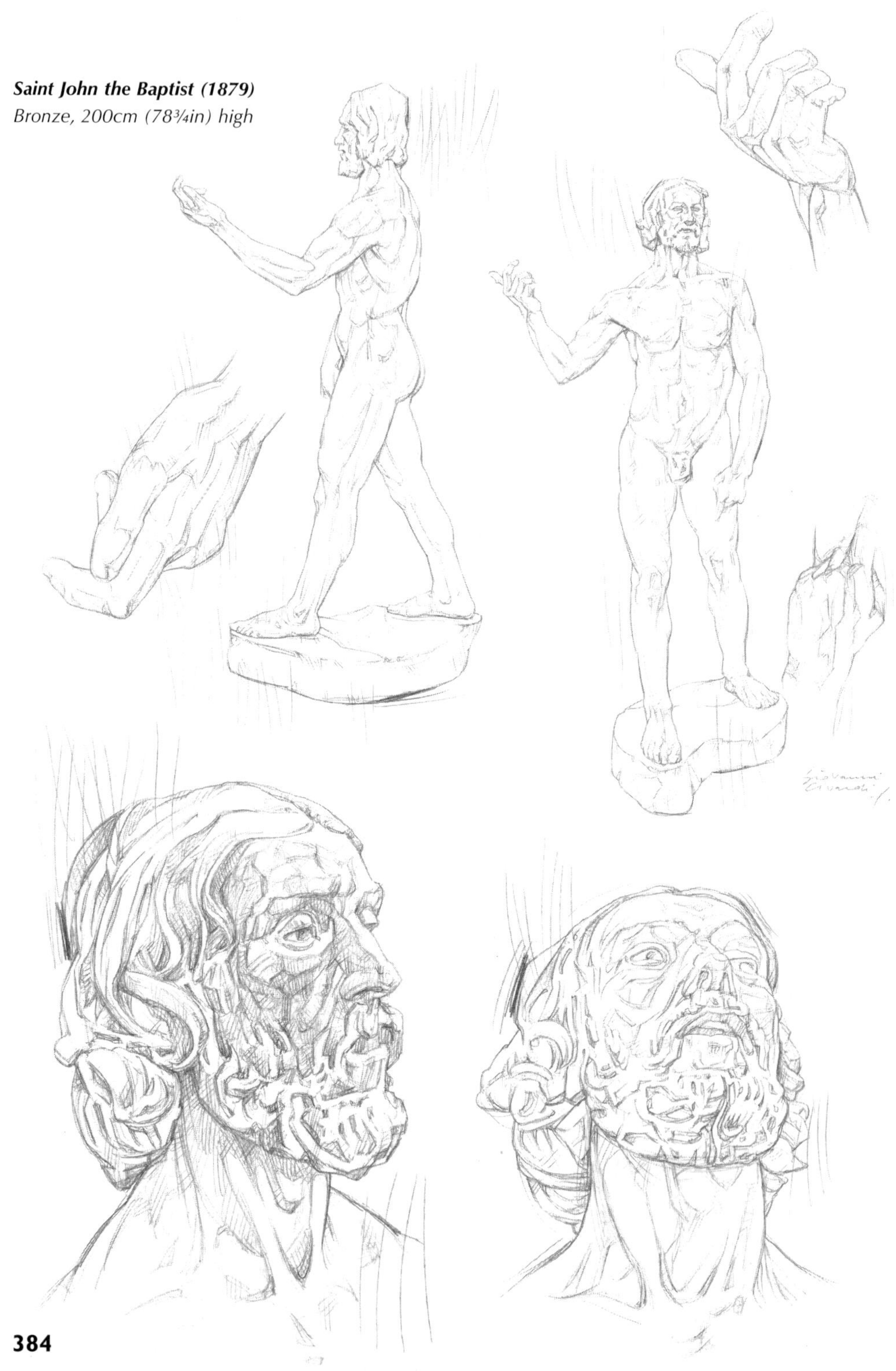

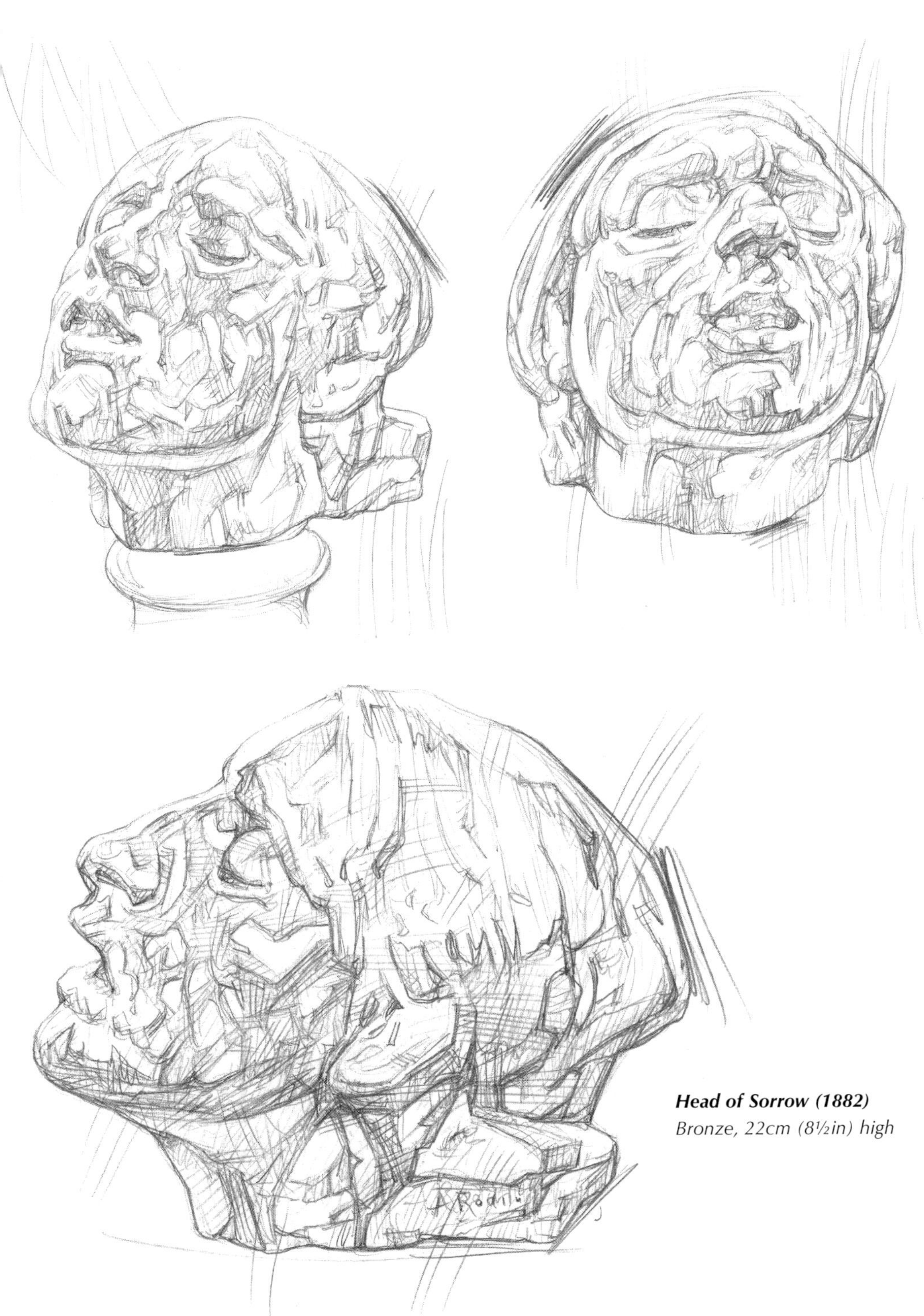

Head of Sorrow (1882)
Bronze, 22cm (8½in) high

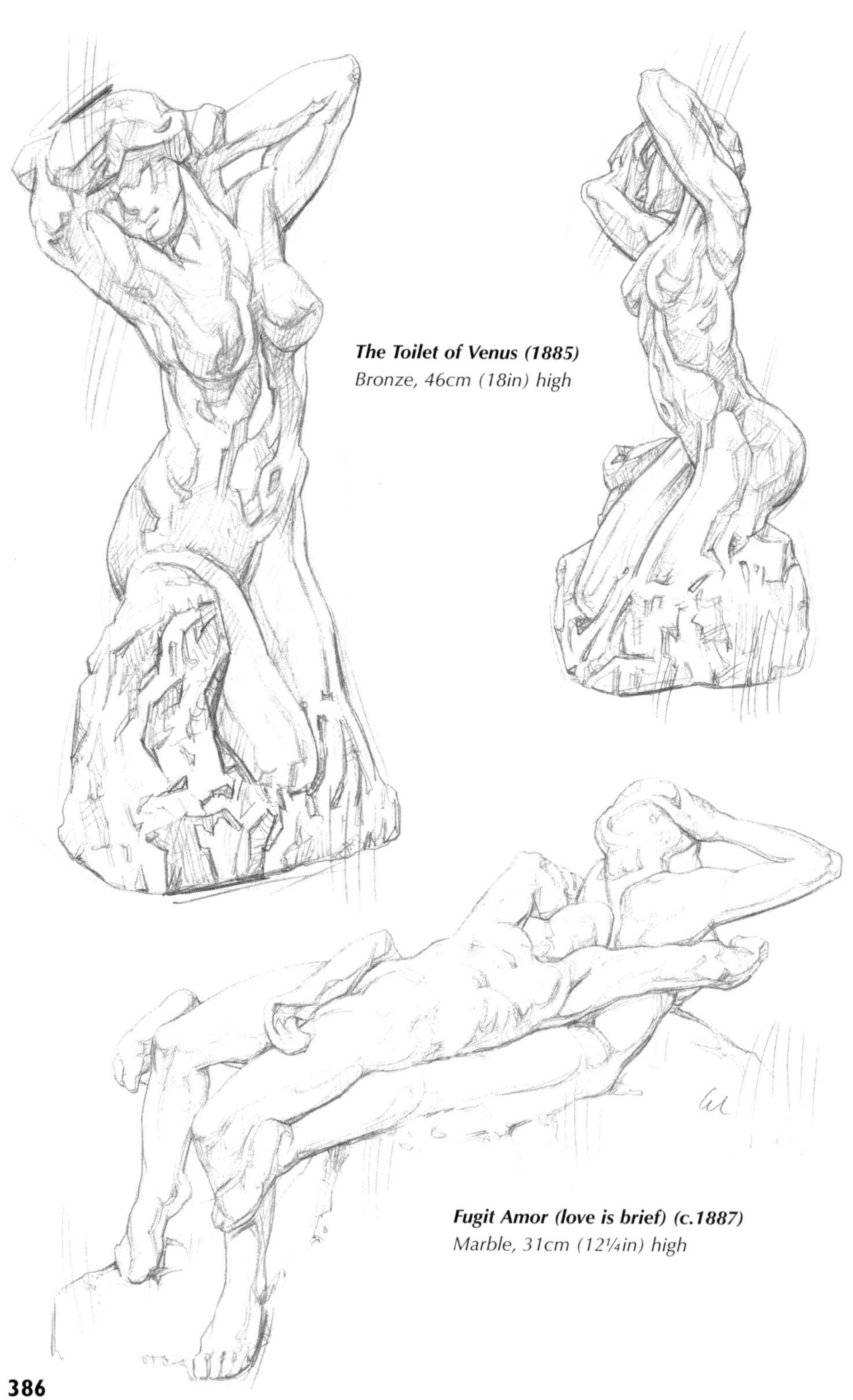

The Toilet of Venus (1885)
Bronze, 46cm (18in) high

Fugit Amor (love is brief) (c.1887)
Marble, 31cm (12¼in) high

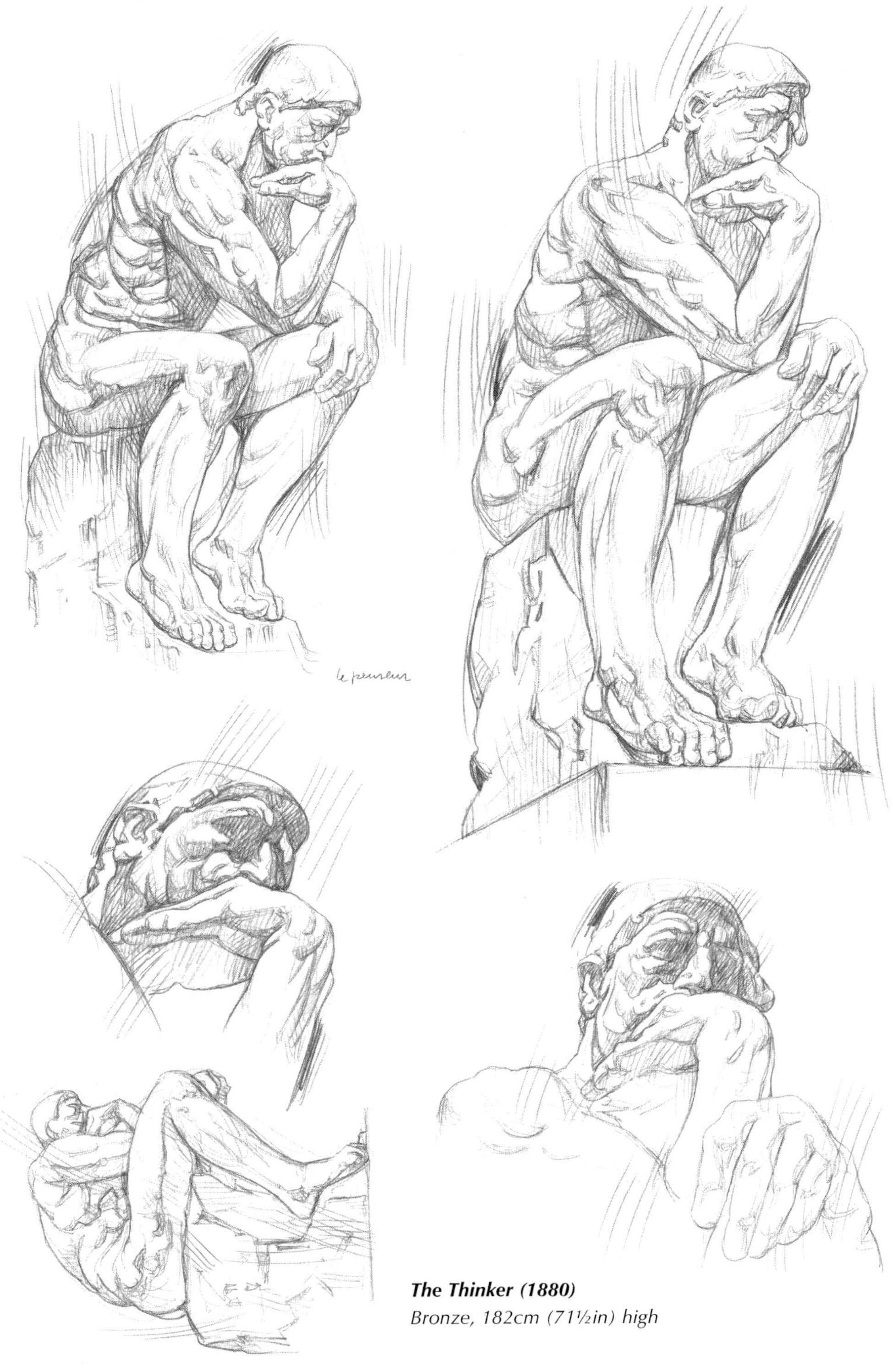

The Thinker (1880)

Bronze, 182cm (71½in) high

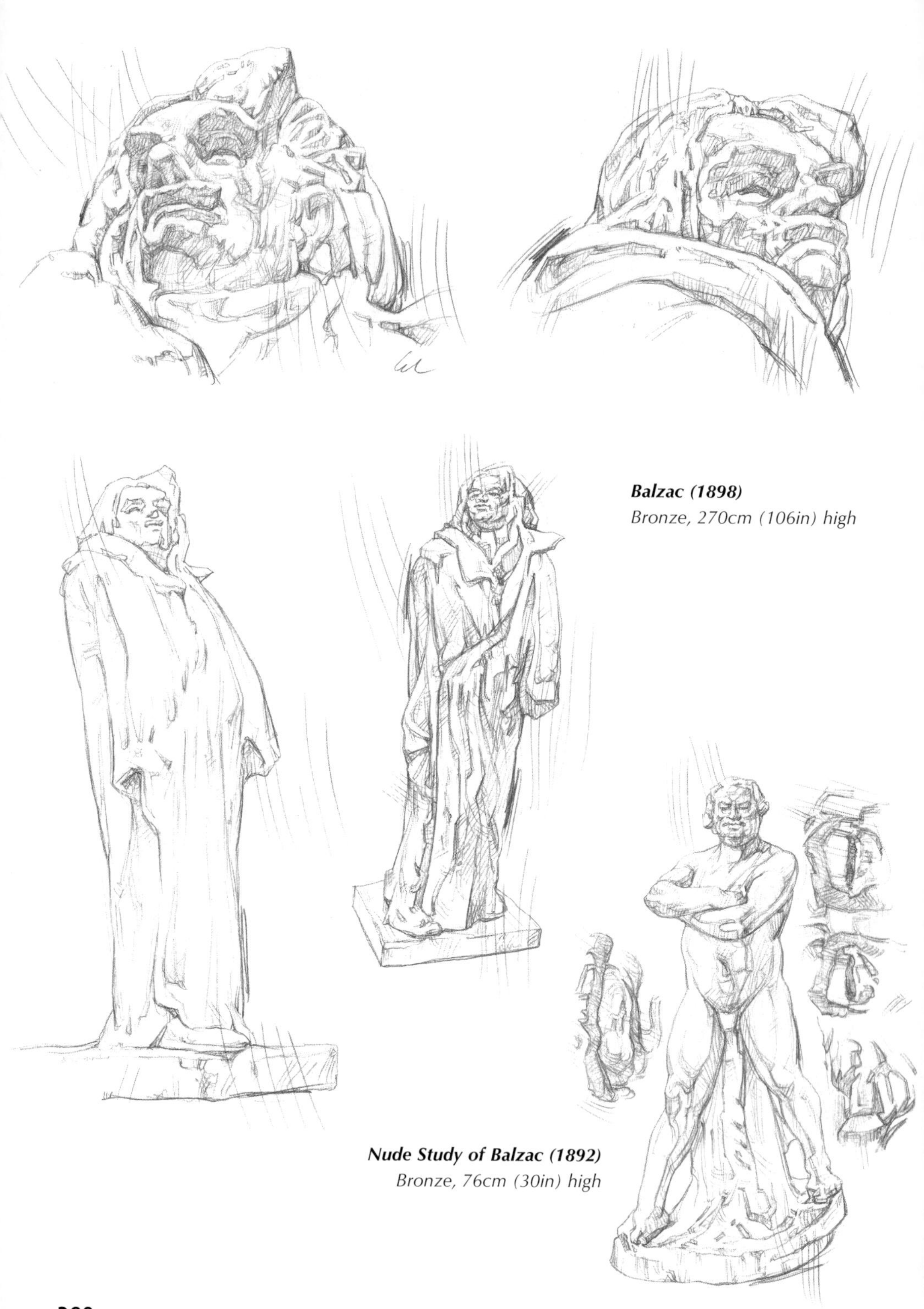

Balzac (1898)
Bronze, 270cm (106in) high

Nude Study of Balzac (1892)
Bronze, 76cm (30in) high

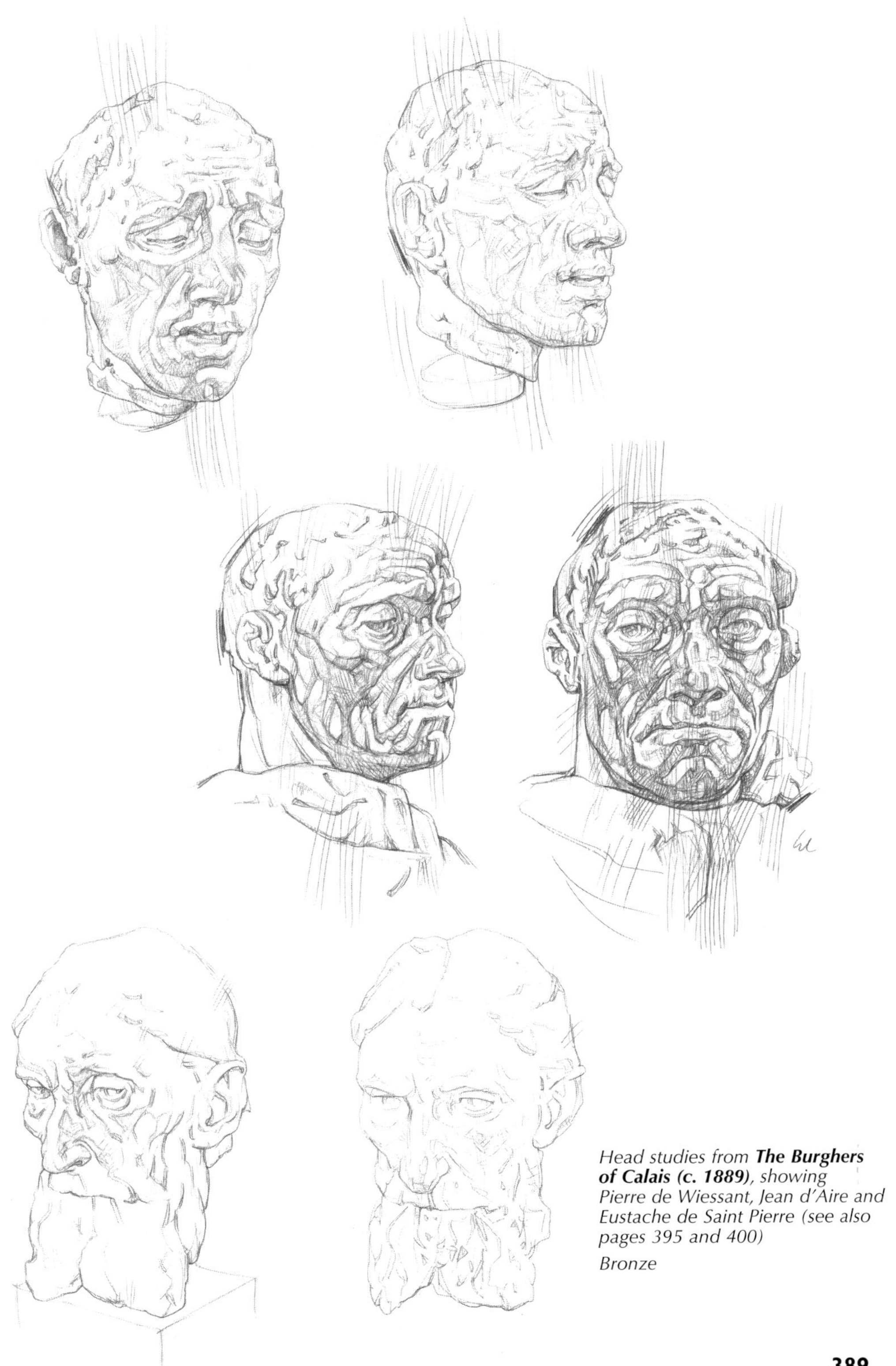

Head studies from ***The Burghers of Calais (c. 1889)****, showing Pierre de Wiessant, Jean d'Aire and Eustache de Saint Pierre (see also pages 395 and 400)*

Bronze

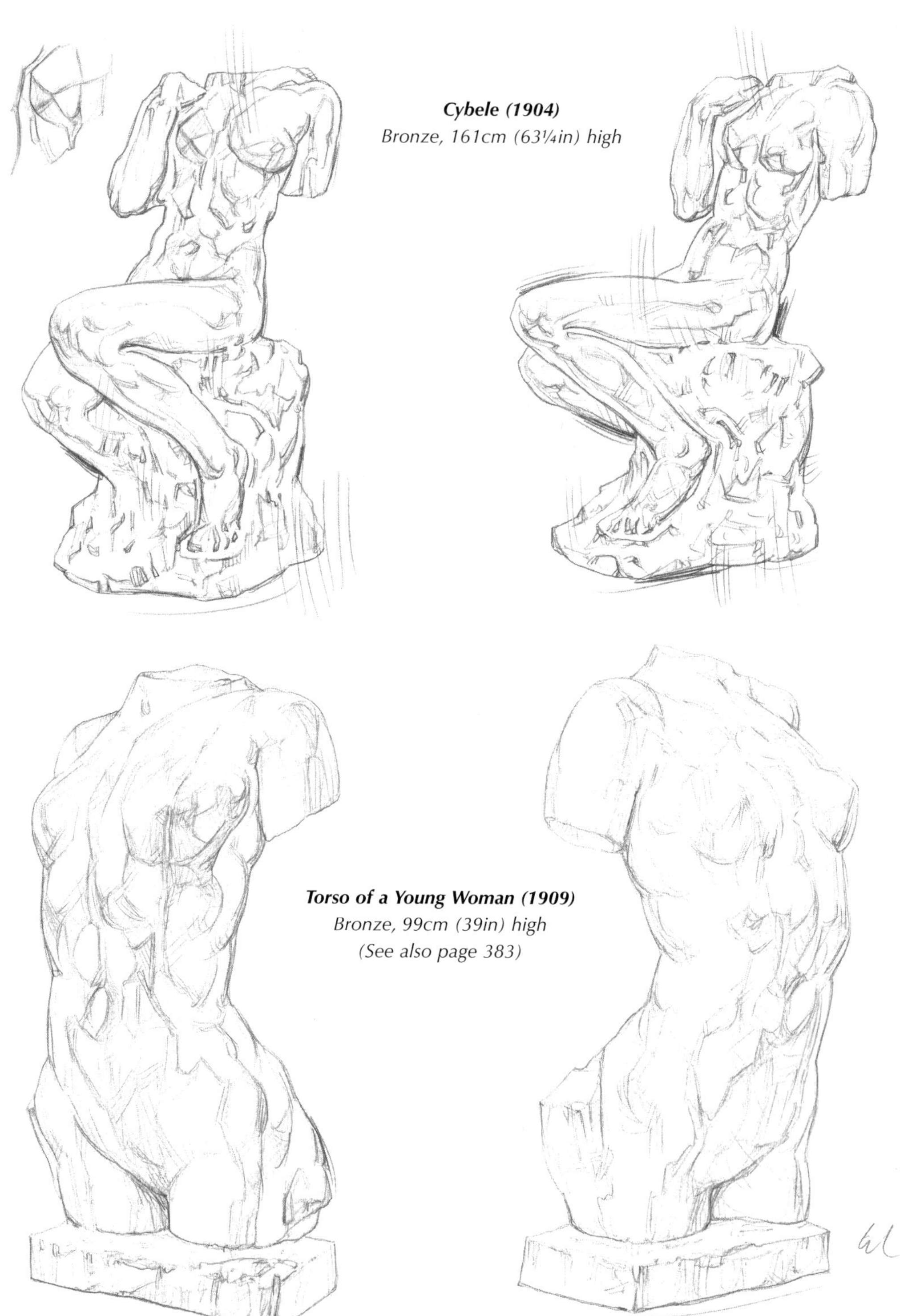

***Cybele* (1904)**
Bronze, 161cm (63¼in) high

***Torso of a Young Woman* (1909)**
Bronze, 99cm (39in) high
(See also page 383)

Ugolino and his Children (1881)
Plaster

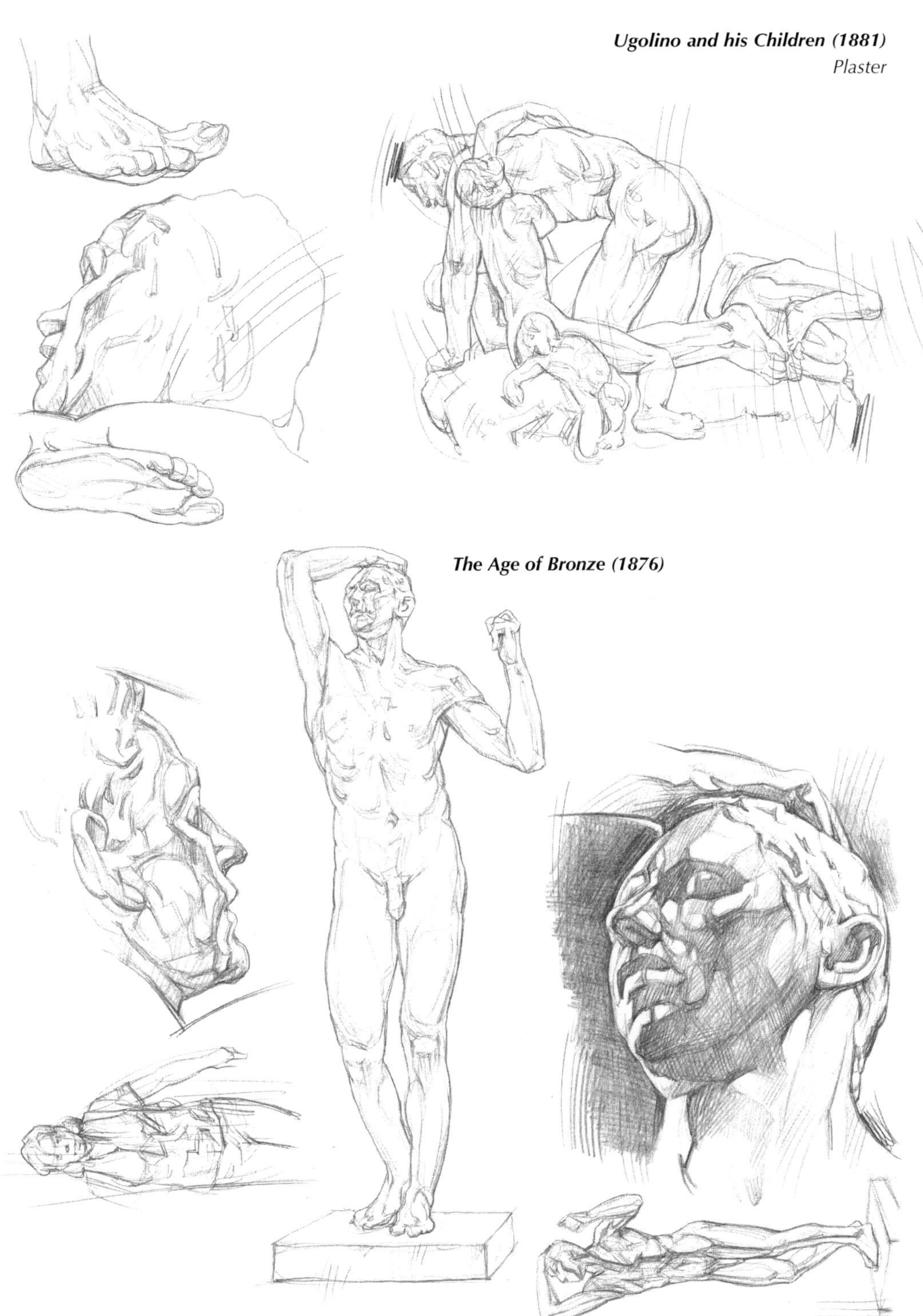

The Age of Bronze (1876)

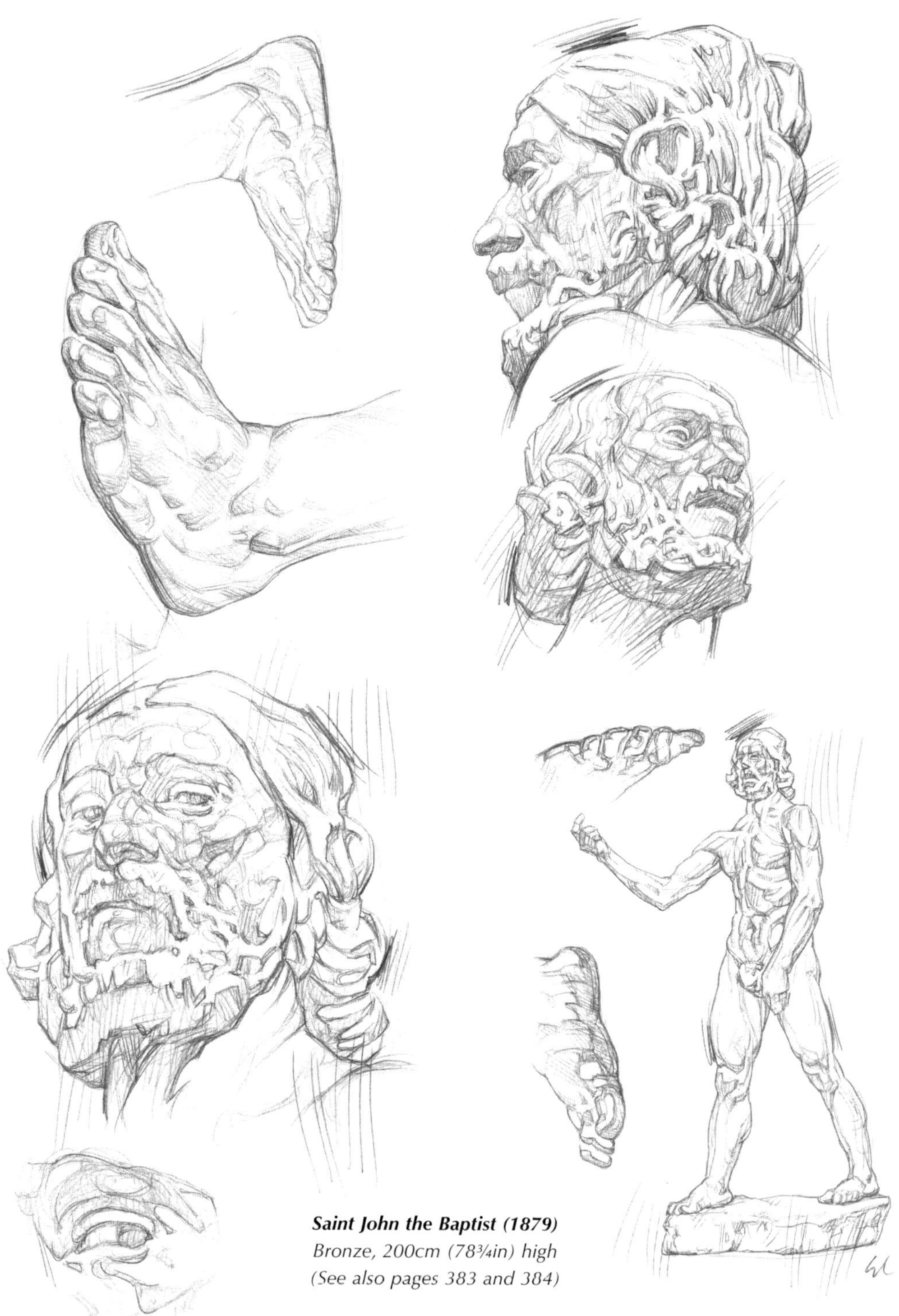

Saint John the Baptist (1879)
Bronze, 200cm (78¾in) high
(See also pages 383 and 384)

Portrait of Jules Dalou (1883)
Bronze, 57cm (22½in) high

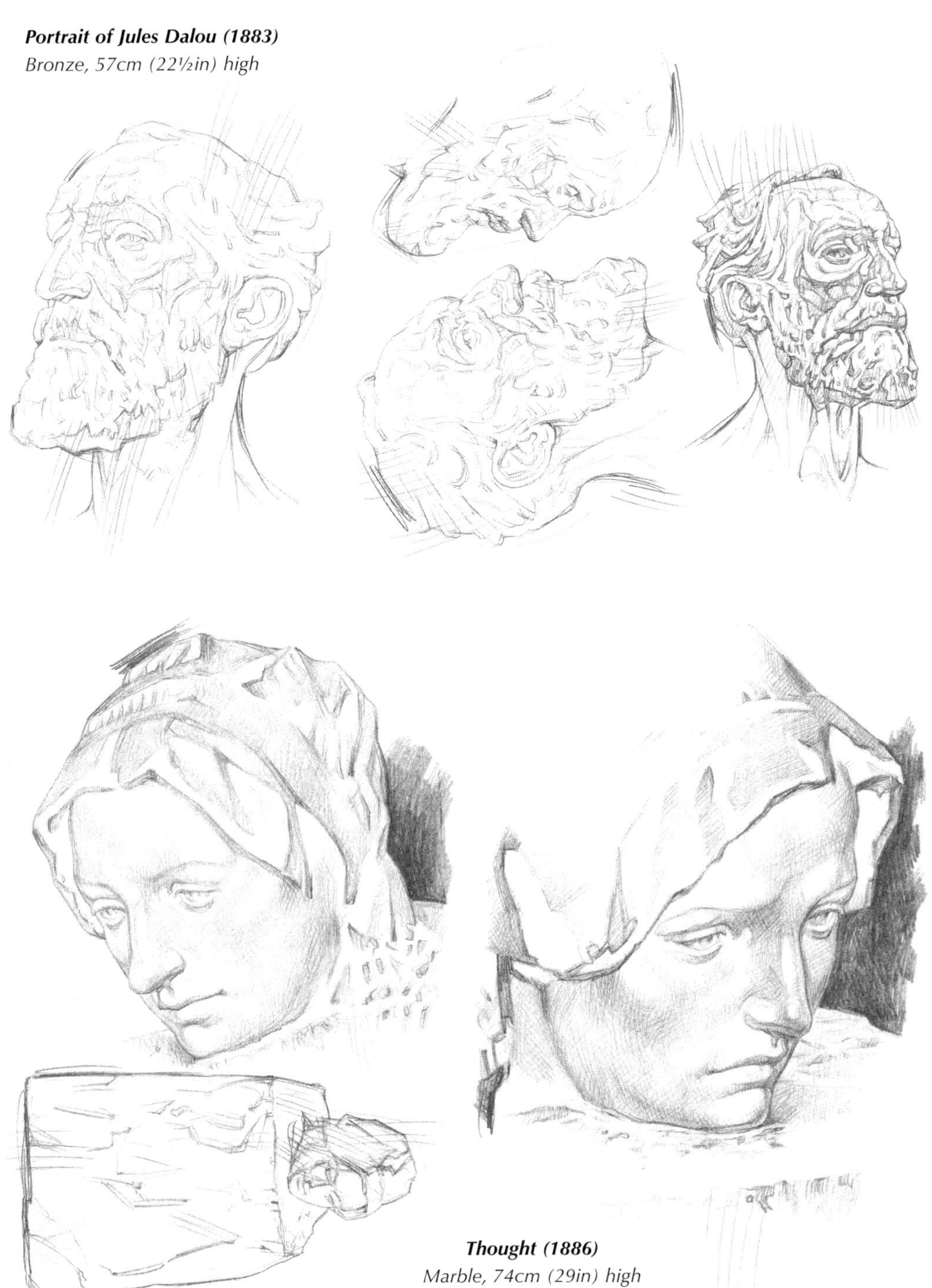

Thought (1886)
Marble, 74cm (29in) high

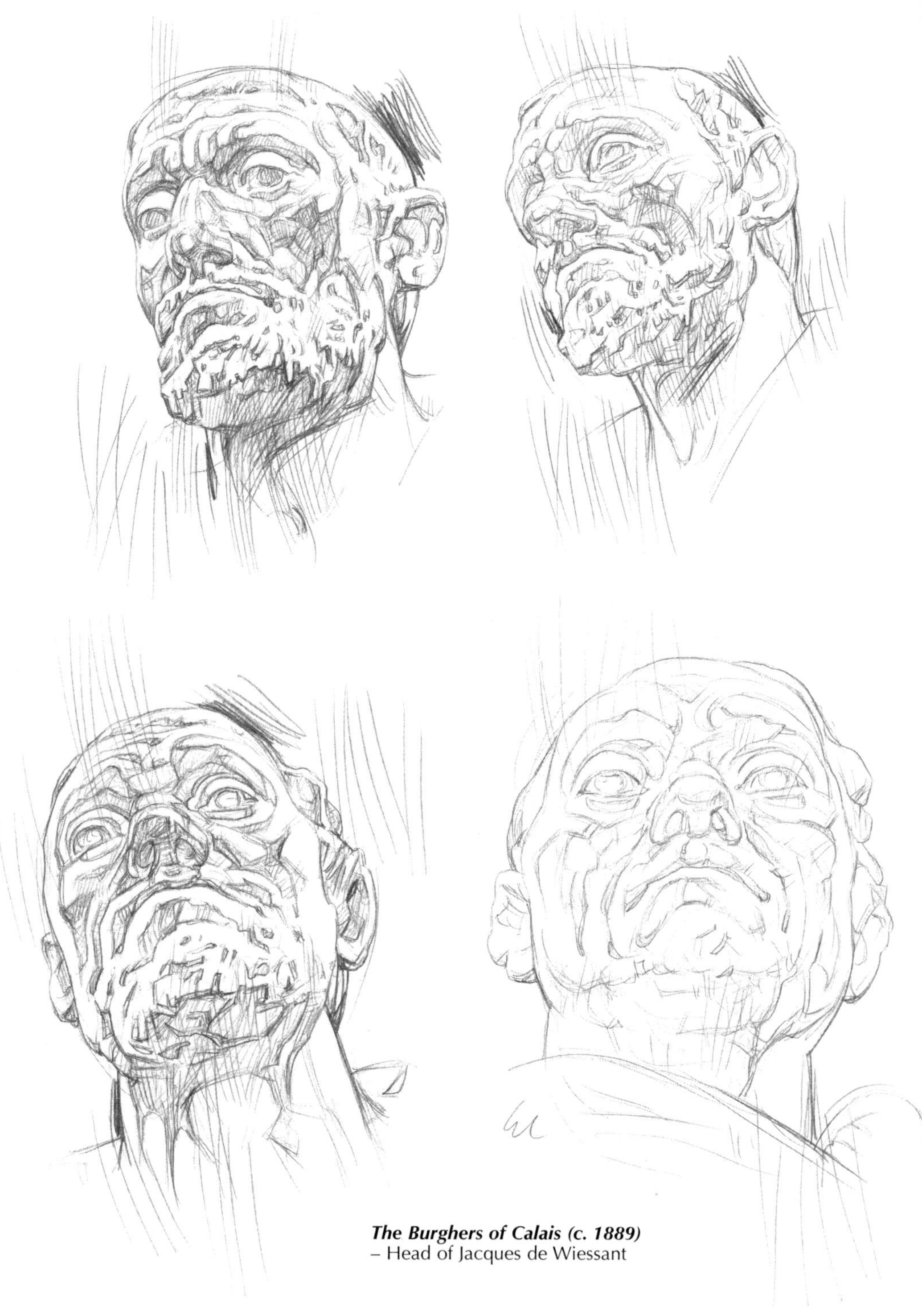

The Burghers of Calais (c. 1889)
– Head of Jacques de Wiessant

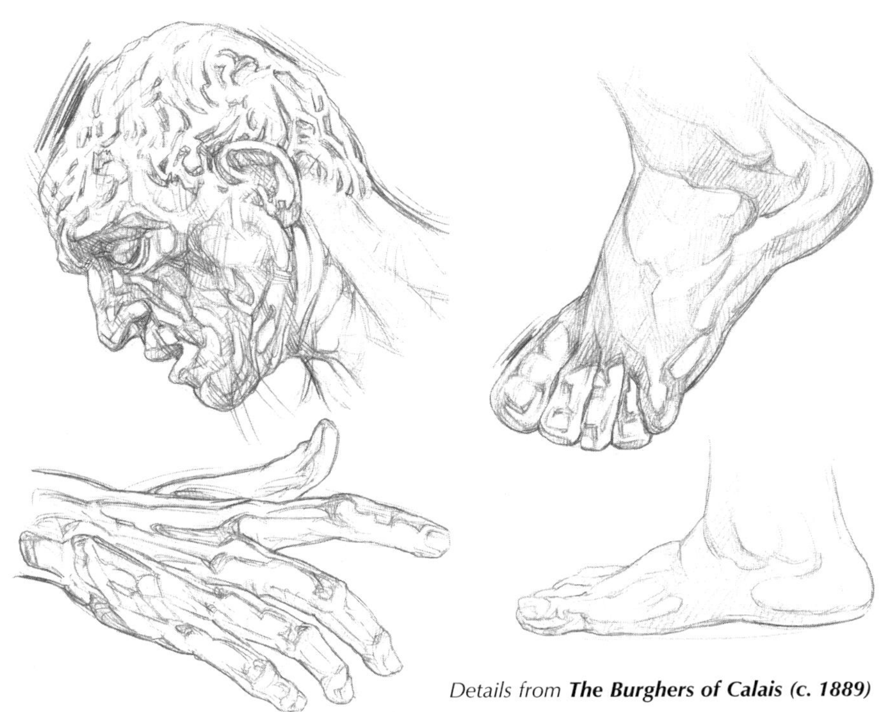

Details from **The Burghers of Calais (c. 1889)**

The Kiss (c. 1888)
Marble, 183cm (72in) high

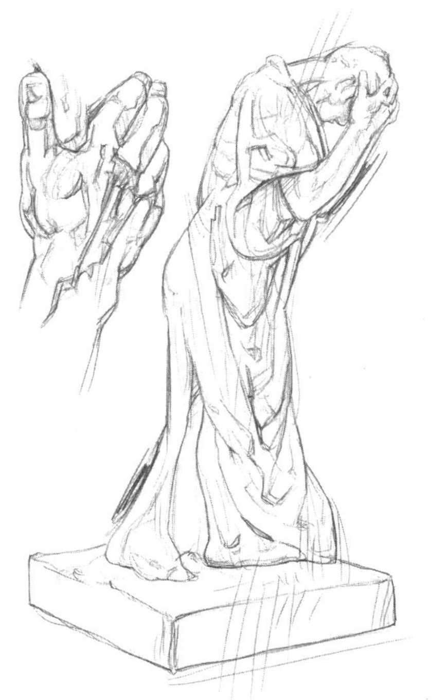

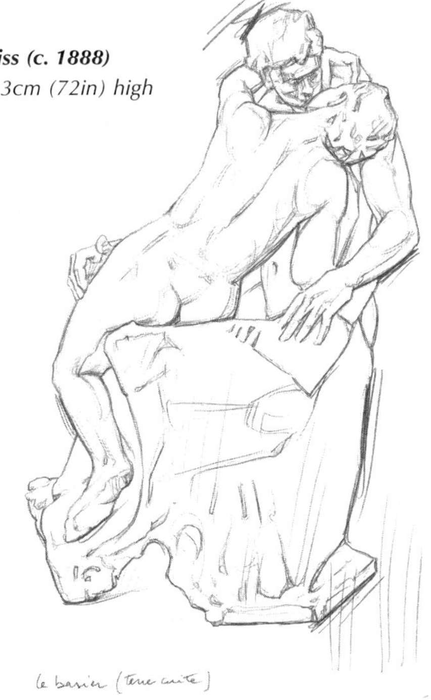

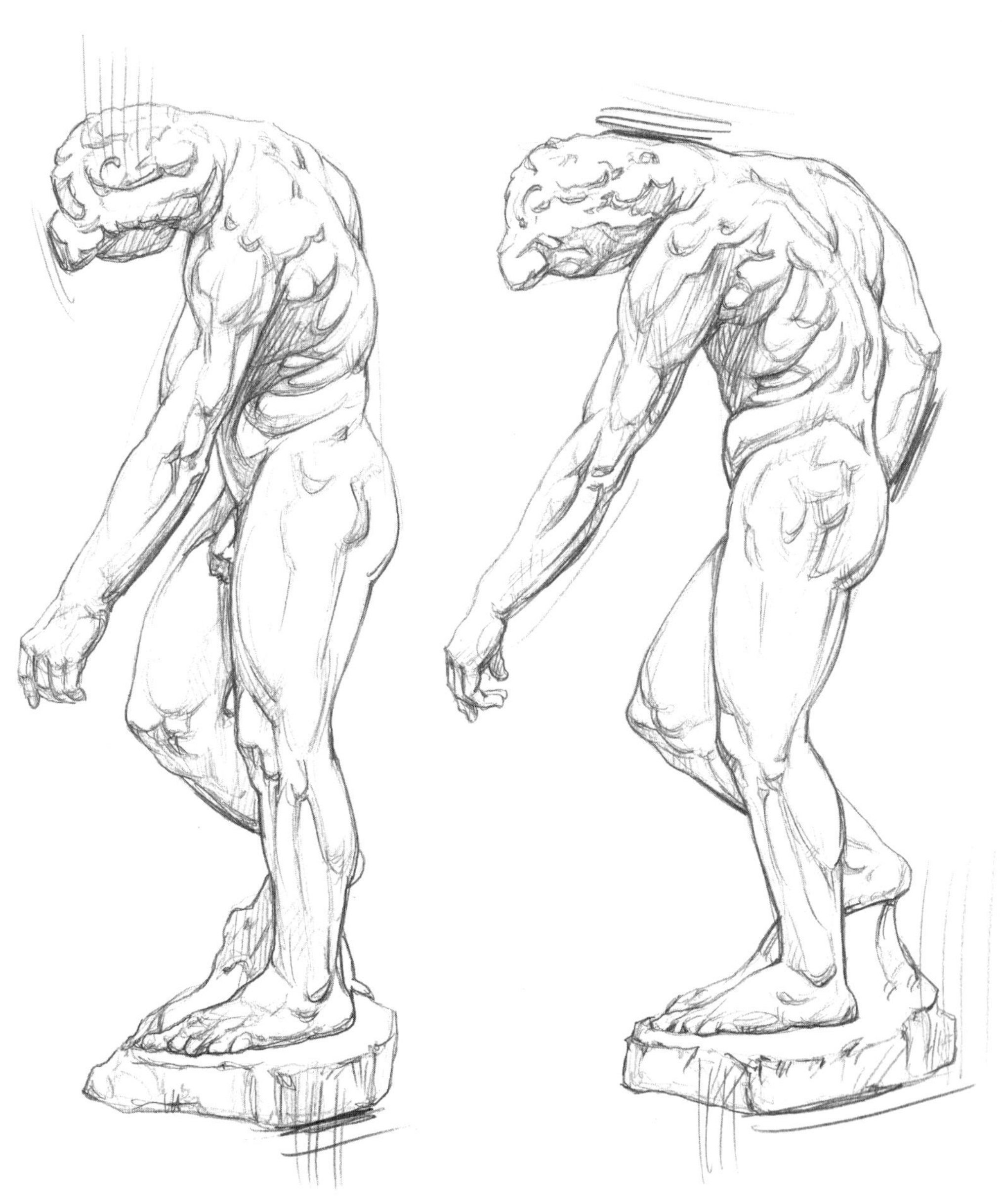

The Shadow (1880)
Bronze, 192cm (75½in) high

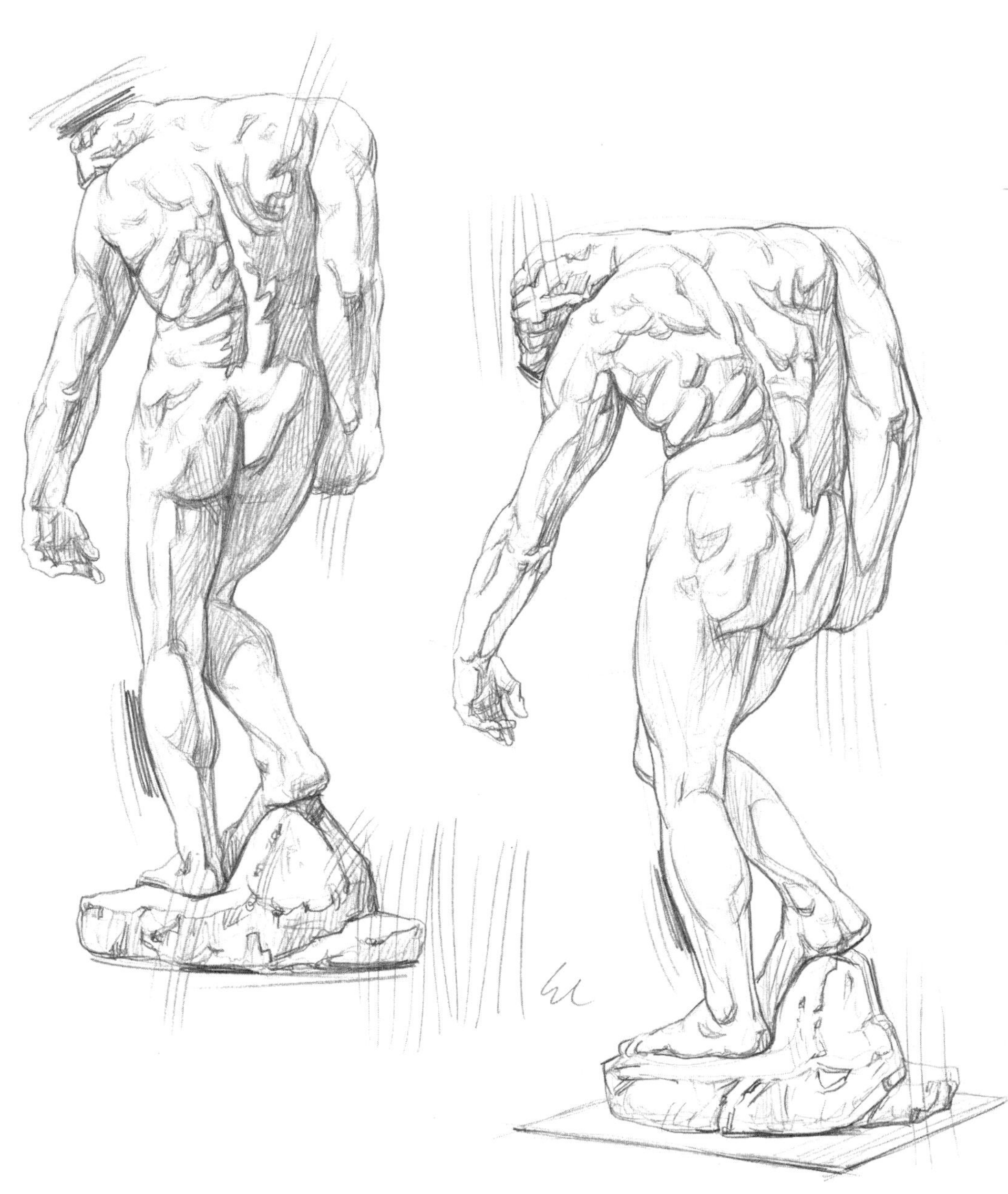

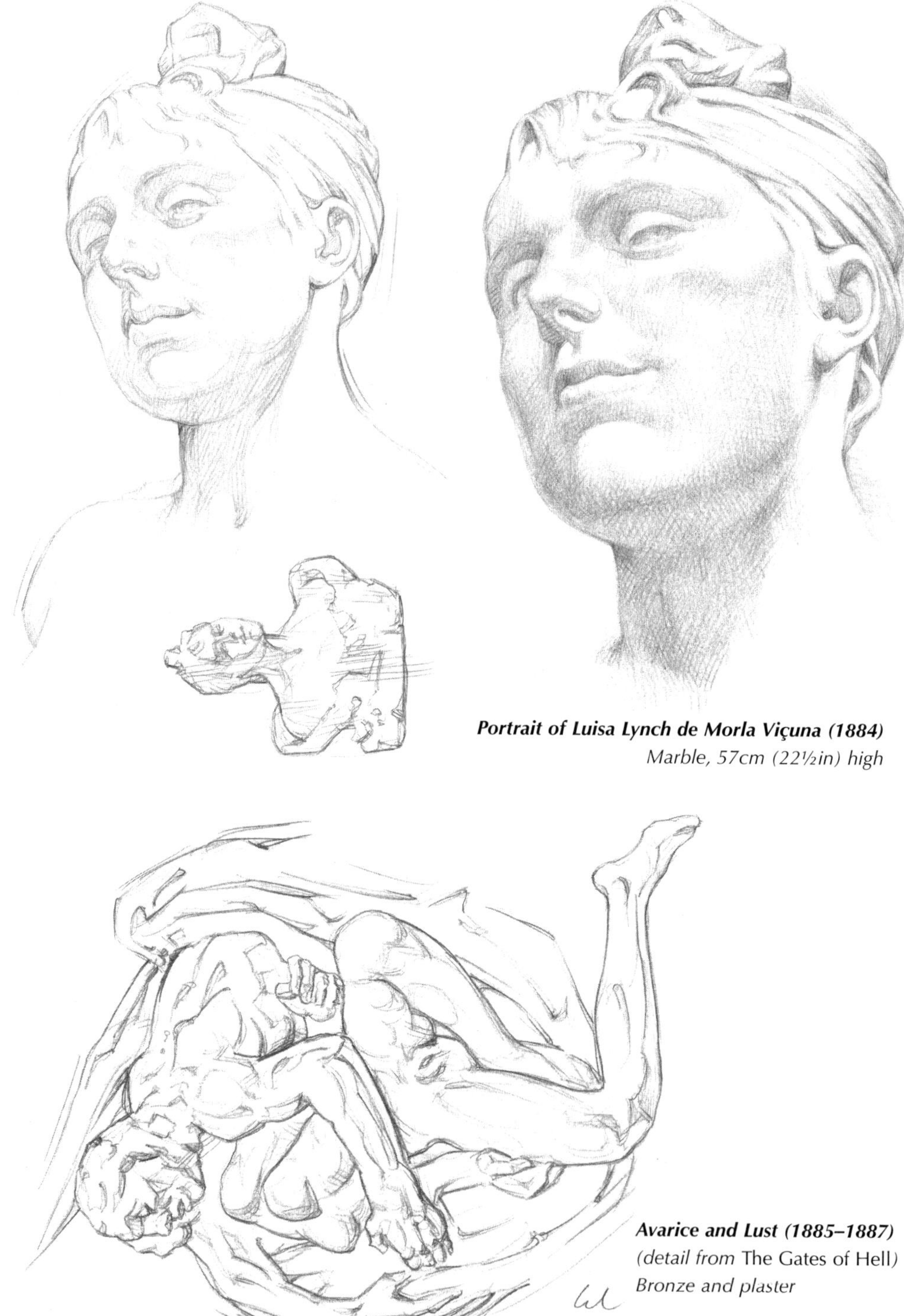

Portrait of Luisa Lynch de Morla Viçuna (1884)
Marble, 57cm (22½in) high

Avarice and Lust (1885–1887)
(detail from The Gates of Hell*)*
Bronze and plaster

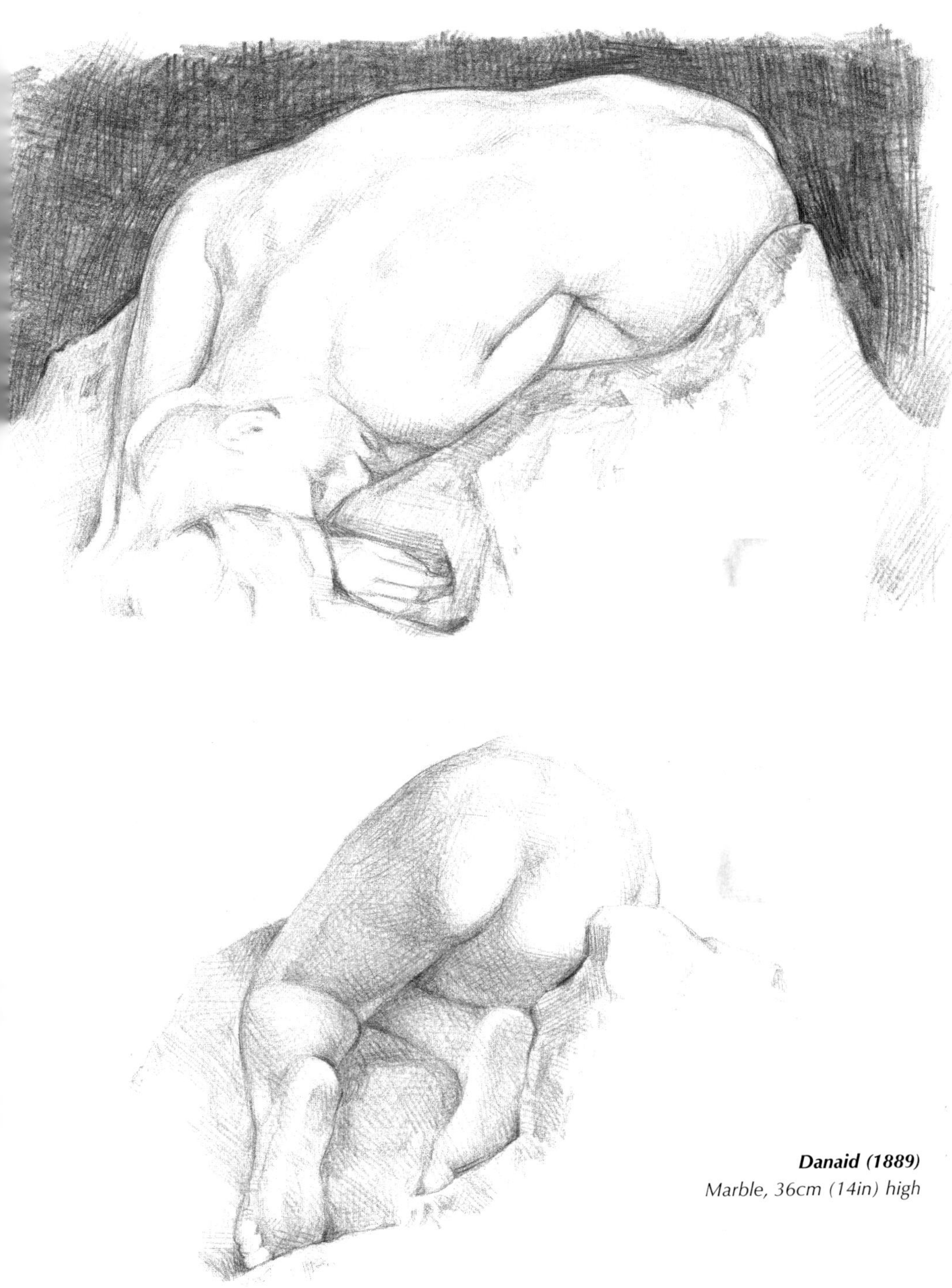

***Danaid* (1889)**
Marble, 36cm (14in) high

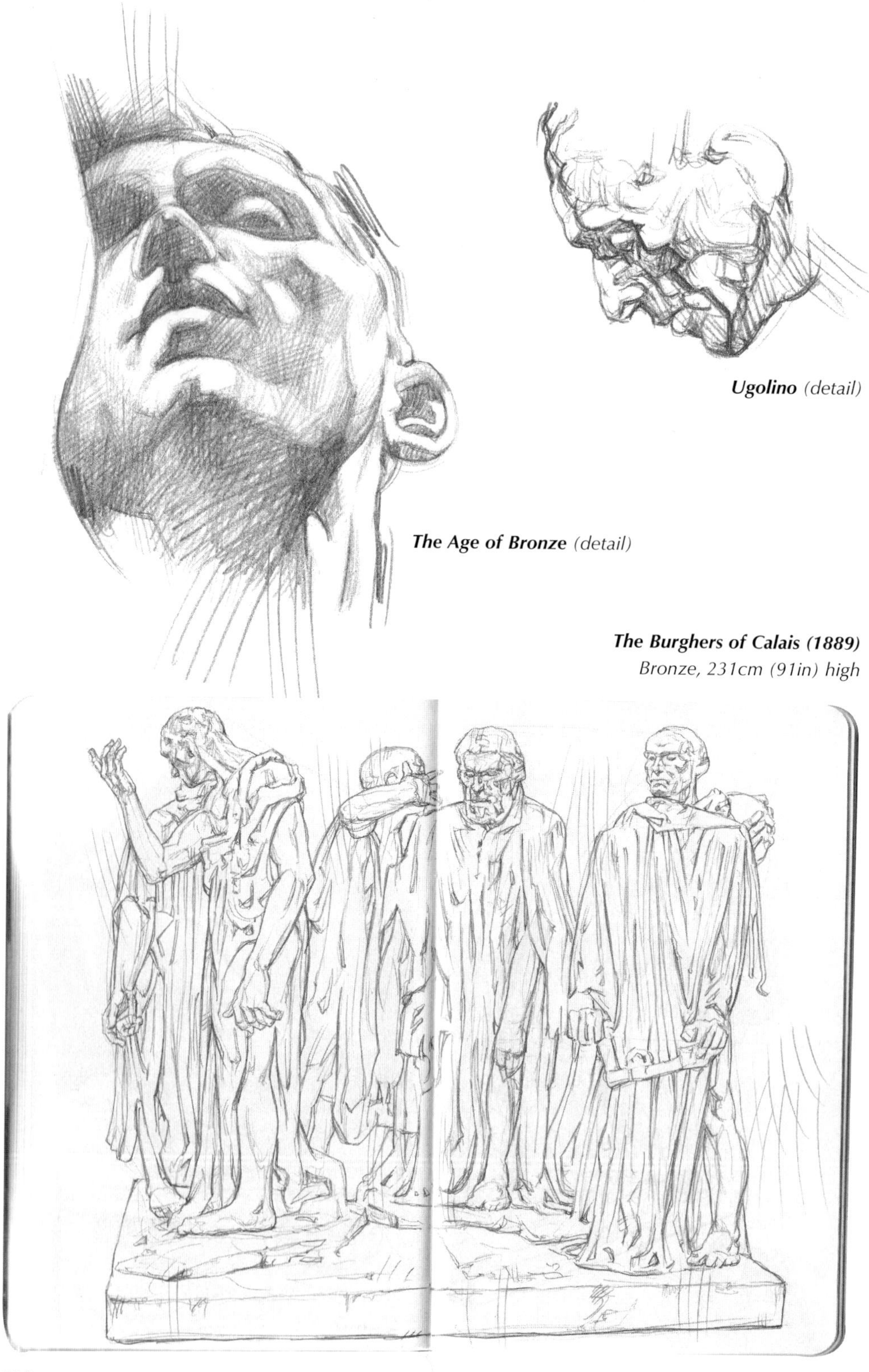

Ugolino *(detail)*

The Age of Bronze *(detail)*

The Burghers of Calais (1889)
Bronze, 231cm (91in) high